S0-AEK-629

A Dictionary of
English Folklore

Dr Jacqueline Simpson was president of the Folklore Society from 1993 to 1996, editor of *Folklore* from 1979 to 1993, and is currently Honorary Secretary of the Folklore Society. Her publications include *Folklore of Sussex*, *Folklore of the Welsh Borders*, and *Scandinavian Folktales*.

Steve Roud is Local Studies Librarian for Croydon and was Honorary Librarian of the Folklore Society for over 15 years. He is the author of *Mumming Plays in Oxfordshire* and has compiled the *Index to the Journal Folklore 1968–1992*.

Oxford Paperback Reference

The most authoritative and up-to-date reference books for both students and the general reader.

ABC of Music
Accounting
Allusions
Archaeology
Architecture
Art and Artists
Art Terms
Astronomy
Better Wordpower
Bible
Biology
British History
British Place-Names
Buddhism
Business
Card Games
Catchphrases
Celtic Mythology
Chemistry
Christian Art
Christian Church
Classical Literature
Computing
Contemporary World History
Dance
Dates
Dynasties of the World
Earth Sciences
Ecology
Economics
Engineering*
English Etymology
English Folklore
English Grammar
English Language
English Literature
Euphemisms
Everyday Grammar
Finance and Banking
First Names
Food and Drink
Food and Nutrition
Foreign Words and Phrases
Geography
Handbook of the World
Humorous Quotations
Idioms
Internet
Irish Literature
Jewish Religion
Kings and Queens of Britain
Language Toolkit
Law
Linguistics

Literary Quotations
Literary Terms
Local and Family History
London Place-Names
Mathematics
Medical
Medicinal Drugs
Modern Design*
Modern Slang
Music
Musical Terms*
Musical Works*
Nursing
Ologies and Isms
Philosophy
Phrase and Fable
Physics
Plant Sciences
Pocket Fowler's Modern
  English Usage
Political Quotations
Politics
Popes
Proverbs
Psychology
Quotations
Quotations by Subject
Reverse Dictionary
Rhyming Slang
Sailing Terms
Saints
Science
Scientists
Shakespeare
Ships and the Sea
Slang
Sociology
Spelling
Statistics
Synonyms and Antonyms
Twentieth-Century Art
Weather
Weights, Measures, and Units
Who's Who in the Classical
  World
Who's Who in the Twentieth
  Century
World History
World Mythology
World Religions
Writers' Dictionary
Zoology

*forthcoming

A Dictionary of

English Folklore

JACQUELINE SIMPSON & STEVE ROUD

OXFORD
UNIVERSITY PRESS

OXFORD
UNIVERSITY PRESS

Great Clarendon Street, Oxford OX2 6DP

Oxford University Press is a department of the University of Oxford.
It furthers the University's objective of excellence in research, scholarship,
and education by publishing worldwide in

Oxford New York

Auckland Bangkok Buenos Aires Cape Town Chennai
Dar es Salaam Delhi Hong Kong Istanbul Karachi Kolkata
Kuala Lumpur Madrid Melbourne Mexico City Mumbai Nairobi
São Paulo Shanghai Taipei Tokyo Toronto

Oxford is a registered trade mark of Oxford University Press
in the UK and in certain other countries

Published in the United States
by Oxford University Press Inc., New York

© Oxford University Press 2000, 2003

The moral rights of the authors have been asserted

Database right Oxford University Press (maker)

First published 2000
First published as an Oxford University Press paperback 2001
Reissued with new covers 2003

British Library Cataloguing in Publication Data

Data available

Library of Congress Cataloging in Publication Data

Data available

ISBN 0-19-860766-0

1

Typeset in Swift and Frutiger
by RefineCatch Limited, Bungay, Suffolk
Printed in Great Britain
by Clays Ltd, St Ives plc

Introduction

The title of this book invites two challenges: What is 'folklore'? And what is 'English' folklore?

As regards the first, 'folklore' is notoriously difficult to define with rigour, and the term now covers a broader field than it did when invented in 1846, linking many aspects of cultural traditions past and present. It includes whatever is voluntarily and informally communicated, created or done jointly by members of a group (of any size, age, or social and educational level); it can circulate through any media (oral, written, or visual); it generally has roots in the past, but is not necessarily very ancient; it has present relevance; it usually recurs in many places, in similar but not identical forms; it has both stable and variable features, and evolves through dynamic adaptation to new circumstances. The essential criterion is the presence of a group whose joint sense of what is right and appropriate shapes the story, performance, or custom—not the rules and teachings of any official body (State or civic authority, Church, school, scientific or scholarly orthodoxy). It must be stressed that in most other respects this 'group' is likely to share in mainstream culture and to be diverse in socio-economic status, interests, etc.; the notion that folklore is found only or chiefly where an uneducated, homogeneous peasantry preserves ancient ways has no relevance to England today, and probably never had.

We have included a broad range of oral genres, performance genres, calendar customs, life-cycle customs, supernatural, and 'superstitious' beliefs. Lack of space forced us regretfully to omit entries on traditional foods, sports, games, fairs, and most obsolete customs; we have also been selective in children's lore, fairies, plants, and superstitions, since excellent books on these topics are available already. Material culture (such as traditional farming, crafts, vernacular buildings, etc.) has been left aside, this being an immense but separate topic. But modern everyday lore is well represented; the *Tooth Fairy counts as well as *Puck, the *Vanishing Hitchhiker as well as Lady *Godiva. On some topics (e.g. *conception, *menstruation, *sex) data are scarce, as earlier scholars ignored these 'unpleasant' matters; we hope these entries will inspire others to fuller research. There are entries for past writers who have contributed significantly to the study of English folklore, but not for those still living (except in so far as it is impossible to separate Iona Opie's work from that of her late husband Peter).

There appears to be no precedent for taking 'England' as the basis for a book covering all folklore genres, although there have been books on, for instance, English calendar customs or dances. Folklorists have either studied a specific county, or have drawn material from all over the British Isles. Indeed, there has always been great stress on Scottish, Welsh, and Irish traditions as richer, more ancient, and more worth preserving than those of England. This became a self-fulfilling theory; the more scholars thronged to study them, the larger grew their archives, and the duller England seemed in comparison.

Moreover, the English have never used folklore to assert their patriotic identity, or even (until recent years) to attract tourists, though certain counties and regions have. Whereas Scotland, Wales, and Ireland have celebrated their traditions with pride, here folklore is seen as something quaint, appropriate to rural backwaters, but irrelevant to nationhood. Whereas virtually every other European country has university departments for folklore studies, with massive archives, English academia has almost unanimously turned a blind eye. The paradoxical result is that the country which invented the word 'folklore' and whose scholars, a hundred years ago, were leaders in the field, is now a neglected area. We have long wished to redress the balance; the fact that our work appears now, at a time when there is some public debate on how 'Englishness' should be defined, is purely coincidental.

Our second reason for excluding Scotland, Wales, the Isle of Man, and the Channel Isles, is that these areas have languages of their own; being unable to read their primary material, we could not have treated them adequately. We are fully aware that the traditions of the whole British Isles (plus Ireland) do have vast areas of overlap, in which separate treatment is unnecessary. However, there are also great historical and cultural differences; any book attempting to combine them would either be vastly longer than the present one, or, in our view, unacceptably shallow. We hope other 'Dictionaries' will be written, by those more qualified than ourselves, to cover those areas.

Similarly, we reluctantly decided not to cover the many ethnic groups now forming part of English society. We could have described large-scale public events such as the Notting Hill Carnival or Chinese New Year dragon dances, but how could we, as outsiders, get access to the more intimate world of family custom and personal beliefs? How, for example, could we know where religious ritual ends and customary practice begins in a Muslim or Hindu wedding? Or distinguish between different types of Chinese medicine? Moreover, various families, generations, or individuals within each ethnic group guard, modify, or reject their traditions in different degrees in reaction to their English environment; the situation is currently too fluid and complex for brief summary. Likewise, it is too early to say whether the policy in multicultural schools of encouraging all children to share one another's festivals will spread into the community, and modify established traditions.

Our intention is to provide a work of reference, not to build theories, of which there have been too many, based on too little evidence. The entries therefore emphasize established dates and facts; speculative interpretations are kept to a minimum. In particular, we view with scepticism theories that items of folklore are direct survivals of pre-Christian religion or magic, since the time-lag between their ascertainable dates and the suggested pagan origins is generally over a thousand years, and alternative explanations are often available.

Similarly, although entries on folk medicine and superstitions sometimes refer to cognate ideas in classical writers, notably Pliny, we must state emphatically that we do not imply that the English items are orally transmitted from equally ancient times; classical medicine and 'science' was known to medieval and early modern compilers of bestiaries, lapidaries, and herbals, through whom it passed to ordinary people. The importance of Greek and Roman authors to English folklore is that their prestige among the educated supported various popular beliefs. The authority of the Bible and Church was even more powerful; it endorsed the reality of ghosts, witchcraft, and demons, while the pervasive influence of its ethics and imagery can be traced in very many legends, practices, and beliefs.

In conclusion, we offer appreciation and thanks to our friends and colleagues whose writings, lectures, and conversation have taught us so much: Gillian Bennett, Julia Bishop, Marion Bowman, Georgina Boyes, Theresa Buckland, E. C. Cawte, Jennifer Chandler, Keith Chandler, Hilda Ellis Davidson, George Frampton, Reg Hall, Gabrielle Hatfield, Michael Heaney, Roy Judge, Venetia Newall, Iona Opie, Roy Palmer, Tom Pettitt, Neil Philip, Doc Rowe, Leslie Shepard, Brian Shuel, Paul Smith, Roy Vickery, John Widdowson, Juliette Wood.

Particular thanks to Caroline Oates (Librarian of the Folklore Society), Malcolm Taylor (Librarian of the Vaughan Williams Memorial Library), and the staff of Worthing Public Library and Croydon Libraries (RTS and Local Studies and Archives).

Thanks also to Gordon Ridgewell for suggesting corrections and additions to various bibliographical and geographical references in the hardback edition (2000), now incorporated into the paperback (2001).

J.S.
S.R.

Abbreviations

BM	British Museum
DNB	Dictionary of National Biography
ED&S	English Dance and Song
EDD	English Dialect Dictionary
FMJ	Folk Music Journal
JEFDS	Journal of the English Folk Dance Society
JEFDSS	Journal of the English Folk Dance and Song Society
JFSS	Journal of the Folk-Song Society
L&L	Lore and Language
N&Q	Notes & Queries
OED	Oxford English Dictionary
[JS], [SR]	Information from the authors' own fieldwork or personal experience

Abbots Ann (Hampshire), see *MAIDENS' GARLANDS.

Abbots Bromley Horn Dance. A unique *calendar custom which takes place in Abbots Bromley, Staffordshire, on the Monday following the first Sunday after 4 September, the day of the village *wakes. The team is made up of six dancers, each carrying a pair of antler horns, a Fool, a man-woman called Maid Marian, a *hobby horse, a Bow-man, a triangle player, and a musician, each wearing a pseudo-medieval costume designed in the late 19th century. The horns which the dancers carry are reindeer antlers, mounted on a wooden head, with a short wooden handle for carrying. Three are painted white with brown tips, and three are brown with golden tips. The horns have naturally caused much speculation, and a radiocarbon dating test carried out on one of them in 1976 gave a mean date of AD 1065 ± 80 years. Reindeer have been extinct in Britain since before the Norman Conquest, but these particular horns could have been imported at any point in the custom's history. The performers spend all day perambulating the parish, sometimes progressing in single file, sometimes following the leader in a serpentine hey-type movement, but every now and then they form up in lines of three (the hobby horse and bowman join in to make it four and sometimes Jester and Maid Marian) facing each other. They go forward and back towards each other a few times and then cross over. It is thought to be unlucky if they do not visit your house or neighbourhood. After the dance, the horns are deposited back in the church, where they will remain until next September. The earliest mention of the custom so far found is in Robert Plot's *Natural History of Staffordshire* (1686), where he mentions the 'Hobby-horse dance' being performed at Christmas, New Year, and Twelfth Night, and Sir Simon Degge (1612–1704) anno-

tated his copy of Plot's book with the comment that he had often seen the dance before the Civil War. An even earlier reference, in 1532, confirms the existence of a hobby horse but does not mention the horns (see Heaney).

Kightly, 1986: 41–3; Hole, 1975: 95–6; Stone, 1906: 16–18; Michael Heaney, *FMJ* 5:3 (1987), 359–60; Theresa Buckland, *L&L* 3:2 (1980), 1–8 (also 3:7 (1982), 87, and 4:1 (1985), 86–7).

Abbotsbury garland day (13 May). Abbotsbury in Dorset has been famous for its *garland day customs for many years, and they still continue, despite major alterations within living memory and before. Changes in the village, such as the decline of the local fishing industry, and the closure of local schools, have effected major changes in the way the custom is carried out, but locals have been sufficiently determined to meet those changes and to ensure its survival. A number of other villages in the area formerly had similar garland customs, but Abbotsbury is the only one that has survived. The way the custom was described in the 1980s was as follows: The children who attend the local school get the day off for the event and they construct two garlands—one of wild flowers and another of garden flowers. The flowers are fixed onto wire frames which are carried on poles. The children go from house to house round the village, displaying the garlands and receiving money, which they keep. Later in the day, the older children who have been at school in Weymouth get home and construct a third, more elaborate garland, which they also take round the houses. Two of the garlands are eventually laid on the local War Memorial (suggested by benefactor Lord Ilchester after the First World War). This is quite different to how things were one hundred years earlier. The custom was first described by Hutchins' *History of Dorset* (1867), and later by C. H. Mayo (1893). At that time the garlands were made and exhibited only by the children of fishing families. The garlands were blessed in a church service and some were rowed out to sea and thrown into the water. The rest of the day was spent in jollification on the beach. Around the time of the First World War, the first non-fishermen garlands appeared, and the number of garlands has since fluctuated a great deal. The local school closed in 1981, and as children no longer get a holiday on Garland Day there has been a tendency to move the custom further to the evening, or to the nearest Saturday.

C.H. Mayo, 'Garland Days', *Somerset & Dorset N&Q* 3 (1893); Peter Robson, 'Dorset Garland Days on the Chesil Coast', in Buckland & Wood, 1993: 155–66; Kightly, 1986: 43; Stone, 1906: 70–1.

adders. There are a number of beliefs about the adder which have been collected across the country, with little variation. It was said to be deaf, on the authority of Psalm 58 ('They are like the deaf adder that stoppeth her ear, which will not hearken to the voice of the charmer'). It can only die at sunset, and if you kill one its mate will come looking for you. Adult female adders swallow their young when in danger, then vomit them up once the danger is past. An adder coming to the door of a house is a death *omen, and to dream of adders means your enemies are trying to do you some secret mischief. In the Fens, it was said they were attracted by the smell of a *menstruating woman (Porter, 1969: 51).

Adders were thought to like milk. A story in *The British Chronicle* of 15 October 1770 concerns a farmer and his wife who, having noticed that their best cow gave little milk, stayed up one night to catch the thief. Just about sunrise they saw 'a most enormous overgrown adder, or hag worm, crawl out of the bush, and winding up one of the cow's legs, apply its mouth to one of the paps'. The man managed to kill it with his cudgel, and the stuffed four-foot long skin could be seen displayed at the farmhouse (quoted in Morsley, 1979: 72).

On the principle that like cures like, adder's oil was prized as a remedy for *deafness and earache; one snake-catcher used to sell it regularly to a chemist in Uckfield (Sussex) at a guinea an ounce in the late 19th century. The way to catch an adder was to shake a silk neck-cloth in front of the snake, which would strike at it and be unable to withdraw its fangs; one could then break its back, slash its skin, and

hang it in a warm place for the fat to drip out as oil.

A shed adder skin could draw out thorns, splinters, or even needles when applied to the other side of the hand or finger. This cure is mentioned by Aubrey (1686, 1880: 38), as well as by 19th- and 20th-century folklorists. He also mentions that 'Sussexians' wear the skins 'for hatt-bands, which they say doe preserve them from the gripeing of the gutts'. Other sources list this as a remedy for a headache. In Cornwall, adder skin sewn to flannel was worn by pregnant women as a belt (Opie and Tatem, 1989: 362–3).

If a man or animal has been bitten by an adder, the best remedy is fat taken from that very adder, but another is to wrap the victim in a fresh sheepskin. Aubrey's cure (*Natural History of Wiltshire* MS in Royal Society) involves the 'fundament of a pigeon applied to the bite-place'. The pigeon will quickly die. Keep putting fresh pigeons to the wound till they stop dying.

adderstone, see *SNAKESTONE.

Addy, Sidney Oldall (1848–1933). A solicitor in Sheffield from 1877 until his retirement in 1905, his real passion was for the dialect, folklore, and history of the Yorkshire/Derbyshire area in which he lived and worked. He was an enthusiastic member of local societies and regular contributor to local journals and newspapers, as well as national publications such as *Notes & Queries* and *Folk-Lore*. Addy joined the *Folklore Society in 1894, having already published enough to make him an acknowledged expert in his area, but soon became disenchanted with the Society's policy which at the time foregrounded reiterative publishing of previously printed works (exemplified by their County Folk-Lore series) and the construction of high theory, at the expense of first-hand fieldwork. Addy was one of several regional folklorists who felt similar frustration, and after urging, unsuccessfully, a new policy of active collection (e.g. in *Folk-Lore* 13 (1902), 297–9) he resigned from the Society in 1905, although he continued to gather and publish material elsewhere. In retrospect, Addy was ahead of his time in the quality of his fieldwork, combining careful observation with interviews and an ethnographic approach, which can be seen in his article on the *Castleton Garland custom published in 1901. Much of his folklore work remains little known, buried in local publications, and would certainly repay collecting together and republishing.

Major folklore publications: *Glossary of Words Used in the Neighbourhood of Sheffield* (1888); *Household Tales and Traditional Remains* (1895); 'Garland day at Castleton', *Folk-Lore* 12 (1901) 394–428; 'Guising and Mumming in Derbyshire', *Derbyshire Archaeology and Natural History Society Journal* 29 (1907), 31–42.

John Ashton, *Folklore Historian* 15 (1998), 5–13; John Ashton, *Folklore* 108 (1997), 19–23; Walter T. Hall, 'The Late Sidney Oldall Addy', *Transactions of the Hunter Archaeological Society* 4 (1937), 221–5.

afterbirth, see *PLACENTA.

alabaster. Powdered alabaster was formerly believed to have medicinal value when made up into an ointment, and was reputedly particularly good for bad legs. It was common for people to chip pieces off church statues for the purpose, with the implication that this holy connection would make the stone even more effective, and many ecclesiastical buildings show mutilated statues at ground level both inside and outside the building for this reason. Correspondents in *N&Q* report that the efficacy of powdered alabaster was recorded in a number of leech-books, as early as AD 900.

N&Q 11s:6 (1912), 129, 175, 234–5.

Alderley Edge (Cheshire). A rocky outcrop near Macclesfield, honeycombed with old mining tunnels. A farmer was once stopped there by a wizard, who insisted on buying his white mare, and led him through huge iron gates inside the rock, where he saw many horses and warriors asleep. These, the wizard explained, would ride out and decide the fate of a great battle to save England, 'when George the son of George shall reign'. Then he paid the farmer from the treasures in the cave, and led him out; the iron gates shut, and no one has seen them since.

The tale has been noted by many local writers from 1805 onwards; it is said to have circulated orally since the 1750s. The earlier versions do not name the wizard and the sleepers; later ones identify them as *Merlin, *Arthur, and his knights. A spring in the rocks was called the Holy Well in the 18th century, and its water was thought to cure women of barrenness; it is now called the Wizard's Well, and used as a *wishing well.

Alford, Violet (1881–1972). An authority of international repute on all forms of folk dancing, and the related music and festival customs. She stressed the similarities to be found over much of Europe, which she believed were due to a common origin in prehistoric ritual. Most of her research was done in France and Spain, especially in the Pyrenees; she was a tireless traveller and a close observer, whose vivid first-hand impressions of customs and performances are of enduring interest even where her theoretic framework is outdated. She was an active member of the EFDSS, organized several major dance festivals, and adjudicated at others; she held strong views on authenticity, and deplored commercial or touristic changes to tradition. She spotted the fragmentary traces of the *Marshfield mumming tradition, stimulated its revival in 1932, and then, characteristically, tried to control the performances.

Her main books are *Pyrenean Festivals* (1937); *The Singing of the Travels* (1956); *Sword Dance and Drama* (1962); *The Hobby Horse and Other Animal Masks* (1978).

See D. N. Kennedy, *Folklore* 82 (1971), 344–50, for a selected bibliography; Lucille Armstrong, *Folklore* 84 (1973), 104–10, and Edward Nicol, *FMJ* (1972), 257–8, for obituaries; Davidson and Blacker, 2001: 151–57.

alien big cats. Since the 1960s, there have been press reports from many areas of large cat-like animals, briefly glimpsed, and assumed by witnesses to be pumas, lions, lynxes, or cheetahs; paw-prints and droppings are sometimes found, and the sightings are often linked to allegedly unusual deaths and injuries among sheep and deer. There were 304 press items drawn from 31 counties in 1997 alone. Interpretation of the evidence is controversial, since alternative explanations are always possible. If exotic animals really are at large, they must be illegal pets, dumped when they grow troublesome, and possibly now breeding in the wild; however, it is unlikely there could be so many as the reports suggest. No foreign feline has yet been captured or killed, apart from one tame puma in Scotland in 1980 and a small swamp cat accidentally run over on Hayling Island (Hampshire) in 1988. Some writers therefore prefer a paranormal explanation; the media adopt an ambiguous attitude, alternating between dread and humour, and favouring emotive terms such as 'beast', 'alien', and 'mystery'.

Many reports are confined to local papers;

others cause nationwide interest and large-scale hunts by police or the army—the Surrey Puma in 1962–6, the Black Beast of Exmoor in 1983, the Beast of Bodmin Moor in 1994–5. The Bodmin case collapsed when investigated by the Ministry of Agriculture (see press reports of 20 July 1995), but further incidents continue; in March 1998 a 'Beast of Essex' was suspected of killing four geese near Epping. Whatever facts may underlie some reports, media-generated interest encourages rumour, misinterpretation, and exaggeration. Hoaxing occurs; a skull 'found' on Bodmin Moor in late July 1995 came from a leopard-skin rug, and some photos simply show domestic cats shot from angles which distort their size.

See also *CATS.

A dossier of press items is held by Paul Sieveking, editor of *Fortean Times*. For a selection of material and a folkloric interpretation, see Michael Goss, 'Alien Big Cat Sightings in Britain: A Possible Rumour Legend?', *Folklore* 103 (1992), 184–202. Janet and Colin Bord, in *Alien Animals* (1980), explain these and other mystery beasts as paranormal phenomena; Di Francis argues in *Cat Country* (1983) that ancient wildcats survive, unrecognized.

Allendale tar barrels. The people of Allendale, Northumberland, welcome the *New Year in a spectacular way with their procession of blazing *tar barrels. During the evening, men in home-made costume (the *guisers) visit the town's pubs and shortly before midnight assemble for the procession which is the focal point of the custom. The barrels are actually one end of a wooden barrel, about twelve inches deep, filled with wood and shavings soaked in paraffin. Once the barrels are alight, the procession follows the town band round the streets and back to the market-place, where an unlit bonfire awaits them. After circling the fire, and at the stroke of midnight, some of the barrels are thrown on to the fire, while others are extinguished and saved for next year, as it is hard to get decent wooden barrels these days. The crowd cheers, and *Auld Lang Syne* is sung. Most of the Guisers spend the rest of the night first footing (see *New Year). According to extensive research carried out by Venetia Newall, the tar-barrel custom is not nearly as old as most people assume it to be, dating only from about 1858. It seems to have started with the band's New Year perambulation of the village. One year, the wind was so strong that it kept blow-ing their candles out, and someone suggested that a tar barrel would be a more effective illumination.

Venetia Newall, *Folklore* 85 (1974), 93–103; Sykes, 1977: 156–9; Kightly, 1986: 44; Shuel, 1985: 190–1.

All Fools' Day, see *APRIL FOOL'S DAY.

All Saints' Day (1 November). Germany and England began celebrating a feast of all martyrs and saints on 1 November in the 8th century, instead of on 13 May, as was done in Rome; eventually the rest of Western Christendom also adopted the November date. Although in itself a joyous festival, it was also the eve of *All Souls' Day, so in medieval times it became customary to pray for the dead on this date. At dusk, torchlit processions and church vigils were held, and bells were rung till midnight. At the Reformation the custom was forbidden, but many people were defying the ban and ringing church bells as late as the 1580s. Later still, in the 18th and early 19th centuries, some villagers in Lancashire and Derbyshire would light small fires in the fields at midnight on All Saints' Day, to see in All Souls, and kneel round them to pray for their dead.

This date falls between *Halloween and All Souls, so in those areas around Shropshire and Staffordshire where *souling was prevalent, All Saints did not have a separate identity but was swamped by these other two festivals. In other areas, however, a range of customs took place on this day, though none of them seems to be widespread, or at least widely reported. At Goadby (Leicestershire) in the 18th century, a children's *bonfire custom is recorded. In Derbyshire it was customary to strew flowers on the *graves of departed loved ones. In Hampshire and the Isle of Wight special cakes were made and eaten. A 19th-century *love divination is reported from Worcestershire as special to All Saints' Day: 'A young woman took a ball of new worsted and holding it in her fingers, threw the ball through the open window at midnight, saying "Who holds?" It was assumed that her future husband would pick up the worsted, mention his name, and disappear' (*N&Q for Worcestershire* (1856), 190).

See also *HALLOWEEN, *ALL SOULS' DAY, and *SOULING.

Wright and Lones, 1940: iii. 121–37.

All Souls' Day (2 November). Also called Soulmas Day, Saumas, etc. This feast was devised by Abbot Odilo of Cluny (d. 1049), to pray for 'all the dead who have existed from the beginning of the world to the end of time'. He set it in February, but it was soon transferred to the day after *All Saints; its sombre associations affected All Saints' Day and ultimately its eve as well, giving rise to many aspects of *Halloween. It is probable that in medieval England, as in many Catholic countries, the dead were believed to leave Purgatory for two or three days, to revisit their homes and seek the prayers of their relatives. In *The Gentleman's Magazine* for November 1784, a correspondent said children at Findern (Derbyshire) lit small *bonfires on the common on 2 November, calling them 'tindles'; adults recalled that the purpose had originally been 'to light souls out of Purgatory'. There are similar reports from Lancashire, but these seem to be isolated examples.

Before the Reformation, it was customary to distribute food and alms to the poor on All Souls' Day as a fee for praying for the dead. Later, *Aubrey describes piles of small cakes set out on this day in Shropshire houses, for visitors to take one; he also gives 'an old Rhythm or saying':

A Soule-cake, a Soule-cake,
Have mercy on all Christen soules for a Soule-cake.

(Aubrey, 1686/1880: 23)

Cakes were long made in many regions, and called 'soul-cake' in some places. The type varies widely from place to place, and even two reports from Whitby (Yorkshire) disagree—'a small round loaf', says one, but 'a square farthing cake with currents on top' says the other.

See also *ANTROBUS SOUL-CAKERS, *MUMMING PLAYS, *SOULING.

Wright and Lones, 1940: iii. 137–45.

amber. Occasionally said to be rubbed on sore eyes and sprained limbs (Henderson, 1866: 113), or worn for chest ailments (*Folk-Lore* 53 (1942), 98). One soldier from the First World War reckoned he owed his life to his amber bead (Lovett, 1925: 13).

Ambleside rushbearing. Not quite so well known as neighbouring *Grasmere, Ambleside, Cumbria, keeps its own version of the rushbearing custom. On the Saturday nearest St Anne's Day (26 July), villagers process to the St Mary's church with men carrying pointed rush pillars, about eight feet tall, while chil-

dren carry rush and flower constructions (the 'bearings') in the shape of harps and so on. A hymn is sung at the market-place, and a sermon preached in the church. Gingerbread is distributed afterwards. A description published in 1892 shows there has been little change in the form of the custom since that time.

Hogg, 1971: 96–7; *N&Q* 8s:2 (1892), 141–2.

Andersen, Hans Christian (1805–75). A Danish shoemaker's son who as a child had heard traditional storytelling 'in the spinning-room or during the hop harvest'. He began writing fairytales in 1835, and continued all his life; the first English translations appeared in 1846. Some, for instance 'The Travelling Companions' and 'Big Claus and Little Claus', follow traditional plots quite closely; others are variations on old motifs, such as 'The Little Mermaid', elaborating the belief that water-spirits may love humans, and may desire to obtain salvation. Many, including the well-known 'Ugly Duckling', are entirely his own creations; almost all are full of pathos and emotionalism. Andersen's influence on the later literary fairytale in England was profound; it pervades the fairytales of Oscar Wilde, and can be felt as early as 1857 in several passages of Dickens's *Little Dorrit*. About a dozen are now among the stock of fairytales which most English children know, and are no longer felt as foreign.

Angels of Mons. During 1915, there were strong rumours that British and French troops had been miraculously protected from the Germans during their retreat from Mons late in August 1914. The earliest allusions are in letters written by Brigadier-General John Charteris on 5 September 1914 and 11 February 1915, though only published in 1931:

[*5 September 1914*] Then there is the story of the 'Angels of Mons' going strong through the 2nd Corps, of how the Angel of the Lord on the traditional white horse, and clad all in white with flaming sword, faced the advancing Germans at Mons and forbade their further progress. Men's nerves and imaginations play weird pranks in these strenuous times. All the same the angel at Mons interests me. I cannot find out how the legend arose.

[*11 February 1915*] I have been at some trouble to trace the rumour to its source. The best I can make of it is that some religiously minded man wrote home that the Germans halted at Mons, AS IF an Angel of the Lord had appeared in front of them. In due course the letter appeared in a Parish Magazine, which in time was sent back to some other men at the front. From them the story went back home with the 'as if' omitted, and at home it went the rounds in its expurgated form. [*At GHQ* (1931), 25–6, 75].

During the spring and summer of 1915 the story flourished in the religious press, whether Spiritualist, Catholic, or Anglican, in parish magazines, and in sermons, before eventually reaching the national press. The accounts are given with heartfelt conviction, but none is a first-hand eyewitness report. The details vary considerably. In some versions there are only two or three angels, in others a whole troop; in some, they are visible to the British soldiers, in others only to the Germans; in some they merely deter the Germans from attacking, in others they actually kill large numbers of them; in some, there is an individual leader of the visionary host, described as a horseman in armour and identified by the English as St George and by the French as the Archangel Michael or as Joan of Arc; in some, 'a strange cloud' comes between the Germans and the British.

Arthur Machen, a leader-writer on The *Evening News*, later maintained that these rumours had all grown out of a story he published in that paper on 29 September 1914, entitled 'The Bowmen'. This tells how an English soldier called on St George for help, and became aware of an army of medieval archers slaughtering the Germans with their arrows; he realizes they are the bowmen of Agincourt. As Brigadier-General Charteris's first letter shows, the legend was current three weeks before Machen's story, so his claim to be its originator cannot be accepted, though he may have genuinely believed he was. Moreover, there are no angels in his story, and no ghostly bowmen in the oral rumours. The latter are best explained as a *contemporary legend which satisfied religious and patriotic needs, and became a powerful and enduring part of the mythology of the Great War.

Kevin McLure, *Visions of Angels and Tales of Bowmen* (Harrogate, 1996); John Harlow, *The Sunday Times* (26 Jan. 1997), 9.

animal disguise. A number of *calendar customs include, or consist of, people dressing up to impersonate animals. See *hobby horses for a general discussion, and for specific examples: *Abbots Bromley Horn Dance, *Antrubus Soul-Cakers, *Hooden Horse, *Minehead Hobby Horse, *Old Horse, *Old Tup/

Derby Ram, *Padstow Hobby Horse, *stag hunt, *straw bears.

Cawte, 1978.

animal infestation. The horror of parasitic infestation is extended in folklore to include the fear that certain types of animal (usually *frogs, *toads, newts, or snakes) could live and grow inside people; allegedly true reports are fairly common from the 18th century to the present day. In most cases, the person is said to have drunk pond or river water containing the eggs or newly hatched young, which then grow in the stomach, causing great discomfort. Typical of the many realistic 'medical' reports is the following, reprinted in *N&Q* from The *North Lindsey Star* of 20 February 1892:

A woman named Jane Rowe, residing at Marazion, in Cornwall, has for several years suffered from violent pains in the stomach, from which she has been unable to obtain any relief, although she has been continually under medical treatment. On Friday evening, after taking some medicine, she had a severe attack of vomiting, in the course of which she threw up a living lizard, from four to five inches in length. Dr. J. Mudge, who has been the woman's medical attendant, has preserved the lizard, which he believes must have been in her stomach for many years. Since the reptile was ejected, Mrs Rowe has been almost entirely free from pain. (*N&Q* 8s:1 (1892), 207)

In some stories, the creature is brought out alive by a simple expedient, on the advice of a 'wise woman': the sufferer must starve for a few days (or, alternatively, eat very salty food), and then bend over a bowl of milk or other tempting morsel. The hungry animal will come out to get some, and can then be caught and killed.

Such stories and beliefs could serve as explanations for chronic dyspepsia and unnatural hunger. In the latter case, the creature in the stomach could be visualised as much bigger and more aggressive. 'He must have a wolf in his stomach' was a common phrase, though it is not always clear what 'wolf' means in such contexts; there is a Yorkshire term 'water-wolf' which seems to refer to some form of super-newt.

The motif of animal infestation remains popular in *contemporary legends. When the 'beehive' hairdo was fashionable, there were stories about girls who neither washed nor combed their hair for weeks, so spiders or bugs bred in it and gnawed into their skulls; more recently, stories about people returning from exotic holidays with a boil, which bursts to reveal hundreds of tiny spiders, or a mass of ant eggs. From antiquity to the mid-19th century, there are accounts (often supported by medical writers) of lice generating spontaneously on or in the human body. The notion that earwigs creep into people's ears if they lie down on the grass, and will there gnaw through your brain, ranges from the 18th century to modern children's lore.

The possibility of animals in the stomach was repeatedly debated in *N&Q*, under the heading 'newspaper folklore' (1s:6 (1852), 221, 338, 446; 1s:9 (1854), 29–30, 84, 276–7, 523–4); also under the heading 'animals living inside people' (9s:7 (1901), 222–3, 332–3, 390–2; 9s:8 (1901), 89–90, 346; 9s:9 (1903), 467–8). See also Gillian Bennett, 'Vermin in Boils: What if it were True?', *Southern Folklore* 54 (1997), 185–95; 'Bosom Serpents and Alimentary Amphibians: A Language for Sickness', in *Illness and Healing Alternatives in Western Europe*, ed. Marijke Guswijt-Hofstra and others (1997), 224–42.

animals. For the folklore of real-life animals, see under each individual species. Two forms can occur: beliefs about the *luck or ill luck the animal brings or foretells, and ideas about its biology and behaviour which, though mistaken, are not superstitious but merely popular fallacies. The latter often have a long history in books as well as oral tradition. Also, pious legends about animals and birds explain their markings or behaviour by association with Jesus (see *donkey, *robin). The haddock and the dory both have a black spot behind each gill, said to be the marks of St Peter's thumb and forefinger as he held the fish to extract a coin from its mouth (Matthew 17: 7)—a tale recorded in the 17th century, but probably medieval.

There are many supernatural creatures in animal form, some being shape-changing *boggarts and *fairies, others human *ghosts, others demonic; each account has to be separately assessed.

Antrobus Soul-Cakers. One of the very few surviving *mumming play teams which have a claim to be traditional, the Soul-Cakers perform their souling play every year at *Halloween and the following two weeks, around the vicinity of the village of Antrobus (Cheshire). As is usual with this type of play, the basic action is that King George and the Black Prince fight, and the latter is killed and brought back to life by a Doctor, and the last characters to enter are the Wild Horse (Dick) and his Driver. The Wild Horse is made up of a real horse's skull, painted black, mounted on a pole, held

by a man bent double under a canvas cover—a construction defined as a 'mast-horse' (see *hobby horse). The Driver's attempts to control his cavortings and misbehaviour are the highlight of the play for many of the audience. A local team is known to have performed up to the First World War, and then lapsed for a while, being revived in the late 1920s at the instigation of Major A. W. Boyd, and it has been regularly performed ever since.

Shuel, 1985: 179–80; Helm, 1981: 69–71; A. W. Boyd, *A Country Parish* (1951), 69–74.

April Fool's Day. The first mention of this custom is a curt note in Aubrey: 'Fooles holy day. We observe it on ye first of April. And so it is kept in Germany everywhere.' (Aubrey, 1686, 1880: 10). It must have reached England from Germany or France in the mid-17th century, and quickly became very popular under the name All Fools' Day; 18th-century writers call it 'universal'. At this period it was an adult amusement; people tried to trick one another into going on ridiculous errands, seeking non-existent objects such as pigeon's milk or a biography of Eve's mother, and so on.

Individual hoaxing of this kind grew rare among adults in the 19th century, but in recent decades impersonal media hoaxes have become popular; every year, press and television produce a crop of plausible, poker-faced absurdities ingeniously disguised as news items. On 1 April 1970 BBC radio broadcast a tribute to a non-existent scholar and philanthropist, in which various celebrities took part. *The Times*, abandoning its rule that hoaxes should be ignored, did report this one; readers were amused, not angry. The idea was increasingly imitated, for example by the *Guardian*'s 1977 account of the delightful but imaginary island of Sans Serif.

Children's tricks can be directed either against adults or against one another. Some are novel, as when some Bradford sixth-formers in 1970 advertised their school as being for sale, but most are traditional in form; they give false warnings and disconcerting news, and mock those who believe them, play simple practical jokes, send people on futile errands (Opie and Opie, 1959: 243–7). As with other children's customs, there is a time limit; anyone attempting a trick after midday is taunted:

> April Fool is gone and past,
> You're the biggest fool at last.

Arbor Day. Until 1995, a large black poplar tree standing in the centre of the village of Aston-on-Clun in Shropshire was permanently decorated with flags suspended from its branches. In that year the old tree died, and since a young one grown from its seeds is not yet large or strong enough to carry the flags, they are currently lashed to railings around it.

The flags are renewed on 29 May (*Oak Apple Day), locally called Arbor Day. As far as is known, the custom began in 1786, to celebrate the wedding of the local squire John Marston. The poplar was called the Bride's Tree; sprigs from it were given to village girls on their wedding day, to ensure a large family. Some authorities assume that the tree-decoration was a previous custom adapted for the occasion, but there is no evidence to back this. The Marston family eventually died out, so Hopesay Parish Council took over the ceremony, and gave it great publicity from 1954 to 1959; unfortunately, the press dubbed it a 'pagan fertility rite', rousing disapproval which nearly led to its abolition. However, it continued, and is still organized by the Parish Council supported by the proceeds of an annual fête.

Michael M. Rix, *Folklore* 71 (1960), 184–5; Tom Chambers, *FLS News* 23 (1996), 14.

art. The study of English regional folk-art styles has been deplorably neglected. Yet visual display has always been essential to many traditional customs; even if the objects created were only to be seen for one day, they had to have an impact. They were skilfully made, showing individual variations within traditionally determined designs.

Folk-art of this kind includes the purely domestic (e.g. *Easter eggs, *Christmas decorations); communal artistic creation (*well-dressing); objects made and displayed by an occupational group, or by children, in expectation of reward (*Jack-in-the-Green, *May garlands, *grottoes, the *poppy show); carts temporarily decorated for seasonal celebrations (*rushbearing, *harvest home); *effigies to be burnt. More substantial objects, designed to be repeatedly used at annual events, include many costumes and masks worn by participants in folk drama, dancing, and pageantry, such as *hobby horses and processional *giants and *dragons. Many are comic, or mock-horrific. A few objects, notably *corn dollies, were displayed for a year and then des-

troyed; the funereal *Maidens' Garlands were meant to be permanent. All were made, not bought; all show the interplay of traditional patterns and individual variation which is the essence of folklore.

In pre-industrial England, most men's crafts were utilitarian, their beauty depending on the match between form and function, rather than ornament; only a few working groups made much use of colour, mainly carters and boatmen. Decorative woodcarving is found on furniture and a few personal items such as pipes, whips, tool-handles, walking sticks, and shepherds' crooks. Certain intricately chip-carved objects were fashioned by men not for their own use but as love-tokens; notable examples are the Yorkshire knitting sheaths, whose shape and ornamentation varies from one dale to the next, and Yorkshire stay-busks (Brears, 1989: 46–62, 75–80; Lambert and Marx, 1989: 20–1).

Women's needlework emphasized ornament; lace-making, smocking, embroidery, tapestry, and beadwork were always popular, among those who could afford the materials. One widespread product was the sampler, a small linen square displaying different stitches in silk or wool, made by children to prove their skill; its centrepiece was lettering, usually expressing piety, surrounded by pictorial decoration. Elaborate satin or velvet pincushions were made as christening presents, shining pinheads forming patterns and a message (e.g. 'Welcome, little stranger'). Women also made sturdy rag-rugs from strips of cloth threaded through hessian in attractive designs, especially in the northern counties (Brears, 1989: 140–51). This region also had a vigorous quilting tradition, using embroidery, patchwork, and appliqué; many nineteenth-century examples survive.

Ornamental objects created by local craftsmen as a means of public communication included carved or painted inn signs and trade signs, ships' figureheads, weathervanes, and tombstones. They were handmade, and offered scope for lively invention within a shared tradition. In recent decades, 'village signs' have become popular in East Anglia.

When discussing material objects in an industrialized society, it is hard to know where to draw the line between 'folk culture' and 'popular culture'. Items such as fairground souvenirs, greetings cards, mourning jewellery, or religious pictures have been factory-made since early Victorian times, and hence fairly standardized; yet they are used as adjuncts to festivities and life-cycle events which are essentially folkloric. Their designs may also be rooted in folk tradition. On this level, folk/popular art has been, and still is, abundant.

Towards the middle of the 19th century, various social groupings began using conspicuous objects, created by industrial techniques, to symbolize their identity. There were large, bright pictorial banners used in street parades by many organizations, religious and secular, especially Temperance Clubs and Trade Union branches. Painted on rubberized silk and adorned with fringes and tassels, they conveyed the aims of the organization through realistic or symbolic figures, mottoes, heraldic devices, and portraits of leaders.

Gaudy decoration characterized the world of popular amusements: music halls, pubs, fairs, and circuses. Here too the 19th century saw an increase of industrial products, but individual craftsmen and amateurs were still active. What is now thought of as a 'Gypsy caravan', a one-roomed dwelling mounted on a horse-drawn cart, originated among fairground showmen of the early 19th century, and was adopted by *Gypsies around 1850. Its multicoloured paintwork, covering every inch of the exterior and much of the internal fittings, constitutes a distinctive artform with scrolls, flowers, and horses as its typical motifs; though such waggons were made by specialist firms, they were exclusively used by two marginal social groups, showmen and Gypsies, and proclaimed their identity.

Another working group using mobile homes was the canal bargees and their families, and they too compensated for cramped quarters by colourful decoration. Canal boat art, first described in 1873, combines geometric designs with flowers and romantic landscapes, applied not only to the boat but to all its furnishings, and even utensils such as basins and pails. The artists were generally the boatbuilders, but sometimes the bargees themselves.

Peter Brears, 1989; Lambert and Marx, 1989; Averil Colby, *Samplers Yesterday and Today* (1964); Anne Sebba, *Samplers: Five Centuries of a Gentle Craft* (1979); John Gorman, *Banner Bright* (1973); M. FitzRandolph, *Traditional Quilting* (1953); Rosemary Allen, *North Country Quilts and Coverlets* (1987); C. H. Ward-Jackson and D. E. Harvey, *The English Gypsy Caravan* (1972); Tony Lewery, 'Rose, Castle and Canal', *Folklore* 106 (1995), 43–56.

Arthur. Arthurian literature is beyond the scope of the present work, as is the problem of Arthur's historical setting. One theme, however, the belief that Arthur is not dead and will return, remained rooted in the popular mind throughout the centuries. The earliest references come from *Celtic areas—a Welsh poem which remarks cryptically, 'A mystery until Doomsday is the grave of Arthur'; a mention of a fight which broke out at Bodmin (Cornwall) in 1113 because some Frenchmen laughed at a local man who assured them Arthur was alive; allusions to an obstinate belief among Bretons that he would return.

By the time Malory wrote, in the 1460s, the tomb at *Glastonbury containing a coffin alleged to be Arthur's was famous, but he does not mention it. Instead, he first says that a ship full of fair ladies bore Arthur away to 'the vale of Avilion' to be healed, but then that they returned that night with a corpse, and asked a hermit to bury it; finally, he says there were many tales, both written and oral, and he cannot decide between them:

No more of the very certainty of his death I never read, but thus was he led away in a ship wherein were three queens. . . . [These] ladies brought him to his burials . . . but yet the hermit knew not in certain that it was verily the body of King Arthur. . . . Yet some men say in many parts of England that Arthur is not dead, but had by the will of Our Lord Jesu into another place, and men say that he shall come again, and he shall win the Holy Cross. I will not say it shall be so, but rather I will say, here in this world he changed his life. But many men say that there is written upon his tomb this verse: *Hic jacet Arthurus, Rex quondam Rexque futurus* ['Here lies Arthur, former King and future King']. (*Morte d'Arthur*, book 21, chapter 7).

Part of this derives from *Geoffrey of Monmouth, who says Arthur was taken by boat to *Avalon, an island paradise where nine queens would heal him. Folk tradition, however, claims he is sleeping in some secret cavern with his knights round him until his country needs him—a tale told of great kings and heroes throughout Europe. It is localized at several places in Britain, the main English ones being *Cadbury Castle (Somerset), Richmond Castle (Yorkshire), and Sewingshields Castle (Northumberland). It tells how a farmer, or a potter, happens upon a secret entrance in the hillside, leading to an underground chamber where Arthur and his knights lie sleeping, surrounded by weapons and treasures, including a sword and a horn. At this point, the man blunders; either he draws the sword but fails to blow the horn, or he runs away without doing either. He can never find the entrance again.

Arthur's name is attached to a number of other sites, sometimes in such a way as to imply that he was imagined as a *giant. There is a huge crag called Arthur's Seat near Sewingshields, a megalith called Arthur's Quoit at Trethevy (Cornwall), and another called Arthur's Stone at Hereford, with dents said to be the marks of his knees. There are also places linked to events in the medieval romances, either in the old texts themselves, or by later speculation. For instance, it is said that Excalibur was thrown into either Looe Pool or Dozmary Pool (both in Cornwall).

Other beliefs, more rarely recorded, are that Arthur leads the *Wild Hunt, and that he lives on as a *raven.

See also *ALDERLEY EDGE, *ROUND TABLE.

Westwood, 1985: 5–8, 18–21, 29, 241–5, 313–15, 370–1.

arum lilies. These are among the *white *flowers considered unlucky to bring indoors or into a hospital. They are much used at funerals, and for church decoration at Easter.

Ascension Day. This marks the ascension of Christ into heaven, and being the fortieth day after Easter Sunday it always falls on a Thursday (hence its other name, Holy Thursday), though the actual date changes yearly. A custom of processing around the parish in order to invoke divine protection and to bless the crops and livestock at this time was adopted by the Church in England in the 8th century, although it had been practised on the Continent for centuries before that time. The three days before Ascension, when the processions took place, became variously known as Rogation, Processioning, Ganging (going), or Cross (from the crucifix carried) days, and the processions themselves could be quite spectacular, carrying crosses, banners, and garlands, and prayers and hymns being given at key points around the parish. There is some evidence that the Rogation customs in some areas had begun to get out of hand and were suppressed, but others continued until they were abolished by the Puritans in the 17th century. In the meantime, however, the relatively secular need for identifying and

maintaining parish boundaries had become apparent, and as this became grafted on to the old religious custom, the better-known *Beating the Bounds developed. In many areas, Beating the whole Bounds of a parish can take a considerable time, and it was deemed sufficient to undertake it sporadically rather than annually. For those interested in the blessing rather than the beating, smaller-scale customs evolved.

Few other customs took place on Ascension Day, although some beliefs connected the Day with water. In many areas it was the day for visiting local holy *wells, either for cures (especially sore eyes) or for luck (*Trans. of the Devonshire Assoc.* 40 (1908), 190–2). A children's custom reported at different times of the year, under different names, involved mixing water from a particular well or spring with sugar or sweets to make a special drink. In some areas this was carried out on Ascension Day and called 'Sugar and Water Day' (see also *Easter, *elecampane, and *Spanish Sunday). Rain which fell on Ascension Day was similarly believed to be special as coming 'straight from heaven', and was collected and stored for medicinal use, and again sore eyes are mentioned regularly. In addition, the popular custom of *well-dressing occurs at Ascension in some villages. Several beliefs about the prevention of *fires had an Ascension Day slant— a piece of hawthorn gathered on the day and brought to you (i.e. not picked yourself) and hung in the rafters is reported from Staffordshire (*Folk-Lore* 7 (1896), 381), whereas in Nottinghamshire it was an egg laid on the day which should be placed somewhere in the roof (Jewitt, *Ancient Customs and Sports of Nottinghamshire* (1852)). In Shropshire, it was believed that rooks take a rest from their nest-building on Ascension Day (Burne, 1883: 218), and in Lincolnshire it was said that to hang sheets out to dry or air on this day was a sure way to bring a death to the family (compare *Good Friday, and *washing) (*The Times*, 8 May 1934). A belief was reported from the West Country in the 18th century (more usually linked to Easter), that the figure of a lamb could be seen in the rising sun (*Gentleman's Magazine* (1787), 718, quoted in Brand, 1849: i. 197).

For other Ascension Day customs, see *HUNTING THE EARL OF RONE, *WELL-DRESSING, WHITBY *PENNY HEDGE.

Wright and Lones, 1938: i. 129–48; Brand, 1849: i. 197–212; Hutton, 1996: 277–9.

Ashbourne Royal Shrovetide Football.
One of the few surviving street *football games
takes place at *Shrovetide in Ashbourne, Derbyshire. The first known mention of the Ashbourne game is in 1683, by Charles Cotton in
his *Burlesque on the Great Frost*, 'two towns, that
long that war had waged being at football now
engaged' but it is likely to be much older than
that. The game is played between two teams,
of indeterminate size, called the Upp'ards and
the Down'ards, i.e. those who live above or
below the Henmore Stream which flows
through the town. Two mills, over two miles
apart, are the respective goals, and the ball can
be kicked, thrown, or carried, but must not be
transported by car. Much of the time the ball is
in the middle of a mass scrum, or 'hug', and
travels very slowly. The balls are handmade in
the village, of stitched leather, and much decorated, but they sometimes get torn to pieces
during the game. Sometimes two, very
occasionally three, games can be played in a
day, and the game is staged both on Shrove
Tuesday and *Ash Wednesday. In the mid-19th
century, there were determined and increasing
attempts to suppress the game altogether and
regular clashes between players and police
occurred. A workable compromise was reached
in 1862/3 when it was agreed to move the game
out of the Market Square and town streets
where it had formerly raged, on to an open site
called Shaw Croft on the edge of town where
the crowds would do less damage. In subsequent years, as long as the game stayed out of
the town, it was left alone by the authorities.

Lindsey Porter, *Ashbourne Royal Shrovetide Football: The
Official History* (1992); Kightly, 1986: 205–6.

ashen faggot. Reported only from the West
Country, this was similar to the *Yule Log custom in that the faggot was brought in with
some ceremony and laid on the fire on
Christmas Eve, but it was made of smaller ash
sticks bound into a faggot with strips of hazel,
withy, or bramble. These strips were watched
carefully as there were beliefs and customs
attached to them. In one report from Torquay
in 1836 farmworkers could demand more
cider from the farmer each time a strip burnt
through, while in families it was customary
for each of the children present to choose a
strip and the one whose strip burnt through
first would marry first. The earliest references
to the custom are from the turn of the 19th
century, much later than those for the Yule
Log; the custom still continues in some

homes, and takes place in some West Country
pubs, such as at Curry Rivel (Somerset).

Wright and Lones, 1940: iii. 213–14, 227; G. R. Willey,
Folklore 94:1 (1983), 40–3.

ash (tree). A traditional cure, recorded in
several counties, for young children with her-
nias; an ash sapling, preferably one grown
from seed and never touched by a knife, was
split down the middle and held open with
wedges, the child was passed through the gap,
and the damaged tree tightly bound up—as its
cleft healed, so the hernia would disappear.
Descriptions of the procedure from the 19th
century include further ritualistic details: it
must be done at dawn, with the child naked
and held face up; or it must be done by *nine
people, from west to east, on nine successive
mornings; or it must be done at *midnight,
nine times, in complete silence. The tree must
not be cut down during the child's lifetime .

The tree's other major use was for curing
lameness, pains, and swellings in cattle, supposedly caused by a *shrew running over
them. A shrew would be thrust into a deep
hole bored into an ash tree, and the hole
plugged up; once the shrew was dead, any
animal whipped with twigs from that tree
would be cured. A famous shrew-ash in
Richmond Park was frequently visited, in the
mid-19th century, by women bringing
sickly children for healing, especially from
whooping cough.

Other beliefs are that snakes cannot bear to
be near an ash, or even its leaves or a stick cut
from its wood; and that anyone carrying ash-
keys cannot be bewitched. A well-known
rhyme predicts how rainy the spring will be
from the relative dates of budding by oak and
ash; another warns that ashes attract
lightning:

> Avoid the ash,
> It draws the flash.

See also *ASHEN FAGGOT, *ASH WEDNESDAY,
*SHREW, *THUNDER. For mountain ash, see
*ROWAN.

Vickery, 1995: 14–19; Opie and Tatem, 1989: 5–8, 355–6.

Ash Wednesday. Some children's seasonal
games used traditionally to begin on this date,
notably *marbles. In Sussex, Hampshire, and
Middlesex up to the 1950s, children brought
an ash-twig with a black bud on it to school;
any who were caught without one would be
pinched or stamped on by the others, up until

noon. Some maintained that it must then be thrown away at once (Vickery, 1995: 17). This must be related to the Catholic ritual of blackening one's brow with ashes, but whether as parody or as misunderstanding of the word 'ash' is impossible to say; it also echoes a *Royal Oak Day custom.

astrology. One of the clearest examples of an item of culture originating among intellectuals, but passing to the peasantry. Throughout much of its long history, it derived its authority from complex mathematics and philosophical speculations; its prestige was high in courts and universities in medieval and Renaissance Europe, and as late as the English Civil War it was still important in political propaganda. Its symbols and concepts were also diffused through cheap printed almanacs, and were used in simplified forms by farmers, magicians, healers, and fortune-tellers (Davies, 1999a: 229–46).

During the 18th and 19th centuries astrology became marginalized, and by the early 20th century had virtually disappeared from public view. However, it was given fresh life by a press stunt in 1930, when the *Sunday Express* invited an astrologer to draw up a nativity chart for the newborn Princess Margaret, and to compile a simple horoscope applying to anyone whose birthday fell that week. Other newspapers copied the idea, encouraging semi-serious curiosity about astrology; like other aspects of the occult, it is currently enjoying a revival.

See also DR JOHN *DEE.

Aubrey, John (1626–1697). Best known now for his *Brief Lives*, published long after his death, Aubrey was an inveterate collector of gossip, trifles, natural history and 'antiquities', and, as such, one of our earliest folklorists. He was, however, much more of a collector than a writer. Only one book (*Miscellanies*) was published in his own lifetime, but he left copious manuscripts which others have put into shape since his death. Aubrey was unique amongst the early antiquaries in that

he was interested in the beliefs, customs, and stories of the people. Amongst his contemporaries he was regarded as gullible, and many since have made the same judgement, but it is not necessary to care whether he *believed* in wonders, only to be grateful that he *recorded* them. He lived in extremely interesting times, and his lifespan covered not only the Civil Wars (1642–8), rule of Cromwell, and the Restoration of the monarchy (1660) but also the Great Plague (1665–6), Great Fire of London (1666), and much more. He appears to have steered clear of the raging political and religious controversies of his time, but as an antiquarian he was particularly aggrieved not only by the Puritan destruction of churches and their contents but also by the changes which were sweeping English society, including wars and literacy: 'Printing and Gunpowder have frighted away Robin-good-fellow and the Fayries' (*Remaines*, 67–8). The two works of particular interest to folklorists are *Miscellanies* (1696) and *Remaines of Gentilisme and Judaisme*, which existed as a manuscript in the British Museum (Landsdowne MSS 231) until published by The Folklore Society in 1880, edited and annotated by James Britten. Both *Miscellanies* and *Remaines* were again published along with a further manuscript entitled *Observations*, as *Three Prose Works*, edited by John Buchanan-Brown (1972).

DNB; Dorson, 1968.

Avalon. *Geoffrey of Monmouth notes briefly in his *History* that King *Arthur 'was carried to the Island of Avalon for the healing of his wounds'; in a later work, *The Life of Merlin*, he elaborates upon this, saying Avalon is ruled by nine sisters, the eldest and wisest being Morgan. It is an earthly paradise, also called The Island of Apples or the Fortunate Isle, where crops grow untended, 'apple trees spring up from the short grass of its woods', and men live for a hundred years or more. Geoffrey obviously associated its name with Welsh *afellenau* = 'apple trees', and with classical descriptions of the Fortunate Islands. Others, however, identified it with *Glastonbury.

Baa Baa Black Sheep. One of the most widely known of our *nursery rhymes whose somewhat oblique words and simple tune have been used as a *lullaby and early-learning song for centuries. The first known publication was in *Tommy Thumb's Pretty Song Book* of c.1744, which shows that the text has hardly altered since. The line 'Three bags full' has become an English idiom in its own right, as a parody of servile agreement to unreasonable demands.

Opie and Opie, 1997: 101.

babies. Certain circumstances at birth were thought to foretell the baby's future character or *luck, e.g. a rhyme about *days of the week, best known in the version:

> Monday's child is fair of face,
> Tuesday's child is full of grace,
> Wednesday's child is full of woe,
> Thursday's child has far to go,
> Friday's child is loving and giving,
> Saturday's child works hard for a living,
> But the child that is born on the Sabbath day
> Is blithe and bonny, good and gay.

A breech birth indicated a trouble-maker ('awkward born, awkward all their lives'); *teeth already visible, a cruel nature; hands open, generosity; a *caul, immunity from drowning. Those born at *midnight on a *Friday, or at the *chime hours, would be able to see *ghosts; those born on a Sunday, or on *Christmas Day, would never be drowned or hanged. Some midwives said the first food to pass the baby's lips should be a spoonful of butter and sugar, to give 'a sweet nature'.

One widespread rule was that the baby's first move should be upwards, so that it 'rises' in life; if possible, this was done by carrying it to a higher storey or an attic, but if there was none, then the midwife should climb on to a stool with the baby in her arms. She should also wrap it in some old shirt or petticoat before putting its proper clothes on, to avert bad luck. In Cumberland, the baby's head was washed with rum for luck, and in Suffolk with gin; everywhere it was (and is) usual to drink its health, which is called 'wetting the baby's head'. In earlier times, *salt, *iron, or *rowan twigs might be put in the cradle as protection against witches and fairies.

In some areas, it was thought wrong to take a baby out of the house before the day of its *baptism. Writers from the late 18th century onwards say that in northern counties when a baby is first taken to visit some relative or neighbour, the latter should present it with 'a cake of bread, an egg, and a small quantity of salt'; if this is not done the baby will grow up poor, but if it is, he/she will be rich and lucky (Hone, 1827: ii, cols. 21–2). Matches, representing light, were sometimes given as well. The corresponding modern custom, now very widespread, also applies to people visiting the house where the new baby lives, and to those meeting it for the first time in the street; the essential gift is now a *silver coin.

Until the baby was a year old, two further rules were common: do not cut the finger- or toenails with *scissors, but bite them off instead, or he/she will grow up a thief; do not allow him/her to look into a *mirror, or he/she will become conceited.

See also *BAPTISM, *CAULS, *CHILDBIRTH, *PREGNANCY.

Radford, Radford, and Hole, 1961: 95–7, 118–19; Opie and Tatem, 1989: 10–13, 274–5.

backwards. The notion that walking backwards is unlucky was occasionally noted in the mid-19th century from the Lancashire/Yorkshire area: '[Lancashire] children are frequently cautioned by their parents not to walk backwards when going on an errand; it is a sure sign they will be unfortunate in their objects' (*N&Q* 1s:3 (1851), 55). Similarly, getting out of *bed backwards brought bad luck.

But recipes for *love divinations, such as making the *dumb cake, commonly require the participants to walk backwards when going to bed, perhaps to heighten the feeling of 'otherness' in the proceedings, or perhaps only to make things more difficult.

In black *magic, to say or do something backwards symbolizes evil intent. Clear instances are a 17th-century *curse with the name of the victim written backwards; and a Lincolnshire tradition that witches must renew allegiance to the Devil annually by walking backwards round a church on *St Mark's Eve (Rudkin, 1936: 73). Nowadays, a common but none too serious idea is that one can raise the Devil by saying the Lord's Prayer backwards.

See also *LEFTWARD MOVEMENT.

Opie and Tatem, 1989: 422.

Bacup Britannia Coconut Dancers. The Coconut Dancers (or Nutters) parade the Lancashire mill-town of Bacup, every *Easter Saturday, performing their dances to the sound of the local silver band. There are eight male dancers, plus a whipper-in who helps to control the traffic. Their processional dance alternates between jogging along the road and a stationary part in which they clap together the wooden 'coconuts' (bobbin tops from the mill) which each dancer has strapped to his hands, knees, and waist. At certain points in the town, the group stops and performs one or more of their five garland dances. Standing in square 'quadrille' formation, each dancer holds a decorated semi-circular hoop above his head. The dancers wear strange colourful costumes and blackened faces. The present team can trace their lineage back to the early 1920s, when their predecessors, based at the Britannia Mill, were taught the dance by the Tunstead Mill Nutters, also from the Bacup area. The first documented reference to the Tunstead Mill Nutters is in 1907, but as this consists of reports of the team celebrating their jubilee, a starting date of 1857 is pretty definite. There are indications that there were other teams around at the time.

Theresa Buckland, *FMJ* 5:2 (1985), 132–49; Shuel, 1985: 45–6.

Baddeley cake. When Robert Baddeley, former chef turned actor, died in 1794, he left £100 for the annual provision of wine and a *Twelfth Night cake to be shared by the current company at the Theatre Royal, Drury

Lane, London. The custom still continues, and every year on 6 January the cast of whichever show is on at the time gathers, still in costume and make-up, in the Grand Saloon where the cake is served by attendants in 18th century dress, and Robert Baddeley is duly remembered.

Shuel, 1985: 127–8; Brian Shuel, *FLS News* 13 (1991), 1–2.

Bainbridge hornblower. The Bainbridge horn is blown every evening in this North Yorkshire town, at 9 p.m., between 28 September and Shrove Tuesday. Unlike the hornblowing custom at nearby *Ripon, the origin of this custom is obscure. Some have tried to link it with Roman times, but it is more likely to date from when Bainbridge was the administrative centre of the Forest of Wensleydale, and the sound of the horn was designed to guide benighted travellers to safety. This would date it to medieval times, but the first known mention is in 1823.

Kightly, 1986: 141; Smith, 1989: 142–5.

baiting, see *BLOOD SPORTS.

Balfour, Marie Clothilde. A collector of folklore in Northumberland and Lincolnshire, the most interesting items being eleven folktales from the latter, published in *Folk-Lore* 2 (1891), 145–70, 257–83, 401–18. Most have no parallels elsewhere, and are tragic and macabre; their supernatural beings (*bogles, *Tiddy Men, *Yallery Brown) are grim, and have to be propitiated with offerings. Mrs Balfour claimed to tell the tales 'exactly as told' to her, but her reliability has been queried (Philip 1992: 156).

Philip, 1992: 150–7, 409–15; Jacobs, 1890/1968: 163–7, 178–80, 185–7, 193–7, 211–14, 224–8; Briggs, 1970–1: A. i. 310–12, 502–5, 577–9; ii. 41–2, 238–40.

ballads. Folklorists view ballads as a subdivision of folk *song, whereas literary scholars are more likely to treat them as a subgenre of poetry. The word 'ballad' is highly ambiguous, but, except in the specialist sense of *broadside ballad, folklorists usually use 'ballad' to refer to the 'traditional ballads' included in collections starting with Thomas *Percy's *Reliques of Early English Poetry* (1765) and later identified and collected together by F. J. *Child in his monumental *English and Scottish Popular Ballads* (5 volumes, 1882–98). Percy provided the first substantial source of ballad material for both scholar and poet, which became enormously influential in literary circles. Similarly, it is difficult to overstate the influence which Child's collection had over the field of ballad studies. His collection of 305 pieces rapidly became regarded as a closed canon and until recently few dared to question it. It is unfortunate that Child died before he could write the major essays which he planned to accompany the texts, as his criteria for inclusion now appear inconsistent, and instead of trying to construct a definition against which particular items can be measured, many later scholars have attempted to arrive at a definition which includes all the pieces in Child's work. They have thus largely failed, and have had to be content with description rather than definition. Nevertheless, the rule-of-thumb definition that a ballad is a 'narrative folk-song' is a useful starting-point. According to Richmond, the ballad

is usually anonymous, it concentrates on a single episode, it begins *in media res*, it is dramatic in its narrative structure, and it is impersonal (objective) in its telling. Moreover, it is always stanzaic, either seven- or eight-stress rhymed couplets or quatrains rhyming a, b, c, b, and generally alternates light and heavy stresses in each line. In addition, a repetition of words, phrases, and stanzas is common, not only in individual ballads but also in the genre as a whole . . . (Richmond, 1989: p. xx).

The corpus includes ballads on a range of topics, which can be roughly classified by subject: Robin Hood ballads, Border ballads (Hunting the Cheviot, Battle of Otterburn), Tragic ballads (Sir Patrick Spens, Cruel Brother, Lord Randal), Enchantment and Fairy ballads (Tam Lin, Thomas Rhymer), and one or two Christian carols/ballads (Cherry Tree Carol, St Stephen and Herod). For many of them the only evidence for their traditional status is in the manuscript collections of the past, while others such as Barbara Allen, The Gypsy Laddie, Lord Bateman, and Lord Thomas and Fair Ellender remained extremely popular and were noted time and again by 19th- and 20th-century folk-song collectors on both sides of the Atlantic.

Ballad scholarship has embraced many analytical perspectives, following the intellectual fashions of the day, including various linguistic, psychological, and literary approaches, and engendered a number of its own bitter controversies, starting with *Ritson's acerbic attack on Percy's editorial standards, and continuing with the 'ballad war' in the early 20th century between the communalists and the individualists who argued over origins and early development (see Wilgus for a summary).

The narrative nature of the ballad ensures that scholars often find it difficult to adhere to national boundaries, and, as Child amply illustrates, the British tradition can be usefully compared with those of other European countries, especially from Scandinavia, while Scotland is generally agreed to have a stronger ballad tradition than England. Much of the best ballad criticism and analysis has emanated from North America, but so much of ballad scholarship came from literary and linguistic quarters that the musical side of balladry was relatively neglected. The indefatigable champion of ballad tunes was Bertrand H. Bronson, who, from the 1950s onwards, attempted to redress the balance with a series of articles and books, culminating in the four-volume set entitled *The Traditional Tunes of the Child Ballads* (1959–72) which stands beside Child's collection as the bedrock of scholarship. Bronson was fond of asking, 'When is a ballad not a ballad?—When it has no tune'.

W. Edson Richmond, *Ballad Scholarship: An Annotated Bibliography* (1989); D. K. Wilgus, *Anglo-American Folksong Scholarship Since 1898* (1959); MacEdward Leach and Tristram P. Coffin, *The Critics and the Ballad* (1961); David Buchan, *The Ballad and the Folk* (1972).

Bampton Morris Dancers. Bampton, Oxfordshire, has one of the best-known *morris traditions in the country, and is one of the few villages which can claim an unbroken tradition (apart from during the First World War) of dancing over the past 150 years. The earliest written reference is in Revd J. A. Giles's *History of the Parish and Town of Bampton* (1847, p. lxv) in a passage which is relatively dismissive of the dancers, but at least proves their existence at that time, and implies an already established tradition. Village tradition claims a much longer history of two, three, or even six hundred years, but although two hundred years is possible given the family traditions involved, the other two figures are unsubstantiated. As with most teams in the area, the traditional time for Bampton morrismen to dance was previously *Whitsun but it is now Spring *Bank Holiday. They dance what scholars term 'Cotswold' morris, with most dances being for six men, carrying white handkerchiefs. They dress in white, bells strapped to their shins, and wearing black hats trimmed with flowers. They also have a 'fool' character, and a cake-bearer who carries a large cake in a tin, impaled on a sword which itself is decorated with flowers and ribbons. Onlookers get a piece of cake when they make a donation. The musician is nowadays a fiddle or melodeon-player, but until the mid-19th century was a pipe and taborer.

Cecil *Sharp included the Bampton dances in the third volume of his *Morris Book*, and from that time on the village morris has attracted visitors from a wide area. This outside attention helped to keep the tradition going when other teams faded away, but the contribution of particular families, and individuals such as William 'Jingy' Wells, Arnold Woodley, and Francis Shergold, in keeping the dance alive must also be acknowledged.

Cecil Sharp, *The Morris Book*, iii (2nd edn., 1924); Keith Chandler, *Morris Dancing at Bampton until 1914* (1983); Keith Chandler, *Musical Traditions* 10 (1992), 18–24; Chandler, 1993.

banging-out. The custom designed to mark the ending of a worker's apprenticeship. See *OCCUPATIONAL LORE and *PRINTING TRADE.

Bank Holidays. The institution of Bank Holidays had a profound effect on the leisure patterns of the working classes, and affected the traditional *calendar in that many customs were pulled from their traditional days to take place on the nearest Bank Holiday. They were introduced to sort out a long-standing problem in the financial world by allowing bills of exchange which fell due on national holidays to be payable on the following day; thus allowing banks to close on those holidays. In addition, they were part of the drive to regularize holidays for working people. The Bank Holidays Act of 1871, strenuously promoted by Sir John Lubbock (later Lord Avebury), stipulated (for England) *Easter Monday, *Whit Monday, the first Monday of August, and *Boxing Day (26 December), in addition to *Christmas Day and *Good Friday which were already holidays under common law. This pattern remained unchanged until the 1970s when the moveable Whitsun was replaced by a fixed Spring Bank Holiday; New Year's Day was added in 1974; and *May Day (or the first Monday in May) was added in 1978. In the late 1980s, a government plan to replace May Day by a later holiday (e.g. Trafalgar Day, 21 October) came to nothing after much public debate.

J. A. R. Pimlott, *The Englishman's Holiday* (1947); *The Times* (various dates throughout 1871); *Encyclopaedia Britannica*.

baptism. Also called christening, this is for most denominations an essential act; many theologians taught that infants dying *unbaptized could never enter Heaven—a doctrine reflected in the unwillingness to give them proper burial. In popular belief it was also assumed that unbaptized babies were in danger from demons, witches, and fairies. At the same time, christening was (and is) a ceremony asserting the baby's membership of a family and social group; the choice of godparents, for instance, often has more to do with social bonding than religious upbringing. Name-giving, accompanied by presents and celebration, ratifies the child's status; the need for such a ritual is so strongly felt that some now wish to devise an official but non-religious ceremony as its civic equivalent.

An interesting custom in working-class areas of Newcastle and Durham was for parents taking a baby to baptism to have with them a paper bag containing a cheese sandwich and a slice of cake, and a *silver coin, and sometimes a *candle and *salt; this had to be given to the first person of the sex opposite to the baby's whom the christening party saw on their way to church, or at the church gate after the ceremony. This was still being done in the 1970s (*FLS News* 11 (1990), 4–6; 12 (1991), 10–13).

In folk tradition, various *taboos and beliefs surrounded baptism. The chosen name must not be used in advance, nor should the baby go out of the house until taken to the church for the ceremony, for it was in danger itself and a possible source of bad luck to others; if the mother's *churching had not yet taken place, she could not attend the christening. The baby should cry when sprinkled with the baptismal water, to show the Devil has been driven out; some said a silent baby would not live long. If several were to be baptized at once, boys must precede girls; in northern counties, it was said that if this rule was broken the boy would never grow a beard, but the girl would (Henderson, 1866: 9). It was widely held that fretful or sickly babies, especially those suffering from fits, would improve in health once baptized.

See also *NAMES, *UNBAPTIZED BABIES.

Radford, Radford, and Hole, 1961: 27–30, 172; Opie and Tatem, 1989: 72–4.

bargest, barguest. This is the name for a particularly alarming shape-changing *bogey animal in the folklore of Yorkshire, Lancashire, and other northern areas, which might be encountered at stiles and in dark lanes, or near churchyards. Sometimes it was only heard, not seen; it howled and shrieked, and to hear it was an *omen of someone's approaching death—possibly one's own. If visible, it might be 'a frightful goblin with teeth and claws', a headless man, a cat, a rabbit, or most often a *Black Dog, whose coming would set all the real dogs in the district chasing after it and howling.

Thomas Wright, *English Dialect Dictionary, s.v.*, and quotations given there; Henderson, 1866: 239.

Baring-Gould, Sabine (1834–1924). Ordained in 1864, he served in several parishes, but in 1881 he appointed himself rector of the estate of Lew Trenchard (Devon) which he had inherited in 1872, and he remained there as squire and parson till his death. In a long and busy life, he was involved in numerous fields and wrote over 200 books, including 40 novels, travel books (West Country, Iceland, France, etc.), archaeology, hagiography, mythology, history, biography, folklore, and folk-song, in addition to hymns (including 'Onward Christian Soldiers', *c.*1864), sermons, and numerous articles, and in his day was a tremendously popular author. Perhaps it is inevitable that in scholarly terms his output is more notable for its quantity than its quality, but in this as in everything his achievements were erratic, ranging from the excellent to the not very good.

Baring-Gould's interests roamed over many aspects of folklore, but it is in his folk-song collections that Baring-Gould made a lasting contribution. He was one of the first of the Victorian folk-song enthusiasts in the field, commencing his collecting in 1888, and publishing *Songs of the West* (1891) and *A Garland of Country Song* (1895). His books inspired others, such as Anne *Gilchrist, to take an interest, but his cavalier attitude to both texts and tunes gave him a bad name with other collectors. Nevertheless, he was one of the few of his generation who showed an interest in the singers as well as the songs, and he left several descriptions of the old men and women from whom he collected and whom he manifestly loved for their own sake. He commented, in his *Reminiscences*: 'To this day I consider the recovery of our Westcountry melodies has been the principal achievement of my life' (quoted in Dickinson, 1970: 123). He also had an extensive knowledge, and collection, of *broadsides and *chapbooks which he put to good use in his historical notes. Cecil *Sharp took Baring-Gould in hand for a revised edition of *Songs of the West* in 1905, the edition which is now accepted as the best, and the two men also collaborated on *English Folk Songs for Schools* (1906). His other song venture was the six-volume *English Minstrelsie* (1895–7), a meandering collection of art, popular, and folk-song, with his valuable and authoritative notes on the songs and often on the performers of bygone days. Baring-Gould left a mass of material when he died and his vast manuscripts are only now being identified and made available.

DNB; Bickford H. C. Dickinson, *Sabine Baring-Gould: Squarson, Writer and Folklorist* (1970); Harold Kirk-Smith, *Now the Day is Over: The Life and Times of Sabine Baring-Gould* (1997); William E. Purcell, *Onward Christian Soldier: A Life of Sabine Baring-Gould* (1957).

Barley-Break. A popular chasing game, mentioned often in literary sources of the 16th to 18th centuries, played either by children or young people of both sexes. The game reconstructed by the Opies involved three mixed-sex pairs of players. One pair stood in the middle of the playing area (called 'hell'), and one pair stood at each end. The two end pairs had to change partners, without being caught by the middle pair, and the latter had to hold hands throughout. An alternative name was 'Last Couple in Hell'.

The earliest mention of the game is found in Henry's Machyn's Diary of 19 April 1557: 'The sam owre master parsun and entryd in-to helle, and ther ded at the barle breyke with alle the wyffe of the sam parryche'. Other early references include Sir Philip Sidney (*Arcadia*, written in 1580s), Shakespeare and Fletcher (*Two Noble Kinsmen*, IV. iii, 1634), and Robert *Herrick (*Hesperides*, 1648). Other descriptions imply different ways of playing and suggest that it derives its name from originally being played in the farmyard around the stacks.

Opie and Opie, 1969:128–30; Gomme, 1884: i. 21–3; Hazlitt, 1905: 28–9.

barring-out. A widespread custom, up to the 19th century, was the 'barring-out' of the schoolteacher by his pupils. On a day sanctioned by custom (but varying from place to place), the pupils contrived to bar the door with the teacher outside, often with his connivance, and refused to let him in until he agreed to their terms, which were usually for a half-holiday, or something similar. By the 19th century the custom was relatively controlled, but in previous generations had been much rougher. On at least one occasion, in Scotland in 1595, a magistrate who was helping the teacher gain access to the school was shot dead by one of the pupils. Not surprisingly, local authorities waged a continual war against such activities and gradually succeeded in taming and, eventually, eliminating the custom.

Rex Cathcart, *History Today* (Dec. 1988), 49–5; Chambers, 1878: i. 238–9; Brand, 1849: i. 441–54; Hone, 1832: 653–4; *N&Q* 187 (1944), 37, 83–4, 218–19.

barrows. Prehistoric burial mounds commonly attract legends. The fact that they are graves was often correctly remembered (or guessed?), but the dating would be inaccurate—they might be linked to Vikings, medieval heroes, or men killed in the Civil War. Long barrows naturally suggested the idea of a giant's grave, as at Castlecarrock (Cumbria). The idea that *fairies live inside them is much rarer in England than abroad, but see *Willy Howe; at Pixies' Mound at Stogursey (Somerset) it is said a passing ploughman once mended a broken tool for the pixies and was rewarded with a delicious cake.

*Treasure legends are numerous, encouraged no doubt by occasional finds of prehistoric gold, and of money buried in later centuries for safety; local names such as Money Hills (Hampshire), Goldenlow (Bedfordshire), and Dragonhoard (Oxfordshire) refer to this, even where the tale itself has been forgotten. But it was also thought that to dig into a mound brought supernatural retribution, either immediately in the form of violent thunderstorms or fearsome apparitions, or in long-term bad luck and illness; tales about this seem to be particularly common in Devon.

Grinsell, 1976.

Barwick-in-Elmet maypole. The site in Yorkshire of what was previously claimed to be the tallest *maypole in the country (86 feet), but Ansty in Wiltshire erected a new one (96 feet) in 1982. Every three years the maypole is lowered and removed from its central village site and carried to a nearby field for refurbishment. The stripes are repainted, and the garlands made of cloth rosettes, ribbons, and artificial flowers are repaired or replaced. The villagers elect three Polemen who take

responsibility for this work and for the re-erection of the pole. On Spring Bank Holiday (previously Whit Tuesday), after an afternoon of games and music, the maypole is carried in procession back through the village and put back where it belongs. Traditionally, a young man would climb up the pole to release the ropes and spin the weather vane with a flourish, but modern-day safety and insurance fears have made this less acceptable.

Dalesman 47 (Jan. 1986), 849–50; 58 (Apr. 1996), 51–2; Shuel, 1985: 34; Kightly, 1986: 162; Sykes, 1977: 58–9.

bats. These feature surprisingly little in the standard folklore collections of the 19th and 20th centuries. There is nowadays a general tendency to associate bats with witches, the Devil, and vampires, although this stems more from modern horror films than from traditional lore. Nevertheless, Ella M. Leather reported that 'witches change themselves into the form of animals, usually bats or black cats' (Leather, 1912: 52). A bat flying against a window or, worse, into a room, is counted as very unlucky or even a death *omen. The most common notion about bats, however, is their alleged tendency to get entangled in women's hair, with the extra problem that the hair has to be cut off to extricate the animal.

Wootton, 1986: 75–7; Opie and Tatem, 1989: 14; *N&Q* 160 (1931), 46, 86, 124, 159.

Bawming the Thorn. 'Bawming' means decorating, and the thorn in question is in the centre of the Cheshire village of Appleton. The tree is duly adorned in late June or early July with ribbons, garlands, flags, and so on, nowadays mainly by local children, who also process and sing, but previously by the villagers *en masse*. Successive revivals and changes have seen the custom tamed. The present tree dates from 1967 when it was planted to replace a predecessor which had been blown down. Unsubstantiated tradition maintains that the first tree on the site was a cutting from the famous *Holy Thorn at *Glastonbury.

Kightly, 1986: 47; Hole, 1975: 81.

bay (tree). There were many uses, both practical and symbolic, for the aromatic evergreen leaves of bay (also called laurel); it was much favoured for festive decoration, but at funerals it expressed the hope of resurrection, since it can revive after dying back to its roots. The herbalist John Parkinson wrote in his *Paradisus Terrestris* (1629), 426:

The bay-leaves are necessary both for civil uses and for physic, yes, both for the sick and the sound, both for the living and for the dead. It serveth to adorne the House of God as well as man, to crowne or encircle, as with a garland, the heads of the living, and to sticke and decke forth the bodies of the dead; so that from the cradle to the grave, we still have use of it.

In Pliny's *Natural History* (AD 77), it is said that laurel guards the doorways of great men's houses, and is never struck by lightning. Both ideas passed into English lore; a bay in the garden was thought to protect the house from lightning and keep away witches, the Devil, or (nowadays) bad luck (Opie and Tatem, 1989: 14; Vickery, 1995: 28). Occasionally bay trees wither for no apparent reason, an *omen of death for rulers (Shakespeare, *Richard II*, II. iv).

bears, see *BLOOD SPORTS, *STRAW BEARS.

Beast of Bodmin, see *ALIEN BIG CATS.

Beating the Bounds. In former times, when the parish was an essential unit of both religious and local government organization, it was imperative that the exact parish boundaries be generally known, agreed, and, most important of all, remembered from generation to generation.The custom of perambulating the parish boundaries, or Beating the Bounds as it is usually called now, thus had a very necessary practical purpose, and the curious practices associated with the event were also usually of practical utility. Perambulations usually took place at *Rogationtide and involved both religious and secular officials, as the boundary custom had been grafted on to a much older one of religious processions on *Ascension Day. Many other local residents took part—each of whom would be able to 'bear witness' in any future boundary dispute—and a number of boys were also taken along, to ensure that the knowledge was passed to future generations. These youngsters were useful in that they could be made to clamber through hedges, wade streams, climb over walls, and so on, to ensure that the whole boundary was properly followed, and various customs grew up whereby the boys were bumped on to boundary stones or whipped at key points, 'to make sure they remember'. They were, of course, remunerated in some way. At other key points the clergy would

preach or lead a prayer—'cursed be he that removeth his neighbour's landmark' (Deuteronomy 27: 17) being a favourite text—and a number of local Vicar's or Gospel Oaks are memories of these places. Once the practical aspects of the perambulations faded, and the ceremonial became increasingly meaningless, most of them died out, although there are still sporadic revivals, especially at the time of centenary celebrations or other important local dates. A handful of places still perform the custom on a regular basis, including St Mary the Virgin and St Michael in the Northgate (both in Oxford) and the Liberty of the Tower of London.

Shuel, 1985: 103–6; Kightly, 1986: 49; Angus Winchester, *Discovering Parish Boundaries* (1990).

beds. Numerous beliefs cluster round this most important piece of household furniture, but only those concerned with getting out of bed have been recorded before the mid-19th century, and by the documentary record, the others are all quite recent. The orientation of the bed is vital. A belief reported so far only from the 20th century cautions against sleeping with the foot of the bed towards the door, which is explained by the fact that coffins are carried out feet first. Placing a bed across, rather than in line with floorboards or ceiling beams was held to prevent sleep and, worse, to prolong the death of a dying person (*N&Q* 4s:8 (1871), 322). This is reported regularly from the mid-19th century and into the 1970s, although fitted carpets and plastered ceilings now disguise the orientation of the woodwork in the bedroom.

Making the bed is also ruled by belief. The most-quoted superstition here is that it is unlucky to turn a mattress on a *Friday, or a Sunday (or both): 'Your mistress says that her bed last night was hard and full of lumps; I'm afraid you did not turn it yesterday.' 'Oh no, Ma'am! Yesterday was Friday: it would turn the luck' (*N&Q* 7s:4 (1887), 246). The predicted result varies from having fearful dreams, or losing your sweetheart, to illness and probable death. Again, this is recorded from 1851 onwards, and would seem likely to have faded out as sprung mattresses became the norm. The latest version quoted by Opie and Tatem, from a Hampshire woman in 1983, maintains that 'if you change the sheets on Friday the devil has control of your dreams for a week'. Several other strictures apply, for example if you sit on the bed of a sick person, you will be the next occupant, and three people must not take part in making a bed.

As already mentioned, getting out of bed correctly was important in earlier times: 'Howe happily rose I on my ryghte syde to day, or blessed me well ... this happye or lucky day' (Palsgrave, *Acolastus*, 1540: 90, quoted by Opie and Tatem: 16), and there are numerous 17th-century literary references to the belief (see Lean). A further belief was that it is lucky to get out of bed backwards, provided it was not deliberate. The first known mention is in Congreve's *Love for Love* (1695) and again there are a number of literary references. Two more bed-related superstitions are included under *feathers and *washing.

Opie and Tatem, 1989: 15–17; Lean, 1903: esp. ii. 20–3.

bees. In medieval, Elizabethan, and Stuart times, bees were regarded as mysterious, intelligent, and holy; their wax was used in church *candles, honey was a biblical image for God's grace and the joys of heaven, poets praised the hive as a model for the perfect society, grouped around its 'king' (it was only in the 1740s that English naturalists admitted the large bee was female). Something of this awe remains in a nursery riddle from the 16th century, with the answer 'a bee':

> Little bird of Paradise,
> She works her work both neat and nice;
> She pleases God, she pleases man,
> She does the work that no man can.

(Opie and Opie, 1951: 82–3)

Folk tradition about bees stresses how easily they might take offence, in which case they would cease to give honey, desert their hives, or die. They had to be treated as members of the household; in particular, they must be told about deaths, births, and marriages in the family, their hives must be appropriately adorned, and they must be given their share of the festive or funereal food. They would then hum, to show they consented to remain.

The *funeral custom is frequently described throughout the 19th century:

My mother, who passed most of her youth in the village of Bakewell in Northamptonshire, tells me that the belief in the necessity of telling the bees everything was very strong there. At the death of a sister of hers, some of the cake and wine which was served to the mourners at the funeral was placed inside each hive, in addition to the crape put upon each. At her own wedding in 1849 a small piece of wedding cake was put into each hive. (*Folk-Lore* 3 (1892), 138)

The ceremony of informing bees of their owner's death is in full force in Ashbourne, Derbyshire, Hinton, Wilts, and even in the highly intellectual city of Oxford. The ceremony is the same in all these places. Three taps are made on the hive with the house-key, while the informant repeats, 'Bees, bees, bees, your master is dead, and you must work for ——', naming the future owner. A piece of black crape is then fastened to the hive. Many bee owners think it politic to inform the bees of the death of a relation; but in this case they never give the name, but the degree of relationship, as 'your master's brother, sister, aunt &c. is dead'. On weddings the bees expect to be informed of the auspicious event, and to have their hive decorated with a wedding favour. (*N&Q* 1s:4 (1851), 308)

Such observations could be paralleled from virtually every part of England; many references will be found in *Folklore* and *N&Q*, besides regional books of folklore. Some localities add minor details; in Shropshire and Somerset, for instance, hives had to be lifted or turned as the coffin left the house, while in some Yorkshire villages bees were formally invited to funerals.

Other common beliefs were that quarreling and swearing would drive bees away, and that they must be spoken to in soft tones. They could not tolerate the presence of an unchaste woman, or one who was *menstruating, but would sting her. In the north of England, it was said they could be heard humming hymns on Christmas Eve (Henderson, 1879: 311). Bees must never be bought with ordinary money, only with a gold coin; they can, however, be safely acquired by gift, loan, or barter. A single bee or bumblebee entering a house means good luck, probably in the form of money.

When bees swarmed, it was usual for the women and children of the household to follow them, making a clatter with pots and pans, which was supposed to induce them to settle, and also let everyone know what was happening; it was accepted that in these circumstances one could go on to someone else's land without being charged with trespassing. It was a bad *omen if the swarm settled on a dead branch, meaning death for someone in the owner's family, or for the person seeing the swarm there.

Hilda M. Ransome, *The Sacred Bee* (1937; reprint, 1986), 211–32; Radford, Radford, and Hole, 1961: 38–40; Opie and Tatem, 1989: 17–21.

beetles. Apart from *ladybirds, beetles do not have much of their own lore in English tradition. The only belief regularly reported (from the 1870s to the present day) is that to kill one brings rain. The beetle also turns up in medicine, as for example in a report from Lindsey (Lincolnshire): a small girl was sent by her mother to ask that if anyone found a beetle—by accident it had to be—could they keep it as her sister had the whooping cough and they wanted to tie it round her neck, so that as it decayed the cough would go too (N&Q 3s:9 (1866), 319). It is more common in England to find spiders used in this context. Udal also reports a Dorset saying that if you kill a black beetle, twenty will come to its funeral, but again this is said of many insects (Udal,1922: 246–7). A letter in N&Q (2s:2 (1856), 83) hints at another beetle belief that is otherwise unrecorded. Some countrymen in the New Forest were seen stoning a stag-beetle to death, and when asked why said that it was the Devil's imp and was sent to do evil to the corn. Unfortunately, no other information is given.

Opie and Tatem, 1989: 21.

begging customs, see *DISPLAY CUSTOMS.

Bellerby Feast. The remnant of the old-style village *feast, the celebrations at Bellerby in North Yorkshire now focus on one day of fun and games. The principal participants dress as clowns and, accompanied by an accordion player, drummer, and helpers, they go from door to door round the village collecting money, cakes, sweets, raffle prizes, and so on. They also stop pedestrians, passing cars, coaches, and whoever they can find to exact contribution. The edibles are distributed to children and other villagers who gather for the purpose around midday, and the money goes to organizing a fête on the day and, later in the year, a children's disco and Christmas party. The custom has changed over the years, and was several times in danger of extinction, but local effort revived interest each time. Its date has moved from the Wednesday after Whitsun to Whit Monday (in 1933) and later to the Spring Bank Holiday. The heavy drinking previously associated with the custom has been toned down, and the event made more family oriented.

Smith, 1989: 78–81; Sykes, 1977: 91–4.

bells. The primary purpose of church and monastery bells was, and is, to remind hearers of a duty of prayer; in medieval times they marked the 'canonical hours' for monks (6 a.m., 9 a.m., midday, 3 p.m., 6 p.m., 9 p.m.), rang before Mass and at certain points during Mass, rang the 'passing bell' when anyone in the parish was at death's door, and tolled for *funerals and the anniversaries of deaths. They also sounded in celebrations and thanksgivings, to honour eminent visitors, at *weddings, and to mark holy days. The choice of which bell or bells to ring, for how long, and in what rhythm, was a code indicating what had occurred. Bells were widely believed to frighten away the demons of the air that cause storms and *thunder.

Much of this continued after the Reformation. Soon, the unique English skill of change ringing evolved, as set out by Fabian Stedman in his *Tintinnalogia* (1668) and *Campanalogia* (1677). The tolling of a single bell was used as a signal to request prayers for a dying person (the 'passing bell'), and also just before a funeral. Parishes developed local codes for the latter—three strokes for a child, six for a woman, nine for a man was common; but Didsbury (Cheshire) did eight for a child, twelve for a woman, sixteen for a man; Marsham (Suffolk) did three for a girl, four for a boy, five for a spinster, seven for a wife or widow, eight for a bachelor, nine for a husband or widower; some places then gave as many strokes as the age of the deceased. Peals were rung for local celebrations, especially weddings, and for public festivals and national events.

Bell-ringing took on a secular role as the Morning Bell, rung in many places at 5 a.m. in summer and 6 a.m. in winter to summon labourers to work, and the curfew at 8 or 9 p.m. to mark the day's end. There are numerous records of benefactors leaving a piece of land to a church, for its rent to pay someone for ringing peals and curfews; at Kidderminster (Wiltshire), Twyford (Hampshire), and elsewhere, legend says the donor's life was saved when the sound of a bell guided him or her home when lost. Bells also signalled the opening of markets, the moment when gleaners could enter a harvested field, and the making of fritters and *pancakes on *Shrove Tuesday.

Many places have a legend telling how a church bell fell into deep water, and could never be recovered. In some cases it fell in accidentally; in others, it was carried off by looters, or demonic forces. Rescue attempts failed because some *taboo was infringed, and the bell sank back. The tale usually concludes by saying that it can still sometimes be heard ringing underwater. Legends about *churches or wicked villages submerged or swallowed up as a *judgement also often include this final detail; so do some traditions about real medieval villages lost through coastal erosion, for example at Dunwich (Suffolk).

Tom Ingram, *Bells in England* (1954); Camp, 1988.

Beltane. This word, variously spelled and meaning 'bright fire' or 'lucky fire', is the Irish and Scottish Gaelic name for *May Day, and is particularly associated with the custom of lighting *bonfires on the eve of the feast, to protect cattle from witchcraft. May Eve bonfires were also common in the 18th century in Devon, Cornwall, Cumbria, and the Isle of Man—areas where *Celtic tradition could have survived. The word 'Beltane' itself, however, is never found in England (Hutton, 1996: 218–25).

Beowulf. This Old English epic of 3,182 lines, probably composed in the 8th century, is set in Scandinavia 200 years earlier and alludes to much semi-legendary history. The hero, an unhistorical figure of superhuman strength, overcomes three monsters. The first two are man-eating ogres (Grendel and his mother), who emerge from a *bottomless pool to ravage the Danish king's halls; the third, a dragon, attacks Beowulf's own Swedish kingdom, and the hero, by then an old man, kills it at the cost of his own life. These themes have obvious affinities with folktales. The burial customs described have been confirmed by archaeology.

The poem was clearly intended for recitation before an aristocratic Christian audience with a special interest in Scandinavian traditions; the style is that of oral formulaic poetry, though the author presumably composed in writing. The story has left no trace in English folklore, except that 'Grendel's Pit' and 'Grendel's Mere' occur as minor place-names in a few pre-Conquest charters (one each in Devon, Middlesex, Staffordshire, Wiltshire, and Worcestershire).

Michael Swanton's *Beowulf* (1978; rev. edn. 1997) conveniently prints text and translation on facing pages.

Berkeley, the witch of. The medieval chronicler William of Malmesbury, writing in the 1120s, tells how, in 1065, a woman living at Berkeley (Gloucestershire) who was skilled in witchcraft was warned by her pet jackdaw

that death was at hand. She begged her family to protect her body by sewing it up in a stag's hide and laying it in a stone coffin fastened with three chains, which must stand in the church for three nights, after which it could be buried. But the plan failed; each night one chain was broken by demons, till finally the Devil dragged her out of the church and set her on 'a black horse . . . with iron hooks projecting over the whole of his back'; she vanished, but 'her pitiable cries . . . were heard for nearly the space of four miles'.

Some elements here point towards folklore themes; the jackdaw may be an early example of a *familiar, while the sinner tortured by riding a demonic horse has links with the *Wild Hunt.

Betley Window. A painted glass window, formerly in Betley Hall, Staffordshire, but now at Leigh Manor, near Minsterley, Shropshire, and dated between 1509 and 1536. The window has twelve roughly diamond-shaped panels which portray, in colour, six dancers, a musician, a hobby horse, a friar, a fool or jester, a female character, and a maypole with the words 'a mery May' across it. The window's content was first brought to the attention of scholars by George Tollett, who contributed a description to Johnson and Steevens's influential edition of Shakespeare published in 1778, as a note to *Henry IV part 2*. It was long thought to be one of the most important pieces of visual evidence regarding the early history of *morris dance, the *hobby horse, and the *May games, but the nature of this evidence is, however, problematic. Some of the figures on the window are so similar to those on a work by the 15th-century Flemish engraver Israel van Meckenhem as to call into serious question their relevance to England, and *Dean-Smith deplores the false conclusions based on the assumption that the figures are English.

E. J. Nicol, *JEFDSS* 7:2 (1953), frontispiece, 59–67; Margaret Dean-Smith, *Folklore* 79 (1968), 161–75.

Bible divination. Reported by folklorists all over the country in only slightly differing forms, the Bible and Key was a popular method of divination. In the version collected by Ella M. Leather in 1909 (1912: 65–6), it is used for three purposes—to discover a lover's name, to name a thief, or to remove a spell. To find a lover, place the key in the Bible on the page containing Ruth 1: 15, with its text 'Whither thou goest I will go'. Close the book and bind it with string. Two people hold up the Bible with their forefingers under the key. As the names of probable lovers are recited, the key will turn at the right name. The only difference when trying to discover a thief is that Psalm 1: 18 is chosen. For removing a spell, place the key on two crossed sticks—one of yew, the other of mountain ash, place them on the text Ephesians 6: 13–15 'Put on the whole armour'. Read these verses nine times and at each repetition a small tear is made in a piece of white paper. Fold up the paper, sew it into the clothing of the person who is bewitched, without their knowledge.

Leather's informants showed an ambivalent attitude to this procedure. They certainly believed its efficacy but were worried that the forces used may not come from the right quarter and that the Church authorities would hardly approve of them using the Holy Book in such a manner. The antiquity of the custom is shown by references in Opie and Tatem, which date back to 1303. Compare also *sieve and shears.

Less complicated, but still relying on the Bible's innate powers, was a *New Year morning custom whereby people who wanted to know about the coming year opened the Bible at random, placed their finger on a verse, without looking of course, and read out the selected chapter. Those assembled then interpreted the prognostication. This could be done at other times, for example when starting on a journey. A variation was to take the Bible to bed on New Year's Eve, and open it in the dark when you first wake (after midnight), mark the place, and read it in the morning (Gurdon, 1893:136–8).

Alternatively, place the Bible 'under your pillow with a sixpence clapt into the book of Ruth (verses 16 and 17, chap.1) and you will dream of your future husband' (Lean 1903: ii. 371), or the last chapter of the Book of Proverbs can be used to divine certain things: each verse indicates the disposition or fortune of the persons born on the number corresponding to the days of the month.

See also *BOOK (DIVINATION WITH).

Opie and Tatem, 1989: 23–5; Henderson, 1866: 195–8; Hone, 1832: 127–8; N&Q 8s:4 (1893), 326; Lean 1903: ii. 343, 371.

Biddenden Dole. A charitable dole which takes place every *Easter at Biddenden, Kent. The legend is that the charity was founded by the sisters, Eliza and Mary Chulkhurst, who were Siamese twins. They were born in 1100, and, at the age of 34, when one died the other refused to be separated from her sister and she died six hours later. They left 20 acres of land to the parish to pay for an annual dole to the poor of bread, cheese, and beer. The story is apparently borne out by the Biddenden Cakes which are distributed each year at the dole. These cakes, which are more like hard biscuits, and reputedly quite inedible, are stamped with an illustration of two women standing close together, with their names and 'Biddenden', and some letters which can be taken to mean 34 years old and 1100. It is quite likely, of course, that the story was invented to explain the cakes rather than the other way round. Edward Hasted (*History and Antiquities of the County of Kent*, 1790) writes that the stamped cakes were only introduced in the mid-18th century.The dole continues to this day every Easter Monday—bread and cheese (and tea replacing the beer) to the needy, and the cakes to all and sundry.

Shuel, 1985: 126; Hole, 1975: 142–4; Stone, 1906: 28–9.

bird droppings. Having bird droppings land on you is, strangely enough, considered lucky. The notion is still current, having been reported regularly in our 1998 *Superstitions Survey, but the first known reference is little more than a hundred years old:

'It's a pity this isn't Easter Day', said he; 'for we say in Cleveland that if a bird drops on you on Easter Day you'll be lucky all the year after'. He added that on Whitsunday, if you don't put on at least one brand-new article of dress the birds will be sure to come and 'drop' on you . . . (*N&Q* 5s:10 (1878), 287)

See also *EXCREMENT.

Opie and Tatem, 1989: 142.

birds. It is widely said to be an *omen, or even a cause, of death if a wild bird enters, or is brought into, a house, or beats against a window (Opie and Tatem, 1989: 25–6); this does not apply to farmyard fowls or caged birds. Some people even avoid having ornaments, pictures, or wallpaper with birds on (Gill, 1993: 67). Certain species, e.g. *robins and *martins, are regarded as lucky, but even they should not come indoors.

There were also various mistaken ideas about the physiology and habits of certain birds, for example that *swans sing before they die, that swallows hibernate under water, that *cuckoos and hawks are the same bird in its summer and winter plumage, etc., many of which originally came from learned writers whose ideas were popularized and entered oral tradition.

See also under the names of particular species, and *GABRIEL RATCHETS.

Swainson (1885) is the basic reference work. Edward A. Armstrong, *The Folklore of Birds* (1958), ranges over many periods and cultures, with little English material.

birth, see *CHILDBIRTH.

birthday cake candles. The now ubiquitous custom of presenting a cake with burning *candles to someone on their birthday—with their age symbolized by the number of candles—appears to be relatively new to England. Several British correspondents in *N&Q* in 1902 describe the custom as common in Germany, and one mentions it as practised in the USA, but they make it clear that the custom was unknown to them in this country.

N&Q 9s:8 (1901), 344–5, 486–7; 9s:9 (1901), 96.

black. Many traditional meanings of black are gloomy: night, death, evil, or the *Devil. Yet *chimney-sweeps are lucky, as is *coal, a black *cat, and (according to some sources) a single black lamb in a flock (Latham, 1878: 8, 10; Opie and Tatem, 1989: 29). The same is sometimes true of Negroes; one account of the Second World War mentions 'an African air-raid warden nicknamed Uncle Sam' who found people believed that because of his colour he was a lucky omen; 'He once calmed a panic in a shelter of 120 people, in the dark, by shining a torch on his face' (Norman Longmate, *How We Lived Then* (1971), 132).

In some seasonal customs, the performers blacken their faces with soot, ashes, or burnt cork (e.g. the *Bacup Coconut Dancers, various *mummers); this is of course a convenient disguise, but since other easily available substances (flour, chalk) were rarely used, it is likely that black was deliberately chosen. The underlying reason may be the idea that dirt is lucky (see *excrement), or it may be because social norms are inverted at festive seasons.

Black Annis. Until recently, there was a cave called Black Annis's Bower in the Dane Hills on the outskirts of Leicester, a local beauty spot and the scene, from 1668 till 1842, of an Easter Monday fair with sports and draghunting. It was said that long ago a skin-clad, blue-faced ogress with 'vast talons, foul with human flesh' had lurked there, preying on sheep and children. A light-hearted poem of the late 18th century mentions her, in a way which implies that the story was well known; other writers give the more likely names 'Anna' or 'Anny'. Correspondents in the *Leicester Chronicle* in 1874 describe how adults used her as a *bogey to alarm their children :

Little children, who went to run on the Dane Hills, were assured that she lay in wait there, to snatch them away to her 'bower'; and that many like themselves she had 'scratched to death with her claws, sucked their blood, and hung up their skins to dry'.

Black Anna was said to be in the habit of crouching among the branches of an old pollard oak which grew in the cleft of the rock over her cave or 'bower', ever ready to spring like a wild beast on any stray children passing below. The cave she was traditionally said to have dug out of the solid rock with her finger nails.

In the 1890s working-class girls in Leicester still spoke of her, calling her 'Cat Anna' and saying she lived in an underground tunnel running from the cellars of Leicester Castle to the Dane Hills. Other children thought she was 'a witch who lived in a tree'.

Billson, 1895: 4–9, 76–7; Palmer, 1985: 218–19.

blackberries. There is a widespread *taboo against picking blackberries after a specified date, sometimes given as Michaelmas (29 September), sometimes as 10 October—which, allowing for the eleven-day calendar shift of 1752, is the same thing. It is said that from then on the berries taste bad because the *Devil has damaged them. Polite versions say he has struck them, kicked them, waved a club over them, or trampled them; less polite ones, that he has spat or pissed on them, which is likely to be the original idea, since blackberries become watery and sour once frost has got at them. The link with Michaelmas is because this feast celebrates the battle in Heaven when Michael the Archangel drove Satan out and hurled him down to earth (Revelations 12); perhaps the joke implies that he landed in a bramble bush, but this is not made explicit.

Brambles send out long shoots which root themselves at the tip, forming an arch. To crawl under this was a cure for various illnesses—most frequently whooping cough, as Aubrey noted (*Remaines*, p. 187), but occasionally hernia, boils, or rheumatism. Horses or cattle injured by a *shrew were also dragged under a bramble arch (Opie and Tatem, 1989: 29, 37; Vickery, 1995: 45–9).

black dogs. The many phantom dogs of local legend are almost invariably large black shaggy ones with glowing eyes; those which appear only in this form are simply called 'the Black Dog', whereas those that change shape often have some regional name such as *bargest, *padfoot, or *Shuck. A few are said to be ghosts, but the majority are either supernatural creatures in their own right or manifestations of the *Devil. They are solitary, unlike the pack of hounds forming the *Wild Hunt (though these too are black); they usually patrol specified lanes, but some are associated with churchyards, streams, pools, gallows sites, and barrows. In some districts (e.g. Lincolnshire) it is said that they are harmless, or even friendly, if they are not disturbed, though in others it is an *omen of death to meet one. Occasionally they guard *treasure, as at Dobb Park Lodge (Lancashire). Another haunted a farm near Lyme Regis (Dorset), to the annoyance of the farmer, who chased it with a poker and accidentally struck the attic wall, dislodging a hidden box of coins (Udal, 1922: 167).

The idea that the Devil may appear as a Black Dog is found in several accounts of witch trials and in other printed sources. A violent storm one Sunday in August 1577 damaged the villages of Blythburgh and Bungay in Suffolk, and a contemporary tract claimed that a black dog of 'horrible shape' accompanied by 'fearful flashes of fire' was seen rushing through both churches, killing or injuring several people; it was 'the divil in such likeness' (Briggs, 1970–1: B. i. 6–8). Another pamphlet of 1638 described the Black Dog of Newgate Gaol which would ride in the cart beside criminals going to the gallows; this was explained as the ghost of a medieval wizard, killed and eaten by starving fellow prisoners.

Black dog legends are common in East Anglia, the northern counties, and the southwest, and occur sporadically elsewhere; there is an extensive listing, including modern eyewitness accounts, in Janet and Colin Bord, *Alien Animals*, 1981: 77–111. A selection is in Briggs, 1970–1: B. i. 4–19. For discussion, see Ethel Rudkin, *Folk-Lore* 49 (1938), 111–31; Theo Brown, *Folklore* 69 (1958), 175–92; Westwood, 1985: 145–9.

black sheep. 'We speak figuratively of the one black sheep that is the cause of sorrow in a family; but in its reality it is regarded by the Sussex shepherd as an omen of good luck to his flock' (*Folk-Lore Record* 1 (1878), 8). A number of other nineteenth and twentieth century references, from Somerset, Kent, and Derbyshire, for example, agree with this assessment of the black sheep, but others say the opposite. 'It was unlucky for the first lamb dropped in lambing season to be black—black twins were more unlucky' (Wiltshire, 1975: 56) and Charles Igglesden (*c.*1932: 105) writes the same for Shropshire, adding that the only way to avoid the bad luck is to cut their throats before they can 'baa'.

Opie and Tatem, 1989: 29.

blade-bone. General *divination using the shoulder-bone (blade-bone) of a sheep has a very long history in Scotland and Wales, with regular references back to 1188 (see Opie and Tatem, 1989: 30), but is apparently rarely recorded in England, apart from in Chaucer's *Canterbury Tales* ('Parson's Tale' (*c.*1395), l. 602). Chaucer's parson is here railing against false swearing and conjuring 'as doon thise false enchauntours or nigromanciens in bacyns ful of water, or in a bright swerd, in a cercle, or in a fir, or in a shulder-bone of a sheep'. Strangely enough, the blade-bone (of either sheep or rabbit) turns up in English sources in the 19th century, in a specific divinatory context, as one of the many ways in which one can see one's future lover or even draw him/her to you: 'Take the blade-bone of a rabbit and stick nine pins in it, and then put it under your pillow, and you will be sure to see the object of your affections' (*N&Q* 1s:6 (1852), 312, from Hull, Yorkshire). Opie and Tatem also identify another reference to the blade-bone in the *Canterbury Tales* ('Pardoner's Prologue', ll. 350–60) which maintains that water in which such a bone has been steeped will have strong veterinary applications.

Opie and Tatem, 1989: 30–1; Lean, 1903: ii. 342, 356, 372.

bleeding. There are many traditional ways of staunching blood; some are practical and physical, such as the covering of a wound with cobwebs (see *spiders), while others rely more on the effect of verbal *charms. The otherwise sceptical Reginald *Scot (1584: book 13, chapter 10) states that a bone from a carp's head was good for staunching blood, although he does not state how this was done. He also names the herb heliotrope as effective (book 13, chapter 6) and gives some charms (book 12, chapter 18), one of which is very similar to that reported by Charlotte Burne 400 years later (1883: 183). Verbal *charms are recorded in most of the regional folklore collections, and were clearly widespread, and there are identifiable groups, such as those which concern Christ being baptized in the River Jordan, and stopping the flow of the water, or those which relate how Christ on the cross was wounded with a soldier's lance.

Many of the recorded examples are for nosebleeds or for unspecified wounds, but the grim reality of medicine relying on words is brought home in a report from the 1880s. A farm labourer who cut his wrist on his scythe was attended by local 'charmers' who claimed to be able to stop the blood, and the delay in getting him to hospital cost him his life (*Daily Telegraph* (7 July 1887); quoted in *N&Q* 7s:4 (1887), 67). Numerous plant remedies, current in East Anglia in the 20th century, are given by Hatfield.

See also: *NOSEBLEED, *KNIVES.

Black, 1883: 76, 79–80, 96–7, 111; Opie and Tatem, 1989: 31–2; Hatfield, 1994: 32–3; Owen Davies, *Folklore* 107 (1996), 20–2; Forbes, 1971: 293–316.

blessing the throats. A service at some Roman Catholic churches and the occasional high Anglican church which takes place every year on St Blaise's Day (3 February) is known as 'Blessing the throats'. The priest takes two candles, blesses them, ties them together with red ribbon to form a cross, and lights them. He then places the candles across the throats of anyone who wants the special blessing, reciting words which mention Blaise removing a fishbone from a child's throat. This process is certainly old, as *Scot (1584: book 12, chapter 14) reports it as 'a charm in the Popish church'. The best-known modern venue is the church of St Etheldreda, Ely Place, Holborn, London, where the ceremony has been performed since its introduction in 1876 (*The Times* (4 Feb. 1928), 9).

Blind Man's Buff. One of the oldest and most consistently popular of traditional games, played in the past by adults (especially at *Christmas family gatherings) as well as children. In basic form, one player is blindfolded, turned around a few times to disorient him/her, and either has to catch other players or to catch and identify them. Earlier names for the

game were Hoodman Blind, and the Hood-winke Play, as a reversed hood is an effective blindfold, and it is clear from earlier descriptions and illustrations that the game could be much rougher than it tends to be nowadays, with the blindfolded player being buffeted by the knotted hoods of the others. The game is first mentioned by name in the 16th century, although Strutt reprints manuscript illustrations dating from the 14th century which are clearly the same game. Samuel Pepys records in his *Diary* for 26 December 1664: 'and so home to bed, where my people and wife innocently at cards, very merry. And I to bed, leaving them to their sport and blindman's buff', and the game is also mentioned regularly in literary sources over the centuries. The Opies give references to foreign analogues, and Gomme supplies rhymes which were used in some versions of the game.

Gomme, 1894: i. 37–40; Opie and Opie, 1969: 117–20; Strutt, 1801 (1876): 499–501.

blood sports. Many of the traditional sports and pastimes of England were what would now be classed as 'blood sports' and have long since been outlawed and suppressed. Badger-baiting, bear-baiting, bull-baiting, *bull-running, dog-fighting, *cock-fighting, and throwing at *cocks are the best known, but there were many more obscure ones such as goose-riding, where a goose with a greased neck was hung up by its feet and horse riders tried to pull its head off as they galloped past, and sparrow–mumbling, where men tried either to remove the feathers or to bite the head off a live sparrow, using only their lips and teeth. As opposed to fox/hare/stag-hunting, angling, and grouse shooting, the historical pattern for each of the popular sports is broadly similar. From the earliest records to about the middle of the 18th century, they were an accepted part of English life, both rural and urban. Admittedly, the Puritans had tried to ban some of them, and there were individual voices speaking out against cruelty, but on the whole Church, State, local authority, and the social élite either supported or at least accepted them, and the general people revelled in them.

The baiting of animals with dogs was very popular, with bull-baiting being the most common and taking place at any time, but particularly popular at *wakes, fairs, elections, and other gatherings. It involved tying a bull to a permanent ring, or stake driven securely into the ground, with about fifteen feet of rope secured to the base of its horns. Dogs were then let loose, one or several at a time, and encouraged to attack or 'bait' the bull. Any dog could be used, but in most places people bred and trained animals for the 'sport'—bulldogs, mastiffs, and so on. As its horns had been blunted, the bull's main defence was to toss the dogs into the air, and the dog-owners were adept at catching them on sloping poles to break their fall. This was clearly popular with the audience—many pictures of the custom choose this part to illustrate. The sport was given legitimacy by the belief that beef from baited bulls was much more tender than from normally slaughtered animals, and in some places local regulations insisted that bulls be baited before being killed (N&Q 9s:9 (1902), 255).

Bear-baiting was just as popular but less common. In its heyday, it had attracted royal support, and had reputedly been introduced to England, from Italy, in the 12th century, and to have been first seen in this country at Ashby-de-la-Zouche in Leicestershire. William Fitz Stephen mentions in London, c.1183: '... or huge bears, do combat to the death against hounds let loose upon them' (Fitz Stephen, c.1180: 58). An illustration of c.1340, from the Bodleian Library, is given by Armitage.

In urban areas, blood sports were indeed big business. Institutions like the Bear Garden at Bankside, Southwark, were famous for their spectacles, and its successor at Hockley-in-the-Hole, Clerkenwell, became a popular byword for animal sports. At Hockley they offered a twice-weekly programme, throughout the year. Bear-baiting, bull-baiting, dog-fighting, were regular fare, but on other occasions one could witness whipping a blindfolded bear, and the baiting of other animals including a leopard, an African Tyger, and a mad ass. On more than one occasion, horse-baiting is mentioned, and Strutt includes a 14th-century illustration of the 'sport' (p. 333). The advertisements often proclaim a forthcoming event as TO THE DEATH! which was clearly far more attractive than just an ordinary baiting. Both John Evelyn (16 June 1670) and Samuel Pepys (14 August 1666) recorded visits to Bankside, although Evelyn did not like it: 'I most heartily weary, of the rude & dirty passetime ... ' Evelyn's distaste seems to be at the start of a new sensibility, but the consensus over blood-sports began to crumble seriously in the mid-

18th century as the isolated voices gradually coalesced into a unified, vociferous, and passionate movement for reform. The reformers attacked the traditional sports on two moral fronts: first was the genuine outrage against cruelty to animals, often set in a Christian context, and second was the concern with the effect that such pastimes would have on the moral character of the working classes. William Hogarth's popular engravings of Four Stages of Cruelty (1751) are good examples of the changing moral climate. They show, in succession, boys torturing small animals, adults mistreating horses and donkeys while, in the background, a bull-running is in progress. This callousness leads to murder and an end on the dissection table. Similarly, a schoolteacher writing in 1833 characterized the workers of Staffordshire, with their penchant for blood sports, as 'ignorant, vulgar, and wicked to excess' (Malcolmson, 1973: 119).

The opposition to blood sports comprised only part of the drive against the leisure pursuits of the working classes in the 18th and 19th centuries. Street *football and mass *November the Fifth celebrations, for example, were also under attack from the new moralists, on the basis that they were violent, drunken, degrading, brutish, and potentially dangerous to respectable people and their property. There was naturally resistance from participants, and these sports became a major moral battleground between the traditionalists and the reformers from the mid-18th to the early 19th centuries, with successes and setbacks on both sides. The reformers won in the end, of course, and major breakthroughs were the formation of the Society for the Prevention of Cruelty to Animals in June 1824 (it added the 'Royal' part in 1840), the Cruelty to Animals Act of 1835, and the Prevention of Cruelty to Animals Act of 1849. It is clear, also, that there were overt class aspects to the reform movements. Sports which had widespread upper- or middle-class support, such as fox-hunting, were either ignored or expressly excluded from the campaigns, and in a case such as cock-fighting it was only when the gentry had largely forsaken the sport that real action was taken against it. Those which can take place in private, such as cock-fighting, dog-fighting, and badger-baiting, still persist.

See also *BULL-RUNNING, *COCK-FIGHTING, throwing at *COCKS.

Malcolmson, 1973; Hutton, 1994; Boulton, 1901: i. 1–34; Edward G. Fairholme and Wellesley Pain, *A Century of*

Work for Animals: The History of the RSPCA (1924); Strutt, 1801 (1876 edn.); John Armitage, *Man at Play* (1977).

blue. In current folklore, blue is either a gender marker for the clothing of baby boys, or a colour associated with loyalty and true love, and hence lucky for brides, who must wear:

> Something old, something new,
> Something borrowed, something blue.

In the days when bridal dresses were not necessarily white, blue was a good colour to choose:

> Marry in blue,
> Your love will be true.

This meaning is derived from the rhyme 'blue/ true', which has been noticed from the Middle Ages onwards; Chaucer refers to blue drapery as a 'signe of trouthe that is in wommen sene' ('The Squire's Tale', l. 645).

blue beads. In his investigations into superstition in London at the time of the First World War, Edward Lovett discovered that all over the capital working-class people wore strings of blue beads around their necks (inside their clothes) as a prophylactic against bronchitis. He was told that these beads were put round the necks of young children, and never taken off for the rest of their lives, and that the custom extended all over the country. A note in *The Hospital* of 25 December 1909 (quoted by Opie and Tatem) and a letter in *N&Q* (160 (1931), 206) confirm Lovett's findings. There are previous examples of *blue being worn as a cure or preventative, in the form of threads or ribbon, although most known examples refer to Scotland.

Lovett, 1925: 81–4; Opie and Tatem, 1989: 33; Black, 1883: 112–14.

Blunt, Janet (1859–1950). The daughter of a General Charles Harris Blunt, Janet spent the first 30 years of her life in India, and returned to England in 1892, settling at Halle Place, Adderbury, Oxfordshire, where she lived for the rest of her life. In many ways the typical educated, middle-class leisured lady of her time, Blunt became interested in the folk *song and *dance movement and about 1910 started collecting songs from local villagers, and arranged for Cecil *Sharp to note the Adderbury morris dances in 1919; she was also an active country dance teacher in the local school and elsewhere. She made little attempt to publish her collection, but her manuscripts

were eventually donated to the *English Folk Dance and Song Society and are now housed in the *Vaughan Williams Memorial Library.

Michael Pickering, *Village Song and Culture* (1982); Michael Pickering, *FMJ* 3:2 (1976), 114–57.

boar's head. Bringing in the boar's head, on a huge plate, was a potent symbol of old *Christmas on a grand scale, popular with Victorian illustrators to evoke a *Merrie England tradition. It survives at Queen's College, Oxford, but certainly existed elsewhere; for example at the Inns of Court, St John's Gate, Clerkenwell, and St John's College, Cambridge. At Oxford, the special 'Boar's Head Carol', first printed in 1521, and existing in numerous versions, is sung as the head is carried in on a silver platter decorated with rosemary, bay, and other plants (see *Oxford Book of Carols*, (1928), No. 19). One legend which explains the custom is that a student was once walking through the forest of Shotover, reading Aristotle as he walked, when he was attacked by a wild boar. With great presence of mind, he rammed the book into the open mouth of the advancing animal and thus choked it to death. There are many other references to boars at Christmas (e.g. Dyer, 1876: 470).

Dyer, 1876: 473–4; Wright and Lones, 1940: iii. 279.

Bodmin Riding. This annual Riding custom was held at Bodmin (Cornwall) on the Sunday and Monday after 7 July (St Thomas a Becket's Day). Accounts over its long history vary, but it involved a horseback procession around the town, carrying two large *garlands, and probably originated as a Guild Riding custom. The earliest documentary evidence of the custom is in the Bodmin parish church rebuilding accounts of 1469–72, and it ceased in the early 19th century, but was revived in 1974.

Pat Munn, *Bodmin Riding and Other Similar Celtic Customs* (1975); Wright and Lones, 1940: iii. 31–2.

bogey, bogy, bogie. In modern folklore studies, the term 'bogey' or 'bogeyman' is applied to any figure deliberately used to frighten others, almost always children, to control their behaviour.

Formerly, the related words bogey, *bogle, *boggart, *bugbear, and their variants were common in rural speech all over England. They were all scarey creatures, whose exact nature was not defined; most collectors (and some informants) classified them as fairies, but there are instances where ghosts and localized minor demons are referred to by the same terms. Examples will be found in most regional collections. Descriptions of their appearance and behaviour differ from one tale to the next, though shape-changing is a standard feature (see *brag, *guytrash). It is not always possible to deduce from the accounts whether they were seriously feared, or whether some informants treated the topic as a joke. Certainly some were famous enough locally to be given individual names and become the subject of humorous anecdotes (Henderson, 1866: 233–9; Harland and Wilkinson, 1867: 49–55).

Sometimes a bogey or boggart replaces the *Devil as the dupe of a deceptive agreeement or competition involving mowing crops; in such tales, naturally, the bogey is represented as extremely stupid. Versions from Northamptonshire and East Anglia are given in Briggs (1970–1: B. i. 26, 28–9, 140; 1976: 31–2).

bogeyman. Any real or imaginary figure used by adults as a threat to coerce children into good behaviour is a bogeyman—often the final function of a belief that adults no longer share. This form of discipline was common until recently, and the figures invoked could be male or female, monstrous or natural, and could range from the Devil to the local doctor or policeman. The threat usually was that the creature would carry the child away, and perhaps eat it, either to punish naughtiness in general or because the child has gone too close to a dangerous spot, stayed out after dark, gone into an orchard to steal fruit, etc. Dickens shows a nursemaid ordering a little girl to go to sleep: 'My goodness gracious me, Miss Floy, you naughty, sinful child, if you don't shut your eyes this minute, I'll call in them hobgoblins that lives in the cock-loft to come and eat you up alive' (Dombey and Son, chapter 5).

See also *BLACK ANNIS, *GOOSEBERRY WIFE, *JENNY GREENTEETH, *HYTERSPRITES, *POLDIES, *TANKERABOGUS.

boggart. In the dialects of northern counties, 'boggart' was a general term for any supernatural being which frightened people, whether indoors or out, without specifying whether it is ghost, malicious fairy, or minor demon. An outdoor boggart might haunt any pit or well or lonely lane; an indoor boggart's behaviour was like a poltergeist's—he would knock, throw stones, break dishes, and so on.

'Nearly every old house had its boggart which played ill-natured tricks on the inhabitants. Singly or in packs they haunted streets and roads, and the arch-boggarts held revels at every three-road-end' (Harland and Wilkinson, 1867: 49). The word is still used for a mischievous ghost.

In some tales, the boggart is attatched to a particular house or family, like a *brownie, but as a nuisance rather than a helper. The most frequent anecdote on this theme is a humorous one, found in several collections from northern counties, and also in Lincolnshire and Shropshire. It tells how a farmer was so pestered by the tricks of a boggart that he and his family decided to move house, much against their will; as they set out, a neighbour asked if they really were leaving. 'Yes, we're moving,' said the farmer. 'Yes indeed,' came the boggart's voice from among the piled-up furniture, 'we're *all* moving.' So the farmer turned the cart round and went home, saying if they were to be tormented anyway, they'd do better to stay in their own old house.

bogle, boggle. A variant on the terms 'boggart' and 'bogy', used for particularly frightening and evil specimens. Mrs Balfour said it was 'a not uncommon theory' in part of Lincolnshire that bogles are really the dead, still able to appear and to act, until the time their corpses are fully decayed (Balfour, 1891: 402). Jessica Lofthouse describes those of north Lancashire and Cumbria as 'spine-chilling' creatures, which could appear as 'a light, a ball of fire, a ghostly shape, a phantom hound or bull or calf, or red hen or black cock'. They guarded buried *treasure, punished the wicked, and 'could uncover the graves of the dead' (North-Country Folklore, (1976), 35).

bones. A belief reported in England and Scotland from the mid-19th century onwards was that it is unwise to burn bones, usually with the reason that your own bones will ache if you do so, and a much earlier notion links burnt bones with toothache (Gospelles of Dystaues (1507), part 2, p. xiii, quoted in Opie and Tatem, 1989: 15). Aubrey (1686: 165) reported that women wear a tooth taken from a skull to prevent toothache, and that 'cunning alewives putt the ashes of ... bones in their Ale to make it intoxicating. Dr. Goddard bought bones of the Sextons to make his drops with. Some make a playster for the Gowte with the earth or musilage newly scraped from the shin-bone.' Many other recorded cures mention the use of skulls.

See also *BLADE-BONE, *WISHBONE, *SKULL, *LUCKY BONE, *CRAMP BONE.

Opie and Tatem, 1989: 35.

Bonfire Night, see *NOVEMBER THE FIFTH.

bonfires. Throughout recorded history, it has taken very little persuasion to get English people to make a bonfire. Not only do fires appear regularly as an integral part of certain *calendar customs such as *November the Fifth, *Queen Elizabeth I's accession (17 November), *New Year, and *midsummer, but a bonfire was also the way the people celebrated national victories and royal occasions, either spontaneously or by order of the appropriate authorities.

November the Fifth and Queen Elizabeth celebrations had definable historical origins, and similar things went on at each:

mighty bonfires and the burning of a most costly pope, carried by four persons in divers habits, and the effigies of two devils whispering in his ears, his belly filled with live cats who squalled most hideously as soon as they felt the fire; the common saying all the while it was the language the pope and the devil in a dialogue betwixt them. (1677: Letter from Charles Hatton describing 17 November celebrations, quoted by Cressy, 1989: 177)

Even before that time, however, bonfires were in use as anti-papal devices and celebrations. About 1536–40, a report written to advise Henry VIII on how to get across to the people the new propaganda against Rome suggested that they should go in procession and make 'bonfyers' to celebrate their escape from its clutches, in a similar way as they celebrated the victory of the battle of Agincourt (quoted in *Journal of the Warburg and Courtauld Institutes* 20 (1957), 176–9).

Midsummer fires, however, are older and of more obscure origin. The important description by the 16th-century chronicler John Stow is detailed under *midsummer. An earlier description, by the 14th-century monk John Mirk, proves to be quoting from continental sources, but his derivation of 'bonfire' from 'bone-fire' is accepted by the *OED*, while others, including John Stow, have presumed the first syllable to be from French *bon* for 'good', or from 'boon', revealing the idea of fire as doing good in itself or as a symbol for good neighbourhood. Adams points out that

in no other European language does the word for bonfire have any connection with bones. Further confusion arises from a range of dialect terms, balefire, banefire, banfire, and so on, which are quite logical localized pronunciations, and the notion that these preserve a memory of an ancient pagan god (Baal) has nothing to support it beyond wishful thinking. Similarly, the fashionable idea that midsummer bonfires in England are survivals of an extensive Celtic tradition has very little to support it, despite the custom's popularity in Ireland and the Isle of Man. Indeed, the paucity of bonfires in Gaelic Scotland and most of Wales argues against a pan-Celtic fire festival.

Nevertheless, there are other indications that fires were considered beneficial in themselves. The so-called 'need fire' is described by Denham, quoting his father, who died in 1843 aged 79:

A disease among cattle, called the murrain, then prevailed to a very great extent through that district of Yorkshire. The cattle were made to pass through the smoke raised by this miraculous fire, and their cure was looked upon as certain, and to neglect doing so was looked upon as wicked. This fire was produced by violent and continued friction of two dry pieces of wood until such time as it was thereby obtained. To work as though one was working for a need fire' is a common proverb in the North of England. (*Denham Tracts*, 1895: ii. 50).

Similar uses of the need fire have been reported more commonly from Scotland and Ireland.

Cressy, 1989; Hutton, 1996; G. B. Adams, *Folklore* 88:1 (1977), 34–8.

book (divination with). A well-attested way of finding out one's short-term future, especially for a particular venture, is to open a book at random and read the first words which come to your eye. Some references stipulate the *Bible for this purpose, which is not surprising, but Virgil seems to have been popular, and many seem to imply that any book will do. In some circles, the use of the Bible in such a 'superstitious' way would anyway have been frowned upon. The one time that the Bible seems to be *de rigueur* is on *New Year's Day, when the coming year can be assessed:

It is usually set about with some little solemnity, on the morning of New Year's Day before breakfast, as the ceremony must be performed fasting. The Bible is laid on the table unopened; and the parties who wish to consult it are then to open it in succession. They . . . must open it at random . . . The chapter is then read aloud and commented upon by the company assembled . . . (Forby, 1830: 400–1)

A correspondent in *N&Q* (2s:12 (1861), 303) reports the custom from Oxfordshire in the 1850s and says it was called 'dipping' (i.e. to 'dip' into the Bible) and must be done before twelve noon on New Year's Day.

St Augustine refers to the haphazard opening of 'the pages of some poet' (*Confessions* (c. AD 397), IV. v), while the earliest English source is *Scot (1584: book 11, chapter 10)— 'Lots comprised in verses, concerning the luck ensuing, either of Virgil, Homer, or Anie other, wherein fortune is gathered by the sudden turning unto them'. The custom is reported well into the 20th century and is still current.

See also *BIBLE DIVINATION.

Wright and Lones, 1938: ii. 40–1; Opie and Tatem, 1989: 35–6.

Book of Sports (1618, 1633). The *King's Declaration of Lawful Sports*, commonly called *The Book of Sports*, was first issued by James I in 1618, as a response to zealous Lancashire justices who had banned all popular sports and games on Sundays. This was but one skirmish in a long and bitter battle over the correct manner of keeping Sunday (the 'Lord's Day') which was not fully resolved until the Puritans achieved complete control in the 1640s. James was caught between the growing power of the Puritans on one side and still potent fears of Roman Catholicism on the other. It was seriously believed that Sunday sports were a Catholic plot: 'It was no small policy in the leaders of the Popish party to keep the people from church by dancing and other recreation even in the time of divine service' (John Barwick, quoted by Tait, p. 562).

The *Book of Sports* attempted a compromise by identifying which sports should be allowed on Sundays, while prohibiting others, and most crucially stipulating that the lawful entertainments must only take place after evening service, and that anyone who had not attended that service (i.e. Catholics) was excluded from this liberty. Those pastimes allowed were listed as:

dancing, either of men or women, archery for men, leaping, vaulting or any such other harmless recreation . . . (such as) . . . May Games, Whitson Ales and Morris-dances and the setting up of Maypoles . . . and that women shall have leave to carry rushes to the

church for the decoring of it, according to their old custom.

Those forbidden entirely on Sundays were bear- and bull-baiting, interludes, and bowling (for the meaner sort of people). Bowling had previously come under fire from those in authority because the popular craze for the game had threatened to eclipse archery as a regular pastime, and there were fears of its effect on the military prowess of the populace.

The *Book of Sports* angered the stricter Puritans and Sabbatarians at the time, and was reissued by Charles I in 1633, in response to a similar hard-line approach to Sundays taken by a group of Somerset magistrates. By this time the Puritan faction was in a much stronger position, and the declaration proved a major focus of bitter debate. Nevertheless, at local level, it helped to strengthen the hands of the authorities by codifying what was and was not allowed, and numerous prosecutions of miscreants followed. There was certainly still much flouting of the law:

And when the people by the book were allowed to play and dance out of public service-time, they could so hardly break off their sports, that many a time the reader was fain to stay till the piper and players would give over; and sometimes the morrice dancers would come into the church in all the linen and scarfs, and antic dresses, with morrice bells jingling at their legs. As soon as common-prayer was read they did haste out presently to their play again. (Quoted in Govett 1890: 120–1)

Govett, 1890 (includes a transcript of the text); Julian Davies, *The Caroline Captivity of the Church* (1992); James Tait, 'The Declaration of Sports for Lancashire (1617)', *English Historical Review* 32 (1917), 561–8; Thomas G. Barnes, 'County Politics and a Puritan Cause Celebre: Somerset Church Ales 1633', *Trans. Royal Historical Soc.*, 5s:5 (1959), 103–22; Underdown, 1985.

bottomless pools. In the Old English epic *Beowulf* the hero dives into a pool so deep that 'no man living knows where the bottom of it may be'. There are many like it in local folklore, some of them being said to lead straight down into Hell, others to have channels linking them to the sea; some really are unusually deep, but others are not—Dozmary Pool (Cornwall) is quite shallow, and owes its uncanny reputation to its isolation. Storytellers provide lively details; they may, for example, say that a fully loaded haywain once overturned into the pool and vanished without trace, or that bell-ropes from a nearby church were tied end to end and still did not touch the bottom.

Such pools may contain a *treasure, a *dragon, a sunken *church, or a whole sunken village, as at Bomere (Shropshire); at *Semerwater (Yorkshire) and Talkin Tarn (Cumbria), a bottomless lake appeared overnight, to swallow up a wicked town. This association with damnation is also illustrated by three small round pits near Darlington (Durham), called *Hell Kettles; Holinshed reported (*Chronicles*, 1577) that 'foolish people' believed they were not only bottomless but boiling, so that the souls of sinners 'haue oft beene harde to crye and yell about them'. A sceptical investigator in the 1690s found they were only 30 yards deep, and cold (Westwood, 1985: 332–3). Bottomless pools are also an appropriate place to which evil ghosts could be banished (Brown, 1979: 24–34).

Burne, 1883: 64–73; Palmer, 1973: 70–1; Simpson, 1973: 38–9; Westwood, 1985: 332–3.

Bourne, Henry (1694–1733). Curate of All-Hallows, Newcastle-upon-Tyne. In 1725 he compiled and published the book *Antiquitates Vulgares, or The Antiquities of the Common People*, in which his purpose was to warn people against popish and heathen rituals which, masquerading as traditional customs, led to 'uncleanness and debauchery', and 'rioting, gaming, and drunkenness'. In so doing, he provided much information for the future folklorist, although his work might have remained unknown but for another Newcastle clergyman, John *Brand, who used it as a basis for his *Observations on the Popular Antiquities of Great Britain* in 1777 and numerous subsequent editions.

Dorson, 1968: 10–15.

Boxing Day, see *ST STEPHEN'S DAY.

box tree. This evergreen plant was formerly used at *funerals as a cheap substitute for the customary *rosemary or thyme (Vickery, 1995: 43). The mourners would each carry a sprig in the procession, and drop it into the grave; sprigs were also sometimes tucked into the winding sheet. The eccentric Major Labellière, who died at Dorking (Surrey) in 1800, arranged for two carts to pass through the town on the morning of his funeral, one laden with sprigs of box and the other with *yew, so that everybody could take one; the crowds were so great that the ten-foot shaft serving as

his grave was half-filled by the greenery thrown on his coffin (Charles Rose, *Recollections of Old Dorking* (1877), 92–8). This presumably explains why it is unlucky to bring box indoors.

boy bishops. In medieval times, most English cathedrals and abbeys, collegiate churches, and schools, used to reverse the structures of hierarchy at midwinter by selecting a young choirboy to act as 'bishop' or 'abbot'. Wearing appropriate robes, he would preside at services, preach a sermon, and lead a procession through the streets blessing the people— during which money would be collected for the upkeep of the institution he represented. His term of office began on *St Nicholas's Day (6 December) and ended on *Holy Innocents Day (28 December); in London and some other towns, he was actually referred to as 'St Nicholas'. The last known example in England was at Gloucester Cathedral in 1558.

Neil Mackenzie, *History Today* 37 (1987), 10–16; Hutton, 1996: 100–4; Wright and Lones, 1940: iii. 194–7; Hazlitt, 1905: 68–71.

brag. A shape-changing *bogey in Northumberland and Durham. Its favourite form was that of a donkey or a horse, to tempt people into mounting it, and then throw them into a pond or a gorsebush and run off 'nickering and laughing' (Wright, *English Dialect Dictionary*, citing a source from 1843). One localized at Picktree could also appear as a calf wearing a neckerchief, a headless man, and, on one occasion, as four men carrying a white sheet; one at Humbleknowe was never seen, but made hideous noises in the night (Henderson, 1866: 233; Brockie, 1886: 52–5).

Brand, John (1744–1806). Curate in several parishes in Newcastle-upon-Tyne, before becoming rector of St Mary-at-Hill and St Mary Hubbard, City of London (1784), where he lived for the rest of his life. Brand was one of the new breed of 18th-century antiquarians who were becoming fascinated by British traditions rather than the primarily classical interests of their predecessors, and he was elected a Fellow of the Society of Antiquaries in 1777, serving as the Society's Resident Secretary from his arrival in London until his death. As were many of his contemporaries, Brand was an indefatigable collector, of books (his library at his death numbered over 10,000 volumes), manuscripts, and, in particular, notes, and the book by which he is now remembered started life as his annotation of an earlier work. A previous Newcastle curate, Henry *Bourne, had published a pamphlet of miscellaneous lore and traditions under the title of *Antiquitates Vulgares, or the Antiquities of the Common People*, in 1725. Brand reprinted this, in 1777, with his own comments and notes, as *Observations on Popular Antiquities*, and from then on began gathering material for a second, expanded edition. For both Bourne and Brand, the material was the remnant of the superstitions foisted on the people by pre-Reformation Catholicism, and thus, although fascinating as evidence, to be held at arm's length. By the time he died, in September 1806, he was still amassing material and his manuscript was sold to publishers hoping to turn it into a book.

The huge task of editing Brand's material into publishable form fell to Sir Henry *Ellis, who had little time to devote to the project, and could do no more than add the new material in the form of footnotes, but, despite its faults, this edition hit the taste of the time, and became one of the standard works to which antiquarians and folklorists turned for source material. Numerous other editions have appeared over the intervening years, including Ellis's three-volume set, *Observations on the Popular Antiquities of Great Britain* (a new edition with further additions) in 1849, and an alphabetically arranged *Dictionary of Faiths and Folklore* edited by W. Carew Hazlitt in 1905, and recently reprinted. It has been said that Brand gave scant credit to Bourne for his pioneering work, but with so many editorial emendations and additions in later editions it is now difficult for the modern reader to ascertain what is by Bourne, Brand, Ellis, or subsequent hands, making the dating of much of the material extremely problematic.

DNB; Dorson, 1968: 13–30.

bread. There are two opposing traditions regarding a loaf with holes in it, or a 'hollow loaf', although neither was noted before the 20th century. A report from West Cornwall held that it meant a death in the family (*N&Q* 10s:12 (1909), 88), while others maintain that if the bread rises too much, so that the loaf has big holes in it, it is a sign that the woman who baked it is going to have a baby (*Folk-Lore* 37 (1926), 297). The 'death' verdict wins by weight of numbers. An older belief maintains that the first loaf out

of the oven should be broken rather than cut, or else the rest will be too heavy.

See also *BREAD AND CHEESE THROWING.

bread and cheese throwing. An annual *Whit Sunday *scrambling custom which still takes place at St Briavels (Gloucestershire), in which bread and cheese is distributed by being thrown from the top of a high stone wall to the waiting crowd below. The ceremony once took place in the church, but changing ideas of appropriate behaviour prompted a move outside, with the throwing being done from the top of the tower, and another move out into the lane where it now resides. The first known record of the custom dates from 1779, but it is presumed to be much older and somehow (although it is not clear how) connected to the preservation of the right of local people to take firewood from a nearby wood. An alternative explanation is that King John stayed at St Briavels castle in or about 1204 and he gave to the village a thousand acres of land stipulating that bread and cheese should be distributed every Whit Sunday to uphold the right.

Although St Briavels is the only surviving example, it was not unique. A report in the *London Magazine* (Dec. 1737, 705) details a very similar custom in Paddington (London), which lasted until 1838. Edwards also reports other bread and cheese doles, but without the scrambling element.

Kightly, 1986: 59; Crawford, 1938: 160–1; *N&Q* 3s:2 (1862), 68–9; 4s:8 (1871), 507; Edwards, 1842: 17–22.

Briggs, Katharine Mary (1898–1980). Born into a family of considerable artistic talent, she was herself a writer of children's fiction; she came relatively late to folklore. Her outstanding contribution was in two fields: *fairy lore, and *folk narratives. Although in both cases her work extended throughout Britain, the amount of purely English material she found was a revelation to those who thought English folklore scarce and unimportant. Initially, her interest was in the folkloric background to the supernatural in Elizabethan and Jacobean literature; her first academic books, *The Anatomy of Puck* (1959) and *Pale Hecate's Team* (1962), examined how far the treatment of fairies and witches by Shakespeare and his contemporaries reflected popular beliefs; in *Fairies in Tradition and Literature* (1967) she extended this discussion to later periods. She made the vigorous and varied fairy traditions recorded by 19th-century folklorists readily accessible in books aimed at a wide audience. The most important are *A Dictionary of Fairies* (1976) and *The Vanishing People* (1978), which offer thorough coverage of British fairy lore and some comparative material from Ireland and Europe.

Her other concern was to disprove the charge that Britain (and more specifically England) 'has no folktales'. Scouring a wide variety of published sources, from medieval to modern times, and drawing on the extensive manuscript collection of F. J. Norton, she brought together previously scattered texts to form a *Dictionary of British Folk-Tales in the English Language*—she knew no Celtic languages, so had regretfully to limit herself to those in English. The result was four large volumes (1970–1); the first two reprint or summarize all known fairytales, animal fables, jocular tales, novelle and nursery tales within her remit, while the other two give an extensive selection of local and historical legends, thematically arranged to illustrate topics typical of English tradition. It is an essential reference work, showing the range of traditional narratives recoverable from printed sources.

Her interest in the art of storytelling (at which she was herself very skilled) brought her into contact with Ruth *Tongue, whom she helped considerably by editing her *Somerset Folklore* (1965); she regarded Tongue as a valuable source for oral folktales, and included many of her stories in a joint work, *Folktales of England* (1965) and in her 1970–1 *Dictionary*. Briggs also wrote on the traditions of her own home area in *The Folklore of the Cotswolds* (1974), and was a frequent contributor to folklore journals.

She played a major role on the Council (later Committee) of the Folklore Society in the 1960s and 1970s, and was President from 1967 to 1970; she was much appreciated as an international lecturer, especially in America. Her warm charm and enthusiastic scholarship inspired all who knew her (Davidson, 1986).

broadsides. Flimsy sheets of paper, sold cheaply in the streets, at fairs, and wherever working people gathered. On them were printed songs, prose accounts of horrible crimes, scandals, newsworthy items, pictures, wonders, tales, religious tracts, parodies, political sqibs, the 'last dying speeches of murderers' sold at the foot of the gallows while the body was still hanging, or any other piece which the printers thought would sell. Given the fact that the printers copied freely from each other and tried to mirror the public's taste, many items included were traditional in their own right, such as the 'Pack of Cards Spiritualized', or the 'Letter from Our Lord Jesus Christ'. From the late 18th to the late 19th centuries, the printers of broadsides were at the decidedly lower end of the trade and, indeed, many of the sheets were appallingly printed, but others gave good value for the cost of a penny or halfpenny, giving two or more songs, with woodcut illustrations (often having little if any connection with the song itself). A typical mid-19th-century sheet would be quarto size (about 10 in. × 8 in.) with two songs and two cuts, but many sellers chopped the sheets in half to make two 'slips', and others sold much bigger sheets which could hold as many as 50 songs—in very small print.

Much of the broadside trade was centred in London, and some printers such as James Catnach, John Pitts, and Henry Such had a national reputation, but there were also important regional centres in Newcastle, Birmingham, Manchester, and Liverpool, and most small towns had a printer who turned out broadsides as and when he or she could. Between them, they churned out hundreds of thousands of sheets.

In the earlier period, from the mid-15th to the late 17th centuries, most sheets were printed by better class printers, in the old gothic script, called 'Blackletter'. In addition to general songs, those engaged in religious and political controversies often used the broadside form to carry on their public debates, and these sheets were much prized by collectors and examples are still preserved in major collections such as the Pepys, Roxburghe, and Bagford.

Devotees of the traditional *Child ballad and many folk *song scholars were particularly scathing about broadside ballads, but much of the evidence used in folk song research is perforce taken from printed examples. Appearance on a broadside is often the only way a song can be dated, and few song researchers have not used broadside texts to complete fragmentary versions they have collected, or to elucidate obscure or incoherent phrases. The exact relationship between traditional song and broadsides has never been quite determined. Certainly, very many of the songs collected from the people have appeared on broadsides at one time or another, and it is also known that many traditional singers learnt songs from print, and some even made collections of their own. Broadsides could be stored away in scrapbooks, passed around from hand to hand until they fell to pieces, or pasted on the wall: 'I will now lead you to an honest ale-house, where we shall find a cleanly room, lavender in the window, and twenty ballads stuck about the walls' (Izaak Walton, *The Compleat Angler* (1653)). A purely oral folk song tradition has probably not existed in this country for centuries. Nevertheless, a minority of songs do not seem to have appeared widely in print and, as broadsides did not give tunes yet song collectors found versions of songs with similar tunes all over the country, an element of orality must have existed, and so we must assume that a flexible mix of print/oral traditions was the norm.

Leslie Shepard, *The Broadside Ballad* (1962); Leslie Shepard, *The History of Street Literature* (1973); Claude M. Simpson, *The British Broadside Ballad and its Music* (1966).

Broadwood, Lucy Etheldred (1858–1929). A member of the Broadwood piano family and thus comfortably off, well connected, and musical, she lived in Sussex and London. Lucy's uncle, John Broadwood, had published a collection of Sussex folk songs in 1843, and she herself started collecting songs in the neighbourhood of the family home. In 1893, her book, *English County Songs*, edited with her cousin J. A. Fuller-Maitland, burst on the musical scene which had just started to take folk song seriously. The book was enormously influential, and immediately placed Lucy Broadwood at the centre of the new movement, and she was thus involved in setting up the *Folk-Song Society in 1898. She served the new society in various capacities—Secretary, Editor, President—for the rest of her life, and thus worked in close contact with all the major figures of the time, including Ralph *Vaughan Williams, Percy *Grainger, and Frank *Kidson, often as their mentor and adviser. Broadwood's scholarship and broad knowledge of a wide range of musical forms were formidable and belie the image of dilettante maiden aunt with which educated women of her era are often dismissed. She continued to collect in Surrey and Sussex and elsewhere in England as opportunity arose, and also made important discoveries in Co. Waterford in 1906 (*JFSS* 3 (1907), 3–38). Although she certainly 'softened' and adapted texts, like most of her contemporaries, her

editorial standards set a high example which influenced the way the Society viewed and presented its material. Lucy Broadwood had problems reconciling the respect she had for the songs and the singers with popularizing movements such as represented by Cecil *Sharp. It is a great pity that she did not publish any sustained pieces of opinion, but mainly restricted herself to annotations in the *Journal of the Folk-Song Society* and in her three books of songs: *English County Songs* (with J. A. Fuller-Maitland, 1893); *Sussex Songs* (with H. F. Birch Reynardson, 1889); *English Traditional Songs and Carols* (1908).

Margaret Dean-Smith, *JEFDSS* 9:5 (1964), 233–68; Ralph Vaughan Williams, *JEFDSS* 5:3 (1948), 136–9; Frank Howes, *ED&S* 30:1 (1968), 14–15; Gammon, 1980: 61–89.

broom. Many people in 19th-century Suffolk, Sussex, and Wiltshire thought that during the month of *May the broom meant bad luck, even death; one must not bring its flowers into the house, nor *sweep the floor with broom twigs:

> If you sweep the house with broom in May,
> You'll sweep the head of that house away,

and:

> Bring broom into the house in May,
> It will sure sweep one of the family away.

The taboo applied, in modified form, to the household broom as well as the plant; it was (and is) thought very unlucky to buy a broom or brush during May, and the rhyme became:

> Buy a brush in May,
> Sweep a friend away.

In medieval and later art, a broom is often the typical attribute of a woman, especially a housewife, in humorous contexts; a misericord in Bristol Cathedral shows a man and his wife tilting, pitchfork against broom. Hence it could be used as social comment:

When local opinion decides that a wife has been absent from home longer than justifiable, a broom, decorated with a ribbon, will be hung over the doorway, or stuck in a chimney or ... window, as an advertisement for a housekeeper. When the man himself puts out the broom, it is understood that he invites his friends to carouse with him during his wife's absence, the broom in this case being equivalent to the bush (the old sign of an inn) ... (Wright, 1928: 25).

See also *BROOMSTICK, *SWEEPING.

Opie and Tatem, 1989: 45–6; Vickery, 1995: 51.

broomstick. Modern artists and fiction writers take for granted that a witch's magic *flight requires a broomstick, but folk tradition mentions other means too, including pitchforks, staffs, plant-stems, hurdles, bowls, and pig-troughs. Two sources which may have helped fix the stereotype are a *chapbook on the famous Lancashire witch trial of 1612, where one woodcut shows a woman, a devil, and a man, all on broomsticks; and Reginald *Scot, who (quoting a French source) said that when witches dance at Sabbaths 'everie one hath a broome in her hand, and holdeth it up aloft'.

Brown, Theo (1914–93). A good recent example of the regional folklorist concentrating on a single area—in her case, Devon and adjacent parts of the West Country. She specialized in first-hand recording of local traditions, folk narratives, and otherworld beliefs; her attitude was that of a serious academic, citing source materials with care. For deeper interpretation she drew on Jungian symbolism, but never let theory obscure or distort the primary material. Her most important book, *The Fate of the Dead* (1979), examines legends about laying troublesome ghosts in relation to the impact of the Reformation on popular religious beliefs. She had planned a full study of the *black dog, but the mass of material she gathered proved unmanageable; a preliminary report appeared in *Folklore* 69 (1958), 175–92.

Much of her work consisted of articles and reviews in *Folklore* and the *Transactions of the Devonshire Association*, pamphlets, and contributions to symposia. She became an Honorary Research Fellow at Exeter University; her lectures there, and to local organizations, encouraged many others to collect folklore.

See Davidson and Blacker, 2001: 247–55.

brownie. Now the standard term for a helpful household *fairy anywhere in Britain, but when first recorded in the early 16th century a dialect word limited to Lowland Scotland and the English Border counties; many of the early descriptions are Scottish. Corresponding beings in areas further south were called *hobs, *pucks, or *pixies. King James VI and I defines the brownie in his *Daemonologie* as a devil 'who appeared like a rough man' and 'haunted divers houses, without doing any evill, but doing as it were necessarie turnes up and down the house'; foolish people thought their homes prospered if they had one.

A vicar of Beetham (Westmorland), making notes on local lore in 1777, stated firmly 'A Browny is not a Fairey, but a tawney colour'd Being which will do a great deal of work for a Family, if used well.' Sir Walter Scott agreed: 'The Brownie formed a class of beings distinct in habit and disposition from the freakish and mischievous elves' (*Minstrelsy of the Scottish Border* (1802–3), 41). In modern scholarly terminology, the category of 'household spirit' to which the brownie belongs is regarded as a subdivision within the fairy species, but one which has very distinctive features of its own. Such beings live alongside humans in their own homes and farms, bringing them luck and helping them in various ways, and there is only one per house; in contrast, other types of fairy are more remote, often dangerous, and often thought of as living in groups.

Beliefs and tales about brownies are everywhere similar. They work by night, doing housework and farm tasks, and their presence ensures prosperity. As a reward, a bowl of cream or porridge, or a small cake, is regularly set out for them, often on the hearth. They punish lazy and slovenly servants by upsetting and breaking things, pinching them as they sleep, and so on; they may also rummage about noisily and create untidiness out of pure fun. Brownies should not be spied on while working, criticized, or laughed at, or they will take offence and either leave for ever (taking the luck of the house with them) or turn into angry and troublesome *boggarts. Occasionally, a brownie is given an individual name; such was the Tawny Boy at Overthwaite (Westmorland) around 1650, and the *Cauld Lad at Hilton (Northumberland).

The most striking tale concerns the gift of new clothes. The first English mention of this comes in Reginald Scot's *Discoverie of Witchcraft* (1584), book 4, chapter 10:

In deede your grandams' maides were woont to set a boll of milke before him and his cousine Robin Goodfellow, for grinding of malt or mustard, and sweeping the house at midnight; and you have also heard that he would chafe exceedingly, if the maid or goodwife of the house, having compassion of his nakednes, laid anie clothes for him, beesides his mess of white bread and milke, which was his standing fee. For in that case he saith,

What have we here? Hemton, hamten,
Here will I never more tread nor stampen.

Immediately thereon he would take himself off and be never seene again.

Versions differ in what explanation (if any) is given for this odd outcome. The Cauld Lad accepted a green cloak and hood with delight, but left at dawn, singing:

Here's a cloak, and here's a hood!
The Cauld Lad of Hilton will do nae mair good!

(Keightley, 1889: 296)

Perhaps, like the Devon *pixy, he now thought himself too grand to work. A Lincolnshire story rationalizes the motif; there, a brownie who had regularly accepted a linen shirt took umbrage when given one made of sacking, i.e. hemp, and sang:

Harden, harden, harden hamp,
I will neither grind nor stamp;
Had you given me linen gear,
I had served you many a year.
Thrift may go, bad luck may stay,
I shall travel far away.

(M. Peacock, *Folk-Lore* 3 (1891), 509–10)

From a functionalist point of view one can say, with L. F. Newman, 'The brownie or hobthrush fitted easily into the old, generous rural economy. He typified the good servant in kitchen, dairy or stable' (*Folk-Lore* 63 (1952), 103–4). Belief in him could be exploited in two ways—by servants, to lay the blame for breakages, untidiness, or odd noises in the night on his mischief-making; by employers, to foster the belief that he would reward those who worked well, and punish the idle. The Elizabethan fairies who, in Bishop Corbet's poem 'The Fairies' Farewell', put sixpence in the shoe of a good maid were probably brownies.

Briggs, 1959 and 1976; Gillian Edwards, *Hobgoblin and Sweet Puck* (1974), 103–121.

bucca, bucca-boo. The Cornish spelling of a Celtic word for various supernatural creatures, usually frightening *bogeys; it is ultimately from the same root as *bogey and *puck. In Cornwall, it was 'a spirit it was once thought necessary to propitiate'; fishermen, tin-miners, and harvesters would deliberately leave a few scraps of their food for him, and spill a few drops of beer. Children were told to stop crying, or the bucca-boo would come and carry them off. Some said there were two buccas, one white and kindly, the other black and dangerous. Fishermen applied the name to a sea goblin of some sort, causing a 19th-century vicar to refer to the bucca-boo as 'the stormgod of the old Cornish'; marks on a certain pile of rocks were said to be traces of fishing nets he stole, turned to stone when he heard a

church choir sing the Creed (Courtney, 1890: 79, 129).

buckets. According to *N&Q* (5s:6 (1876), 24), it was the custom for the mother of a newly christened baby in 19th-century Cumberland to give a tea to her neighbours. When they were ready to leave, a bucket was placed in the doorway which all the women had to jump over. If they stumbled or tripped it was taken as a sign that they were pregnant. Over 50 years later, but referring to the 'old days', another reference to Cumberland (*Folk-Lore* 40 (1929), 279) describes a similar situation but with the different detail that the bucket held a lighted candle, and if the draught of a woman's skirts put the candle out 'it was taken as an omen she would be the next to require the midwife'. Another variant was for a besom to be placed across two buckets, and jumped over. The link between pregnancy and the domestic bucket is confirmed by a comment from a young Yorkshire woman reported in Opie and Tatem—'Jump over a bucket to bring on labour'.

Opie and Tatem, 1989: 46.

bug, bugbear. A widely used word in medieval and Elizabethan English for a *bogey or anything which scares people; the simple 'bug' is now obsolete, though its compound 'bugbear' is still well known.

building trade. One of those *occupations which had a rich variety of traditional customs and beliefs, but as there has been no systematic collection or study devoted to them our knowledge of them is patchy. The overriding principle for most seems to be the same the country over—at certain key points in the building the workers expected a ceremony of some sort, and money for a drink.

What passes for building trade lore nowadays are 'official' customs such as cutting the first turf, laying a foundation stone, and topping out. The latter has been particularly popular since the 1960s, and few major construction projects are completed without a gathering of company officials, local dignitaries, and newspaper photographers on top of the new building to perform some ceremony such as laying the last brick. This custom has some roots, as there are earlier references to the workers hoisting a bush, or a flag, to the roof of a completed building.

A personal experience recounted in 1900 details some beliefs of the time:

My little boy of four years old was taken one day lately to see the house now in building for us in Barnet. It had already been arranged that he should formally lay the date-stone when it was ready, but he wanted to be able to help at once, so the workmen good-naturedly let him lay a brick. As he was leaving the house afterwards, the head bricklayer called after the nurse, 'the little boy will have no luck with the stone if he don't wet the brick!'. When she told me this, I took back the child later in the day with a small coin to give to the friendly bricklayer who had superintended his work, and I found the words 'no luck' scribbled upon the brick he had laid. On our next visit to the house, we found that the words had been smudged out, but after the laying of the date-stone, which we were careful to 'butter' with a variety of coins, we noticed that even the smears were carefully washed off. In my native district (the borders of Shropshire and Staffordshire) this would have been called 'paying his foot-ale'. The builder of our house tells us that when the first chimney is finished he himself will have to give the men a pint of ale apiece, after which they will hoist a flag on the roof-tree. If they do not get the ale, they will very likely hoist a black flag, and perhaps even refuse to continue the work. (*Folk-Lore* 11 (1900), 457–8)

A follow-up letter in the same journal describes a 'rearing', common in the northern counties, which was a supper given to the workmen when the roof principals of a house were fixed (*Folk-Lore* 12 (1901), 104).

See also *SHOES and *CATS.

bull-baiting, see *BLOOD SPORTS.

bullbeggar. In North Country and West Country dialects, a term for any frightening supernatural figure. In Reginald *Scot's *The Discoverie of Witchcraft* (1584), it comes at the head of a mixed list of scary creatures: 'Our mothers' maids have so fraied us with bull beggers, spirits, witches, urchins, elves . . . and other such bugs that we are afraid of our owne shadowes' (p. 153).

bull-running. One of the well-known popular *blood sports of the past, although it apparently took place in only a few locations, and is often confused with bull-baiting which was much more widespread. Bull-running involved letting a bull loose in the streets of a town, if necessary goading him with dogs and sharp sticks to encourage him to rampage through the streets just for the fun of the chase for all concerned. The best-known example was at Stamford (Lincolnshire), which obtained its celebrity by inspiring one of the first successful campaigns by the Royal Society for Prevention of Cruelty to Animals after the passing of the Cruelty to Animals Act in 1835. The local people had been fighting hard to keep their custom since at least 1788, when the first attempt to ban it had taken place, but the bull-running was finally suppressed in 1839.

The other known example of bull-running was at Tutbury (Staffordshire), where the custom was bound up with a curious organization called the Court of Minstrels, apparently founded in the 14th century. The minstrels had the privilege of one bull a year from the local Priory (and after dissolution from the Duke of Devonshire), which was 'run' in the town and which they could keep if they could catch it before sunset. Originally, it was only the minstrels involved, but later the local people were permitted to join in and it developed into a contest between Staffordshire and Derbyshire men, as the town is on the border between the two counties. The bull-running lapsed in 1774. An origin story states that John of Gaunt, who rebuilt Tutbury castle, married a Spanish princess in 1374, and he started the bull-running to make her feel at home.

The description of bull-running in Birmingham, published in the *Victoria County History: Warwickshire*, ii (1908, 416–17) appears to be based on one from Stamford and is not evidence for the custom in Birmingham (see *N&Q* 185 (1943), 82).

Malcolmson, 1973; Hone, 1827: i. 741–3; Brand, 1849: ii. 63–5, Chambers, 1878: ii. 225–6, 574–6; Edward G. Fairholme and Wellesley Pain, *A Century of Work for Animals: The History of the RSPCA 1824–1924* (1924), 75–9; F. W. Hackwood, *Staffordshire Curiosities and Antiquities* (1905), 110–17.

burial, irregular. Traditionally, outcasts in life were outcasts in death. In early modern England, 'The infliction of damage upon the corpses of executed criminals—the quartering of traitors, and the use of dissection upon murderers—historically constituted a deliberate judicial breach of society-wide norms and values . . . the deliberate mutilation or destruction of identity, perhaps for eternity' (Richardson, 1987: 28–9). The same could be said of gibbeting, and of the *skins of sacriligious robbers nailed to church doors, like vermin to barn doors.

Religious burial was also refused to *suicides and the excommunicate, symbolizing their damnation, and to *unbaptized babies, whose status was ambiguous. Jews, Nonconformists, and Roman Catholics were not admitted to Anglican churchyards, and used private burial grounds until public cemeteries were established. Another solution was to bury the rejected person on his own land; the *Hereford Journal* of 19 June 1783 reported the discovery of a skeleton in a paddock near Grantham, under a stone inscribed: 'Here lies the body of Zacharias Laxton, deceased the 27th of August, 1667, being for his excommunication denied the usual place of burial.'

Many Romano-British and Anglo-Saxon corpses have been discovered decapitated (the head often between the feet), laid face down, crushed under large boulders, bound, or dismembered; some are in normal cemeteries, others in boundary earthworks. The latter may have been criminals, buried at execution sites; their remoteness 'probably reflects the desire to banish social outcasts to the geographical limits of local territories' (Reynolds, 1998). At Sutton Hoo (Suffolk), the practice continued into the 10th or 11th centuries at the site of a gallows (Carver, 1998: 137–44). Such treatments could also be rituals to stop them returning as *undead; indeed, both intentions may be present, since executed criminals, having died by violence, would be thought likely to 'walk'.

Belief in the effectiveness of prone burial persisted remarkably long. On 29 July 1915 a letter to *The Times* describes how British soldiers were impressed by the evil expression on a dead German's face: 'Later, I found our men burying him most carefully—face downwards. You know why. If he began digging his way out he would only go deeper' (reprinted in *Folk-Lore* 27 (1916), 224–5). On 30 July 1915, the *Daily Chronicle* reported what must surely be the same incident, with the soldier's explanation: 'If the beggar begins to scratch, he will scratch his way to the devil. It's an old belief in our district, and it took our fancy' (quoted in *N&Q* 11s:12 (1915), 118).

Suicides also received dishonorable burial. From medieval to modern times, English law distinguished between those guilty of 'self-murder' and those 'of unsound mind'. By Church law, the former could not be laid in consecrated ground, nor could the burial service be read over them; the latter were allowed these rites, but were often placed on the *north side of the churchyard. Until 1823, 'self-murderers' were buried in a roadway (not necessarily at a *crossroads), to be trampled underfoot. A stake was often driven through the body to pin it in its grave; its top was sometimes left visible, as a deterrent (MacDonald and Murphy, 1990: 44–9, 137–9). Broken pottery, flints, and stones might be thrown in (Shakespeare, *Hamlet*, v. i) as a further mark of disgrace, or perhaps a precaution against ghosts.

Roadside and crossroads burials are a fairly common topic for local legend, as is the idea that a particular tree grew from a stake driven through a corpse, or from a seed laid in its mouth—e.g. Dab's Elm near Winchcombe and Maud's Elm in Swindon (both Gloucestershire), grown from the stakes of suicides.

Some unconventional burials were freely chosen; William Chambers's *Book of Days* (1864) lists several examples from the late 18th century of men buried on hilltops, in woodland, or in fields (i. 804–5, ii. 627–8). In 1800, the coffin of a notorious eccentric, Major Peter Labellière, was lowered head first into a deep grave like a well, on Box Hill in Surrey (*The Gentleman's Magazine* 70: 2 (1800), p. 693); it was said he expected the world to turn topsy-turvey on *Doomsday, so he would then be the right way up. Such graves become a topic for storytelling; run round them seven times, it is often said, and the ghost will jump out. Isolated towers, obelisks, and follies are sometimes alleged to cover odd burials, e.g. of a man on horseback, or holding a bottle of wine; the macabre here blends with humour.

It is said of various legendary *wizards and local heroes that they cheated the Devil by promising he could have their souls whether they were buried inside or outside the church, and then getting themselves buried in the thickness of its wall, i.e. 'neither in nor out'.

Merrifield, 1987: 71–6; David Wilson, *Anglo-Saxon Paganism* (1992), 77–86; Andrew Reynolds, *British Archaeology* 31 (Feb. 1998), 8–9; Martin Carver, *Sutton Hoo: Burial Ground of Kings?* (1998); MacDonald and Murphy, 1990.

burial, normal, see *FUNERALS.

burial with grave-goods. In pagan burials and cremations, the dead body was often (though not invariably) accompanied by jewellery, weapons, food, and drink, and sometimes a horse or dog, presumably its possessions in life. Christianity abolished the custom for ordinary people, but allowed priests, monks, and nuns to be buried in their religious vestments and habits, and bishops and abbots to have their rings and croziers with them. Throughout the Middle Ages and beyond, there was always a conflict between the urge towards the humble anonymity of a shroud, and the wish to dress a corpse in clothing appropriate to its status. Recent clearances of over 2,000 18th- and 19th-century coffins from vaults of London churches produced a good many wedding rings, but only two cases of men buried in normal clothing: one in military uniform, one a dandy in fashionable dress, with wig and cane (Litten, 1991: 73). Nowadays shrouds are still common, but many people prefer clothes, which can be anything from high-quality nightwear to one's wedding dress or a favourite suit.

In modern times, it is normal at military and state funerals for flags, items of uniform, insignia, etc., to be laid on the coffin; they may or may not go with it into the grave. The same may be done for other occupational symbols, as when the friends of an old bargeman who was being buried at Havant (Hampshire) in 1994 laid his cap and a small anchor on the coffin at the end of the service (*FLS News* 22 (1995), 13). It is fairly common for small personal possessions such as photographs to be slipped into the coffin or dropped into the grave; even more frequently, suitable objects are laid on graves, either after the *funeral or on anniversaries and festivals.

Archaic customs such as animal sacrifice and food offerings occasionally reappear; Lovett stated that in the London working classes early in the 20th century, it was 'by no means rare' for pets to be killed at the death of their owner; he notes two instances—a little girl's canary laid in her coffin, and an old woman's cat buried in the garden on the day of her funeral, 'so that the old dear might have her best friend with her' (Lovett, 1925: 35, 48). In 1928 at Paignton (Somerset), a woman who used to put chickens, pigeon pies, fruit, and wine on or in her family vault sued the local council because they had forbidden her to do so, saying this constituted a 'nuisance'. She lost her case (*Daily Express*, 21 Mar. 1928 and 11 Nov. 1928).

See also *FUNERALS, *GRAVES.

Burne, Charlotte Sophia (1850–1923). An interest in the local history and antiquities of her adopted county of Shropshire led her to folklore, but the defining moment came when her notes were shown to Miss Georgina Jackson in the early 1870s. Jackson had for many years been working on a projected book on Shropshire dialect, and had collected much folklore in the process, but failing health prompted her to hand the projects to Burne for completion. The latter thus brought out the planned *Shropshire Word-Book* (1879) and, after adding a great deal of her own material, *Shropshire Folk-Lore* (1883), which proved to be one of the best of the *regional folklore collections and is still in demand today. Burne also joined the *Folklore Society in 1883, and was soon involved on its Council and in various organizing roles, editing the journal *Folk-Lore* (1899–1908) and serving two terms as the Society's President (1909–10). In her first presidential address (*Folk-Lore* 21 (1910)) she claimed, probably correctly, to be the first female president of a learned society in Britain. She continued to contribute numerous articles and notes to folklore journals and to local Shropshire/Staffordshire periodicals for the rest of her life, and her other major publication was the second edition of the influential *Handbook of Folk-Lore* (1914), for the Folklore Society.

Burne's particular forte was fieldwork, in contrast to her fellow folklorists who were primarily library scholars and thinkers, basing their theories on other people's books and manuscripts. *Shropshire Folk-Lore* demonstrated the wealth of material waiting to be collected, and also identified an important practical role available to those interested in the subject but unable to indulge in high theory. She became an advocate of fieldwork, urging systematic collecting programmes, offering advice on how to go about it, and urging high standards of documentation. In the process, she experimented with methods such as the geographical mapping of *calendar custom variants, which were later to be adopted as normal practice. At the time of her death, she was working, with the Society's 'Brand Committee', on an ambitious plan to publish a new comprehensive survey of customs, to serve as an updated and expanded edition of *Brand's *Observations on Popular Antiquities*.

Burne's major articles were 'The Collection of English Folk-Lore', *Folk-Lore* 1 (1890), 313–30; 'The Value of European Folklore in the History of Culture', *Folk-Lore* 21 (1910), 14–41; 'The Scientific Aspects of Folklore', *Folk-Lore* 22 (1911), 14–32.

Obituary: *Folk-Lore* 34 (1923), between pp. 99 and 100; Dorson, 1968: 318–22; Gordon Ashman, *Talking Folklore* 1:1 (1986), 6–21 and in Davidson and Blacker, 2001: 33–44; Simon J. Bronner, *Folklore Women's Communication* 24 (1981), 14–19.

Burning Bartle. An apparently unique *calendar custom which takes place on the evening of the Saturday after St Bartholomew's Day (24 August) in West Witton (North Yorkshire). A larger-than-life *effigy (known as Bartle) is constructed of combustible material and is paraded down the village street followed by a crowd of local people. At certain houses, Bartle is halted, while his bearers declaim the following lines:

> At Pen Hill Crags, he tore his rags
> At Hunter's Thorn, he blew his horn
> At Capplebank Stee, he brak his knee
> At Grassgill Beck, he brak his neck
> At Waddam's End, he couldn't fend
> At Grassgill End, he made his end,

and the assembled people cheer heartily. At the far end of the village, Bartle is first stabbed and then burnt, while the crowd sings. Nothing is known about the custom's origins, although one local legend seeks to explain it: Bartle represents a local pig thief who was chased, captured, and killed by an irate populace. The chant, with its local place-names, is cited as evidence of the chase. It is most likely, however, that the name Bartle simply reflects the day (St Bartholomew's Day), which is the logical day for local festivities as it is the feast day of the parish church. That said, however, we are no nearer understanding the origin or purpose of the custom, as its provable history only dates from the late 19th century.

Smith, 1989: 119–22; *N&Q* 200 (1955), 127–8; Kightly, 1986: 59–60.

burns. A spoken *charm for curing burns and scalds has been recorded from various parts of England. The Shropshire version ran:

> There was three angels came from the west,
> The one brought fire and the other brought frost,
> The other brought the book of Jesus Christ.
> In the name of Father, Son and Holy Ghost, Amen.

(Burne, 1883: 183–4)

From Fittleworth (Sussex), there is more information about the associated ritual. The words, there called a 'blessing', could only be used on a Sunday evening by one particular woman, who would bow her head, blow on the burn, and murmur:

> There came two Angels from the north,
> One was fire and one was Frost.
> Out, Fire; in, Frost.
> In the name of Father, Son, and Holy Ghost.

(Latham, 1878: 35–6)

bus tickets. Fieldwork by Iona and Peter Opie in the 1950s revealed a cluster of beliefs concerned with the humble bus or tram ticket. Children all over the country reported various ways in which the serial number printed on the ticket could be interpreted, the simplest being that if the numbers added up to 21 it was lucky for you and should be kept. More complex ways of calculating the number revealed the initials of your future spouse, when you would be married, and so on. Several reported the use of the rhyme more usually associated with *magpies: 'One for sorrow, two for joy', etc. Ticket customs are still carried out by some children (SR).

Opie and Opie, 1959: 329–34; Opie and Tatem, 1989: 50.

butterflies. In William Hone's *Table Book* (1827, I, col. 678), a young woman describes having recently seen, in a Devonshire lane, 'a man running at full speed, with his hat in one hand, and a stick in the other'; he was trying to kill a butterfly, the first he had seen that year, because 'they say that a body will have cruel bad luck if a ditn'en kill a *furst* a zeeth'. In Lincolnshire, anyone who crushed the first butterfly of the year underfoot would crush all his enemies that year. A related omen was that if the first butterfly you see is white, you will eat white bread all year (implying enough money for good food); but if it is brown, then you will eat brown bread, i.e. be unlucky and poor (Opie and Tatem, 1989: 51).

Butterflies and moths were associated with death, sometimes merely as *omens, sometimes as the soul or *ghost (Opie and Tatem, 1989: 266–7). In Devon and parts of Yorkshire they were thought to be souls of *unbaptized babies (Radford, Radford, and Hole, 1961: 77–8).

See also *WASPS.

Butterworth, George Sainton Kaye (1885–1916). One of the most promising of the Edwardian generation of musicians interested in folk music, his work was sadly curtailed by his death in France in August 1916. He came to folk music through his acquaintance with Ralph *Vaughan Williams, and with characteristic energy and enthusiasm started collecting songs in 1906 and continued to do so until the First World War. His manuscripts (now at the *Vaughan Williams Memorial Library) contain over 300 songs, collected in various counties, although he is best known for his work in Sussex. In 1911, he joined the *English Folk Dance Society and became a disciple and collaborator of Cecil *Sharp, collecting and editing *morris, *sword, and country dances at his behest and helping with several of his books; he was also an energetic member of Sharp's demonstration dance team. Butterworth's interests as a musician prompted him to use some of the material he collected in his own compositions, and he published a number of pieces which included traditional themes, although he destroyed many of his unpublished manuscripts while in the army. Two of his best-known pieces, *A Shropshire Lad* and *Banks of Green Willow*, are still heard regularly today.

George Butterworth, *Folk Songs from Sussex* (1913); Michael Dawney, *FMJ* 3:2 (1926), 99–113; Russell Wortley and Michael Dawney, *FMJ* 3:3 (1977), 193–207; Ian Copley, *George Butterworth: A Centennial Tribute* (1985); *DNB*.

cabbages. The method of *love divination by means of a cabbage (kail) stalk pulled at random from the ground is best known by the note to Robert Burns's poem 'Halloween' (1787), and would seem exclusively Scots and Irish if it were not for isolated English references such as Ella M. Leather's note from Herefordshire: 'If a girl go into the garden on this night (Halloween), and cut a cabbage, as the clock strikes twelve, the wraith of her future husband will appear' (Leather, 1912: 64). Cabbages also had various uses in folk-medicine, although again the Irish and Scots examples outweigh the English in number and variety. Vickery records a reference from Cambridge in the 1960s which recommends a cabbage-leaf tied round a swollen knee, and from Devon in the 1990s to drink cabbage-water as a cure for colds, flu, headache, and especially hangovers.

Vickery, 1995: 57–9; Opie and Tatem, 1989: 53.

Cadbury Castle. Two early antiquaries, John Leland (1542) and William Camden (1586), claimed that this site, a large Iron Age hill-fort about twelve miles from *Glastonbury in Somerset, was the Camelot where King *Arthur often held court; this contradicts Malory, who identified Camelot with Winchester. Local people had told Leland that Arthur 'much resorted' to Cadbury, and that Roman coins and a silver horseshoe had been found there. Stories current in the 1890s were fuller. It was then being said that the hill was hollow, with a golden gate that opened on *Midsummer Eve to show the king and his court feasting inside; at every full moon Arthur and his men rode round the hill to water their silver-shod horses at a nearby well. Some antiquaries visiting the fort at this period were asked by a local man if they had come 'to take the king away'.

calendar. The English calendar is based on that devised by Julius Caesar, the 'Julian calendar'. It has twelve months, beginning on 1 January, but as the Christian Church disapproved of the wild festivities held by pagan Romans around that date it chose 25 March, the Feast of the Annunciation, as New Year's Day; some countries adopted this for civic purposes too, but not all. In England, the year was held to begin either on 1 January or 25 December up to the late 12th century, when 25 March was chosen instead; the two systems ran concurrently till 1751, with calendars and almanacs using 1 January, but legal and official documents using 25 March. The year reckoned in the latter way was called the 'Year of Grace'.

Astronomically, the Julian calendar was faulty, being based on a slightly mistaken estimate of the length of a year. As centuries passed, it became visibly out of synch with the astronomical solstices and equinoxes, and in 1582 Pope Gregory XIII directed that that year be shortened by ten days, reorganized the method of reckoning leap years, and restored 1 January as New Year's Day. Catholic countries adopted this 'Gregorian calendar', but Protestant ones did not, though the mathematician Dr *Dee argued as early as 1583 that England too should make an adjustment, preferably of eleven days. At last, in 1750, Parliament decreed that the year 1751 would end on 31 December, and that in 1752 September would be shortened by eleven days, with 2 September being followed immediately by 14 September. (The tax year, however, was not changed, and still starts on 5 April, eleven days after the old New Year date of 25 March).

The 'loss' of eleven days worried many people, and some were upset that festivals would no longer be held on the 'right' date, i.e. precisely twelve months after they were last held (see *Holy Thorn). An 'Old Style' date is eleven days later than the adjusted calendar; thus 10 October is an Old Style equivalent to

Michaelmas (29 September), while 6 January is *both* the Feast of the Epiphany or Twelfth Night in its own right (New Style) *and* the Old Style equivalent of Christmas (25 December).

Quarter Days were four dates marking the beginning or end of legal contracts, especially between landlord and tenant or employer and employee. In England they were Lady Day (25 March), Midsummer Day (24 June), Michaelmas (29 September), and Christmas Day.

calendar customs. Those which take place once a year, at a particular date or season; also called seasonal customs. Examples are bonfires on *November the Fifth, *wassailing apple trees on *Twelfth Night, or sending *valentine cards on 14 February. They are thereby distinguished from *life-cycle customs and *occupational customs.

The folklore calendar is complex, since it is a combination of several historically independent systems. Scientific calculation plays hardly any part; even *Midsummer Day, 24 June, is not identical with the astronomical solstice, while the midwinter festivities have always stretched across a range of dates in late December and early January, and the equinoxes are totally ignored. From the mid-13th century there is evidence that 1 May (*May Day) was regarded as marking the beginning of spring in England, as it does over much of Europe; its counterpart, 1 November, is more composite, since it seems to draw part of its significance from the start of an old Celtic cattle-rearing year, and part from two major Church festivals, *All Saints Day and *All Souls.

One extremely important factor is the annual cycle of food production, which itself varies according to the crop and the climate; arable farming sets a different pattern from stock-breeding or fishing or fruit-growing. Each of these generated festivals to mark the beginning of major activities (ploughing), or more often their ending (*sheep-shearing, *harvesting). The cycles of dearth and abundance, of hard work and leisure, also affected festivals, both positively and negatively; for instance, the abundance of corn, beer, and meat in late autumn favoured them, whereas in summer they were impossible until the vital work of harvesting and haymaking was finished.

Equally important was the Church calendar, supplying not only the major cycle of Advent, *Christmas, *Shrove Tuesday, *Lent, *Good Friday, *Easter, *Ascension, *Whitsun, and

Corpus Christi, but also (especially before the Reformation) a series of saints' feasts on fixed dates. These determined the patronal feast of the local church (see *church ales and *wakes), and/or the date of the local fair. Some saints were the patrons of particular guilds or trades, so their feasts were celebrated by these craftsmen throughout the country; thus, cobblers observed *St Crispin's Day and blacksmiths *St Clement's, and were still doing so late in the 19th century. Other saints' days were the occasion for 'visiting' and 'display' customs which continued after the reason was forgotten; *catterning, *thomasing, and *grottoes are examples.

Superimposed on the natural and the ecclesiastical calendar come the turning-points of the legal year (*New Year's Day, the Quarter Days); the official commemorations of national events, of which at least two (*Oak Apple Day and *November the Fifth) developed folkloric traits; civic and academic celebrations; and *Bank Holidays set on arbitrary dates but attracting traditional pageants, sports, etc., to themselves. It should also be remembered that the reform of the calendar in 1752 caused the 'loss' of eleven days; this led some people to claim that 6 January was the 'real' or 'old' Christmas Day, and to transfer certain beliefs and customs to that date. A dating which now looks arbitrary can sometimes be better understood by making an eleven-day adjustment (see *blackberries, *grottoes).

At present, the traditional calendar is undergoing exceptionally rapid changes. Many customs have been moved from their traditional dates to the nearest weekend, or even to the nearest Bank Holiday, for the convenience of performers and spectators. May Day and Whitsun are both threatened by the establishment of Bank Holidays on nearby Mondays; Whitsun has succumbed, but so far popular attachment to May Day itself remains strong. Traditional foods once linked to one special day, such as hot cross buns, chocolate Easter eggs, and mince pies, now appear in the shops about two months ahead of time. On the other hand, some new dates are becoming prominent, and new ways of celebrating old ones are devised.

Apart from considering their dates, calendar customs can be usefully classified in a number of ways. One is to identify the people involved as participants or performers: does the performance involve everyone in the village, or a particular age-group, sex, occupation, area, religion, or interest? A further method is to analyse the characteristics of the performance itself—drama, singing, disguise, display, and so on—and of the place where it occurs.

'Display' customs are those where the participants have made or gathered something which they display to a potential audience, usually in the hope of receiving something for showing it; children's *grottoes, *garlands, or *poppy shows are examples.

In 'visiting' customs, the participants visit people's homes or other buildings (e.g. shops, pubs) to carry out their performance, either indoors or outside, depending on the type of custom. They thus give the same performance over and over again at different locations, but the journey from one place to another is not part of the performance. *Mumming plays, *souling, and *clementing are examples. In some cases the visit itself is explicitly claimed to bring luck, either generally (e.g. *first footing) or for specific items (e.g. wassailing trees, cattle, crops), but by no means always. The performance can be of many kinds, including drama or display, but in most cases the visitors sing a song and hope for money, food, or drink in return. In a few customs, such as thomasing, it is simply the visiting which elicits generosity, for no real performance is involved.

'Processional' customs are those in which the performance continues while moving from place to place, as in a parade, though the performers may also halt at certain points to perform particular static actions. *Helston Furry Dance is a good example, since the dance itself processes through the town, as does the *Padstow Hobby Horse. The *Bacup Coconut Dancers are another example because even though they perform static dances they also dance on their way from one place to another. The *Abbots Bromley dancers sometimes walk normally as they go from farm to farm, or sometimes progress in a winding single file, i.e. processionally.

'Static' customs are stationary, so that the audience comes to the custom rather than vice versa; *well-dressing is an example, as are children on a street corner asking for 'a penny for the Guy'.

All books on regional folklore include a section on calendar cusoms. For an extensive collection of illustrative texts, historically arranged, see Wright and Lones, 1936–40; for a thorough historical analysis, see Hutton, 1994 and 1996. For introductory accounts of major customs, see Hole, 1976; Pegg, 1981; Shuel, 1985. Sutton 1997 combines detailed recent fieldwork with archive material for a single area.

calendars. 'Calendars received about Christmas time should not be hung on the wall till the new year, as it is unlucky to do so' was noted from a Birmingham informant and published in *Folk-Lore* (45 (1934), 162). Other examples of the same belief are given by Opie and Tatem, including one where it was considered unlucky even to display the next month before it arrived. This appears to be based on the idea that to do so would tempt fate.

Opie and Tatem, 1989: 53.

Camelot. In French medieval romances, Camelot was one among several towns where King *Arthur regularly held court, but unlike the others (London, Carlisle, Caerleon) it has come to symbolize the glamour of Arthurian times. Its name corresponds to *Camulodonum*, the Roman forerunner of Colchester, the ruined walls and gateways of which were still conspicuous in the 12th century, but medieval writers were unsure of the identification. Malory said it was Winchester; the Elizabethan antiquaries Leland and Camden more tentatively suggested *Cadbury Castle (Somerset).

candle auctions. 'Auction by candle' or 'sale by inch of candle' was one of the normal ways in which auctions were organized until about the turn of the 18th century. There are two main variations. In one a short candle (usually about an inch) is lit and bidding continues until it goes out, and the last bid made before it goes out is the one that stands. Alternatively, a pin or nail is stuck into a lighted candle, and the bidding stops when it falls out. Samuel Pepys provides excellent historical perspective: '6 November 1660—To our office, where we met all for the sale of two ships by an inch of candle (the first time that ever I saw any of this kind)', and there are further references on 28 February 1661, 9 April 1661, and 3 September 1662.

Although the practice was new to Pepys, it had been in operation since at least the 15th century, and was sufficiently reputable to be the stipulated method in, for example, the Act for Settling the Trade to the West Indies

(1698). Candle auctions have survived in a number of places, always concerned with *land tenure and annual leasing arrangements. At Hubberholme, North Yorkshire, a sixteen-acre field called the Poors Pasture, left over from the local enclosure, is auctioned on the first Monday night in January. The vicar and churchwardens are in charge, and the bidders cannot actually see the candle's progress. Church Acre meadow in Aldermaston, Berkshire, is let every three years by candle (and pin) in December. Stowell Mead, seven and a half acres at Tatworth in Somerset, is let annually on the Tuesday following 6 April. Church Acre, Chedzoy, Somerset, is let every 21 years (and this claims to be the oldest candle auction in the country). In Leigh, Dorset, the 'aftergrass' (i.e. autumn and winter grazing) of two meadows is let in the same way.

Brian Learmount, *A History of the Auction* (1985); Kightly, 1986: 65–6; Hole, 1975: 127–8; Sykes, 1977: 50–1, 163.

Candlemas (2 February). This is the English name for a religious festival, the last of the Christmas cycle, which celebrates the Purification (i.e. the *churching) of the Virgin Mary 40 days after the birth of Jesus, in accordance with Jewish custom. It necessarily falls on 2 February, the fortieth day after 25 December. It began in Byzantium in the 4th century, and was established in Rome by the 7th century; it has no connection with the Irish feast of Imbolc on 1 February.

Candlemas was important in the medieval Catholic calendar; each parishioner attended Mass and joined a procession, bringing a *candle as an offering to the church. Other candles were blessed and then taken home, to be kept as protection against *thunderstorms, demons, and sickness, and lit by the beds of the dying. Elaborate processions and liturgical dramas were devised, using candles to symbolize Christ, the Light of the World; at Beverley (Yorkshire), a woman 'nobly dressed and adorned as the Queen of Heaven' carried a doll representing the Infant Jesus, while other parishioners represented Joseph, Simeon, Anna, and angels, the latter carrying 24 large candles. These rites were suppressed after the Reformation, but in Dorset and Nottinghamshire there are occasional 19th-century references to people lighting candles in their own homes on this day, or exchanging them as gifts.

In the 17th century, the Eve of Candlemas marked the end of the Christmas season.

*Herrick wrote three poems on the topic, noting that sports and dainty foods were at an end, the remains of the *Yule Log quenched and set aside till the next year, and all decorative greenery removed.

Duffy, 1992: 15–22; Hutton, 1996: 139–43.

candles. In religious ritual, candles express a widespread symbolism whereby light is equated with goodness and spirituality—specifically, in Christianity, with Christ as the Light of the World. In all Catholic and many Anglican churches, there must be two alight during all services; they feature in the communal liturgy at Advent, *Candlemas, and *Easter; they are often used in processions and *baptisms, and placed beside deathbeds and coffins. They also are a material expression of individual prayer; hence the customs of buying a small candle (or its modern equivalent, a night-light) and leaving it to burn before an altar or statue, and carrying candles during vigils of mourning or protest. Paradoxically, they also express celebration, so have a place on *Christmas trees, *birthday cakes, and dinner tables.

In medieval Catholicism, candles blessed by a priest (especially at Candlemas) were kept at home to protect the house against demons, *witchcraft, and thunderstorms, and to be lit for the sick and dying; they were one of the commonest gifts offered in *pilgrimage; people left money to ensure that lights would burn in front of specified altars, crosses, or statues in their parish church, especially during Mass (Duffy, 1992: 16–22, 134, 146–9; Finucane, 1977: 95–6).

Religious ritual is recalled in the idea that solemn cursing involves 'bell, book, and candle', and stories about ghost *laying where the exorcist's candle must be kept alight. An ingenious variation of the latter concerns the ghost of 'Old Coles', who haunted a road between Bransford and Brocamin (Worcestershire): twelve parsons trapped him one dark night in a nearby pool, by the light of an inch of candle, bidding him stay there till the candle burnt out—and, to make sure he does, they threw the candle into the pool and filled it in (Hazlitt, 1905: 458).

Occasionally candles were used in *magic; in 1843 a Mrs Bell in Norwich was said to have stuck a candle with *pins in order to immobilize the arms and legs of a man she had quarrelled with (Hole, 1973: 91). Henderson reports two love *spells, the first being from Durham, where a servant girl who kept a candle stump studded with pins explained, 'It's to bring my sweetheart. Thou see'st, sometimes he's slow a-coming, and if I stick a candle-end full o' pins it always fetches him.' His second account is from Buckinghamshire:

Damsels desirous of seeing their lovers would stick two pins through the candle they were burning, taking care that the pins passed through the wick. While doing this they recited the following verse:

It's not this candle alone I stick
But . . . .'s heart I mean to prick
Whether he be asleep or awake
I'd have him come to me and speak.

By the time the candle burned down to the pins and went out, the lover would be certain to present himself. (Henderson, 1879: 172-3; cf. Opie and Tatem, 1989: 55-6).

Henderson's informant thought this dangerous. Of three girls she knew who had used this spell, one did marry the man but was very unhappy; a second was harangued by her lover when he arrived, as 'no tongue could tell what she had made him suffer' by summoning him, and he immediately left her.

One of the regular *Halloween games was to hang a short stick from a rafter, with an apple fixed to one end and a lighted candle to the other. With their hands tied behind their backs, the players attempt to bite the apple while avoiding the singeing candle. Strutt reproduces two illustrations from 14th-century manuscripts showing games where people are sitting on a pole above a large bowl of water, holding candles which they must manipulate carefully to avoid losing their balance (*Sports and Pastimes of England* (1801; 1876 edn. by William Hone, 503-4).

See also *BLESSING THE THROATS, *CANDLE AUCTIONS, *CANDLEMAS, *HAND OF GLORY.

cante fable. A technical term for spoken prose narratives interspersed with short songs conveying crucial information (e.g. magical utterances, riddles, threats, etc.). English *folktales often contain verses, but they are not sung; one of the few references to a true cante fable performance is by W. H. Jones, who noted in 1889 that he had recently heard a version of The Frog King from a storyteller in Holderness, who used 'a traditional air' (unspecified) for the frog's calls:

Come bring me my supper,
My own sweet, sweet one

and

Come, let us go to bed,
My own sweet, sweet one.
(Philip, 1992: 95-6)

Cap o' Rushes. This Suffolk *fairytale was contributed to the *Ipswich Journal* in 1878 by Mrs Anna Walter-Thomas, from memories of how her nurse used to tell it some twenty years earlier. It belongs to an international type known as 'Catskin' (part of the *Cinderella cycle), but has rationalized the magic elements. It tells how a man with three daughters asks each one how much she loves him; the youngest answers, 'I love you as fresh meat loves salt', so he angrily drives her away. Disguising herself in a hooded cloak of rushes, she takes work as a kitchenmaid and hides her own fine clothes. Some time later, she secretly goes to a grand dance being held nearby, looking so lovely that her master's son falls in love with her, but she slips home unnoticed. This happens twice more, and though the third time he gives her a ring he still cannot learn who she is, and falls ill with longing. By dropping the ring into his gruel she reveals herself, and they marry. She orders the food at the wedding feast to be cooked without salt, which causes her father, who is among the guests, to understand just how essential salt is, and repent of his injustice to her; they are reconciled.

Jacobs, 1894/1968: 34-6; Briggs, 1970-1: A. ii. 387-9; Philip, 1992: 122-6.

cards, playing. Invented in the 14th century, and a popular pastime ever since for both pleasure and profit. It is hardly surprising that numerous superstitions concerning card-playing have been reported, including, for example: sitting *cross-legged, changing or turning your *chair, being the first to touch the two of clubs, and even possessing a piece of hangman's rope (*N&Q* 4s:1 (1868), 193; 4s:12 (1873), 41; *Gentleman's Magazine* II (1832), 491-4). Since at least the 17th century, card-playing was particularly popular at Christmas, and even those who did not play the rest of the year would take a hand or two at the festive season. 'The country-maid leaves half her market, and must be sent again if she forgets a pack of cards on Christmas-eve . . .' (Hone, 1827: 804, quoting Stevenson, *Twelve Mouths*, 1661). Card-playing was also prevalent at *funerals and wakes, even on the coffin itself (Henderson, 1879: 55).

The popular view of cards has long been ambivalent, however, as there has always been an awareness of the moral and spiritual danger involved in handling them. Not for nothing were they termed by many 'The Devil's Picture-Books', either in earnest or in uneasy jest. Playing on Sundays was particularly frowned upon (N&Q 4s:10 (1872), 377). A moralistic story, known all over Europe in various versions, reflects this ambivalence by relating how members of a card-playing party suddenly realize that they have been joined by the Devil. This is often told as a developed tale, but also exists in more modest form:

(The Devil's) partiality for playing at cards has long been proverbial, both in Lancashire and elsewhere. A near relative of the writer firmly believed that the devil had once visited their company when they had prolonged their play into Sunday. How he joined them they never rightly knew, but (as in the Danish legend respecting a similar visit) his presence was first suspected in consequence of his extraordinary 'run of good luck'; and a casual detection of his cloven foot completed the dispersion of the players. (Harland and Wilkinson, 1882: 81; see also Puhvel, 1975)

Some cards were generally thought to be unlucky, the Four of Clubs, Queen of Spades, and Ace of Spades, are usually the ones quoted in this context, while others had individual names: Four of Clubs (Devil's bedpost), Four of Hearts (Hob Collingwood), Ace of Diamonds (Earl of Cork), Nine of Diamonds (Curse of Scotland), Six of Hearts (Grace card), Queen of Clubs (Queen Bess), Four of Spades (Ned Stokes), Jack of Clubs (a Sunderland Fitter), and so on. Each has a story (or several stories) to explain it.

Lean, 1902–4; Opie and Tatem, 1989: 56–7, 68, 109–10, 189, 382–3, 449; Chambers, 1878: i. 281–4; Martin Puhvel, Folklore 76 (1975), 33–8; N&Q 5s:12 (1879), 426, 473; 185 (1943), 199, 262–3, 294).

Carpenter, James Madison (1888–1984). A Harvard-trained scholar who conducted extensive fieldwork in Britain between 1928 and 1935. While here, he amassed a staggering amount of material including 1050 *Child ballads (with 850 tunes), 500 sea songs and *sea shanties, 1,000 lyric folk-songs, and 300 *mumming plays, from England, Wales, and Scotland, noting items by ear and hand but also using a dictaphone to record many of the tunes. His collection is now housed in the Library of Congress, but remains largely unpublished. A microfilm copy of most of the material is lodged at the *Vaughan Williams Memorial Library, London.

Special issue of FMJ 7:4 (1998); Quarterly Journal of the Library of Congress 30:1 (1973), 68.

cars. Fine examples of living beliefs about good and bad luck. Some owners hang all sorts of *charms and *mascots from the driving mirror or from their key-rings; *green cars are rarely seen, because this colour is widely feared—yet, oddly, British racing cars were traditionally green. *Red, on the other hand, is safe and lucky. Beliefs about *numbers are readily applied to cars; recently there have been press items about a supposedly unlucky Ford Capri with the 'Satanic' *number 666 in its registration (Telegraph (15 Feb. 1997); Mirror (31 July 1998)). If a car persistently gives trouble, some say 'it must have been made on a *Friday'.

A good many *contemporary legends involve cars. Two of the earliest to be identified are the famous *Vanishing Hitchhiker (a pathetic ghost story), and 'The Stolen Corpse', a macabre joke about holiday-makers who try to smuggle the body of an elderly relative home on the roof-rack, only to have both car and corpse stolen. There are others about cars in which a suicide occurred, where bloodstains or a stench of death remain permanently; about maniacs and murderers either lurking inside one's car or trying to enter it when parked; about ghost cars haunting roads where they crashed; about ghostly hands gripping the steering-wheel. Old tales about witches immobilizing horse-drawn vehicles are echoed by modern ones where a car is inexplicably halted by a UFO.

There are innumerable anecdotes about drivers and driving, and about particular makes of car; some are mocking, while others, especially about the Rolls Royce, express awed admiration (Sanderson, 1969: 246–7). Back window stickers are a good medium for jokes, either against oneself ('When I grow up, I'm going to be a Porsche', seen on a Mini), or against other drivers ('This may be small, but it's mine, it's paid for, and it's ahead of yours').

Stewart Sanderson, Folklore 80 (1969), 241–52. For discussion based on American versions, see Jan Brunvand, The Vanishing Hitchhiker (1981), and The Choking Doberman (1984).

Castleton Garland. This takes place on *Oak Apple Day (29 May) in Castleton, Derbyshire, and in itself is unique although there are other *garland customs. The main event is a procession, led by the King and the Lady, on horseback, dressed in Stuart-looking costume, and, until 1955, the part of the Lady was played by a man dressed as a woman. Also in the procession are costumed Attendants who lead the horses, a number of village schoolgirls, dressed in white and carrying flowers and coloured ribbons, and a band. The centre of attention, however, is the Garland. This is made annually by each of the village pubs in turn. It is a large bell-shaped structure made up of a circular metal rim with upright wooden lathes meeting at the top. The whole thing is covered in garden and wild flowers and is large enough to fit over the King's head, with the aid of straps to rest on his shoulders. A separate, smaller bunch of flowers, called the Queen, is fixed to the top, and the complete garland is over three feet high. The procession sets off round the village, stopping outside each of the pubs, where the schoolgirls dance, and they then proceed to St Edmund's Church. The Queen is removed, and the Garland is then hoisted up the church tower by ropes and fixed to a pinnacle, where it will stay for a few weeks. The girls dance round a maypole set up in the village square. The King then places the Queen on the village war memorial, while the band plays the Last Post.

The earliest known reference is in the Churchwardens' Accounts of 1749, with a payment for 'an iron rod to hang ye Ringers Garland in'. The custom was organized by the church bell-ringers until 1897, and it was they who did the dancing. The war memorial visit, and the maypole, were introduced in 1916. As discussed elsewhere, *Royal Oak Day is the day of celebration for the restoration of the monarchy in the person of Charles II in 1660. There are numerous oak-motifs at Castleton, the church tower is decorated with oak branches, many of the locals wear oak-leaves, and the modern costumes reflect the Stuart theme. However, most authorities presume that the custom is a hybrid of Royal Oak Day and a *Jack-in-the-Green custom, and there is no doubt that the King looks remarkably similar to a Jack when he is underneath the Garland. However, Boyes argues persuasively for an origin in a village *rushbearing custom, and she also documents the major changes which the custom has undergone over time.

S. O. Addy, *Folk-Lore* 12 (1901), 394–430; 13 (1902), 313; Georgina Boyes, in Buckland and Wood, 1993: 105–18;

Geoff Lester, *Castleton Garland* (1972); Shuel, 1985: 32; Kightly, 1986: 67–8.

caterpillars. Make but few appearances in English lore, in most cases as one of the many small creatures who must be sacrificed to cure someone of whooping cough or, in at least one instance, the ague. The usual procedure is to tie the caterpillar in a bag round the neck of the afflicted person, or carry it in their pocket, and as it wastes away so will the malady. This was reported well into the 20th century. Charlotte Burne (1883: 239) reports from Shropshire that it was considered lucky if a hairy caterpillar crawls on you. However, according to the play *Wily Beguiled* (1606), '. . . how now caterpillar, It's a sign of death, when such vermin creep hedges so early in the morning'. In some quarters, the caterpillar was believed, particularly by children, to be poisonous (*N&Q* 5s:6 (1876) 462; 5s:7 (1877) 53, 237).

Opie and Tatem, 1989: 64.

cats. Beliefs concerning cats, especially *black ones, are numerous and often contradictory (Opie and Tatem, 1989: 57–62, 241). On the whole, black cats are lucky in England, and therefore appear on greetings cards and as *charms; however, informants from several counties say it is unlucky if one crosses your path, especially on the way to work, or if it sits with its back to you. Occasionally, the belief is found that *white cats bring bad luck. Dreaming of cats is usually interpreted as a warning that someone is being spiteful or treacherous towards you.

Perfectly normal feline actions, such as washing behind the ears or rushing wildly about the house, are thought to foretell rain or gales; the matter was debated in *N&Q* in 1889, with some correspondents saying it was true, but 'the paw must go right over the outer side of the ear', or the cat must 'place the paw behind the ear, and work it to the front right over her head, more as if she was brushing her hair than washing herself' (*N&Q* 7s:7 (1889), 309–10). A later issue (169 (1935), 202) adds: 'To discover from which side the wind will come it is necessary to observe the direction in which the cat is looking while scratching the earth.' Drowning a cat at sea will raise a strong wind, which in most circumstances is reckoned unlucky. All kittens born in May should be drowned, for they will be bad mousers, unlucky, good-for-nothing, and fond of bringing snakes into the house.

The idea that cats could be witches' *familiars is found in writings and trial reports of the 16th century, and has now become a cliché. But they were only one among many animals of which this was said; similarly, though there are references to witches changing into cats, *hares are mentioned more often. There is no evidence from England of regular large-scale massacres of 'satanic' cats, or of burning them in Midsummer bonfires, as sometimes occurred in Europe. They were occasionally used for demonic 'special effects'—in 1677 a *bonfire for *Queen Elizabeth's Day consumed the effigy of 'a most costly pope ... his belly filled with live cats which squalled most hideously as soon as they felt the fire', supposedly representing a dialogue between Pope and Devil (Cressy, 1989: 177).

Various cures involving the death or mutilation of a black cat are recorded in the 17th and 18th centuries: its head, burnt to a powder, was supposed good for eyeache, and blood from its cut-off tail or ears for shingles and erysipelas; the whole tail, buried under the *threshold, kept sickness away. *Styes were healed by stroking them *seven or *nine times with a black cat's tail—hopefully, still attached to its owner.

According to old medical theory, cats' blood and brains are poisonous, and their very presence harmful to man; the evidence cited in support sounds typical of allergy:

there is in some men a natural dislike and abhorring of cats, their natures being so composed, that not onely when they see them, but being neere them and vnseene, and hid of purpose, they fall into passions, fretting, sweating, pulling off their hats, and trembling fearefully, as I have knowne many in Germany ... and therefore they haue cryed out to take away the Cats. (Edward Topsell, *A History of Foure-Footed Beastes*, (1608), 106)

Topsell also thought that if a child got a cat's hair in his mouth, it would stick there, and cause wens or *king's evil. It was commonly said that a cat must never be allowed near a baby in its cot, lest it lie on the child and 'suck its breath'; this fear is still current, and not unreasonable, since the weight of a large cat might smother an infant. It was also thought wrong to let a cat into a room where a corpse was laid out, for if it jumped on to it, it would bring death to others (Opie and Tatem, 1989: 63–4). Some said a cat would never settle in a house while there was an unburied corpse there (*Denham Tracts*, 1895: ii. 74).

The dried-up corpses of cats are quite often found hidden away in cavities in the walls of old *buildings, and though some may have accidentally got trapped there, many are set up in lifelike attitudes, some even holding a dead rat or mouse. Traditionally, this was said to be done to scare mice away, just as dead vermin would be nailed to a barn door 'to warn others'; however, some folklorists interpret the custom as a survival of *foundation sacrifices, or as intended to repel witches' familiars in the form of *mice (Margaret M. Howard, *Man* (Nov. 1951), 149–5; Merrifield, 1987: 129–31). Small mutilated wooden cat-figures were found in the 1950s hidden in two old Essex houses, one accompanied by a piece of newspaper dated 1796; perhaps they too brought protection (*N&Q* 197 (1952), 367).

See also *ALIEN BIG CATS.

catterning, see *SOULING.

Cauld Lad of Hilton. According to Surtees's *History and Antiquities of Durham* (1820), this was the ghost of a stable lad, killed by one of the Barons of Hilton in an outburst of temper, who haunted Hylton castle; he worked like a *brownie by cleaning up untidy kitchens, but would also mess up anything which was already tidy. In order to get rid of him, the servants gave him a cloak and hood, which he put on gleefully, and then vanished, as brownies do. However, he was still sometimes heard wailing in and around the castle, where there was one room called 'the cauld lad's room' and never used except in emergencies.

Henderson, 1866: 229–30; Keightley, 1889: 296–7; Westwood, 1985: 334–6.

cauls. A belief repeatedly recorded from the 16th century to the present day is that when a baby is born with a caul (a 'mask', 'veil', or 'sillyhow') covering the face (also called a 'mask', 'veil', or 'sillyhow'), it must be kept for luck; whoever has one will never drown. This is a case of like-cures-like: 'for as a caul is removed from the head of a newly born child to save it literally from being suffocated by moisture, it became regarded as a charm against drowning by any who carried one beneath their clothing' (Lovett, 1925: 52). Formerly, cauls were often advertised for sale, for once sold they protected the new owner. In 1799, as much as 30 guineas was being asked, but prices fell steadily during the 19th century, and by the early 20th century had dropped to a few shillings, though rising to three or four pounds during the First World War (Forbes, 1966: 106–7).

Another belief is reported from Liphook (Hampshire):

An old woman told my niece lately that her brother was so born, and so potent was the influence of the caul that when his mother tried to bathe him he sat upon the surface of the water, and if forced down, came up again like a cork. There seems no doubt that this was fully believed and related in all seriousness. The mother had kept the caul stretched over a sheet of note paper, and whenever her son was in danger it became wet and soft, but it remained dry and like a dried bladder so long as he was safe. It got destroyed somehow, and soon after that the brother, a sailor, was shipwrecked and drowned. (*N&Q* 9s:3 (1899), 26)

It was very unlucky to lose or throw away a caul; in one case in early 20th-century Somerset a toddler drowned soon after his mother had been persuaded to throw away his caul, and 'almost everyone in the village' thought this was the reason (Hole, *Folk-Lore* 68 (1957), 412). It was also said that someone whose caul was lost would become a restless wanderer.

Opie and Tatem, 1989: 66–7; Forbes, 1966: 94–111. Most regional collections mention this belief, as do contributors to many issues of *N&Q*; letters in the *Daily Mail* on 26 Aug. 1996 showed it is still current.

Cecil Sharp House. Built by public subscription in memory of founder Cecil *Sharp, to serve as the national headquarters of the *English Folk Dance Society, and (from 1932) the *English Folk Dance and Song Society, the House was opened on 7 June 1930. The building was badly damaged in the Second World War, and reopened on 5 June 1951. It houses the important *Vaughan Williams Memorial Library. Address: 2 Regents Park Road, London NW1 7AY (Tel: (0207) 485 2206).

ED&S 16:1 (July 1951); 17:6 (June 1953), 188.

Celtic influence. The folklore of regions where Celtic languages are spoken (or were until recently) is particularly abundant and well documented; this is true of Ireland, the Scottish Highlands, Wales, and Cornwall. What is uncertain is whether this merely reflects the fact that they were less affected than England by 19th-century economic changes, and hence kept their traditions relatively stable, attracting more attention from folklore collectors; or whether it implies deep-rooted differences in ethnic culture going back to prehistoric times. Most Victorians, steeped in nationalist and racist assumptions,

took for granted that Celtic-speaking Iron Age Britons differed sharply from the Germanic Anglo-Saxons in religious and artistic temperament, and that these differences persisted in their descendants. Contrasting stereotypes were established: Celts were mystical, poetic, and 'superstitious'; Anglo-Saxons pragmatic and unimaginative.

This has become something of a self-fulfilling prophecy, especially among non-academic writers, to whom Celts seem mysterious and awe-inspiring in a way that other early peoples do not. Where similarities exist between a fairly localized custom or belief in England and a more widespread one in a Celtic area, many are tempted to see the former as inherited from native Britons rather than incoming Anglo-Saxons, or as due to contact with neighbouring Celts. The problem with this theory is not that the proposed Celtic parallels do not exist, for in most cases they do, but that the true distribution of the item under discussion may be much wider. Irish and Scottish folklore is easily available for comparison, whereas that of France, Germany, or Scandinavia is known only to specialists; what seems 'Celtic' when viewed from an English perspective may in fact be due to a wider inheritance of European traditions rather than to direct influence of Britons on Anglo-Saxons.

The calendar custom most commonly claimed as Celtic is *Halloween, long celebrated in Ireland, Wales, and Highland Scotland, by a medieval combination of the ancient Irish festival *Samhain with the Christian *All Saints and *All Souls' Days. There are isolated allusions in Lancashire and Derbyshire (see *All Souls, Day and Halloween), but its spread in 19th- and 20th-century England was fostered by Scottish, literary, and American influences. Celtic origins are also claimed for *May Day and *Midsummer, which Bede does not list among Anglo-Saxon festivals; it is true that all Celts celebrated these dates, but so did the medieval French (whose influence on English culture was immense) and most other continental countries.

In the sphere of belief and ritual, it has been argued that holy *wells and *wishing wells are updated versions of sacred healing waters venerated by the Britons, and their offerings made in shafts, pits, and wells; the similarities are strong, though on the Continent such practices were not limited to Celtic peoples, and could have been familiar to Anglo-Saxons too. Some think that when *skulls and stone *heads are regarded as luck-bringers, this derives from the way early Celts displayed severed heads and carved stone heads as magical protectors; others, that some bogeys such as *Black Annis are related to British divinities. A Celtic origin was long accepted for the *Uffington White Horse, which now turns out to be even older; the dating of hill figures at *Cerne Abbas and *Wilmington is currently under debate. It was long thought that the *sheela-na-gig was an archaic fertility charm with strong Irish connections, but modern research shows it belongs to the history of European church art. The idea that *circling to the *right (sunwise) brings good luck, but circling to the *left is linked to *witchcraft and *curses, is predominantly Scottish and Irish (Opie and Tatem, 1989: 383–6); the fact that it is now well known in England can count as a Celtic influence, albeit a recent one enhanced by popular books and films.

One of the aims of this book is to contest the facile prejudice that 'the English have no folklore'; naturally, the authors, while not denying that Celtic influence is probable in certain cases, do not regard it as an automatic explanation for everything eerie, magical, or picturesque in this country.

Centre for English Cultural Tradition and Language (CECTAL), see *NATIONAL CENTRE FOR ENGLISH CULTURAL TRADITION (NATCECT).

Cerne Abbas Giant. On a hillside above Cerne Abbas, Dorset, stands the figure of a giant, 55 metres (180 feet) high, waving a huge knobbed club, and with an erect penis measuring 26 feet (7½ metres). Its age is hotly disputed. There is no reference to it before 1694, when churchwardens' records show a payment of three shillings 'for repaireing of ye Giant'. John Hutchins in his *History of Dorset* (1774) described it as 'a modern thing, cut out in Lord Holles' time' (i.e. 1641–66), and this unromantically late dating could be the true one. However, there undoubtedly were medieval *hill figures elsewhere, while the one at *Uffington is prehistoric, so a medieval or even a pre-Conquest date for the Cerne Abbas figure is arguable. A silt-luminosity test, as at Uffington, would settle the debate.

Assuming him to be old, the main theory about the Giant views him as a Romano-British representation of Hercules, dated about AD 200, since Hercules wielded a club.

Resistivity tests hint that there was once something hanging from his extended left arm, which could have been the lion-skin of Hercules. Alternative suggestions are mostly Celtic: that he is the Irish god called the Dagda, or the Gaulish thunder-god Taranis, both of whom wield clubs, or that the object in the left hand was a severed head. The Saxon thunder-god, Thunor, has also been proposed.

Like other hill figures, this giant needed periodical scourings to maintain his visibility, and in the 18th century these were being done every seven years. They sometimes went beyond mere maintenance—at some stage, someone elongated the penis (Grinsell, 1980). There may be a link between the scourings and the May Day games formerly held in a prehistoric enclosure on top of the same hill; but this is uncertain, as hilltop games were common.

In view of the giant's notable physique, it is not surprising to hear various versions, more or less discreet, of a belief that he can confer fertility. Already in the 19th century it was being said that 'if a girl sleeps on the giant she will be the mother of many children', and in 1922 J. S. Udal, in his *Dorsetshire Folk-Lore*, explicitly stated that a man and woman wanting children should make love on the giant's penis; writing in 1968, H. S. L. Dewar found it was then common for women and girls to 'visit the figure and perambulate his frame' to get a husband, to keep a lover true, or to have children. The practice continues—during the 1990s *Wicca groups have held ceremonies there for infertile couples, who then follow Udal's prescription.

Marples, 1949: 159–79; Leslie Grinsell, *Antiquity* 54 (1980), 29–33; J. H. Bettey, *Antiquity* 55 (1981), 118–21; Rodney Castleden, *The Cerne Abbas Giant* (1996).

chain letters. A relatively recent phenomenon, but one which already has its own traditional mixture of continuity and variation which makes it an interesting folkloric genre. The essence of a chain letter is that each recipient is required to copy it a number of times and forward those copies to others, thus making an ever-growing chain. Many examples do no more than this, but the more complex types include a list of names and addresses with instructions what to do. You should send something (money, a postcard, or whatever is dictated) to the person at the top of the list. Before forwarding it the required number of times, you should add your name to the bottom of the list of names and addresses given in the letter, and omit the top one. Depending on how many copies each recipient is instructed to make, everyone involved should receive a large number of letters in return as their name climbs to the top of the list, provided nobody breaks the chain. The earliest example so far found is handwritten on a postcard, postmarked 15 July 1916:

Endless chain of prayer. O Lord we ask thee to bless our soldiers & sailors & keep them in the hollow of thine hand & bring them to rest with thee for thou art our refuge & helper in time of trouble & we would ask thee to give us peace in our time send thine help from above Amen. This is to be sent all over the world. Send it & see what will happen. It is said in olden times, that he who wrote it would be free from all misfortune send it to 7 persons & on the 7th day you will receive great joy. Do not send more than one a day. Commence when you receive this. Please do not break the chain.

It is interesting to note the very real poignancy of a chain of prayer for soldiers and sailors in the midst of the slaughter of the First World War juxtaposed with the promise of good luck.

Throughout its short history, the chain letter has attracted strong criticism. The promise of good fortune is often linked with the explicit threat of misfortune if one does not obey the instructions, and some people are upset by these threats. Indeed, many believe that chain letters are now actually illegal. Modern examples, mostly aimed at children and in an apparent effort to circumvent the worrying threat, appeal to the better nature of recipients by stressing the length of time the chain has been going, and saying that they hope to get into the *Guinness Book of Records*. The genre has also been utilized for political and pressure-group ends—Greenham Common Peace Camps and Nuclear Disarmament chain letters in 1986, for example, and likewise humorous spoofs circulate from time to time, including a feminist one which asked women to send their husband to the woman on the top of the list and in *x* days they would receive 149 men in return, and one of them at least must be better than the one they sent. In recent years, new communications technologies have been utilized and there are now the chain E-mail and chain fax.

Folklore Society Library Cuttings Collection; Opie and Tatem, 1989: 67–8. For the 'Saviour's Letter' as an 18th century chain, see Davies, 1999a: 126–30.

chairs. A mixed collection of beliefs focus on chairs. A well-attested idea known to *card-players is that you can 'turn your chair and change your luck'. In many cases this was taken literally and the chair turned round three (or more) times, others simply changed chairs. This notion is first reported in the early 18th century, and relatively regularly well into the 20th century. In another context, however, turning a chair round in someone else's house means you would quarrel (Hone, 1832: 126). Still current, even if only jokingly, is the idea that young women should avoid sitting on a chair which has just been vacated by a pregnant woman, as they will soon become pregnant if they do. This is frequently heard in modern offices which have young female staff, but it is difficult to gauge how old it is as, apart from one reference in Opie and Tatem, it seems to have escaped the notice of folklorist writers. In the experience of the present editors it was certainly extant in the 1960s if not before. Another chair belief, reported here from Lincolnshire: 'When having a meal with an acquaintance, do not push your chair under the table when you get up, or you will not come there again for a meal' (*Folk-Lore* 44 (1933), 196). Opie and Tatem include a similar report collected in Yorkshire in 1963. Knocking over a chair is also deemed ominous—'You won't be married this year' in 1738, but in 20th-century hospitals it meant that a new patient, or emergency case, would soon be arriving.

Opie and Tatem, 1989: 68–9, 318; Lean, 1903: ii. 42, 158, 321, 573.

changelings. In societies where the belief in *fairies was strong, it was held that they could steal human babies and substitute one of their own race; the latter would never thrive, remaining small, wizened, mentally abnormal, and ill-tempered. A baby whose defects were not obvious at birth but appeared in the first year or two could thus be explained as not truly human. In 16th- and 17th-century England, such an infant was called either a 'changeling' or an 'auf' or 'oaf'—a variant of 'elf', defined by the *OED* as 'a goblin child . . . left by the elves or fairies; hence a misbegotten, deformed or idiot child'.

They were often ill-treated, as this supposedly drives changelings away. In Cornwall, for instance, one should 'put the small body upon the ashes pile and beat it well with a broom, then lay it naked under a church-way stile . . . till the turn of night; and, nine times out of ten, the thing will be took off and the stolen cheeld put in his place'; alternatively, lay it on the hearth beside a thickly smoking fire (Bottrell, 1873: 202). In 1843 a Penzance man was charged with letting one of his children be cruelly treated by a servant; the child had been put up a tree and left there for over two hours on a cold winter night (*The West Briton* (14 July 1843)).

By the 19th century, accounts of alleged changelings are rare. From Kington (Herefordshire) comes the sole English example of a tale well known in Scotland, Ireland, and abroad, telling how a changeling was detected and expelled; it was told by a woman who said she had heard it from another woman, 'who knew that it was true'. It begins realistically:

A woman had a baby that never grew; it was always hungry, and never satisfied, but it lay in its cradle year after year, never walking, and nothing seemed to do it good. Its face was hairy and strange-looking. One day the woman's elder son, a soldier, came home from the war, and was surprised to see his brother still in the cradle . . .

The soldier then begins brewing beer in an eggshell, which startles the changeling into saying: 'I'm old, old, ever so old, but I never saw that before!' The soldier takes a whip and drives it out, and at once the stolen human reappears, now grown to a fine young man (Leather, 1912: 46–7).

Briggs, 1976: 69–72; Susan S. Eberly, *Folklore* 99 (1988), 58–77.

chapbooks. For over two centuries, from the 17th to the 19th, street literature in the form of chapbooks and *broadsides provided the basic reading matter of the poor in Britain. Chapbooks were paper-covered booklets, usually of eight to 24 pages, and they were cheaply, often crudely, printed in their hundreds of thousands by specialist printers all over the country and sold in town streets, at country fairs, and by travelling hawkers for a halfpenny or a penny a time. They contained ballads, romances, folk tales, jokes, riddles, superstitions, news both true and fabricated, reports of trials, grisly murders, last dying speeches of condemned criminals, amazing wonders, sermons, squibs, catchpennies, and whatever else the printers and hawkers thought would take the public fancy. Whenever possible they were illustrated by woodcut illustrations. Chapbooks also provided the

first real children's literature, and they proved an excellent means by which folklore could be disseminated across the land. Favourite items were reprinted again and again over the years. Most towns had their printers, but London was the acknowledged centre of the trade. Edinburgh-born James Boswell records in his *London Journal* for 10 July 1763:

some days ago I went to the old printing-office in Bow Church-yard kept by Dicey, whose family have kept it fourscore years. There are ushered into the world of literature *Jack and the Giants, The Seven Wise Men of Gotham*, and other story-books which in my dawning years amused me as much as *Rasselas* does now. I saw the whole scheme with a kind of pleasing romantic feeling to find myself really where all my old darlings were printed. I bought two dozen of the story-books and had them bound up with this title, *Curious Productions* . . .

Leslie Shepard, *The History of Street Literature* (1973); John Ashton, *Chapbooks of the Eighteenth Century* (1882); Roger Thompson, *Samuel Pepys' Penny Merriments* (1976).

Chappell, William (1809–88). A member of the successful music publishing family, William Chappell became a well-known 'gentleman scholar', and the leading historian of popular music in his day. He founded the Musical Antiquarian Society (with G. A. Macfaren and Edward Francis Rimbault) in 1840, and published *A Collection of National English Airs* (2 vols, 1838–40). This was revised and expanded into his most enduring work, *Popular Music of the Olden Time* (2 vols., 1855–9). Later folk song collectors such as Cecil *Sharp were dismissive of Chappell's work because he paid little attention to traditional tunes, but his thorough knowledge of popular music and his high standard of scholarship make his books indispensable for tracing the history of printed songs and tunes. A revised edition of *Popular Music*, edited by H. E. Wooldridge (1893), was not successful.

Introduction to the Dover reprint of *Popular Music* (1965); Claude M. Simpson, *The British Broadside Ballad and its Music* (1966).

charities. In former times, it was quite common for people to leave money in their wills for the relief of the local poor or other good causes. The care of the poor was viewed as a local affair and many bequests were for purely altruistic motives, but in pre-Reformation times there was the added bonus of ensuring that people gathered to pray for your soul, and as this became forbidden, 'being remembered' became a major factor. Some benefactors sought to set up lasting memorials to themselves by arranging for a perpetual charity, and this needed a regular supply of money and some form of trustees. The money was often supplied by leaving land for the purpose, which could either be rented out or its crops sold to finance the charity. Some benefactors indulged themselves with strange complicated bequests, laying down many rules and regulations, and often stipulating that the charity be distributed over their grave. Over the years, however, social changes have often made a nonsense of the charity, and the money involved has usually become negligible. Of more interest to folklorists, however, is that the original documentation has often been lost and the charity has become *a custom*. Small changes have crept in, and what may have made sense at the beginning has lost any rational explanation. In the absence of real information (or, in some cases, in the absence of any *interesting* information) legends have been created to explain, and as these are necessarily *post facto* creations, they fit the bill nicely. These legends then begin a life of their own. Lack of space precludes the inclusion of most surviving charities, but see Shuel, 1985; Kightly, 1986; H. Edwards, *A Collection of Old English Customs and Curious Bequests and Charities* (1842).

charivari, see *ROUGH MUSIC.

Charlton Horn Fair. One of London's most popular fairs, until it was discontinued in 1872, famous for its obsession with *horns. In its heyday in the 18th century, visitors flocked to the fair in their thousands carrying or wearing horns and every stall was decorated with them. Every sort of horn imaginable, and everything possible made of horn, was for sale, and even the gingerbread men had horns. An origin legend provides a neat reason for the horn motif. King John was out hunting on Shooter's Hill, and he stopped to rest at a miller's house. The only person home was the miller's attractive wife and she and the king were just 'kissing' when the miller returned and caught them. He drew his dagger, threatening to kill them both, but when he realized who he was dealing with, he wisely asked for some other recompense instead. The king therefore granted him all the land visible from Charlton to the river beyond Rotherhithe, and also the right to hold a fair every 18 October (St Luke's Day). The miller's jealous neigh-

bours gave the name Cuckold's Point to the river boundary and they started wearing horns at the fair as a derisive gesture. See *HORNS for an examination of the connection between horns and cuckoldry/adultery.

Needless to say, no charter from King John can be found. In an early reference to the fair, in Kilburn's *Survey of Kent* (1659), it already has the Horn nickname, and a previous mention takes the horns, if not explicitly the fair, back to 1598. Although we cannot pinpoint its starting date, there is a more prosaic theory about the horns connection. The 18th of October is St Luke's Day, and St Luke is the patron saint of the local parish church. In medieval pictures, Luke is invariably seen in writing posture, with a horned ox or cow prominently displayed. It is likely that the carrying of a large pair of horns, on a pole, indicated the opening of St Luke's Fair. Given the popular connection between horns and cuckoldry, the origin story was concocted later to fit the known facts. Be that as it may, the people who visited the fair made a point of wearing horns if they could, and many appeared in fancy dress, with sexual *cross-dressing a common theme. William Fuller, for example, relates how his landlady's clothes were spoilt by horseplay, while he was wearing them (William Fuller, *The Whole Life of William Fuller* (1703), 122, quoted by Muncey, *c.*1935: 76). Many other writers denounced the fair for its rudeness and indecency, or, as Daniel Defoe called it 'the yearly collected rabble of madpeople' (*A Tour Through the Whole Island of Great Britain* (1724–1726)).

Brand, 1849: ii. 194–5; Hone, 1826: i. 693–4; R. W. Muncey, *Our Old English Fairs* (*c.*1935), 74–8.

Charlton-on-Otmoor Garland. In another variation on the *garland theme, a wooden cross on the rood-screen of the parish church at Charlton-on-Otmoor, Oxfordshire, is decorated with box and yew leaves, making it look more like a person than a cross. This greenery is replaced twice a year—1 May and 19 September (the patronal feast day). On May Day, local children also go to the church, in procession, carrying a long rope-like garland made of leaves and flowers, and each also carrying a small cross made of flowers (see Shuel for photograph), and these are used to decorate the church. There is a church service, and they sing the May Garland song. The cross, which is always referred to as 'she' or 'my lady' is presumed to be the remnant of the pre-Reformation custom of having saints' images in the church which were taken out and carried in procession round the parish on set days. It is known that two images formerly stood on the rood screen—one of St John and the other of the Virgin Mary. These vanished at the Reformation, but the villagers replaced them with two hooped garlands, although it is not recorded how they managed to get away with that. The larger of the two garlands was still carried, once a year, to what had been a local Priory for blessing, while the other was carried round the village. One garland disappeared, and the other was replaced by the present cross.

Shuel, 1985: 31, 35; Kightly, 1986: 123; Hole, 1975: 59.

charmers. Certain men and women were thought to have the gift of healing a specific disease or injury in humans or farm animals, for example *bleeding, *burns, *king's evil, *warts, or ringworm. For some, the gift was inborn, notably in the case of a *seventh son or daughter; more often it depended on a secret verbal *charm and ritual learnt from an older healer—usually a relation who was near to death. Each charm cured only one trouble, and the charmer rarely knew more than one or two. A third group were those owning a material object such as a *snakestone, which would be lent out when needed.

Methods used were various. Many charmers stroked the injured area with a hand wetted with their own spittle (preferably when fasting); others blew on it; for warts, looking at them or counting them might be enough. All these actions might be accompanied by prayer or by verbal charms, uttered mumblingly and low. Some charmers undertook healing at a distance and by telephone, provided they knew the name of the person or animal to be treated and the nature of the trouble. They and their patients regarded this as a natural God-given ability; they must therefore be distinguished from *cunning men, who used magic to combat the effects of witchcraft.

Occasionally, charmers turned 'professional' and charged for their services, especially in towns (see *seventh son), but most took no money, believing this would destroy their power; however, they would acccept hospitality or a gift-in-kind if tactfully offered. Their livelihood was usually farming, or one of the rural crafts such as smithying; women charmers were of equivalent social status.

There are many references to charmers in 19th-century sources, and some were still practising well within living memory.

Davies, 1996 and 1998; Theo Brown, *Folklore* 81 (1970), 37–47.

charms (material). The etymology of the word 'charm' (from Latin *carmen*, 'a chant') shows that in medieval times it meant verbal formulas (see next entry), but in modern languages it is far more widely applied. All the varied objects which are worn, carried, or displayed to bring good luck and success, or to avert bad luck and evil powers, are popularly called 'lucky charms' or *mascots (see the latter for a selection); one can also say actions are 'charms' when done to produce magical results, for example turning a coin on hearing the first cuckoo, to have money all year.

Certain objects were carefully guarded as healing charms, and lent out to those who needed them—*eaglestones for women in labour, beads and *holed stones for sore eyes, *Irish stones and sticks against snake bites.

charms (verbal). In a general sense, all traditional spoken formulas to bring good luck or good health are charms, apart from explicit prayers such as 'God bless her and all who sail in her', said when launching a ship. So are those that turn aside evil, like the rhyme to be said on seeing a *magpie.

Healing charms form a distinctive subtype, of medieval origin, often noted by collectors. Practitioners called them 'blessings'; they were uttered in a whisper, and often accompanied by ritual actions—making the sign of the cross; stroking, breathing over, or spitting on the sufferer; rubbing with different coloured rags or threads, etc. A few come straight from the Bible; thus one way to staunch *bleeding is to repeat: 'And when I passed by thee, and saw thee polluted in thine own blood, I said unto thee when thou wast in thy blood, Live; yea, I said unto thee when thou wast in thy blood, Live' (Ezekiel 16: 6). More widespread are those which recount some pseudo-biblical event as precedent; for example, that Christ miraculously stopped the Jordan, as in this charm from a Shropshire blacksmith's notebook early in the 19th century:

Our Saviour Jesus Crist was borne in Bethalem was Baptsed of Jon in the river of Jordan. God commanded the water to stop & it stoped so in his name do I command the blood to Stop that run from this orrafas vain or vaines as the water Stoped in the river of Jordan in the name of the Father Stop blud in the name of the son stop blood in the name of the Holeygst not a drop more of blud proceduth Amen Amen Amen—to be sed 3 times or if the case be bad 9 times and the Lords praier before & after holding your rithand [= right hand] on the place and marck the place thus + with your midel finger. (Davies, 1996: 20).

Similar examples are the 'St Peter' charm against *toothache, the 'Angels' charm against *burns, the 'St George' charm against the *nightmare. In all cases, it is implied that the power whereby the holy personage resisted or defeated evil will be available to heal the present sufferer; often the formula includes words of command supposedly uttered at the original event and now used by the healer, enhancing his authority, and ends with a religious phrase:

> There came two Angels from the north,
> One was fire and one was Frost.
>   Out, Fire; in, Frost.
> In the name of Father, Son, and Holy Ghost.
>
>   (Latham, 1878: 35–6)

Those against recurrent troubles such as toothache and ague were written down and given to the sufferer, sometimes on sealed paper which must not be opened and read; he or she would then carry the paper permanently, to prevent recurrence. Several medieval charms against ague stipulate that the words be written on a leaf, or on a communion wafer, and eaten; this was to be done three days running (Forbes, 1971: 296–7). Medieval and Elizabethan charms made copious use of names of God, Jesus, and angels, in garbled Latin, Greek, or Hebrew, plus scraps of Biblical quotations, usually in Latin. Some seemingly gibberish words, such as AGLA, were acronyms for religious phrases—in this case, for the Hebrew for 'Thou art powerful and eternal, O Lord'—though the users probably did not know it.

A charm against sprains, known in many countries, is especially interesting as one of the few with demonstrably *pagan origins. It tells how Christ healed his horse's sprained leg with the words, 'Bone to bone, sinew to sinew, vein to vein'; in an early medieval German version, it is Balder's horse which is hurt, and the god Woden who heals it. Here, and in many other cases, the crucial formula is made memorable by rhythmic phrasing, repetition, rhyme, or alliteration.

A number of elaborate Anglo-Saxon verse charms have been preserved; one is against 'elf-shot' (see *elves); another, which involves making a paste from *nine herbs and includes mention of both Christ and Woden, is effective against nine evil spirits, nine poisons, nine plagues, and nine snakes; another is not against sickness, but to 'mend thy fields if they will not produce well, or if sorcery or witchcraft has harmed them'. It is extremely complicated; the farmer must cut four sods by night, wet them with holy water in which he has mixed honey, milk from every cow, and leaves from every kind of plant on his land, and take them to church for four Masses; then replace them in the field, bow nine times towards the east, recite various prescribed prayers, and eventually put incense, fennel, salt, soap, and seeds on his plough with the words:

> Erce, erce, erce, mother of earth,
> May the Almighty, the everlasting Lord, grant thee
> Fields growing and flourishing . . .
> And may it be guarded against all evils,
> Witchcrafts sown throughout the land.

Whether 'erce' is a proper name, or just a nonsense word chosen as a half-rhyme for 'earth', is not known.

See also *CHARMERS.

Forbes, 1971: 293–316; Davies, 1996: 19–32; Davies, 1998: 41–52; Theo Brown, 'Charming in Devon', *Folklore* 81 (1970), 37–47. Many regional folklore collections contain one or two charm texts from the 19th century. For early examples, see Storms, *1948; Bonser, 1963; Hunt, 1990.

charm wands. A name sometimes given to ornamental glass objects shaped as *rolling-pins or small walking-sticks, in which either the glass itself has a multicoloured twisting pattern, or the object is filled with beads, threads, or coloured seeds; it implies they were intended as protection against a witch's *evil eye. They were also sometimes said to draw infections to themselves, thus protecting people in the house from sickness if they were wiped daily (Radford, Radford, and Hole, 1961: 94–5). They date from the late 18th and 19th centuries, and are now collected as antiques.

cheese rolling. In this annual custom a large round Double Gloucester cheese is set off rolling down a very steep hill at Cooper's Hill, near Brockworth (Gloucestershire). People chase after it—themselves running, tumbling, rolling, and bouncing—and the one who gets to the bottom first wins the cheese. There is usually no shortage of runners. There are several cheeses, and therefore several races, including one for females only. The custom formerly took place on Whit Monday, but is now held on the Spring Bank Holiday. Its origin and development are not known, but there are references at least as far back as the early 19th century. The locals even managed to keep the custom going during the food rationing of the Second World War, and in 1998, when the custom was banned by the local authority because of safety fears, a few dedicated traditionalists came out early on the day to chase one cheese down the hill and thus 'keep the tradition going' (*Daily Telegraph* (26 May 1998), 3); it resumed officially in 1999. The Cooper's Hill custom is a unique survival, but cheese rolling certainly took place elsewhere. Thomas Hughes' *The Scouring of the White Horse* (1859), for example, mentions the custom taking place at Uffington in the 18th and 19th centuries.

Shuel, 1985: 17, 24–5; Kightly, 1986: 70–1.

Child, Francis James (1825–96). By far the most important figure in *ballad studies, his work still dominates the field. Born in Boston, Mass., Child enrolled as a student at Harvard College in 1842, and stayed there, as teacher, for the rest of his life, becoming Harvard's first Professor of English in 1876. Child had already edited books on ballads and early poetry, when he encountered Svend Grudtvig's *Danmarks Gamle Folkeviser* (1853–90), and realized the potential for further work on the subject. After the Civil War Child, with characteristic thoroughness, set out to investigate all known sources of British ballad material. Aware of the poor quality of previous scholarship and the reputation that ballad collectors and editors had for tampering with the texts, he was determined to trace original manuscripts and early printed material and his success on this score is evidenced by the fact that Harvard has the best collection of ballad source material in the world, and his name is still synonymous with ballad scholarship 100 years later. The five volumes of Child's *English and Scottish Popular Ballads*, published between 1882 and 1898 represent his life's major achievement, and it is difficult to overstate their influence. Not only did he gather all the known key primary material and bring his own considerable knowledge and scholarship to bear on the material, but he single-handedly defined the

scope of the genre, and the 305 ballads he selected rapidly became a closed corpus available for further study but not amenable to extension or diminution. Successive ballad scholars have suggested a handful of other items which could perhaps have been included, but the majority have accepted the corpus without demur. While this has had certain administrative benefits, there is no doubt that this situation has had a stultifying effect on ballad studies for many years.

Child's scholarship is indeed impressive. For each ballad, he gives several texts, with extensive comparative commentary which discusses motifs and plots on an international scale. When he died he had finished editing the ballad texts and commentaries, and his pupil and colleague George L. Kittredge saw the last parts through the press. Unfortunately, Child did not have time to write the proposed introductory essays on balladry, and this lack of a definitive word from the acknowledged master has bedevilled ballad scholarship ever since, particularly in the realm of definition. By modern standards, Child's one major failing was that as a literary scholar he was little interested in the music of the ballads, but this shortcoming was more than compensated by Bertrand H. Bronson's *The Traditional Tunes of the Child Ballads* (4 vols., 1959–72).

English and Scottish Popular Ballads in five volumes (1882–1898); G. L. Kittredge, 'Francis James Child' in volume i of *English and Scottish Popular Ballads*, pp. xxiii–xxxi; Sigurd Bernhard Hustvedt, *Ballad Books and Ballad Men* (1930); Tom Cheesman and Sigrid Riewerts, *Ballads Into Books: The Legacies of Francis James Child* (1997).

childbirth. Books on British folklore are sadly inadequate on this topic. This must be due partly to women's natural unwillingness to discuss intimate details openly, and partly to their fear that traditional practices would be scorned as 'superstitious' or unhealthy by middle-class researchers; moreover, until recently folklorists rarely published any 'unpleasant' material they encountered. Certain related topics were freely mentioned (e.g. the harelip, the *caul), but not childbirth itself.

Some English information comes from Protestants confiscating relics, including those to help women in labour; thus, a Bristol convent had a red silk 'girdle of Our Lady' and a white 'girdle of Mary Magdalene' (Forbes, 1966: 125), which would have been lent to women to tie round their waists, to speed delivery and guard against evil forces. Continental evidence shows cords and ribbons blessed during *pilgrimage were similarly used, and *candles lit. Some late medieval verbal *charms from English sources are lengthy adjurations to the baby itself, in Latin, urging it to come out of the womb: 'Christ said, Lazarus, come forth! . . . O child, whether alive or dead, come forth, because Christ calls thee to the light' (Forbes, 1971: 302–3).

Early treatises on midwifery, such as that ascribed to Trotula, a woman gynaecologist in 11th-century Cordoba, Nicholas Culpeper's *A Directory for Midwives* (1653), Jane Sharp's *The Midwives' Book* (1671), and her *The Compleat Midwife's Companion* (1724), were intended for educated readers, and some of their prescriptions require expensive ingredients—powdered ivory, coral, or pearl, for example (Forbes, 1966: 76–7). But information from these books, adapted to suit simpler households, spread into the wider community, either orally or through family 'recipe' notebooks—for example the use of *eaglestones, and the idea that during pregnancy a male child lies more on the right. Sometimes learned writers incidentally reveal current 'vulgar' practices by sneering at them; Culpeper, discussing prolapse of the womb, remarks: 'My own Magnetick Cure is this. Take a common Bur leaf (you may keep them dry if you please all year) and apply to her Head, and that will draw the womb upwards . . . whereas the vulgar way of Cure is to push it back, bind it in, and fumigate.' Citing this, Mary Chamberlain (1981: 191) comments acidly that manipulation plus antiseptic fumigation might work, but a leaf on the head never would.

Until well into the 19th century childbirth was generally a neighbourly affair, supervised by a local midwife whose knowledge came from experience rather than formal training, and attended by the pregnant woman's female relatives and friends—a situation where traditional advice and beliefs would flourish. According to a Warwickshire journalist in the 1940s, having many people present used to be thought a protection against *changelings (M. H. Powis, *Birmingham News* (13 November 1944)); the distribution of the *'groaning cheese' reflects communal jollity after a safe delivery. But when women of the upper and middle classes turned increasingly to doctors and trained registered midwives, so by the late 19th century only working-class mothers

called in 'the handywoman'; by the mid-20th century, home births were rare.

See also *BABIES, *CAULS, *CONCEPTION, *PLACENTAS, *PREGNANCY.

Chamberlain, 1981, examines the history of women as healers and midwives, including oral information from London and East Anglia in the early 20th century. Forbes, 1966, has chapters on several birth-related topics, using learned sources. Cf. Gélis, 1991; his material is French.

Childermas, see *HOLY INNOCENTS' DAY.

children's folklore. This, or child-lore, is the generic term used to refer to children's own folklore, as distinguished from folklore-about-children or folklore taught to children by adults (e.g. *nursery rhymes). Children as a social group clearly have a very wide range of cultural traits and material, which mirror the adult world, but the fact that much of their learning is done through informal channels, and that they have genres, such as games and rhymes, which are lacking in the adult world, makes them a particularly rewarding area of research for the folklorist. Early folklorists took it as read that children preserve in their games and rhymes the serious practices of previous adult generations, and were thus quick to see survivals of bride-capture, funeral customs, or foundation sacrifice. It is true that echoes of adult traditions can be found in children's lore, but there is rarely any evidence that these date back more than three or four hundred years at the most, and the notion of survival from ancient times has long been discredited.

The first English scholar to take a real interest in children's lore was J. O. *Halliwell, whose *The Nursery Rhymes of England* (1842) and *The Popular Rhymes and Nursery Tales of England* (1849) presented hundreds of children's rhymes, songs, narratives, and other verbal lore to an adult audience for the first time and provided the basis for most subsequent discussion in that area. Alice Bertha *Gomme's *Traditional Games of England, Scotland and Ireland* (1894/98) did a similar thing for games, on a more systematic basis, collecting a huge mass of material. Individual studies continued to appear, but it was not until the post-war work of Iona and Peter *Opie that other genres were brought into the folklorist's net. The Opies published a string of books which immediately became standard works, including *The Oxford Dictionary of Nursery Rhymes* (1951, new edition 1997), *Lore and Language of Schoolchildren*

(1959), *Children's Games in Street and Playground* (1969), *The People of the Playground* (1993), and *Children's Games with Things* (1997). *Lore and Language*, in particular, widened the horizons of child-lore researchers to include *superstitions, *calendar customs, nicknames, taunts, jokes, *riddles, *truce terms, and so on.

It is a recurrent characteristic of the adult view of children's lore that it is always believed to be on the verge of extinction. This is partly because adults confuse change with decline, but also because they seem to lose the ability to recognize play unless it is highly structured and overtly rule bound.

See also *CLAPPING RHYMES, *COUNTING-OUT RHYMES, *HALLOWEEN, *CHILDREN'S GARLANDS, *MISCHIEF NIGHT, *NURSERY RHYMES, *SINGING GAMES, *SKIPPING (1), *TRUCE TERMS.

Brian Sutton-Smith, *The Folkgames of Children* (1972); Brian Sutton-Smith *et al.*, *Children's Folklore: A Source Book* (1995) (includes Rosemary L. Zumwalt, 'The Complexity of Children's Folklore' (pp. 23–48)); Andy Sluckin, *Growing Up in the Playground: The Social Development of Children* (1981); Sandra McCosh, *Children's Humour* (1976).

chime hours. There was a belief in some parts of England that those born at certain hours could see ghosts. The crucial time was generally said to be *midnight—a *Friday midnight, according to Dickens (*David Copperfield*, chapter 1). But in Somerset and East Anglia people spoke of being 'born in the chime-hours', a term alluding to the old monastic hours of night prayer, which some churches marked by bell-ringing even after the Reformation; at Blaxhall (Suffolk) these were 8 p.m., midnight, and 4 a.m. (Evans, 1956: 216–17). In Sussex, though the term 'chime hours' is not mentioned, the belief was that 'those born at three, six, nine or twelve o'clock' would be able 'to see much that is hidden from others' (Wales, 1979: 56); these are the daytime hours of monastic prayer. Ruth *Tongue said that in Somerset it was the period from Friday midnight to cockcrow on Saturday; she claimed (incorrectly) to be a 'Chime Child' herself.

chimney-sweeps. That sweeps bring luck is implied by the *Jack-in-the-Green, known since the late 18th century, and is explicitly stated in many texts from the 1880s to the present. On seeing a sweep in the street in his working clothes and with his face blackened, one had to bow, raise one's hat, curtsey, or call out a greeting; some of the references show that this belief was particularly strong among

coachmen and race-goers (Opie and Tatem, 1989: 71–2).

Still common is the custom of having a sweep outside the church at a *wedding to kiss the bride and shake hands with the groom, generally interpreted as a means of ensuring *fertility. A recent press report (*Sunday Telegraph* (28 Dec. 1997), 17) states that sweeps can earn £60 for this, as against £25 for a cleaning job, and that many do two or three weddings every weekend; they generally attend in pairs, wearing top hat and tails, carrying their brushes, and with their faces blacked. They claim that George II decreed that sweeps would 'bring good luck to the land' after his life was saved by one who managed to halt his carriage horses when they bolted, and that this is generally known: 'Old people have always come up to us in the street and touched us for good luck, and since the National Lottery began everybody has been doing it.'

See also *BLACK, *JACK-IN-THE-GREEN.

christening, see *BAPTISM.

Christianity. The religion which has shaped English culture for the past 1,500 years is Christianity, whether in its Catholic or its Protestant form; much English folklore embodies Christian ethics, echoes biblical themes, or presents a modified, secularized version of what was once a religious custom or festival. This ought to be self-evident, but folklorists have often neglected the obvious while pursuing archaic origins. They would brush aside as unimportant any element which did not spring from the distant past; moreover, many Victorians knew little about medieval Catholicism, and despised what they did know. Today, academic folklorists have a sounder historical sense, and build their interpretations on documentary evidence, not cross-cultural analogies. Regrettably, many current writers for the popular market are less rigorous. Greatly admiring prehistoric *paganism, and wishing to prove it survived under a veneer of Christianity, they repeat the Victorian error by regarding intervening centuries as irrelevant except in so far as selected items can be made to support the argument for continuity.

In fact, medieval and early modern Christianity deeply affected folklore. Most old *calendar customs (with the important exceptions of *May Day and *Midsummer) are 'holidays' related to 'holy days'; to Catholics, there is nothing inappropriate in having secular amusements alongside church-going. Later, *Queen Elizabeth Day and *November the Fifth were deliberately created by Church authorities to celebrate Protestant deliverances from Catholic threats. However, Puritan Christianity usually opposed festivals, on four grounds: that it was wrong to consider any day (except Sundays) as more significant than another; that most festivals involved 'popish' doctrines or practices; that religion and merrymaking should be kept apart, with the few approved holy days, for example Easter, being stripped of secular elements; and that the merrymaking was reminiscent of classical paganism. At the Reformation, and again in the 17th century, Puritans campaigned to destroy calendar customs; so did some Victorians, disapproving of the associated drunkenness, brawls, and sexual opportunities. Thus, whereas medieval Christianity encouraged lively communal celebrations, later religious opinion often opposed them.

In some respects, Christianity offered strong support for folklore. Scriptural texts were cited by educated writers well into the 17th century as proving the reality of certain supernatural beings—*ghosts, *witches, *giants, *dragons, and of course demons—thus strengthening and prolonging popular belief in them. The great abundance of traditions about ghosts and witches in 19th-century folklore may reflect the seriousness with which the Church had discussed them two centuries earlier, as well as their enduring importance as an explanation for subjective experiences. In contrast, *fairies lacked biblical endorsement, which may be one reason why belief in them dwindled to a pleasant whimsy. Folk *medicine and verbal *charms drew heavily on religion; to the users, this legitimized them, despite the opposition of Protestant clergy. Similarly, *churches, churchyards, and *graves were credited with various healing and magical powers because of their sanctity, as were sacraments. Many beliefs that are older and more widespread than Christianity nevertheless fitted easily into its framework; *dreams, *omens, and *ghosts, for example, could all be viewed as sent by God with warnings or information.

Fairytales and other narrative genres intended as entertainment usually have no overt religious content, though their morality is generally compatible with principles of justice and kindness. *Legends, however, often do,

either directly or by implication. Particularly common are stories, supposedly true, which describe God's *judgements on sinners and providential protection of the virtuous, and stories involving the *Devil; saints also feature in a few local legends. Others carry traditional moral messages—murder will out, ill-gotten gains never prosper, pride comes before a fall, and so on—which are of course not unique to Christianity, but have long been associated with it.

See also *CHURCHES, *CROSS, *PAGANISM, *PILGRIMAGES, and *SAINTS.

Christingle. This popular pre-Christmas service for children was introduced in the Church of England in the late 1960s, in imitation of a custom of the Moravian Church in Britain and America dating from the 18th century. Children are given oranges decorated with fruit, nuts, and a candle, to symbolize the earth, the fruits of the earth, and Jesus the Light of the World. The word comes from German dialect *Krist Kindl* = 'Little Christ Child', via its American corruption *Krisskringle*.

Christmas. By far the most popular festival in England today, imposing itself even on those whose religious or political beliefs would normally rule out Christian celebrations; the greatest pressure is to conform for the sake of the children, who are swamped by advertisements, shop displays, and peer pressure. Thanks largely to the inadvertent genius of the Victorians who reinvented it (see below), Christmas is now an astonishingly successful and cohesive blending of religious and secular elements, which operates on many levels; there is space within its framework for people to choose activities and meanings according to their individual tastes and needs.

Thus, we may or may not go to church; we can have an angel, or a fairy, or a teddy bear on the tree; we can make decorations, or buy them; they can be a tasteful construction of holly and fir-cones, or a riot of tinsel and flickering lights; we can send religious, humorous, political, or risqué cards, or charity cards, or (by agreement with friends) none at all, donating the money to charity; we can play board games or charades with our grandparents or computer games with our children; we can watch Snow White videos, or the Queen's Speech; we may get drunk, or have just one glass of sherry—and we will still be within the parameters of 'normal' Christmas behaviour.

The one thing that is extremely hard to do with Christmas is to ignore it.

Within this broad consensus, there are degrees of conformity, the two main variables being whether the family is religious or not, and whether children are present. Childless couples and persons living alone often prefer to go to a hotel or guest-house, among strangers, but with the same festive spirit as others create at home. Major elements in the standard modern image of Christmas are: it is family centred; it is child centred; presents are exchanged; homes, churches, shops, and streets are decorated, according to loose but definable rules; food is special and plentiful, again following loose rules; greeting cards are exchanged, and everyone we meet is verbally wished 'Happy Christmas'; carols are sung or heard everywhere; many who do not regularly go to church attend special services; the season is universally declared to be one of 'peace and good will'.

Christmas has a complex and much debated history. There is no scriptural clue to the date of Christ's birth; the Early Church celebrated it (if at all) on 6 January, and the first document setting it on 25 December is a Roman calendar of AD 354. Possibly it was a conscious takeover of a Roman festival, 'The Birthday of the Unconquered Sun', honouring Mithras and other sun-gods. This dating had become standard throughout Western Europe well before Augustine's mission to England; it was not devised to match Anglo-Saxon midwinter festivals. The Council of Tours (AD 567) ruled that the twelve days from the Nativity to the Epiphany would be a work-free period of religious celebration, and this became English law in AD 877. The word 'Christmas' itself only appears in 1038; previously the festival period had been called *Yule, a native word for the midwinter season.

Medieval manorial records show villeins were not required to work during the Twelve Days; the lord of the manor provided a communal feast, and his tenants and subjects gave him gifts, normally farm produce. The pattern was varied; some wealthy landowners apparently kept open house, feeding and entertaining all comers, while others concentrated on their own local people. By Tudor times, Christmas at court and on the estates of the nobility was characterized by increasingly splendid banquets, balls, plays, masques, and mummings, often co-ordinated by a 'Lord of Misrule'.

This officials (also found at Oxford and Cambridge Colleges, the Inns of Court, and some civic corporations, such as the City of London) combined the roles of planning committee, master of ceremonies, jester, and mock king; sometimes he was accompanied (or replaced) by an Abbot of Unreason, who parodied the Church in the same way as the Lord parodied the court. They are first mentioned (under various titles) in the 15th century, and were conspicuous at the courts of Henry VIII and Edward VI; at the accession of Mary (1553) they vanished from the court, and rapidly went out of fashion elsewhere, except among young men at the universities and Inns of Court. A far less expensive domestic equivalent, the 'King of the Bean' chosen by lot on *Twelfth Night, remained popular. To Victorians, the Lord of Misrule, despite his relatively brief and socially exclusive existence, came to symbolize a jovial role-reversal for which there is little or no evidence.

Throughout the 16th and 17th centuries Puritans waged a well-documented campaign against saints' days and other religious festivals, as unscriptural and as encouraging gluttony, drunkenness, sexual licence, and public disorder. In the 1640s Christmas became a major target; in June 1647 Parliament finally banned Easter, Whitsun, and Christmas, but each successive year of the Puritan reign saw major disturbances in various parts of the country, and increasingly draconian enforcement. John Evelyn's *Diary* for 25 December 1657 records his own arrest for attending a Communion service in London: '... the Chapell was surrounded with souldiers; all the communicants and assembly surpriz'd & kept prisoners by them ... These wretched miscreants held their muskets against us as we came up to receive the Sacred Elements, as if they would have shot us at the altar ...' This policy proved counter-productive; the fate of Christmas became a rallying-point for anti-Puritan feeling, and a symbol of lost freedoms. After the Restoration most aspects of the celebration were revived, though with wide variations in the degree of lavishness even by the wealthy. As the festival was now no longer a bone of contention, documentary sources become fewer.

The diaries of 18th- and early 19th-century rural clergy take little notice of Christmas, though regularly noting money distributed to the poor around this time. Bell-ringing is sometimes mentioned, and drunkenness complained of. The tradition of charitable hospitality was still strong; thus William Holland, a Somerset parson, on 25 December 1799, had:

dinner by myself on spratts and fine woodcock. The kitchen was tolerably well lined with my poor neighbours, workmen, &c. Many of them staid till past ten o'clock and sang very melodiously. Sent half-a-crown to our Church Musicians who had serenaded the family this cold morning at five o'clock. (Holland, ed. Jack Ayres, 1984)

Many traditional *visiting customs occurred at this season: *mumming of various kinds, *sword dancing, *Hooden Horses, *Old Tup, *Plough Stots, *wassailing, and *waits (Wright and Lones, 1940: iii. 209–79). This concentration may reflect the importance of midwinter festivals in the remote past, but practical factors were important too; there was a lull in farmwork, potential audiences had gathered in gentry households, and the tradition of Christmas hospitality and generosity ensured a good welcome for performers. At least one custom, *thomasing, was specifically aimed at soliciting alms.

What is regarded as the archetypal Christmas was forged in the second half of the 19th century by popular writers such as Charles Dickens and Washington Irving, using a combination of indigenous elements, imported ones, and new ones, in response to a widespread opinion that Christmas was no longer what it had once been, and something should be done. Their reinvention harked back to a romantic ideal of the lost golden age of *'Merrie England'—perhaps specifically to Walter Scott's description of a medieval baron's Christmas in his best-selling poem *Marmion* (1808). Key elements in their vision were the Lord of Misrule, Boar's Head, Yule Log, and the squire's lavish display of hospitality in his 'baronial hall'. Models for more homely celebration were sometimes sought abroad. As early as 1821 a correspondent in the *Gentleman's Magazine* (pp. 505–8) praised a Christmas custom in the north of Germany 'which cannot be too strongly recommended and encouraged in our own country': children make or buy little presents for their parents and each other, which they lay out on Christmas Eve under 'a great yew bough' in the parlour, decked with tapers and streamers; next day the parents bring presents for the children (reprinted in Gomme, 1884: 97–102). Written twelve years before Victoria married Albert, this shows court influence was not the only

route by which German models impinged on English customs.

This 'new' Christmas evolved gradually by an astute combination of existing elements (e.g. carols, mince-pies, holly and mistletoe, candles, ample food and drink, hospitality to neighbours) with recent importations and inventions (presents, crackers, turkey, greetings cards, the tree, Father Christmas/Santa Claus as gift-bringer), each of which has its own history, as outlined in the entries listed below. But many of these took a long time to filter down to the poorer sections of society; it can be argued that the 'Victorian' Christmas only became truly the norm after the Second World War.

Some commentators describe this reinvention as if it had been consciously aimed at taming the working classes and imposing 'respectability' on their boisterous and drunken traditions. Concern for public morals was certainly one factor, but commercialism was powerful too; cheap illustrated periodicals spread the fashion, and industry was eager to supply cards, toys, and other presents. It is significant that the new elements are conspicuously secular; the stress on charity was the only one with real religious underpinnings.

See also *ASHEN FAGGOT, *CHRISTMAS CARDS, CRACKERS, DECORATIONS, FOOD, PRESENTS, SUPERSTITIONS, TREE, *FATHER CHRISTMAS, *HOLLY, *HOLY THORN, *MISTLETOE, *MUMMING, *MUMMING PLAYS, *ST STEPHEN'S DAY, *SANTA CLAUS, *SQUIRREL HUNTING, *SWORD DANCES, *TWELFTH NIGHT, *WASSAILING, *WAITS, *YULE.

Wright and Lones, 1940: iii. 230–73; Golby and Purdue, 1984; Weightman and Humphries, 1987; Hutton, 1994 and 1996; Chris Durston, *History Today* 35 (Dec. 1985), 7–14; Underdown, 1985.

Christmas cards. These emerged in the mid-19th century, combining an older custom of sending *New Year verses to friends with the new emphasis on Christmas. The first was designed by John Calcott Horsley, at the instigation of Henry Cole, in 1843. A large central panel shows a family sitting with wine glasses in their hands, and a banner saying 'A Merry Christmas and a Happy New Year to You'; two side panels show a man and woman giving alms to the poor. Though this card was too expensive to be commercially successful, the idea gradually spread, and by the 1860s cheap cards were generally available. Religious symbolism is strikingly absent; family gatherings, dancing, eating, winter scenes, holly, and Christmas trees were the standard fare. An advertisement in the *Illustrated London News* of 17 November 1883 lists 27 categories of design, of which only two were remotely religious.

George Buday, *The History of the Christmas Card* (1954).

Christmas carol singing. Nowadays there are carol concerts in schools and churches in the run-up to Christmas, and groups of carol-singers can be found in shopping centres or visiting homes and pubs in the evenings to collect money for charity. Earlier, singers would have been earning money for themselves, but by the 20th century this was mainly limited to children, and has now apparently died out. There was a very strong and long-standing custom of serenading people in their homes early on Christmas Day; this could be done by informal groups (sometimes not very well), but in the 19th century was more usually an organized activity of the church choir or of the *waits, where these existed. Some writers use that term for all perambulating singers and musicians. A few carols in the current repertoire are traditional folk-songs ('God Rest You Merry Gentlemen', 'As I Sat on a Sunny Bank', 'The Holly and the Ivy'), but most were composed by Victorian or later musicians.

See also *WAITS.

Christmas crackers. According to Tom Smith's, the leading cracker manufacturers in Britain, crackers were invented by their founder, a London confectioner, in 1847. Smith's idea was based on French bon-bons, sweets wrapped in screwed-up coloured paper, to which he added first a motto and then the characteristic snapper, inspired by a crackling log on his fire; it was an immediate success. However, it should be noted that the *OED* gives two slightly earlier references (1841 and 1844) to people 'exploding a cracker bonbon' or 'pulling' one, implying a rather more complex history.

Tom Smith Group, *A History of the Cracker* (booklet *c.*1997).

Christmas decorations. Decorating houses and churches with evergreens is an old custom; London streets were decorated too, in John Stow's time (Stow, 1598 (1602): 123). Churchwardens' accounts throughout the 16th century record payments for holly and ivy, and at Westminster as late as 1647 'for rosemarie and baies that was stuck about the church'; other sources add cypress, laurel, box, and yew (Brand, 1849: i. 522–3). In homes, the centrepiece was the Kissing Bush (Bough or Bunch), known all over England from the 18th century until superseded by the *Christmas tree. Basically, it was constructed from two hoops at right angles, intertwined with ivy and holly, and fixed to the ceiling; from it hung apples, oranges, streamers, sugar mice, and, most importantly, a sprig of *mistletoe.

More elaborate decorations became fashionable in Victorian times, including greenery festooned over mirrors and pictures, and, later, paper garlands, hanging confections, and seasonal mottoes embroidered or picked out in artificial flowers. German influence is likely here; Hannah Cullwick, maid to a London family, thought it 'a German way' when a fellow servant put up paper festoons and coloured candles for Christmas in 1871 (Cullwick, *Diaries*, ed. Liz Stanley, 1984: 184–5). Tinsel, baubles, and other artificial adornments are now ubiquitous.

Traditions differ sharply on when to take decorations down and what to do with them. *Twelfth Night is generally mentioned nowadays, though some say they must be removed on this date, others on its eve. In earlier records, they stayed up till *Candlemas (2 February). Once taken down, many sources state the evergreens should be burnt—especially the mistletoe, according to Charles Igglesden, otherwise 'all who have kissed beneath it will be foes before the end of the year' (Igglesden, *c.*1932: 69–70). Others insist they should never be burnt. Occasionally, they were fed to cattle.

See also *HOLLY, *MISTLETOE.

Opie and Tatem, 1989: 76; Brand, 1849: i. 519–25.

Christmas food. It has always been traditional to eat well at Christmas, but the fare has changed over the years and become more standardized, with a decline in regional variation. Leaving aside the lavish banquets in royal and noble households, whose swans, peacocks, and boars' heads were not found lower down the social scale, three meats dominate. Roast beef was the staple fare from the 17th century to the 19th, with 'roast beef and plum pudding' so frequently mentioned as to be a cliché; thereafter, goose for the poor and turkey for the wealthy was the norm. Turkey slowly spread down the social scale, becoming in the 20th century the unchallenged Christmas bird.

The iced cake was originally a *Twelfth Night speciality, many other traditional cakes being eaten at Christmas in various regions (see, for example, Brears, 1987: 177–8; Morris, 1911: 217). Mince-pies are first recorded by this name in 1600, and frequently mentioned throughout that century (and ever since). At that time they were oblong or coffin-shaped, which John Selden (*Table-Talk*, 1686), and later writers, said represented the manger at Bethlehem; this is unlikely, as they were actually called 'coffins' (Dyer, 1876: 458–9). Plum pudding, or the synonymous plum porridge, is also regularly recorded from the 17th century onwards; the current idea that everyone in the household must stir it and make a wish first appears in the mid-19th century (N&Q 2s: 12 (1861), 491).

Brand, 1849: i. 526–32; Hone, 1827: i, 819–20.

Christmas presents. Essential to the modern Christmas, these came to the fore in the 1840s and 1850s, replacing a much older tradition of *New Year gifts between adults which by then was in decline. The rapid upsurge of Christmas gift-giving had several concurrent causes: the growing child-centredness of the festival; the example of Germany, where small presents were associated with the *Christmas tree, the availability of mass-produced toys, especially imported from Germany. At first most presents were for children, but those for adults became ever more popular during the rest of the 19th century. It must be stressed, though, that these were upper- and middle-class habits, which the less well-off could not afford; numerous people who grew up in the first half of the 20th century attest that their Christmas presents at that time were still a handful of nuts and sweets, an orange, and, if they were lucky, a new sixpence.

Some families pin up pillowcases as receptacles for small presents, but most use a stocking. It is not certain when this began, nor whether it is a native or imported custom. Henderson, in 1866, noted that 'The old custom of hanging up a stocking to receive Christmas presents . . . has not yet died out in the North of England', and that friends of his did it 'without the excuse of a child to be surprised and pleased' (Henderson, 1866: 50). Yet others writing in 1879 and in the 1880s reported it as unfamiliar (see *Santa Claus).

One can probably assume continental influence.

See *FATHER CHRISTMAS, *SANTA CLAUS.

Christmas superstitions. Most regional collections report a belief that at midnight on Christmas Eve cattle kneel to welcome the Holy Child, and bees buzz, or hum the Hundredth Psalm (e.g. Harland and Wilkinson, 1882: 253). During this night *cocks crow, and 'the powers of darkness can have no evil influence on mankind' (Udal, 1922: 51; cf. *Hamlet* I. i).

Babies born on Christmas Day are fortunate, either in general, or because they cannot be drowned or hanged, or cannot see ghosts and spirits. Brand (1849: i. 478–80) quotes a long poem from a manuscript of c.1525 setting out for each day of the week what it will mean if Christmas falls on that day, as regards the weather and events of the coming year, and the destiny of children born on that Christmas Day. It was also an appropriate time for *divinations, though less so than the *New Year; in 19th-century Yorkshire a girl who had been kissed under the mistletoe would take a berry and a leaf to her room, swallow the berry, prick the man's initials on to the leaf, and stitch it inside her corset to keep him true (Blakeborough, 1898: 69).

Some New Year beliefs applied to Chrismas Day too, including the taboo on taking *fire out of the house or borrowing from neighbours, and the custom of *first footing, especially in Herefordshire (Leather, 1912: 108–9). Many households 'let Christmas in' by opening doors early in the morning and saying 'Welcome, Father Christmas' or the like. A handful of sources call it unlucky to bring new shoes, or new leather into the house (Opie and Tatem, 1989: 230, 350). More common, from the mid-19th century to the present, is the idea that you will have as many happy months in the coming year as you eat mince-pies—in different houses, most say (Opie and Tatem, 1989: 248–9).

See also *ASHEN FAGGOT.

Opie and Tatem, 1989: 74–8.

Christmas tree. It is generally assumed that this indisputably German custom was introduced to Britain by Queen Victoria's husband, Prince Albert, but this is only partly true. The British royal family had had regular Christmas trees since the days of Princess Charlotte of

Mecklenberg Strelitz, who married George III in 1761, and Victoria had been brought up knowing them (see Miles). Other families with German connections had them too. But it was certainly due to active promotion by Victoria and Albert that the fashion for trees spread so remarkably fast, at least among the better-off. From 1845 to 1855 the *Illustrated London News* featured Christmas trees more and more, including the famous picture of the royal family round its tree at Windsor in 1848, though the accompanying article still labels this 'a German custom' (*ILN* Christmas Supplement (1848), 409–10). By 1854, a Suffolk farmer's wife, Elizabeth Cotton, could simply record in her diary, 'Had a Christmas tree for the children'. However, there were many working-class families, well into the 20th century, who could not afford one; they improvised, or did without.

Delia Miles, *Country Life* (3 Dec. 1992), 60–3; Golby and Purdue, 1984; Weightman and Humphries, 1987.

church ales. A feature of the medieval traditional calendar which lasted well into the 17th century but which at various times became a major focus of religious, moral, and political contention, and has been described as 'a crude precursor of today's sedate parish fete' (Barnes, 1959: 106). In essence, as the name implies, the ale was originally a local festive gathering involving food, drink, and entertainment, organized, or at least supported, by the church, and held to raise money for the church. These ales were mainly held in spring or summer, and were thus often called May games, Whitsun ales, Summer games, or, after a feature discussed below, King game or Robin Hood game. Nevertheless, ales could be held at any time, and there could be a series of them throughout the year, or they could be held for specific fund-raising purposes, such as the annual 'Cobb ale' in Lyme Regis (Dorset) which helped maintain the harbour wall (the Cobb) which was essential to the town's economic well-being. (Underdown, 1985: 57). They could even be organized as benefits for individuals—'Bid-ales', or 'Clerk-ales' (for the parish clerk). It is clear that the word 'ale' was used for any get-together or feast.

Most of our early information about church ales comes from churchwardens' and other parochial accounts, which provide numerous bare bones but little flesh. Fuller descriptions appear from the 16th century in the writings of those opposed to the ales, usually on religious grounds, and in the works of poets and playwrights when they begin to construct the romanticized rural idyll with which literature would abound for the ensuing centuries, and both sides give a biased picture. Exactly what went on at the earlier ales varied from place to place and over time, but the key elements of food, drink, and music, mentioned in the accounts, connect with the opposing voices which concentrate on gluttony, drunkenness, and the moral dangers of men and women dancing together. The food and drink were supplied by the church, or contributed beforehand by parishioners, for which officers and a local committee could be elected, and equipment such as spits, kettles, and so on, belonging to the parish was available for their use. Ales would also attract people from neighbouring parishes, and there are records of organized reciprocal visits, and also some instances of parishes staging joint events.

One of the first areas of contention between traditionalists and reformers was the siting of the ale. It is clear from the earliest records that it was customary for celebrations to take place in the churchyard, or even in the church itself. Throughout the period from about 1220 to the 1360s there were repeated, and eventually successful, attempts to banish the festivities from holy ground, and also to forbid the active involvement of the clergy (see Heales for examples).

The feature of the games which has excited most interest in folklore circles was the election of a King and Queen or Lord and Lady, to preside over the festivities, and, in some cases, the presence of particular characters such as *Robin Hood. To get the matter into some perspective, however, Hutton estimated that of 104 parishes for which he could find records of ales, only 17 per cent had a King or Lord, and a further 20 per cent a Robin Hood—little over a third all together. Of those which had a King/Lord, only three mention a Queen or Lady. *Frazerian writers have been quick to see these figures as remnants of nature or fertility spirits, but there is no evidence to support this view. They are better seen as examples of the medieval tendency to put people in charge of festive events—compare, for example, the *Twelfth Night King of the Bean, or the *Lord of Misrule. These temporary rulers were elected beforehand to preside over the celebrations, and in some cases they could be fined if they refused. One set piece in the event was the procession of the King/Lord, with retainers, in full state and dressed in suitable costume. There is no evidence that these ceremonial positions were treated as parody or burlesque in the way that *mock mayors certainly were, but appear to have been treated with good-humoured respect and dignity. Nor is there evidence of a reversal of roles, such as in the *boy bishop ceremonies, where social inferiors take charge of their superiors for a specified time. Spring ales in particular were also notable for their bowers and use of greenery.

As with other traditional festivals, church ales came under increasing pressure from Puritans and other moral reformers from the mid-16th century onwards, who attacked them on a variety of linked fronts, religious, moral, and legal (the maintenance of public order), and in particular the staging of entertainments on Sundays. Many Puritans were convinced that church ales were remnants of popery (which, in a sense, was true, as they were indeed survivals of pre-Reformation ways). Ales had their supporters, however, in the shape of many traditional churchmen (partly because of the church's financial interest in their continuance), those who believed in the old ideal of community, as well as those with political leanings which became increasingly polarized between Royalists and Parliamentarians. Richard Carew, for example, defended ales in his *Survey of Cornwall* (1602: 141) on the grounds of the good fellowship they engendered, and the innocent pastime raising money for good causes, but this is a far cry from the description by Kethe in 1570: '. . . the multitude call (Sunday) their revelyng day, which day is spent in bullbeatings, bearebeatings, bowlings, dicyng, cardyng, daunsynges, drunkennes and whoredome . . .' (quoted in Hazlitt, 1905: 126).

The struggle for control was carried out at local level, and, throughout the first decades of the 17th century, parishes up and down the country replaced church ales by church rates as a more seemly way of raising money for the church. In many places this transition was accompanied by sharp local conflict, but the trend was clear, and even though the older customs received something of a boost with the issue the king's *Book of Sports* in 1618 and 1633, they were increasingly seen as old-fashioned and inefficient. With the Restoration of the monarchy in 1660, there was a much-publicized return to the old pre-Puritan

days, but although local wakes and revels were quickly revived, most churchmen were content to leave the routine raising of money for the church in the hands of the rate-gatherers rather than the ale-sellers and *hoglers. Nevertheless, some were transformed into other celebrations, such as the *Whitsun ale.

Underdown, 1985; Thomas G. Barnes, 'County Politics and a Puritan Cause Célèbre', *Trans. of the Royal Historical Soc.*, 5s:5 (1959), 103–22; Hutton, 1994; Alfred Heales, 'Early History of the Church of Kingston-upon-Thames', *Surrey Archaeological Collections* 8 (1883), 103–9.

churches. As appears in many entries in this book, a remarkable number of English *calendar customs are associated with churches, even though they now contain no religious elements. Sometimes, their dates link them to saints' days; sometimes, as with *ales, *wakes, and *rushbearing, they were a way of raising funds for the church and supplying its needs. The further back one explores the historical record, the more one sees church buildings functioning as centres for community events, secular as well as sacred, while for individuals they were places where major life-cycle rites were held, and the dead visibly commemorated; unlike castles and manor houses, they were used by all classes, not merely the élite. Their interiors, brightly painted and crammed with statues, murals, lamps, candles, draperies, and votive offerings, gave work to local craftsmen; in some regions, notably East Anglia, wholesale rebuilding and modernization of churches was undertaken as a proud statement of economic prosperity.

Symbolically, a church could represent its whole community—a fact neatly expressed by various taunting rhymes in which 'steeple' and 'people' are jointly mocked:

> Dirty Tredington, wooden steeple,
> Funny parson, wicked people.
>
> (Gloucestershire)

It is also notable that traditions about coastal villages abandoned to the encroaching sea commonly have the poetic detail that the church can still be glimpsed under water, or that its bells still ring in stormy weather. Along the Welsh Border, there is a cluster of legends about lakes and pools in which villages were miraculously engulfed because of some crime or impiety, and again the loss of the church is stressed (Burne, 1883: 64–73; Leather, 1912: 11).

A type of legend found throughout England

purports to explain why a church comes to stand where it does, by alleging that supernatural events guided the builders; naturally, such tales generally apply to those which are inconveniently sited in relation to the village they serve. Sometimes the story has religious overtones; just as cows, wandering freely, brought the Ark of the Covenant to an appropriate halting-place (1 Samuel 6: 8–14), so the site for Clodock Church (Herefordshire) was indicated when oxen drawing St Clydawg's bier stood still (Leather, 1912: 214). More often, it is said that the work had been started elsewhere, but every night what had been built by day was torn down, and the stones shifted—by fairies, or the Devil, or an invisible force—till the builders gave in and adopted the new site. Animals can play a role here too: at Winwick (Lancashire) the builders mistakenly thought they were raising their church on the precise spot where St Oswald died, but a pig carried the stones away one by one in its mouth to the right place, so a pig is carved on the church wall.

Some churches have structural oddities which call for explanation—for instance, when the weight of shingles twists a spire like a corkscrew. At Chesterfield (Derbyshire), where the effect is very pronounced, there are at least two stories to account for it: that the *Devil, enraged by the *bells, wrenched the spire round as he flew past; or, that a bride who was a virgin was arriving for her wedding, and the spire, amazed at her unheard-of virtue, turned to stare at her, and got stuck. At West Tarring (Sussex) the twist is only slight, yet enough to cause a story that the architect made an error in his plans, and flung himself off the spire (or off Beachy Head) in despair at the sad result [JS].

Large boulders near a church are sometimes said to be missiles which the Devil vainly aimed at it, the most dramatic example being the huge prehistoric stone at Rudston (Humberside); in other cases, he is said to have kicked a church, or attempted to fly away with it, or flood it, or drop a hill on it. Such tales are now jocular, but probably began as religious propaganda, since the Devil constantly attacks the Church but can never defeat it (Matthew 16: 18). It is sometimes suggested that they refer particularly to local conflicts with paganism at the Conversion; in itself, the motif might well be that old, but the churches where it is now found (both here and in Europe) are not exceptionally ancient—it is

the presence of a nearby rock which sparks the tale.

Churches and churchyards being eerie places, especially by night, they figure frequently in magical and divinatory rituals. The oldest and most serious was watching in the church porch on *St Mark's Eve to see who would die that year. In Lincolnshire, Herefordshire, Cambridgeshire, and Sussex in the early 20th century, it was said of various village churches that anyone who ran round the building seven times on a moonlit night (or, at *midnight) and then peered through the keyhole (or *whistled through it, or dropped a pin through) would see the Devil (Rudkin, 1936: 71–3; Leather, 1912: 40; Porter, 1969: 337; Simpson, 1973: 66). A *love divination for young men in the 17th century, still known in Shropshire in the late 19th, was to go to a churchyard at midnight with a drawn sword and circle the church nine times (or three times), saying 'Here's the sword, but where's the scabbard?', after which the destined girl would appear (*Mother Bunch's Closet Newly Broke Open*, 1685, ed. G. L. Gomme, 1885: 18; Burne, 1883: 177).

Lead cut from the windows or guttering of a church, water dripping from its roof, dust from its altar, and chips of stone from its carvings have all been regarded as having healing power (Opie and Tatem, 1989: 78, 81, 94).

See also *BELLS, *CHRISTIANITY, *GRAVES, *PILGRIMAGES.

churching. Jewish law stated that women were under taboo after childbirth, because of pollution by blood, until ritually cleansed by a priest (Leviticus 12: 1–8); Mary obeyed this rule after the birth of Jesus (Luke 2: 22–4). Modern liturgies stress thanksgiving, but medieval symbolism still implied impurity, for the women came to church veiled, 'without looking at the sun or sky', or other people, till they had been blessed with holy water, and given a candle. Traces of this attitude remained in the refusal of some Anglican clergy, even as late as the 1950s, to let a woman take Communion before she had been churched (Sutton, 1992: 68).

In popular belief, a woman who went out of her own house before being churched would bring bad luck on anyone she met, or any house she entered, and often on herself too. It was still common in many areas in the 1950s for vicars to be asked to perform the rite for a non-churchgoing woman, so that she would be free to go shopping or visit friends (Radford, Radford, and Hole, 1961: 100). In other places, 'being churched' did not refer to a special ritual but to the first time a woman attended a normal Sunday service after giving birth; in Yorkshire in the 1980s, women who never normally went to church or chapel would slip in for a few minutes during a service as soon as they were fit to walk, for otherwise nobody would let them into their houses—it would be 'asking for trouble' (Clark, 1982: 115, 122–4; Gill, 1993: 26–7).

churchyard, see *GRAVES.

cigarettes. The belief that it is very unlucky to light three cigarettes from one match is still extremely well known. The popular explanation is that it is a soldier's superstition: in the trenches, an enemy sniper would use the light made by a match to locate a target. Keeping the match burning to light three cigarettes gave him time to take proper aim and fire, whereas two would not. The superstition certainly came to be widely known during the First World War, and the earliest concrete reference is a letter from Private Bradstow published in *N&Q* in 1916. Various commentators have written that the belief was held during the Boer War (1899–1902), while others place it in the Crimean War (1853–6), but with no evidence for their assertions. None of the standard folklore collections published before the First World War mentions it. There have been various attempts to connect this belief with older ones concerning three *candles, but this is unlikely. Cigarette packets feature in a children's superstition/custom. Iona and Peter Opie (1959) report that children in the 1950s, and before, on finding packets of particular brands—Black Cat, Player's Navy Cut, Churchman's Tenner are mentioned—stamp on them and say a rhyme, for example:

> Black cat, black cat, bring me luck
> If you don't I'll tear you up

Opie and Tatem, 1989: 55, 82; *N&Q* 12s:1 (1916), 208, 276; 12s:9 (1921), 528; 12s:10 (1922), 38–9, 116; Opie and Opie, 1959: 222–3.

Cinderella. The oldest known version of this famous European and Asiatic *fairytale is Chinese, from about AD 850, translated by Arthur Waley (*Folk-Lore* 58 (1947), 226–38); but the story as it is now known is always based on *Perrault's French 'Cendrillon' (1697), translated into English by Robert Samber (1729).

Native English versions probably once existed, for a Scottish one, 'Rashin Coatie', discovered by Andrew *Lang in 1878, is clearly independent of Perrault—the heroine is helped by a magical 'little red calf' which enables her to appear in church three times at Christmas in fine clothes and satin slippers, instead of her ugly cloak of rushes; a prince sees her and tries to catch her as she slips out before the service ends. Twentieth-century versions have been found among Gypsies in Lancashire and Scotland (Philip, 1989: 60–9, 161–74). *Cap o' Rushes is also related, though less closely.

See Marian Roalfe Cox, *Cinderella: Three Hundred and Forty-Five Variants of Cinderella, Catskin, and Cap o' Rushes* (1893), and Anna Birgitta Rooth, *The Cinderella Cycle* (1951). Neil Philip's *The Cinderella Story* (1989) gives 24 versions with commentary, including the British Gypsy ones. Perrault's text is in Philip, pp. 10–16; also in Opie and Opie, 1974: 117–27.

circles, circling. Symbolically, a circle can stand for perfection, wholeness, or a boundary (protective or confining); circling round something can be a way of honouring or blessing it, or, conversely, of receiving blessing or power from it. Circling can also summon a supernatural being—it is one of the commonest English local traditions that if you run round a specified mound, tree, cross, grave, church, or stone at a specified time and/or a specified number of times without stopping, you will raise a *ghost, or the *Devil; the condition is less easy than it seems, since running round a small object causes giddiness, and round a large one is exhausting. The circle as boundary is exemplified by the common instruction in manuals of *magic to draw a circle round oneself as protection against spirits summoned, or to conjure the spirit into a circle which will confine it; more prosaically, it appears also in the Devonshire belief that a snake cannot escape a circle drawn round it with an ash stick (Bray, 1838: 95).

See also *LEFTWARD and *RIGHTWARD MOVEMENT.

civic customs. Those which are performed as part of the ceremonies of local government. The history of local government in England is highly complex and littered with responses to special local circumstances, many of which became the stuff of folklore as the reasons faded but the form continued. The Municipal Corporations Act of 1835 was the first attempt to introduce a uniform system of local authority and swept away many of the remnants of previous practice, but a few customs still remained. Examples which still continue range from the spectacular Lord Mayor's Show in London, to the homely 'weighing the mayor' ceremony at *High Wycombe, and the *scrambling for coins at *Rye (Sussex) and Durham, and the *Hungerford Hocktide ceremonies in Berkshire.

Kightly, 1986: 77–9; 'Curious Corporation Customs', *New Penny Magazine* 55 (1899), 125–8.

clapping games. Most are played by two girls standing face to face and clapping their own and each others' hands in a set pattern and in time with a chanted or sung text. To the uninitiated, the process seems dextrous and complex, but the movements are relatively few and repetitive and can be picked up quite quickly. Most junior school girls in England will know a half a dozen clapping games, and the overall repertoire is not large, perhaps 20 to 30. The more innovative, however, will adapt other rhymes if necessary. Clapping games were certainly known in earlier periods but seem to have lost favour from about 1900 to after the Second World War. Since then they have enjoyed a renaissance, probably under American influence, and are now an integral part of the playground game repertoire.

An example of a clapping rhyme is

Have you ever, ever, ever, in your long-legged life
Seen a long-legged sailor with a long-legged wife.

No, I've never, ever, ever, in my long-legged life
Seen a long-legged sailor with a long-legged wife.

(Successive verses replace 'long-legged' with 'knock-kneed', 'bow-legged', etc.)

Opie and Opie, 1985, 440–80.

Clare, John (1793–1864). Born in Helpston, Northamptonshire, the son of a farm labourer, he lived virtually all his life in his home county, although the last 20 years were spent in mental asylums. By dint of his own effort he became a well-known poet, with four collections published in his own lifetime. He drew heavily on his observations of nature and village life and custom for the matter of his poems, and his work is thus an excellent source of information on early 19th-century customs and *superstitions. His autobiographical writings (published in 1983) also contain much useful material. Clare was particularly interested in *song and music, and collected items from his parents, neighbours, and local

Gypsy families. His four collections were: *Poems Descriptive of Rural Life* (1820); *The Village Minstrel* (1821); *The Shepherd's Calendar* (1827); *The Rural Muse* (1835), and others have since been published from his manuscripts.

George Deacon, *John Clare and the Folk Tradition* (1983); Eric Robinson, *John Clare's Autobiographical Writing* (1983).

clementing, see *SOULING.

clipping the church. A widespread but relatively under-researched custom. 'Clipping', in this context, means 'To embrace, fondle, encircle with the arms' (*EDD*) and this custom involves people holding hands and encircling their local church. The best-known example is at *Painswick in Gloucestershire, where it is now a church-organized custom, carried out by children, but earlier versions were less tightly organized. In most places it was a *Shrovetide or *Easter Monday custom. The known geographical distribution is inconclusive: most common in Somerset and Wiltshire, but also reported from Gloucestershire, Worcestershire, Birmingham, Shropshire, Derbyshire, and West Yorkshire. No reference has been found earlier than the early 19th century, although a correspondent in Hone's *Every-Day Book* (i. 431) published in 1825, writes 'When I was a child, as sure as Easter Monday came, I was taken to see the children clip the churches', which would probably carry the record back into the 18th century. Other features should be noted. Partridge (1912) brings attention to a number of instances where church clipping is associated with *Thread the Needle. Another noteworthy feature is that in some reports the clipping was accompanied by much joyful shouting and cheering, and/or the blowing of tin trumpets. Some accounts specifically state that the clippers had their backs to the church while clipping it. It is clear that there is much further work to be done to map and document this custom.

J. B. Partridge, *Folk-Lore* 23 (1912) 196–203; *Word-Lore* 1 (1926), 257; 2 (1927), 30, 55, 131, 166–7, 218; Wright and Lones, 1936: i. 20–1, 121; 1940: iii. 65, 70; *N&Q* 5s:5 (1876), 226, 316; 5s:6 (1876), 308, 436, 520–1; 5s:7 (1877), 38; 5s:9 (1878), 367; 7s:1 (1886), 329, 420, 486.

clocks. Until recently only found in wealthy homes, or on public buildings. Nevertheless they became the subject of several superstitions, from the 1820s onwards. The basic one is that a clock will stop at the very moment its owner dies; the first example given by Opie and Tatem is also one of the most dramatic, for it refers to a clock in the Houses of Parliament having stopped on 27 January 1820, 'being nearly the hour at which HM King George the Third had expired'. A clock stopping inexplicably, or striking the wrong hour, could be *omens of some death soon to occur. Parallel to these beliefs is the custom that as soon as someone dies any clock in the room (or, according to some, all the clocks in the house) must be deliberately stopped, to symbolize the fact that time has now ceased for that person.

If the church clock strikes the hour during a wedding, within a year the bride or groom will die, though if the timing is such that the bride hears the chime while still *outside* the church, that brings good luck. Similarly, if it strikes while a hymn is sung at a Sunday service, this foretells death within a week for someone in the parish; a town clock striking while the church bells are ringing, foretells a fire. In Devon around 1900, it was even thought unlucky to speak while a clock is striking (Opie and Tatem, 1989: 84–6).

Clodd, Edward (1840–1930). By profession a banker, he was an excellent example of the part-time Victorian folklorist: widely read, articulate, and intelligent, making major contributions to the scholarship of the time while holding down a demanding full-time job in a completely different field. Clodd was a founding member of the *Folklore Society (1878), having already published books on cultural evolution (*The Childhood of the World*, 1873) and religion (*The Childhood of Religions*, 1875). Following the debate opened by Darwin, Huxley, and *Tylor, Clodd steadily became more openly agnostic as he pursued folklore in search of early humans' mental development, and was particularly dismissive of spiritualism and occultism, so fashionable at the time, and of the Society for Psychic Research and Andrew *Lang's psycho-folklore. Clodd was elected the Folklore Society's President in 1895 and 1896, and in his second Presidential Address (*Folk-Lore* 7 (1896), 35–60) presented a highly contentious paper which caused an immediate furore in the Society and elsewhere, by comparing the 'savage' materials with which folklorists were by now abundantly familiar with Christianity and pointing out not just the connections or vague similarities, but 'the persistence of barbaric ideas and their outward expression throughout the higher cul-

ture' (p. 47). Sacramental bread and wine, miraculous conception and virgin birth, the second coming, exorcism, holy water, saints, were all cited as examples. Unrepentant, he also commented, 'if in analysing a belief we kill a superstition, this does but show what mortality lay at its core' (p. 42). It had been, in fact, only a matter of time before these ideas were voiced, as many of the leading folklorists and scientists of the period had been moving in the same direction. They had already been hinted at by *Frazer (*The Golden Bough*) and *Hartland (*The Legend of Perseus*), but Clodd had the courage to say them out loud, on a public platform. As expected, the Christian press roundly denounced him in terms varying from the misguided fool to the Anti-Christ, and he remained a *bête noire* for many Catholic writers for the rest of his life. A number of Folklore Society members tried, unsuccessfully, to prevent the publication of the address in the journal, and some, including ex-Prime Minister Gladstone, resigned from the Society in protest, but others publicly or privately applauded his courage and agreed with his interpretation. The fuss gradually subsided, and the lengthy obituary in the Society's journal does not even mention the affair. Despite his controversial views, Clodd was a popular and respected member of the folklore fraternity, but outlived most of his generation.

Other books by Clodd include: *Myths and Dreams* (1885); *The Story of Creation: A Plain Account of Evolution* (1888); *Tom Tit Tot: An Essay in Savage Philosophy in Folk-Tale* (1898); *Magic in Names and Other Things* (1920).

Obituary (with bibliography) by A. C. Haddon, *Folk-Lore* 40 (1929), 183–9; Dorson, 1968: 248–57.

clothes. Many beliefs focus on new clothes, and there are several times when it was good to wear them for the first time. One was *New Year, on the principle that whatever you did on that day would affect the rest of the year, while others swore by *Easter. If you could not manage new garments, you could at least spruce up the old ones, as Samuel Pepys recorded in his *Diary* for 30 March 1662: 'Easterday: Having my old black suit new-furbished, I was pretty neat in clothes today—and my boy, his old suit new-trimmed, very handsome.' The third important time for new clothes was *Whitsun: '(Cleveland, Yorkshire) . . . on Whitsunday, if you don't put on at least one brand-new article of dress the birds will be sure to come and "drop" on you . . .' (*N&Q* 5s:10 (1878), 287). It was also believed that to wear new clothes first on a Sunday was very good, as they would last twice as long if you did, but it was unlucky to wear them first on a Friday. When someone you knew was wearing new clothes for the first time you should pinch them, for luck, or else greet them with the formula 'Health to wear it, Strength to tear it, And money to buy another' (Wright, 1913: 224).

The second area of focus was on untoward or unusual things happening: 'I lately heard that apron-strings unfastened mean either "He loves you very much", or as a variation, "Someone is thinking about you"'. So wrote a correspondent to *N&Q* in 1940 (179: 302). These two related meanings have been given to apron strings suddenly coming untied since at least the mid-19th century, although in the first mention of the phenomenon quoted by Opie and Tatem (from Scotland) it was clearly a bad omen. Other sources mention the garter as the recalcitrant item, but do not agree on its meaning. In the 16th and 17th centuries it was considered unlucky, while in several 19th-century sources it is a sign of the thoughtful sweetheart. But S. O. Addy reports from York-shire that 'if a woman loses her garter in the street her lover will be unfaithful to her' (Addy, 1895: 98).

It is still said to be unwise to mend clothes while wearing them, an idea which has been reported regularly since 1850, often in rhyme (Lean, 1902: ii. 158; Igglesden, *c.*1932: 174), and how you dress yourself in the morning can be significant: 'If you put a button or hook into the wrong hole while dressing in the morning, some misfortune will occur during the day' (Henderson, 1879: 113). Putting something on inside out has been considered ominous at least since 1340, but opinions have again var-ied on what it means. In earlier times it was a token of bad luck (Scot, 1584: book 11, chapter 15), but for most the opposite was true as long as you let it be and did not turn the offending article the right way round (*Connoisseur*, 13 Mar. 1755). In certain circumstances, however, it was definitely advisable to turn some item of clothing inside out. This was a sure way of breaking the spell if you had been *pixy-led or beguiled by the *fairies in some way, and in many calendar customs, such as *guising or *mumming by children, it was standard prac-tice to turn your jacket inside-out in lieu of other costume to wear.

Another belief, reported from the mid-19th century onwards from various parts of the country (e.g. Leather, 1912: 89; Wright, 1928: 21) was that dead people's clothes, if given away, wore badly and soon deteriorated. Many beliefs focused on particular items of clothing. A notion reported twice early in the 20th cen-tury (Hertfordshire in 1914, and Gloucester-shire in 1915), maintains that if the hem of a woman's skirt accidentally becomes turned up, she will receive a present or some other form of good luck (*Folk-Lore* 25 (1914), 372; 26 (1915), 210). On the other hand, if a girl's petticoat or slip is seen to be showing beneath her dress it was a sure sign that her father loved her more than her mother, 'perhaps because it is plain that her mother does not attend so much to her dress as she ought to' (Chambers, 1878: ii. 322). In post-Second World War Britain, there were a number of traditional remarks said about women whose slip was showing, either as a coded message said by a female friend, or shouted derisively by boys: 'S.O.S. (Slip on show)', 'It's snowing in Paris', 'Your washing is hanging out', or the incomprehensible but very widely reported 'Charley's Dead' (see Eric Partridge, *A Diction-ary of Catch Phrases* (2nd edn., 1985, 47, 175, 383). A woman in Surrey in 1959, however, commented, 'If any of the staff are showing a petticoat they are accused of husband hunt-ing' (Opie and Tatem, 1989: 303).

See also *SHOES; *SHOELACES; *DRESSMAKING; *WEDDINGS; *WASHING.

Opie and Tatem, 1989: 4–5; Lean, 1903: ii. 28, 158, 220, 226, 236, 328, 452; *N&Q* 11s:8 (1913), 288–9, 336–7, 377; 11s:9 (1914), 136, 157.

clover. The first English reference to the *luck of the four-leafed clover dates from 1507: whoever finds one and keeps it reverently can know 'for all so true as the gospell y^t he shall be ryche all his life' (Anon., *The Gospelles of Dys-taues*, part 2, p. xv). Others say it brings luck in love, or a long healthy life. Nowadays plants producing four-lobed leaves are commercially grown, and the leaves encased in plastic are sold as charms.

A charm reported twice from East Anglia in the 1850s involves 'a clover of two', i.e. a piece with only two leaves: if a girl puts one in her shoe, the next man she meets (or someone of the same name) will be her husband (*N&Q* 1s:6 (1852), 601; 1s:10 (1854), 321).

coal. A lucky substance. It is regularly brought as one of the traditional gifts in *first footing on *New Year's Eve; some say this guarantees a warm hearth for the year, others that the main point is 'black for good luck' (cf. *black). In Herefordshire around 1900, 'a box of coal and a plate of salt should be the first things taken into an empty house, before moving any furniture in' (Leather, 1912: 86). There are references from the 1950s to the luck of carrying a lump of coal in one's pocket, and to making a wish when picking one up in the road and throwing it over one's shoulder (Opie and Tatem, 1989: 89); now that coal fires are so rare, these customs must have died out.

See also *MIDSUMMER COAL.

cockatrice. This legendary creature, first described by classical authors, remained acceptable to the educated till the 17th century. Belief in it was reinforced by the fact that 'cockatrice' is used several times in the King James Bible to translate one of the Hebrew words for 'serpent'. It was supposed to have the head and legs of a cock, but the body and tail of a small dragon; it was venomous, and could kill people with its deadly glance. It was said to come from an egg laid by a *cock (or from a duck's egg) hatched out by a *toad.

According to legend, the monster could only be killed by tricking it into seeing itself. At Saffron Walden (Essex), a knight is said to have donned crystal armour to destroy a cockatrice; at Wherwell (Hampshire), where a man lowered a mirror of polished steel into the creature's den, it fought its reflection till exhausted (Simpson, 1980: 40–1).

cock-fighting. Particularly popular at *Shrovetide, but found at any time of year, either on an *ad hoc* basis or in specially constructed cock-pits which featured a raised circular platform in the centre and tiered benches for spectators. Fighting cocks were specially bred and trained, and successful ones fetched high prices, and the sport enjoyed widespread support from all levels of society. The earliest reference links cock-fighting with schoolchildren:

each year upon the day called Carnival ... boys from the schools bring fighting-cocks to their master, and the whole forenoon is given up to boyish sport; for they have a holiday in the schools that they may watch their cocks do battle (Fitz Stephen, *c.*1183: 56)

and there are numerous references in literary and historical sources to the 'cock-penny',

which the master could exact from each of the boys in order to provide for the sport.

Sporadic attempts to ban the game, from the 14th century onwards, seem to have been ignored, and the wide support is still evident in 1761 when 'an hostler in his apron often wins several guineas from a lord' (quoted Malcolmson, 1973: 50). However, as the voices of protest gathered against *blood sports in the mid-18th century, cock-fighting came in for increasing levels of criticism and attempts at abolition. It was specifically banned in the 1835 Cruelty to Animals Act, but continued quite openly in a number of areas, and still takes place in secret.

Wright and Lones, 1936: i. 24–6; Malcolmson, 1973; Edward G. Fairholme and Wellesley Pain, *A Century of Work for Animals: The History of the R.S.P.C.A. 1824–1924* (1924), 75–82.

cocking a snook. The most common name for the gesture formed by holding the thumb to the tip of the nose and spreading the fingers. Sometimes varied by waggling the fingers, or by adding the second hand (a 'double snook'). Also called 'taking a sight', 'cocking a snoot', or the 'Shanghai gesture', its meaning ranges from mocking to rude, although in the present day its use is considered childish. Unlike most gestures, cocking a snook is found, with a similar meaning, across the whole of Europe. The gesture is described in the writings of François Rabelais in 1532, but its first known unmistakable depiction is in *La Fête des fous*, a drawing by Pieter Brueghel of 1560. It is not clear how far back the gesture dates in England. References are relatively common in England in the 19th century, almost always referring to schoolboys, and Hone (1832: 33) writes that it 'suddenly arose as a novelty within the last twenty years among the boys of the metropolis'. A correspondent in *N&Q* (5s:3 (1875), 298), however, gives a reference to a 1702 publication, *The English Theophrastus*.

See also *GESTURES, *THUMBS, *V-SIGN.

Morris, 1979: 25–42; Archer Taylor, *The Shanghai Gesture* (FF Communications No. 166, 1956); *N&Q* 5s:2 (1874), 166, 234, 255–6, 299; 5s:3 (1875), 39, 119, 298, 376; correspondence in *The Times* (9–23 July 1936).

Cockle-Bread. In the 19th and 20th centuries, Cockle-Bread was a children's game in which one squats on its haunches with hands clasped beneath the thighs, while others grasp its arms and swing it to and fro. This action was often accompanied by a rhyme:

My granny is sick and now is dead
And we'll go mould some cocklety bread
Up with the heels and down with the head
And that's the way to make cocklety bread.

Earlier references, however, show both rhyme and action with a more serious purpose. John *Aubrey (1686: 43–4) notes:

Young wenches have a wanton sport, which they call moulding of Cocklebread; viz. They gett upon a Table-board and then gather up their coates with their hands as high as they can, and then they wabble to and fro with their Buttocks as if they were kneading of Dowgh with their A——, and say these words:

My dame is sick and gonne to bed
And I'le go mowld my cockle-bread . . .

The dough thus kneaded would be baked and the bread given to the object of the young woman's fancy, which would thus ensure his undying love for her. Cockle-Bread is also mentioned in George Peele's play *The Old Wives Tale* (1595) and Richard Brome's *Jovial Crew* (1652).

Gomme, 1894: i. 74–6; *EDD*, 1898: i. 685.

cocks. A cock crowing at daybreak drives away *ghosts and evil spirits, and even Satan, as in the legend of the *Devil's Dyke. Henry *Bourne noted in his *Antiquitates Vulgares* (1725), chapter 6, that:

It is a received tradition among the Vulgar, That at the Time of Cock-crowing, the Midnight Spirits forsake these lower Regions, and go to their proper Places. . . . Hence it is, that in Country-Places, where the way of Life requires more early Labour, they always go chearfully to Work at that Time; whereas if they are called abroad sooner, they are apt to imagine everything they see or hear, to be a wand-ring Ghost.

Crowing at unusual times generally meant death or ill luck—except on *Christmas Eve, when cocks crow joyfully all night (Shakespeare, *Hamlet*, I. i). But a cock crowing at the door only meant that vistors would shortly arrive. Cocks on church spires guarded the building and the graveyard, and would crow on Doomsday to wake the dead (Opie and Tatem, 1989: 90–1; Radford, Radford and Hole, 1961: 108–9).

It was thought that cocks might occasionally lay eggs, a belief based on the fact that old hens sometimes develop male plumage and behaviour, yet still lay small, sterile eggs; this was regarded as ill-omened, and the egg would be broken, for fear it hatched into a *cockatrice (Blakeborough, 1898: 149; Forbes, 1966: 1–22).

A 'cockstride' was a country term for a tiny distance; it was used of the increase of daylight in early January, as in John Ray's *A Collection of English Proverbs* (1678): 'At twelf-day the days are lengthened a cock-stride.' In some legends about *laying ghosts the banished spirit is said to be creeping home at the rate of one cockstride per year.

See also *COCK-FIGHTING.

cocks, throwing at. A number of traditional sports, called 'cock-threshing', 'throwing at cocks', 'cock-running', were particularly popular at Shrovetide. In its basic form a live cock, or hen, is tied by one leg to a stake or other immovable object. Players take it in turn to throw heavy sticks at the bird, and the one who kills it wins it. The game existed at least since 1409, when the Corporation of London was trying to stop youths exacting payment from passers-by to fund their activities, but it is clearly much older and involved all levels of society, including royalty. Over the years, however, it gradually became the province of the lower classes and children. Schoolchildren were typically allowed to play the game at Shrovetide, with the schoolmaster's assistance, although *cock-fighting was more common in this context. So prevalent was the game that Cesar de Saussare, a French visitor in 1728, warned,

It is even dangerous to go near any of these places when this diversion is being held; so many clubs are being thrown about that you run the risk of receiving one on your head. (Quoted in Malcolmson, 1973: 48–9)

'Threshing the fat hen', mentioned by Tusser in 1580, involved a live hen suspended from a man's back, with straw stuffed into his clothes to protect him, and some horse bells attached. Players were blindfolded, and had to kill the bird by hitting it with sticks (Hone, 1827: 123–4). Alternatively, a cock was placed in a specially made earthen vessel, with its head and tail protruding from the pot, which was then suspended across the street about twelve feet above the ground (c.1760, Hone, 1827: 126).

These cock-based customs were the first of the *blood sports to come under sustained pressure for abolition, partly because they were deemed particularly unsporting, but also because by that time the game was a purely working-class activity. By the end of the 18th century the custom was regarded as nearly extinct, with Quainton (Buckinghamshire) being cited as the last place it occurred, in 1844. A memory of the sport continued in the form of throwing sticks at lead figures (made in the shape of a bird, animal, or man) and trying to knock it over. This could be a fairground game, or boys could own their own leaden 'cocks' and play at the game (Hone, 1827: 127).

Hone, 1827: 122–5; Malcolmson, 1973: 48–9, 118–22; Hutton, 1996: 153–9; Wright and Lones, i. 1936: 22–4; Dyer, 1876: 65–9.

coffee grounds, see *TEA.

coffins. One of the paradoxes of folk *medicine is that objects connected with death are deemed curative. In several parts of England, from the late 18th century to the end of the 19th, there are references to *rings made out of 'the handles of decayed coffins', or their hinges, or their lead lining, worn to prevent *cramp, fits, or rheumatism. In Shropshire, the ring was 'made of three rings taken from three coffins out of three several churchyards' (Opie and Tatem, 1989: 91).

coins. The belief reported most regularly about coins is that a holed or bent coin is lucky. The coin with a hole is mentioned from the 1830s to the 1950s. The *Poole and Dorsetshire Herald* of 11 February 1847 details how a local shopkeeper had kept all holed coins she had received over the counter, in the belief that they were special and should only be used for holy purposes (reprinted in Morsley, 1979: 305). Edward Lovett, collector of First World War beliefs, described meeting a soldier who showed him an old farthing with a hole in it, which he carried as his mascot. Also lucky was a bent coin, such as the 'crooked sixpence' of the nursery rhyme, but this is recorded from a much earlier date, being mentioned (as 'bowed silver' or 'bowed groat', etc.) by playwrights from the 16th century onwards (see Lean), often in the context of a gift, as for example in the description by John Foxe of the martyrdom of Alice Benden at Canterbury, in 1557: 'A shilling also of Philip and Mary she took forth, which her father had bowed and sent her when she was first sent to prison', and similar gifts were reported into the late 19th century (*N&Q* 1s:10 (1854), 505). Finucane (1977: 94–5) reports numerous examples of coin-bending in medieval times, in confirmation of a vow, when in

danger, as part of a cure, or for general good luck. In each case the bent coin was offered to a saint.

Most other coin beliefs have been short-lived or at least have escaped being recorded more than once or twice, except in the case of *fishermen who used to cut a slit in one of the cork floats of their nets, reputedly to let Neptune know they were willing to buy the fish they caught, and the widespread practice of placing a coin under the mast of any new boat—'for luck'.

See also *GOLD for the use of gold coins in folk-medicine.

Lovett, 1925: 13–14, 54–5, 70–1; Opie and Tatem, 1989: 92–3; Lean, 1903: ii. 44–5, 134–5.

Colchester oyster fishery. The town of Colchester in Essex owns all the oyster beds on the river Colne by virtue of a grant in the 12th century by Richard I. The start of the oyster season on 1 September is thus marked by the Mayor, Town Clerk, and other officials setting out by boat into Pyefleet Creek, to assert their ownership and officially start the season's dredging. The Town Clerk reads the proclamation (dated 1256) which states that the oyster beds have belonged to Colchester 'from the time beyond which memory runneth not to the contrary'. The loyal toast is given in gin and gingerbread, and the Mayor pulls up, and eats, the first oyster. A few weeks later, about 20 October, they stage a great Oyster Feast in Colchester's Moot Hall, where about 400 people consume thousands of oysters.

Kightly, 1986: 82; Hole, 1975: 106–7; David Cannadine, 'The Transformation of Civic Ritual in Modern Britain: The Colchester Oyster Feast', *Past and Present* 94 (1982), 106–30.

colours. In English folklore, the main significant colours are *black, *white, *red, *green, and to a lesser extent *blue. The ascribed meanings, however, do not form a systematic code, nor are they self-consistent; each colour is considered individually, not in parallel or contrast to others in a set, and each can carry either good or bad meanings, according to context. In some cases rhyme determines the meaning, notably in the association of blue and 'true'.

Various more coherent codes associated with religion, astrology, and alchemy in the medieval and early modern period, were known to at least some sections of the community. The traditional Catholic liturgical colours were: white for the feasts of Christ, Mary, and saints that are not martyrs; red for martyrs; violet in penitential seasons; black on Good Friday and at funerals; green at all other times (the system was modified in the 1960s). Catholics also associate blue with the Virgin Mary.

A powerful modern code is the red/amber/green of traffic controls, according to which red = 'danger/stop', and green = 'safety/go ahead'.

colt-pixy. A Hampshire name for a mischievous *fairy, which takes the shape of a horse and neighs to the horses of travellers, leading them astray into bogs (Briggs, 1976: 78–9). In Somerset, acccording to Ruth Tongue (1965: 119), it also attacks boys who steal apples from orchards.

comets. As with spectacular *storms and winds, whenever a comet appears, it is bound to portend great events. Tacitus thought so, and Bede in the 8th century agreed—'Comets are long-haired stars with flames, appearing suddenly, and presaging a change in sovereignty, or plague, or war, or winds, or floods' (*De Natura Rerum* (*c*.725), xxiv). Queen Elizabeth I was reputedly above such things (Hazlitt, 1905: 142), but John Evelyn was not sure. He noted in his *Diary*, 12 December 1680: 'They may be warnings from God, as they commonly are for-runners of his animadversions . . .'

Opie and Tatem, 1989: 93; *N&Q* 11s:1 (1910), 448; 151 (1926), 224, 267

conception. Until modern times, conception was a topic fraught with anxiety. For a married woman to be childless was a disgrace and disaster—but unwanted pregnancy could be disastrous too. Traditional advice on how to conceive (or avoid conceiving) must have been copious, though little has been recorded in print; early folklorists and their informants probably avoided the subject as unseemly. In general terms, it is known that medieval women went on *pilgrimages and visited holy *wells to cure barrenness, and that the 'luck' of various folk customs could include human fertility, but personal measures are very rarely mentioned. Nowadays, there is less reticence; the information which follows was easily gathered orally and by a questionnaire in 1998.

A waxing *moon and a rising *tide were thought to favour conception, and the full moon was best of all [JS]; Lincolnshire women interviewed in the 1980s stated:

We were told by our mothers and grandmothers: have intercourse when the tide is coming in, the sea will wash it in.

We used to say, do it when it was a full moon, (but) I think really you could do it any time and get a baby.

If you live on the coast, do it when the tide is going out and the sea will take it all away. (Sutton, 1992: 53, 93)

Some believed the time of conception had physical results; in Kent in the 1950s a girl with a facial birthmark was told she must have been conceived during an eclipse, and her red-haired brother that his parents must have made love during the mother's period [JS].

It was thought that a death in a family would soon be followed by a conception, the child coming, according to an old saying, 'to replace the one lost'; also, that if a childless couple adopts a baby, the woman will very shortly become pregnant. Position during intercourse was thought important, the deeper the penetration the likelier conception. Some held that position could determine the baby's sex: 'A woman from Hackthorn (Lincolnshire) remembers her mother's advice in the 1930s: "Lay on your right side when doing it and you'll have a boy, lay on your left if you want a girl"' (Sutton, 1992: 54). The same advice was given in the so-called *Aristotle's Masterpiece* ((1684), book I, chapter 2), which recommends continuing to lie thus when sleeping, for at least a week. It was said that if the mother's 'system' was acid, she would conceive a girl, but if alkaline, a boy; women would adjust their diet accordingly, and use douches of boracic acid, or bicarbonate of soda [JS].

Two common fallacies among young girls were that you cannot become pregnant the first time you have intercourse, nor if you do it standing up [JS]. To urinate or take violent excercise straight afterwards was thought to be a safeguard; girls would make themselves cough or sneeze, jump about—or jitterbug. Various strange contraceptive methods were used. One was to insert one's wedding ring into the womb and leave it there; this is known to have been practised in London some 50 years ago [JS]. Another, recorded from East Anglia, depended on contact with death; the woman might hold a dead man's hand for two minutes—some said, by opening up a new grave—or put a coin which has lain on a corpse's mouth under her pillow, thus averting pregnancy while it was there, or, according to others, for ever after (Porter, 1969: 11–12; Sutton, 1992: 92). In the north of England around 1850, it was commonly thought that if a woman bore twins of which one was a boy and the other a girl, she would never get pregnant again (Denham Tracts, 1890: II, 30).

Plants reputed to prevent conception or cause abortion included *parsley, pennyroyal, *nettles, and saffron (Hatfield, 1994: 17–20); aloes and purgatives were also used as abortifacients, as was gin (preferably hot), and vinegar in which twelve pennies of church money had been steeped for two or three days (*Folklore* 69 (1958), 113). Violent excercise, especially throwing oneself downstairs, was also thought effective.

See also *CHILDBIRTH, *MENSTRUATION, *PREGNANCY.

conjurer. Until it was appropriated by fairground and stage performers, this word was used for *wizards and *cunning men who could conjure up demons and spirits, and lay ghosts.

conkers. The popular name for the horse-chestnut, and for the game played with them suspended on a string. The history of the game is not quite as clear as it could be, but its outlines are known even if the precise dating is unclear. The name appears to derive from a previous game called 'conquerors' or 'conquering', in which snail shells are squeezed together, point to point, to see which will break first. The earliest description of this game was written by Robert Southey in 1821, recalling his childhood near Bristol in 1782. In parallel with this game, however, another existed from at least the mid-17th century in which hazel-nuts or cob-nuts were strung and knocked together, in the same way as our modern conkers. By the 1850s, horse-chestnuts and walnuts are mentioned, but the earliest known unambiguous reference to horse-chestnuts being used dates from the *Every Boy's Book* of 1856. It is clear that this game was not nearly as well known in the second half of the 19th century as one would expect from its ubiquity in the 20th. As Vickery points out, the entries in Britten and Holland's *Dictionary of English Plant-Names* (1878–86) imply that the game was known in certain parts of the country only.

The modern game of conkers is replete with its own etiquette and terminology, including the scoring by which a victorious conker takes on the score of its defeated opponent (e.g. if a ten-er beats a six-er it becomes a seventeen-er, $10 + 6 + 1$). Your opponent can stamp on your conker if you drop it unless you shout 'Bagsie no stampsies' first; a 'cheesecutter' was a conker with a flat side; the cry to claim first hit varies from place to place but always has to rhyme with 'conker':

> Iddy iddy onker, my first conker
> Iddy iddy oh, my first go

As with other children's games there are periodic worried questions whether the game of conkers is dying out, and there are also adult competitions during the season which are well reported in the national press.

Opie and Opie, 1969: 227–32; Vickery, 1995: 189–97.

Contemporary Legend. Founded in 1991, this is the annual journal of the International Society for Contemporary Legend Research, covering all aspects of the genre, and using examples from many countries, including England. ISCLR also publishes a biannual newsletter, *Foaftale News*, reporting current items in the media, on the internet, etc.

contemporary, urban legends. From the 1940s onwards, folklorists became aware of a 'new' type of folktale—frightening, macabre, and/or amusing anecdotes going round orally, and sometimes in newspapers. These fitted the *legend genre because the tellers presented them as really true (and often genuinely believed they were) and the hearers accepted this. But whereas legends as previously defined had mostly been collected from country-dwellers, and were always set in the past, these were common in cities and were about things alleged to have happened very recently, within a few weeks of the telling. Their plots often turned upon some typically modern behaviour or invention—baby-sitting, hitchhiking, takeaway food, microwave ovens, kidney transplants, etc.—and reflected the fears and moral judgements of today's society. Collectors therefore labelled them 'contemporary', 'urban', or 'modern' legends; a more flippant term is 'foaftale', an acronym based on the way narrators claim the adventure happened to 'a *friend of a* friend' of theirs. The label 'urban' is much used by journalists and the public, but slightly misleading, for they circulate throughout a whole country; 'contemporary' is now widely preferred.

With the exception of some ghost stories (notably the *Vanishing Hitchhiker), their content is not supernatural but bizarre, violent, and gruesome—a grandmother's corpse is stolen from a car roof-rack; a madman decapitates a motorist who has left his car, and bangs the head on the car roof; a serial killer, disguised as an old woman, hitches a lift, but is detected by his hairy hands; someone with Aids deliberately infects others, and leaves a message saying so; a takeaway chicken portion is really a rat. Others, more light-hearted, involve sexual and social humiliations (nudity, open flies, farting, etc.) in complicated and barely credible circumstances; these are basically narrative jokes, sometimes presented as such, while other tellers believe them utterly: 'This is very funny, but this is absolutely true. It was my aunty's neighbour who we knew very well . . . ' (Bennett, 1988: 13–14).

Initially the sinister stories seem persuasive because of their mundane setting, and because they grow out of a more diffuse body of beliefs, prejudices, and experiences current in the community. The tellers generally give convincing details of time and place, saying they heard of the occurrence from someone who knew the people it happened to; the hearers do not know that the event has allegedly also happened in many other places, thus casting doubt on which account (if any) is factual. However sincere an individual teller is, and however fully he/she trusts his/her informant, somebody back along the line of transmission consciously created an effective tale, which others transferred to new locations, adapting the details to suit. The process by which contemporary legends appear, spread, are updated, and develop new variations by recombining older elements, can thus be regarded as a speeded-up version of the dissemination of *migratory legends.

Such a widespread genre can be studied from several angles. Scholars concerned with folk narrative produce accurate transcripts of actual tellings, and study the rhetorical strategies of the narrators. Others trace the history of particular plots and themes, and identify legends which were told as contemporary in previous centuries. Others use sociological and psychological approaches to show their

significance and relevance in the community.

The legends being international, Jan Brunvand's influential American collections of texts and commentaries are relevant: *The Vanishing Hitchhiker* (1981), *The Choking Doberman* (1984), *The Mexican Pet* (1986), *Curses! Broiled Again* (1989), and *The Baby Train* (1993). For British collections designed for the popular market, see Rodney Dale, *The Tumour in the Whale* (1978) and *It's True, It Happened to a Friend* (1984); Paul Smith, *The Book of Nasty Legends* (1983) and *The Book of Nastier Legends* (1986); Phil Healey and Rick Glanvill, *Urban Myths* (1991), *The Return of Urban Myths* (1993), and *Urban Myths Unplugged* (1994). Verbatim recordings of current teenage versions are included in Wilson, 1997.

Bennett and Smith, 1993, is an annotated international list of texts and scholarly studies; a selection of major essays is reprinted in Bennett and Smith, 1996. Papers have appeared in many folklore journals, both here and in America, and in the following volumes: Smith, 1983; Bennett, Smith, and Widdowson, 1987; Bennett and Smith, 1988; Bennett and Smith, 1989; Bennett and Smith, 1990. This series has now been replaced by the journal *Contemporary Legend*.

coopering trade. One of the old established trades which had its own set of *occupational customs, concentrated on key points in the worker's life, such as entering the trade, coming of age, qualifying, and so on. Given the trade, the barrel naturally features in most of the customs, with the victim being placed in one and rolled around the yard or factory, but other features such as covering him with shavings and beer, and making a great deal of noise, are common to most trades which have such ceremonies. 'Trussing the Cooper', to celebrate the end of an apprenticeship, is illustrated in *Picture Post* (30 November 1946), 16–17, and essentially the same procedure is also described in the *Independent on Sunday* (28 June 1998), 28, as still being practised. Photographs published in Drake-Carnell, 1938: plates 106–7, depict a similar process to celebrate an apprentice's twenty-first birthday at a Birmingham brewery.

J. Geraint Jenkins, *Gwerin* 1:4 (1957), 149–60.

coral. Coral beads hung round babies' necks were seen by some as purely decorative, and coral teething rings as purely practical; however, others believed coral warded off evil, as Reginald *Scot noted in 1584:

The corrall preserveth such as beare it from fascination or bewitching, and in this respect they are hanged about children's necks. But from whence that superstition is derived, and who invented the lie, I know not: but I see how readie the people are to give credit thereunto, by the multitude of corrals that be employed. (*Discoverie of Witchcraft*, 1584: book 13, chapter 6).

Some elaborate children's corals of the 18th and 19th centuries, silver mounted and with bells attached, have a tapering and twisting shape reminiscent of Neapolitan phallic horns, famous as charms against the Evil Eye; it may well be that the superstition, like the substance itself, is imported.

Corby Pole Fair. Held in Corby, Northamptonshire, on Whit Monday, the fair claims to have been founded by charter of Queen Elizabeth I in 1585, in gratitude for an incident in which locals rescued her from a nearby bog into which she had somehow wandered. Needless to say, no such charter can be found, but Charles II did confirm the fair in 1682, and it is now held every twenty years. The distinctive feature from which the fair gets its name involves the barring of local roads and exacting tolls from anyone who wants to pass. Anyone who refuses to pay, or commits any other misdemeanour, is carried through the fair on a pole (or, if female, on a chair) and placed in the stocks. Compare *Riding the Stang.

Kightly, 1986: 87; Hole, 1975: 163; Stone, 1906: 1–4.

cork. The belief that cork keeps *cramp at bay has been recorded a number of times since the 1850s, and is still current. Sufferers place the substance under their pillow or between the sheets, or even wear home-made cork garters or cork between their toes (*Folk-Lore* 62 (1951), 268). Another letter published in *N&Q* (12s:3 (1917), 449) asks why it is believed that wearing cork will keep off a heart attack, but no other report has been found to corroborate this idea. A completely different notion leads to the keeping of champagne corks, popped at some significant time, 'for luck', often with a slit cut in the cork and a coin placed in it. Opie and Tatem list examples back to the 1950s, and the custom is still widely observed at weddings, major birthday parties, and so on.

Opie and Tatem, 1989: 69, 96.

corn dollies. A modern craft form based loosely on traditional figures made of straw, previously connected with *harvest customs. Many references to harvest figures exist, under various names (Corn baby, Corn maiden, Kern baby, etc.), and the treatment of the figures also varied from place to place. Sometimes the image was large enough to be carried in triumph on a pole or in pride of place on the last load, but in others it was a more homely affair apparently made more for its decoration than for its representational features. Some were hung up in farmhouse or barn till the following year, others were displayed in the church at the harvest festival, while some places had a tradition whereby the figure could be sent to mock a nearby farm which had not finished its harvest. Some were rough and ready, others well crafted. Corn figures, like harvest customs in general have not received the detailed attention they deserve because writers have been content to adopt the discredited *Frazerian theory of corn spirits and fertility and have thus needed to enquire no further, so their distribution and function remains unclear. The custom of making corn figures had virtually died out in England well before the Second World War, but was revived in modified form, by a number of enthusiasts, under the generic name of 'corn dolly' as a rural heritage handicraft in the 1950s and 1960s. Minnie Lambeth, the wife of the Curator of the Cambridge Folk Museum, was one of the leading lights of the new movement, and she produced the first practical manuals, *A Golden Dolly: The Art, Mystery, and History of Corn Dollies* (1963, enlarged 1969) and *Discovering Corn Dollies* (1974). The craft 'corn dollies' have evolved far beyond the original traditional styles.

Iorwerth C. Peate, *Folklore* 82:3 (1971), 177–84; Porter, 1969: 123–4; *Folklore* 79:3 (1968), 233–4; *Folk-Lore* 15 (1904), 185.

corpse candles, lights. One of the *omens warning of impending death was the appearance of small faint lights flitting about near the home of the person fated to die, or along the road by which the funeral will reach the churchyard; they might also be seen hovering over the place where the grave would be dug. In areas bordering on Wales, where the belief was particularly common, they were called 'corpse candles', and in Sussex 'corpse lights'; the 19th-century Sussex folklorist Charlotte Latham found the belief was widespread, but thought glow-worms might account for it (*Folk-Lore Record* I (1878), 49–50).

Cottingley fairy photographs. Five photos taken in 1917 and 1920 by two teenage girls at Cottingley (Yorkshire) purported to show fairies dancing in a nearby glen; they convinced Edward Gardner, a prominent Theosophist, and Sir Arthur Conan Doyle. Over 60 years later, the girls admitted to a hoax, originally simply meant to deceive their family (*Yorkshire Evening Post* (19 Mar. 1983); *The Times* (9 Apr. 1983)). The photographic process itself had not been faked, but the objects photographed were painted cardboard cut-outs pinned on to bushes. The photos and related documents fetched £22,000 at auction in July 1998.

For the original report, see Sir Arthur Conan Doyle, *Strand Magazine* (Dec. 1920), 436–8; and Edward L. Gardner, *Fairies: A Book of Real Fairies* (1945; many reprints). For fuller discussion, see Geoffrey Crawley, 'The Astonishing Affair of the Cottingley Fairies', published in ten parts in *The British Journal of Photography* (1982–3); Cooper, 1990; Paul Smith, in Narváez, 1991: 371–405.

counterspells. Some traditional measures against *witchcraft were general defences, e.g. *horseshoes, *hagstones, various plants hung at the door, the sign of the *cross, a bent *coin laid in the churn, etc. But if a particular witch's curse had already taken hold, aggressive procedures were needed to break it; there are numerous accounts of these from Tudor times to within living memory, from all parts of England.

The simplest and best known was to 'draw blood above the breath', i.e. to scratch the witch's face to make it bleed; this was widely used in the 17th century, suspected women being forced to submit to scratching, on the assumption that those bewitched would then recover, and the witch lose her power. Illegal assaults still occurred in Victorian times. At Stratford-upon-Avon in 1867 a man made 'a frightful gash' in a woman's cheek, saying, 'There, you old witch, I can do anything with you now'; at Long Compton (Warwickshire) in 1875 a woman of 80 was killed with a pitchfork by a man who thought she had bewitched him (Palmer, 1976: 83–4). Symbolic violence was also thought effective: to stab the witch's footprint or shadow with a *nail, preferably a coffin-nail, or to burn straw from her thatch, would break her power.

By casting a spell, the witch had created a magical link with her victim, which could be used in reverse to punish her. Thus, in 1626 a woman recalled how, as a servant in Hull, she had been told by her mistress to 'clap the churn-staff to the bottom of the churn' and lay her hands across the top of it, because a woman thought to be a witch had come to the house to spoil the butter-making; the woman was immediately fixed to the spot, and after six hours 'fell down on her knees and asked forgiveness, and said her hand was in the churn, and she could not stir before (the) maid lifted up the staff of the churn'. On another occasion, the girl's mistress being ill, she was told 'to take a horseshoe and fling it in her dame's urine, and as long as the horseshoe was hot, the witch was sick at the heart' (Sharpe, 1996: 160). These principles were remembered for generations. In Sussex in the 1930s, it was said that if a waggon was halted by witchcraft, one must flog the wheels or cut notches on them; one man who did, saw the witch come out of her cottage 'a-yellin' an' sloppin' blood, and for every notch on the spokes there wor a cut on her fingers' (Simpson, 1973: 71).

The commonest way of exploiting this link was to apply heat to the object bewitched, so as to burn the witch. If cream could not be churned to butter, one should dip a red-hot poker or horseshoe in; a sick person's *urine should be boiled in a *witch bottle, or made into a cake and baked hard, or buried; his or her excrement should be thrown into a fire; if a farm animal died, its *heart should be cut out, stuck with *pins, and thrown in the fire or put up the chimney to dry slowly; or its carcass burnt, to save the rest of the livestock. Occasionally, an animal would be burnt alive; *The Times* of 3 July 1810 reported (p. 3) that:

At a village about two miles distant from Burton, in Kendal, a farmer had lately several of his calves die of the distemper; some of his credulous neighbours persuaded him that they were bewitched; and a cunning woman told him, that nothing would thrive about his house till the witch was burnt, and that the most effectual mode of breaking the enchantment was to cause a calf to be burnt alive. This plan was accordingly adopted on Friday the 11th ult., and a fire was kindled for the purpose on an adjacent moss, whither the poor victim (a fine heifer calf) was taken in a cart, and placed on the burning pile. Two men and a servant-woman were the barbarous executioners, who held the animal on the fire, one by its legs, another by its tail, and the third by its head; it however escaped from them several times, and was again and again committed to the flames.

See also *CUNNING MEN, *HAG-RIDING, *HEARTS AND PINS, *URINE, *WITCH BOTTLES.

counting. It has long been considered unlucky to count things too accurately—it is tempting fate to announce (even to yourself) the exact number in case it makes you lose some. 'Don't count your chickens before they are hatched' is an oft-quoted maxim even today. The references given in Opie and Tatem show that the fear of counting stretches back at least to biblical and classical times, but British examples only appear from the 18th century, and the majority of illustrations given by them are from Scotland. Nevertheless, English *card-players are particularly advised against counting their winnings at the card-table, and on a similar principle: 'A Suffolk shepherd . . . will seldom willingly tell even his master the number of lambs born until the lambing-season is over for fear of bad luck' (*Folk-Lore* 54 (1943), 390). The only thing one should definitely count is *warts, as from the mid-19th century to the present day this has been a standard way of getting rid of them.

See also: *COUNTING-OUT RHYMES; *SHEPHERDS' SCORE; *STANDING STONES; *WEIGHING.

Opie and Tatem, 1989: 101–2.

counting-out rhymes. Used by children (and sometimes adults *sotto voce*) to make a random choice between options but particularly to choose who will be 'it' in a game. The children stand in a circle or line, and one child points to each in turn in the rhythm of the chanted rhyme and either the one pointed to on the last word is 'it' or, more usually, is eliminated from the count and the process is repeated until there is only one left. As such it is normally accepted as a fair method of choosing, but in the hands of a skilful practitioner the outcome can be manipulated to a certain degree. There can be few people in Britain who do not know a variant of:

> Eenie meenie minie mo
> Catch a nigger by his toe
> If he hollers let him go
> Eenie meenie minie mo.
>
> [SR]

The offensive word in the second line, under pressure from parents and teachers, is usually rendered now as 'beggar' or other two-syllable word, much to the annoyance of those who believe that our traditional lore should not be changed for mere 'political correctness'. There

is evidence, however, that the 'nigger' word was imported relatively late from the USA, with 'chicken' or 'tinker' being the older British form (Opie and Opie, 1997: 184–6). The first line turns up in dozens of other counting-out rhymes, and is also found in German, Austrian, and a French-Canadian version, but the middle two lines are first reported in 1888 (from Scotland). English children have a wide range of rhymes from which to choose:

> One potato, two potato, three potato, four
> Five potato, six potato, seven potato, more
> One bad spud!
>
> [SR]

is common all over Britain, USA, Canada, and Australia, but does not seem to have been reported before 1885 (in Canada). A number of rhymes start with the words 'Ip dip', and indeed many children refer to the process as 'dipping':

> Ip dip sky blue
> Who's it not you

is a simple version, but more common nowadays (but rarely published) is:

> Ip dip dog shit
> Fucking bastard silly git
>
> (Norbury, Croydon, 12-year-old girls, 1986)

See also *SHEPHERDS' SCORE.

Bolton, 1888; Abrahams and Rankin, 1980; Opie and Opie, 1969: 17–61.

country dance, see *DANCE.

coven. In medieval English, this word, a variant of 'convent' and derived from Latin *conventus*, 'assembly', had no link to witches; it meant either a gathering of people (number unspecified), or a community of thirteen monks and their abbot, modelled on Christ and his apostles. However, in Scotland from about 1500 it was occasionally applied to a witches' meeting, possibly by association with the similar-sounding word 'covin', meaning a plot or a group of plotters; in 1662 a Scottish witch, Isobel Gowdie, said in her confession that 'ther is threttein persones in ilk coeven'. A second example of this usage occurs in the deposition of a Northumbrian girl called Anne Armstrong, a witness in a witch trial in 1673; she spoke of witches attending the sabbath in 'coveys' of thirteen (Sharpe, 1996: 279). The term remained rare until it was picked up by Sir Walter Scott in his *Letters on Demonology and Witchcraft*, 1830.

In 1922 Margaret *Murray launched the theory that witches were always organized in groups of thirteen where the leader impersonated the Devil, and alleged that trial records showed several such groups, including five in England. When checked by historians, her figures turned out to be wrong; she had manipulated information in her sources to achieve the desired number. Though the idea of organization by covens is now rejected by scholars as unhistorical, it is widely taken for granted in fiction and journalism; it is also central to the organization of the *Wicca movement.

cowslip. Cowslip balls were made by hanging the flower heads from a string and tying the ends. Children would toss them to each other, reciting, as the ball gradually fell to bits:

Tissty-tossty, tell me true,
Who am I going to be married to?
Tinker, tailor, soldier, sailor,
Rich man, poor man, beggarman, thief.

In Lincolnshire, women attempted to throw these balls over a house (presumably having weighted them), which some said was 'to keep away evil, the devil'; others hung bunches in cowsheds to keep witches out (Sutton, 1997: 105–6).

cradle, pram. A number of beliefs cluster around the cradle and, by extension, the pram. Rocking an empty cradle is regularly reported, from the early 19th century onwards, as resulting in a new baby arriving soon, and is still current in the idea of advice not to push an empty pram. It is also considered by many that to have a cradle or pram in the house before the baby is born is to tempt fate and run the risk of bad luck, while the underlying fear is the baby being born dead or dying young. This notion is first reported in the 1890s, and is still regularly mentioned, although it is nowadays acceptable to buy one, but it should not be delivered to the house in advance of the birth. Other, less common, beliefs can be quoted. Referring to the north of England in the mid-19th century, Denham reported, 'In all sales either under distraint for rent or common debt, it is an ancient and invariable custom to leave the cradle unsold, and the original owner is at liberty to repossess it' (*Denham Tracts*, 1891: ii. 40). In Yorkshire, new parents were warned that a cradle must be paid for before the baby

sleeps in it, otherwise it 'will end its days lacking the means to pay for its own coffin' (Blakeborough, 1898: 114–15). An annual Candlemas custom at Blidworth (Nottinghamshire) involved the vicar rocking the last-baptized infant in an old cradle bedecked with flowers and surrounded by candles, before the altar. The custom was revived in 1923, although it is locally believed that it dates back to the 13th century (Wright and Lones, 1938: ii. 123–4).

Opie and Tatem, 1989: 103, 315–16.

cramp. Numerous cures for cramp have been recorded, some with an alleged physical basis, while others are purely magical. Forbes gives several examples of verbal *charms, including the following from a schoolboy Samuel Coleridge Taylor:

The devil is tying a knot in my leg
Mark, Luke, and John, unloose it I beg
Crosses three we make to ease us
Two for the thieves, and one for Christ Jesus!

A widespread belief in a particular animal bone, carried in the pocket or placed under the pillow, to prevent or cure cramp has a long history, and is still found. In the earliest references, in the 16th century, it was a bone from a hare: 'The lytle bone in the knee ioynt of the hinder legge of an hare, doth presently helpe the crampe if you touch the grieved place therewith. Often proved' (Lupton, 1579: i. 87; quoted in Opie and Tatem) and Reginald *Scot (1584: book, 13 chapter 10) agreed. By the 19th century the effective bone was usually the patella, or knuckle-bone of a sheep.

See also *CRAMP RINGS, *CORK, *EELS.

Forbes, 1971: 293–316; Black, 1883: 27, 86, 95, 154, 156, 175, 182, 199; Lean, 1903: ii. 491–3; Opie and Tatem, 1989: 104.

cramp rings. From the reign of Edward III to that of Mary Tudor, monarchs used to bless a plateful of gold and silver rings every *Good Friday at the altar of the Chapel Royal, rubbing them between their fingers; thanks to the royal healing touch (cf. *king's evil), they could cure epilepsy, cramp, or palsy, provided they were 'given without money or petition', as Andrew Borde noted in his *Breviary of Health* (1557, fo. 166).

This royal ritual either developed from, or inspired, a less élitist one described in a manuscript of *c*.1400 (MS Arundel 275, fo. 23b). Five silver pennies must be taken from the Mass-offerings on Good Friday in five different churches; these 25 coins must be laid before a crucifix while five 'Our Fathers' are said in honour of the Five Wounds of Jesus, for five days running, and then hammered into a ring inscribed with 'Jesus of Nazareth' and the names of the Three Wise Men.

After these customs had been abolished in the reign of Elizabeth, people took to making rings for themselves, to cure fits or rheumatism, out of metal that was in some way special. The most popular method was to collect 12 or 30 pennies, each from a different person, and ask a clergyman to exchange them for a shilling or a half-crown from the collection plate; this 'sacrament *silver' was then made into a ring. There are references to this in Hereford in the mid-17th century, in Berkshire in the 18th, and in several 19th-century regional collections. In Cheshire, the ring could be made from a shilling obtained by begging a penny each from twelve people of the sex opposite to the sufferer (Moss, 1898: 166); in Essex and Devon, from nine sixpences, and in Suffolk from twelve scraps of broken silver, all to be got in the same way (Radford, Radford, and Hole, 1961: 293–4; Opie and Tatem, 1989: 327–8). In Yorkshire, pieces of lead cut from *coffins were used; in Shropshire and Devon, coffin nails— 'three nails taken from three coffins out of three several churchyards' (Burne, 1883: 193).

crickets. The belief that a cricket singing in the house means something is well attested from the early 17th century onwards, but there is no consensus whether it is good or bad. John *Melton (1620: 46) was quite clear: 'It is a signe of death to some in that house, where Crickets have been many yeeres, if on a sudden they foresake the Chimney Corner', whereas only 30 years later, Nathaniel Homes (*Daemonologie* (1650), 59) maintains that death is foreshadowed 'of a cricket crying in an house, where was wont to be none'. Charles Dickens titled one of his stories *The Cricket on the Hearth* (1846) in which there is no equivocation, 'To have a cricket on the hearth is the luckiest thing in all the world!' Charlotte Burne (1883: 238) sums it up in her work on Shropshire lore: 'The cricket on the hearth appears somewhat in the light of a domestic familiar, or household bogy, sometimes regarded as a "lucky" inmate and sometimes as quite the reverse.'

Opie and Tatem, 1989: 104–5.

Cromwell, Oliver. Chiefly remembered in folk tradition as a destroyer. A considerable number of castles and manor houses, especially in Yorkshire and Lincolnshire, are said (incorrectly) to have been destroyed or severely damaged by Cromwell's cannon-fire; an even larger number of churches, in several different counties, are said to have been desecrated by Cromwell (or Cromwell's men) stabling horses there. Presumably as a result of this violent and destructive reputation, Cromwell became a *bogey figure. Flora Thompson mentions in her *Lark Rise to Candleford* (1945) that in Oxfordshire in the 1880s 'the older mothers and grandmothers still threatened naughty children with the name of Cromwell. "If you ain't a good gal, old Oliver Crummell'll have 'ee!" they would say, or "Here comes old Crummell!" ' (chapter 14).

His sudden death on 3 September 1658, at the height of his power, made a deep impression on the popular mind. Shortly before, on the night of 30/31 August, there had been a great gale, and it was soon being said that the two events were connected— indeed, that the *storm had come on the very night Cromwell died. Such signs were ambiguous; they could mark the death of a great hero, or of a sinner bound for Hell. In the case of a regicide the latter was more likely, and became the accepted interpretation in folk tradition.

To add to the drama, Cromwell's body was exhumed from Westminster Abbey after the Restoration in 1660 and decapitated, the head being displayed at Westminster Hall, and these events too are said to have been accompanied by storms. The body may have been secretly buried in Red Lion Square in Holborn, London, or taken by his daughter to her home at Newburgh Priory and laid in a vault there; it is said that any attempt to open this vault to establish the truth will lead to disaster.

Alan Smith, *Folklore* 79 (1968), 17–39.

cross. The many ways in which material representations of the cross, and the gesture of prayer and blessing called the Sign of the Cross, are used in official religious rituals need not be listed here. At the level of folk custom and belief, the cross functions as a powerful protection against evil, and hence as a way of ensuring luck. Children draw a cross on themselves with thumb or finger (generally licking it first) as a form of oath, saying 'Cross my heart and wish I may die!' To draw it on one's shoe is said to cure cramps, and revive a foot that has 'gone to sleep'; Coleridge recalled this from his schooldays, with the rhyme:

> Foot, foot, foot is fast asleep!
> Thumb, thumb, thumb in spittle we steep!
> Crosses three we make to ease us,
> Two for the thieves and one for Jesus!

(*Table Talk* (1835), ii. 59)

There are many references to marking bread-dough and cake mixtures with a cross before baking, to keep the Devil and witches away, so that they rise properly in cooking; other foods were sometimes protected in the same way. No witch could step over sticks or straws laid crossways, or enter through doors or chimneys where a cross had been carved; the symbol was therefore common on *witch posts and *threshold patterns.

cross-dressing. Despite the Biblical prohibition against cross-dressing, 'The woman shall not wear that which pertaineth unto a man, neither shall a man put on a woman's garment: for all that do so are abomination unto the Lord thy God' (Deuteronomy 22: 5), men dressing as women (and occasionally the other way round) is a recurrent feature of traditional customs, including *morris dance, *mumming plays, *occupational customs (especially mock weddings), *Molly dance, *sword dance, *Castleton Garland, *Abbots Bromley Horn Dance, and even the Lady *Godiva procession, and is regularly mentioned as a feature of other events such as *Charlton Horn Fair, and private Christmas parties. Some folklorists pronounced that cross-dressing had a ritual, fertility-enhancing function, but there is no evidence of this, and the practice has other more prosaic features which are sufficient to explain its presence and continuity. Until the 17th century women were routinely debarred from taking part in all performance milieux, including the legitimate stage, and this prohibition would have been even stronger in the realm of customs which involve heavy drinking, rough horseplay, and fighting. A further reason is that in our society men dressed as women have been regarded as inherently funny, allowing scope for ribaldry and innuendo which normal social mores would hardly allow if women were taking part.

crossing fingers. The act of crossing the *fingers (i.e. middle finger over index finger)

'for luck', or to ward off ill luck (e.g. after walking under a *ladder) is one of our most well-understood *gestures, although we may often say it—'I'll cross my fingers for you'—rather than actually carry out the action. Morris shows that the gesture is understood by some on mainland Europe but is only commonly found in Britain and parts of Scandinavia. Given its ubiquity in this country, it is surprising to find that the earliest reference found by Opie and Tatem only dates from 1912 (Leather, 1912: 88), where it is already linked to the ladder superstition. See *thumb for an older gesture, of similar protective nature. One sphere in which crossed fingers are still taken seriously is in the school playground, used as a protective action to accompany a *truce term to obtain temporary respite in a game. One of the popular explanations for the gesture's origin is that it dates from classical times when Christians were persecuted for their religion, and crossing the fingers was a secret way of invoking the cross. Given its late appearance, restricted distribution, and the fact that crossed fingers bear no relation to the shape of a cross, the explanation is completely unfounded.

See also *CROSSING LEGS, *FINGERS, *GESTURES, *THUMBS, *TRUCE TERMS.

Opie and Tatem, 1989: 109; Morris, 1979: 15–24; Opie and Opie, 1959: 122–5, 142–53, 211–17.

crossing legs. John Aubrey commented in 1686: 'To sit cross legged or with our fingers pectinated, shutt together, is accounted bad. Friends will psuade us from it. The same conceit was religiously observed by ye ancients as is observable from Pliny', and also 'When one has ill luck at cards, 'tis common to say that somebody sits with his legges acrosse, and brings him ill luck' (Aubrey, 1686: 111, 199). Most other reports, from before his time until the present day, report crossed legs as a way of ensuring good luck, especially at cards, or (in 1671) girls wanting luck in the lottery by 'praying cross-legg'd to S. Valentine'. In two specific situations, however, crossed legs must definitely be avoided—while someone else is giving birth and, according to a note in *Folk-Lore* (33 (1944), 390–1), at a spiritualist seance.

Compare *CROSSING FINGERS.

Opie and Tatem, 1989: 109–10.

crossroads. Traditionally felt to be uncanny places, likely to be haunted; this may be due to their ambiguous nature (belonging to two or more roads at once), and is certainly reinforced by their association with death and punishment.

Until 1823, English law required that suicides be buried in the highway; crossroads were generally chosen, and the corpse was often staked—a ritual of public disgrace, to deter others. According to local stories, some witches were similarly treated, while crossroads burials of executed criminals are known from Anglo-Saxon times. Those chosen were usually outside the town boundaries, probably symbolizing expulsion of the wrongdoer. Some have speculated that they might also confuse the ghost of the deceased, who could not then return home to haunt.

Crossroads also feature in magical cures. In Shropshire, grains of wheat rubbed against *warts were left there in the hope that some passer-by would pick them up; in Suffolk, the remedy for ague was:

You must go by night alone to a cross-road, and just as the clock strikes the midnight hour you must turn yourself about thrice and drive a tenpenny nail up to the head in the ground. Then walk away backwards from the spot before the clock is done striking twelve, and you will miss the ague; but the next person who goes over the nail will catch the malady in your stead. (Gurdon, 1893: 14).

crows. Generally regarded as unlucky, and as *omens of death, especially if they croak persistently near a house, or fly low over its roof. Occasionally, the number of crows seen at once is important, as with *magpies; in Leeds in the 1860s it was said 'When one crow is seen, it is a sign of bad luck; two, of good luck; three, of death; and four, of a wedding' (Opie and Tatem, 1989: 111).

'Crying Boy' painting. Apparently out of the blue in October 1985, the tabloid newspaper *The Sun* ran a story about a popular painting, which they dubbed 'The Crying Boy', being cursed or jinxed. In a series of articles, they built up the story that the picture was very bad luck to those who owned it, and that it somehow caused fires, but was untouched when everything else in the room was burnt. A number of readers wrote in agreeing that the picture was cursed, although some claimed that it was actually good luck when paired with the 'Crying Girl' painting. When the newspaper offered to destroy any pictures sent to them (paradoxically on a giant bonfire), they 'came flooding in'. The item made the

national television news, but by March 1986 seems to have been forgotten. It will be interesting to note whether any previous examples of this belief come to light, or if the newspaper concocted it, and whether it continues without the help of the media. Either way, it is an excellent example of how the mass media play a major role in creating and spreading modern folklore.

See also *PICTURE.

Main articles: *Sun* (24, 25, 26 Oct. 1985); (12, 13 Nov. 1985); (24 Feb. 1986).

cuckoos. The arrival of cuckoos is the signal that spring has come; various April dates are called 'Cuckoo Day' in different parts of the country: 14th in Sussex, 15th in Hampshire and Northamptonshire, 20th in Worcestershire, and so on. These are dates of local fairs, and there is often a tradition that an old woman goes to the fair and lets a cuckoo out of her bag or apron (Wright and Lones, 1938: ii. 177–8).

A good deal of light-hearted rivalry surrounds the question of when and where the first cuckoo is heard, and many letters on the topic have been published in *The Times* over the years. *Omens were drawn from the first call heard: lucky if to your right, unlucky if to your left or behind you, or if you have not yet eaten; if you have money in your pocket at the time, you will have plenty all year (especially if you turn it or jingle it), but if not, you will stay poor; if you are in bed, this forebodes an illness, unless you start running at once; if you are standing on grass, that bodes well, but if on earth or stones, you will be dead before next spring. The number of calls you hear shows how many more years before you die, or before you marry. Another divination, first mentioned in 1579, was to look inside your shoe on hearing the first call, for in it would be a hair of the same colour as that of whoever you were fated to marry.

There was a custom among some 19th-century workmen, especially Shropshire colliers, to stop work on hearing the first cuckoo, claim the day as a holiday, and go off to drink ale or beer out of doors, to welcome the bird. This custom was called 'Wetting the Cuckoo', or 'Cuckoo Foot-Ale' (Wright and Lones, 1938: iii. 20). It was kept up at Hoffleet Stow (Lincolnshire) within living memory:

In the 1920s and 30s it was the custom to welcome in the spring. When we heard the first cuckoo of the spring call we would take a barrel of beer into the spinney or wood where it was calling.... that's where the ale was drunk, in the centre of the wood.... There we drank the health of the cuckoo with the new cuckoo ale. (Sutton, 1997: 80–1)

At Mere (Wiltshire) in the 16th century the *church ale was held in spring and its master of ceremonies was entitled 'Cuckoo King' (*Folklore* 18 (1907), 340–1).

The cuckoo's habit of laying eggs in the nests of other birds explains why its cry was regarded, in medieval and Elizabethan times, as mocking cuckold husbands—they would have to bring up another man's child. In folksong, 'cuckoo's nest' is sometimes a term for a woman's genitals.

Cuckoos are also associated with stupidity; in northern dialects 'gowk' means both 'cuckoo' and 'fool', and *April Fools are often called April Gowks. 'You're cuckoo' is still a slangy way of saying 'You're crazy'. Or it may be the humans who are stupid, as in the old joke about the men of Borrowdale (Westmorland/Cumbria), who are said to have built a wall to imprison the cuckoo, so that summer would never end; the bird flew out, skimming the top, at which one exclaimed, 'By gow! If we'd nobbut laid another line o' stanes atop, we'd 'a copped him.' The same is said about the people of *Gotham; also of Wing (Leicestershire), which has a pub called the Cuckoo Inn, offering further opportunities for wit.

James Hardy, *Folk-Lore Record* 2 (1879), 47–91; Swainson, 1885: 109–22; Opie and Tatem, 1989: 112–14.

cunning men, women. From the medieval period almost to the present day, there have been people who were employed by others to practise magical skills on their behalf, and were paid in money or small gifts, thus usefully supplementing the income from their regular occupations. Frequent complaints by the educated classes indicate how popular they were. In a sermon in 1552, Bishop Latimer lamented: 'A great many of us, when we be in trouble, or lose anything, we run hither and thither to witches or sorcerers, whom we call wise men ... seeking aid and comfort at their hands' (*Sermons* (1844), 534). In 1807, Robert Southey could still say: 'A Cunning-Man, or a Cunning-Woman, as they are termed, is to be found near every town, and though the laws are occasionally put in force against them, still it is a gainful trade' (*Letters from England*, p. 295).

It is impossible to arrive at any figures, but anecdotal evidence indicates that they were quite common throughout the 19th century, and in some country areas in the first half of the 20th century. There were various popular names for them: wizards, conjurers, sorcerers, *charmers, wise men/women, cunning men/ women, the latter two being the most widespread. 'White witch' was a term more used by outsiders than by practitioners and their clients. 'Conjurer' implied the ability to summon and dismiss devils or spirits—a power claimed by some rural magicians, such as Jenkyns of Trelleck (Monmouthshire) (Wherry, 1904: 76–81).

Cunning men were called upon to heal sickness in humans or animals, to detect and punish thieves, look into the future, give information about people far away, cast horoscopes and tell fortunes, and to procure love; perhaps their most important function, and certainly the most dramatic, was to diagnose *witchcraft, identify the witch, and defeat her by their own *counterspells. Some claimed their power was inborn and hereditary, but many others used manuals of fortune-telling and/or astrology, and handwritten collections of herbal recipes and magical formulas; the predominantly illiterate clientele were awed by such displays of book-learning. Several regional folklore collections give reminiscences about famous individuals such as the cunning man named Wrightson who lived at Stokesley (North Yorkshire) around 1810 (Henderson, 1866: 177–82; Brockie, 1886: 21–5; Blakeborough, 1898: 187–92). He was the *seventh son of a seventh daughter, and appeared to have clairvoyant powers, though some thought him a fraud, and 'his private character was said to be very bad'; Blakeborough says he favoured counterspells 'of the heart-frizzling, pin-sticking, wickenwood and bottery-tree order'.

The educated classes criticized or mocked the influence of such persons throughout the whole period; they could be prosecuted under the Witchcraft Act of 1736, which, while denying that magic had any reality, imposed penalties on anybody who publicly claimed to practise it, this being regarded as a form of fraud. Such prosecutions were rare, and were generally brought by dissatisfied clients who thought themselves cheated, rather than by the police.

Thomas, 1971: 177–252; Sharpe, 1996: 66–70; Maple, 1960; Davies, 1997; Davies, 1998; Davies, 1999 6: 27–91.

cures, see *MEDICINE.

curses. Although invoking God's power to curse is generally done by the clergy, in previous centuries some lay people who believed themselves deeply wronged would utter a ritualized curse, kneeling on their bare knees in some public place in the presence of witnesses. Records of a Hereford diocesan court describe how in 1598 one man cursed another on his knees in the churchyard, 'praying unto God that a heavy vengeance and a heavy plague might light on him and all his cattle', and in 1614 a woman cursed a man she believed had killed her husband, 'and prayed to God that his house, his children and all he had were one wild fire' (Thomas, 1971: 506–8). Psalm 109 was called 'the cursing psalm' for its vidictive words; it was said that if a dying man recited it while thinking of someone who had wronged him, the latter was doomed (Bottrell, 1873: 227–33).

There was a widespread belief that when monastic estates were confiscated at the Reformation the monks laid the curse of God on those who received them; they and their descendants suffered financial disasters (since 'illgotten gains never prosper'), and sometimes untimely deaths and personal misfortunes. These ideas were widely discussed in books and pamphlets from the 17th century onwards, notably Henry Spelman's *The History and Fate of Sacrilege*, published in 1698; the fourth edition, in 1895, was updated with further local traditions (Thomas, 1971: 96–104).

Cursing through black magic was greatly feared, and is mentioned in many *witchcraft trials and traditions. Occasionally, material objects are found which definitely prove that someone had been turning theory into practice. In 1899 a lead tablet was found buried in Lincoln's Inn, bearing invocations to the moon and the wish that Ralph Scrope (a Governor of the Inn in 1570–2) should never succeed in anything he did. Two more, also probably of the 1570s, were dug up from a barrow on Gatherley Moor (North Yorkshire); they had astrological symbols and rows of figures, and a curse that several members of a family named Philip should 'come presently to utter beggary', and 'flee Richemondshire' (Hole, 1973: 92–3). Another, found in a cupboard at Wilton Place near Dymock (Gloucestershire) in 1892, and now in Gloucester Museum, was also designed to drive away its victim. At the top is the name 'Sarah Ellis', written backwards in 17th-century script; then come complex designs and some numbers, all referring astrologically to the moon, and then the curse itself, which invokes eight demons, the first being one linked to the moon: 'Hasmodait Acteus Magalesius Ormenus Leius Nicon Minon Zeper make this person to Banish away from this place and Countery amen. To my desier amen' (Merrifield, 1987: 147–8).

In 1960, an 18th-century doll was found hidden in a house in Hereford, with a written curse pinned to its skirt: 'Mary Ann Ward. I act this spell upon you from my holl (whole) heart wishing you to never rest nor eat nor sleep the resten part of your life I hope your flesh will waste away and I hope you will never spend another penney I ought to have. Wishing this from my whole heart' (*Hereford Times* (22 Jan. 1960)).

No doubt others too vented their anger in similar ways, using whatever magical rituals they knew; a more recent development is the belief that *Gypsies can lay potent curses.

daisies. The daisy features in a light-hearted *love divination, the petals being plucked off singly with the words 'He loves me, he loves me not' till all are gone, the last one deciding the issue. Daisy-chains are made by slitting the stem with a thumb-nail, threading another through it, and repeating the process; since modern lawns have few weeds, the game is getting rarer. It was said that spring had truly arrived if one could set one's foot on seven (or nine, or twelve) daisies at once (Vickery, 1995: 100–2).

dance. A standard basic distinction in folk dance scholarship is between 'ceremonial' and 'social' dance. Ceremonial dances are performed by a special group within the community for display at special times, in special costume (as, for example, *morris dance, *sword dance, *Molly dance, *Bacup Coconut Dance, and the *Helston Furry Dance) or as an integral part of a *calendar custom performed only on certain occasions (such as *Wishford Magna, *Padstow Hobby Horse, and the *Shaftesbury Byzant). Social dances, on the other hand, are performed in everyday situations by both sexes, without special training beyond knowing the basic steps and movements. This entry will concentrate on social dance.

In the sphere of social dance, the notion of a separate identifiable English 'folk' dance repertoire is difficult to sustain. It would be difficult to find a dance form which is not 'traditional', that is, informally learnt, passed on, and practised. More than most cultural forms, dances have moved up and down the social scale, have gone in and out of fashion, and undergone revival at different times, and at any given historical moment there were several possible dance repertoires existing side by side, as now. The 19th century, for example, was dominated by new dance crazes introduced from the Continent, including the Quadrille, a lively square dance for four

couples, which arrived from France in 1816 (although it was based on earlier English country dances) and several 'round' or couple dances such as the Waltz (1812), the Polka (1844), and the Schottische (1848). Each of these was characterized by its own musical rhythm, and the Waltz and Polka in particular took the middle classes by storm, with thousands of new tunes and variations flooding the market. Each took its time filtering down the social scale. Quadrille dancing underwent a vigorous revival in the late 19th century in middle-class circles. Since the late 19th century, new dances have tended to come from America rather than Europe. What the ordinary working village or town dweller was dancing before these fashionable new dances arrived is still open to some debate.

The usual assumption, based largely on the writings of Cecil *Sharp, is that the indigenous English folk dance was what became known as the 'country dance'. The key difference between the old country dances and the new couple dances is that while in the latter couples progress independently round the room, repeating a short sequence of specified steps, in the country dances couples are included in a particular formation (circle, square, lines, etc.), and they perform a series of figures and steps in co-operation with other couples. Sharp started trying to collect country dances in rural areas about 1907, with only limited success:

In the village of today the polka, waltz and quadrille are steadily displacing the old-time country dances and jigs, just as the tawdry ballads and strident street-songs of the towns are no less surely exterminating the folk-songs. (Written in 1909; Sharp: i. 9)

There is abundant evidence from literary and historical sources that 'country dances' had been extremely popular at court and other fashionable balls, particularly in the

17th century. Samuel Pepys, for example, recorded a ball in the presence of the king and queen on 31 December 1662; after a bransle and a coranto: '... very noble it was and a great pleasure to see. Then to country dances: the King leading the first which he called for: which was, says he, 'Cuckolds All a-Row', the old dance of England ...' Sharp's basic assumption was that these fashionable 'country dances' were the existing vernacular village dances, tidied up and developed for the court and the ballroom, while they also continued in their natural habitat, the remnants of which he had hoped to find in the villages. He used early dance manuals, in particular John Playford's *English Dancing Master*, first published in 1650 and then in sixteen other editions until 1728, to attempt a reconstruction of earlier 'country dance' forms. The problem is that there is no real proof that the courtly country dances were taken from the village at all, but may have been largely invented for the court, and only loosely based on the 'folk' dances of the time. What evidence there is concerning the latter points to people dancing in circles, linked lines (moving in serpentine fashion), heys, or weaving in and out when two lines met, and a *thread the needle movement as the line passed under an arch made by two dancers holding up their hands. The first uses of the term 'country dance' (from 1579 onwards) rarely give clear information but seem to refer to these types of dances. It was probably these which Queen Elizabeth I was delighted to watch the 'country people' dancing at Warwick in 1572, but by 1600 she was present to 'see the ladies dance the old and new country dances' (*JEFDSS* 3:2 (1937), 93–9). It seems likely, but at present still unprovable, that the new fashionable figured country dances were invented at court, probably using Italian models, and simply utilizing the lively music of the older English folk dances. These new country dances only filtered down to village level at a later date. Thomas Hardy, for example, offers some corroboration. According to him, there were two classes of people in the Dorset villages of his youth and his parents' time (i.e. the first half of the 19th century); the tradespeople, freeholders, upper servants in one group, and the labourers and lower servants (work people) in the other, and the two had quite distinct gatherings at which they rarely mixed. The 'country dances' were the regular fare of the respectable tradespeople, while the work people had different dances, 'which were reels of all sorts, jigs, a long dance called the "horse-race", another called "thread-the-needle", &c. These were danced with hops, leg-crossings, and rather boisterous movements' (*EFDS News* (Sept. 1926), 383–5; *JEFDS* 2s:1 (1928), 52–6). He maintained that 'country dances' were introduced to the tradespeople class in the village in about 1800, and the work people were extremely reluctant to take them up. Sharp was disdainful of town-dwellers' traditions, but a detailed account of London costermongers' 'tuppenny hops' in the 1840s, written by Henry Mayhew, gives weight to Hardy's view. These events included jigs, hornpipes, polkas, and country dances, 'the last mentioned being generally demanded by the women' (Henry Mayhew, *London Labour and the London Poor* (1861), i. 12; a much shorter version was contributed by Mayhew to the *Morning Chronicle* (27 Nov. 1849), letter XII).

Both Mayhew and Hardy indicate the factor which is missing in most accounts of 'folk' dancing, in that at least in the 18th and 19th centuries, and probably before, an extremely common form of dance for the working classes, both rural and urban, was 'stepping' or 'stepdancing'. In its basic form, this involved 'the rhythmic beating and scuffling of the feet on the floor' (Hall, 1990: 77) and could be performed solo, or in pairs facing each other, in threes or fours, with alternate sequences of stationary stepping and changing places or doing a figure of eight, the latter being the basic form of dance called a 'reel'. Stepping could be done any time, any place, providing there was music and a reasonably suitable floor, and there are descriptions of people taking barn doors off their hinges to dance on. It could also be taken seriously enough for competitions to be organized, often dancing on a farm cart, with the musician and judges with their backs to the dancers to avoid favouritism. In some parts, stepping developed into clog-dancing (also mentioned by Mayhew), in which the wearing of clogs with metal tips gave a more satisfying aural dimension. Regional styles of clogging developed (e.g. Lancashire and Westmorland), and champion dancers were famous enough to appear on the local music hall stage.

Until recent years, studies of dance history have usually concentrated on the dance forms themselves, and have largely ignored the social context, the venues and events, and, most importantly, the style of dancing. What little information we have in these spheres must be gleaned from other sources, such as novels and newspapers. The Mayhew description quoted above is unusually informative, while Thomas Hardy includes several descriptions of 19th-century rural dance events in his novels. His short story, *Absentmindedness in a Parish Choir* (1891) revolves around the fact that the same musicians played for dances and in church, and other works include dancing at a Christmas party (*Under the Greenwood Tree* (1872) part 1, chapters 7, 8), the social gradations of an outdoor village dance (*The Return of the Native* (1878) book 4, chapter 3), the innocent dance of the girls in the fields on May Day (*Tess of the d'Urbevilles* (1891), chapter 1), and many more. Dance venues and settings can be categorized according to the social class of the participants; the degree of formality involved; the social cohesion of the group (family, friends, work colleagues, strangers); the physical venue (pub, hired village schoolroom, village hall, commercial ballroom), and so on. Other regular venues not already mentioned include dancing-booths at fairs, where couples paid for each dance they wished to do, while in some areas a peripatetic dancing-master might stay a few weeks in the locality, giving lessons and organizing a social at the end of his stay.

The 'country dance' was vital for Sharp as the basic social dance in his planned revival movement, and he formed the *English Folk Dance Society* (EFDS) in 1911 to help spread the message. While country dances continued to fade from the village repertoire, the EFDS produced dedicated enthusiasts and dance teachers for whom country dancing at clubs, festivals, and garden parties became a normal hobby pursuit, and Sharp also succeeded in getting country dancing accepted on to the school curriculum. Throughout the inter-war years, country dancing remained a regular hobby pursuit of thousands of enthusiasts up and down the country, but had no appreciable effect on the mass popular culture which took its various dance crazes from America. Some revivalists continued Sharp's work and collected further traditional dances, and, indeed, discovered that some 'country' dances were still danced in amongst other dance forms, at village socials in many places in the country. After the Second World War the *English Folk Dance and Song Society* (as it had become in 1932) was shaken by a sudden national craze for American square dancing and, a few years later, on the back of the *song revival, a boom in interest from a younger generation of enthusiasts. The new revival deliberately shunned the 'plimsoles and gymslips' image of the pre-war dance scene, and created a much livelier movement. The terminology changed—the word 'ceilidh' (under various spellings) was adopted from Ireland, coming to mean a much livelier type of event than a 'country' or 'folk' dance implied. At the time of writing, however, the term 'barn dance' is used by most lay people, while 'ceilidh' is mainly restricted to the cognoscenti. There is still a thriving barn dance/ceilidh scene in England, as one of many types of vernacular dance forms from which people can choose. There are specialist clubs and festivals in most parts of the country, and the EFDSS continues to co-ordinate and encourage. It is also quite common for non-specialist groups, such as sports and social clubs, PTAs, staff associations, churches, and so on, to organize occasional barn dances as social events, and many people also choose to have barn dancing at their wedding receptions, as it is ideal for all-age gatherings. The basic repertoire of these events is usually based loosely on the old country dances, with some newly composed dances on the same lines, and often a few similar dances from America, Scotland, and Ireland. Thus the repertoire is deliberately revived/contrived, but the informal gathering—the event itself—has many claims to be termed 'traditional'.

Reg Hall, *I Never Played to Many Posh Dances: Scan Tester, Sussex Musician* (1990); Cecil J. Sharp, *The Country Dance Book* (6 parts, 1909–22); Belinda Quirey, *May I Have the Pleasure: The Story of Popular Dancing* (1976); Cecil Sharp and A. P. Oppé, *The Dance: An Historical Survey of Dancing in Europe* (1924); Julian Pilling, *FMJ* 1:3 (1967), 158–79; Anne-Marie Hulme and Peter Clifton, *FMJ* 3:4 (1978), 359–77; Theresa Buckland, *FMJ* 4:4 (1983), 315–32; Derek Schofield, *FMJ* 5:2 (1986), 215–19; Melusine Wood, *JEFDSS* 3:2 (1937) 93–9; Melusine Wood, *JEFDSS* 6:1 (1949), 8–12; J. P. Cunningham, *JEFDSS* 9:3 (1962), 148–54.

dandelions. The commonest belief about dandelions is that picking their flowers causes bed-wetting—hence its alternative name 'peebed' or 'pissabed'. But there is no taboo against picking the seed-heads, called 'dandelion clocks'; children blow the seeds away, counting the number of puffs needed, and claiming that this tells them the time, or the number of years before marriage. They may also recite the divinatory 'Loves me, loves me not', or 'This year, next year, sometime, never'

(Vickery, 1995: 102–5). Another pastime was reported in Victorian times:

Dandelion chains are made with the flower stalks only. The supple hollow stalk, denuded of its flower, is bent in a circle, and the smaller end is pushed for about half an inch into the larger. A circle is thus formed, its size depending upon the length of the stalk. This is the first link of the chain. Link is added to link, and the only limits to the length of the chain are the paucity of dandelions and the persistency of the child making it. Some children make necklets of the chain. (N&Q 9s:7 (1901), 397; cf. 474, 511 and 9s:8 (1901), 70, 232, 466)

Rubbing with dandelion juice is a well-known traditional remedy for *warts, and dandelion tea is believed good for indigestion and as a spring tonic (Hatfield, 1994: 54, 56, 58).

Dando's dogs, dandy-dogs. In Cornwall, the *Wild Hunt was said to be due to the Devil carrying off a wicked priest named Dando who went hunting on Sundays. Since then, he and his dogs are seen or heard galloping across the moors on stormy nights. An alternative name was 'the Devil's dandy-dogs'; a man who was chased by a pack of them, all breathing fire, had the presence of mind to kneel and pray, at which they fled (Hunt, 1865: 220–3).

Davy Jones. Among modern sailors, 'Davy Jones' is an imaginary figure supposed to lurk on the seabed, where he collects wrecked ships and anything thrown or dropped overboard; to be buried at sea is to 'go to Davy Jones's Locker'. He is first mentioned in 1751, in Smollett's novel *The Adventures of Peregrine Pickle* (chapter 15), in a way which shows he was well known as supernatural and ominous. Wanting to scare an officer, a sailor dresses up in an ox-hide and a leather mask stretched over a shark's jaws; it has broad glasses for eyes, lit up with rushlights, and a firework between its teeth. The officer takes this for Davy Jones, exclaiming: 'I know him by his saucer-eyes, his three rows of teeth, his horns and tail, and the blue smoak that came out of his nostrils.' Smollett adds that this fiend 'presides over all the evil spirits of the deep, and is often seen in various shapes, perching among the rigging on the eve of hurricanes, shipwrecks and other disasters'.

Alan Smith, in Davidson and Chaudri, 2001: 91–100.

days of the week. For practitioners of high *magic, the days of the week had astrological and mythological meanings; it would be appropriate for spells aimed at obtaining power or wealth to be done on Thursday (Jupiter's day), and love spells on Friday (day of Venus). There was nothing like this at the popular level; only two days were individually characterized—Sunday as holy (see *Sabbath-breaking), and *Friday as unlucky. However, there are rhymes linking the luck of days with *babies, *fingernails, *washing, and *weddings.

dead man's hand. A traditional cure for cysts, wens, scrofula, goitre, and ulcers was the touch of a dead man's hand—preferably, as Reginald Scot wrote in 1584, one who has died an untimely death. *Aubrey knew of a man's wen and a child's hunchback cured by this means (Aubrey 1686/1880: 198). Margaret Courtney noted instances in 19th-century Cornwall where the cure was used for persistent sore eyes, for a 'peculiar tuberous formation' on a child's nose, and for a sore on a child's leg; she was told that 'there is no virtue in the dead hand of a near relation', presumably because that would be too easy of access (Courtney, 1890: 152–3).

Throughout England, the hand of a hanged man was thought to be especially effective. People went to public executions and paid the hangman to let them rub the corpse's hand across their swellings as it hung on the gallows; in 1785, Boswell saw 'four diseased persons . . . rubbed with the sweaty hands of malefactors in the agonies of death'.

In the Fens, where families were large and poverty acute, it was thought that if a woman held the hand of a dead man for two minutes, she would not become pregnant during the next two years (Porter, 1969: 11–12, Sutton, 1992: 92).

See also *HAND OF GLORY.

Opie and Tatem, 1989: 99–100; Radford, Radford, and Hole, 1961: 124–6. Mabel Peacock, *Folk-Lore* 7 (1896), 268–83, includes European parallels.

deaf and dumb fortune-teller. Occasional literary references in the 18th and 19th centuries indicate that deaf or dumb people were particularly sought after as fortune-tellers. This is confirmed in a Scottish example reported in N&Q (1s:12 (1855), 488), and in the 1718 Diary of Revd John Thomlinson (published in *Six Northern Diaries* (Surtees Soc., vol. 118), 1910), but most clearly in an entry in the Overseers account book of Wyke Regis (Dorset) for February 1754: 'Gave to two dumb women with a pass being fortune tellers, 1s.' (Dorset County Record Office). A trial reported in *The Times* ((24 Sept. 1863), 4, 6) records how a deaf and dumb Frenchman known as 'Dummy', and feared for his powers, died at Sible Hedingham, Essex, after being repeatedly 'swum' in the local river.

deafness, earache. A regular cure for deafness or earache in English folklore is to apply a hot *onion to the ear, or to drip its juice into the ear, although some sources claim that garlic, figs, or even leeks can be used for this purpose. Another substance used is the froth of a snail pricked with a pin. Less obviously medicinal, however, is the further instruction which is sometimes mentioned, that the ear should also be stuffed or covered with 'black wool', the significance of which is not explained. Yet another infallible cure is to use *adder fat. Correspondence in *N&Q* (5s:9 (1878), 488, 514; 5s:10 (1878), 57) reveals some confusion about field–poppies in this context. A writer claims that a local name for the flower in Derbyshire was 'Ear-ache' because that is what would happen if you put one to your ear. A reply from Lincolnshire claimed they were called 'Head-aches', which happened if you sniffed them. A third writer claimed, however, that poppies were effective in *curing* pains in the ear (see also under *poppy).

See also *EELS.

N&Q 11s:3 (1911), 69, 117, 171; 11s:11 (1915), 68, 117–18, 247–8, 328, 477; Hatfield, 1994: 36–7; *Denham Tracts*, 1895: ii. 294–5; Black, 1883: 117, 158, 161, 193.

Dean-Smith, Margaret (1899–1997). The stepdaughter of Arnold Dunbar-Smith (1866–1933), a well-known architect within the Arts and Crafts movement, and thus brought up in an artistic and intellectual circle which influenced her later interests in music and literature. She worked in bookselling and libraries, and her first contact with folklore came with the *English Folk Dance Society in London in the early 1920s, and after the war she took on the important task of organizing the library of the *English Folk Dance and Song Society (now the *Vaughan Williams Memorial Library). At the same time she started writing a string of influential articles in the journals of that society (which she edited from 1947 to 1950), the Folklore Society, and others. In many ways, Dean-Smith was a direct descendant of the 19th century folklore-

antiquarians who sought to explain literary material by reference to folklore, while she sought to understand and elucidate folklore by tracing literary examples, but unusually for her generation she was equally at home with a number of genres including dance, song, music, drama, and literary history, and wrote also on fairy-lore, calendar customs, and other topics. Her indispensible series on John Playford's *English Dancing-Master* (1943–5) displayed considerable bibliographic, literary, and musical knowledge, and her delightfully titled article 'The Pre-Disposition to Folkery' (1968) sought to explain the flowering of interest in 'folk' material in England in the late 19th century by tracing international currents and fashions of romanticism and nationalism back to the 18th century and beyond. Her views on the *mummers play, although only expressed in a handful of articles, greatly influenced Alex *Helm, and through him the post-war generation of traditional drama scholarship.

Dean-Smith's works include (with E. J. Nicol), 'The Dancing Master 1651–1728', *JEFDSS* 4:4 (1943), 131–45; 4:5 (1944), 167–79; 4:6 (1945), 211–31; 'The Preservation of English Folk-Song and Popular Music', *JEFDSS* 6:2 (1950), 29–44; *A Guide to English Folk Song Collections 1822–1952* (1954); 'The Life-Cycle or Folk Play', *Folklore* 69 (1958), 237–53; 'An Un-Romantic View of the Mummers' Play', *Theatre Research* 8:2 (1966), 89–99; 'The Pre-Disposition to Folkery', *Folklore* 79 (1968), 161–75; 'The Ominous Wood: An Investigation into some Traditionary Sources of Milton's *Comus*', in Venetia Newall, *The Witch Figure* (1973), 42–71.

Obituary by Malcolm Taylor: *FMJ* 7:3 (1997), 388–92.

death. Beliefs and customs surrounding death are well documented at all periods and most social levels. Historical and literary writings amply describe those of the educated classes, while folklorists recorded any beliefs or practices among the 'folk' which were not part of official religion, or which struck them as differing from middle-class norms in an archaic or picturesque way. There is almost invariably a section on death and *funerals in books on regional folklore, where the customs described vary very little; quotations illustrating the 'superstitious' beliefs can be conveniently found in Opie and Tatem (1989) under the relevant headwords.

Formerly, it was widely believed (and to some extent still is) that *dreams and *omens provide forewarnings of death, for oneself or another; there was a great variety of the latter, mostly drawn from the behaviour of animals and birds, or from simple household occurrences such as a picture falling, sudden creaking or rapping sounds, and so on. For the bereaved, such events hold great emotional significance, which may, paradoxically, be comforting; they suggest that death is part of a destined plan, not a mere accident. Also, until fairly recent times, there was a strong religious emphasis on the value of a 'good death', i.e. one fully prepared for, as opposed to a swift and sudden one; in this context, forewarnings were a blessing.

It was believed that certain things would ease, and others hinder, the process of dying. In many parishes, a church *bell was rung as death drew near, the purpose of this 'Passing Bell' being to remind people to pray for the dying; in earlier times, it would also have been thought to drive away demons. An ebbing *tide and a waning *moon hastened death, but a pillow stuffed with *feathers of pigeons or wild birds made it painfully slow, and should be removed. If the *bed stood across the floorboards, rather than parallel to them, this too prolonged the agony, and it should be shifted. There are several references in folklore collections to relatives helping someone who was dying 'hard' by jerking the pillow away, lifting him out of bed and on to the floor, or even throttling him with tape, but some seem suspect, since they all end with the same words: 'He went off like a lamb'. A more detailed account comes from the Fens, and refers to the late 19th century; the village nurse would speed death by laying the dying man's head on a special black pillow, making him unconscious with opium and gin, and then jerking the pillow away (Porter, 1958: 119).

As soon as death occurred, doors and windows must be opened, to give the soul free passage; in Warwickshire the main door of the house remained ajar, night and day, until the funeral, because the deceased's spirit is still nearby, and must be able to enter or leave at will (N&Q 170 (1936), 231). Some people also put out the *fire and stopped the *clocks, presumably to mark the transition from time to eternity. A common custom of the 19th century was to turn *mirrors and pictures to the wall, or cover them with cloth; this was usually said to be for fear that someone looking into them should see the ghost, or the corpse, reflected there.

Until well into the 20th century, people normally died at home, where the corpse spent the interval between death and the *funeral. The laying-out, which was done by hired women (often midwives), involved washing the body, closing its eyelids and weighting them with pennies until they stiffened, holding the mouth shut by a bandage beneath the chin, and tying the feet together. The washing was symbolic as well as practical; in 1980 a Suffolk woman explained, 'the washing is so that you're spotless to meet the Lamb of God' (Richardson, 1987: 19). The body would then be dressed in a shroud and white stockings, or stitched into a winding-sheet; in both cases, the face remained visible until just before burial. Sprigs of *rosemary, *yew, *box, or *rue were often tucked into the shroud; flowers might also be displayed in wealthier households. A more curious custom was to lay a pewter dish of *salt on the breast of the corpse, or beneath the bed where it lay; occasionally, a piece of turf might be used instead (Leather, 1912: 120; Burne, 1883: 299). This was said to prevent the corpse swelling.

From medieval times to the early 18th century, it was usually considered essential, as a mark of respect, that the body should never be left alone in the room, even for a few moments, or be left in the dark; after that period, the custom gradually weakened among the upper classes, but country people and urban poor still often observed it. It was called 'watching' the dead, and required only one or two people to sit quietly near the corpse; it is not the same as the lively social *wake, which is rare in English tradition. On the other hand, 'viewing' the dead was common—indeed, almost obligatory—for both adults and children until the 1920s and 1930s; those who had known the deceased came to offer condolences to the family, and spend a few moments looking at the body, usually also touching or kissing it; this would ease grief, and ensure that one would not dream of, or be haunted by, the dead person.

The effect, however, was not always soothing. A contributor to N&Q in 1914 remembered being taken 'as a frightened child' to view a body in a Derbyshire village. It was laid out with its feet on a Bible, a sprig of box in its folded hands, and a plate of salt on a green turf on its breast:

Round the chin was a white cloth tied in a knot on the top of its head, and the 'laying-out woman' was in the act of laying two penny-pieces on the eyelids; but she could not make them keep in position. This frightened me most of all, for the right eye seemed to be glaring at me; and the woman said to the rest in the room, 'He's lowkin' fer th'next un.' (*N&Q* 11s:11 (1914), 296–7)

See also *BURIAL, *FUNERALS, *SIN-EATING, *WAKES (2).

There is an excellent summary of this subject in Richardson, 1987: 3–29. See also Radford, Radford, and Hole, 1961: 126–31; Puckle, 1926; Clare Gittings, *Death, Burial and the Individual* (1984); Litten, 1991: 143–52.

Dee, Dr John (1527–1608). A learned mathematician, astrologer, and Hermetic philosopher, who had a high reputation both at the court of Elizabeth I and on the Continent. However, many people believed him to be a 'conjurer', i.e. one who raised evil spirits; the influential Protestant writer John Foxe made this accusation as early as 1563, and it was repeated at intervals throughout Dee's life and beyond. In 1583, a hostile mob plundered his home and burned his books in his absence. Dee's work was in fact a pious form of Renaissance ritual 'high' magic, which involved summoning angels and questioning them through a medium who could see them in a crystal; the diaries in which he recorded these sessions were posthumously published in 1659, with a hostile preface by Meric Casaubon, who insisted such spirits could only be devils. By the 19th century it was widely believed that Dee and his medium Edward Kelly had been necromancers who desecrated graves in attempts to speak with the dead.

Peter J. French, *John Dee: The World of an Elizabethan Magus* (1972); Edward Fenton (ed.), *The Diaries of John Dee* (1999).

Denby Dale Pie. On special occasions, the people of Denby Dale, West Yorkshire, bake a pie—eighteen foot long, six foot wide, and eighteen inches deep. The 1964 pie, to celebrate royal births, contained three tons of beef, one and a half tons of potatoes, and half a ton of gravy, and 30,000 people had a piece. The money raised built the village hall, known as Pie Hall. The occasions chosen are nothing if not eclectic. The first great pie was made in 1788 to celebrate George III's recovery from his mental illness, the next was for the Battle of Waterloo (1815), and another for the repeal of the Corn Laws (1846). The 1887 version, for Queen Victoria's Jubilee, was found to be bad when opened, and a replacement had to be baked in a hurry. The 1896 pie was a jubilee

for the 1846 one, and in 1928 it was to raise money for the local Infirmary. In 1988 they baked a bicentenary pie, and held parades, funfairs, and helicopter rides, and 50,000 people bought £1 tickets to ensure a piece of the pie. A similar custom took place in the 19th century at Aughton (Lancashire) (*N&Q* 7s:2 (1886), 26).

David Bostwick, *Folk Life* 26 (1987/8), 12–42; Smith, 1989: 125–9; Kightly, 1986: 100.

Denham Tracts. Michael Aislabie Denham (died 1859) a general merchant of Piercebridge, Durham, was early in the field of folklore collecting, and he died before the new movement had become fashionable. As with many of his generation, Denham's interests were wide and he collected coins and other physical antiquities as well as less tangible beliefs, proverbs, rhymes, and sayings in Northumberland, Durham, Cumberland, Westmorland, Isle of Man, and Scotland. The mass of material which he gathered was published in a series of limited circulation booklets and leaflets, newspaper articles, and other ephemeral formats. The nature of these publications has made them very difficult to obtain, and we would know hardly anything of him if many of them had not been collected and reprinted by the *Folklore Society as *The Denham Tracts: A Collection of Folklore by Michael Aislabie Denham*, edited by James Hardy (London: David Nutt, 1892–5, 2 vols.) which immediately became a standard source for material on the northern counties of England.

Derby Ram, see *OLD TUP.

Devil. In folk traditions, the Devil is sometimes a powerfully evil tempter and destroyer, sometimes a stupid enemy whose plans fail through his own clumsiness, or because he is outwitted by ordinary humans. Broadly speaking, the stupid Devil is found in *local legends where he hurls rocks, builds bridges, digs hills, etc., but is thwarted; in stories about magicians who obtain his services but elude his power; and in comic tales where he is tricked, or loses a wager. The powerful Devil features in moralistic tales; in traditions about *witchcraft; and in accounts of sinister and inexplicable events like the apparition of the *Mowing Devil or the *Black Dog at Bungay. By bringing sinners to a bad end he is the instrument of God's *judgements. His name should not be mentioned—'Talk of the Devil and he'll appear' has been proverbial since the 17th century. He may appear as a *black dog or a black cock; if in human form, he wears black clothes.

Though contradictory, both ideas spring from medieval Christianity, which taught that though the Devil constantly attacked the individual with temptations, his overall strategy was ultimately futile, since Christ had already defeated him. Stories on the pattern of the *Devil's Arrows may have been meant to teach this lesson through concrete imagery, since the planned destruction of a church invariably fails, and nobody is harmed by it. Landscape features ascribed to the Devil are unproductive ones (tracts of stony or sandy soil, ravines, rocky mountains, large boulders), for all good things come from God. Many minor place-names, and some names of animals and plants, involve the Devil, generally indicating that the place or creature is ugly, unfit for cultivation or for human consumption, or eerie (Wright, 1913: 203–4).

Briggs, 1970–1: B. i. 43–155.

Devil's Bridge. A fine 15th-century bridge spanning the Lune at Kirby Lonsdale, Cumbria/Westmorland, is said to have been built by the Devil in one night, as a favour to an old woman whose cow had strayed to the far side of the river, on condition that he could carry off the first living thing that crossed it. At dawn the old woman arrived, with a dog hidden under her cloak; she tossed a bun on to the bridge, and the dog rushed after it. Furious at being cheated of human prey, the Devil clawed at the coping stone of one arch (the marks are still there), and disappeared. The tale was first recorded late in the 18th century, but fits an international pattern. There are similar tales elsewhere in England (Briggs, 1970–1: B. i. 52, 86–9).

Devil's dandy-dogs, see *DANDO'S DOGS.

Devil's Dyke. A deep gash in the north slopes of the Downs near Hove, East Sussex, is said to have been dug by the Devil, who wanted to let the sea through to drown low-lying villages with many churches. He had to finish the work in one night, but was tricked into thinking dawn had come, and flew off. The first recorded account, a humorous poem, says an old woman deceived him by letting a candle shine through a sieve like the rising sun, and

making her cockerel crow (William Hamper, *Gentleman's Magazine* 80 (1810), 513–14); later literary variants give the credit to St Cuthman or *St Dunstan, but in oral tellings the old woman is the usual heroine. The tale is typical of the international theme of the Devil being duped, often by weak or marginalized humans, and danger narrowly averted (Simpson, 1983).

Devil's hoofprints. On the night of 8/9 February 1855, during an unusually severe winter, long trails of prints appeared in the snow in at least 30 different places in Devon. Each was about 3½ inches long by 2½ inches broad, resembling a donkey's hoofprint, and some seemed cloven; they were said to have crossed roofs, high walls, and haystacks, adding to the supernatural impression. The first known press report, from Dawlish, says that the marks had 'caused an uproar of commotion among the inhabitants in general', and that 'several of the very superstitious' were saying 'it must be the marks of Old Nick', while others blamed 'some monkey which has escaped a travelling menagerie with something on its feet' (*The Western Luminary and Family Newspaper for Devon, Cornwall, Somerset & Dorset* (13 Feb. 1855)).

The story was taken up in *The Times* (16 Feb. 1855) and the *Illustrated London News* (24 Feb. 1855, 3 Mar. 1855, 10 Mar. 1855), the latter being particularly detailed. Explanations offered were naturalistic, if implausible; over the years, badgers, rats, cats, a variety of birds, a kangaroo, a toad, and groups of Gypsies on stilts have been suggested. A further burst of interest in *N&Q* many years later led people with personal memories of the event to speak of the general excitement and consternation felt at the time (*N&Q*, 7s:8 (1889), 508–9; 7s:9 (1890), 18, 70).

Theo Brown, *Report & Transactions of the Devonshire Association* 82 (1950), 107–12; 84 (1952), 163–71. An extensive discussion, reprinting all original and secondary sources, is Mike Dash, *Fortean Studies* 1 (1994), 71–150.

Devil's Kettles, see *HELL.

Devil's Knell, see *RINGING THE DEVIL'S KNELL.

dipping, see (a) *BOOK (DIVINATION WITH), (b) *COUNTING-OUT RHYMES.

display customs. This term has been invented here to define a range of customs which involve children making something, and then displaying their handiwork by standing with it in the street, or visiting friends and neighbours, hoping for a reward of money, sweets, food, or whatever they could get. Many previous writers called them simply 'begging' customs, but this is unjustifiably insulting; there is a strong and long-lasting tradition that this is a legitimate way for children to get pocket money and treats, sanctioned by custom. Included under this heading would be *grottoing, 'penny for the guy' (see under *November the Fifth), and many others, including some where what is displayed is their own fanciful costume, as in *trick or treat. Some former adult customs were also displays, for example the *milkmaids' garland.

divinations, see *LOVE DIVINATIONS, *ST MARK'S EVE, and *WRAITHS. See also *BIBLE, *BOOK (divination with), *FORTUNE-TELLING, *SIEVE AND SHEARS, *TEA, COFFEE.

Dobbs, dobby, dobie. These are regional nicknames for various supernatural beings, probably short for 'Robin'. Dobbs was used for a *brownie in Sussex, dobby in Yorkshire and Lancashire, and dobie in Northumberland. The latter was proverbially stupid, according to Henderson (1866: 209). However, according to Francis Grose (late 18th century), a dobie was a wild moorland spirit who could control deer, and jumped upon travellers. Outdoor ghosts were also sometimes called 'dobbies' in Lancashire (Bowker, 1883: 152); some haunted the sands and coves of Morecambe Bay. In County Durham, the Shotton Dobby appeared at births or deaths in the village, as a goose, dog, horse, donkey, or cow (Brockie, 1886: 50–1). In the Yorkshire Dales, *holed stones are called 'dobbie stones'; small ones are hung at doors and windows, larger ones built into drystone walls.

Doggett's Coat and Badge Race. This sculling race of over four miles, down the Thames from London Bridge to Chelsea, has been staged every year since 1715, apart from during the two world wars. It was founded by Thomas Doggett, actor-manager at the Haymarket and Drury Lane theatres who, when he died in 1721, left money to form a trust to perpetuate the custom, which later handed over responsibility for organization to the London Fishmongers' Company in association with the Company of Watermen and Lightermen, who still run the event. The race was for six Thames watermen who had just completed their apprenticeship to compete, every 1 August, for a prize of a splendid orange coat and even more splendid badge, the latter representing 'liberty'. This all had a political meaning at the time, as Doggett was a staunch supporter of George I and the new house of Hanover. The first of August was the day of George I's accession to the throne, the orange and the horse motif on the badge also represented the royal family. The race was sufficiently well known to form the background to a ballad-opera by Charles Dibdin, entitled *The Waterman, or The First of August*, first produced at the Haymarket in 1774. An account of the race and a biographical sketch of Doggett can be found in Hone (1827: ii. 531–3). Some changes have been made over the years. The coat is now red. The boats have gradually become smaller and lighter and the date is fixed more by the state of the tides than by Doggett's original decree. Late July is usually the time now. Most important of all, for the racers, they now move *with* the tide rather than against it. When there were too many applicants, the six were chosen by lot, but now there are eliminating heats. The winners wear their coats at subsequent races, where they act as stewards, and on other ceremonial occasions on the Thames.

Hone, 1827: ii. 531–3; Shuel, 1985: 145–8; Kightly, 1986: 101–2; Stone, 1906: 51.

dogs. It is commonly believed that dogs can sense anything uncanny, and show terror if forced to pass a haunted spot; if they howl for no reason, especially at night, it 'portends death, either in the house nearest to which they howl or to some of their kith and kindred' (*Denham Tracts*, 1892: ii. 55), or is a general sign of evil being about. A spayed bitch, however, may drive off uncanny forces:

I believe all over England, a spaied bitch is accounted wholesome in a House; that is to say, they have a strong beliefe that it keeps away evill spirits from haunting of a House; e.g. amongst many other instances, at Cranborn in Dorset about 1686, a house was haunted, and two Tenants successively went away for that reason: a third came and brought his spaid bitch, and was never troubled. (Aubrey, 1686/ 1880: 53)

There are many supernatural dogs in English folklore—*black dogs, the dogs of the *Wild Hunt, the Devil as a dog, *Grim, and various shape-changing bogey-beasts, for example *guytrash, *padfoot, and *Shuck.

donkeys. Donkeys, proverbially stupid, obstinate, and over-sexed, were despised, yet the cross on their backs was a holy marking, since Jesus rode a donkey. Nineteenth-century sources credit them with healing powers; children suffering from whooping cough, measles, fevers, or rickets were passed *three or *nine times over and under a donkey, or made to wear or swallow hairs from this mark (Opie and Tatem, 1989: 122–3).

Doomsday. Early Christians expected Doomsday to occur when the world was 6000 years old; since Creation was then reckoned at 5200 BC (not at 4004 BC, the date proposed in the 17th century), Doomsday was due around AD 800. Bede, writing in the 720s, criticised *rustici*, 'country folk', for frequently asking him how many years were left before the sixth millennium ended (*De Tempore Ratione*, cited in Thompson, 1996: 32). However, there is no evidence of millenial panic in 1000 or 1033.

Doomsday is of course inseparable from the concept of the Second Coming and the establishment of a just and godly world. These ideas have strong political implications; they were conspicuous in England during the Civil War and Commonwealth, but after the Restoration lost all prestige (Thomas, 1971: 140–6). Doomsday preoccupations periodically recurred at the level where popular religion and folklore meet, causing anxiety about 'signs' such as comets and earthquakes. There was panic in 1794 when a currently famous prophet, Richard Brothers, announced that God would destroy London by earthquake on 4 June 1795, and again in 1881, because of a fake prophecy attributed to *Mother Shipton.

Some, thinking it important that their corpses should be complete and intact, ready for resurrection on Doomsday, arranged for their amputated limbs to be buried with them (*Folk-Lore* 11 (1900), 346; 18 (1907), 82; 19 (1908), 234; 21 (1910), 105, 387), or even their *teeth. Gibbetting, burial in quicklime, and anatomical dissection, were viewed with horror on the assumption that they would prevent resurrection, and hence salvation (Richardson, 1987: 28–9).

One curious notion occasionally recorded (and parodied by Swift in *Gulliver's Travels*, part I, chapter 6) was that the earth would turn upside down on Doomsday. One person, a

Major Labellière, was indeed buried head down on Box Hill (Surrey) in 1800, allegedly so as to be the right way up on Doomsday; whether this really was his motive is uncertain. The same is said (almost certainly falsely) about the burial of a Mr Hull in a tower on Leith Hill (Surrey) in 1772; of a miller on Highdown Hill (Sussex) in 1794; and of the Revd J. H. Smyth-Piggot, leader of an unorthodox sect, buried in a garden at Spaxton (Somerset) in 1927. Some who hear and repeat these rumours take them seriously; for others, they are jokes.

See also *NUMBER 666.

J. F. C. Harrison, *The Second Coming: Popular Millenarianism* (1979). For discussion of the year 1000, and the growth of modern beliefs about the millennium, see Damian Thompson, *The End of Time: Faith and Fear in the Shadow of the Millennium* (1996).

Douce, Francis, (1757–1834). Although he studied for the law, he did not practise long as his lifelong passion for literary research soon prevailed. For a time he was keeper of manuscripts at the British Museum, which gave him access to such key sources as the Lansdowne and Harleian collections. Although he only published one major study, and that a literary one, Douce's name is cited as a major influence by all the leading figures of the generation of antiquarian-folklorists which emerged in the late 18th and early 19th centuries. Everybody knew him and was grateful for his help—he lent books and manuscripts from his own vast collection, answered queries, introduced people to others, suggested lines of enquiry and annotated collections. *Brand, *Strutt, *Thoms, *Hone, *Ellis, all proclaim their debt, and he also worked with Irish and Scottish folklore writers such as Thomas Keightley and Sir Walter Scott. Douce's one major publication, *Illustrations of Shakespeare and of Ancient Manners* (1807), set the scene for a generation of Shakespearian scholars, such as *Halliwell, who would comb early books and manuscripts for elucidatory material, and turn up a great deal of folklore in the process.

DNB; Dorson, 1968: 57–61.

dragons. Throughout the medieval and early modern periods, dragons were accepted as real but rare beasts. The Bible mentions fiery serpents in Exodus, and a great dragon symbolizes the Devil in Revelations 12; many writers on natural history also described various strange reptiles, including winged serpents, on the authority of Pliny, Aristotle, and others. Myths, hero legends, saints' legends, and heraldry all exploited the concept of this dramatic monster. Pre-Conquest heroic dragon legends are lost, apart from that in *Beowulf*. Religious ones are more common, the most influential being that of *St George. In Church art and writings, dragons always stood for evil, but in the secular world they also symbolized ferocity in battle, and hence were often adopted as heraldic crests.

Model dragons were a fairly common feature of religious and civic pageantry in late medieval and Tudor/Stuart times, of which only *Snap at Norwich survives. Civic account books at Newcastle-upon-Tyne in April 1510 record the purchase of twelve yards of canvas, nails, spars, and straps for building a dragon (presumably for *St George's Day), and payments for building it, painting it, and 'going with' it; also the purchase of thick twine and candlewax—perhaps to give it glowing eyes and jaws. The Midsummer Show at Chester, a large and spectacular affair, is known to have included a two-man fiery dragon in 1564 and again in 1610 when it pursued *Green Men, spat fire, and 'died' dramatically. Although the hero of the *mumming play is often St (or King) George, it is extremely rare for a dragon to appear among his adversaries there.

Dragon-slaying is a theme in several English *local legends, for example at Brent Pelham (Hertfordshire), *Mordiford (Herefordshire), *Lambton (County Durham), Lyminster (Sussex). Only twice does St George appear as the hero: once at Dragon Hill beside the White Horse of *Uffington, and once at Brinsop (Herefordshire), where the church is dedicated to him and boasts a fine carving of his feat. More often, the hero is alleged to be the founder, or an early member, of some important landowning family nearby, who was rewarded with a title or great estates, for example Sir John *Lambton, or Sir Piers Shonks at Brent Pelham. Often the heroes are sturdy working men, who do not usually kill their dragon in open combat, but by cunning tricks. Among the devices used are poisoned or indigestible food, hiding inside a spiked barrel, or using a spiked dummy as decoy (the dragon wounds himself by attacking it); rolling a large stone into the beast's open jaws; kicking it in the vent. Again, the hero's reward is practical, not romantic; treasure hoards and endangered maidens are absent in this genre. Local place-names, church carvings, and ornate medieval tombstones may be used as 'proofs' of the story, but the attitude towards it is often humorous. One Yorkshire tale is now known only through an anonymous farcical poem, 'The Dragon of Wantley', printed in 1699 (Simpson, 1980).

dragon's blood. A useful and powerful ingredient in *love divination and other spells, used in a number of ways, but usually involving the fire: 'Buy a pennyworth of dragon's blood from a chemist, sprinkle the powder in the fire any night when the clock is striking twelve, and your future husband or wife will appear . . . ' (Billson, 1895: 59–60). It was being used in this way well into the 20th century (*N&Q* 12s:10 (1922), 248). Joseph Wright's *English Dialect Dictionary* glosses Dragon's Blood as the herb Robert (*Geranium Robertianum*); A. R. Wright (1928: 69) defines it as 'the resin from the *Calamus draco* and certain other trees, used chiefly in varnish-making'.

Drake, Sir Francis (1540?–96). According to West Country folklore, Drake was a *wizard—a notion possibly taken from the Spaniards, who believed in all seriousness that the Devil helped Drake in battle. The fact that his surname means 'dragon' added to his prestige. In the 1830s Devon people said he could turn chips of wood into fireships, draw a river from Dartmoor to Plymouth, and fire a cannonball straight through the earth from the Antipodes, to warn his wife that he was still alive and she must not remarry. This cannonball is still displayed at Combe Sydenham Hall; it is said always to return if shifted, and to roll about at times of national danger. Other tales are that he once built a barn with the Devil's help, and that his ghost drives a hearse on stormy nights, drawn by headless horses and followed by headless hounds.

The most famous Drake legend is a modern one concerning his drum, kept at Buckland Abbey. A rousing poem written by Henry Newbolt in 1895 and set to music in 1904 by C. V. Stanford, says that when Drake lay dying he ordered that his drum should be taken home to England, and promised that if it were struck when invasion was threatened, he would return to drive off the enemy. There is nothing to show that this 'tradition' existed before Newbolt wrote. In 1916 another poet, Alfred Noyes, added a further marvel: that the drum need not be struck by human hand, for it sounded of its own accord. This legend was exploited as patriotic propaganda in both world wars, and it is claimed that drum-beats have indeed been heard, for example at the evacuation of Dunkirk.

Hunt, 1865: 230; Bray, 1836: ii. 170–3; both are summarized in Briggs, 1970–1: B. i. 138–9; ii. 38–9. For the drum, see E. M. R. Ditmas, *Folklore* 85 (1974), 244–53.

dreams. The idea that dreams convey true information and/or foreshadow future events is widespread, so it is rather puzzling that folklore collections do not give it much space. Perhaps the very fact that it was current at all social levels (and endorsed by the Bible) prevented Victorian scholars from regarding it as *folk*lore, except in *love divinations. In fact, popular publications show there was (and is) a lively interest in dream interpretation as a form of *fortune-telling, taught through manuals listing numerous items and their meanings. They often exploit obvious associations of ideas:

LIPS. To dream of thick, unsightly lips, signifies disagreeable encounters, hasty decisions, and ill temper in the marriage relation. Full, sweet, cherry lips, indicates harmony and affluence. To a lover, it augurs reciprocation in love, and fidelity. (Gustavus Hindman Miller, *What's in a Dream?* (1901), reprinted as *The Dictionary of Dreams* (1983), 357)

Some alternate between this method and the rule that 'dreams go by contraries':

GRENADIER. For a girl to dream of a grenadier denotes a civilian husband in the near future.
GREYHOUND. You will win more than a race despite keen rivalry.
GRIEF. This indicates joy and merry times. (Anon, *The Mystic Dream Book* (Foulsham: n. d.), 86)

The older manuals are notable for their many gloomy interpretations, and if taken seriously could have caused considerable anxiety; the compilers also favoured moral admonition:

SEA FOAM. For a woman to dream of sea foam, foretells that indiscriminate and demoralizing pleasures will distract her from the paths of rectitude. If she wears a bridal veil of sea foam, she will engulf herself in material pleasures to the exclusion of true refinement and innate modesty. She will be likely to cause sorrow to some of those dear to her, through their inability to gratify her ambition. (Miller, 1901/ 1983: 500)

At a far more serious level, many people recall that they themselves, or others known to them, have had warning dreams whose meaning only became clear later on, when death or misfortune struck. For some, it is a rare experience; others are thought to have a psychic ability, akin to *second sight, which brings such dreams regularly. A Cheshire woman in 1981 said:

I've never experienced it myself, but I have a friend, a colleague, and she does, and I know she does! She has dreams, and she'll come in and say very vividly, and she knows what's happened and it does come to happen! It may not be soon. And it's happened a lot of times with her. I've known it happen with her. She might dream of, say a fire, or a national disaster—something like that—and it does come to happen. She comes in some mornings quite bothered when she's had one of those dreams very vividly. . . . (Bennett, 1987: 134)

These personal accounts of ominous dreams are underpinned by strong beliefs and emotions; one reason they rarely appear in folklore collections may well be a concern for privacy in both informant and collector.

dressmaking. One of those trades which has declined considerably over the second half of the 20th century. The occupational lore of professional dressmakers is not well recorded, although the three sources listed below provide some information, including:

to jump over a dress when finished is a certain means of preventing its return for alterations. Dressmakers will not fit with black pins, nor tack with green thread. Care is taken not to bring bad luck on a bride by staining the bridal dress with blood from a pricked finger. 'Unpick on Monday and you unpick all the week'. It is a sign of the worker's own wedding coming soon if she accidentally sews one of her own hairs into a garment of a trousseau. If by chance, in trying on, a new garment is pinned to the customer's other clothes, it is reckoned that each pin so attached means that a year will elapse before her marriage. (Wright, 1928: 36)

See also *CLOTHES, *WEDDINGS, *PINS.

Wright, 1928: 36; Christina Hole, *Folk-Lore* 68 (1957), 411–19; E. M. L., *Folk-Lore* 25 (1914), 371.

drowning. This has attracted a number of beliefs and customs, the most widespread being that anyone born with a *caul will never drown. It was considered unwise to save someone from drowning; at best they will turn into your enemy, at worst the sea will take you instead. It was also believed that the rescuer of a drowning person would afterwards be legally responsible for maintaining that person, or that anyone who pulled a drowned body from the water was liable to pay for his/her funeral. Still extremely widespread is the notion that a drowning person will surface three times before succumbing, and that one's life flashes before one's eyes in the process.

In popular belief, there are several ways of finding the bodies of drowned people. One is to float a loaf of bread, loaded with a quantity of mercury, across the pond or river, and it will stop over, or near to, the place where the body lies (N&Q 6s:8 (1883), 367, 435–6), a method which goes back at least to the 1580s. Another way of locating the corpse is to fire a gun across the water, which will bring the body to the surface. Sailors believed that the concussion of the shot bursts the gall bladder of the drowned body and thereby makes it float (Denham Tracts, 1895: ii. 72). A variation on this principle was to fill bottles with gunpowder and contrive to explode them under water (N&Q 5s:9 (1878), 478). A number of other long-standing beliefs existed about drowned bodies. It was thought that a body found floating on the water cannot have been drowned but must have been a murder victim, already dead before being placed in the water, on the premiss that drowned bodies sink. N&Q (167 (1934), 297, 336–7; 168 (1935), 214) cites a court-case of 1699 in which this belief is cited as evidence. Corpses were, however, believed to rise on the ninth day after drowning (when their gall bladder broke), and it was also maintained that males floated face up, while females floated face down. Thomas Browne devotes a chapter of his *Pseudoxia Epidemica* (6th edn. (1672), book 4, chapter 6) to refuting these notions.

Opie and Tatem, 1989: 34, 127; N&Q 8s:2 (1892), 48; 161 (1931), 164, 230, 337–8; Lean, (1903), ii. 615–16.

Druids. Late in the 16th century, scholars became intrigued by accounts of the Druid priesthood by classical authors. Some stressed the barbaric cruelty of their human sacrifices, but others saw them as virtuous sages; the latter view became increasingly popular. *Aubrey, though regarding Druids as semi-savages, was the first to suggest cautiously that they might have built *Stonehenge; in the 1740s William Stukeley enthusiastically adopted this theory and extended it to other monuments. Soon local historians were claiming that not only megaliths but various natural rock formations were Druids' altars, and these ideas passed into place-names and folklore, especially in Cornwall.

The first modern Druidic Order was created in the 18th century; the motive was Welsh patriotism, and the model Freemasonry. There are now nearly twenty. They practise pantheistic nature worship, holding seasonal rituals on Primrose Hill (London) and at prehistoric sites, especially at Midsummer at *Stonehenge.

See also *MISTLETOE, *SNAKESTONE.

Stuart Piggott, *The Druids* (1968); Miranda Green, *Exploring the World of the Druids* (1997).

dumb cake. One of the specialist forms of *love divination, named after its central elements—the making of a special cake while maintaining absolute silence. Precise details vary, but the overall pattern is remarkably similar across the country and over the two or three hundred years since its first recorded mention in the 1680s. An unvarying characteristic is that the process to be undergone is complex and difficult to achieve successfully. In most cases, the making of the cake must be a joint effort by several people, usually young women but not exclusively so. Other recurring motifs are the use of a high proportion of salt, the scratching of initials on the pieces, and sometimes the placing of the cake under the pillow. Earlier recipes for the cake itself are generally more testing to the participants' resolve, including, apart from the salt, soot and even urine. Some mention the measuring of the ingredients in thimbles or egg-shells, presumably to make the cakes easier to eat. The times when this ceremony are usually reported are those traditional to love divination: *midsummer, *St Agnes' Eve, and *Halloween, and *Christmas Eve. Opie and Tatem identify the first two references in 1685: *Mother Bunch's Closet* (where it is called 'Dutch Cake'), and G. Sinclair, *Satans Invisible World Discovered* (referring to the Scottish Highlands), and, from available references, the custom does not much seem to have survived the end of the 19th century. Henderson (1879: 90–1) gives a detailed description.

Opie and Tatem, 1989: 127–8.

Dunmow flitch. At Great Dunmow, Essex, a custom now takes place every year which can definitely trace its history back at least 600 years. In the earliest known form, any man who had been married for more than a year without ever regretting it or wishing himself single could apply to Little Dunmow Priory and, if he could prove his assertion, claim a flitch of bacon from the Prior. If successful, he was carried in procession, in a special chair on poles. Recorded instances of successful claimants are few and far between—1445, 1467, 1510, 1701 are the first four. But the custom must be much older, as both William Langland (*Piers Plowman*, c.1360–99) and Chaucer (*Tale of the Wife of Bath*, c.1387) mention it in a matter-of-fact way. The 1701 occasion was the first time that wives are mentioned as having a part to play, and also a formally constituted jury to hear the case. After 1751, the custom lapsed until a novel by Harrison Ainsworth, entitled *The Flitch of Bacon*, published in 1854, gave the trial the publicity which resulted in the revival which continues today. There have of course been numerous changes, in particular the tone of today's proceeding is decidedly comic, parodying a real trial, whereas previously it was serious. The custom is not quite unique, as there are references to a similar one at *Wichnor in Staffordshire, and there are analogous customs on the European mainland. Its ultimate origin at Dunmow is probably as a manorial land-holding custom, but of this there is no real proof.

Francis W. Steer, *The History of the Dunmow Flitch Ceremony* (1951); Shuel, 1985: 120–3.

dwarves. Traditional rural English speech rarely, if ever, uses the term 'dwarf' for a supernatural creature, even though in the 19th and 20th centuries it has become very familiar in literature as the preferred translation of various German, French, and Scandinavian words for sturdy gnome-like beings living underground or in forests.

eaglestones. Reputed the finest amulets for use in pregnancy and *childbirth, they are mentioned in English sources from at least the 13th century, though many of these will be basing their knowledge directly on Pliny (*Natural History* (AD 77), XXXVI. xxix). Also known as *Aetites*, they were hollow stones, often brown and egg-shaped, containing sand or small pebbles rattling inside; it was said they could only be found in eagles' nests, and that without them the birds could not produce young. Worn round the neck or on the left arm, they would act like a magnet to hold the foetus in place and prevent miscarriage; English tradition adds the instruction (not given by Pliny) to tie them inside the left thigh during labour, thus quickly drawing out the baby and the placenta, but then remove them at once, for fear of bleeding or prolapse.

They were expensive, and families lucky enough to own one were expected to lend it around; in 1662 Dr Bargrave, Dean of Christchurch, Canterbury, wrote of one he had bought from an Armenian in Rome:

It is so useful that my wife can seldom keep it at home, and therefore she hath sewed the strings to the knitt purse in which the stone is, for the convenience of the tying of it to the patient on occasion, and hath a box to put the purse and stone in. It were fitt that the Dean's (Canterbury) or vice-dean's wife (if they be marryed men) should have this stone in their custody for the public good, as to neighbourhood; but still, that they have a great care into whose hand it be committed, and that the midwives have a care of it, so that it shall be the Cathedral's stone. (cited in Forbes, 1966: 67)

Similarly, it is known that a friend of the Countess of Newcastle lent her one in 1633 (*N&Q* 12s:12 (1923), 189), and that a Norfolk family in 1881 had one as an heirloom (*N&Q* 6s:3 (1881), 327).

Forbes, 1966: 64–71; C. N. Bromehead, *Antiquity* 21 (1947), 16–22; Opie and Tatem, 1989: 129.

earnest money, see *GOD'S PENNY.

ears. The idea that your ear or cheek burning or itching is a sign that someone is talking about you is still generally known, if not actually believed. The belief is of considerable age, being included by Pliny (*Natural History*, (AD 77), XXVIII). In Britain, Chaucer is the first to mention it (*Troilus and Criseyde*, II. i), and it turns up regularly in the written record from then on, with little alteration. It is generally agreed that the right or left mean different things, 'When the lefte cheek burnes, it is a sign somebody talkes well of you; but if the right cheek burnes it is a sure sign of ill' (Melton, 1620: 45). 'In the case of the right ear I have been advised to pinch it, and the person who is speaking spitefully of me will immediately bite his or her tongue' (Hampshire, *N&Q* 7s:10 (1890), 7). Other reported remedies to get back at the talker are to wet the ear with your finger, tie a loop in a piece of string or leather lace, tear up a tuft of grass and throw it away, or tie a knot in the corner of your apron (Opie and Tatem, 1989: 130–1; *N&Q* 12s:2 (1916), 310, 413).

Ringing in the ear is also widely held as significant, although it is not recorded much before the mid-18th century. It is usually believed to be of ill omen, presaging bad news, and is thus called the 'dead-bell' or 'news-bell': 'What a night of horrors! . . . I've had the news-bell ringing in my left ear quite bad enough for a murder, and I've seen a magpie all alone!' (Thomas Hardy, *Far from the Madding Crowd* (1874), chapter 8). Alternatively, if you get a ringing in your ear, immediately ask someone to give you a number. Translate that number into a letter of the alphabet, which will be the first letter of the name of the person whom you will marry, or who is thinking about you. The first recorded instance of this is from Oxfordshire in 1865 (*N&Q* 3s:8 (1865), 494) and Opie and Tatem report it still current in the 1980s.

The size and shape of ears are thought worthy of notice, although references are too scattered and various to provide a consensus: 'Small ears denote generosity, well-curled ones a long life' (Lean, 1903: ii. 307). 'Will someone tell me why ears that lie flat against the head are said to be a sign of good breeding?' (N&Q 167 (1934), 391), and the curious idea that anyone with ears that stick out is nicknamed 'Pontius Pilate' (N&Q 167 (1934), 352).

Until recently it was generally agreed, even by many in the medical profession, that piercing one's ears improved the eyesight:

When I was a house-surgeon (about 1881) at the Royal National Hospital, Margate, I several times pierced the ears of children suffering chronic ophthalmic conditions as a remedial measure, doing it by the order of the visiting surgeons. (N&Q 11s: 3 (1911), 294)

A more elaborate idea was reported in the Exeter and Plymouth Gazette for 15 March 1877 (quoted by Radford) in which a Braunston woman went from house to house collecting pennies towards the cost of earrings to cure a sight problem, in the belief that they would only be effective if she collected money solely from men and did not say 'please' or 'thank you' when asking. The notion of the opposite sex in cures and superstitions is relatively common.

The two groups which had formerly a near monopoly on male earrings were Gypsies and sailors. Both had the usual traditions about eyesight, but it was also said that sailors' earrings would save them from drowning, while others argued that should a sailor be drowned and washed up on some foreign shore, his gold earrings would pay for a proper Christian burial (FLS News 22 (1995), 16; 23 (1996), 7–8)

N&Q 5s:8 (1877), 361–4, 453–4; 9 (1878), 133, 156) gathers together numerous classical and biblical references to earrings (and, incidentally, noserings); N&Q 11s:3 (1911), 149, 171–2, 235, 294; 4 (1911), 481–2; 153 (1927), 248; Radford, Radford, and Hole, 1961: 146–7; Opie and Tatem, 1989: 176–7.

See also *DEAFNESS and EARACHE.

Opie and Tatem, 1989: 128–30.

east. Normally, churches have the main altar at the eastern end, and altars in side chapels set against east walls; some early Christian writers recommend those praying out of doors to face east, as the rising sun symbolizes God (or Christ) as the Light of the World; it was also thought that when Christ returns on *Doomsday he will appear like a blaze of lightning in the east (Matthew 24: 27). These beliefs affected the layout of burials, both inside churches and in churchyards; for preference, graves should lie east-and-west, with the body facing eastwards.

Easter. The death and resurrection of Jesus Christ is the central defining event of the Christian religion, and the time appointed to celebrate it would clearly be the most important festival in the ecclesiastical calendar. Holy Scripture defines the time as early spring, around the time of the Jewish Passover festival, but it was not until the 8th century that Britain and western Europe finally settled on the standard still in use today—the first Sunday after the moon has reached its fullest point after 21 March.

It has never been clear why the English language calls this season Easter when all other European languages (apart from one early German medieval dialect) call it by a variant of 'Pasch'. Bede says pagan Anglo-Saxons called the fourth month of the year Eosturmonath after a goddess 'Eostre', 'for whom they were accustomed to hold festivals at that season' (De Temporum Ratione, 13), and this is frequently quoted as established fact. However, since there is no other mention of her in any of the numerous sources of information about Germanic heathenism, some scholars doubt Bede's asertion, suggesting instead that he or his informants created the goddess by speculative 'back-formation' from a pre-existing, and perplexing, name for a season. The word is certainly related to 'east', and to ancient words meaning 'dawn' in various languages. April may have been regarded as the dawn of the year. Whether Bede was right in thinking the season was personified as a goddess is more doubtful—especially since the 'goddess Hreda' whom he gives as the explanation for the name of March (Rhedmonath) is equally unconfirmed by other sources—but on balance many are willing to accept it (Wilson, 1992: 35–6; Newall, 1971: 384–6).

In the medieval church, there were numerous customs and duties carried out at Easter including extinguishing and renewing all the lights, 'Watching the Sepulchre' (Duffy, 1992: 29–37, 436, 461; Andrews, 1891: 111–19), the decoration of churches, and the performance of plays and pageants dramatizing appropriate biblical events, but these were swept away with the Reformation (Wright and Lones, 1936: i. 95; Brand, 1849 edn: 157–9).

In the secular sphere, the most abiding Easter custom is the giving and eating of *Easter Eggs, but in the past numerous games and customs also clustered around the season. As with the other spring festival at *Whitsun, Easter was a favourite time for *church ales, revels, and other outdoor celebrations, with sports and games to the fore. For Londoners, Greenwich Park was a favourite place of resort on Easter and Whitsun Mondays, where thousands of people gathered and an unchartered fair sprang up to cater for them. Numerous other fairs and gatherings were held up and down the country.

Easter was one of the occasions when it was felt essential to have new *clothes, or at least some item of new dress, the other times being *New Year and *Whitsun. This idea is first recorded in the 16th century, and is mentioned by Shakespeare in *Romeo and Juliet* (III. i). Samuel Pepys indicates that in his day the fashions changed at Easter:

She did give me account of this wedding today, its being private being imputed to its being just before Lent, and so in vain to make new clothes till Easter, that they might see the fashions as they are like to be this summer. (*Diary*, 15 Feb. 1667)

If you did not wear new clothes you would have bad luck or birds would drop on you or, in one account, dogs would spit at you, and the belief lasted at least into the 1970s and is probably still to be found (Opie and Tatem, 1989: 131). It was also customary to wear new gloves at Easter, and they were thus a favourite present on the Saturday, especially from tenants to their landlords and young men to their sweethearts.

A widespread and deeply held belief was that the sun dances for joy at dawn on Easter Sunday. There are numerous reports of people making up parties and ascending local high points to watch the sun rise, and that they saw it spinning, jumping, or rocking to and fro. It was said that if you did not see it happening the Devil was deliberately obstructing your view, or that you were not sufficiently devout. More rare, but found particularly in the West Country, was the notion that you could see the figure of a lamb, or a lamb and a flag, in the sun on this day. The belief first appears in the documentary record in the 17th century, in Sir John Suckling's 'Ballade Upon a Wedding' (1646) but was already sufficiently well known for the arch-sceptic Sir Thomas Browne to feel the need to refute it—'We shall not, I hope, disparage the Resurrection of our Redeemer, if we say the sun does not dance on Easter Day' (Browne, 1672 edn.: book 5, chapter 22) but this did nothing to diminish its popularity (Opie and Tatem, 1989: 131–2).

A customary game which, like *Lifting and other customs, pitted males against females, was reported from Yorkshire, Northumberland, and Co. Durham in the 18th and 19th centuries. On Easter Sunday, youths tried to waylay young women and steal their shoe-buckles, or even their complete shoes. The women retaliated on Easter Monday by taking the men's hats or caps. Both sides met that evening, or the next day, and a small sum was exacted to redeem their belongings, which was then used to fund an evening of eating and drinking. As is usual with such customs, strangers were not exempt, and anyone passing through the village on these days was likely to be stopped by the young people and a small sum demanded in lieu of shoe, spurs, or hat (*Gentleman's Magazine* (1790), 719; Dyer, 1876: 167–8).

A children's custom which appeared at different times in different areas, and under a variety of local names, took place in Derbyshire on Easter Sunday and Monday. At Tideswell, they called it 'sugar-cupping', and children went to the spring at nearby Dropping Tor, where they mixed the water with sugar to make an Easter drink (Hone, 1827: 226). At Castleton and Bradwell it was 'Shakking Monday' and they used peppermint, and children at Little Hucklow mixed water from the Silver Well with broken sweets. Compare also similar customs under *Spanish Sunday, *Ascension Day, and *elecampane. Nineteenth-century children at Evesham (Worcestershire) used to play *Thread the Needle through the streets on Easter Monday.

As noted under *hares, there is no evidence of a connection between that animal and the putative Germanic goddess Eostre, although the link with Celtic peoples is reasonably well attested. It cannot be shown, nor is it likely, that Celtic beliefs such as these survived the Germanic and Nordic invasions and subsequent Christianization of the English. Nevertheless, there are a number of later connections between Easter and hares which are difficult to explain. In Leicestershire there was an annual 'hare hunt', and the surviving *hare pie and bottle kicking custom at Hallaton. In Warwickshire, a manorial custom reported in the 18th century at Coleshill set young men trying to catch a hare on Easter Monday. The *Folk-Lore Journal* (5 (1887), 263–4) quotes *The Calendar of State Papers* (Domestic Series) (4th series, VIII: 23): '1620, April 2. Thos. Fulnety solicits the permission of Lord Zouch, Lord Warden of the Cinque Ports, to kill a hare on Good Friday, as huntsmen say that those who have not a hare against Easter must eat a red herring'. But none of the accounts of special foods for Easter mentions hare; for example, Samuel Pepys records eating hare three times but never at that season. Charles Billson (*Folk-Lore* 3 (1892), 441–66) accumulates much of the evidence for a long-standing connection, although he is characteristic of his time in being too ready to invoke totemism as an explanation. It is clear that further work needs to be done on the subject.

See also *GOOD FRIDAY.

For other customs which take or took place at Easter, see *BACUP BRITANNIA COCONUT DANCERS, *BIDDENDEN DOLE, *CLIPPING THE CHURCH, *HALLATON HARE PIE AND BOTTLE KICKING, *LIFTING, *MIDGLEY PACE-EGGERS, *PACE EGGS.

Wright and Lones I, 1936: 85–122; Hutton, 1996: 179–213; Brand I, 1849: 157–84.

Easter eggs. Eggs have been linked to Easter for centuries throughout Europe, partly to symbolize new life, and partly because of their seasonal abundance; they must not be eaten during Lent, so those not used for hatching were available, preserved or hardboiled, as Easter food. In northern England they were called 'pace eggs', 'peace eggs', or 'paste eggs', corruptions of *pasche*, the Latin-based medieval word for Easter, here confused with *pax* = 'peace'. *Aubrey described how children from poor families went from house to house asking in rhyme for eggs to celebrate the death of *Jack o' Lent. The custom was called *pace-egging, and persisted until late in the 19th century; in the Wirral (Cheshire), one of the rhymes was still remembered in the 1930s (Hole, 1937: 77–8).

Also in the north, Easter eggs were decorated by various techniques, the simplest being to dye the egg a single colour by hardboiling it with onion peel (dark yellow, golden brown), gorse blooms (light yellow), cochineal (red), spinach or grass (green), or coffee grounds (dark brown), and then scratch the dye away to leave a white pattern or an inscription. Alternatively, the pattern or writing could be applied in melted wax, which resists the dye. The most subtle method, still practised in Northumberland and Cumberland, is to collect small leaves from wild plants, press them against the egg, wrap it in bits of old cloth whose dye will run, and boil; the leaf patterns stand out white against the softly coloured ground.

At Carlisle on Easter Monday crowds of children gathered in a field to play a game like conkers: two eggs would be tapped together, end to end, till the shell of one cracked, whereupon it was forfeit to the owner of the uncracked egg. There were many places where children would roll coloured hardboiled eggs down a hillside, a sloping path, or the beach, until they cracked, and then eat them; the custom is still kept up on a large scale at Preston (Lancashire), and Derby, but elsewhere died out after the Second World War. Some families attached religious symbolism to these customs, saying eggs were dyed red to honour the blood of Jesus, or rolled because of the stone rolled away from the tomb, or hidden in gardens because Mary Magdalen searched for Jesus in a garden (Sutton, 1997: 75–7).

A more domestic game was for parents to hide eggs in the garden for children to discover; this is still done with chocolate eggs (a major feature of the festival throughout the 20th century). The 'Easter Bunny' is a recent arrival, probably due to American influence. In several German-speaking regions of Europe an 'Easter Hare' comes by night to lay eggs for which children search; the first German reference is from 1572. In America, settlers of German descent kept the tradition alive, and hence spread it to a wider American public; they also made Easter cakes in the shape of a hare, which reveal the underlying joke—the hare is shown 'laying', i.e. excreting, its egg-shaped droppings (Newall, 1971: 323–6 and ill. 13a).

Wright and Lones, 1936: i. 76, 87–91, 114–15; Newall, 1971: 281–5 and plates XXII and XXIII; Hole, 1976: 62–6; Hutton, 1996: 198–203.

Ebernoe Horn Fair. This small Sussex village's fair on 25 July gets its name from the sheep which is roasted whole, and shared out, although the main activity of the day is a cricket match between Ebernoe and a neighbouring village team. The man who scores the most runs on the winning side is presented with the horns of the ram. Earlier sources speak of general sports and games on the day, but the cricket has been featured since at least the 1920s. It is known that the fair was revived in 1864, but for how long it had been dormant is not known, nor is the date of its origin. A feature of the modern custom is the singing of the 'Horn Fair' song, which was probably not written about Ebernoe, but has now been adopted. *Charlton, for example, had an infinitely more famous Horn Fair.

See also *HORNS.

A. B. (Arthur Beckett), *Sussex County Magazine* 2 (1928), 331, 338; Stanley Godman, *Sussex County Magazine* 29 (1955), 320–3, 29 (1955), 403, 501; Hilary and Ailsa Cripps, *Sussex Life* (July 1968), 39–40.

Edenhall, the Luck of. In the Victoria and Albert Museum is a delicate painted and gilded glass beaker, made in Syria in the middle of the 13th century. How and when it reached England is unknown, but some verses of 1729 mention it by name, and indicate it was a cherished heirloom of the Musgraves of Edenhall in Cumbria. Its leather case is inscribed with IHS, a Catholic monogram for *Iesus Hominum Salvator* ('Jesus, Saviour of Humanity'), probably implying that it was once used as a chalice.

Later, in 1791, an article in *The Gentleman's Magazine* gave the legend of its origins:

Tradition . . . says, that a party of Fairies were drinking and making merry round a well near the Hall, called St Cuthbert's well; but, being interrupted by the intrusion of some curious people, they were frightened, and made a hasty retreat, and left the cup in question; one of the last screaming out:

If this cup should break or fall,
Farewell the Luck of Edenhall!

This story follows the pattern of a *migratory legend about how a precious cup or drinking horn was stolen from *fairies and then given to a church, or to a great lord (see *Willy Howe). If the Luck of Edenhall was indeed a Catholic chalice, this would be a perfect cover story to explain the politically risky act of keeping it.

Two other families in Cumbria keep heirlooms called 'Lucks': a glass bowl at Muncaster, said to have been given by the saintly Henry VI; a brass dish at Burrel Green with a Catholic Latin inscription, allegedly given by a fairy or a witch.

Edric the Wild. A Saxon lord owning land along the Welsh Border at the time of the Norman Conquest, who became a focus for several legends. According to Walter *Map, he kidnapped a most beautiful fairy woman, whom he saw dancing and singing with her sisters in a hall in a forest. She agreed to marry him, on condition he never alluded to her past; some years later he broke this promise, and she vanished instantly. Soon after, he died of grief.

In later folklore, Edric himself took on supernatural characteristics. Charlotte Burne was told that he and his fairy wife and all their followers were still alive, deep in the Shropshire lead mines, and would not die till all the wrongs done by the Normans are righted. Miners would hear them knocking where the best lodes ran. 'Now and then they are permitted to show themselves. Whenever war is going to break out, they ride over the hills in the direction of the enemy's country, and if they appear, it is a sign that the war will be serious' (Burne, 1883: 25–9). Charlotte Burne's informant, a miner's daughter, said her father had seen Edric riding out in Napoleon's time, and she herself before the Crimean war. More modern books on Shropshire lore mention people who claim sightings in 1914 and 1939.

eels. A common belief was that a long black horsehair thrown into a running stream instantly becomes a live eel or water snake. William Harrison, *The Description of England* (1587: 321) provides an early reference, although he reserved judgement on the truth of the matter, and in the early 19th century the author of the *Denham Tracts* (1895: ii. 29) admits to trying it himself as a boy in the north of England. Correspondence in *N&Q* (7s:2–4 (1886–7)) under the heading 'Animated Horsehairs' indicates that this had been a very widely held notion in England, Scotland, and elsewhere, at all levels of society well into the late 19th century.

A different correspondent in *N&Q* reported a belief in eels as a cure for *deafness. A woman at Lochleven, who was putting live eels into a bag, told him they were being sent to England to cure a lady of her deafness, and that this was a regular occurrence. Asked if she herself believed in the cure, she answered, 'Od, I dinna ken, sir, but thae English doctors shud ken'. (*N&Q* 5s:9 (1878), 65). A more generally reported medical use of eels was (and perhaps still is) to wear their skins as a garter as a

preventative for *cramp, or a cure for rheumatism. Enid Porter (1969: 47, 67, 72, 86–7) gives
a full description of how to prepare the skin,
plus other eel lore, and Opie and Tatem (1989:
132) give references starting in 1684. A further
belief, not confined to Britain, asserts that
eels, like fish, are killed by *thunder (*N&Q*
10s:2 (1904), 331–2).

effigies. These appear in a number of English
customs, rarely being treated with respect,
and nearly always ending up being burnt. The
best known in modern times are concerned
with *November the Fifth, ranging from the
home-made domestic guy to the spectacular
processional constructions satirizing public
figures displayed at *Lewes (Sussex). Other
regular effigies include *Burning Bartle at
West Witton (Yorkshire) and, in previous
times, Burning *Judas in Liverpool. The parading of an effigy could also be a relatively
spontaneous customary way of showing group
displeasure at local or national events. Carica-
tures of the offending parties were common in
*rough music ceremonies, and, for example, at
Sherborne (Dorset) on the news of the proclamation of Charles II in May 1660, effigies of
Cromwell and Bradshaw were subjected to a
mock trial, dragged through the streets,
hacked to pieces, and thrown on a bonfire
along with the arms of the Commonwealth
(Underdown, 1985: 271). In much earlier
times, some effigies had a much more respectable role in *civic events such as the Lord
Mayor's Show and *midsummer watch processions, where *giants and *dragons were
particularly popular characters, and before
the Reformation statues of saints would also
have been paraded around the parish on patronal feast days and other special occasions, as
on the Continent.

See also *JUDAS; *JACK O LENT; *QUEEN
ELIZABETH I'S ANNIVERSARY; *ST DAVID'S DAY;
*SALISBURY GIANT.

eggs. It was thought very unlucky to take
eggs into or out of a house after sunset. There
were rules about setting them to be hatched—
it should be done with a waxing *moon, but
not on a *Friday or Sunday; there should be an
odd number, preferably *thirteen, for an even-
numbered clutch would produce cockerels
only. In some coastal areas, it was thought that
eggs set at ebb-tide produced hens, and those
at the flood cockerels. The abnormally small
yolkless egg sometimes produced by old hens

were believed to be cock's eggs. They were
very unlucky; if hatched, they would produce
a *cockatrice, so they were thrown over the
roof.

A form of girls' *divination, known since the
17th century and usually done on *Midsummer Day, was to drop egg-white into water and
observe what shapes it made; these foretold
one's destined husband's occupation (Opie
and Tatem, 1989: 135). Another, done on *St
Agnes' Eve in Northumberland, was to fill an
empty eggshell with salt and eat it, shell and
all, and then go to bed backwards; the future
husband would be seen in a dream (Radford,
Radford, and Hole, 1961: 144).

In Sussex, it was thought unlucky to bring
the eggs of wild birds indoors, though strings
of them were hung on outbuildings in spring
(why, is not said) (Latham, 1878: 10); more
commonly, it was unlucky to take *robins'
eggs.

See also *EASTER EGGS, *PRIMROSES.

eggshells. In his *Vulgar Errors* (1686), Sir
Thomas Browne noted:

to break an egg after ye meate is out we are taught in
our childhood . . . and the intent thereof was to prevent witchcraft; lest witches should draw or prick
their names therein and veneficiously mischiefe ye
persons, they broke ye shell. . . . This custome of
breaking the bottom of the eggeshell is yet commonly used in the countrey. (Browne, *Pseudodoxia
Epidemica* (1686), v. xxii, para. 4)

Others, including Reginald Scot in 1584, had
heard say that witches sailed in eggshells; thus
by driving the spoon through the shells one
was 'sinking the witch boats' and preventing
shipwrecks. Children were still being taught
this in the 1930s; a poem written in 1934 runs:

Oh, never leave your eggshells unbroken in the cup,
Think of us poor sailor-men and always smash them
up,
For witches come and find them and sail away to sea,
And make a lot of misery for mariners like me.

(Gill, 1993: 97)

Newall, 1971: 80–7; Opie and Tatem, 1989: 135–6.

Egremont Crab-Apple Fair. Egremont in
Cumbria claims to have held its fair every year
since its charter was granted in 1267 (except
for during the two world wars). The day, the
Saturday nearest 18 October, is a series of
events rather than a continuous fair, starting
with a greasy pole which locals are invited to
climb to claim the joint of meat (or money)

fixed to the top. Later in the morning a lorry is driven round the streets while men throw apples to the crowd—they used to be crab-apples, but more edible varieties are now distributed—and during the day there are children's races, wrestling, dog races and shows, and much else. The evening includes bizarre events such as a pipe-smoking contest, sentimental song singing competition, and what they claim to be the World Champion *Gurning Competition.

Shuel, 1985: 14–16; Kightly, 1986: 98–9; Sykes, 1977: 125–6.

elbows. As with other parts of the body, an itching elbow is significant. It is mentioned by *Scot (1584: book 11, chapter 13) as one of 'an innumerable multitude of objects, whereupon they prognosticate good or bad lucke'. Unfortunately, he does not tell us what this particular one means. Neither is Shakespeare very clear: 'rub the elbow at the news of hurly burly innovation' (*Henry the Fourth Part 1* (c.1597), v. i). It is only with 17th-century authors that we understand that an itching elbow means that you will, or should, change your bedfellow. Much more recent is the idea, reported in Opie and Tatem, that if you bang your elbow accidentally, you should also knock the other one, for luck.

Opie and Tatem, 1989: 136–7; Lean II, 1903: 285–6.

elder. Traditional attitudes towards the elder are contradictory. Many people thought it evil, and would never lop it, bring its flowers into the house, or make tools from its wood; to burn it would bring death, or the Devil, into the house. Its shade was thought to poison all other plants, and even humans sleeping nearby; also, a gash from an elder stick supposedly never heals, and babies rocked in elder-wood cradles always die young. Some said this was because *Judas hanged himself on an elder, others that it is 'a witch-tree' (cf. *Rollright Stones). In some districts anyone about to cut elder wood asked permission, though the formula used had a trick in it: 'Owd Gal, give me of thy wood, and Oi will give some of moine, when Oi graws inter a tree' (or, 'when I am dead', in other versions).

In contrast, others thought it sacred, because the Cross was made of elder wood; it would never be struck by lightning, and one near a house would drive away all evil, especially witches. Its leaves or twigs, carried in the pocket, were a defence against witchcraft

and a cure for rheumatism; a necklace of its twigs prevented fits.

Elderflower tea and elderberry wine were good for coughs, colds, and fevers, and the bark boiled in milk for jaundice; the leaves were used in poultices and ointments, for example for grazes and for eczema. The smell of the leaves repels flies and wasps, so elder bushes were planted outside the windows of dairies and larders, and round outdoor lavatories.

Vickery, 1995: 118–26; Hatfield, 1994; Opie and Tatem, 1989: 127–9.

elecampane. The roots of this plant were widely used in folk medicine and particularly veterinary medicine—for curing hydrophobia in cows and skin diseases in horses and sheep. In Wiltshire, at least, the plant was called 'Horseheal' (Wiltshire, 1975: 18). For human use, the traditional ways of processing the plant often involved mixing with sugar, honey, or wine. In this form it eventually became available as a sweet, and the name lived on even after the plant ceased to be an ingredient:

So now its medical virtues are forgotten, and it is sold merely as a candy in confectioners' shops, with no more of the plant in it than there is of barley in what is now sold as barley-sugar.

One writer in *Notes & Queries* equates elecampane with the liquorish-concoction made and drunk by children on a special day in certain parts of the country (see under *Spanish Sunday).The other way in which the plant is remembered, after a fashion, is in the Doctor's speech in many versions of the *mummers play, in which the name is garbled in all manner of ways (such as Allikan-pane or Hokumpokum-hellican-pain) but it is quite clear that elecampane was the 'original' word used.

Vickery, 1995: 126; N&Q 4s:5 (1870), 595; 4s:6 (1870), 103, 205, 264; 4s:7 (1871), 243, 314.

elephant statuettes. Ebony statuettes of elephants in graded sizes were popular mantlepiece ornaments in the first half of the 20th century; it was said they had to face the door of the room, otherwise the good luck they gave would turn to bad.

Ellis, Sir Henry (1777–1869). All his working life was spent in major libraries and archives, at the Bodleian and the British Museum. He was a leading figure among the literary-antiquarians of his day, and was Secretary for the Society of Antiquaries for 40 years from 1814. For folklorists, Ellis's main claim to fame is that he undertook the daunting task of editing the mass of material collected by *Brand for a second edition of his *Observations on Popular Antiquities*. Ellis managed this by 1813, publishing a two-volume set, but without grasping the nettle of arrangement, and the work rapidly became famous for its irritating lack of clear structure and footnotes upon footnotes. Nevertheless, the new edition immediately became a standard work in the burgeoning antiquary-folklore field, being referred to as 'Brand-Ellis' by later writers, and Ellis returned to the subject with a new three-volume edition, better organized, and with additional material, in 1849.

Dorson, 1968: 17–20, 22–4; *DNB*.

elves. In Old English, *ælf* was the general all-purpose term for a *fairy; after the Conquest, however, the French 'fairy' partially replaced it, though Chaucer and Shakespeare still used them interchangeably, and 'elf' seems to have faded out of rural usage in most of England (though not in Yorkshire). It kept a place in literary English, however, so it now sounds both more archaic and more elegant than 'fairy'.

Elves must have been regarded as helpful in some contexts, otherwise *ælf* would not have been used as an element in personal names, e.g. Ælfred and Ælfwine. On the other hand, Anglo-Saxon medical textbooks and collections of healing charms refer to 'elf sickness', 'water-elf sickness', and 'elf shot'; the latter could afflict horses, cattle, or humans, and was thought to be caused when elves shot them with small darts. Prehistoric flint arrow heads were long known as 'elf arrows' or 'elf bolts'. Elves were also blamed for tangling human hair and horses' manes during the night ('elf locks'), and for 'riding' humans and horses by night, causing nightmares, sweating, and restless sleep.

The Anglo-Saxon charms against such afflictions are interesting texts. Some rely on prayers and psalms, regarding the troublesome elf as a demon to be exorcized; others mix religious and non-religious elements:

If a horse be elf-shot, then take a knife of which the haft is the horn of a fallow ox, and on which are three brass nails, then write upon the horse's forehead Christ's mark and on each of the limbs thou mayest feel at; then take the left ear, and prick a hole

in it in silence; this thou shalt do, then take a staff, strike the horse on the back, then it will be whole. And write upon the horn of the knife these words, *Benedicite omnia opera domini dominum* (All ye works of the Lord, bless ye the Lord). Be the elf what it may, this has power against him as a remedy.

One, in verse, describes how she-elves have plunged their spears in a victim, and the healer's counter-attack; he is to boil up feverfew, red nettle, and plantain with butter, and plunge a knife in the mixture, reciting a lengthy chant with the repeated adjuration, 'Out, little spear, if herein you be!'

Wilfred Bonser, *Folk-Lore* 37 (1926), 350–63; full translation of the verse in R. K. Gordon, *Anglo-Saxon Poetry* (1926), 94–5.

English Dialect Survey. The result of the sustained enthusiasm and effort of two linguists, Harold Orton (1898–1975) and Eugen Dieth (1893–1956). When Orton was appointed to the Chair of English Language and Medieval Literature at Leeds University in 1947, it provided them with a base from which to launch an ambitious survey of the dialects of England, designed to amass an archive of accurate and authentic data, and to provide material for the publication of a linguistic atlas. Aware of the limitations of previous work on dialect in England, they used trained fieldworkers, standard questionnaires, and professional dialectological principles, and between 1948 and 1961 the team conducted fieldwork in 313 rural locations. The 'Survey of English Dialects' was the name of the publishing programme launched in 1962, which published a number of books of findings in tabular form, and the cherished *The Linguistic Atlas of England*, edited by Harold Orton, Stewart Sanderson, and John Widdowson, in 1978. Other atlases based on the Survey material followed. In addition to the collecting and publishing, Orton was instrumental in forging dialect studies into an academic discipline, and more than 100 student theses on dialect were completed at Leeds University in his time. He retired in September 1964, although he continued to play an active part in the publication programme, and having laid the foundations of what became in October that year the *Institute of Dialect and Folklife Studies under the direction of Stewart Sanderson.

Harold Orton, 'How We Say and What We Play', *The Village* 8:1 (1953), 26–31; Craig Fees, *The Imperilled Inheritance: Dialect and Folklife Studies at the University of Leeds 1946–1962* (1991); S. F. Sanderson, 'Folklore Material in the English Dialect Survey', *Folklore* 83 (1972), 89–100.

English Folk Dance Society. The foundation of the EFDS was formally proposed by Cecil *Sharp, seconded by Alice *Gomme, at a public meeting in December 1911, and the Society lasted until 1932 when it amalgamated with the *Folk-Song Society to form the *English Folk Dance and Song Society. Sharp had been actively collecting traditional dance since 1906, and had already published the first parts of his *Morris Book* (1907), *Country Dance Book* (1909), and *Sword Dances of Northern England* (1911). His public disagreements, and growing competition, with Mary *Neal prompted him to form a Folk Dance Club in 1910, which resulted directly in the formation of the EFDS the following year. Sharp's agenda at the time was heavily influenced by his differences with Neal, which were adopted wholesale by the new Society, in particular his stress on 'artistic' rather than 'philanthropic' principles. He believed that the newly discovered dances should be brought back to the people by way of trained professionals rather than enthusiastic amateurs. What distinguished the EFDS from the existing *Folklore Society and Folk-Song Society was that it had from the beginning 'a policy of active propaganda with a view to restoring traditional arts to popular use' (Croft, 1927: 3), but only on Sharp's terms. His views openly dominated the Society until his death in 1924, when he was succeeded as Director by Douglas *Kennedy, and it took years for Sharp's influence to begin to wane.

The Society immediately set out a programme of training, holding classes, granting certificates, lecturing, and demonstrating on a nationwide basis, as well as organizing country dance parties, balls, and festivals, and attracted thousands of enthusiasts, particularly amongst schoolteachers. Until the First World War, the activities of its members were viewed by the general public as mildly eccentric, but continued work brought wider public acceptance during the 1920s and 1930s, although the movement was never able to shake off the rather fussy, precious, serious-minded reputation it had gained. Development was also hindered by the fact that many of Sharp's most promising disciples, such as R. J. E. Tiddy and George *Butterworth were killed in the war. Ironically, considering the birth of the Society in Sharp's disagreement with Neal and her supporters, there were factions within the EFDS who believed that the Society should concentrate

less on certificates and more on enjoyment, and this viewpoint gradually became accepted as the inter-war years progressed. When amalgamation with the Folk-Song Society was mooted in 1932, there were some in the latter organization who feared that their relatively academic membership interests would be swamped by the hobby dancers, and this tension remained a major force in the development of the new combined Society.

The Society published a *Journal*: 2 volumes, 1914–15; second series 4 volumes, 1927–31.

Derek Schofield, *FMJ* 5:2 (1986), 215–19; W. D. Croft, *JEFDS* 2s:1 (1927), 3–16; Douglas Kennedy, *FMJ* 2:2 (1971), 80–90.

English Folk Dance and Song Society. The EFDSS was formed in 1932 by the amalgamation of the *Folk-Song Society (founded 1898), and the *English Folk Dance Society (EFDS) (founded 1911). At that time, the two societies had a number of leading figures in common, including Ralph *Vaughan Williams and Maud *Karpeles, who felt that the two bodies had sufficiently compatible aims to combine to make a stronger organization. Since then, the EFDSS has been the leading institution in the *song and *dance field in England, and has also contributed significantly to their performance, collection, and study and is still active in promoting and co-ordinating activities and publications at a variety of levels.

The fact that the EFDSS has come under constant criticism since its inception, from one group or another within and outside its membership, cannot be ignored, and some of its problems can be seen in the original amalgamation plan. Even at that time there were voices who argued against the venture—Alice *Gomme, for example—who feared that the primarily recreationally minded and much larger EFDS would swamp the more scholarly minded Folk-Song Society, and until the post-war song revival this looked as if it might be true. With notable exceptions, the rank-and-file membership remained polarized into dance people and song people, with the former numerically stronger. However, not only were there dance and song camps, but there were also within each camp those whose primary interest was in research and others whose interest was in performance; and within the performance camps there were those who wished to perpetuate the styles and repertoire of the past in a relatively strict form, while others believed in artistic freedom and development. Added to this, there have been other areas of debate—whether women should be allowed to dance the *morris, for example, or whether the Society should be solely concerned with English traditions. The potential for conflict within this complex of attitudes and agendas is obvious, and tensions have periodically flared into open conflict.

It also cannot be denied that the Society has been slow at times to understand the major changes taking place at large in the song and dance movements and has always appeared slightly behind the times and therefore slightly irrelevant. It is perhaps expecting too much of an organization dedicated to the preservation of traditional cultural forms to be at the cutting-edge of cultural change, but the new *revival which came into being in the 1950s and blossomed in the next two decades appeared to many to be taking place in spite of the EFDSS rather than because of it.

On the more positive side, the EFDSS, by its continued existence, has provided a focal point for much of the enduring work carried out in song and dance, and has acted as a channel for information exchange between its members and the outside world, in addition to providing thousands of ordinary enthusiasts with the opportunity to indulge in dance and song activities which would not have existed otherwise. The Society has provided recordings and dance instruction manuals to countless schoolteachers and other bodies and has thus helped to provide the materials and foundations of each new revival, and a small but respectable catalogue of books and sound recordings of traditional song has been issued over the years. Without its continued work little would have survived to be revived. The Society's journal, the *Journal of the English Folk Dance and Song Society* (1932–64), continued as the *Folk Music Journal* (1965 to date), is a major repository of material in its own right, and has developed into an internationally-respected scholarly publication; and the magazine, *English Dance and Song* (1936 to date) also provides an essential outlet for less formal articles, reviews, and notes. The *Vaughan Williams Memorial Library has the best collection of song and dance material in the country, and has developed into an essential information resource for scholars, with a deservedly high reputation for the support it gives to research. The EFDSS is based at *Cecil Sharp House, 2 Regents Park Road, London NW1 7AY (Tel.: 020 7485 2206).

Espérance Morris Guild, see MARY *NEAL, CECIL *SHARP.

Ethnic. A short-lived home-made periodical, subtitled 'A Quarterly Survey of English Folk Music, Dance and Drama' compiled and published by Mervyn Plunkett, Reg Hall, and Peter Grant. The first issue was dated January 1959 and the fourth and last came in Autumn the same year. In an aggressive style, *Ethnic* championed the collection and study of authentic traditional style and repertoire in contradistinction to what its editors saw as a burgeoning *revival movement based on false principles, little knowledge, and cosy middle-class fashion. The magazine included several important articles based on first-hand experience (such as one on May Day at *Padstow in issue number three, and several on particular singers and musicians) and its criticisms are also useful for evidence of a critical time in the post-war development of folklore studies and the folk-song and dance revival.

ethnic jokes. The English are not alone in having an active repertoire of jokes which rely for their point on negative ethnic stereotypes, as all European countries have their joke cycles about particular groups. In earlier times, the groups singled out for ridicule were more likely to be the inhabitants of a local town or village—*Gotham, for example—but this has gradually given way to jokes about particular nationalities or ethnic groups, although different regions still hold stereotyped views about others. There is a range of stereotyped traits assigned to particular groups in jokes, but the most common is stupidity, presumably because it has much wider comic possibilities than, say, meanness or avarice. In England, jokes or humorous tales depicting the Irish as stupid were circulating at least as early as 1739 when some were printed in *Joe Miller's Jests* (see Halpert and Widdowson, 1996: 647–53), and were taken abroad by Canadian, American, and Australian settlers, where they also flourished. Jokes and tales about the Irish have existed ever since, and there is no doubt that racist stereotypes are perpetuated in this way, but as two of Sandra McCosh's English informants said: 'we have nothing against the Irish; my father and his father were Irish. They're just *supposed to be stupid*' (McCosh, 1976: 120).

See also *FOOLS, WISE MEN OF *GOTHAM.

Christie Davies, *Ethnic Humor Around the World: A Comparative Analysis* (1990); Christie Davies, 'Fooltowns: Traditional and Modern, Local, Regional and Ethnic Jokes About Stupidity' in Gillian Bennett, *Spoken in Jest* (1991), 215–35; Sandra McCosh, *Children's Humour* (1976); Herbert Halpert and J. D. A. Widdowson, *Folktales of Newfoundland* (1996), ii. 647–53.

Evans, George Ewart (1909–88). One of the founders of Oral History in Britain, he was the son of a shopkeeper in the mining village of Abercynon in Glamorgan. He came to Suffolk in the 1930s to work as a teacher and writer, and after the war he discovered a field which absorbed him, and his readers, for the rest of his life. After hearing his Blaxhall neighbours, Robert and Priscilla Savage, a retired shepherd and his wife, using dialect and country words which Evans recognized from his reading of 16th-century poets, he realized the long tradition of farming and village ways which was about to be swept away as the last generation who had used horse-power and hand tools gradually faded away. In a series of highly readable books based on his researches, mainly in Suffolk, Evans wrote about this rural heritage, gradually refining a methodology which combined interviewing with wide reading, and he became a passionate advocate for '... getting history directly from the people, and going about introducing the technique to schools, continuing education classes, and groups in universities all over Britain' (*Spoken History*, p. xiii). From the first book, Evans always put his living informants centre-stage and this feature caught the attention of a rising generation of social historians who went on to forge the new field of Oral History.

Books by Evans: *Ask the Fellows Who Cut the Hay* (1956); *The Horse in the Furrow* (1960); *The Pattern Under the Plough* (1966); *The Farm and the Village* (1969); *Where Beards Wag All* (1970); *The Leaping Hare* (with David Thomson) (1972); *The Days We Have Seen* (1975); *From Mouths of Men* (1976); *Horse Power and Magic* (1979); *Spoken History* (1987); *The Crooked Scythe: An Anthology of Oral History* (1993). Also his autobiography, *The Strength of the Hills* (1983).

Gareth Evans, *George Ewart Evans* (1991); Alun Howkins, *Oral History* 22:2 (1994), 26–32; Obituary by Trefor Owen, *Folklore* 99:1 (1988), 126.

evergreens. A high proportion of the plants important in folk customs are evergreen—a fact which can be seen either in practical or symbolic terms. Folklorists have usually highlighted the latter, suggesting that at winter festivals they represented the unconquered life-force, and at funerals immortality. This may be so, though early sources offer little direct evidence, and what there is does not always bear out the theory; *holly, for instance, is celebrated in a well-known medieval carol because its features recall aspects of Christ's birth and life, while *rosemary proverbially was 'for remembrance'. The herbalist Willam Coles, in his *The Art of Simpling* (1656: 64–5), thought lasting memory was the key concept:

Cypresse Garlands are of great account at Funeralls amongst the gentiler sort, but Rosemary and Bayes are used by the Commons both at Funeralls and Weddings. They are all plants which fade not a good while after they are gathered and used (as I conceive) to intimate unto us, that the remembrance of the present solemnity might not dye presently, but be kept in minde for many yeares.

However, availability must also have been an important factor; weddings and funerals occur at all seasons, so it was possible to make evergreens a standard feature of these occasions, but not always flowers.

See also *BAY, *BOX, *HOLLY, *IVY, *MISTLETOE, *ROSEMARY, *YEW.

evil eye. The belief that certain people can inflict disease or death simply by a glance was accepted by the educated throughout medieval and Elizabethan times, as it had been by Pliny and other classical authorities. Scientists held that vision was an active process, in which the eye emitted rays, and that envy or anger made these rays destructive; Francis Bacon, in his essay 'Of Envy' (*c*.1600), says the emotion causes 'an ejaculation or irradiation of the eye', inflicting a 'stroke or percussion' on the person envied.

In common speech, the action was called 'overlooking', and it was generally regarded as *witchcraft, consciously used. Writing in the 1890s in Somerset, Elworthy said the stories about it there were 'almost infinite', and 'one of the commonest of everyday facts'. Sick pigs were said to be 'overlooked', and so were sick children; it was taken for granted they would die, so no effort was made to cure them. Certain protective charms designed to attract, deflect, or confuse a witch's gaze, including *witch balls, *horse brasses, and *threshold patterns, reveal a fear of overlooking; however, spoken curses and physical actions are more frequently mentioned than mere looking in English accounts of witchcraft.

There are occasional English references to the idea, common in Mediterranean countries, that those with the evil eye cannot control it. *Aubrey mentions a man who accidentally overlooked his own cattle (Aubrey 1686/1880: 80); there is an account from Yorkshire of a man who kept his eyes fixed on the ground so as not to harm anyone, and another who made sure he looked at a pear tree first thing every morning, so that it would take the brunt of his power (Radford, Radford, and Hole, 1961: 155).

Elworthy, 1895/1958, is a valuable introduction, and there is a collection of essays in *The Evil Eye: A Casebook*, ed. Alan Dundes (1992), but neither uses many English examples.

excrement. Colloquial speech abounds in references to defecation and associated organs and processes. Until recently they were regarded as a form of obscenity and were taboo in general society, so becoming a powerful mark of communal solidarity within the subgroups (usually male and/or juvenile) which did use them among themselves. Currently, they are freely uttered across a far wider range of society than at any previous period in England. Used in anger, they shock or insult, but they are also often deployed for humorous effects; they are common in minor verbal genres such as riddles, playground rhymes, and limericks, where the humour may consist either in uttering the offensive word or cleverly avoiding it. Many jokes and idioms exist in both a coarse and a polite version—as an expression of incredulity, 'My foot!' is acceptable anywhere, but 'My arse!' is not.

Beliefs about actual excrement are few. To step accidentally on dog dirt or a cowpat is said to bring good luck, as attested by two 17th-century proverbs: 'muck is luck', and 'shitten luck is the best'. Some say the reason some burglars befoul the scene of their crime is as a charm to ensure they will not be caught (*N&Q* 11s:1 (1910), 296–7).

In folk *medicine, a poultice of cow-dung in brown paper was used to induce local warmth, for example for easing rheumatic pain. Since at least the early 17th century, it was thought that to throw somebody's excrement into a fire, or plunge hot iron into it, would cause violent bowel pains and fever; mothers were cautioned against harming their babies in this way, while doctors, on the same principle, placed the patient's excrement in cold water to cool a fever. As with *urine in a *witch bottle, the principle could be exploited as a *counterspell (Opie and Tatem, 1989: 141–2).

See also *BIRD DROPPINGS.

exorcism. Exorcizing demons from possessed persons has always been regarded as a task for specialist clergy, and though it played a part in some witchcraft cases (Thomas, 1971: 477–92), it is rarely mentioned in folklore. Exorcism of *ghosts, however, was (and still is) frequently practised at the request of people whose houses seem unpleasantly haunted; it is also a common topic in local legends (see *laying).

eyebrows. English folklore is convinced that eyebrows which meet are indicative of a person's character, but it cannot decide whether it is good or bad, and the honours are about even either way. For example: 'It's a good thing to have meeting eyebrows. You'll never know trouble' (various places) (*N&Q* 1s:7 (1853), 152); 'People with meeting eyebrows are thought fortunate fellows (Durham)' (Henderson, 1879: 112). On the other hand: 'Those who have the eyebrows met are witches and warlocks ... unlucky to meet someone whose eyebrows met on New Years Day' (*Denham Tracts*, 1892: i. 325, 340), and 'They whose heaire of the eye browes doo touch or meete together, of all other are the woorst. They do shewe that he or she is a wicked personne ... ' (Lupton, *Thousand Notable Things* (1579), quoted by Opie and Tatem).

Opie and Tatem, 1989: 143–4; *N&Q* 185 (1943), 41–2; 186 (1944), 77, 123, 298–9.

eyelashes. A number of folklore collections since the mid-19th century have included instructions for 'wishing on an eyelash'. From Shropshire: 'If an eyelash comes out, put it on the back of the hand, wish, and throw it over the shoulder. If it leaves the hand the wish will come true' (Burne, 1883: 268). A Cornish schoolgirls' version dictates that the lash must be placed on the tip of the nose, and blown off (*Folk-Lore Journal* 5 (1887), 214).

Opie and Tatem, 1989: 144.

eyes. Itching on many parts of the body is held to be ominous, and the eye is no exception. The meaning here is relatively stable, its first documentary appearance in Shakespeare's

Othello ((1604), IV. iii) : '. . . Mine eyes doth itch, Doth that bode weeping?' The belief is recorded regularly from then on, although sometimes embellished with a choice of eyes—right to cry, left to laugh, or the other way round. Long before these English examples, however, Theocritus (*Idylls*, *c.*275 BC) wrote 'My right eye itches now, and shall I see my love?'. The eyes can also be significant in other ways; by their colour, size, shape or other detail they can betray a person's true character, or simply be unlucky or even dangerous in their own right. Cross-eyed or squinting people are most often singled out in this respect: 'A person that is blear-eyed, googled and squinting signified malice, vengeance, cautell and treason' (*Shepherd's Kalendar*, 1503) or 'People who squint are said to be of a penurious disposition, but punctual in their dealings' (both quoted by Lean). Most references simply state that it is unlucky to meet a cross-eyed person, although some maintain that it is all right if they are of the opposite sex to you.

For the widespread belief that certain people can inflict harm simply by their glance, see under *EVIL EYE. See also *EYEBROWS; *EYELASHES.

Opie and Tatem, 1989: 143; Lean, 1903: ii. 20, 193, 201, 311.

fables. Short comic tales making a moral point about human nature, usually through animal characters behaving in human ways. The great majority are first recorded in Ancient Greece or India; they became very popular in medieval Europe in both oral and literary versions, especially those about the trickster Reynard the Fox. By now, many are regarded as traditional English tales, their foreign origins forgotten.

face. Certain physical features are persistently, and irrationally, seen as clues to inner character: a high domed forehead indicating intelligence, a receding chin stupidity and cowardice, a jutting jaw bad temper, close-set eyes dishonesty, thick lips sensuality, etc. The size of a man's nose and a woman's mouth are said to correspond to that of their sexual organs—sometimes seriously, often in jest.

Some minor forms of *fortune-telling were based on the face. The presence and position of *moles and dimples was considered significant; E. M. Wright collected the following predictions of poverty or wealth, of which the first two were still known in 1958:

> A dimple in your cheek,
> Your living to seek
>
> (Yorkshire)
>
> A dimple in your chin,
> You'll have your living brought in
>
> (Yorkshire)
>
> If you've a mole above your chin
> You'll never be beholden to your kin
>
> (Shropshire)

and also a Lancashire belief that a mole on the side of the nose was a sign that the Devil has marked you for his own (Wright, 1913: 224). Others reported that 'it is the opinion of nurses that babies who have dimples have short tongues, and will lisp' (N&Q 5s:9 (1878), 466).

See also *EARS, *EYEBROWS, *EYELASH, *EYES, *MOLES, *MOUTH, *NOSE.

Opie and Tatem, 1989: 119, 288; Lean, 1903: ii. 1. 284–5.

fainites, see *TRUCE TERMS.

fairies. The basic European repertoire of beliefs and tales about fairies is less fully preserved in England than in the Celtic areas of Wales, Ireland, and Highland Scotland, though much of it was well known here in the 17th century, and later. Unfortunately it has been overshadowed by literary portrayals, medieval, Shakespearian, or modern; the rural lore collected by regional folklorists made little impact on public awareness until the 1960s and 1970s, when Katharine *Briggs brought all the evidence together, demonstrating its coherence and power.

Folklorists generally use the term 'fairy' rather loosely, to cover a range of non-human yet material beings with magical powers. These could be visible or invisible at will, and could change shape; some lived underground, others in woods, or in water; some flew. Some were believed to be friendly, giving luck, prosperity, or useful skills to humans who treated them respectfully; many were regarded as troublesome pranksters, or, in extreme cases, as minor demons; sometimes they were blamed for causing sickness, stealing human babies, and leaving *changelings. Human adults might be invited (or abducted) into *fairyland.

Fairies can be divided into two major groups: 'social' fairies, imagined as living in communities and pursuing group activities such as dancing and feasting; and 'solitary' fairies, of which some (the *brownie type) attach themselves to human households as helpers and luck-bringers, while others (the *bogey/boggart type) haunt an open-air site, often as a more-or-less serious threat to passers-by. But it is not always clear-cut; *pixies, for example, can be either 'social' or 'solitary', while *Robin Goodfellow behaves equally readily as prankster or helpful household sprite. Conversely, informants sometimes insist on rigid separations between categories; a brownie, for instance, might be regarded as a quite different creature from a fairy, and a shape-changing apparition like the Yorkshire *guytrash as something different again—which, from a functionalist point of view, is true enough. The number of local words for species and sub-species, and for individuals, is considerable. The original English term for the whole species was *elf, but in Middle English this was largely replaced by 'fairy', borrowed from French.

The clergy, whether Catholic or Protestant, usually insisted that all such creatures could only be devils; many realized their similarity to the fauns, satyrs, nymphs, etc., of classical mythology, which they also regarded as demons. In popular belief, however, fairies were fitted into the Christian frame of reference in ways which left them morally ambiguous; in Cornwall, they were said to be angels who refused to side either with God or with Lucifer when the latter rebelled, and so, being 'too good for Hell and too bad for Heaven', were thrown down to earth and lived wherever they happened to fall. Alternatively, they could be identified with *ghosts—either of the dead in general, or of special categories such as *unbaptized infants. The latter was commonly said of the *Will-o'-the-Wisp.

Belief in the household brownie (or pixy, or puck) was closely linked to farming; he threshes corn, tends horses, herds sheep, churns butter, cleans the kitchen, and so on, like an ideal farm servant. He also brings prosperity, and can take it away again if offended; he punishes anyone who mocks him, and those who work badly. The *knockers had a similar role in tin and lead mining, but not in coal mines, indicating that this belief had faded by the time the latter industry was established.

The Anglo-Saxon charm against *elves shows how they were once dreaded for the diseases they inflicted; there are scattered indications that the fear persisted, to some extent, into Tudor and Stuart times. There are records of village healers seeking to cure children 'haunted with a fairy' by prayer and by magic measurements (Thomas, 1971: 184). On the other hand, people claiming unusual powers might say they had been granted them by fairies; there are instances of 16th- and 17th-century healers using ointments and powders alleged to be fairy gifts, or saying fairies enabled them to identify witches (Thomas, 1971: 186, 248, 266, 608–9). More sophisticated magicians used rituals to conjure up fairies, hoping to obtain great wealth, or occult secrets (Thomas, 1971: 236–7, 608–9, 613).

In the final stage of fairy-lore, belief is deliberately instilled by adults (who do not themselves share it) as a way of controlling children and ensuring their safety by threats of danger from a *bogey figures, e.g. *Jenny Greenteeth, *hytersprites, or *poldies. This strategy was still used in the upbringing of some people now in middle age, but probably no longer is. A more amiable item of fairy-lore for children is that fairies take away shed *teeth, leaving money instead (see *teeth and *Tooth Fairy).

Briggs, 1959, 1967, 1976, 1978; Thomas, 1971: 606–14. For narratives embodying the beliefs see Briggs, 1970–1: B; Philip, 1992: 307–36. Narváez 1991 contains valuable recent papers on various special topics.

fairy godmother. A kind fairy godmother is already a feature of the story of *Tom Thumb in 1621, but the later familiarity with such a figure depends on two fairytales, Cinderella and Sleeping Beauty, which reached England from France late in the 18th century. In Cinderella, the protective godmother replaced the magical animal which helped the heroine in older oral versions, commonly associated with her dead mother. She entered stage tradition, and was imitated in literary children's stories; she is now a stock figure in popular imagination.

fairyland. Beliefs about *fairies imply that their world lies close alongside the human world, often underground; it is a place of beauty and luxury which humans normally cannot reach, or even see. Some, however, may enter it by accident, for instance by stepping into a fairy ring; others may be invited, or abducted, by the fairies. The theme is relatively rare in England, though common in Scotland and Wales, and is chiefly found in areas of *Celtic influence. Four elaborate and rather romantic stories from Cornwall are in Bottrell (1873: 173–85) and Hunt (1865: 114–18, 120–6). Three concern girls who go to work for a fairy master as nursemaid to his child, and eventually return home; in the fourth, a man loses his way on the moors and finds himself in a house where fairies are feasting and dancing, and where he might have been held captive for ever if a girl, formerly human, had not warned him neither to eat nor drink there. An oral tale from Wigmore (Herefordshire), collected in 1909, tells how a girl joined a fairy dance and vanished for a year, which to her seemed only a day (Leather, 1912: 45–6).

See also *AVALON, *HERLA, *ORFEO.

fairy loaves. A name for fossil sea-urchins, because their plump domed shape, with five lines at the apex, resembles a small round loaf. They are found in chalky downland; they were said to be lucky, and whoever finds one should spit on it and toss it over his left shoulder. In Suffolk, where they were usually polished with black lead, it was said people who kept one in the house would never lack bread. They were also called *shepherd's crowns, and were sometimes used as *thunderstones.

fairy photographs, see *COTTINGLEY.

fairy rings. Circle dancing (carol) was the norm in medieval society, but later English dances were so different that dancing in a ring came to seem not merely old-fashioned or childish but uncanny, associated with *fairies or witches. When circles of lush, dark green grass were seen in meadows, they were said to mark the place where fairies had danced, and anybody who set foot in one risked being carried off. Such rings are caused by underground fungi, which at times produce visible toadstools; they persist for years, getting steadily larger, and grazing animals avoid them. No serious belief now attaches to them; at most, a vague idea that it is unlucky to step into one, or, contrariwise, that one can make a wish (Vickery, 1995: 130).

fairytales. This is the usual English term for a group of oral narratives centred on magical tests, quests, and transformations, which are found throughout Europe and in many parts of Asia too. They are defined by their plots, which follow standard basic patterns, and have been classified by Antti Aarne and Stith Thompson, *The Types of the Folktale* (1961); their function is to be oral entertainment for adults as well as children, and telling them well is a skilled art. The term 'fairy tale' only appeared in the 18th century, almost certainly as a translation of the French *Contes des Fées*, the title of a book by Madame d'Aulnois pub-

lished in 1698 and translated into English the following year. It is universally understood, but not in fact accurate, since many of the best-loved stories have no fairies in them, though magic abounds; consequently some scholars prefer the terms 'Wonder Tales' or 'Magic Tales'.

Native English fairytales must once have been abundant, but unfortunately at the very period when someone might have thought of collecting them and transferring them from orality to print, a flood of foreign tales appeared—first the French ones of Charles *Perrault (1697), Madame d'Aulnois (1698), and Madame de Beaumont (1756), then the German ones of the Brothers *Grimm (1812, and subsequent editions), and the Danish ones of Hans *Andersen (at intervals between 1835 and 1872). Selections from these were quickly translated and cheaply printed; by now established favourites such as Cinderella, Bluebeard, Sleeping Beauty, Puss in Boots, Beauty and the Beast, The Frog Prince, Red Riding Hood, Snow White, Rumpelstiltskin, Rapunzel, The Tinder Box, and The Little Mermaid are totally absorbed into English culture, together with a few items from the *Arabian Nights*, notably Aladdin.

The English fairytales which did get printed in chapbooks were humorous ones (*Jack and the Beanstalk, *Jack the Giant-Killer, *Tom Thumb), except for the more magical *Three Heads in the Well. Later, Victorian collectors found some oral examples, including *Tom Tit Tot and *Cap o' Rushes from Suffolk, the *Small-Tooth Dog from Derbyshire, and the *Rose Tree from Devon. However, the great majority of fairytale texts recorded in Britain were found either in Scotland and Wales or among Gypsy storytellers; the typical English narrative genres are the jocular anecdote, the horrific anecdote (e.g. *Mr Fox), and the *local legend. However, current research among teenage schoolchildren shows that some evolve personal versions of fairytales and tell them orally to their peer group (Wilson, 1997: 255–60).

The best collection is Philip, 1992, with accurate texts and valuable introduction and comments; see also Briggs, 1970–1: A. i and ii, with some texts summarized; Jacobs, 1890/1968, with texts often reworked. All three collections include other genres of folktale besides the fairytales. Baughman 1966 is a catalogue of all versions known at that date, and their sources. Opie and Opie 1974 gives authentic texts of the 24 best-known tales and discusses their sources and histories.

fakelore. The idea of 'fakelore' came to the fore in the 1960s when academic folklorists, primarily in America, began to take note of occasions where traditions were being invented or appropriated either for direct commercial gain (e.g. the rise of commercial 'folk singers' or the branding of mass market foods), tourism (e.g. the creation of 'wishing wells', or the appointment of 'town criers'), social control (see *Merrie England), nationalism, political legitimization, or simply to satisfy an apparent societal need for a definable but safe heritage. The term was rapidly extended to cover the creation and fostering of a false picture of the traditional culture, usually by culturally dominant groups, most clearly enunciated in the field of 'folk-song', but also in other genres. European scholars have tended to use the related term 'folklorism'.

The term is sometimes inappropriately applied to the use of folklore motifs by political cartoonists, advertisers, and others with a message to convey. By its very nature, 'folklore' is a shared system of symbols and meanings, and traditional motifs can therefore serve to set a scene or carry a meaning that native readers/viewers will immediately understand, although outsiders will be baffled.

See also *MERRIE ENGLAND, *REVIVAL, *TOURIST LORE.

Venetia Newall, *Folklore* 98:2 (1987), 131–51; Violet Alford, *Folklore* 72 (1961), 599–61; Dave Harker, *Fakesong: The Manufacture of British Folksong, 1700 to the Present Day* (1985); G. Legman, *The Horn Book* (1964), esp. 494–521.

familiars. Minor demons who, at Satan's command, become the servants of a human wizard or witch. It is one of the distinctive features of English *witchcraft that these spirits were very often thought to take the form of small animals, such as would be found around farms and homes; some witches claimed to have received them directly from the Devil, others from a relative or friend. One account of 1510 concerns a schoolmaster at Knaresborough (Yorkshire), who allegedly kept three spirits in the form of bumble bees and let them draw blood from his finger; he was attempting to locate treasure by magic. According to a pamphlet of 1566, two women on trial at Chelmsford (Essex), had successively owned a white spotted cat named 'Satan'; in return for a drop of blood, it had brought them possessions and caused people who had offended them to fall sick and die. The first woman had been given 'Satan' by her grandmother when she was 12 years old, with instructions to feed him on bread and milk and keep him in a basket—unusual luxury, probably, for an Elizabethan cat. In such cases, there seems no reason to doubt that the animals described did actually exist, and became the subject of gossip and suspicion.

Many other references can be found; there were said to be familiars in the forms of *cats, dogs, *toads, *mice, rabbits, flies, or grotesque creatures of no known species. They were commonly called 'imps', a word which combined the meanings of 'child' and 'small devil'. They were thought to suck blood or milk from the witch, causing growths on her face or body which looked like nipples; by the 17th century these were generally thought to be near the genitals or anus.

In rural tales and beliefs of later centuries, mice and toads are the familiars most commonly mentioned. Supposedly the witch sent them to bring misfortune on her enemies; in Somerset tales, witches are quoted as threatening, 'I'll toad 'ee!' It was believed that a witch could not die before passing them on to someone else, thus transferring both her power and her guilt. In anecdotes from Sussex and Essex in the 1930s, people alleged that mice had appeared at the deathbed of some local wizard or witch of a previous generation, who persuaded a reluctant relative to 'inherit' them. At West Wickham (Cambridgeshire) it was said that in the 1920s a witch tried to rid herself of her imps by putting them in the oven, but it was she, not they, who got burned; eventually they were buried with her (Simpson, 1973: 76; Maple, 1960: 246–7).

Thomas, 1971: 445–6, 524–5; Sharpe, 1996: 70–4.

farisees, pharisees. In the dialects of Herefordshire, Suffolk, and Sussex, fairies were called 'farisees', to the amusement of educated listeners, who assumed the term arose through stupid confusion with the Pharisees of the Bible, and often spelled the word accordingly. It is simply a reduplicated plural, like 'waspses' for 'wasps', or 'ghostses' for 'ghosts'.

Farthing Bundles. A custom which has lost much of its original *raison d'être* but which is still carried out on special occasions is the distribution of Farthing Bundles at Fern Street School Settlement, Bow, in East London, which was founded by Clara Grant in 1907. In addition to numerous practical philanthropic schemes, Farthing Bundles were distributed to children every Saturday:

Farthing bundles are full of very human things such as children love, e.g. tiny toys of wood or tin whole or broken, little balls, doll-less heads or head-less dolls, whistles, shells, beads, reels, marbles, fancy boxes, decorated pill boxes, ballroom pencils, scraps of patchwork, odds and ends of silk or wool, coloured paper for dressing up, cigarette cards and scraps.

The bundles were so popular, attracting thousands of children each week, that ways of controlling the numbers were sought. From 1913, to be eligible, children had to pass, without stooping, under a purpose-built wooden arch fixed on a frame, although the height of this arch had to be raised twice over the years as improving living standards resulted in taller children. Changing populations and circumstances rendered the bundles increasingingly anachronistic, and the last regular distribution was made in 1984.

R. Beer and C. A. Pickard, *Eighty Years on Bow Common* (1987).

fate. Though folklore is much concerned with *luck, it also recognizes the power of fate—but not an arbitrary or malevolent fate. On the contrary, traditional beliefs and practices imply that the circumstances of one's life and death were laid down in advance as part of an orderly plan determined by the Will of God. Occasional glimpses of the future could come unsought to anyone through *omens or premonitory *dreams, sent as forewarnings. Deliberate divination seems usually to have been tolerated when practised by young girls with an eye on love and marriage; however, the 'church porch watch' on *St Mark's Eve (and other dates) to learn who would die during the coming year was viewed with fear and disapproval. Opinion on the morality of *astrology and *fortune-telling was divided.

Some folktales teach how useless it is to try to evade fate. One (from Minster-in-Shippey, Kent) tells how a man killed his horse because of a prophecy that it would cause his death—and so it did, much later, when he kicked its skull, cut his foot on a splintered bone, and died of blood-poisoning (Westwood, 1985: 97–9).

Father Christmas. The earliest evidence for a personified 'Christmas' is a carol attributed to Richard Smart, Rector of Plymtree (Devon) from 1435 to 1477 (Dearmer and Williams, *Oxford Book of Carols* (1928), no. 21, 41–3); it is a sung dialogue between someone representing 'Sir Christmas' and a group who welcome him, in a way suggestive of a *visiting custom:

> Nowell, Nowell, Nowell, Nowell!
> 'Who is there that singeth so?'
> 'I am here, Sir Christëmas.'
> 'Welcome, my lord Sir Christëmas,
> Welcome to us all, both more and less,
>   Come near, Nowell!'

Sir Christmas then gives news of Christ's birth, and urges his hearers to drink:

> 'Buvez bien par toute la compagnie,
> Make good cheer and be right merry.'

There were *Yule Ridings in York (banned in 1572 for unruliness), where a man impersonating Yule carried cakes and meat through the street. In Tudor and Stuart times, 'Lords of Misrule' called 'Captain Christmas', 'The Christmas Lord', or 'Prince Christmas' organized and presided over the season's feasting and entertainments in aristocratic houses, colleges, and Inns of Court. A personified 'Christmas' appears in Ben Jonson's court entertainment *Christmas his Masque* (1616), together with his sons: Misrule, Carol, Mince Pie, Gambol, Post-and-Pan, New Year's Gift, Mumming, Wassail, and Baby Cake. He protests against an attempt to exclude him:

Why, gentlemen, do you know what you do? Ha! Would you have kept me out? Christmas, Old Christmas, Christmas of London, and Captain Christmas? . . . Why, I am no dangerous person . . . I am Old Gregory Christmas still, and though I am come from Pope's Head Alley, as good a Protestant as any in my parish.

The need to defend seasonal revelry against Puritan accusations of Popery became more urgent some decades later. Pamphleteers continued the device of personifying Christmas, as in *The Examination and Tryall of Old Father Christmas* (1658) and *An Hue and Cry after Christmas* (1645). Echoing this tradition, Father Christmas acts as presenter in many versions of the *mumming play, with such opening lines as:

> In comes I, old Father Christmas,
> Be I welcome or be I not?
> I hope old Father Christmas
> Will never be forgot.

The Victorian revival of Christmas involved Father Christmas too, as the emblem of 'good cheer', but at first his physical appearance was variable. He had always been imagined as old and bearded (in a masque by Thomas Nabbes (1638) he is 'an old reverend gentleman in furred gown and cap'), but pictures in the *Illustrated London News* in the 1840s show him variously as a reveller in Elizabethan costume grasping a tankard, a wild, holly-crowned giant pouring wine, or a lean figure striding along carrying a wassail bowl and a log. One famous image was John Leech's illustration for Dickens's *Christmas Carol* (1843), where the gigantic Ghost of Christmas Present, sitting among piled-up food and drink, wears exactly the kind of fur-trimmed loose gown of the modern Father Christmas—except that it is green, matching his holly wreath.

Towards the end of the 1870s, he developed a new role as present-bringer for children, in imitation either of European *St Nicholas customs, or of the American *Santa Claus, or both. By 1883, a French visitor to England mentions, as a matter of common knowledge, that he comes down chimneys and puts toys and sweets in stockings. In view of the German influence on the British Christmas, it may be significant that in Southern Germany the saint was accompanied by a gnome-like servant, usually dressed in a red, brown, or green hooded garment, carrying a small fir tree and a bag of toys. Father Christmas's costume became more standardized: it was almost always predominantly red, though Victorian Christmas cards do occasionally show him in blue, green, or brown; in outdoor scenes he often wore a heavy, hooded knee-length coat and fur boots; he carried holly, but the holly crown became rarer.

Nowadays Father Christmas is almost always associated with children's presents rather than adult feasting. His authentic dress is a loose, hooded red gown edged with white; however, he now often wears a red belted jacket and tasselled floppy cap imitated from Santa Claus, and has acquired Santa's reindeer sledge and nocturnal habits.

See also *SANTA CLAUS.

Father's Day. This celebration, on the third Sunday in June, has no basis in tradition; it was invented in the 1970s in imitation of *Mothering Sunday/*Mother's Day, for commercial profit. Greetings cards and gifts are given.

feasts, see *WAKES (1).

feathers. A belief, widely attested in the 19th century, was that if certain feathers other than those of domestic poultry, ducks, and geese were used in stuffing a pillow or a featherbed, any dying person lying on them would linger in agony. Correspondence in several early issues of *N&Q* showed slight local variations: pigeons were blamed in Cheshire and Northamptonshire, wild birds of any species in Cornwall, game birds in Sussex and Surrey. Similar ideas are recorded from other parts of England throughout the century. The remedies were equally traditional; either the pillow was pulled out from behind the dying man's head in such a way that he fell backwards, or he was lifted out of bed entirely and laid on the cold floor. Various informants told horrified collectors how well it worked:

Look at poor Muster S., how hard he were a-dying; poor soul, he could not die ony way, till neighbour Puttick found out how it were. 'Muster S.,' says he, 'ye be lying on geame feathers, mon, surely,' and so he were. So we took'n out o' bed and laid'n on the floor, and he pretty soon died then! (*N&Q* 1s:5 (1852), 341)

Conversely, 'Instances have been recorded where some such feathers have been placed in a small bag, and thrust under the pillow of a dying man to hold him in life till the arrival of some expected relation' (Wright, 1913: 277).

feet. English lore is apparently much less concerned with feet than its Scots, Irish, and Manx neighbours. The only belief which has predominately English examples is that if your sole itches or tickles you will tread strange ground. This is reported first in 1755, and was still current at least in the 1950s, and is one of the many beliefs concerned with itching parts of the body. A notion reported in 1878 (*N&Q* 5s:9 (1878), 286, 476) is that where two toes are partially joined, called 'twin toes' they are reputed to be lucky, although it is not stated how this luck will be manifested. It is also said that all important journeys should start on the right foot, and many accounts of the custom of first footing at *New Year stipulate that the first-footer should not be flat-footed.

See also *SHOES.

Opie and Tatem, 1989: 165–7.

Fenny Poppers. A *calendar custom which

celebrates the building of St Martin's, the parish church (1730), and takes place at Fenny Stratford, Buckinghamshire, every 11 November. The money for the church was raised and donated by the then Lord of the Manor, Dr Browne Willis, and he also left money for an annual feast and the firing of the Fenny Poppers. These Poppers are six cast-iron cannon-like objects which are filled with gunpowder and set off with a long red-hot iron rod, with deafening effect. The event takes place in the recreation ground (having been moved from the churchyard), and the Poppers are fired three times (noon, 2 p.m., and 4 p.m.), by the vicar, the verger, and the churchwardens.

Compare *OTTERY ST MARY.

Hole, 1975: 139; Shuel, 1985: 187–8; Kightly, 1986: 114–15.

fernseed. In Elizabethan times the seed of ferns was thought to be invisible, except for a few moments around *midnight on *Midsummer Eve, when it could be seen falling to the ground; anyone who could catch some in a pewter plate would be invisible while he carried it. In 19th-century Lancashire, 'It is said that young people went to Clough, near Moston, to gather silently the seeds of "St John's fern" on the Eve of St John's Day, to gain the affections of those maidens who would not accept their attentions' (*Transactions of the Lancashire and Cheshire Antiquarian Society* 25 (1907), 69). In Lincolnshire, *St Mark's Eve was called 'the Devil's Harvest' because ferns were said to bud, blossom, and yield seed, all between midnight and 1 a.m., and the Devil would harvest it; anyone who caught some between two pewter plates would become as wise as the Devil (J. A. Penny, *Lincolnshire N&Q* 3 (1892–3) 209).

fertility. The central theory of *Frazer's *The Golden Bough* was that much European folklore preserved rituals from archaic vegetation cults, in which men and women ensured fertility of trees and crops by having sexual intercourse at seasonal festivals; also, that this fertility corresponded magically to the virility of the local king or chief priest, who would be killed and replaced while still in the prime of life, to guard against any risk of impotence. This did not convince anthropologists (Ackerman, 1987), but had a huge impact on novelists, popular writers, and journalists throughout the 20th century, as its bloodthirsty and sexual content gave it great appeal. Of all the

Victorian mythological theories it is the only one still remembered; it has been so widely publicized that performers themselves now often believe their local custom to be 'a fertility rite', and say as much to enquirers. Certainly, bawdy humour is common in festive contexts, but for this very reason is more likely to be spontaneous, rather than a ritual survival from a remote culture.

Among agricultural customs actually recorded in England, some do explicitly aim at ensuring success for crops or fishing (see *Plough Monday, *wassailing apple trees), and many others bring a more vague and general good luck, and/or joyfully celebrate natural processes such as the return of spring or the completion of harvest.

For beliefs concerning human fertility, see *CERNE ABBAS, *CONCEPTION.

fetches, see *WRAITHS.

Fig Sunday. A nickname for *Palm Sunday, formerly common in Hertfordshire and Northamptonshire, where figs were eaten on this day, because Christ had wanted to eat some when travelling to Jerusalem (Mark 11: 12–14) (Wright and Lones, 1936: i. 58–9).

fingernails. The little white specks, sometimes seen on the nails of the left hand, signify gifts on the thumb; friends on the first finger; foes on the second; lovers on the third; a journey to be undertaken on the fourth. This meaning given to specks on the nails was so widely known that many people called the marks 'gifts' or 'presents'. The first documentary evidence for the belief occurs in Ben Jonson's play *The Alchemist* ((1610, I. iii) and Sir Thomas Browne was sceptical about it as one of his 'vulgar errors' (*Pseudodoxia Epidemica* (1672 edn.), book 5, chapter 23). The belief was still being reported at least as late as the 1960s. Other meanings have been given to the marks, however. In *Melton's *Astrologaster* ((1620), 45), he writes '. . . to have yellow speckles on the nailes of ones hand is a great signe of death'.

A widely reported and relatively constant belief about babies' nails is that you must not cut them before the child is a year old, the mother must bite them off to keep them short. If you ignore this advice, the child will grow up to be a thief. The first written references occur in the mid-19th century (e.g. *Denham Tracts*, 1895: ii. 24) and it was still being reported in the 1980s. A slightly different idea was noted from a Dorset woman and included in *N&Q* (1s:4 (1851), 54): she was seen cutting her children's nails over an open Bible, and was asked why, 'I always, when I cut the nails of my children, let the cuttings fall on the open Bible, that they may grow up to be honest. They will never steal, if the nails are cut over the Bible!'

Removable parts of the body such as *hair and fingernails are particularly useful for anyone wishing to harm you with any form of *witchcraft and should therefore be disposed of carefully. On the other hand, their intimate association with the person means they are also useful in cures. The idea that it matters when you cut your nails is also as old as the 16th century. Most authorities agree that Monday is the best day, and Friday and Sunday should be avoided at all costs. Some have a useful rhyme such as the following from East Anglia:

Cut them on Monday, you cut them for health
Cut them on Tuesday, you cut them for wealth
Cut them on Wednesday, you cut them for news
Cut them on Thursday, a new pair of shoes
Cut them on Friday, you cut them for sorrow
Cut them on Saturday, see your true-love tomorrow
Cut them on Sunday, the devil will be with you all
  the week

(Forby, 1830: 411)

Nails should also be cut at the waning of the *moon, and at sea should only be pared during a storm (otherwise it will cause one).

See also: *FINGERS; *HAIR.

Opie and Tatem, 1989: 273–6; Lean, 1903: ii. 267–8, 292–3 (and others).

fingers. Traditionally, different fingers had different attributes and uses. The forefinger was considered 'poisonous' and therefore should never be used for applying ointment to a cut or bruise; in contrast, the ring finger, especially that of the left hand, was known in the 15th century as 'leche man', i.e. 'doctor', since doctors always used it to stir, taste, and apply their medicines. These ideas were still remembered in 19th-century Somerset: 'The ring-finger, stroked along any sore or wound, will soon heal it. All the other fingers are poisonous, especially the forefinger' (*N&Q* 1s:7 (1853), 152). Another old idea, still current, is that a vein runs straight from this finger to the heart, and that that is why engagement and wedding *rings are worn there.

The little finger, rarely functioning alone for practical purposes, is used in a playful ritual: when two people say the same thing simultaneously, they link little fingers and make a wish. Among children in the 1950s, when two have had an argument they would link little fingers and shake their hands up and down, chanting:

Make up, make up, never do it again,
If you do, you'll get the cane.

Another children's custom, of the 19th century, was for boys to pinch the little finger of girls, and vice versa; if they screamed, it meant they couldn't keep a secret—and as boys pinched harder than girls, it followed that girls couldn't keep secrets (*N&Q* 5s:6 (1876), 108, 214, 337–8).

Finger gestures currently in use include *crossing fingers for luck or to avert bad luck; thumbing one's nose (also called *cocking a snook or 'five finger salute') as mockery, usually among children; thumbs up for approval, or to indicate that all is well; the defiant, sexually insulting *V-sign ('two-finger salute'); the more strongly obscene raising of the middle finger, of American origin. Two gestures known in Elizabethan England were 'the fig', in which the thumb is thrust between clenched fingers as a sexual insult, and 'the horns', made by extending the forefinger and little finger while clenching the rest, as a taunt to a cuckold. Nobody now uses them here, but little pendants showing hands in these positions can be bought as lucky *charms, because in parts of Europe the 'fig' and 'horns' gestures are used not only as insults but to avert the evil eye and bad luck.

See also *FINGERNAILS, *HAND, *THUMBS.

Opie and Tatem, 1989: 149.

fire (domestic). The domestic fire has attracted a bewildering number of beliefs, and most of the standard folklore collections include several, which are often contradictory and are normally concerned with the fire's behaviour being lucky or unlucky, or with divination. Opie and Tatem list nine superstitions about the fire's behaviour, although only one or two of them date from before the 19th century. If you discover the fire still alight from the night before, you will hear of an illness (Shropshire/Staffordshire servant-maid, quoted in *N&Q* 6s:9 (1884), 137), but fire burning on one side of the grate only could be considered even worse: '... all the fires in the house burnt only one side of the grate, which she considered a sure sign that a death would shortly occur in the family' (Essex: *N&Q* 8s:9 (1896), 225). Nevertheless, in Herefordshire this could mean a wedding (Leather, 1912: 87).

An extremely widespread practice reported regularly from the 18th to the later 20th centuries, was to place a poker against the bars of the fire-grate to induce the fire to burn briskly. It was widely stated that the poker and top bar of the grate made a cross which kept the devil (or other interfering forces) away from the fire. Rationalists tried to argue that the poker helped to cause a beneficial draught. You must not poke someone else's fire unless you have known them for seven years—first reported in 1880, but a writer in 1938 claimed to have known it for 70 years, and added the rider 'or been drunk with him three times' (*N&Q* 174 (1938), 142). 'If a servant be trying to light a fire and it will not burn, she will frequently say "Oh dear, my young man's in a temper!" If by chance the fire-irons are all at one end of the fender it is a sign of a quarrel' (Leather, 1912: 87). Approaching the middle of the 20th century, fires could still be problematic for domestic staff:

The housemaid watches a newly-lighted fire and does all she can to prevent it parting in the centre. For should it happen that the embers suddenly break into two parts, it portends she will lose her situation. She also believes that if a fire roars it is the sign of a row in the house, while there is a somewhat similar saying about a fire—'When it burns without blowing, You'll have company without knowing'. (Igglesden, c.1932: 174)

One of the few beliefs which can be shown to be older is the idea that if the fire collapses towards an observer, it means he/she will suffer someone's anger, which Opie and Tatem report from 1668. Another sign that a stranger is coming is the presence of flakes of soot on the bars of the grate, first mentioned in the mid-18th century. Much older and more widespread is the belief that fire should not be taken out of the house—to be avoided at any time, but particularly bad at certain seasons such as *Christmas and *New Year. Opie and Tatem start their list of examples with a 7th-century Irish manuscript, and a late 12th-century source, and it was still being reported well into the 20th century.

Opie and Tatem, 1989: 150–6, 313.

firedrake. This word, literally meaning 'fiery *dragon' in Old and Middle English, was used in Elizabethan times for streaks of fire cross-ing the sky (i.e. meteorites), and sometimes also for the *Will-o'-the-Wisp or *corpse candle.

fires (accidental). Various objects were thought to have magic power to preserve a house from fire if hung from the rafters or placed in the roofing, for example eggs laid on *Ascension Day and a hawthorn twig gathered on the same day, and buns baked on *Good Friday. *Houseleeks growing on the roof were protective too. As one of the dangers of thunderstorms is that lightning may strike a building and set it alight, the various plants and objects listed as warding off *thunder are also, indirectly, protections against certain types of fire.

first footing, see *NEW YEAR.

fish falls and frog showers. For nearly 2,000 years, and from nearly every part of the world, there have been reports of showers of rain which contained large quantities of live frogs, fish, or other creatures, and the reports still occur with quite startling regularity. An early reference to Weymouth in *The Travels of Peter Mundy in Europe and Asia, Volume 3 part 1: 1634–1637* ((1919), 10–11) concerns, unusually, small snails, and implies that it was a regular occurrence and that the people found them in their hats because they 'dropp out of the ayre', and Reginald *Scot (1584: book 13, chapter 18) provides another early English reference. Numerous other writers mention the subject, including Izaac Walton (*Compleat Angler* (1653)) and Samuel Pepys (*Diary*, 23 May 1661). The phenomena could be taken as more than a simple wonder, as a Restoration newspaper rails against the 'lying faction' who report false 'prodigies' such as that 'in several places in England it lately rained blood, frogs and other animals . . .' (*Kingdom's Intelligencer* (30 Dec. 1661), quoted in Picard, 1997: 270). Most are second hand, but sometimes the account is from an eyewitness (*N&Q* 8s:6 (1894), 191). Various explanations have been put forward, including an early belief that the sun draws up frogspawn, which then hatches in the clouds. Modern theories usually involve some sort of localized waterspout or whirlwind which sucks up the contents of a pond or other body of water and deposits them at a distance, but this still leaves many questions unanswered. *Forteans revel in this type of phenomenon: widely reported, suitably mysterious, on the edge of science but not (yet) accepted by the scientific establishment. We can thus claim fish falls, and related phenomena, as still in the realms of folklore, at least for the time being.

Michell and Rickard, 1977: 12–19; Michell and Rickard, 1982: 72–88; N&Q 8s:6 (1894) 104–5, 189–91, 395; 8s:7 (1894), 437, 493.

fishing industry. Two of the main reasons usually cited as favourable to the growth of superstition are dangerous working conditions and the degree on which success/failure is affected by 'luck' rather than skill. Fishing has clearly fulfilled both these criteria, in abundance, for centuries, and even the introduction of new technologies has not altered the basic nature of the business, and fishing communities have a reputation for being extremely superstitious. Beliefs clustered around various parts of the life, both on shore and at sea, but at the risk of stating the obvious, it must be stressed that not all fishermen were or are superstitious, or to the same degree. In addition, none of the beliefs cited are unique to the fishing community, they all turn up in some guise or other in other trades or communities, particularly, it seems, in the mining industry.

Fishermen had to be particularly careful what happened to them on their way down to the boat. It was considered unlucky for a seaman to meet a woman on his way to the quay, few fishermen would allow a woman on board a ship, and they were not allowed down to the quay to see the boats off (although they could be there to welcome them home). It was also bad to meet a clergyman or see a drowned animal. Seeing a rabbit, hare, or pig was unlucky, as was a squinting person, but meeting a *hunchback or an idiot is lucky. Despite these dangers, it was very unlucky to turn back after you had set off from home—even looking back was avoided.

Sailing on a *Friday was avoided if possible, and beginning a voyage on *Friday the Thirteenth was out of the question. But the worst day of all, was *Holy Innocents Day (28 December), which is not surprising considering the story of the slaughter of innocent children after which it is named. While at sea there were numerous prohibitions to be considered. Talking in plain terms about the size of a catch was to be avoided as tempting fate (compare *counting), and many words were avoided altogether. One of the strongest

taboos was the word 'pig', and fishermen and their families would go to extraordinary lengths to avoid saying the actual word. They would use synonyms such as 'porker', or spell it out, but no remotely satisfying suggestion for an origin for this has been advanced. Paradoxically, Gill points out that many families in fishing areas actually kept pigs. The word was taboo, no part of a pig should be taken on board, to see a pig on the way to sailing was unlucky, but the animal itself on shore was not forbidden or even feared.

Carrying a corpse on board ship was avoided if at all possible, and if it was absolutely necessary it had to lie across the ship (not end on) and should leave the ship before any of the crew. *Coins figure in more than one custom. All new vessels had to have a coin beneath the mast, and many fishermen would cut a slit in the cork floats on a net and insert a coin to pay for their catch. Most ships had a *horseshoe nailed to the mast, and a knife stuck into a mast would encourage a fair wind.

Many seamen share the belief with the general population that possession of a child' *caul will protect you from drowning, and they naturally have a vested interest in possessing one. There was a curious tendency in past times for seamen to be unable to swim. This was perhaps based on an idea that to learn would be to tempt fate, or that if the sea wants to take you it will not be cheated and there is nothing you can do to prevent it.

That *whistling can be very dangerous is a belief shared with other professions. At sea it was believed that it conjured up a wind, of which much could be disastrous, although in sailing days a little judicious whistling might be necessary if you were becalmed. There was also a hint that whistling attracted the attention of unwelcome forces which were best left alone. A whistling woman was a particular anathema. Seamen were careful not to put certain items upside down—a bowl or hatch cover, for example—as this would cause a boat somewhere to capsize. On shore or at sea, the ringing sound made by a *glass accidentally knocked must be stopped immediately or another sailor would be washed overboard.

It was not only the fishermen themselves who were circumscribed by superstition, but their families at home had to be careful in certain actions. Wives must never *wash the man's clothes on sailing day (or other inauspicious days such as New Year's Day) or she will 'wash him overboard', families must not wave him goodbye, or even say anything as final as 'goodbye'. Do not point to ships, or count them, or watch them sail out of sight, and so on. In fishing communities, these worries were well understood, and women would be as careful to avoid meeting a seaman as he would to meet them.

It is still considered extremely unwise to change the name of a boat, as it brings bad luck to the vessel and its crew. R. L. Stevenson's novel *Treasure Island* ((1881), chapter 11) is the first to mention the idea, but, as Gill points out, it is far from uncommon for fishing trawlers to undergo a name-change. Ships which are bought second-hand by other companies, and whole fleets which were taken over, have regularly had their names changed, as did ships which were requisitioned in the two world wars. Similarly, some companies use the same name for a succession of vessels. Nevertheless, the seamen themselves dislike the practice, and often blame a name-change for subsequent ill luck (Opie and Tatem, 1989: 33; Igglesden, *c*.1932: 116–19).

On a lighter note, the mackerel fishermen of Sussex, and their families, had a celebratory feast every year on the day the season started, which was often *May Day or just before. The celebration was called 'Bendin' in', which may refer to the custom of bending the nets or may be a corruption of the word Benediction (see, for example, Simpson, 1973:117–18). There are various records from round the country of the sea, the boats, the men, the fish, etc., being blessed at the beginning of the fishing season. Another regular feature is for the fishing boats to be decorated with *garlands.

See also *SEAFARING CUSTOMS AND BELIEFS.

Christina Hole, *Folklore* 78 (1967), 184–9; Shaw Jeffrey, *Whitby Lore and Legend* (enlarged edn., 1923), 137–43; Gill, 1993.

fivestones. Under a variety of names and a fair degree of difference in the basic equipment required, fivestones has a definite claim to date back at least to Ancient Greece and Rome, and more than likely to Ancient Egypt. There is probably no country in the world that does not have a version, and there is also indication that they were used for adult gambling (similar to dice-throwing) and even divination. The original game used knucklebones or astragalus, the ankle bone of a cloven-hoofed animal, or pebbles, but artificial ones have been made out of just about every possible material, including pottery, metal, stone, chalk, wood, and plastic. The game has several features which have ensured its continuance. The equipment is basic, cheap, and extremely portable, it can be played at a range of levels from beginner to expert, it can be played solo or competitively by two or more players. The true heart of the game, upon which all variations are built, is that the player holds the stones in his/her hand, throws them up, turns the hand over and catches as many as possible on the back of the hand. In many cultures, and at various times, it has been considered a game mainly for females, but this is certainly not the case in all places or throughout its history. In England, since about the 1930s, there have been two basic variations available. Terminology varies, but one is Fivestones—five pale-coloured cubes made of a chalky substance, or wood—while the other is Jacks—a number of metal star-shaped objects, with a rubber ball. Main local names are: Bobber and Kibs, Chucks, Chuckies, Clinks, Dibs, Dabs, Fivestones, Gobs, Jacks, Jinks, Snobs.

Opie and Opie, 1997: 56–72; Gomme, 1894: i. 122–9.

floral dance, see *HELSTON FURRY DAY.

flowers. Nowadays, flowers play an important role in social behaviour, and are commercially available all year; they are gifts expressing affection, gratitude, celebration, congratulation, mourning, or apology, and are used as decoration at both personal and public events. *Weddings and *funerals would be inconceivable without them.

The use of flowers in medieval and Tudor times is well documented, especially in courtly circles, where fashionable men and women wore chaplets of leaves and flowers on their heads (a custom suriving in the modern bridal wreath, and in daisy chains). Scented flowers or petals were strewn on floors, together with herbs and rushes, and carried in processions; strewing was a feature at both weddings and funerals. Churches were garlanded with fresh greenery and flowers at summer festivals, as with *evergreens at other seasons, and clergy sometimes wore wreaths—in 1405 the Bishop of London wore a chaplet of red roses in St Paul's for the feast of that saint (Goody, 1993: 155).

The link between flowers and religious ceremonies was broken at the Reformation. From the 16th to the mid-19th centuries there were no flowers in churches, and mourners carried *rosemary or *rue, not blossoms, at funerals. More research is needed to show when, and by what stages, they returned; in 1884 one writer referred to a growing 'pretty custom of sending wreaths for the coffins of deceased friends', encouraged by the example of Queen Victoria and the Royal Family (Vickery, 1995: 144–5). Probably there were local variations; Charlotte Burne said that in north Shropshire it had long been customary to put roses and wallflowers inside the coffin, but that laying wreaths visibly on top of it, and then on the grave, had only begun in the 1870s (Burne, 1883: 299). Writing of Cheshire, Fletcher Moss is even more precise: 'In my memory it was considered heathenish to put flowers on graves or in them, and I believe it was on my father's grave, in December 1867, that the Rector of Didsbury first consented to having plants or flowers planted on a grave' (Moss, 1898: 18–19).

Towards the end of the Victorian period, 'floral tributes' in fancy shapes were introduced, and are still made; some are symbolic, such as a broken column or the gates of Heaven, but most represent things associated with the deceased, from a teddy bear to a racing car, or spell a name. Nowadays, mourners sometimes place an individual flower on the coffin during the funeral service. It is common to put flowers on graves on the anniversary of death, and at *Christmas, *Mothering Sunday, or *Easter; to plant a rose bush in the crematorium grounds; and to leave bouquets as *memorials at the sites of fatal accidents or murders.

The traditional festivals of spring and summer generally involve greenery and flowers; the entries for *May Day, *maypoles, *Abbotsbury Garland, *Castleton Garland, *rushbearing, and *well-dressing describe some of the ways they are used, and many other references will be found throughout this book. Nowadays the blossoms are mostly garden grown, but in earlier times gathering them in woods and fields was itself part of the fun.

Until the Second World War, wild flowers featured largely in the *display customs of country children, notably the *May garlands, and in their games, for example making *cowslip balls, *daisy chains, *dandelion clocks— indeed, as a (male) correspondent wrote to N&Q in 1901:

We made chains of daisies, buttercups, 'dandies', daffadowndillies, haws, cankers, crab-apples, 'slaws', cob-nuts, and many other things. We decorated pet lambs and each other with these chains, which were often combinations of flowers, stalks, and berries. Buttercups and daisies were the favourites, dandelions being shunned somewhat ... (N&Q 9s:8 (1901), 70)

However, many wild flowers were thought to cause bad luck, sickness, or death if they were brought indoors, and children were discouraged from picking them; a survey organized by Roy Vickery in 1982–4 found that some 70 species had this reputation. There is also a widespread modern taboo on having red and white flowers together in a vase without any of another colour, especially in a hospital; it is said to be an omen of death.

Vickery, 1995 and 1985; Tony Walter, Folklore 107 (1996), 106–7. For an international perspective, see Goody, 1993.

FLS News. A newsletter for members of the *Folklore Society, begun in 1985 and appearing twice a year. It contains many notes and queries.

flying. Magical flying is featured in stories about *fairies, *wizards, and *witches, but differently in each case. Fairies, who in authentic folklore are never imagined as winged, were generally thought of as sweeping along in the wind by their innate power, but are sometimes said to utter the magic words 'Horse and Hattock!', to need a magic cap, or to ride on straws, sticks, or plant-stems. Wizards, such as *Jack o' Kent, achieve flight simply by forcing the Devil to carry them on his back, for the point of such tales is to show the hero domineering over evil beings. But witches, both in legend and in real-life trials, were thought to fly by sitting on some household object such as a broom, pitchfork, hurdle, or pig-trough, having smeared it (or themselves) with magic ointment. According to Francis Bacon's Silva Sylvarum (1608), it was made from the fat of children's corpses, mixed with the juices of sleep-inducing plants, 'Hen-Bane, Hemlock, Mandrake, Moonshade (or rather Nightshade), Tobacco, Opium, Poplar-leaves, etc.' There are many such recipes; all include at least one highly poisonous, soporific, and hallucinogenic plant. It has been repeatedly noted by commentators that these ingredients, absorbed through the skin, could cause hallucinations.

foliate head. An ornamental motif common in sculpture and woodcarvings in churches from the Norman and Gothic periods is a male head with leafy sprays growing from its mouth and/or eyes, or partially covered by leaves, like a man peering out from a bush. Art historians call this a foliate head; in English over the last twenty years it has been constantly called a *Green Man, a term first applied to it by Lady Raglan in 1939, whose authentic meaning was quite different.

Examples are very numerous in England, and no complete listing exists, though several researchers are hoping to compile one (*FLS News* 23, 24, 25 (1996-7)); they are found on arches, capitals, corbels, roof bosses, choir-stalls, misericords, chancel screens—anywhere where rich ornament was desired, and secular or humorous themes allowed. Usually they are just one among many non-religious motifs in a decorative scheme; for example, on the doorway of Kilpeck Church (Herefordshire), the choir-stalls of Winchester Cathedral, the passage to the chapter-house at York Minster, and many others.

Their history is well established. They reached England early in the 12th century from France, as part of a repertoire of grotesque figures in the style called 'Romanesque' on the Continent and 'Norman' in England; typical examples can be seen at Kilpeck (Herefordshire) and Iffley (Oxfordshire). The continental Romanesque foliate heads, though stylized and distorted, were ultimately derived from the dignified leaf-masks of late Roman art, representing gods and supernatural beings (Oceanus, Silenus, Dryads, etc.). When Gothic style replaced Norman, foliate heads became ever more varied, subtle, and realistic, some being strikingly beautiful, while others had the glaring eyes and snarling mouths of demons; identifiable leaves were shown, with oak, hawthorn and ivy being particularly favoured. The carvings thus combined two favourite subjects of medieval artists, foliage and the human face, and were very popular from the 13th to the 15th centuries.

Interpretation is far more problematic than history. Medieval writers expound the moral and religious symbolism of many art motifs in considerable detail, but only one ascribes a moral meaning to greenery—the theologian Rabanus Maurus (784–856) said leafy sprays symbolized fleshly lusts and depraved men heading for damnation, and cited texts from Ezekiel and Job in support (Basford, 1978: 12). The heads themselves vary greatly in expression; some look serene, others gloomy, angry, threatening, mocking, sick, or anguished, and some also stick out their tongues. It is most unlikely that they all conveyed the same meaning, and no source ascribes any name to them. Throughout Britain, their context has been distorted by the Protestant destruction of the sacred images to which they were originally subordinated. For example, a foliate head supporting the pedestal of a saint's statue might have been 'read' as meaning that holiness is achieved by subduing mere nature; now that the head alone survives, it assumes an independent importance its carver never intended.

Modern theories begin with Lady Raglan's literalist view that medieval artists only drew what they had seen in real life—in this case, she claimed, a leaf-clad mummer like a *Jack-in-the-Green enacting a spring fertility ritual. She is followed by Sheridan and Ross (1975) who see secretly surviving paganism as the explanation, not only for this but for many motifs in medieval art; this idea, though it lacks supporting evidence and contradicts the known history of the motif, is currently the favourite among popular writers and neo-pagans.

Others think symbolism more likely. Weir and Jerman suggest that early Romanesque 'foliage-spewers' represented sins of speech, but that also, in certain positions such as doorways, some may have been regarded as guardians of the building; Gothic ones may have been affected by folkloric beliefs about woodland spirits (Weir and Jerman, 1986: 106, 148-50). Basford (1978: 12, 19) is chiefly struck by the devilish features of some heads, and the air of grief or sinister foreboding on others; she says the latter symbolize how death rules the natural, as opposed to the spiritual, world—a major theme in medieval thought. Anderson (1990) also stresses nature, but in an optimistic ecological sense, where death is always followed by rebirth, and humanity's union with nature is a desirable goal.

See also *GREEN MAN.

The initiating paper is Lady Raglan, *Folk-Lore* 50 (1939), 45–57. For extensive discussion, see Basford, 1978/1996; Weir and Jerman, 1986; Anderson, 1990; Sheridan and Ross, 1975. Recent comments include Bob Trubshaw, *At the Edge* 4 (1996), 25-8; contributions to *FLS News* 23, 24, 25 (1996–7); Brandon S. Centerwall, *Folklore* 108 (1997), 25–34.

folk dance, see *DANCE.

Folk Life. Launched in 1963, *Folk Life* is the journal of the *Society for Folk Life Studies, and since 1973 has borne the subtitle 'A Journal of Ethnological Studies'. *Folk Life* covers all parts of the British Isles, as well as including some articles from abroad, and many of its contributors are museum professionals. Although the core of most volumes concentrates on the physical side of traditional life; crafts, buildings, tools, costume, farming techniques, transport, and domestic life, for example, the journal has also included many important articles on less tangible folklore topics such as custom, narrative, and medicine, and it remains one of the few essential journals for British folklorists to read. From its inception, a feature of the journal has been its excellent photographs and other illustrations. Editors: J. Geraint Jenkins (1963–79), William Linnard (1980–90), Roy Brigden (1991–).

Folk Life Society, see *SOCIETY FOR FOLK LIFE STUDIES.

Folk-Lore Journal. The journal published by the *Folk-Lore Society from 1883 to 1889 (seven volumes altogether), replacing *Folk-Lore Record* and in turn replaced by *Folk-Lore.

Folk-Lore Record. The first journal published by the *Folk-Lore Society, and thus the first journal in the world to be devoted solely to the subject. *Folk-Lore Record* ran for five volumes, 1878 to 1882. It was succeeded by the *Folk-Lore Journal, and later by *Folk-Lore* and *Folklore.

Folklore Society. The Folk-Lore Society was founded in January 1878 (it kept the hyphen till 1968), and was thus the first society in the world devoted to the subject. There had been protracted correspondence in *N&Q* in 1876–7, initiated by Eliza *Gutch ('St Swithin'), calling for such a body to be formed. After some hesitation over the definition of its remit, a group of already well-known figures, including W. J. *Thoms and George Laurence *Gomme, took up the challenge and announced the formation of the Society (with 107 members); its journal, *The *Folk-Lore Record*, was launched in February 1879. In the first issue, the Society's object was defined as 'The preservation and publication of Popular Traditions, Legendary Ballads, Local Proverbial Sayings, Superstitions and Old Customs (British and foreign) and all subjects relating to them' (*Folk-Lore Record* 1 (1878), p. ix). The music, dancing, and

material culture excluded from this official agenda nevertheless had a place in the personal work of some members, and sometimes in the pages of the journal; eventually they became the remit of the *English Folk Dance Society, the *Folk-Song Society, and the *Society for Folk Life Studies.

Initially, the Society's aim was to publish books and a journal; members met only once a year, the work being carried on by a Council which met at intervals. There were occasional lectures in the 1880s, more regular ones from the 1890s onwards. For the first 30 years of its existence, the Society was a forum for intellectual discussion between well-known scholars, who debated their theories hotly, even acrimoniously, in its publications and meetings, which were often reported in the daily and weekly press. Many debates concerned very broad issues, approached in a scientific spirit: the origin of mythology, the relationship between folklore and the minds and lives of primitive humanity, and/or contemporary 'savages', the cultural diffusion of traditions. The goal was, and long remained to cover the topic worldwide, and over the whole span of history. One high point of this first phase was the Society's hosting of the International Folk-Lore Congress of 1891.

Large publication programmes were launched, resulting in many books of lasting value. Work began on several ambitious schemes: to collect all English proverbs and collate them with their foreign analogues; to classify and analyse all British 'popular customs and superstitions'; to collect folktales, on a worldwide scale, and tabulate them according to their main plots and incidental traits; Gomme's plan for a 'Dictionary of British Folk Lore'. Most of these wide-ranging plans remained unfinished, for lack of manpower and/or money. With hindsight, one can see it might have been wiser to focus research more sharply on Britain itself, but the Society's policy had always been to view its subject from an international perspective, not an insular one.

As the 20th century dawned, the Society began to lose impetus as founder members died or retired, and the Great War killed many who might have replaced them. After 1918 professional academics turned more to the new subjects of anthropology and sociology which were gaining the foothold in universities which folklore had failed to achieve. Matters cannot have been helped by the fact that the most prominent 'heavyweight' now associated with the Society was *Frazer, whose old-fashioned methods were disapproved of by professional anthropologists. Nevertheless, a Committee (led first by Burne, then by Hartland, then by A. R. Wright) worked throughout the war and on into the 1920s and 1930s on a major undertaking begun in 1910, a survey of British *calendar customs to update *Brand; this was eventually published in eight volumes between 1938 and 1946, covering England, Scotland, Man, and Orkney and Shetland.

Between the wars, the FLS carried on as a minor learned society consisting largely of amateurs, though still attracting individual academics from diverse fields (e.g. E. O. James and S. H. Hooke, experts on the history of religions, and the Modern Greek scholar R. M. Dawkins). *Folk-lore* continued to be published, and though much of the theoretical basis for its contents at this period is questionable, it still provided a wealth of primary detail, as well as many sound and stimulating articles. But the amateurishness showed; many contributors pursued pet topics of their own, without reference to what others were doing even in this country, let alone abroad; others uncritically echoed dubious theories of the previous generation, especially Frazer's on *fertility. Folklore study in England gradually gathered a negative reputation for unsound reasoning, lack of intellectual rigour, ahistorical assumptions, and general pottiness.

The Second World War brought a major logistic and financial crisis. That the Society survived at all, and continued to produce its journal, albeit much reduced in size, is due to a very small group of enthusiasts who gave their time and money to keep it afloat. Unfortunately this led to a concentration of power in the hands of a well-meaning, financially generous, but domineering and blinkered Treasurer-cum-Secretary, Mrs Lake Barnett, who contrived to block virtually all suggestions for growth and new undertakings throughout the 1950s and early 1960s.

Meanwhile, folklore in general was enjoying a revival of public interest, in part linked to the folk *song and *dance revivals. New trends in scholarship emerged from the 1950s onwards; in particular, the work of Iona and Peter *Opie opened fresh fields, switching attention to the young, and to the present day; that of Katharine *Briggs combined literary and folkloric expertise; that of E. C. Cawte and Alex *Helm brought factual accuracy to the study of folk drama and guising. A new era for the Folklore Society opened in 1967, when a 'revolution' on its Council led to Katharine Briggs becoming President and Venetia Newall Secretary; together, they worked vigorously with the support of an efficient Committee to re-establish the book publications programme, renew links with scholars in America and Europe, reinstate regular conferences, and update the Society's image by becoming more visibly active. A definite trend from the 1970s onwards was the increased interest members showed in living British traditions, and in modern forms of folklore such as *contemporary legend. Publications and conferences have reflected this well.

The Society's Library and Archives, which began as a single bookcase in 1892, has grown into an excellent resource for the study of folklore, past and present; it contains many volumes and journals otherwise unobtainable in this country. Successive Editors of the journal *Folklore* have set higher standards for contributors, and it is now a respected scholarly publication, while the newsletter *FLS News* provides a lively informal vehicle for the exchange of information and material. Publication of books and pamphlets has once again been active in recent years.

The office and reference library are at The Warburg Institute, Woburn Square, London, WC1H 0AB (Tel.: 020 7862 8564); the lending library and archives are at University College, Gower Street, London WC1E 6BT.

Dorson, 1968; A. R. Wright, *Folk-Lore* 39 (1928), 15–38; Allan Gomme, *Folk-Lore* 63 (1952), 1–18; Sona Rosa Burstein, *Folklore* 69 (1958), 73–92; E. O. James, *Folklore* 70 (1959), 382–94; Katharine M. Briggs, in *Animals in Folklore*, ed. Hilda R. Ellis Davidson and W. M. S. Russell (1978), 4–20; J. R. Porter, in *Folklore Studies in the 20th Century*, ed. Venetia Newall (1978): 1–13; Davidson, 1986: 143–7; *Folklore* 98 (1987), 123–30.

Folklore (the journal). The early history of the Folklore Society's periodical was summarized by Allan Gomme (*Folk-Lore* 63 (1952), 6–7). Initially it appeared annually as *The *Folk-Lore Record* (1879–82); then monthly as *The *Folk-Lore Journal* (1883–4), a method entailing 'a great deal of effort and no very marked success'; then quarterly, still as *The Folk-Lore Journal* until 1890, when the simple title *Folk-Lore* was adopted, at the suggestion of Joseph *Jacobs (the hyphen was dropped in 1958). During the Second World War it came close to extinction, but survived thanks to the devoted work of E. O. James; despite various financial crises, it regained its pre-war size. Publication changed from quarterly to twice-yearly in 1976, then annual in 1993; in 2000 it returned to two issues per year. Jacobs was Editor from 1890 to 1893, after which responsibility was shared by a Publications Committee. From 1899, the succession runs: Charlotte *Burne, 1899–1908; A. R. *Wright, 1909–14; W. Crooke, 1915–23; A. R. Wright, 1924–31; E. O. James, 1932–55; Christina *Hole, 1956–78; Jacqueline Simpson, 1979–93; Gillian Bennett, 1994– .

The journal, like the Society, took the whole of folklore worldwide as its remit, and also explored adjacent disciplines for material which might have a bearing on it. Consequently, it printed many papers discussing comparative religion and myths, supernatural themes in ancient and medieval literatures, and anthropology, thus reflecting the very diverse interests of its readers. At the same time, it was always a place where factual accounts of newly discovered items, large or small, could be permanently recorded; there are many such contributions, which have become increasingly valuable as time goes by, whereas some of the more speculative discussions are now only of historical interest. The diversity of the contributors, and the fact that folklore was not a university subject, meant that the journal never became dominated by a single school of thought, methodology, jargon, or interpretative theory; it was always addressed to a scholarly but non-specialized readership.

In 1986 a survey showed that most individual members of the Folklore Society found exotic anthropological material remote from their concerns, and wished *Folklore* to concentrate on British traditions, and on European or North American material which offered closely relevant contexts or parallels; it seemed probable that the needs of those reading it through academic libraries would be similar. A shift of emphasis duly occurred, but editorial policy remains broad-based, and has recently been strengthened by setting up an International Advisory Board.

Cumulative indexes to *Folklore* have been published up to 1992. These are: Wilfred Bonser, *A Bibliography of Folklore* (1961); Wilfred Bonser, *A Bibliography of Folklore for 1958–1967* (1969); Steve Roud and Jacqueline Simpson, *An Index to the Journal Folklore, Vols. 79–103, 1968–1992* (1994). For comments on the history of the journal, see E. O. James, *Folklore* 70 (1959), 382–94; Jacqueline Simpson, *Folklore* 100 (1989), 3–8.

folklore (the word). Writing in *The Athe-* *naeum* on 22 August 1846, the antiquarian W. J. *Thoms invited readers to record 'the manners, customs, observances, superstitions, ballads, proverbs . . . of olden time . . . what we in England designate as Popular Antiquities or Popular Literature (though by-the-by it is more a Lore than a Literature, and would be more aptly described by a good Saxon compound, Folk-Lore—the Lore of the People).' The word thus casually tossed out caught on, and has been adopted into many other languages; its crispness is an advantage, but its implications pose problems. Until recently, 'folk' was not used inclusively, but restricted to lower-class and relatively uneducated rural communities, whose life was thought to be static, untainted by urban sophistication, and thus likely to preserve archaic items. Tradition was defined as information or custom handed on unchanged over many generations; the present was of little interest in itself, only valued as a pointer to the past. 'Lore' too was a restrictive concept; it covered oral genres, beliefs, and behaviour, excluding all that comprises material culture: crafts, tools, working practices, buildings, furnishings, decorative arts, etc.

These points show up plainly in Charlotte Burne's definition in *The Handbook of Folk-Lore* (1913), 1:

The word . . . [is] the generic term under which the traditional Beliefs, Customs, Stories, Songs and Sayings current among backward peoples, or retained by the uncultured classes of more advanced peoples, are comprehended and included. . . . In short, it covers everything which makes part of the mental equipment of the folk as distinguished from their technical skill. It is not the form of the plough which excites the attention of the folklorist, but the rites practised by the ploughman when putting it into the soil . . .

It was not till the 1950s and 1960s that these assumptions were widely questioned in England. The mould was then decisively broken through the work of the *Opies on present-day *child-lore, the discovery of *contemporary legends, and a change of direction among those studying customs and performance genres to take account of their social, economic, and functional aspects.

The present authors see folklore as something voluntarily and informally communicated, created or done by members of a group (which can be of any size, age, or social and educational level); it can circulate through whatever media (oral, written or visual) are available to this group; it has roots in the past, but also present relevance; it usually recurs in many places, in similar but not quite identical form; it has both stable and variable features, and evolves through dynamic adaptation to new circumstances. The essential criterion is the presence of a group whose joint sense of what is right and appropriate shapes the story, performance, or custom—not the rules and teachings of any official body (State or civic authority, Church, school, scientific or scholarly orthodoxy).

Boyes, 1993; Gillian Bennett, *Oral History* 4 (1993), 77–91.

Folk Music Journal. Annual journal of the *English Folk Dance and Song Society from 1965, replacing the *Journal of the English Folk Dance and Song Society*, and the leading British vehicle for the serious discussion of folksong, music, and dance material. Successively edited by Dr Russell Wortley (1965–71), Michael Yates (1972–80), Dr Ian Russell (1981–93), Dr Julia Bishop (1994–7), and Michael Heaney (1997–). The contents of the *Folk Music Journal* reflect a move away from the collectanea approach of its predecessors towards more scholarly articles and reviews; a trend which still continues.

folk-song, see *SONG.

Folk-Song Society. Founded at a meeting of sixteen interested parties in London on 16 May 1898, which included Alice Bertha *Gomme, Kate Lee, A. P. Graves, J. A. Fuller Maitland, and Laura A. Smith. At the Society's formal inaugural meeting on 16 June 1898, Lucy *Broadwood and Frank *Kidson, who would both play a significant role in the Society's development, were added. The Society's 'primary object' was ' . . . the collection and preservation of Folk Songs, Ballads and Tunes, and the publication of such of these as may be advisable'. Meetings were to be held, at which papers would be read and discussed, which would include 'vocal and instrumental illustrations' (Keel, 1948: 111). It should be noticed that from the start the tone of the Society was academic—collection and study, rather than performance and teaching were the objectives. The first four Vice-Presidents chosen—Sir John Stainer, Sir Alexander Mackenzie, Sir Hubert Parry, and Dr Villiers Stanford—demonstrated the intended standing of the new Society in the respectable musical establishment of the late Victorian era.

The Society's annual *Journal* was launched in 1899, and for the rest of the Society's existence it served as the major source of raw material for the folk-song movement. A pattern soon evolved which was adhered to for many years. The proof sheets of the songs chosen for inclusion were circulated to members of the Committee, and their comments invited, and Frank Kidson in particular provided historical information from his own vast library. The journals thus included not only the songs themselves, but important comparative and analytic comments by the collectors themselves and a range of experts, but no unified editorial commentary. As time went on, articles began to appear beside the collections of songs, but they were always in a minority.

Despite its roster of distinguished names, the Society had got off to a somewhat shaky start. Already in 1900 there were discussions on the need to increase the subscription, and by 1904 it had almost ground to a halt. The main problem was the protracted illness, and death in 1904, of the Secretary, Kate Lee, who had been the driving force from the start. In that year, Lucy Broadwood took over as Secretary, Cecil *Sharp and Ralph *Vaughan Williams joined and reinvigorated the Committee, and the Society was set fair for a re-launch and increasing popularity and influence. Folk-song collecting became all the rage for budding English musicians until the outbreak of the First World War, and the membership soon included Percy *Grainger, George *Butterworth, Edward Elgar, and Edvard Grieg amongst others.

Throughout its life, the Society resisted suggestions to change its name to include the words 'English' or 'British', but its journals actually included very little that was not collected in the British Isles, and the bulk of the material was English. Nevertheless, important contributions on Irish, Manx, and Scots song were published from time to time. Until the war, individual members were busy collecting, giving lectures, demonstrations, and concerts, and were active in promoting folk-singing through local music competitions, and so on. The Society itself, however, still had no structure, no unified voice, no Director to speak on its behalf, and could only act as a medium of exchange, not as a driving force. The Society was hit badly by the war, with several of its promising younger men being killed, and its continued existence was only ensured by the unflagging efforts of Kidson, Broadwood, Anne *Gilchrist, and a handful of others.

By the late 1920s, the collecting boom was over, most of the founders and leading figures had died, Sharp (1924), Kidson (1926), Broadwood (1929), and the feeling amongst many of those who were left was that the collecting work had been done—no new songs would be found, only variants. An approach from the *English Folk Dance Society for the Folk-Song Society to join them in *Cecil Sharp House was considered by a joint Committee and, despite some strong reservations voiced by Lady Gomme, the combined *English Folk Dance and Song Society came into being on 31 March 1932.

The leading members of the Folk-Song Society were primarily interested in the tunes of the songs, and this is reflected in the contents of the *Journal*, especially in the earlier years. Tunes were published exactly as they were noted, but texts were often not printed, or only one or two verses would be given. By tacit agreement, if not overt policy, the Society's definition of folk-song was narrow. Hardly anything which had an identifiable author, however far back in time, was accepted for publication in the *Journal*, and 'modal' tunes had a far greater chance of inclusion than others. Nevertheless, the pages of the *Journal* include a vast amount of material on British folk-song which would otherwise not have been published, and it is this which is one of the two main legacies left by the Society. The other is the thread of interest in traditional song which continued into the new English Folk Dance and Song Society, and thereby into the post-war second *revival and through to today.

Frederick Keel, *JEFDSS* 5:3 (1948), 111–26; Wilgus, 1959; Ian Olson, *ED&S* 57:1 (1995), 2–5; E. A. White, *An Index of English Songs Contributed to the Journal of the Folk Song Society* (1951).

folktales. This term can be used either broadly or narrowly. In the broad sense it applies to all prose narratives following traditional storylines, which are told orally, or were so told in previous generations. It thus covers *fairytales, *legends of all types, *memorates, *fables, *tall tales, and humorous anecdotes. The original author is always unknown; in the rare cases where an individual who shaped the current version has been identified, the tellers are unaware of this (e.g. *The Three Bears). Most

tales seem to have been formed by recombining traditional elements ('motifs') and/ or transferring an established plot ('tale-type') from one hero, or one location, to another.

The narrow definition restricts itself to the avowedly fictional narratives in the above list, excluding legends and memorates, since these claim to be true. From an English point of view, this is regrettable, since legends make up a very high proportion of our corpus of traditional narratives and still circulate vigorously, while memorates are a major source for the study of current beliefs.

The basic catalogue of folktales in the narrow sense is *The Types of the Folktale* by Antti Aarne and Stith Thompson (1961); see also Stith Thompson's *The Folktale* (1977). Its system was applied to British material in Baughman, 1966; it is used in the works of Katharine Briggs and other recent British folklorists.

See also *CONTEMPORARY LEGENDS, *FABLES, *LEGENDS, *MEMORATES, *STORYTELLING, *TALL STORIES.

fools. Laughing at stupidity and craziness is a basic, universal form of humour, well represented in English tradition. The language is rich in inventive semi-proverbial phrases to express just how daft someone is, from the medieval jeer that he or she would 'shoe a goose' or 'cut off the branch he's sitting on' to the modern 'he's a couple of sandwiches short of a picnic'; the nonsense world of *nursery rhymes is full of jokes about silly or impossible acts and topsy-turvy situations. Visually, the theme can be recognized in medieval art and sculpture, where grotesque figures pulling faces and/or engaging in undignified or ludicrous actions were surely intended as fools.

Whole communities and ethnic groups have been labelled fools, and made the topic for cycles of jokes; older examples (often called 'noodle' or 'numskull' tales) relate to people from specified villages or rural districts, for example the Men of *Gotham and the Wiltshire *moonrakers, more recent ones to certain immigrant groups, especially the Irish. In some contexts, notably in schools and workplaces, custom allows practical jokes aimed at making people look foolish, and this is especially true on *April Fools' Day.

Until fairly recent times it was socially acceptable to laugh at the behaviour of those born 'simple-minded', at the mad, and at freaks. From medieval times till the reign of

Charles I, there are ample records of fools, jesters, and dwarfs at court and in wealthy households; some of the fools were undoubtedly 'innocent', i.e. half-witted, while others were skilled entertainers, with a repertoire of bawdy and/or slapstick humour and witty repartee lightly masked as 'folly'. 'Jest books', i.e. collections of stock anecdotes about the cleverness (or stupidity) of fools, circulated as popular literature. Some are sheer fiction, such as those about the legendary Marcolf who supposedly disputed with Solomon; others describe real people, such as Henry VII's fool Will Somer, and may contain accurate reminiscences alongside the inventions. As is well known, the professional fool-as-entertainer is also an important figure on the stage, from Elizabethan plays to modern circus clowns and cinema comedians.

See Clouston, 1888; Welsford, 1935; Billington, 1984; Christie Davies, in *Spoken in Jest*, ed. Gillian Bennett (1991), 215–35; Malcolm Jones, *Folklore* 100 (1989), 201–17.

fool's errand, see *APRIL FOOL, *OCCUPATIONAL CUSTOMS.

football. Traditional football games had virtually no rules, no limit on the number of players, and goals, if they existed at all, could be a mile or more apart. In most cases, the opposing 'sides' were drawn from different parts of the town or from different trades. In London, and other big cities, it was specifically a game of the apprentices. Throughout its known history there have been repeated attempts to abolish or modify the custom, and most of the earliest references are concerned with trying to suppress what must have been an already well-established tradition. In the long-drawn-out struggle between the authorities and the players, the former were bound to win in the end, but it took centuries to achieve. The documentary record starts in *c.*1183 with William Fitz Stephen's account, which includes no hint of societal disapproval:

After dinner (at Shrovetide) all the youth of the City goes out into the fields to a much-frequented game of ball. The scholars of each school have their own ball, and almost all the workers of each trade have theirs also in their hands. Elder men and fathers and rich citizens come on horse-back to watch the contests of their juniors, and after their fashion are young again with the young . . . (Fitz Stephen, *c.*1180: 56–7)

Published disapproval started in 1314, when it was prohibited in the City of London, and from then on regular attempts were made to ban it, and Puritan reformers such as Stubbes (1583: 184) inveighed against the game, and the authorities attacked the game on various fronts. Firstly, the popularity of such 'pointless' games drew young men away from other more rational and necessary pursuits, particulary archery, and secondly the violence and lawlessness involved held moral dangers both for the individual and society in general. The third factor was the danger to property and trade which was a potential result of allowing rough, mass sports in narrow streets and city centres. An early casualty was the game at Chester, which was abolished in 1539. Opposition at other places went less smoothly. Throughout the 17th and 18th centuries there are records of particular communities' games coming under increasing pressure and one by one they were suppressed, or modified out of all recognition. In Manchester in 1608 and London in 1615, Worcester in 1743, Bolton in 1790, the pattern was very similar. By the mid-19th century, there was still a number of examples alive and kicking and in each case the custom was hotly contested between the supressors and the players, with a key turning-point coming with the Police Act of 1840. The game at Derby was gone by 1849, Kingston-upon-Thames (Surrey) by 1868, and Dorking (Surrey) by 1909. The Kingston-upon-Thames case is an example of just how difficult it was to reform or suppress a custom until all the influential people in the community united against it. The first attempt to suppress it came in 1799, but the game lasted until 1868.

The origin of the game remains obscure. Although the vast majority of instances took place at *Shrovetide, there seems to have been no formal church involvement. Players from various parts of the country explained that the game started when locals were kicking around the severed head of a Dane (or other invader).

See also *ASHBOURNE, *HALLATON BOTTLE-KICKING, *HAXEY HOOD GAME, *HURLING.

Malcolmson, 1973; Hutton, 1996: 154–7; Hole, 1949: 50–2; Matthew Alexander, 'Shrove Tuesday Football in Surrey', *Surrey Archaeological Collections* 77 (1986), 197–205.

footing. One of the commonest features of *occupational customs, found in many trades, which required a newcomer to a firm, or a colleague ending his apprenticeship, to pay for drinks, or an entertainment for the other workers. Usually called 'paying one's footing' and sometimes referred to as 'foot-ale'. See also *building trade.

Hazlitt, 1905: 242; *EDD*.

Forteans. Forteans are followers of Charles Hoy Fort (1874–1932), an American writer whose books, *The Book of the Damned* (1919), *New Lands* (1923), *Lo!* (1931), and *Wild Talents* (1932), explored the realms of 'strange phenomena' which science could not explain, had declared impossible, or had refused to countenance. A magazine entitled *The News* was launched in Britain in 1973, which changed its name in 1976 to *Fortean Times: The Journal of Strange Phenomena*, and is now the leading periodical in the field, published bi-monthly. A more heavyweight journal, *Fortean Studies*, was launched in 1994, and there have also been a number of books and booklets from the same stable. The Fortean movement includes a wide range of viewpoints, from outright believers to scientific sceptics, and their typical fare includes UFOs, alien abductions, crop circles, sea serpents, dreams, government conspiracies, strange coincidences, mystery animals, ghosts, poltergeists, spirit forces, and so on, and there is clearly a great deal of overlap with contemporary folklore studies, at least in terms of subject-matter if not always in approach.

fortune-telling. The urge to know one's future takes many forms. Children count cherry stones or daisy petals, adults observe *omens and interpret *dreams; formerly, young women performed *love divinations on set nights such as *Halloween or *St Agnes' Eve to find out who they would marry. Fortune-telling, however, involves more complicated systems which require interpretation, either by a paid professional, or by learning from handbooks. *Astrology, palmistry, and numerology were known in the Middle Ages; cheap booklets explaining them were readily available from the 16th to the 20th centuries. The 18th century saw the beginnings of fortune-telling by playing-cards, and by reading *tea leaves and coffee grounds; the late 19th century brought Tarot and crystal-gazing, and the 20th century the I Ching and various newly invented systems using fanciful cards, runic symbols, and so forth. Since the 1960s, interest in such things has greatly increased (Davies, 1999a: 130–42, 246–70).

foundation sacrifice. When bones, or pots presumably once containing food or drink, are found under the foundations of Roman sites in Britain, they are interpreted as ritual offerings to bring luck to a new *building. Other examples come from Anglo-Saxon sites, both before and after the conversion, and the series continues into medieval and early modern times with sporadic finds of animal skulls and bones under doorways, in boundary ditches, built into walls, under bridges, etc. (Merrifield, 1987: 50–7, 116–21, 186). If the object is inside a wall or ceiling space, it is not usually possible to decide whether it was deposited during construction of the building, or later, for example as protection against suspected *witchcraft; *shoes and mummified *cats are the most frequent finds.

See also *HORSES, *HOUSE, *THRESHOLD.

foxgloves. In 1870 the naturalist James Britten launched the theory that 'foxglove' means 'glove of the Little Folks' or fairies, since the flower is called 'witches' thimbles' in North Country dialect, and 'fairy's petticoat' in Cheshire. This pretty whimsey has often been repeated, but reference to the *Oxford English Dictionary* and the *English Dialect Dictionary* shows it to be nonsense. The word is attested from AD 1000 onwards, always as 'fox-' and never as 'folks-'; there are several other plants with 'fox' in their names; in Norway, the flower is called *revbjelde*, 'fox-bell'. Nor is there any instance of 'folk' being used without any defining adjective to mean 'fairies'.

There are few traditions about foxgloves. In north Devon they are said to have sprung up wherever the blood of St Nectan, a locally revered saint, dripped on the ground after he was beheaded; one Staffordshire man stated, in 1917, that 'I don't like them, missus; they mean war. Them foxgloves is soldiers.'

They are one of the few plants whose curative properties have been tested and accepted by orthodox medicine. A scientist named William Withering was asked, in 1775, to examine a herbal drink used in Shropshire to cure dropsy, and correctly identified foxglove leaves as its most effective ingredient. This led to the scientifically controlled use of digitalin to treat various types of heart disease—although, wrongly used, foxgloves can also cause fatal heart failure.

Frazer, Sir James George (1854–1941). An anthropologist who held that all human societies have evolved through similar stages of magical and religious belief. These he established by comparing ancient mythologies with the beliefs and rituals of tribal societies in Africa, Australia, or the Americas, and with recent folk customs—since the latter, he claimed, contained items surviving from earlier stages, albeit corrupted and misunderstood. This non-historical cross-cultural approach was typical of his period; it is now rejected as invalid by anthropologists and folklorists, but its influence can still be seen in many popular works.

Frazer's major book was *The Golden Bough*, on which he worked throughout his life; the first edition (1890) was in two volumes, the second (1900) in three, the third (1911–15) in twelve. Modern readers often use the one-volume abridgement (1922), where the arguments stand out more clearly, stripped of their massive footnotes and many examples; this is a pity, since the data remain valuable even where the interpretations are obsolete.

The Golden Bough was widely acclaimed, and influenced several major poets and novelists in the inter-war years; to the general public, it remains the best-known, and most emotionally persuasive, study of myth and folklore. Frazer launched the idea of a sacred king who had to be killed when he grew old, because his virility was identified with the life-force of the crops; he stressed the importance of the annual cycle of vegetation, and especially cereal crops, which he linked to the myths of dying-and-rising gods in Near Eastern religions; he distinguished usefully between 'imitative' and 'contagious' *magic; he had much to say about taboos, tree-worship, human and animal sacrifice, scapegoats, fire-festivals, and much else. The logical links between these many topics are weak, and the accumulated data sometimes hardly relevant to the theories they are meant to support; his speculations regularly go far beyond what the evidence will bear, and he sometimes adds to the confusion by allowing incompatible interpretations to coexist. But his dramatic ideas and colourful, emotive style were most persuasive, and his influence endures; whenever '*fertility cults' are offered as an explanation of folk custom, an echo of Frazer can be heard.

Ackerman, 1987; Dorson, 1968: 283–8.

Friar Tuck. Companion of *Robin Hood in some sources from 1475 onwards, Tuck may have originally been an independent comic figure based on the medieval stereotype of a disreputable friar—fond of fighting, hunting, and wenching. He is almost certainly the unnamed friar in a play in William Copland's edition of *The Gest of Robin Hood* (1560), who beats Robin in a fight and is invited into the outlaw band, where he is delighted to be given a woman (unnamed, but possibly *Maid Marian):

> She is a trull of trust,
> To serve a frier at his lust,
> A prycker, a prauncer, a tearer of sheets,
> A wagger of ballockes when other men sleeps.

Friar Tuck is also often mentioned as a character in Elizabethan *morris dances, usually linked to Maid Marian.

Dobson and Taylor, 1976: 208–14; Knight, 1994: 61–2, 101–5.

Friday. The belief that Friday is an unlucky day goes back to the Middle Ages, and is widely attested. As early as 1390 Chaucer wrote 'And on a Friday fell all this mischance', and throughout the 18th, 19th, and 20th centuries there are ample references to people thinking this a bad day on which to do business, travel, move house, start a new piece of work, be born, or get married (Opie and Tatem, 1989: 167–9). This is probably an indirect consequence of the old Catholic rule that Fridays are a day for penance. It is still very strong, and has some specifically modern developments, for instance that Friday is now thought to be a day on which many road accidents occur. Similarly, if a car or machine frequently breaks down, it may be said that 'It must have been made on a Friday', though here the implication is not always superstitious; sometimes what is meant is that the workmen, eager for the weekend, were too slapdash.

The night between Friday and Saturday is also significant. Dreams that come then are trustworthy; a current saying runs:

> Friday's dream on Saturday told
> Is bound to come true, be it never so old.

In *David Copperfield* (chapter 1), Dickens says that babies born at *midnight on a Friday night are fated to be unlucky and will be able to see *ghosts; according to Ruth *Tongue, they have even wider powers:

In the early years of this century, old people in West Somerset still firmly believed that children born after midnight on a Friday and before cockcrow could see and talk to ghosts and fairies, and come to no harm. They also had power over black witchcraft, and could cure ailing animals and plants. . . . I have found that the fact that I was myself so born has been an Open Sesame to many carefully guarded secrets. (*Folklore* 69 (1958), 43)

See also *FRIDAY THE THIRTEENTH, *GOOD FRIDAY.

Opie and Tatem, 1989: 71, 125, 167–9.

Friday the thirteenth. The widely current idea that Friday the thirteenth is unlucky is a modern combination of two older beliefs: the medieval fear of *Friday, and a comparatively recent dislike of *thirteen. The latter was first recorded at the end of the 17th century, in the limited context of people sitting at a meal; it became more common in the late 19th century, and especially in the 20th. The two ideas are not found in combination before the beginning of the 20th century, but the reputation of Friday the thirteenth is now thoroughly established, and constantly reinforced by the media.

Opie and Tatem, 1989: 169, where the earliest record of the belief is from *N&Q* in 1913.

frog showers, see *FISH FALLS.

funerals. A great deal is known about English funerary customs through the centuries, both in their religious and their social aspects. Naturally, the picture is fullest for the better-off classes, but since Victorian folklorists were interested in life-cycle customs, certain aspects of lower-class funerals which struck them as archaic or quaint are regularly described, especially for rural districts. Their descriptions, however, are not total; they are apt to omit aspects which, being standard procedure in their own class too, did not by their definition count as *folk*lore, notably the purely religious ritual. Some things often went unmentioned because of their very familiarity, such as the rule that a corpse must be carried feet first, whether inside a coffin or not.

In medieval times, each parish had a burial guild, which supplied bearers to carry the corpse; the coffin, however, was parish property, and the corpse would be buried in its shroud, the coffin being taken back for re-use. After 1552, the *Book of Common Prayer* required the service to take place out in the churchyard, leading to the invention of the lych-gate and the portable bier. Responsibility for organizing the funeral rested with the family, apart of course from the service itself. By mid-Victorian times the middle classes had handed over their arrangements to professional undertakers, but working-class funerals were still basically personal affairs until the 20th century. Despite local variations, the following account in 1914, recalling childhood memories of village life in Derbyshire, can be taken as typical of 19th-century rural custom:

On the day of burial a table was set outside the cottage door, on which were set a bowl of box and yew sprays, a plateful of bread (each slice cut in four), half a cheese, a plateful of plum cake, a bottle of home-made wine, a large jug of beer, and various glasses and wine-glasses—most of the latter, as well as the white table-cover, having been lent by my mother. When the funeral-folk assembled about the door, having been bidden by the 'laying-out woman', the bowl of box and yew sprays was offered round, and each person took a piece. Then a tray of funeral cakes was brought out of the house in packets. Each packet contained two cakes wrapped in white paper, on which was printed a suitable verse of poetry. Each guest, including also the bearers, was presented with a packet.

When this part of the ceremony was over, the table was cleared and the coffin brought out of the house and laid upon it—open, so that friends might take the 'last look'. The funeral man (undertaker) then closed and screwed down the lid, produced from a large box a number of 'weepers and scarves' with which he decked the relations as mourners, and arranged the procession to the grave. As a rule there were two sets of bearers, for the churches were distant, and all the village folk had to walk. After the service each person stepped to the graveside for a last look (a formal matter not to be omitted), and the sprigs of box and yew were dropped on to the coffin. The whole party with the parson (if he was willing) then returned to take tea in the house.

Whilst they were away all the death-tokens had been removed, the windows set open, and the pictures, looking-glasses and furniture stripped of the white cloths with which they had been covered from the time of the 'laying-out' to the departure of the body. The talk at the tea-table was of the dead and others who had predeceased him, and the room was a gossips' rally until the eatables and drinkables were consumed and the company dispersed. In the arrangements there were many variations according to the age, sex, and station of the dead. (*N&Q*, 11s:11 (1914), 296–7).

In this account, the food and drink was displayed before the coffin left the house, recalling an older custom common along the Welsh Border, and in the Midlands and northern counties (especially Yorkshire), where mourners ate around the coffin before setting out for the church. Sweet biscuits, cakes, bread and cheese, wine, and beer were served; a share was sometimes given to the poor, in the house or at the graveside. The custom derives from two pre-Reformation rites: taking Communion at the Requiem Mass, and giving alms to the poor so that they too would pray for the dead. Its continued symbolic importance among Protestants is well attested; in 1671, for instance, a French visitor described how at the funeral of a nobleman in Shrewsbury relatives and friends assembled in the house to hear a funeral oration from a clergyman, during which 'there stood upon the coffin a large pot of wine, out of which everyone drank to the health of the deceased, hoping he might surmount the difficulties he had to encounter in his road to Paradise' (Burne, 1883: 309–10). In Derbyshire in the 1890s it was said that at a funeral 'every drop you drink is a sin which the deceased has committed, you thereby take away the dead man's sins and bear them yourself' (Addy, 1895: 123–4); in Herefordshire around 1910, a man was urged, 'But you must drink, sir. It is like the Sacrament. It is to kill the sins of my sister' (Leather, 1912: 121).

In a simple 'walking funeral', as described above, the bearers were friends and relatives, and chosen, if possible, to reflect the status of the deceased: older people, especially if married, would be carried by married men; unmarried girls by young women (or young bachelors, if the road to the church was a long one); babies and little children by older children in white. They were generally given black gloves, scarves, and hatbands. In more elaborate funerals, a pall (hired from the parish or the undertaker) covered both coffin and coffin-bearers, its hem being held by pall-bearers. Funerals of the wealthy and the nobility were far more lavish; they involved long processions of mourners (at first on foot, later in carriages), increasingly elaborate horse-drawn hearses, displays of black plumes and velvet drapes, richly lined coffins, attendant 'mutes', and so forth. At the opposite end of the scale was the 'pauper's funeral'—a cheap coffin pushed on a hand-cart, as remembered in the children's rhyme:

> Rattle his bones over the stones,
> He's only a pauper whom nobody owns.
>
> (Thomas Noel, "The Pauper's Drive")

An odd but widespread notion, whose origin

has never been explained, was that any path along which a corpse was carried thereby became a public right-of-way. In some localities, there were traditions that the funeral procession must approach the church by a *rightward circuit, or take one particular road rather than another, or pause at specified spots on the way. Gentle rain was welcome, as a token of God's mercy and blessing, but a *storm boded ill for the dead man's soul; so did any untoward accident, for example the coffin slipping, or horses finding it hard to draw the hearse.

During the First World War, public ceremonial at upper- and middle-class funerals was much reduced, and did not reappear thereafter; nevertheless, some close-knit working-class communities in cities kept up lavish Victorian customs, such as the hearse drawn by horses in black canopies, with ostrich plumes on the roof. Press reports and photographs of such funerals still occasionally appear. The use of *flowers has increased, both as professional wreaths at the funeral itself, and as informal tributes at the *grave or roadside *memorial. The post-funeral buffet meal is as important as ever, though now more often held in a hotel or pub than at home.

Cremation has increased sharply since the 1930s, and is now chosen for about 70 per cent of deaths; in many cases it consists of a service in the crematorium chapel rather than in the deceased's own church (if any). Currently, in reaction against the impersonality of traditional funerals and cremations, a trend towards variation and individuality can be seen in, for instance, the choice of music and readings, and the display of objects symbolizing the life of the deceased person. At the Anglican funeral of a morris dancer, his hat lay on the coffin, and the men of his side danced in the aisle (Walter, 1990: 16); during the requiem for a Catholic nun in 1998, the Latin grammar she had used as a teacher was put on the coffin, alongside her Bible and a rose (JS). Other recent developments are the popularity of memorial services some months after the death, to mark the public aspects of a person's career and achievements; funerals for stillborn babies and miscarriages, very different from former attitudes towards the *unbaptized (Walter, 1990: 271–80); and new rituals devised by *Wiccans and other neo-pagan groups.

See also *BEES, *BELLS, *BURIAL, *DEATH,

*FLOWERS, *GRAVES, *MOURNING, *SIN-EATING, *WAKES.

There are many books on upper- and middle-class funerals. They include J. S. Curl, *The Victorian Celebration of Death* (1972); Gittings, 1984; Litten, 1991; Puckle, 1926.

There is no single study of folk customs at funerals, but sections on them appear in most regional books. The current situation is assessed in Walter, 1990.

Furry Dance, see *HELSTON FURRY DAY.

Gabriel Hounds, Ratchets. In northern counties, the name Gabble or Gabriel Ratchets was applied to a strange yelping sound heard in the sky at night, supposedly a death *omen. The name, first recorded around 1665, implies a link with the dogs of the *Wild Hunt, 'ratchet' being an old word for a type of hound. In Cleveland, the explanation given was that 'a gentleman of the olden times was so strangely fond of hunting that, on his deathbed, he ordered his hounds all to be killed and buried at the same time and in the same tomb as himself', and therefore he and they still hunt as ghosts (J. C. Atkinson, *The Gentleman's Magazine* (1866), part II, 189); in Derbyshire, that a squire persisted in hunting on Sundays, and once drove his pack into a church, for which sin he is condemned to ride out on stormy nights for ever (*N&Q* 11s:5 (1912), 296–7). Some informants, however, spoke of spectral birds with glowing eyes which showed themselves (singly) to those who had a friend or relative close to death, shrieking mournfully; others, of ghosts of *unbaptized babies flitting round their parents' homes.

It is generally agreed that the sounds are really bird cries: curlews, widgeon, teal, or wild geese. 'Gabble' is a good word for this noise, which would explain the name; however, 'Gabriel' is supported by a Derbyshire belief from the mid-19th century that 'the angel Gabriel was hunting . . . [the damned] and that the cries were uttered as the lash of the angel's whip urged them along' (*N&Q* 7s (1886), 206).

Joseph Wright, *The English Dialect Dictionary* (1898–1905).

gallows, gibbets. A number of beliefs and customs clustered around the gallows, the hangman's rope, and even the body of the executed person. The wood of the gallows itself was prized for its curative properties, as it was believed effective against the ague and *toothache. The earliest references show that for the ague, a piece was worn or carried as an amulet, as noted by Sir Thomas Browne in his *Pseudodoxia Epidemica* ((1650; 6th edn. 1672), book 5, chapter 23) 'when for amulets against agues we use the chips of gallows and places of execution'. From the 19th century on, the emphasis is on splinters of the wood being placed in the mouth to cure the toothache. Attention also focused on the rope used in the hanging. Reginald Scot (1584: book 12, chapter 14) reports 'A charme for the headach: Tie a halter about your head, wherewith one hath beene hanged', and a century later John Aubrey (1686/1880: 198) confirms its practice, commenting that the hangman makes a profit by selling pieces of the rope. This belief had been held in classical times, and continued to be reported in England well into the 20th century. In addition to being good for headaches, the rope was held to be generally lucky, especially by *card-players. The body of the hanged person was also valuable, the touch of the corpse's hand was used to cure swellings (see *dead man's hand) and the *hand of glory was much prized by burglars. *Mandrakes were believed to grow especially beneath the gallows ' . . . arising from fat or urine that drops from the body of the dead' (Browne, 1672: book 2 chapter 6).

See also *HANGMAN'S STONE; *SKIN (HUMAN).

Opie and Tatem, 1989: 172, 189.

Gardiner, George Barnet (1852–1910). A Scot who made an important contribution to the study of English folk-song by his enthusiastic collecting activities in the early 20th century. From 1904 to 1909, he spent a great deal of time in the field, particularly in Hampshire (at the suggestion of Lucy *Broadwood) but also in Cornwall, Somerset, and Wiltshire. Gardiner concentrated on the texts and enlisted the help of trained musicians, such as H. Balfour *Gardiner (no relation), H. E. D. *Hammond, Charles Gamblin, and C. F. Guyer. His manuscripts, containing 1,460 songs (1,165 with tunes) are lodged in the *Vaughan Williams Memorial Library. A selection of his songs appeared in the *JFSS 3 (1909), 249–304, in his Folk Songs from Hampshire (1909); and in James Reeves, The Everlasting Circle (1960).

Frank Purslow, FMJ 1:3 (1967), 129–57; Stephen Lloyd, H. Balfour Gardiner (1984), 34–52.

Gardiner, Henry Balfour (1877–1950). One of several young English composers who caught the craze for folk music in the first years of the 20th century. Between 1905 and 1907 he assisted George Barnet *Gardiner (no relation) in collecting forays in Hampshire, as the latter lacked the necessary musical skill to note the tunes. Balfour Gardiner noted over 100 items, some of which were published in Folk Songs from Hampshire (1909), and the manuscripts of which are in the *Vaughan Williams Memorial Library.

Stephen Lloyd, H. Balfour Gardiner (1984), 34–52.

Gardner, Gerald Brosseau (1884–1964). A flamboyant and assertive personality, he was a seminal figure in the creation of modern paganism. He had developed an interest in anthropology and the occult while working in Malaya as a tea and rubber planter and a Customs officer, and on retiring to England in 1936 he made this his prime preoccupation.

In Hampshire in 1939 he joined what he claimed was a witch coven preserving unbroken medieval traditions, and from 1951 onwards he publicly promoted a fertility religion of the type now called *Wicca. He recruited members into an organized initiatory cult of several grades, for which he composed rituals and spells under the title A Book of Shadows; his system shows similarities to Freemasonry, and to ceremonial magic as practised by the Hermetic Order of the Golden Dawn, Aleister Crowley, and others in the early 20th century. His Witchcraft Today (1954) is the foundation of Wicca; he also set up a Museum of Witchcraft at Castletown (Isle of Man). He always insisted that he had learnt about witchcraft through initiation, not from books, but both his theories and his rituals are clearly influenced by earlier writers, including Margaret *Murray (Hutton, 1999: 225).

His work has been assessed by Ronald Hutton (1999: 205–52). See also the accounts by Doreen Valiente (1973, 152–8; 1989, 35–62), and J. L. Bracelin, Gerald Gardner: Witch (Octagon Press, 1960).

garlands. Together with similar constructions of flowers and greenery, garlands are common elements of English customs, whether carried around the village on May Day, hung up as Christmas decorations or on Maypoles, carried at weddings and funerals, and even worn on the head as at Castleton, Derbyshire, and although individual customs may not be very old, garlands in general have a long history:

Three ornaments belong principally to a wife. A ring on her finger, a brooch at her breast, and a garland on her head. The ring betokens true love, as I have said, the brooch betokens cleanness in heart and chastity that she ought to have, the garland betokens gladness and the dignity of the sacrament of wedlock. (Dives and Pauper, c.1405–10; spelling modernized)

Less well-known examples of 19th century garlands include prizes at games in Yorkshire, and as a fishing industry custom where returning Whitby whalers fixed 'a garland or hoop fluttering with ribbons' from the masthead (Gutch, 1901: 57).

See also *ABBOTSBURY GARLAND DAY, *CASTLETON GARLAND DAY, *CHRISTMAS DECORATIONS, *FUNERALS, *MAIDENS' GARLANDS, *MAY DAY, *MAYPOLES, *RUSHBEARING, *WEDDINGS.

Brears, 1989: 178–203.

Garratt, Mayor of. Probably the most famous of the *mock mayors, even though the last recognized Mayor died in 1810. Garratt was a small hamlet between Wandsworth and Tooting, now in South London but then in the county of Surrey. The election of the Mayor of Garratt always took place at the same time as the real election for Parliament, and its function as parody was always its main raison d'être. The first recorded election took place in 1747, and local public house landlords supported the event for the extra custom it brought. Within a few short years, thousands were flocking to Garratt, from London and elsewhere, and even fashionable society paid regular visits. Samuel Foote wrote a successful play, The Mayor of Garret, in 1763, which helped to publicize the event. The candidates were as flamboyant as possible, in dress and behaviour, and adopted silly names such as Lord Twankum, Squire Blow-Me-Down, and speeches and processions were made, as in real elections. Most of the candidates were from humble origins—watermen, cobblers, gravediggers, barbers, sweeps, and so on, but some became well-known characters in their own right: Sir John Harper, Sir Jeffrey Dunstan, and Sir Harry Dimsdale (not their real names) among them. The event gradually lost the support of both fashionable visitors and locals, perhaps because the crowds were getting too large or the humour had begun to wear thin. Dimsdale was the last recognized Mayor and he died in 1810. Sporadic attempts to revive the custom failed.

Anthony Shaw, *The Mayor of Garratt* (1980); Hone, 1827: ii. 410–33; Gomme, 1883: 208–9.

Gawain and the Green Knight. This fine poem, written in the West Midlands in the later 14th century, not only has a plot centred upon a shape-changing giant but is rich in details of interest to folklorists. The Green Knight's brusque entry at Arthur's *New Year feast, bearing a *holly branch, is suggestive of the masquerades and games common in medieval households at that season; the beheading challenge he proposes has folktale analogues; his home in a hollow knoll recalls legends in which prehistoric barrows are linked to giants. His colour and ability to survive decapitation have provoked speculation about seasonal symbolism and vegetation spirits. Unfortunately, it is impossible to tell how much of this is due to the English poet drawing on customs and tales from his own culture, how much to his immediate source (a French poem now lost), and how much to the remote sources of the basic story, which were Celtic.

Text ed. J. R. R. Tolkien and E. V. Gordon, *Sir Gawain and the Green Knight* (1925; many reprints). Full translation in J. R. R. Tolkien, *Sir Gawain and the Green Knight, Pearl and Sir Orfeo* (1975).

geese-dancing, see *GUISE-DANCING.

Geoffrey of Monmouth (?1100–55). A Benedictine monk attached to the household of Robert, Earl of Gloucester; in 1152 he became Bishop of St Asaph. His *Historia Regum Britanniae*, written c.1136, claims to be a history of all the kings of Britain from Brutus, the founder of the realm and great-grandson of Aeneas of Troy and Rome, to Cadwallader (d. 689); the reign of *Arthur is the centrepiece of the work, and Geoffrey's account, which was accepted as historically valid by most of his contemporaries and successors, was a major influence on

the development of Arthurian romances throughout Europe. His *Vita Merlini* (c.1150) was equally important as a source for legends about *Merlin, and for prophecies attributed to him. Geoffrey drew on older historians, notably Bede and Nennius, and may have known Welsh traditions now lost; however, a high proportion of what he says, not merely about Arthur but about many alleged early kings and heroes of Britain, seems to have no basis outside his own imagination.

Gervase of Tilbury (c.1150–c.1220). Born at Tilbury in Essex, he was a lawyer and cleric who lived most of his life abroad in the service of various rulers and prelates, notably the Emperor Otto IV, for whom he wrote, probably about 1211, a compendium of history, geography, and natural history which he called *Otia Imperialia* ('Imperial Relaxations'). One section is devoted to 'The Marvels of Each Province' of England, 'marvels' (*mirabilia*) being defined as natural phenomena that cannot be explained, as opposed to miracles due to God's intervention. They include items which would now be classed as legend or superstition.

Gervase is thus an important source for medieval English folklore. He gives a Gloucestershire variant of the tale of the stolen fairy goblet (cf. *Willy Howe); he describes little working goblins in patched clothes, who are generally helpful but also lead travellers astray—clearly akin to *Puck and *pixies; he tells of a swineherd who entered the Peak cavern and reached a pleasant Otherworld where harvesting was in progress, though in the human world it was winter. He has heard of Arthur's Knights as a ghostly *Wild Hunt, and of a demonic hound with fiery jaws appearing during a thunderstorm in a forest near Penrith. He believed that two remarkable events had occurred within his lifetime which proved that 'the sea is higher than the land', indeed that it is 'above our habitation . . . either in or on the air' (a medieval theory based on the reference in Genesis 1 to 'waters above the firmament'). The first took place outside a Gloucestershire church one foggy Sunday, when people coming out of Mass saw an anchor caught on a tombstone, with its rope stretching up into the sky; a sailor came swarming down it and tried to free the anchor, but seemed to choke in human air and soon died as if by drowning. The church kept the anchor for all to see. The second event concerned a merchant sailing from Bristol to Ireland who accidentally dropped his knife into the sea; it fell straight through the skylight of his own house, back in Bristol, landing on the table in front of his wife.

C. C. Oman, *Folk-Lore* 55 (1944), 2–15.

gestures. Excellent examples of folklore. They are learnt informally, by observation and example, there is no official or authoritative canon by which they are judged, and they rely on a shared and agreed symbolic meaning between gesturer and recipient. They also vary over time, and from place to place, and attract origin theories and stories.

See *COCKING A SNOOK, *CROSSING FINGERS, *THUMBS, *TRUCE TERMS, *V-SIGN.

Jan Bremmer and Herman Roodenburg, *A Cultural History of Gesture* (1991); Morris, 1979.

ghosts. English folklore of all periods is full of references to ghosts, and there is a widespread current belief that the dead can reveal their presence to the living, and that some people are better able than others to perceive them. First-hand experience stories on this theme are abundant today, and probably always have been. Some describe how the teller felt that someone he/she loved was nearby to comfort or advise, though dead; others describe fears and distress experienced in some uncanny place, interpreted as due to unpleasant ghosts, whose identity is usually unknown. Folklore collectors have not published much primary material of this kind, partly out of respect for their informants' privacy, and partly because it is 'personal', not 'communal, traditional' (Bennett, 1987: 17–19); however, newspaper files and books on psychic phenomena have numerous examples.

Communal tradition shapes our expectations of how ghosts manifest themselves. Hence even a memorate is likely to include details highlighted because they fit a stereotype (e.g. a drop in temperature, sounds of footsteps, an animal refusing to approach the eerie place), and these become more numerous as the story spreads into the community as rumour. There it may become linked to other anecdotes about haunting set in the same house, road, etc., which ultimately may coalesce into a *local legend. The latter are found everywhere, in great numbers; some are purely oral, others pass to and fro between orality and print, since there is a keen market

for books and pamphlets on the ghost-lore of particular towns or districts, which perpetuate older tales and publicize new ones. Monks, nuns, Roman legionaries, named historical personages, and nameless White and Grey Ladies, abound now in stately homes and old buildings throughout the land, to the delight of tourists.

Evidence for beliefs and tales of past centuries is patchily distributed, and often transmitted through educated writers who had some axe to grind; there are marked differences from one period to another. Among Anglo-Saxons, violent *burial customs indicate fear of the malevolent *undead. Some remarkable tales written down by a monk in 14th-century Yorkshire (James, 1922) concern tormented souls who roam about in terrifying shapes—several appear as grotesque animals (or even 'a whirling heap of hay with a light in the middle of it'), while others are undead corpses which must be held down by force. All find peace through posthumous absolution of their sins. The *Lyke-Wake Dirge, though only recorded in the 17th century, also describes purgatorial punishments.

After the Reformation, in order to debunk Purgatory, some Protestants redefined all alleged apparitions of ghosts as devils in disguise, but others thought this went too far. Much learned writing in the 16th and 17th centuries is focused on this debate, eventually won by those who held that ghosts must be possible, though rare—to deny it was to be a 'Sadducee' (i.e. one who denies the afterlife), and hence an 'atheist'. Books setting out this view included Joseph Glanville's *Saducismus Triumphatus* (= 'Sadduceeism Crushed', 1681), and Richard Baxter's *The Certainty of the Worlds of Spirits* (1691); they include many contemporary accounts of apparitions seen by members of the aristocracy, gentry, and educated persons, whose status gave them authority. *Aubrey collected similar anecdotes, though without polemical purpose. A few of these ghosts seem motiveless, but most appear for helpful reasons: to ensure their debts are paid and wills correctly executed, to denounce a murderer, to warn a friend that he will die soon, as *wraiths announcing their own deaths. These spectres behave with dignity, and are not horrific or dangerous. Glanville and Baxter also describe noisy, invisible, stone-throwing spirits of the type later called *poltergeists, but as demons, not ghosts.

Eighteenth-century intellectuals generally

mocked belief in ghosts as ignorant superstition—'a received Tradition among the Vulgar' and 'Legendary Stories of Nurses and Old Women', as Henry *Bourne, a clergyman of Newcastle-upon-Tyne, put it in his *Antiquitates Vulgares* (1725). Drawing on oral rural material, he presents ghosts as frightening and/or grotesque, never as helpful: they wander from midnight to *cockcrow, especially in and around churchyards; they haunt houses where they died, often by violence; they may appear as spectral cows, dogs or horses, and as fiery or headless shapes. As good Christians, people should not believe such things, but they do, and by talking of them make them more persuasive:

Nothing is commoner in *Country Places*, than for a whole Family in a *Winter's Evening*, to sit round the Fire, and tell Stories of Apparitions and Ghosts. And no Question of it, but this adds to the natural Fearfulness of Men, and makes them many Times imagine they see Things, which really are nothing but their own Fancy. (Bourne, 1725/1977: 76–7).

The regional folklorists whose collections began appearing in Victorian times amply confirmed that these beliefs were widespread, recording them with amusement or amazement as examples of 'superstition' which they themselves definitely did not share. They also included lively, dramatic *local legends about *laying ghosts, *phantom coaches, *skulls, *black dogs, *boggarts, *barguests, etc. There is often a note of humour in these, and a good deal of storytelling skill, though how far it derives from the informant and how far from the folklorist's retelling is hard to guess. A better testimony to the strength and seriousness of the underlying communal tradition is Charlotte Latham's account (from Fittleworth, Sussex, in the 1860s) of children spontaneously pouring out their ghost-lore:

A short time ago there was committed to me the teaching of a Sunday School class composed principally of tradesmen's children, who, on my asking them if they knew what was meant by their 'ghostly enemy', one and all replied, 'Yes, a spirit that comes back from the grave; ' and as they showed an eagerness to tell me everything they knew upon the subject, I allowed them to go on. They then spoke all at once, and quite overwhelmed me with the stories of what their fathers, mothers, brothers, or relations, in whom they placed implicit trust, had seen. Some spirits were reported to walk about without their heads, others carried them under their arms, and one, haunting a dark lane, had a ball of fire upon its

shoulders instead of the natural finial. (Latham, 1878: 19).

Paradoxically, while Victorian folklorists made no attempt to record personal narratives about first-hand ghostly sightings from working-class informants, psychical researchers and spiritualists at the same period began collecting them in abundance, mostly from middle-class sources, and seeking empirical verification. One result, which has fed back into current popular belief, was a theory redefining apparitions as not involving the actual presence of dead persons, but merely some kind of mental flash-back whereby the percipient 'sees' a past event 'imprinted' on the surroundings by the emotional energy it once generated. This period also saw a rising fashion for fictional tales of the supernatural, often with macabre and malevolent ghosts, which in turn led to the hugely popular horror films of the 20th century, which have raised renewed fear of the occult power of the dead.

Current belief takes such varied forms that it is impossible to generalize about it. A mourner finding private consolation in feeling the presence of a loved one; tourists enjoying a 'ghost-walk' in an ancient city; a frightened family getting their house exorcized; people using an ouija board, seriously or in fun; people avoiding a reputedly haunted wood; people talking with affectionate pride of the 'grey lady' sometimes seen in their old house; youngsters sharing a culture of 'spooky' horror tales and personal or family experiences—all are concerned with the dead, but beyond that, have little in common.

See also *LAYING GHOSTS, *PHANTOM COACHES, *PHANTOM SHIPS, *ST MARK'S EVE, *UNDEAD, *VAMPIRES, *WRAITHS.

For the evolution of ideas among the educated, see Finucane, 1982; Thomas, 1971: 587–606. Brown 1979 discusses folkloric material from the West Country and the impact of the Reformation. Bennett, 1985, 1987, and 1999, describes fieldwork among bereaved women in 1981. For current teenage ghost lore, see Wilson, 1997. Virtually all regional folklore collections have a section on ghosts, and there is a glut of books presenting stories about hauntings from a believer's point of view.

giants. The word 'giant' has two senses. In the first, it merely refers to a human being considerably larger and stronger than others; in the second, to an alien being who is not only monstrously large but also (usually) malevolent towards humans, and (often) remarkably stupid. In the first sense, several English heroes became 'giants' in local folklore, as when King *Arthur is alleged to have lifted the capstone of a megalithic tomb at Dorstone, and *Robin Hood to have formed two hills when he dropped two sacks of earth he was carrying (both tales are from Herefordshire). Various local heroes too were said to have been abnormally large, for example Piers Shonks of Brent Pelham and the robber *Jack o' Legs at Weston (both in Hertfordshire), *Little John, and Tom *Hickathrift of Wisbech (Cambridgeshire).

The non-human giant has steadily declined through the centuries from a monster to a figure of fun. In *Beowulf, Grendel and his mother are bloodthirsty threats to humanity, seriously presented as such by the poet; in medieval romances, however, it has become mere routine for a knight to slay a giant; while in local legends it is claimed that the actions of long-ago giants created certain types of landscape feature, though their plans were generally foiled by their own clumsiness and stupidity. They hurled rocks at churches, but missed; carried stones for building, but dropped them; killed one another in stone-throwing battles, or by accident when tossing tools across a valley. However, the giant *Wade and his wife did succeed in building 'Wade's Causeway' across Wheeldale Moor (North Yorkshire); it is in fact a Roman road. Legends about giants are particularly common in Cornwall, and have been since medieval times; *Geoffrey of Monmouth says Corineus, first human ruler of the region, chose it precisely because wrestling against giants was his favourite sport. Giants and giant-killing were a popular subject for *chapbook tales, the best known being *Jack the Giant-Killer and *Jack and the Beanstalk.

Several of the older *hill figures represented giants. The *Cerne Abbas Giant and the Long Man of *Wilmington still exist, but one *Gogmagog at Plymouth and another near Cambridge are lost, as is an anonymous figure which Aubrey says was on Shotover Hill, near Oxford, before the Civil War. On Kingsland Common outside Shrewsbury there was a turf-cut *maze with a giant's face cut in the centre; at the annual Shrewsbury Show in the 18th and 19th centuries, one sport (called the Shoemakers' Race) was to run the maze and leap on to the giant's eyes (Burne, 1883: 456). This must surely be linked to the well-known local legend of the Welsh giant who set out to bury Shrewsbury under a huge spadeful of earth, but was tricked by a clever cobbler into

thinking the town was still many miles away, so that he abandoned his plan, dropping the earth, which formed the Wrekin hill (Burne, 1883: 2–4).

In medieval, Elizabethan, and Jacobean times, effigies of giants were conspicuous in courtly and civic pageants. The London *Gogmagog figures and the giants in the Midsummer civic parades at Chester and Coventry are well documented; records of Newcastle-upon-Tyne show frequent payments from the 1550s to the 1590s for the upkeep of 'Hogmagog' and his coat, though it is not said on which date this effigy was displayed. At Chester in 1495, there was a whole family group of them: giant, giantess, and two daughters. Such figures were constructed from wood, wickerwork, and buckram, and lavishly dressed and painted; they were carried through the streets by a man hidden under their robes. The original official intention may have been to symbolize savage forces tamed by civilization (as in the Gogmagog legend), but in practice these town effigies were regarded with pride, amusement, and affection. Only one processional giant survives in England (unlike Belgium and France, where there are many); this is the *Salisbury Giant, now in the museum there (Cawte, 1978: 29–35; Shortt, 1982).

Local legends involving giants can be found in many regional collections; in Briggs, 1970–1; and in Westwood 1985. There is a lively round-up of Cornish tales by Barbara Spooner, 'The Giants of Cornwall', *Folklore* 76 (1965), 16–32. For hill figures, see Marples, 1949:159–212. For civic processional giants, see F. W. Fairholt, *Gog and Magog* (1859), 50–63; J. Hemingway, *The History of Chester* (1831), i. 199–206; J. J. Anderson (ed.), *Records of Early English Drama: Newcastle upon Tyne* (1982); Hugh Shortt, *The Giant and Hob-Nob* (Salisbury Museum, 1982); Cawte, 1978: 29–35.

Gilchrist, Anne Geddes (1863–1954). Born in Manchester, she was always interested in music and was already knowledgeable on musical topics when she came across the folk *song movement, first by reading Sabine *Baring-Gould and then by contact with Frank *Kidson. She joined the Editorial Board of the Folk-Song Society in 1906, and continued to serve in that capacity for nearly 50 years. Anne Gilchrist was one of the triumvirate of acknowledged experts (the others being Lucy *Broadwood and Kidson) to which members of the Society could turn for advice and information, and between them they held a vast store of historical and comparative knowledge, and Anne in particular was an excellent correspondent and unstinting mentor to anyone who sought her help. She was particularly expert in early psalm and hymn tunes, and could often identify a requested tune from memory alone. Unlike the other two, however, Gilchrist wrote no books, and her contributions to the subject are all in the form of articles and notes appended to songs published in the Society's *Journal* and in other journals including *The Choir* and **Folklore*. She was also a collector, mostly in her home area, and her collection covered a variety of genres, including singing games, sea shanties, Lancashire rushcart and morris tunes, pace-egging songs, ballads, carols, and nursery songs. She was awarded an OBE in 1948 for her services to folk song and dance scholarship, and her papers are now deposited in the *Vaughan Williams Memorial Library, as described by Margaret Dean-Smith, *JEFDSS* 7:4 (1955), 218–27.

Selected articles by Gilchrist include: 'Let Us Remember', *ED&S* 6:6 (1942), reprinted in 54:3 (1992), 8–9; 'Sacred Parodies of Secular Folk Songs', *JFSS* 3 (1937), 157–82; 'Songs and Tunes from the Clague Collection [Isle of Man]', *JFSS* 7 (1924–6), 117–94, 203–76, 281–347; 'The Folk Element in Early Revival Hymns and Tunes', *JFSS* 8 (1928), 61–95.

Obituaries: *JEFDSS* 7:3 (1954), 202; *ED&S* 19:2 (1954), 68–9.

glasses, drinking. A relatively recent idea is that a ringing glass is connected to drowning sailors. The first documented reference so far found is in 1909 (*N&Q* 10s:12 (1909), 310), but it was certainly well known soon after that:

Have you ever noticed the effect upon a dinner-party should anyone hit a glass and make it ring? Nothing less than an interruption in conversation—a momentary silence—relieved only when the culprit placed a finger on the rim 'to save a sailor from drowning'. (Igglesden, *c.*1932: 26)

Opie and Tatem, 1989: 173–4.

Glastonbury. The prestige of Glastonbury Abbey is based on medieval legends. The earliest, in the late 10th century, is a claim that the first church on the site (which actually is no older than the 7th century) predated the arrival of the earliest missionaries. By the 13th century, it was being said that this had been built in AD 63 by twelve disciples of Jesus, led by *Joseph of Arimathea. Simultaneously, a secular legend developed, namely that Glastonbury was the mysterious *Avalon to which *Arthur was taken. In 1191, at the request of Henry II, the monks dug between two tall stone shafts in their graveyard, and found a hollow oak deep in the earth, containing the bones of a gigantic and much wounded man, and of a woman whose golden hair crumbled to dust as soon as someone touched it. Fixed to a stone in the grave was a lead cross saying (in Latin) 'Here lies buried the renowned King Arthur with Guinevere his second wife, in the Isle of Avalon'.

The discovery was useful to the Abbey, hard pressed for funds after a fire in 1184 had destroyed many of its buildings and all its relics; it may also have had a political aspect, discrediting the Welsh and Breton tradition that Arthur had never died. The bones were laid in a black marble mausoleum before the high altar, where they remained till the Abbey was destroyed at the Reformation. The lead cross survived the destruction; Camden's *Britannia* (1590) includes a sketch of it, with a shorter inscription omitting Guinevere, but the object itself is thought to have been lost in the late 17th century. A cross found in 1982 at Forty Hall, Enfield was probably a replica; the finder refused to reveal where he had rehidden it (*The Times* (15 Jan. and 22 Mar. 1983)).

Glastonbury Tor was said in a 16th-century Welsh life of St Collen to be a fairy hill, inside which lived a sinister lord of the Otherworld called Gwyn ap Nudd, who also figures in Welsh Arthurian tales. The Tor is topped by a ruined church, and the terracing along its slopes might possibly be a *maze. On the slopes is a *Holy Thorn, descendant of the original one which stood near the Abbey in 1500.

In modern times the reputation of Glastonbury has grown greatly. Both Roman Catholics and Anglicans hold services and pilgrimages at the Abbey; the spring near the Tor associated with the *Grail legend and used as a spa in the 18th century is now a centre for pilgrimage and healing, tended by the Chalice Well Trust; in the 1930s, the artist Katherine Maltwood claimed that the landscape of a ten-mile area south-east of Glastonbury formed patterns representing the Zodiac. The whole New Age movement of 'alternative' mysticism sees Glastonbury as a major spiritual centre.

Rahtz, 1993; A. Gransden, *Journal of Ecclesiastical History* 27: 4 (1976), 337–58.

Glastonbury Thorn, see *HOLY THORN.

gnomes. This name for dwarfs living underground is not part of folk tradition; it is a Latin word invented by the 16th-century Swiss alchemist Paracelsus in a treatise on four species of elemental beings: nymphs in water, sylphs in air, salamanders in fire, and *pigmaei* or *gnomi* in the earth. The first English writer to adopt it was the poet Pope, in *The Rape of the Lock* (1714). Gnomes became more common in 19th- and 20th-century literature, especially for children, where illustrators gave them the standard appearance of dwarfs in Swiss and German folklore, including a red cap. They were often said to be mining for metals and precious stones.

The first gnome figurines for gardens were small porcelain ones imported from Germany in the late 1860s by Sir Charles Isham, to decorate a large rockery at Lamport Hall (Northamptonshire) imitating a mountain landscape, in which they represented mining dwarfs. Terracotta gnomes were fashionable in late Victorian times; modern mass-produced ones are generally regarded with affectionate mockery.

goats. It was a long-standing custom, which lasted well into the 20th century and may even still be carried out, for farmers to keep a goat with their cattle. It is usually stated that the presence of the goat helps prevent abortion in cattle and generally acts as a calming influence. Some say that the goat eats certain plants which are harmful to cows and thus protects them, while at least one Durham farmer maintained that goats kill and eat adders. The correspondent to *Notes & Queries* who reported the latter was sceptical until he saw it happen with his own eyes. Several sources state that it is the smell of the goat which is beneficial. Virtually all the examples of this practice which can be geographically located come from the Midlands or north of the country, with Gloucestershire being the most southerly example. This may be an accident of documentation, or may reflect the true distribution. Its age is also open to question, as Opie and Tatem give the first known reference as *c.*1840, but it is likely to be much older than that. There is surprisingly little other English lore concerning goats. Hazlitt reported a belief that 'they are never to be seen for twenty-four hours together, and that once in that space they pay a visit to the devil in order to have their beards combed' which he claimed was common in England and Scotland. Another tradition is that diamonds will be softened by no other substance than goat's blood, and

Lean quotes three 16th and 17th century literary references to this idea.

Opie and Tatem, 1989: 174; *N&Q* 3s:9 (1866), 118, 330; 11s:11 (1915), 452, 500–1; 12s:1 (1916), 16; 12s:3 (1917), 310; Lean, 1903: ii. 605–6; Hazlitt, 1905: 278.

goblin. A general term for fairy creatures of malicious or evil nature, especially if small and ugly; it can also be used for minor demons. The word is derived from medieval French.

Godiva, Lady. The wife of Earl Leofric of Mercia, and a devout and generous patron of churches and abbeys, she was Lady of Coventry in her own right. She died in 1067 and about a 100 years after her death, Roger of Wendover, a monk of St Alban's, told how this 'saintly countess . . . beloved of God', inspired by the Trinity and the Blessed Virgin, begged her husband to free Coventry from tax, until, angry at her persistence, he told her that if she rode naked across the crowded market-place, he would grant her request. She agreed, but let her hair hang loose, so that 'her whole body was veiled except her fair white legs'. Her husband 'counted this a miracle', and lifted the tax. Later versions, beginning in the 16th century, switch the emphasis from holiness to cleverness; Godiva, it was now said, asked the magistrates to make everyone stay indoors with closed windows as she rode by, which they did, so 'her husband's imagination [was] utterly disappointed'. By 1659, a new character had been added to the legend: Peeping Tom, struck blind for trying to see the naked Godiva.

Historians are agreed that Godiva and Leofric were real people, who may well have remitted some unpopular tax, but the tale shows influence both from saints' legends (pious wife contrasted with cruel husband, modesty miraculously protected), and from folklore motifs. There are several other English local traditions in which some grant or privilege is said to have been won for the community by a great lady's willingness to undergo a humiliating ordeal: to walk barefoot, or ride naked, or crawl on hands and knees round a piece of land which she wishes her husband to donate to charity, for example at *Tichborne (Hampshire) and *St Briavels (Gloucestershire). These may of course be imitations of the Godiva tale, being recorded far later; however, the motif of a clever woman who fulfils seemingly impossible or intolerable conditions by a trick is old and international. So too is the punishment of curiosity by blinding.

During the Middle Ages Coventry held an annual eight-day fair in Corpus Christi week, which included miracle plays and a procession; after the Reformation, this was replaced by a civic pageant at Midsummer, which was suppressed during the Commonwealth but lavishly revived in the reign of Charles II. From 1678, there are records of a 'Lady Godiva' appearing in the pageant; at first the role was taken by a boy, but from 1765 there was a real woman (fully dressed) on a white horse. Meanwhile, a life-size wooden figure of a man in Tudor armour, the original function of which is unknown, had become famous as 'Peeping Tom'; it was carried in the annual procession, and between whiles displayed in various houses and hotels. It is currently in the Cathedral Lane Shopping Centre. The rowdiness and ribald humour of the occasion drew Victorian disapproval, but parades continued intermittently until the 1960s, and were revived in 1996.

The story of Lady Godiva and Peeping Tom is a great favourite, not merely in Coventry but as a part of English popular culture, the combination of virtue, sexual titillation, and earthy humour having proved irresistible.

Joan Lancaster, *Godiva of Coventry* (Coventry, 1967); Hilda R. E. Davidson, *Folklore* 80 (1969), 107–21; Palmer, 1976: 134–9.

God's penny, luck money, earnest money. Three separate but linked customary practices are concerned with the exchange of money between individuals. At least from the medieval period onwards, the handing over of 'God's penny' (which could be any amount above a penny) was one of the ways in which two traders sealed a bargain, and was thus the equivalent to a binding deposit given by the buyer. The name possibly derives from an earlier belief that this sum should be given to the Church as a voluntary donation. 'Earnest money' was usually a sum given to a new servant or farmworker on being hired by a new employer. Having accepted the earnest, the employee was bound to turn up for work at the agreed date. The same principle applied to the King's Shilling given to a new recruit to enlist him into the army. However, as the name implies, 'earnest money' (i.e. the concept of a promise) could be used to apply to the buying of goods or to the securing of staff, so the terminology can be confusing (see, for example, Thomas Dekker's *The Shoemaker's Holiday* (1599), iii. 1). There were a number of local terms for earnest money, including Arles or Erles in the northern counties and Fasten or Festing money elsewhere.

Luck money was something different. This was a sum of money given back by the seller, to the buyer, on the completion of a deal, for luck. Hard-fought attempts by farmers and manufacturers to eradicate the practice which are reported throughout the 19th century showed how prevalent and ingrained the custom was. Numerous reports also indicate that it was necessary to *spit on the money if you wanted its luck to be effective, and this custom was still being reported in certain quarters late in the 20th century.

F. J. Snell, *The Customs of Old England* (1911), 232–8; *N&Q* 5s:7 (1877), 488; 5s:8 (1878), 37–8 376–7; 9s:11 (1903), 127, 196, 254, 358; 157 (1929), 454–5; 158 (1930), 31; Opie and Tatem, 1989: 233–4.

Gogmagog (or Gog and Magog). In the Middle Ages and in Tudor England, there are several allusions to a giant called Gogmagog, or a pair of giants called Gog and Magog, living in Cornwall when Brutus, legendary founder of Britain, first arrived there. Geoffrey of Monmouth, in his *Historia Regum Britanniae* (1136), spells the giant's name as Goemagot and says he was defeated in wrestling by Brutus's friend Corineus, who threw him off the cliffs of Plymouth Hoe at a spot called Goemagot's Leap.

These names are biblical; in Ezekiel 38–9, it is prophesied that 'Gog from the land of Magog' will invade Israel but be defeated, while in Revelations 20 'Gog and Magog' will be among the hosts of the Antichrist. It has sometimes been suggested that the curious spelling in Geoffrey's text represents some *Celtic Cornish name which he misunderstood. It is, however, far more likely to be due to the fact that his book (first written in Latin) circulated in Norman French for about a century before being translated into English; if spoken as four syllables, *Go-e-magot* is identical in sound with the French form of the biblical names, i.e. *Got et Magot* (the ts are silent).

At some unknown date, but before the close of the 15th century, Plymouth celebrated the defeat of Gogmagog by cutting a figure of him on the slope of the Hoe, and periodically scraping it clean; town records from 1486 onwards call it 'Gogmagog'. But Carew's *Survey of Cornwall* (1602) speaks of two figures wielding clubs, one bigger than the other, and divides the name as 'Gog Magog'. A few years later, however, the smaller figure was being called 'Corineus'. The site was destroyed when the Citadel was built in the reign of Charles II.

There was another turf-cut giant at Wandlebury Camp, near Cambridge, in 1605, but how much older it may have been is unknown; the surrounding hills were called 'the Gogmagog Hills' by Cambridge students in Elizabethan times, and they may have been the cutters of the figure. It was still visible in the 1720s.

In Tudor times, a new version of Geoffrey's tale evolved. Brutus, it was now said, captured the Cornish Gog and Magog alive, brought them to London, and chained them to the gate of his palace as porters. Effigies of giants were used on royal occasions; a male and female pair greeted Henry V on London Bridge in 1415, while 'Gogmagog and Corineus' welcomed Mary Tudor and Philip of Spain in 1554, and Elizabeth in 1559. They regularly appeared in the Lord Mayor's pageants and Midsummer Shows, and were displayed in the Guildhall as defenders of the city, and the nation. The names alternated between 'Gogmagog and Corineus' and 'Gog and Magog', the latter gradually ousting the former.

Naturally, the effigies had to be periodically renewed, and were not always of the same type—in 1605 they were stalking on stilts; in 1672 they were fifteen feet tall, seated in chariots, and 'moving, talking, and taking tobacco as they ride along, to the great admiration and delight of all the spectators'. In Cromwell's time they were destroyed, but at the accession of Charles II a fresh pair appeared. These, made from wickerwork, perished in the Great Fire of London; the next pair had their 'entrails' eaten up by rats; their fine wooden successors, carved in 1708, were too heavy to move, and remained in the Guildhall. Children were assured that 'every day, when the giants hear the clock strike twelve, they come down to dinner'. Portable wickerwork figures, fourteen feet high and copied from the wooden ones, were again made for the Lord Mayor's Show of 1827. The wooden giants of 1708 were destroyed in an air-raid in 1940, and replaced in 1953 by a fresh pair, which still stand in the Guildhall.

Hone, 1827: ii, cols. 609–17; F. W. Fairholt, *Gog and Magog: The Giants in the Guildhall* (1859); Robert Withington, *English Pageantry* (1918–20), i. 58–64; Marples, 1949: 204–12; Westwood, 1985: 23–4, 109–12, 167–70. T. C.

Lethbridge's reconstruction of the Cambridge figure(s) is set out in his *Gogmagog: The Buried Gods* (1957), but neither his methods nor his results have won acceptance.

gold. Thought to have healing properties, especially for sore eyes and styes, which should be rubbed with a wedding ring (the only gold object most families were likely to possess). Gold *earrings were also thought to strengthen the eyes, and, among sailors and fishermen, to prevent one from drowning. *Aubrey says some people of his time tied gold *coins to ulcers and fistulas; he wonders whether the cure worked because 'gold attracts mercury' or because older gold coins 'were printed with St Michael the Archangel, and to be stamped according to some Rule Astrological' (Aubrey, 1686/1880: 206). Similarly, a letter written during the Plague of 1665 advises: 'Friend, get a piece of angell gold, if you can of Eliz. coine (y^t is ye best) wch is phylosophicall gold, and keepe it allways in yor mouth when you walke out or any sicke persons come to you' (Opie and Tatem, 1989: 175). In such cases, the power resides both in the metal and in the symbolism of its design.

For good luck at sea, sailing boats often had a gold sovereign set in the socket under the mast; the custom was common till about 1914, and is still sometimes followed. It has precedents from ancient Rome (Smith, *FLS News* 26 (1997), p. 12). Lovett found that fishermen from several towns used to ram a coin into the cork float of a drift-net, to break a run of bad luck in fishing, and held that 'in the old days' it would have been a gold one (Lovett, 1925: 54–5).

Goldilocks, see THE *THREE BEARS.

Gomme, Alice Bertha (1852–1938). Born Alice Bertha Merck, she married George Laurence *Gomme in 1875 and became Lady Gomme when he was knighted for his work with the London County Council in 1911. Alice Gomme was a founder-member of the *Folklore Society in 1878 and a leading figure in its activities for 60 years, serving on its Council from 1912 to 1938. In retrospect, her contribution was often overshadowed by that of her husband who held much higher-profile positions, produced numerous books and articles, and contributed to the major theoretical debates which shaped the early days of Folklore Studies. Accounts of Alice Bertha stress her supportive nature and her tact (e.g. *Folk-

Lore 49 (1938), 93–4) and it is true that she successfully ran a busy household and brought up their seven sons, but, in addition to the decades of service given to the Folklore Society, Alice made a number of significant contributions to scholarship, and her interests were wide ranging and her knowledge formidable.

One of her first forays into the public limelight came in October 1891, when she was Secretary for the Entertainment Committee for the prestigious International Folk-Lore Congress, held in London, and surviving correspondence shows clearly that she was the main organizer of the Conversazione, which included a major exhibition of folklore items, an exhibition of local cakes and other food, performances of children's *singing games, a *mumming play, songs, dances, and tales. The event was a tremendous success, particularly the games performed by children from her local Barnes Village School, and has been hailed as the first act of the folk *revival (see Boyes). Two of the featured items grew into major research interests for Alice, children's games and traditional food. Her two-volume work on the *Traditional Games of England, Scotland, and Ireland* (1894–8), compiled mainly from correspondence with contributors from all over the country, but also from her own collecting, presents a wealth of detailed information on games of the mid- to late 19th century, which is still used as a source-book today. As befits a member of her generation, Lady Gomme followed the basic *survivals theory, although not slavishly, and the commentary in *Traditional Games* is somewhat dated, but the material itself is still as interesting as the day it was collected. The books were planned as the first volumes in an ambitious 'Dictionary of Folk-Lore' project, but no other titles in the series ever saw the light of day. She also published several popular-market books of singing games, some in co-operation with Cecil *Sharp. Most of Alice's output was in the form of notes and short pieces for the journal *Folk-Lore*, on a range of subjects including medicine, harvest customs, mumming plays, and folktales, but she also contributed widely to newspapers and magazines, and this material still needs to be identified and gathered together. She was also active in a number of other organizations, including the London Shakespeare League, Folk Cookery Association, *Folk-Song Society, and the *English Folk Dance Society, and she lectured widely.

Alice Gomme's work includes *The Traditional Games of England, Scotland and Ireland* (2 vols, 1894, 1898); *Games for Parlour and Playground* (1898); *Children's Singing Games* (2 vols., 1894); (with Laurence Gomme) *Old English Singing Games* (1900); *British Folk-Lore, Folk-songs, and Singing Games* (1916); (with Cecil Sharp) *Children's Singing Games* (5 vols., 1909–12); 'Boer Folk-Medicine and Some Parallels', *Folk-Lore* 13 (1902), 69–75, 181–2; 'The Green Lady: A Folktale from Hertfordshire', *Folk-Lore* 7 (1896), 411–14; 'The History of England in a Cooking Pot: Folk Recipes and Kitchen Magic', *Morning Post* (4 Mar. 1931).

Georgina Boyes, in Davidson and Blacker, 2001: 65–83; M. Gaster, *Folk-Lore* 49 (1938), 93–4.

Gomme, George Laurence (1853–1916). Knighted in 1911 for his work on the Metropolitan Board of Works (which he joined in 1873) and the London County Council. He was extremely knowledgeable about London, and published several works on the history of the city as well as being instrumental in seminal initiatives such as the Survey of London (1894 onwards) and the identification and preservation of important buildings. He also lectured at the London School of Economics on municipal organization. Gomme was a key figure in the group who founded the Folklore Society in 1878, and was one of its leading members till his death, serving in various capacities, including Secretary, Director, and President (1890–4). His interests in folklore were broad, but combined with his interest in history and municipal administration, his key field was the development of village and community life, and the idea that ancient racial divisions in the British Isles could be traced in the surviving folklore of the people. This *survivals theory formed the basis of several books and important articles, but was challenged at the time by several colleagues, and is now universally discredited. Nevertheless, his legacy lives on in his organizational work in founding the Society, the numerous books and journals edited by him (including *Antiquary* (1881–8), *Camden Library*, *Archaeological Review* (1888–9), and an important series of reprints from the *Gentleman's Magazine*), and his insistence that folklore be treated as a science and be pursued with scientific rigour. Gomme married Alice Bertha Merck (see A. B. *Gomme) in 1875, who was the leading authority on children's games, and their son Allan also served as President of the Society.

Gomme's major books on folklore and

ethnology are *Primitive Folk-Moots* (1880); *Folk-Lore Relics of Early Village Life* (1883); *The Village Community* (1890); *Handbook of Folk-Lore* (1890); *Ethnology in Folk-Lore* (1892); *Folk-Lore as a Historical Science* (1908).

Obituaries: by Alfred C. Haddon, *Man* (June 1916), 84–7; by Edward Clodd, *Folk-Lore* 27 (1916), 111–12; *The Times*, 25 Feb. 1916, 5; [Alice B. Gomme], 'Bibliography of the Writings of the Late Sir Laurence Gomme on Anthropology and Folklore', *Folk-Lore* 27 (1916), 408–12; Francis A. de Caro, *Journal of the Folklore Institute* 19 (1982), 107–17; Richard M. Dorson, *The British Folklorists: A History* (1968), 220–9; Sona Rosa Burstein, *Folk-Lore* 68 (1957), 321–38.

Good Friday. It is startling that this, the most mournful day in the Christian calendar, is a cheerful Bank Holiday, and a traditional date for various games such as *skipping and *marbles. Traditionally, it was the day for certain tasks in the vegetable garden, notably planting potatoes and peas, and sowing parsley; some thought the Devil had no power to spoil crops planted on this holy day, but there was probably also the practical reason that men were free to work for their own benefit. However, this was not true everywhere; in North Yorkshire in the 1860s, 'great care (was) taken not to disturb the earth in any way; it were impious to use spade, plough or harrow . . . a villager . . . shocked his neighbours by planting potatoes on Good Friday, but they never came up' (Henderson, 1866: 61–2).

For women, the main taboo was on washing clothes; it would bring extreme bad luck, even death, and moreover anything hung out to dry would be spotted with blood—baking, in contrast, was very beneficial. Some said this was because Jesus, on the way to Calvary, cursed a woman who threw dirty water at him, but blessed one who gave him bread (M. Murray-Aynsley, *Symbolism of East and West*, (1900), 162).

Throughout England, special buns, marked with a cross, were made on Good Friday and eaten toasted for breakfast; they were referred to as 'Cross buns' or 'Good Friday buns'. There are references to the custom early in the 19th century, so phrased as to imply that it had been current for several generations (Opie and Tatem, 1989: 177). The modern unvarying phrase 'hot cross buns' derives from the 18th-century street vendors' cry:

Hot Cross Buns! Hot Cross Buns!
Give them to your daughters, give them to your sons!
One a penny, two a penny, Hot Cross Buns!

Some of the loaves and buns were baked for many hours, to dry out completely; they never went mouldy, but would keep for a year or more, and were grated and used as medicine, especially for diarrhoea. Also, Hone noted:

In the houses of some ignorant people, a Good Friday bun is still kept 'for luck', and sometimes there hangs from the ceiling a hard biscuit-like cake of open cross-work . . . to remain there till displaced on the next Good Friday by one of similar make; and of this the editor . . . has heard affirmed, that it preserves the house from fire. (Hone, 1827: i. 31)

There are occasional Victorian references to *fishermen's wives giving their husbands a bun to take to sea to avert shipwreck (Henderson, 1879: 82; Simpson, 1973: 112); the maritime link and the custom of permanent display find dramatic expression in the *Widow's Son Bun Ceremony.

There are a few records from the 1920s of a belief that an egg laid on Good Friday will keep fresh all year, and (from Somerset) that a *fire can be extinguished by throwing such an egg into it (Opie and Tatem, 1989: 178); there are many European parallels to this idea, showing that it is no mere imitation of the bun belief (Newall, 1971: 232–7).

See also *CRAMP RINGS, *MARBLES, *SKIPPING.

gooding, see *THOMASING.

gooseberry wife. A species of *bogey peculiar to the Isle of Wight, whose function was to guard gooseberry bushes from marauding children, in the form of a large furry caterpillar (Wright, 1913: 198).

Goosey Goosey Gander. A well-known *nursery rhyme, still in circulation although perhaps losing favour because some of its imagery is not considered quite right for today's children. Historically speaking, this rhyme seems to have less textual cohesion than most nursery rhymes, and there is evidence that this standard modern text is actually two older rhymes spliced together. The first four lines are quoted in 1784, and first printed *c*.1790, while the last four are of similar age but are often found in a traditional rhyme addressed to the cranefly.

Opie and Opie, 1997: 224–6.

gorse. Gorse bushes can produce one or two flowers at any time of the year; hence the common saying, 'When the gorse is not in bloom, then kissing's not in fashion'.

Occasionally it is included among the *flowers regarded as unlucky and not to be taken indoors, lest it bring death into the house. On the other hand, in 19th-century Cornwall it was customary to tie a sprig of gorse to the door of the house early on *May Day morning, and whoever did so would get a plate of bread and cream and a drink of skimmed milk for breakfast (*Folk-Lore* 7 (1886), 225).

Gotham, the Wise Men of. Many English villages were mocked for alleged stupidity, but only Gotham, seven miles from Nottingham, was famous well beyond its neighbourhood. There is a brief allusion to 'the foles of Gotam' in a 15th-century play, and a whole cycle of jokes about them was printed in a mid-16th-century *chapbook, *Merrie Tales of the Mad Men of Gotham*, versions of which continued to appear up to the early 19th century.

The jokes about Gothamites are drawn from the common international stock of tales about *fools. They tried to fence the *cuckoo in, so that summer would never end; when an eel got into their fishpond, they tried to kill it by drowning it; one of them burnt his house down to get rid of a wasp's nest in the thatch; another, riding home with a sack of meal, slung it across his own shoulders to spare the horse, but did not dismount; after twelve went fishing, one of the group counted to check nobody was missing, but since he forgot to count himself he made it eleven, so they were sure someone must have drowned. However, some tellers claim all this foolishness was deliberately put on, to stop King John from setting up a hunting lodge in the village—if so, the men of Gotham were wise after all!

Clouston, 1888; Alfred Stapleton, *All About the Merry Tales of Gotham* (1900). Selected texts Jacobs, 1898/1968: 279–82; Briggs, 1970–1: A. ii. 349–61.

Grail. There are no old folk traditions about the Holy Grail, though it is prominent in French Arthurian literature from the late 12th century onwards, where it is usually, but not invariably, linked to the Last Supper and Crucifixion, the Eucharist, and *Joseph of Arimathea. In English Arthurian romances it lies hidden in a mysterious castle somewhere in Britain, guarded by descendants of Joseph or of one of his companions; Arthur's knights try to obtain it, but in vain. Although the story suited medieval piety, Church writers never adopted it; eventually, late in the 15th century, *Glastonbury Abbey claimed to possess a

relic brought by Joseph, but it was of a different form: two silver flasks, one containing Christ's blood and the other his sweat.

Some scholars have argued that *Celtic myths about magic cauldrons underlie the medieval texts. There has been much interest in the Grail in the 20th century, mainly as a mythical and magical, rather than a Christian, symbol; it could therefore be said to have passed from literature into current English folklore. A Victorian belief is that it lies in a spring of reddish water near Glastonbury Tor, which since 1886 has been called 'Chalice Well', though medieval records show the name as *Chalcewelle*, meaning 'Chalkwell'; another theory, known since 1907, identifies it with a wooden drinking bowl kept in a private house at Nanteos in Wales. Both spring and bowl are said to have healing powers; in the 1750s the spring was a popular spa.

Grainger, Percy (1882–1961). Born in Melbourne, Australia, he was something of a childhood prodigy, giving concerts from the age of 12. He came to English folk *song, after hearing a talk by Lucy *Broadwood, with characteristic energy and enthusiasm, noting 435 songs between April 1905 and August 1909, including children's singing games and sea shanties, most notably in Lincolnshire, but also in Gloucestershire, London, Worcestershire, and Warwickshire. He was only one of several musicians in the field at the time, but was unique in the techniques he adopted and in his belief that the collector should note a whole tune, as scientifically as possible, to identify all the small nuances of rhythm and tone used by the best singers in their performances. For this reason he advocated the use of the phonograph, and 216 of his wax cylinders still survive (in the Library of Congress) as a unique record of traditional singing of the Edwardian period. He even persuaded the Gramophone Company to issue recordings of one of his best Lincolnshire singers, Joseph Taylor of Brigg. Grainger's advocacy of the gramophone did not meet with universal approval amongst the folk-song establishment, although several others did experiment with the new technology, but his detailed and complex attempts to annotate the tunes on paper received even less support. In this he was ahead of his time, and his methods later became commonplace in the field of ethnomusicology. Grainger also collected songs in Denmark, and from the Maori in New Zealand.

Grainger's piano arrangements of traditional *morris dance tunes such as 'Country Gardens' and 'Shepherds Hey' made him a household name.

Percy Grainger's work includes 'Collecting with the Phonograph' and 'The Impress of Personality in Traditional Singing', *JFSS* 3:3 (1908), 147–66. Songs collected by Grainger are published in *JFSS* 3:3 (1908), 170–242; *FMJ* 2:5 (1974), 335–51 (plus correction in 3:2 (1976), 171); *FMJ* 6:3 (1992), 339–58.

Jane O'Brien, *The Grainger English Folk Song Collection* (1985); Jane O'Brien, *ED&S* 44:2 (1982), 18–20; Michael Yates, *FMJ* 4:3 (1982), 265–75; John Bird, *Percy Grainger* (1976); Obituaries: *JEFDSS* 9:2 (1961), 113–4; *Journal of the International Folk Music Council* 14 (1962), 147–9.

Grasmere rushbearing. A *rushbearing custom which has survived in symbolic form in Grasmere, Cumbria, even though the church was paved in 1840. Token rushes are carried on a special linen sheet, held by six girls (the Rush Maidens), dressed in green, while others are made into elaborate shapes (called rushbearings), some as large as four or five feet tall, and carried in procession to the church. Traditional shapes for the rushbearings include harps, crosses, maypoles, and St Oswald's crown and hand. The latter is the patron saint of the parish church, and he was so good to the poor in his lifetime that St Aidan blessed his hand and prayed that it might never perish. The custom formerly took place in July, but was moved in 1885 to bring it in line with St Oswald's Day (5 August). After the procession round the village, and a church service, the rushes and rushbearings are placed on shelves in the church, and there they stay for a few days until collected by their owners. Children are given pieces of gingerbread stamped with St Oswald's name. The earliest mention of a rush custom at Grasmere is a payment of 1s. in 1680, 'For ale bestowed on those who brought rushes and repaired the church'.

Hole, 1975: 86–7; Shuel, 1985: 86–7; E. F. Rawnsley, *The Rushbearing in Grasmere and Ambleside* (1953); Gertrude M. Simpson, *The Rushbearing in Grasmere and Ambleside* (1931).

graves. From the Middle Ages through to the mid-17th century, most people were buried in simple graves marked (if at all) by a wooden cross, or under a plain flagstone of the church floor; only the élite received inscribed tombstones, effigies, or brass plaques. It was normal for graves to be reopened after some years, any remaining bones removed to an ossuary, and the ground reused for fresh burials. 'Perpetual graves' became common from the 1650s onwards, each with its carved and inscribed stone(s), offering an opportunity for local traditions of funerary art to develop, and for long, individualistic epitaphs and memorial verses. Elaboration and individualism were very marked in Victorian cemeteries; since the Second World War, however, Church authorities and town councils have curtailed the permitted choices, both in the design of headstones and in the wording of epitaphs. The rigidity of their rules may be one reason for the current liking for intensely personal *memorials at the scenes of tragic deaths.

Visiting and tending graves is a custom which varies greatly from one family to another. Some people visit weekly, or even daily; a far larger number visit at specific dates, especially in the days leading up to *Mothering Sunday, *Easter, and *Christmas, bringing cards and seasonal flowers or a holly wreath. Personal dates (birthdays, wedding anniversaries, the anniversary of death) may be similarly observed. In municipal London cemeteries, some graves of young children are decked at Christmas with floral teddies and Father Christmases, or with actual toys, and helium balloons tied nearby (*FLS News* 21 (1995), 9–10). However, there are also very many people who cannot or will not tend graves.

The traditional orientation of graves, still observed in most churchyards though not in municipal cemeteries, is towards the *east in readiness for *Doomsday. There are generally fewer on the ill-omened *north side of the church. All graves, marked or unmarked, must be treated respectfully; to tread on one is both wrong and unlucky, and also to pick flowers growing on one. A grave prepared for a Monday funeral should not be left open on the Sunday, for then someone else will shortly die; boards should be laid across it. When sextons digging new graves unearth bones from older burials, some rebury them where they lie, others in the strip of ground right against the church itself, where the soil is too shallow for normal graves [JS].

In folk *medicine, contact with death was regarded as curative; teeth from *skulls prevented toothache, moss growing on them cured plague and headaches, and parts of *coffins were good for various ills. In Cornwall in the 1850s, dew from 'the grave of the last young man buried in the churchyard' was gathered at dawn to cure a swollen neck (*N&Q* 1s:2 (1855), 474–5). The strangest belief, recorded from Sussex and Lincolnshire in 1868 and 1933 respectively, was that if a child inclined to bed-wetting is made to urinate into an open grave, or on to the grave of a child of opposite sex, this will stop the habit (Latham, 1878: 49; *Folk-Lore* 44 (1933), 204).

Graves are sometimes found, singly or in groups, on hilltops, in woods, or by the roadside. Reasons for such unorthodox locations vary; some were private burial grounds for Quakers or Nonconformists, denied access to Anglican churchyards, or for aristocratic landowners and their households; some for individuals who had personal motives to choose a particular spot. Roadside graves, if unmarked, are often said to be those of *suicides, or of highwaymen hanged, gibbetted, and eventually buried, at the scene of their crimes; these traditions may be well founded. Some are kept neat and have flowers regularly laid on them by *Gypsies and others; these include a Highwayman's Grave near Beckhampton (Wiltshire), the Boy's Grave near Newmarket (Suffolk), and Jay's Grave near Haytor (Devon), where a suicidal girl is laid. Legends naturally proliferate; the Betty of Betty's Grave, at a crossroads near Poulton (Gloucestershire) is variously called a suicide, a murder victim, a witch, a sheep-stealer, or a woman who dropped dead after a mowing competition (Chetwynd-Stapylton, 1968).

See also *BURIALS, *FUNERALS, *SUICIDES, *UNBAPTIZED INFANTS.

Great Devon Mystery, see *DEVIL'S HOOFPRINTS.

green. The idea that green is unlucky has grown steadily from the late 18th century (when it is first recorded) to the present day, spreading from Scotland and the northern counties to the whole of England. Originally it applied only to clothes, but by the late 19th century a Sussex folklorist could write: 'I have known several instances of mothers absolutely forbidding it . . . in the furniture of their houses' (Latham, 1878: 12), and nowadays those who fear green generally apply the taboo to objects of any kind, for example curtains, cars, or bicycles.

Two ideas are particularly well documented: that to wear green brings death into one's household ('Wear green, and you'll soon wear

black' is a common saying), and that green should never be worn at weddings—especially not by the bride. The reason given in some sources is that it symbolizes being forsaken, or betrayed:

> Those dressed in blue
> Have lovers true;
> In green and white,
> Forsaken quite.
>
> (Henderson, 1866: 21)

or:

> Oh, green is forsaken, and yellow forsworn,
> But blue is the prettiest colour that's worn.
>
> (*N&Q* 9s:8 (1901), 193; 9s:9 (1903), 33)

Yet another rhyme, still known and quoted by older people, is:

> Married in green,
> Ashamed to be seen.

This is usually taken to mean that the bride is pregnant and/or has had other lovers; in Elizabethan slang, 'to give a girl a green gown' was to seduce her and make love in the fields.

There has been much speculation as to why such a pleasing colour, associated with nature and living growth, has acquired this reputation. One possibility is that green stands for death, because graves lie under grass. The favourite explanation (originally Scottish) is that 'green is the *fairies' colour' and they punish anyone who wears it—though it has to be said that no traditional legend actually recounts this, and that fairies do also often wear brown or red. Regardless of whether this is the true explanation or not, it now very regularly accompanies the belief.

However, green has more positive associations too. Greenery and *evergreens are used in many seasonal customs as signs of joy and celebration, and the colour can stand for youthful vigour, spring or summer, hope, and the beneficent aspects of nature. It is also one of the two easiest colours to produce from vegetable dyes (the other is brown), so green cloth was much used in medieval and Tudor times; it should not be assumed that every personage wearing green in a ballad or folktale is necessarily a magical being.

See also *FOLIATE HEAD, *GREEN MAN, *JACK-IN-THE-GREEN, and *WILD MAN.

John Hutchings, *Folklore* 108 (1997), 55–63.

Green Children, The. According to two medieval chroniclers, Ralph of Coggeshall and

*William of Newburgh, two children were found near a pit at Woolpit (Suffolk) in the reign of King Stephen; their skin was greenish, nobody could understand their speech, and the only food they would eat was beans. One, a boy, soon died; the other, a girl, was healthier and learned to eat other food, thus losing her green colouring. She became a servant in a knight's household. Having learnt normal speech, she explained that she and her brother came from an underground world where the sun never shone and everyone was green. She was baptized, but 'was rather loose and wanton in her conduct'. Ralph, a local man, heard the story directly from her employer; William, living in Yorkshire, probably got his information from Ralph, though he gives further details, for example that the children's world was called 'St Martin's Land', and its inhabitants were Christian.

Nowadays, many local people have come to associate this medieval tale with the much later story of the *Babes in the Wood, and a village sign was erected in 1977, showing the Babes. Some writers take it to be fairy lore (Briggs, 1976: 200–1).

Green Gravel. A children's *singing game, reported from all over the country whose haunting tune and strange imagery have intrigued folklorists and children alike.

> Green gravel, green gravel, the grass is so green
> The fairest young damsel that ever was seen
> O Mary, O Mary, your true love is dead
> He sent you a letter to turn round your head . . .

This is the earliest known version, collected in Manchester in 1835 (Opie and Opie, 1985: 240). The players join hands and walk round in a ring, singing the words. At the end of the text, the one who is named stays in the ring but turns to face outwards. The whole thing begins again and another child is named. Versions were still being collected in English playgrounds into the 1980s.

Opie and Opie, 1985: 239–42; Gomme 1894: i. 170–83.

Green Man. Readers will seek in vain for any mention of 'The Green Man' in pre-war folklore collections and studies, for the present-day use of the phrase to designate a *foliate head was only invented in 1939 (see below), and the various authentic uses of the term in English folklore were obscure, and of little interest to folklorists at that time.

The first and most important relates to civic pageants in Tudor and Stuart times, which were preceded by 'whifflers', whose role was to drive back the crowds, and so make space for the main procession to pass. These were costumed as what Elizabethans called Savage Men or *Wild Men, covered in shaggy hair, or in leaves. The latter type were commonly called Green Men. Thus, at Chester in 1610, a St George's Day pageant had: 'ii men in greene leaves set with work upon their other habet [garments] with black heare & black beards very owgly to behould, and garlands upon their heads with great clubs in their hands with fireworks to scatter abroad to maintaine way for the rest of the show'. Later in the same pageant, 'two Disguised, called Greene-men, their habit Embroydered and Stitch'd on with Ivie-leaves . . . [with] huge black shaggie Hayre, Savage-like, with Ivie Garlands upon their heads, bearing Herculian clubs in their hands' fought 'an artificiall Dragon, very lively to behold' (Harleian MS 2150 fo. 356, quoted by Centerwall, 1997). At the Lord Mayor's Show of 1686 there were 'twenty Savages or Green Men, with Squibs and Fire-works, to sweep the Streets, and keep off the Crowd' (Matthew Taubman, *London's Yearly Jubilee*, 1686: 12–13; quoted by Centerwall, 1997: 26).

Tudor court masques and entertainments sometimes included performers dressed in moss and ivy; the sources call them 'Wild' Men, but from the descriptions they could equally well be called 'Green' (see quotations at *Wild Man, Woman).

Also in the 17th century, the Distillers' Company had as its heraldic arms the 'Green Man and Still', in which the supporters were naked, club-bearing, shaggy figures. An undated quotation attributed to John Bagford (1650–1716) says: 'They are called woudmen, or wildmen, thou' at thes day we in ye signe [trade] call them Green Men, couered with grene boues . . . a fit emblem for those that use that intosticating licker which berefts them of their sennes' (quoted by Centerwall, 1997: 27). Aubrey too mentions 'The Wild Man' and 'The Green Man' interchangeably as 'not uncommon' names for London inns, with signs showing 'a kind of Hercules with a green club and green leaves about his pudenda and head' (Aubrey, 1686/1880: 134–5, 177). The design was still used on 18th-century pubs, but by the 19th century its meaning was seemingly forgotten, and it had been almost invariably replaced by the more popular figure of Robin Hood or a forester dressed in green (Larwood and Hotton, 1866: 221–2). Nowadays, thanks to the influence of the books discussed below, several 'Green Man' pubs have repainted their signs yet again to show either a head peering through leaves, or a *Jack-in-the-Green.

In 1939, however, in an article in *Folk-Lore*, Lady Raglan invented a new use for the phrase, applying it to the type of ornamental church carving previously always called a *foliate head—a face with leaves growing from it, or leafy twigs emerging from its mouth. She explained how a vicar had shown her one and had suggested that: 'it was intended to symbolise the spirit of inspiration, but it seemed to me certain that it was a man and not a spirit, and moreover that it was a "Green Man". So I named it, and the evidence that I have collected to support this title is the reason for this paper.'

This was pure speculation, unbacked by evidence, and it is by no means clear what she meant by the term, or why she put it in quotation marks and gave it capitals (she was unaware of the Tudor and Stuart references to leaf-clad masqueraders in pageants). She further asserts this to be identical with '... Jack-in-the-Green, Robin Hood, the King of the May, and the [Castleton] Garland ... the central figure in the May-Day celebrations throughout Northern and Central Europe'. In accordance with Frazerian theory, she goes on to speculate that because the *Castleton Garland is drawn up the church tower on a rope, the man wearing it (and consequently all 'Green Men') would have once been hanged as a spring sacrifice. Thus items with widely different functions and histories were conflated on the basis of a single visual trait, leafiness.

Despite the fragility of Lady Raglan's argument, her term was adopted for foliate heads in several books on church art by M. D. Anderson in the 1940s and 1950s, in the authoritative series of *Buildings of England* guides by Nikolaus Pevsner, and finally as the title for a scholarly and influential study of foliate heads by Kathleen Basford (1978), which in turn served as a starting-point for many subsequent writers and an inspiration to artists. Brandon Centerwall has recently argued that the term is correct after all, and that the leafy whifflers of pageantry were meant to represent the foliate heads in churches. The aura of mystery in the name and its harmony with current ecological concerns have endeared it to many, and 'the Green Man' will probably prove to be an unshakable element in the popular concept of 'folklore'.

See also *CASTLETON GARLAND, *FOLIATE HEADS, *JACK-IN-THE-GREEN, *ROBIN HOOD, *WILD MAN.

Lady Raglan, *Folk-Lore* 50 (1939), 45–57; Basford, 1978/1996; Roy Judge, in *Colour and Appearance in Folklore*, ed. John Hutchings and Juliette Wood (1991), 51–5; Brandon S. Centerwall, *Folklore* 108 (1997), 25–34.

gremlins. A subspecies of *goblin which evolved early in the 20th century, probably during the First World War; certainly their existence was acknowledged (with dismay) by members of the RAF during the 1920s. They are reported to be anything from six inches to two feet in height, greenish or grey, sometimes with horns or hairy ears, and wearing a wide variety of colourful and eccentric clothing. Their original speciality was causing otherwise inexplicable malfunctions in the engines, electrical circuits, and other operational parts of aircraft, drinking up petrol, and tampering with landing strips on airfields. They have since diversified, and apply their expertise to virtually any type of machinery, the more complex the better; one group has become skilled in producing misprints. They often laugh uproariously at the success of their activities, a trait which may indicate kinship to *Puck and *Robin Goodfellow.

Accounts of the appearance and behaviour of gremlins circulated orally among British airmen stationed in Malta, the Middle East, and India during the 1920s and 1930s; the first printed record seems to be a poem in the journal *Aeroplane* on 10 April 1929. They were much discussed, both orally and in print, in the RAF and the Fleet Air Arm in the Second World War. Interest in them spread to the civilian press (e.g. *Punch* (11 Nov. 1942), *Spectator* (1 Jan. 1943), several issues of *N&Q*, 1943), and reached America (*New York Times Magazine* (11 Apr. 1943), *Time* (28 Sept. 1943)). In recent years, they have become the subject of cinematic investigation by Joe Danke which revealed hitherto unknown aspects of their biology, metabolism, and personalities (*Gremlins*, 1984, and *Gremlins II*, 1990).

The origin of the word 'gremlin' itself is obscure. RAF tradition links it with Fremlins beer, though opinions differ as to whether this is because the first gremlin seen was a goblin swimming in a tankard of Fremlins, or because it appeared to a group of officers who were drinking Fremlins and reading Grimm's Fairy Tales simultaneously.

When speaking or writing about gremlins,

it is essential to present the information with as much ingenious detail as possible, and to preserve an attitude of total conviction.

John W. Hazen in *Funk & Wagnalls Dictionary of Folklore, Mythology and Legend*, ed. Maria Leach (New York, 1949; 3rd edn. 1972), 465–6; Gillian Edwards, *Hobgoblin and Sweet Puck* (1974), 209–24; P. Beale, *Concise Dictionary of Slang and Unconventional English* (1989).

Gretna Green. The reputation of this Scottish village as a place where runaway English couples could marry dates from 1754, when clandestine marriages were forbidden throughout England, only those where banns had been published or a special licence obtained being valid. The law did not apply to Scotland, so couples hastened to various villages just across the Border, where they could be instantly married by simple declaration in front of witnesses. At Gretna, the best known, the ceremony took place in the toll-house till 1826, and thereafter in the village hall; it could be conducted by anyone—toll-keeper, ferryman, innkeeper, blacksmith—but popular memory remembers the blacksmith alone, alleging that the couple had to join hands over the anvil, while he waved his hammer over them. In 1856 Scottish law was amended to require three weeks' residence from couples seeking marriage, so instant weddings were no longer possible, but Gretna's well-publicized romantic image still draws many to marry there.

Grim. Several names of prehistoric landscape features such as earthworks, hill forts, and flint mines, include the element 'Grim-'. The name Grimsditch occurs in eleven counties (in some, more than once); Grimsbury twice; Grime's Graves, Grimspound, and Grim's Hill once each. Presumably this Grim was a supernatural entity—perhaps Woden, since his Scandinavian equivalent, Odin, had 'Grimr' as a secondary name, and since the massive earthwork Wansdyke (Wiltshire) was undoubtedly named for him. However, there is also an Anglo-Saxon noun *grima*, meaning 'goblin' or 'spectre', so the situation is not clear-cut. Jennifer Westwood suggests that 'it is a question of scale', awe-inspiring features being ascribed to the god, small ones to the goblin (Westwood, 1985: 69–72).

The *chapbook *Life of Robin Goodfellow* (1628) has among its characters a 'Fairy Grim' who boasts that he frightens many people by crying like a screech-owl at sick men's windows, that some call him the *Black Dog of Newgate,

and that when young people are making merry he comes in 'in some feareful shape' to scare them away and steal their food. The Yorkshire 'church grim' lurked inside the building, but would 'maraud abroad' in stormy weather; it might toll the death-knell at midnight, and peer from a window during funerals, showing by its expression whether the dead person was saved or damned (Wright, 1913: 194). It also sometimes showed itself as a death warning, in the form of a black dog.

Grimm, Jacob (1785–1863), **and Grimm, Wilhelm** (1786–1859). The Brothers Grimm were figures of major importance for folklore studies throughout Europe, but it is only relevant here to speak of their impact in England. Their famous joint collection of *fairytales, the *Kinder- und Hausmärchen*, appeared in 1812–14, and was first translated into English in 1823. They are now thoroughly absorbed into the part-oral, part-printed traditions of English children; they include such famous stories as 'The Frog Prince', 'Snow White', 'Rapunzel', 'Little Red Riding Hood' (also told by *Perrault), 'Hansel and Gretel', and 'Rumpelstiltskin'.

The principles set out by the Grimms strongly affected the development of folklore studies. They urged fidelity to the spoken text, without embellishments, and though it has been shown that they did not always practise what they preached, the idealized 'orality' of their style was much closer to reality than the literary retellings previously thought necessary. They believed folklore expressed the true spiritual and moral values of a nation, faithfully preserved by the uneducated rural population, and that it consisted largely of broken-down fragments of ancient myths and religious beliefs. Noticing that the same tale recurs in variants from distant periods and places, they argued that this implies descent from a shared prehistoric culture.

Another important collection, until recently little known to English-speaking scholars, was their *Deutsche Sagen* (1816–18; 2nd edn. 1865–6); it covers historical and local legends and those about supernatural beings, which provide many parallels to English legends about fairies, witches, hauntings, treasures, etc. Jacob Grimm's *Deutsche Mythologie* (1835; final edn. 1875–8) was an erudite discussion covering the folklore and medieval writings of all Germanic countries, encouraging folklorists to interpret supernatural beings (e.g. *water-spirits, or the *Wild Hunt) as former divinities.

There are many translations of Grimms' *Fairy Tales*; the best are Jack Zipes, *The Complete Fairy Tales of the Brothers Grimm* (1987); and David Luke, *Jacob and Wilhelm Grimm: Selected Tales* (1982). *Deutsche Sagen* was edited and translated by Donald Ward (with excellent notes and assessment) as *The German Legends of the Brothers Grimm* (2 vols., 1981). *Deutsche Mythologie* was translated by J. S. Stallybrass as *Teutonic Mythology* (3 vols., 1880–3). The only full-length biography in English is that by Ruth Michaelis-Jena, *The Brothers Grimm* (1970).

groaning cake (or cheese). In the northern counties, women recovering from *childbirth were given rich fruitcake, gingerbread, and Cheshire cheese, and female neighbours were invited in to share it, as part of the celebration. Several writers from the late 18th to the late 19th centuries mention a form of *divination, similar to that done with wedding cake, but more boisterous. Slices of the cake or cheese would be cut into chunks by the new father, tossed in the midwife's smock, and given to unmarried girls so that they could put them under their pillows and dream of their future husbands (Opie and Tatem, 1989: 183). Sometimes, another slice was given to the first person of opposite sex met on the road as the child was taken to its *baptism (Radford, Radford, and Hole, 1961: 175).

In Cambridgeshire, the term was differently used; it referred to a pain-killing cake which included gin and crushed hemp seed (cannabis) among the ingredients, which midwives gave women in labour (Porter, 1969: 13).

grottoes. An annual *display custom, which lasted well into the 1950s and 1960s, in which children constructed 'grottoes' on the pavement and solicited coins from passers-by. Some authorities give 25 July (St James's Day), while others maintain that early August was the proper time, a probable explanation being that St James's Day *Old-Style* is 5 August. The grottoes were made of oyster shells, although some say they should be scallops. Scallop shells are the accepted symbol of St James, and early August was when the oyster season started and millions of oysters were consumed in London during the season (at four a penny). An old proverb is often quoted—'He who eats oysters on St James's Day will not want money'. The earliest known reference to grottoes is in *Time's Telescope* for 1823 (190–1):

On St James's day (O.S.) large quantities of oysters are eaten by Londoners, but their children are content to use the shells for building grottos and to illuminate these by means of rush-lights. The children ask passers-by for contributions to the grottos. This is an annual custom, but it lasts several weeks, to the annoyance of pedestrians. (Quoted by Wright and Lones, 1940: iii. 40).

The earlier form of grotto was a beehive-shaped pile of shells, perhaps two or three feet high, with a small opening or tunnel at ground level in which was placed the light or candle, although at least one description places the candle on top of the pile. Other forms comprise a box, or just an area of pavement marked out and decorated with flowers, beads, broken glass and china, cut-out pictures, or anything to make it 'pretty'. The accompanying rhyme, by which the children hope to gain recompense for their artistic endeavours, varied from place to place:

> Please remember the grotto
> Me father has run off to sea
> Me mother's gone to fetch 'im back
> So please give a farthin' to me!

> (Rose Gamble, *Chelsea Child* (1979), 105–9,
> remembering Chelsea in the 1920s)

Most of the descriptions refer to grottoing as a London custom, but other reports from Essex, Kent, Hampshire, Sussex, and Swansea bear witness to its wider occurrence. The custom seems to have been particularly tenacious around Mitcham, Surrey. It is possible that grottoing still lingers in the 1990s, perhaps in the privacy of the home, but it has probably gone the way of most children's 'street display' customs.

Good illustrations in *Illustrated London News* (2 Aug. 1851), 137–8; and Merton Library Service, *Merton in Pictures Book 3: Mitcham Fair* (1991), 9. Wright and Lones, 1940: iii. 40; Folklore Society Cuttings Collection.

Guise Dancing. A *calendar custom, apparently unique to Cornwall, which took place during the period between *Christmas and *Twelfth Night and lasted well into the 20th century in the Penzance area and possibly elsewhere. Descriptions vary considerably, but the core of the custom was young people from the villages around to visit the town dressed in all sorts of strange costume or fancy dress, with *cross-dressing particularly popular, and many with blackened faces. Impromptu dances and games took place, and, in some descriptions, hard drinking and fighting. The custom is variously called 'Goose', 'Geese', or 'Geeze Dancing', and although this has caused some confusion it is clear that this reflects local pronunciations of 'Guise', a word which is used in various parts of the country for customs which involve dressing up or disguising (see *guising). In some reports, the Guise Dancers performed the local *mumming play, but it is most likely that this is a combination of what in most cases were two distinct customs.

Jenkin, 1934: 176–81; Wright and Lones, 1938: ii. 56–7; Hunt, 1881: 394.

guising. One of the regularly used local words, in various parts of Britain, for customs which involve disguise or dressing up and for the participants in those customs. Thus in Staffordshire and northern counties the guisers performed the local *mumming play, in Cornwall there was a fancy-dress custom called *Guise Dancing, and in Yorkshire the guisers would force entry to the mell–supper *harvest celebrations.

gurning, girning. The competitive making of grotesque faces, usually with the face framed by a horse-collar. It was previously popular at many fairs and other gatherings, but gurning's only surviving traditional venue appears to be at *Egremont Crab-Apple Fair, where they claim to have the World Champion Gurning Competition. Wright's *English Dialect Dictionary* gives several, clearly related, meanings for the word, such as 'to show or gnash the teeth in rage or scorn; to snarl as a dog; to look savage, distort the countenance; to speak in a snarling, surly tone; to show the teeth in laughing; to grin; to speak with a grimace or chuckle'. The earliest reference cited is from 1685, and nearly all the other pre-1800 quotations are Scottish rather than English. Pulling faces has long appealed to English humour, as can easily be seen on gargoyles, misericords, and other minor items of comic carving in medieval churches.

N&Q 176 (1939), 226, 267, 303, 413.

Gutch, Eliza (1840–1931). Born Eliza Hutchinson in Lincolnshire, she became Mrs Gutch (as she was widely known) when she married York solicitor John James Gutch in 1868. Mrs Gutch was a founder member of the *English Dialect Society (1873) and of the *Folklore Society (1878). Indeed, it was her suggestion in *Notes & Queries (5s:5 (1876), 194) that a new society be formed that led to the foundation of the latter. She contributed large amounts of material on Lincolnshire and Yorkshire to Joseph Wright's *English Dialect Dictionary*, and

was well known to readers of *N&Q* for her hundreds of contributions, spread over 70 years, under the pseudonym 'St Swithin'. Mrs Gutch was one of several Victorian women who made immense contributions to folklore and dialect studies but who, because they did not write major articles or books, are largely forgotten. She was extremely well read and her forte was as supplier of information and source material to those who needed it, such as in the *N&Q* columns and in the three books which she edited for the Folklore Society's County Folklore series which gave her the opportunity to gather and make available material from a wide range of sources.

Mrs Gutch's work includes *County Folklore: Examples of Printed Folk-Lore Concerning the North Riding of Yorkshire, York and the Ainsty* (1901); Mrs Gutch and Mabel Peacock, *County Folklore: Examples of Printed Folklore Concerning Lincolnshire* (1908); Mrs Gutch, *County Folklore: Examples of Printed Folk-Lore Concerning the East Riding of Yorkshire* (1912).

Obituary in *Folk-Lore* 41 (1930), 301; Eileen Elder, ' . . . But Who was Mrs Gutch?', *Newsletter of the Society For Lincolnshire History and Archaeology* (Jan. 1988), 23–6; Eileen Elder, 'Two Lincolnshire Folklorists: Mrs Gutch and Miss Mabel Peacock', *Lincolnshire Life* (Oct. 1988), 24–5.

Guy Fawkes Night, see *NOVEMBER THE FIFTH.

Guy of Warwick. Now virtually forgotten, Sir Guy of Warwick was once famous enough to be counted one of the Nine Worthies of the World; his story first appears as a Norman-French poem of about 1200, though he is alleged to have lived in the reign of Athelstan. He fought against Saracens abroad and Danes at home, killed giants and dragons, married an Earl's daughter, and became a hermit who begged, unrecognized, at the doors of his own castle. Later versions in *chapbooks and street *ballads added his fight against the Dun Cow and an equally monstrous boar. In the 17th century visitors to Warwick Castle were shown an arras depicting Guy's exploits, various huge weapons and other items (implying Guy was gigantic), and the grotto where he lived as a hermit; other sites displayed bones supposedly from the monstrous cow and boar. Some of the Castle weapons are still on show, and pub names and local place-names still recall the legend (Palmer, 1976: 130–4).

R. S. Crane, *Publications of the Modern Language Association of America* 30 (1915), 125–94. For two texts of the 1790s, see John Simons (ed.), *Guy of Warwick and Other Chapbook Romances* (1998), 51–70.

guytrash, gytrash. A frightening shape-changing apparition, usually in animal form, in the folklore of northern England. It was described by Branwell Brontë (d. 1848) in his unpublished fragment *Percy* as 'a spectre not at all similar to the ghosts of those who were once alive, nor to fairies, nor to demons' which appears mostly as 'a black dog dragging a chain, a dusky calf, nay, even a rolling stone'; at the house where his tale is set, the gytrash was known as 'an old, dwarfish and hideous man, as often without a head as with one, moving at dark along the naked fields'. Branwell's biographer, Winifred Gerin, confirms that this is an authentic tradition linked to Ponden House, and adds that this gytrash could also take the shape of a 'flaming barrel bowling across the fields', and appeared as an omen of disaster to the family there.

In Charlotte Brontë's *Jane Eyre* ((1847) chapter 12), the heroine, hearing a horse approaching towards dusk, remembers her nurse's tales about 'a North-of-England spirit, called a Gytrash, which, in the form of horse, mule or large dog, haunted solitary ways, and sometimes came upon belated travellers, as this horse was coming upon me'. She then sees a black-and-white dog, 'a lion-like creature with long hair and a huge head', which also reminds her of a gytrash; in fact, of course, both dog and horse are perfectly normal animals belonging to Mr Rochester.

Another possible form is that of a large cow; to see it is an omen of death, for oneself or another (Wright 1913: 194).

Gwerin. Founded in 1956 as a 'half-yearly journal of Folk Life' by its editor Iorwerth C. Peate (1901–82), *Gwerin* was the first periodical devoted to the subject of folk life in Britain, and paved the way for the *Society for Folk Life Studies' journal *Folk Life* which continues to this day. The word 'gwerin' is Welsh for 'folk', but the journal took the whole of the British Isles, and beyond, as its brief. As befits the field which it helped to define, *Gwerin* provided a much-needed focus for museum workers and others from related disciplines who were beginning to take a serious interest in folk life, to describe and discuss traditional ways of life. The last issue was vol. 3, no. 6 (1962).

Gypsies. Since the Romantic period, Gypsies have had a glamorous image for writers and artists outside their communities, evoking ideas of freedom, exotic passion, mystery, and a life close to nature. In folk tradition, however, the stereotyping is negative; Gypsies are seen as dangerous outsiders; they are likely to seduce respectable women, for example in the well-known song about the grand lady who left her husband and child to follow a Gypsy (F. J. Child, *English and Scottish Ballads*, no. 200). They are suspected of cunning and dishonesty in their work as horse-traders, scrap merchants, and street sellers, and feared for their reputed power to cast spells, *curse, and bless—a reputation they themselves fully exploit.

Real or pretended Gypsies have long made their living as *fortune-tellers (Davies, 1999a: 258–65). The first law against them in England, in 1530, condemns their 'greate subtyll and crafty meanes' of deceiving people through palmistry; in 1620 John *Melton noted in his *Astrologaster* how 'figure-casters' (i.e. drawers of horoscopes) 'would appear in the villages in the likeness of Gypsies ... and that they might be thought to come of the issue of that sun-burnt generation, they with herbs and plants ... (would) discolour their faces, and then for bread, beere, bacon, cheese, but especially for money, would undertake to tell poore maid-servants their fortunes'. Gypsies still work as fairground fortune-tellers, using palmistry, the crystal ball, or cards; they visit many towns to sell 'lucky' white *heather in the streets, where they offer instant fortune-telling. The old request to 'cross the Gypsy's palm with silver' has now become 'Give us gold, dearie', meaning a £1 coin, or even 'Give us paper, dearie' [JS]. The rumour of a 'Gypsy curse' surfaces occasionally, for instance to explain a football club's repeatedly poor results.

The other long-established dread was of their kidnapping children. Flora Thompson describes in *Lark Rise to Candleford* ((1945), chapter 2) how it scared her to see any Gypsies, 'for there was a tradition that once, years before, a child from a neighbouring village had been stolen by them'. This fear seems to have died away, though 'I'll give you to the Gypsies' was a threat used to naughty children within living memory.

The real lifestyle and customs of Gypsy families are virtually unknown to the English public, apart from the lavish *funerals of their most respected members—invariably dubbed 'Gypsy Kings' or 'Queens' by the press. Folklorists are aware that some have kept the art of formal *storytelling, and fine *fairytales were collected from them in England early in the 20th century (Philip, 1992: pp. xvii–xx), and are still being collected in Scotland.

For the Gypsies' own history and traditions, see J. Okely, *The Traveller-Gypsies* (1983); D. Mayall, *Gypsy-Travellers in 19th-Century Society* (1988); Angus Fraser, *The Gypsies* (2nd edn., 1995); F. H. Groome, *Gypsy Folk-Tales* (1899); *The Journal of the Gypsy-Lore Society*.

Hagmena, see *NEW YEAR.

hag-riding. This term refers to a frightening sensation of being held immobile in bed, often by a heavy weight pressing on one's stomach or chest. It is now recognized medically under the name 'sleep paralysis'; it can be accompanied by the sense of an alien presence, and by visual hallucinations. In folklore, it was thought of as a magical attack, though whether by demonic incubus, ghost, harmful fairy, or witch varied according to place and period. Where the term 'hag-riding' was used it usually implied that a witch was to blame, and in 19th-century Dorset and Somerset several people were prosecuted for physically attacking elderly women who, they alleged, had 'hagged' or 'hag-ridden' them, in order to break their power by drawing blood (Davies, 1997: 37–9).

The commonest counter-charm was a *holed stone above the bed; however, one Somerset man in 1862 slept with a nail-studded board tied to his chest, so that if the hag who had plagued him came again, 'she won't sit there long!' (Davies, 1997: 47). A Hampshire woman used to hang a scythe over her children's bed (N&Q 10s:7 (1907), 157).

When horses were found sweating and exhausted in the morning, it was thought that witches or fairies had ridden them all night, and tangled their manes; this too was called hag-riding, and could be prevented by hanging a holed stone over their stalls, round their necks, or at the stable door. Hooks and shears were effective too (Herrick, *Hesperides* (1648), no. 892).

hagstone. A widespread name for a *holed stone, when used to prevent *hag-riding; the word is first recorded by Francis Grose (A Provincial Glossary, 1787).

hair. This makes many appearances in *superstitions, cures, tales, popular errors, and *divination. One should be particularly careful in the disposal of hair after cutting or brushing, as such removable parts of the body can be used in *witchcraft against you. Birds must also be prevented from using your hair to make their nests, as this would mean a headache, or if a magpie, death within a year, so the only safe method of disposal is to burn it (Opie and Tatem, 1989: 184). Most *regional folklore collections include examples of the divinatory use of hair. When it is thrown on the fire, for example, if it burns brightly then a long life is to be expected, but smouldering means the opposite. A single hair drawn between the nails of finger and thumb indicates the character of its owner.

A belief reported from the 17th century to the present day is that if a person's hair grows into a low point over the forehead, like a peak, she/he will be widowed soon—hence the name 'Widow's peak'. Schoolchildren had a particularly useful belief: if you place a single hair across the palm of your hand, it will split the cane with which you are being chastised, or at least it will considerably lessen the pain felt (Harland and Wilkinson, 1873: 225; N&Q 11s:11 (1915), 277–8). See also *onion for a similar idea. Also, 'In my childhood I used to be told that if you swallowed a long hair it would twine about your heart and kill you' (N&Q 8s:10 (1896), 47), an image which is surprisingly old, being found in Thomas Middleton's play, *The Witch* (IV. i): '. . . let one of her long hairs wind about my heart, and be the end of me.'

Porter (1969: 81–2) gives several recipes for traditional hair care from Cambridgeshire, including tobacco and pepper to cure ringworms, and the use of goose grease or bear's grease to keep hair healthy. A Lincolnshire woman, however, swore by hedgehog fat for this purpose (Sutton, 1992: 147) and many writers comment that *rosemary leaves make an excellent hair tonic or rinse. Since at least the 16th century it was thought essential to comb your hair the right way (Lean, 1903: ii. 24), and if you want your hair to grow back thick and luxuriant, it must be cut when the *moon is waxing. It was considered unlucky to cut hair on *Friday, and *Good Friday was the worst day of all to do it; a baby's hair should never be cut until it is twelve months old (N&Q 2s:12 (1861), 500).

There has been a long-standing prejudice against *red hair in Britain since at least c.1200. At best, red-haired people were considered unreliable and hot-tempered, and archetypal evil people such as *Judas Iscariot and Cain were usually depicted with red hair and beard. Another explanation sometimes given is that the Danish invaders had red hair, and red-haired children were sometimes quoted as evidence of their mother's infidelity (Harland and Wilkinson, 1873: 225; N&Q 12s:2 (1916), 128,196–7, 239, 379; 12s:5 (1918), 194, 218; Opie and Tatem, 1989: 325–6).

A regularly reported cure for whooping cough is to take a hair from the afflicted child, place it between two slices of bread, and give them to a dog to eat. The dog will get the cough and the child will be cured (Porter, 1969: 90, and many others). Two widespread 'popular errors' concerning hair are the beliefs that hair could continue to grow after death, and that a person's hair could turn white overnight through extreme fear or mental anguish. The latter idea still turns up as a motif in some *contemporary legends. See the correspondence in N&Q 4s:6 (1870); 4s:7 (1871); 6s:6 (1882); 6s:7 (1883); 6s:8 (1883); 6s:9 (1884); 7s:2 (1886); 7s:3 (1887); 7s:4 (1887); 7s:7 (1889); 10s:9 (1908); 10s:10 (1908).

Opie and Tatem, 1989: 184–6, 325–6, 445–6.

Hallaton Hare Pie and Bottle-Kicking. At Hallaton, Leicestershire, they have an *Easter Monday custom involving a hare pie, which is not made of hares, and a bottle-kicking game where the objects are not bottles and are not kicked. The pie and the bottle-kicking may have been two customs at one time, but now they are inextricably linked as two elements in a day-long village celebration. The day starts with a church service and blessing of a locally made pie, traditionally called the hare pie but nowadays made of beef. As hares are out of season at Easter, it is unlikely that it ever did contain that animal, and an 1892 account

speaks of mutton, veal, and bacon. Half of the pie is distributed to participants at the churchyard gate, while the other half heads a procession through the village out to the Hare Pie Bank. Also in the procession are three men, each holding aloft a small iron-hooped wooden barrel, called the bottles. At the Bank, the rest of the pie is broken up and thrown to the crowd to be *scrambled for. Then the serious bottle-kicking game commences. Two of the bottles are filled with ale, the third is not. Like the street *football games described elsewhere, the bottle-kicking is played between two teams, ostensibly people from Hallaton on one side and from nearby Medbourne on the other, but in reality anyone not from Hallaton has to play for Medbourne—which gives the latter a tactical advantage. There are virtually no rules, and much of the play involves the bottle disappearing in a mass disorganized scrum, while occasionally a player manages to break free and run for the goal. The goals are a stream at one end and a hedge at the other, and a game can last for hours. Once a goal is scored, the second bottle is brought into play and if the score is even the third will be used as a decider. The origin is, as usual, unknown, although it is known that at some date a plot of land called Hare Crop Leys was bequeathed to the local rector on condition that he use the rent to provide two hare pies, a quantity of ale, and two dozen penny loaves for the Easter Monday custom.

Kightly, 1986: 56–7; Shuel, 1985: 165–6; Wright and Lones, 1936: i. 117–18; Hole, 1975: 47; Crawford, 1938: 151–2; Stone, 1906: 43–5.

Halliwell-Phillipps, James Orchard (1820–89). A prolific editor of literary-antiquarian works, and an avid dealer in rare books and manuscripts, although for most of his life he was so short of money that he was forced to sell off his collection on a number of occasions, and for a while in 1843–4 he was under suspicion for handling manuscripts stolen from Cambridge University Library. Originally plain 'Halliwell', he added the -Phillipps in 1872. Many of his publications were issued in short print-run pamphlets and are now extremely hard to locate. From the 1840s onwards, he increasingly concentrated on Shakespeare scholarship, and he broke new ground in the meticulous use of local archives and unpublished material, for which he is justly renowned to this day.

Halliwell did much service to the fledgling

folklore scholarship in his editing of early printed materials, chapbooks, and so on, but he also compiled several books which are more directly relevant and still used as sources. The first was *The Nursery Rhymes of England, Collected Principally from Oral Tradition* which he edited for the Percy Society in 1842. This did not contain much in the way of scholarly apparatus, being mainly a collection of texts, but it had an immediate popular sale, and went through several editions in a very short time. For modern-day scholars, it marks the start of the serious study of *children's folklore and *nursery rhymes. His second book of this type, *Popular Rhymes and Nursery Tales* (1849) extended the coverage further into narrative, and included more commentary. Between them, these volumes covered, as well as nursery rhymes, proverbs, riddles, counting-out rhymes, games, tongue-twisters, songs, and tales such as Jack and the Giants, The Story of Mr. Fox, and Chicken-Licken. Halliwell was well placed to provide excellent historical analogues for many of the items which he included, and this wide reading also shows in another essential folklore work, sandwiched between his nursery rhyme books, the *Dictionary of Archaic and Provincial Words, Obsolete Phrases, Proverbs, and Ancient Customs from the Fourteenth Century* (1846), which again is still a very useful reference tool for the modern researcher. An example of how the skills of the literary antiquarian were brought into the service of folklore is his *Illustrations of the Fairy Mythology of A Midsummer Night's Dream*, published by the Shakespeare Society in 1845.

DNB; Dorson, 1968: 66–74.

Halloween (31 October). The eve of a major Catholic festival, *All Saints (1 November), assigned to this date in the 8th century; next comes *All Souls (2 November), instituted c.1000 AD as a day to pray for the dead. In England since the 19th century, and increasingly in the 20th century, it has acquired a reputation as a night on which ghosts, witches, and fairies are especially active. Why this should be is debatable.

Currently, it is widely supposed that it originated as a pagan Celtic festival of the dead, related to the Irish and Scottish *Samhain (1 November) marking the onset of winter, a theory popularized by *Frazer. Certainly Samhain was a time for festive gatherings, and medieval Irish texts and later Irish, Welsh, and

Scottish folklore use it as a setting for supernatural encounters, but there is no evidence that it was connected with the dead in pre-Christian times, or that pagan religious ceremonies were held (Hutton, 1996: 360–70).

Anglo-Saxon texts never mention this date. Bede notes that the native name for November had been *Blod-monath*, 'Blood Month' (when surplus livestock was slaughtered to save fodder, and some offered as sacrifices), but does not pinpoint one day as significant. From the Middle Ages through to the 19th century, there is no sign in England that 31 October had any meaning except as the eve of All Saints' Day, when bells might be joyfully rung (as also on Christmas Eve and Easter Eve). Mournful tolling marked All Souls' Day, as a call to prayer for the dead. Reformers naturally objected to both, and under Elizabeth I 'the superstitious ringing of bells at Allhallowtide, and at All Souls' Day, with the two nights before and after' was prohibited (Strype's *Annals* quoted in Hazlitt, 1905: 299). But prayer for the dead proved tenacious; there are scattered references from the 16th to the early 19th centuries to people praying in the open fields at night by the light of straw torches or small bonfires, especially in Lancashire and Derbyshire (Wright and Lones, 1940: iii. 109; Hutton, 1996: 372–4). Contrary to popular opinion, the link with fire is fairly late in England, the first allusion being from 1658, though implying a well-established custom: 'On All-Hallow e'en the master of the family anciently used to carry a bunch of straw, fired, about his corn' (Sir William Dugdale, quoted in Hutton, 1996: 373). Early folklorists overstressed this aspect, pursuing solar symbolism and a parallel to the *Beltane fires.

Folklore collections of the later 19th and 20th centuries make remarkably little mention of Halloween in England (as against Scotland), and what there is comes mainly from northern counties. Most quote Scottish sources, especially Robert Burns's poem 'Halloween', and it may well be that some customs detailed below were imported from Scotland to England through literary influences and fashions in Victorian times. Writing in the 1950s, Iona and Peter Opie demonstrated that Halloween was popular among children living to the north and west of a boundary running roughly south-west from the Humber to the Welsh border and then down the Severn, while those to the south and east hardly even noticed it (they celebrated *November the Fifth instead). Modern factors have eliminated this distinction, but its former presence supports the suspicion that Halloween was originally Scottish.

The most common 19th-century references are to love *divinations. All over the country, young people would lay two nuts (in some areas, two apple pips) side by side in the fire, named after themselves and their loved ones, to see whether they exploded or not; in the south, it was generally held that a loud pop was a good sign for the match, but northerners regarded this as bad. As on so many other nights, girls would put something under their pillows to dream of husbands: *rosemary and a crooked sixpence (Addy, 1895: 80), or, in Herefordshire, a sprig of churchyard *yew (*Folk-Lore Journal* 4 (1886), 111). An eyewitness account from Norfolk describes five men sitting all night round a pitchfork on which was placed a clean white shirt, believing that the sweetheart of one of them, 'were she true to him', would enter and remove it (Major Charles Loftus, *My Life 1815–1849* (1877), 302–3; quoted in Wright and Lones, 1940: iii. 114–15). For other Halloween divinations, see *cabbage, *dumb cake, *sage, *three dishes.

Apples and nuts, readily available at this time, were a traditional Halloween food (hence its other name, 'Nut-Crack Night'), and appear in several old games now revived for children's parties. Players have to catch in their teeth apples floating in water, or hanging from a string, or balanced on a heap of flour. Whereas Scottish children disguised themselves and went house *visiting, English ones more commonly attended a fancy dress party indoors; they also traditionally played at scaring people with lanterns of hollowed turnips or swedes, carved into faces and with lighted candles inside (cf. *Punkie Night). In Yorkshire, they called this *Mischief Night and played tricks on all and sundry.

Halloween is one of the few festivals whose popularity has increased, not declined, in recent years. Since about 1980, the media have shown growing interest, shops are full of scary masks and witches' hats, and children have taken to roaming the streets in costume, knocking on doors, saying a rhyme, and expecting money or sweets. They use pumpkins, not turnips, as lanterns. A hundred years ago, children's *visiting customs of this type were commonplace, but they have

declined so sharply that this new variant is surprising. It is clear from the use of the American term 'Trick or Treat' that it was a direct import from America, familiar to children from comics, cinema, and TV; a contributory factor was the tendency of schools and British children's TV, at about the same time, to present it as a safer alternative to Guy Fawkes Night. There have been howls of protest in this country against the Americanization of British culture, the danger to children out at night, and/or the alarm caused to the elderly. Most vociferous is the backlash from fundamentalist Christians, and even many mainstream clergy, arguing that celebrating supernatural evil forces is morally dangerous, and the fact that it is 'fun' makes it worse. Neo-pagans added fuel to this fire by claiming Samhain is older than All Saints, and was hijacked by the Church. At the time of writing, this moral battle still rages, and many schools have opted to ignore Halloween, for the sake of peace.

See also *ALL SAINTS, *ALL SOULS, *ANTROBUS, *SOULING.

Wright and Lones, 1940: iii. 107–20; Hutton, 1996: 360–85; Opie and Opie, 1959: 268–76; Roger Homan, *British Journal of Religious Education* 14:1 (1991), 9–14.

Hamer, Frederick (1909–69). A keen *morris and country dancer and an active member of the *English Folk Dance and Song Society and the *Morris Ring, from the 1930s, and he made several important contributions on morris traditions in Northamptonshire. He later came to folk *song collecting and, despite becoming totally blind in 1952, started tape-recording singers in Bedfordshire, Lancashire, Shropshire, and elsewhere, and compiled a valuable collection from areas not well covered by others. Examples of his recordings were issued on *Garners Gay* (EFDSS LP 1006, 1971), and *The Leaves of Life* (Vaughan Williams Library Cassette No. VWML 003, 1989). His tape-recordings are now lodged at the *Vaughan Williams Memorial Library.

Hamer's main publications are 'The Hinton and Brackley Morris', *JEFDSS* 7:4 (1955), 205–17; 'May Songs of Bedfordshire', *JEFDSS* 9:2 (1961), 81–90; 'Thoughts of a Folk Song Collector', *ED&S* 31:3 (1969), 88–9; 'A Song Seeker Found', *ED&S* 28:1 (1966), 19–24; *Garners Gay: English Folk Songs Collected by Fred Hamer* (1967); *Green Groves: More English Folk Songs Collected by Fred Hamer* (1973).

Obituary by Kenneth Loveless: *FMJ* 2:1 (1970), 71–2.

Hammond, Henry Edward Denison (1866–1910) and **Hammond, Robert Francis Frederick** (1868–?). The Hammond Brothers are remembered for their folk-song collecting in Dorset, which they undertook at the suggestion of Lucy *Broadwood. Henry had been introduced to folk-song by George B. *Gardiner, and he assisted the latter on some of his own trips, noting the tunes for which Gardiner was not sufficiently well trained. The Hammonds struck out on their own, and between 1904 and 1907 they noted 648 songs, the manuscripts for which are now in the *Vaughan Williams Memorial Library. A selection of their songs appeared in the *JFSS* 3 (1907), 59–139; their own *Folk Songs from Dorset* (1908), and (texts only) in James Reeves, *The Everlasting Circle* (1960); also Frank Purslow's *Marrowbones* (1965), *The Wanton Seed* (1968), *The Constant Lovers* (1972), *The Foggy Dew* (1974).

Frank Purslow, *FMJ* 1:4 (1968), 236–64.

hand of glory. The first mention of a 'hand of glory' in English (1707) refers to a piece of *mandrake root, kept as a charm to make coins multiply; this corresponds to medieval French *maindegloire*, a corruption of Latin *mandragora* 'mandrake'. The French word, however, sounds exactly as if it meant 'hand of glory', so it is commonly applied to a magical torch made from a dead man's hand to cast people into deep sleep. This is first described, though not named, in 1440, when a Coroner's Court at Maidstone (Kent) was told that a burning candle held in the hand of 'a dead man that has lain in the earth nine days and nine nights' will ensure that 'they that sleep shall sleep, and they that wake shall not move, whatever thou do' (Opie and Tatem, 1989: 100).

This charm was said to be much used by thieves; variations are recorded from *Aubrey to the early 20th century—the *Ashton-under-Lyme Reporter* of 22 April 1905 says many a burglar feels sure 'that if he can possess himself of a candle made from the body of a young woman, he will never see the interior of a gaol' (*FLS News* 17 (1993), 15). An actual hand, reputed to have been used in this way, is in Whitby Museum (Yorkshire), together with 'A True Receipt for the Pickling and Claiming of a Hand of Glory, and likewise the Making of a Glory Candle' from a North Yorkshire manuscript book of 1823. It must be cut from the body of a criminal on the gibbet; pickled in salt and the urine of man, woman, dog, horse,

and mare; smoked with herbs and hay for a month; hung on an oak tree three nights running, then laid at a crossroads, then hung on a church door for one night while the maker keeps watch in the porch—'and if it be that no fear hath driven you forth from the porch . . . then the hand be true won, and it be yours'. The candle is made from animal and human fat, with a wick of threads from a hangman's rope, and only milk or blood can quench it. This has continental parallels, notably in a French book of spells called *Le Petit Albert* (1722).

An allegedly true story, current in the 19th century, tells how a burglar, having tricked his way into a house, lit a hand of glory, saying 'Let those who are asleep be asleep, and let those who are awake be awake.' But one servant girl was secretly watching him, while pretending to be asleep, and foiled his plot by dousing the hand in milk (Henderson, 1866: 201–2; Radford, Radford, and Hole, 1961: 179–80; Philip, 1992: 199–200).

hands. The idea that if your hand itches you are about to receive money has been around for at least 400 years, and is still current, and is clearly allied to the metaphor of an itchy hand for avarice, which is equally old. Shakespeare provides the earliest known reference (*Julius Caesar* (*c*.1599), IV. ii). Shortly afterwards, *Melton (1620: 46) wrote, 'When the palme of the right hand itcheth, it is a shrewd sign he shall receive money'. Later references distinguish the two hands—left to receive money, right to pay it out—or give further advice:

> If your hand itches
> You're going to take riches
> Rub it on wood, Sure to come to good
> Rub it on iron, Sure to come flying
> Rub it on brass, Sure to come to pass
> Rub it on steel, Sure to come a deal
> Rub it on tin, Sure to come agin

(*Folk-Lore Record* 1 (1878), 240; from Suffolk)

See also *DEAD MAN'S HAND, *FINGERNAILS; *FINGERS; *GESTURES; *HAND OF GLORY, *THUMBS.

Opie and Tatem, 1989: 186; Lean, 1903: ii. 283–4.

hangman's rope, see *CARDS, PLAYING, *GALLOWS.

Hangman's Stone. There are over a dozen places in England with a large boulder called the Hangman's Stone, or a gate called Gallows

Gate, all explained by the following tale:—a sheep-stealer was carrying a live sheep home with its legs tied together, when he stopped to rest against the boulder (or gate); the sheep slipped and struggled, causing the rope to twist round his neck and throttle him. Thus fate ensured that he would be hanged for his crime.

The earliest record is in Thomas Westcote's *A View of Devonshire in 1630* (1845), referring to Combe Martin. Other sites include Boxford (Berkshire), Beer (Devon), Hampnett (Gloucestershire), Rottingdean (Sussex), Barnburgh (Yorkshire), and Allandale (Northumberland), where the boulder is called the Wedderstone (from 'wether' = 'castrated ram'), and there is a rhyme:

> When ye lang for a mutton bone
> Think on the Wedderstone.

Leslie Grinsell, *Folklore* 96 (1985), 217–22.

Hardy, Thomas (1840–1928). Born in Dorset, and working first in architecture, Thomas Hardy became one of the most popular novelists and poets of his day, and his work is still highly regarded. Many of his most popular works were set in a semi-fictional 'Wessex', and included rural dwellers and workers which were described with affection and little condescension. Hardy took a keen and deliberate interest in local customs and other folklore, and often wove such material into his stories; occasionally merely as local colour but often as essential elements in the story; for example, when Eustacia Vye boldly takes a part in the local *mumming play in *The Return of the Native* (1878), and the *rough music episode in *The Mayor of Casterbridge* (1886). Hardy was himself a fiddle-player and his descriptions of *dances and dance events are particularly evocative, and his manuscripts contain traditional tunes noted by himself.

Ruth Firor, *Folkways in Thomas Hardy* (1931).

hares. From the Middle Ages onwards, hares have been considered unlucky. It is a bad omen if one crosses one's path, especially at the start of the day's work or of a journey; if one runs through a town, a house will burn down; no dead hare should be taken on board a fishing-boat, nor the word 'hare' spoken at sea. If a *pregnant woman meets a hare, her baby will be born with a 'harelip', unless she immediately tears her petticoat. This is recorded first in Thomas Lupton's *A Thousand Notable Things* (1579); an earlier book, *Gospelles of Dystaues* (1507), warns women against eating hares, for the same reason: 'Ye sholde not gyve to yonge maydens to ete the heed of a hare . . . and especyll to them that be wyth chylde for certaynly theyr chyldren might haue clouen lyppes.'

However, hares can bring luck or good health. Samuel Pepys carried a hare's foot in his pocket against colics, while others thought it prevented cramps and rheumatism, or protected against witchcraft (cf. *rabbits). Countrywomen often soothed fretful babies by feeding them hare's brains to eat (*N&Q* 6s:1 (1880), 34; 6s:4 (1880), 406, 457–8). One man joining the Navy in 1939 took a hare's foot as mascot (Evans and Thomson, 1972: 234).

In folklore, witches were commonly said to turn into hares; there was a widespread anecdote about a man who vainly hunted a hare which escaped into the house of an old woman—who was found panting hard. But if the hare's leg was bitten by the hunter's dog, or broken with a stone, or shot with a silver bullet, the witch would be found wounded in the same way; this, some said, took away her power (Brockie, 1886: 2–5). In Yorkshire, the hare was occasionally thought to be a *familiar rather than the witch herself; when it was killed with a *silver bullet, the witch cried out in grief (Henderson, 1866: 166–7; Blakeborough, 1898: 203). Both belief and story are in most regional collections, and persisted till the 1930s (Evans and Thomson, 1972: 164; Simpson, 1973: 69–70).

In the west of England white hares were said to be ghosts of forsaken girls, haunting their seducers; one caused her ex-lover's death by scaring his horse (Hunt, 1881: 377). In one Lincolnshire tale the Devil, in the form of a three-legged hare, causes the death of a boy who is playing at hanging himself, by distracting his companions at the crucial moment so that they fail to release him (Gutch and Peacock, 1908: 63).

Nowadays, many writers claim that hares were sacred to the Anglo-Saxon goddess Eostre, but there is no shred of evidence for this; Bede, the only writer to mention Eostre, does not link her with any animal. For Celtic Britons, we have Julius Caesar's authority for saying hares were sacred and provided omens for Boudicca before a battle.

See also *EASTER, *EASTER EGGS.

Opie and Tatem, 1989: 189–94.

Hartland, Edwin Sidney (1848–1927). A solicitor in Swansea and later Gloucester, who served as President of the Folklore Society, 1899–1901. His primary folklore interest was in the *folktale and he rapidly became one the country's leading experts in that field. His publications include *English Fairy and Other Folk Tales* (1890), an anthology of texts, and *The Science of Fairytales: An Enquiry into the Fairy Mythology* (1891), which attempted a theory of the subject, based firmly in the ruling doctrine of *survivals and the belief that the expert can identify and apply the rules governing folklore. Hartland's *tour de force* was the influential three-volume *The Legend of Perseus: A Study of Tradition in Story, Custom and Belief* (1894–6). In this he followed the conviction that tales encapsulate custom and belief of the past, and by tracing a particular story and its analogues across the world and across time, the folklorist can seek to understand the primitive mind of our ancestors. As his researches into folklore and anthropology deepened, Hartland moved away from a primarily narrative base to a more ethnological concern with primitive societies and the origins of religion, although he always used evidence from myths and legends in his argument. Further books include: *Primitive Paternity: The Myth of Supernatural Birth in Relation to the History of the Family* (2 vols., 1909), *Ritual and Belief: Studies in the History of Religion* (1914), and *Primitive Society: The Beginnings of the Family and the Reckoning of Descent* (1921). As did others of his generation, Hartland clashed publicly with Andrew *Lang in the journal *Folk-Lore* in 1898 and 1899. Another title, *County Folklore: Gloucestershire* (1892), although simply a slim gathering of previously printed material, is a source-book still useful today.

Obituaries by A. C. Haddon (including bibliography), *Folk-Lore* 37 (1926), 178–92, and by R. R. Marett, *Folk-Lore* 38 (1927), 83–5; Dorson, 1968.

harvest customs. Numerous customs and traditions clustered around harvest time, the vital climax of the agricultural year in arable areas. Many were extremely localized, and much could depend on the character of the farmer, the type of crop, and other individual circumstances, but some broad patterns can be discerned. While some farmers kept personal control of the work, on many farms the harvest was supervised by an experienced worker (often the farm foreman) who was elected by his fellow workers and 'contracted'

with the farmer for the job. He usually bore some honorary title—Lord of the Harvest, for example, and his Deputy was the Lady of the Harvest. Once a contract covering payment (in money, food, and drink) had been agreed between employer and workers, the men were left to get on with the job. The harvesters regulated their work with traditional voluntary rules, some serious and some playful or parodic, and also claimed the right to levy a fine ('largesse') on anyone else who entered the field, and even on strangers who passed by on adjacent paths or roads. On many farms they also exacted monetary contributions from the main tradespeople who dealt with the farmer. The Lord would normally lead the mowing, dictate the pace of the work, and decide when breaks were to be taken.

On many farms there were ways of marking the approaching end of the harvest, and the consequent release from the hard work and tension involved. Some customs focused on the last sheaf or last patch of crops still standing, and the cutting of this was made into a game, or was accompanied with a degree of ceremony. 'Crying the Mare' in Herefordshire is an example of a game, in which the last patch of standing corn was tied up and the men tried to cut it by throwing their sickles from a distance (Leather, 1912: 104–5). In other areas the 'mare' was fashioned into a rough figure and sent to taunt a neighbouring farmer who had not yet finished his harvesting. 'Crying the Neck' is the generic term for customs in which the last sheaf is greeted with a triumphant shout (*The Times* (28 Sept. 1934), 10).

There are a widespread references to images or figures being made and paraded around, although this was far from universal and again the examples vary considerably from place to place. It was called the Harvest Queen, Kern Doll, Kern Baby, Ivy Queen, and so on. 'Their last load of corn they crown with flowers, having besides an image richly dressed . . .' (Paul Hentzer, 1598; quoted in Hutton, 1996: 333–4). The figures could be small crafted shapes, or semi-human effigies, paraded around the field or placed on the waggon with the last load. Sometimes, the figure was hung up in barn or farmhouse till next year. These figures were often not made from 'the last sheaf', as many writers assume, as they were manufactured in time to *accompany* the cutting of the last sheaf. Modern *corn dollies are a revival and extension of these figures.

A major focus of attention was the triumphant bringing in of the last load from the fields, called by a local name such as Horkey Load or Hock Cart. The waggon and horses were usually highly decorated, children would ride on top, the farmworkers would accompany the load with much shouting and cheering. A recurrent feature was the use of water—thrown over the cart and workers by others waiting in hiding, or from the upstairs windows of cottages as they passed through the village (N&Q 4s:10 (1872), 286–7, 359, 524).

The most important post-harvest event was the Harvest Supper, variously called the Harvest Home, Mell Supper, Horkey Supper, and so on. The farmer would provide a feast for the workers—and usually for their families as well—in celebration of their achievement. The feast was an integral part of the package of remuneration expected by the workers. The exact nature of the event would vary from place to place, with one key variable being whether the farmer and family stayed for the whole evening or left after the meal, and in many cases local dignitaries would also be invited. Writers from Victorian times onwards have tended to romanticize the Harvest Home, stressing the egalitarian nature of employer and worker sitting down together with no class distinction, but this is only partly accurate, as the rigid social hierarchy of farmwork could not be laid aside so easily. Arthur Beckett (*Spirit of the Downs* (1909)) summed it up as an '. . . event, celebrated for heavy feeding, curious songs, and big drinking feats'. The Supper had its traditional songs and games, such as that addressed to the farmer

> Here's a health unto our master
> The founder of this feast . . .

which in many versions neatly combines sycophancy with calls for more drink, while others were the type of song/game which gets funnier as participants get more drunk (e.g. *Sussex Archaeological Collections* 14 (1862), 186–8). There were numerous other local variations, such as a visit from the *guisers—men in heavily disguised costumes who would turn up and gatecrash the *mell suppers in the north of England. At a Lincolnshire farm in the early 19th century, the 'Old Sow' would pay a visit. This was two men dressed in sacks, but the sow's head would be filled with furze cuttings which would prick the people it approached (N&Q 8s:9 (1896), 128).

One last activity in the field remained, as women and children were permitted to go gleaning, or collecting whatever leftover crops they could find in the fields. This was an extremely important economic customary right, with strict local control over who was allowed to glean, and for how long, and in many areas a church bell was tolled (the 'gleaning bell') to signal the start, or the farm bailiff stood by the field gate, watch in hand, to announce the time and ensure nobody got an unfair start on the others.

Numerous descriptions of harvest customs exist, but the material is piecemeal, and still awaits detailed attention from competent scholars. The harvest effigies, for example, were made and treated in very different ways in different areas, and 'crying the mare' could mean cutting the last sheaf or sending a horse to mock your neighbours. For nearly a century, the study of harvest customs has been stultified by the tacit acceptance of J. G. *Frazer's theories about 'corn spirits'. Few folklorists have bothered to analyse this material as they all assume that the origin and background has already been demonstrated. Frazer's ideas have long been discredited (see Hutton, 1996: 335–6), but we still need to move on to a post-Frazer era.

Wright and Lones, 1936: i. 182–90; Hutton, 1996: 332–47; Evans, 1956: 85–96; Evans, 1969: 69–70, 80–2, 124–5; Jenkin, 1934: 149–64; Bushaway, 1982: 107–66.

harvest festivals. The modern Harvest Festival, so well known to churchgoers and schoolchildren, where the church or school stage is piled high with produce and thanks are given in prayer, sermon, and hymns, is often thought to be ancient but owes its origin to Victorian reforming zeal. Revd R. S. Hawker, vicar of Morwenstow in Cornwall, invented it in 1843, and as the idea was just right for the mood of the times, Festivals spread rapidly throughout the country. The custom obviously has intrinsic values of its own which commended it to other congregations, but there were some ministers who also saw in the new Harvest Festival a way of replacing the older farm-based *Harvest Supper celebrations which were sometimes an excuse for excessive drinking, eating, and dancing.

Hole, 1975: 89–91.

Hatherleigh Tar Barrels. Hatherleigh, Devon, has a regular carnival and funfair which has grown out of an older village *revel, but on the same day it has a spectacular *tar-barrel custom. The night before the first Wednesday after 5 November, participants drag two sledges, each with three barrels on, to the top of the town, accompanied by supporters and the Hatherleigh Jazz Band in fancy dress. The barrels have already been prepared, with sufficient tar and other flammable materials to make a good blaze. At dawn on the Wednesday, one sledge is set alight and dragged at speed round the streets of the village. At 8.30 p.m., after the normal events of the day, the second sledge is similarly raced around the streets and finally on to a bonfire.

Shuel, 1985: 188–9; Sykes, 1977: 138–41.

hawthorn. Traditional beliefs concerning the hawthorn are contradictory. One particular tree, the *Holy Thorn of Glastonbury, was regarded as sacred since it blossomed at Christmas; its real or reputed descendants are pointed out with respect. A few others had individual names or tales: one, called Beggar's Bush, used to stand on the boundary between Sutton Coldfield and Birmingham, and was said to mark the spot where a beggar was found dead, lying partly in one parish and partly in the other, and so was buried where he lay. Doble's Thorn, at St Giles-in-the-Heath (Cornwall), is said to be where a treasure was found by a man led by a dream, like the *Swaffham Pedlar; Cornishmen thought that whenever people buried treasure they planted a thorn over it.

Under its alternative name of 'may', hawthorn was frequently mentioned as one of the trees from which branches were taken to decorate houses on *May Day. Early texts can be ambiguous, since any tree used for this purpose might be called a 'may-bush', whatever its species; Aubrey, however, is quite clear: 'At Woodstock in Oxen, they every May-eve goe into ye Parke, and fetch away a number of Hawthorne-trees, wch they sett before their dores, 'tis pity that they make such destruction of so fine a tree' (Aubrey, 1686/1880: 118 n.). Related to this was a Suffolk custom, mentioned in 1830 as old but disused, that any farm servant bringing hawthorn in full bloom into the house on May Day would get a dish of cream for breakfast.

In Herefordshire farms it was customary on *New Year's Day to burn a hawthorn 'bush', i.e. a branch whose twigs had been forcibly bent into a thorny globe, which had hung in the kitchen for a year as a luck-bringer. It was burned in the wheatfield in a straw fire, to protect the future crop from evil spirits, witches, and the disease called 'smut'. Then a new 'bush' would be made, and singed on the embers of the old one (Leather, 1912: 92). Another farming custom based on the protective power of hawthorn is that of hanging a cow's or mare's *placenta on a thornbush. This was seen in Hampshire in 1939, with the explanation that it would prevent fever in the cow (Vickery, 1995: 170); and again in Bilsdale (Yorkshire) in 1998, to bring luck to the newborn foal (Jan Ekermann, *FLS News* 28 (1998), 8).

On the other hand, hawthorn blossom is the most widely dreaded of all unlucky *flowers; over 500 contributors to a survey on flowerlore in the 1980s reported that bringing it indoors would cause a death, a major illness or accident, or some form of serious ill luck. In many cases they themselves had been rebuked for doing this. This taboo is sometimes linked to the idea that hawthorn blossom stinks of death or of the *plague, first mentioned by Francis Bacon in 1627 (*Sylva Sylvarum*, § 912) and still common among countrymen in the 19th century. This has a scientific basis; one species, *Crataegus monogyna*, has a chemical in its blossoms identical to one in decaying meat, and so smells of corpses.

Opie and Tatem, 1989: 242–5; Vickery, 1995: 166–72.

Haxey Hood. Unique among England's *calendar customs is the Haxey Hood game in Lincolnshire, played every year on 6 January, although it bears some relationship to the *football games played elsewhere. The game is organized by thirteen officials, called Boggins, including a Fool. From New Year's Eve, the Boggins have been round the neighbourhood pubs, singing, collecting money to defray costs, and announcing the forthcoming game. At two o'clock on the 6th, they gather at the church gate. The Fool tries to run away and is caught and brought back. He makes a speech, standing on a convenient stone, and he is 'smoked' with the aid of burning straw placed behind him. They then troop off to the field, which is halfway between the two communities of Haxey and Westwoodside. Here, the preliminary games are played. The Boggins have twelve 'hoods', rolls of sacking, which are thrown up one by one and the players have to get hold of them and carry them off the field, past the Boggins who are placed round the edge. Once this has been achieved the main hood is brought out, this one made of heavy rope, covered in leather and about eighteen inches long. This is thrown up and immediately disappears into the 'sway', a huge mass of men which moves slowly, almost of its own accord, towards one of the two pubs which are the 'goals'. There is no running, throwing, or kicking, just this huge scrum. Hours later, when it reaches a pub, and the landlord touches the hood, the game is over. The pub keeps the hood till next year.

The locals have a well-developed legend to explain the game's origin. One day, Lady de Mowbray was out for a ride on 6 January and the wind caught her scarlet hood and whisked it away. Thirteen local labourers saw the Lady's distress and each tried to catch the hood and return it to her. Their antics so amused her that she granted half an acre's land to each of the men on condition that they re-enacted the scene every year. None of this is likely to be historically accurate, but at least it makes more sense than the theories of pagan sacrifices invented by recent 'authorities'. The Mowbray incident is said to have taken place hundreds of years ago, but the earliest description of the game so far found only dates from 1815.

Jeremy J. Cooper, *A Fool's Game: The Ancient Tradition of Haxey Hood* (1993); Shuel, 1985: 166–7; Venetia Newall, *Folk Life* 18 (1980), 7–23; Mabel Peacock, *Folk-Lore* 7 (1896), 330–49; Ethel H. Rudkin, *Lincolnshire Folklore* (1936), 90–7.

hazel. In England, there is no lore about the hazel as a tree, though its twigs were said to make good dowsing rods. The *nuts are used in *love divinations, and 'going nutting' or 'gathering nuts' are euphemisms for love-making.

heads. These make fine trophies; they are easy to preserve and mount, and convey well the characteristics of the living animal. A skull, especially of a horned or antlered beast, is equally impressive. Finest of all is the head or skull of a human enemy, killed in battle or executed, and publicly displayed. From the antlers on the gables of Heorot in *Beowulf* to the fox-mask in a huntsman's study, from the stag's head paraded in *As You Like It* to the reindeer skulls of *Abbots Bromley, from the heads of traitors on Tower Bridge to human *skulls preserved in old houses, from *horse skulls under buildings to those used for *hobby horses, English traditions are full of heads.

There is ample evidence that Germanic and Celtic peoples used heads as sacrifices and believed they had magical powers, which may mean that English head customs are pagan survivals. Yet one can also argue that the intrinsic qualities of a head make it a natural symbol (of knowledge, vigilance, power, honour, etc.), not tied to any specific religious system. Similar ambiguity attends images of heads or faces on buildings, armour, pottery, etc. Many cultures have considered them magical protections, but they also make effective ornamental motifs. So were the monster-heads, gargoyles, and grimacing faces on medieval churches just amusing decoration? Or were they aggressive guardians, keeping demons away?

The problem recurs in modern contexts. In West Yorkshire and Derbyshire, crudely carved stone heads and faces can be seen on capstones of bridges and arched gateways; over doors and windows and on gables of farmhouses; on the surrounds of springs and wells; or set in drystone fieldwalls. The main period of production seems to have been the 17th century, but local stonemasons in the 19th and early 20th centuries made many too. From verses left by one carver in 1828, it appears they were called 'the old man's face'; sometimes they were regarded as protective and luck-bringing, sometimes just made for fun. They are still being made. In 1971, the landlord of the Sun Inn at Haworth (Yorkshire) had one put over the main door to end a haunting, explaining: 'There is a local tradition that these were put on buildings when a workman had been killed on the site before the work was completed, and they are supposed to ward off evil spirits. I feel now that I have quashed any ideas of ghosts for good' (*Yorkshire Evening Post* (21 Oct. 1971)). Recent writers often explain this tradition by the importance of severed heads in *Celtic belief; a few go further, claiming some extant heads are prehistoric artefacts reused in modern contexts. Current interest in them is reflected in anecdotes which have sprung up over the last 30 years or so, often strongly believed, of ill luck and menacing presences dogging those who remove one from its proper place; even when the supposedly evil head turns out to be modern, as happened in at least two cases, the story persists.

See also *SKULLS.

The major discussion of the Celtic head-cult is in Anne Ross, *Pagan Celtic Britain* (1967), 94–171; briefer accounts appear in most subsequent books on Celtic religion. For the stone heads, see Brears, 1989: 32–44; Sidney Jackson, *Celtic and Other Stone Heads* (1973); John Billingsley, *Stony Gaze* (1998).

healers, see *CHARMERS, *CUNNING MEN, *SEVENTH SON, DAUGHTER.

healing, see *CHARMS (VERBAL), *MEDICINE.

hearts and pins. Sticking *pins into an animal's heart is a symbolic aggressive action, much used in *counterspells throughout England. If farm animals were dying and witchcraft was suspected, one should cut out a heart, stick it with pins, nails, or thorns, and boil or roast it, or hang it in the chimney. This should be done just before midnight, in complete silence, with doors and windows barred; some accounts add that a verse from the Bible was read, but do not say which. The ritual would cause intense pain to the witch, who could only get relief by lifting her own spell. Witchcraft against humans could be similarly broken by the use of a hen's, pigeon's, hare's, or toad's heart; these were also used aggressively in love magic, to force a reluctant lover into marriage, or to take revenge on an unfaithful one. In North Yorkshire, the heart was sometimes buried in a churchyard, not burnt (Blakeborough, 1898: 151). There are detailed accounts from 19th-century Yorkshire and Durham (Henderson, 1879: 181–8, summarized in Opie and Tatem 1989: 195–6; also Brockie, 1886: 11–15, 26–8); one instance was recorded in London about 1902 (Lovett, 1925: 67). Some pigs' hearts stuck with pins, found in the chimneys of old Somerset cottages, were given to Taunton Museum (Elworthy, 1895: 53–5).

There have been modern instances of the procedure, which is fairly widely known from books and the media. Sheep's hearts pierced with thorns were found nailed to church walls in several Norfolk villages in the winter of 1963/4, together with human images and magic symbols (Valiente, 1973: 193–4); a cow's heart impaled with nails was sent through the post during a campaign of magical harassment in Lewes (Sussex) in 1997 (*Fortean Times* 102 (Sept. 1997), 38–41).

heather. The idea that white heather is lucky reached England as part of a Victorian enthusiasm for Scottish traditions, and is now known everywhere. A winter-flowering var-

iety is deliberately grown for sale on Burns Night in January, and *Gypsies sell both real heather and substitutes in the streets of many English towns in summer (Vickery, 1995: 396–7).

he (children's game), see *TIG.

hedgehogs. It was widely believed that hedgehogs sucked cows' udders; old churchwardens' accounts record payments of a few pence per head for killing them. There was vigorous debate between those who called this 'a venerable superstition', possibly caused by seeing hedgehogs curled up alongside sleeping cows for warmth, and those who thought it true (*N&Q* 6s:8 (1883), 32–3, 117–18, 217; 12s:4 (1918), 140; 12s:5 (1919), 105, 160–1, 304). It was also thought that hedgehogs sucked birds' eggs, and would carry off fallen fruit on their bristles, or even climb trees to get it; also, that they would block up any opening of their burrows on the side from which the wind would next blow. In Yorkshire hedgehogs were sometimes said to be *familiars, or witches in animal form; such a hedgehog would run as fast as a hare, and could never be caught or shot (Blakeborough, 1898: 198).

A saying, 'Off we go again, as the Hedgehog said to the Devil', is explained by the following *fable: a hedgehog once wagered he could outrun the Devil in racing up and down a ditch at night. He curled himself up at one end, while a second hedgehog did likewise at the other; the Devil rushed to and fro, but at either end of the ditch he always found a hedgehog there, saying 'Off we go again!' Eventually, the Devil dropped dead with exhaustion (Leather, 1912: 357).

Hedley Kow. A very mischievous, but not dangerous, shape-changing *boggart which used to plague the villagers of Hedley (Northumberland) by his many tricks (Henderson, 1866: 270–1). A farmer mistook him for his own horse, a milkmaid for her favourite cow, an old woman for a bundle of straw; in each case he caused unexpected trouble, and then vanished with a loud guffaw. He could even turn into the likeness of a girl, to trick her sweetheart into following him till he ended up knee-deep in a bog.

Hell. There is no particular 'entrance to Hell' in English topographical lore, only a general, and sometimes humorous, assumption that Hell lies underground. *Bottomless pools allegedly go right down to Hell. At Tunstall (Norfolk) there is a boggy pool called Hell Hole, which often has bubbles rising in it; it is said that after Tunstall church burned down, the vicar and churchwardens quarrelled over who would have the bells, so the Devil carried them down to Hell, and the bubbles show they are still sinking. Near Darlington (County Durham) are three 'bottomless' pits called, since the 16th century, the Hell Kettles or Devil's Kettles, supposedly filled with scalding water to boil the souls of sinners. Legend claims the owner of the field where they lie was once carting hay on St Barnabas's Day (11 June), and when someone rebuked him for impiety he retorted:

> Barnaby yea, Barnaby nay!
> A cartload of hay, whether God will or nay!

At this blasphemy, 'instantly he, his carts and his horses, were all swallowed up in the pools, where they may still be seen, on a fine day and clear water, many fathoms deep!' (*Denham Tracts*, 1892: i. 79).

Helm, Alex (1920–70). One of the most important figures in the study of *calendar custom and dance in post-war England. He served as a major in the Ordnance Corps, and spent the rest of his working life as a teacher. At the suggestion of Margaret *Dean-Smith, Helm edited the papers of T. F. *Ordish, the 19th-century collector of *mummers plays, which revealed the wealth of untouched material on traditional drama, and, with characteristic energy and scholarship, he launched into compiling a comprehensive index of material, with colleagues Dr E. C. Cawte and Dr Norman Peacock, and the work on this index consumed his spare time for the rest of his tragically shortened life. Some of the fruits of the work were presented in: E. C. Cawte, Alex Helm, R. J. Marriott, and Norman Peacock, 'A Geographical Index of the Ceremonial Dance in Great Britain', *JEFDSS* 9:1 (1960), 1–41; *English Ritual Drama* (1967). E. C. Cawte, *Ritual Animal Disguise* (1978), and many later writers have also been indebted to the gathering and indexing work of Helm and his colleagues. Helm's work had enormous influence on the next generation of custom researchers in England, by demonstrating that the *mummers' play was worth taking seriously, by advocating the geographical approach, and

by showing that a great deal of information still remained to be discovered. His contention that the customs were best studied as ceremonies or rituals (rather than, for example, by the literary approach adopted by E. K. Chambers) became widely adopted and is still influential today, although it in turn has come under criticism from later writers.

Helm's early death prevented him from writing the projected works which would synthesize this wealth of material, although some of his writings have been published posthumously. His papers are held by University College London. Much of Helm's published output was thus in the form of articles, but he also produced a number of invaluable booklets which made texts and descriptions available to potential practitioners and folklore students alike, including: *Five Mumming Plays for Schools* (1965); *Six Mummers' Acts* (with E. C. Cawte) (1967); *Cheshire Folk Drama* (1968); *The Chapbook Mummers' Plays* (1969); *Eight Mummers' Plays* (1971); *Staffordshire Folk Drama* (1984).

Additional selected publications include 'The Cheshire Soul-Caking Play', *JEFDSS* 6:2 (1950), 45–50; 'The Rushcart and the North-Western Morris', *JEFDSS* 7:3 (1954), 172–9; 'The Mummers' Play', *Theatre Notebook* 18 (Winter 1963/4); E. C. Cawte, Alex Helm, and N. Peacock, *English Ritual Drama: A Geographical Index* (1967); *The English Mummers' Play* (1980).

Obituaries: Margaret Dean-Smith, *Folklore* 81 (1970), 63–4; E. C. Cawte, *FMJ* 2:1 (1970), 72–3.

Helston Furry Day. A town-wide celebration such as Furry Day at Helston, Cornwall, is made up of many parts, but the core of the public day is organized by a special Committee and consists of a series of processional dances through the streets of the town—and sometimes through the shops and houses lining the streets—led by the Town Band playing the *Furry Dance* tune. At seven o'clock in the morning on 8 May there is a relatively informally dressed dance, previously called the Servants' Dance, in which those who will be busy working for the rest of the day join in. Later in the morning is the Children's Dance (introduced in 1922) with local schoolchildren dressed in white but with coloured headbands for the girls and school ties for the boys. The Twelve o'clock Dance is the best known, with women in colourful summer dresses and big hats and their partners in grey top-hats and black morning-coats, and all with a lily-of-the-valley buttonhole. This dance is led by the Mayor or other local dignitary and participation is only by invitation of the Committee. An elegant ball is held in the evening.

Other aspects of the custom include the Hal an Tow, and trips to the local countryside to gather greenery to decorate the town. The Hal-an-Tow has a less than respectable past. This was a none-too-sober perambulation of the town, singing a song in which the words of the verses are sufficiently obscure to have excited the vivid imaginations of amateur folklorists for decades—concerning as they do Robin Hood, the Spaniards, Saint George, and Aunt Mary Moses—but whose chorus is pretty clear, given the time of year:

> For we were up as soon as any day, O
> And for to fetch the summer home
> The summer and the May, O
> For summer is a come, O
> And winter is a gone, O.

This part of the proceedings had been dropped in the 19th century, but was deliberately reintroduced, in suitably cleaned-up form, in 1930 at the instigation of the Helston Old Cornwall Society, and is now acted out in the street in costume.

The earliest known reference to Helston's custom is in the *Gentleman's Magazine* (60:1 (1790) 520), which identifies nearly all the essential elements which have survived to the present day, in particular the day-long event, bringing in the greenery, the Hal an Tow song and procession, dancing in the streets and houses, and, most importantly, the juxtaposition, if not actual combination, of the rougher working-class elements and those of the more elegant and refined gentry. Without this latter description it would have been easy to dismiss the 'elegance' of the modern custom as a prime example of Victorian prettification of the customary calendar.

The custom has had its ups and downs and at certain points in the 19th century almost disappeared. It is certain that its continued existence owes a lot to key individuals (such as those who formed the Old Cornwall Society) who regarded such customs as essential to the area's identity and who lent their vocal support at opportune moments. Certainly, since the turn of the 20th century, the custom has gone from strength to strength. There has been much argument about the derivation of the name—or rather names—given to the custom. It seems clear that the word *furry* is a dialect term related to 'fair'. The local parish church is dedicated to St Michael, and 8 May being St Michael's Day argues for *furry day* as meaning little more than the *fair day*, commonly held throughout England on the day of the local patron saint. The word *flora* or *floral*, used by locals and visitors alike, may have been introduced by early 'authorities' who liked to link our customs with Roman festivals, but the word so well sums up the spring greenery and flowers which decorate the town, and its inhabitants, that its aptness probably guarantees its continuance.

Jill Newton, *Helston Flora Day* (1978); Wright and Lones, 1938: ii. 247–51; H. Spencer Toy, *The History of Helston* (1936), 368–79; Stone, 1906: 56–8.

hemp seed divination. One of the most-often quoted *love-divination procedures, first described in *Mother Bunch's Closet* (1685):

Carry the seed in your apron, and with your right hand throw it over your left shoulder, saying thus— 'Hemp-seed I sow, hemp-seed I sow, And he that must be my true love, Come after me and mow'. And at the ninth time expect to see the figure of him you are to wed, or else hear a bell.

The process varies little from one account to another, although some say you will see a coffin rather than hear a bell, and it either means 'you won't marry' or 'you will die'. Some versions prescribe *Midsummer's Eve as the proper time to do it, while others say *Christmas, *St Mark's Eve, *Halloween, or any night at midnight.

Aubrey (1686: 95); *Folk-Lore Record* 1 (1878), 33; Henderson, 1879: 104–5; *Denham Tracts*, 1895: ii. 278; *Folk-Lore* 34 (1923), 324.

herbs. Plants grown, or collected from the wild, to be used medicinally or as flavourings; herb gardens were a feature of medieval monasteries, and of country households for several centuries. Wild plants have presumably always been gathered, as was still being done well into the 20th century by many country people, some of whom were locally famous for home-made remedies with which they treated their neighbours. In *Mary Barton* ((1848), chapter 2), Mrs Gaskell describes a Manchester woman who would walk far to the fields to gather 'all manner of hedgerow, ditch and field plants, which we are accustomed to call valueless, but which have a powerful effect either for good or for evil [abortion?], and consequently are much used among the poor'; these she hung up to dry in her hovel.

Several Anglo-Saxon manuscripts give

instructions on the medical uses of herbs, sometimes with accompanying verbal *charms, prayers, and ritual actions; they were presumably used by monks. For the early modern period, there is relevant material in botanical and medical books such as John Gerrard's *The Herball* (1597) and Nicholas Culpeper's *The Physical Directory* (1649) and *The English Physician* (1652), though much of it came from continental sources. John Wesley's *Primitive Physic or an Easy and Natural Method of Curing Most Diseases* (1747) gives many herbal cures, and was frequently reprinted in the 18th and 19th centuries. But the great bulk of herbal knowledge must always have been passed on orally, and in home-made 'recipe' books listing ointments, poultices, infusions, distillations, fumigations, and oils for use on humans or animals.

For early herb-lore, see Bonser, 1963; Hunt, 1990. For a detailed modern regional study, see Hatfield, 1994. See also Vickery, 1995; Barbara Griggs, *Green Pharmacy: A History of Herbal Medicine* (1981); Chamberlain, 1981; Agnes Arber, *Herbals* (1912; 3rd edn., 1986). Most local folklore collections and many books on country life include some information on the topic.

Herla. Around 1190, Walter *Map included a tale about an otherwise unknown King Herla, allegedly 'one of the most ancient British kings', in his *De Nugis Curialum*. Herla entered a palace inside a hill at the invitation of a red-bearded, goat-footed, hairy dwarf; he thought he spent a mere three days there, but was away 200 years. Returning to the human world, he and his men found that they crumbled to dust if they touched the ground, so they dared not dismount, and 'this King Herla and his band still hold on their mad course, wandering eternally without stop or stay'— until they plunged into the Wye in the first year of Henry II's reign, and never appeared again.

Map goes on to describe 'nocturnal companies and squadrons ... engaged in endless wandering in an aimless round', silent, and including people known to be dead; they had even been seen by day, but when pursued and challenged 'rose up into the air and vanished suddenly'. This sinister company was known as 'the household of Herlethingus'—probably an Anglo-Saxon phrase meaning 'the troops of Herla'. Other medieval writers knew variants of this belief, and of this word. One tells of a great crowd of the tortured ghosts of sinners, some on foot and some on horseback, the 'household of Herlechinus'; another talks of the Hell-bound 'troops of Herlewin'. Although hunting is not involved, these spectral hosts are medieval forerunners of the *Wild Hunt.

Westwood, 1985: 156-7, 251-3.

Herne the Hunter. In Shakespeare's *The Merry Wives of Windsor* (1597), two women decide to make a fool of Falstaff by getting him to disguise himself as a ghost at midnight in Windsor Park, where:

> There is an old tale goes, that Herne the hunter,
> Sometime a keeper here in Windsor Forest,
> Doth all the winter time, at still midnight,
> Walk round about an oak, with great ragg'd horns;
> And there he blasts the trees, and takes the cattle,
> And makes milch kine yield blood, and shakes a chain
> In a most hideous and dreadful manner.

(IV. iv)

An inferior text of 1604 has different lines here (unlikely to be by Shakespeare), including the idea that the ghost is used as a *bogey:

> Oft have you heard since Horne the hunter dyed,
> That women, to affright their little children,
> Says that he walkes in shape of a great stagge.

Shakespeare was probably referring to authentic legends which the local audience would have known; a tree in Windsor Park was pointed out as 'Falstaff's Oak' or 'Herne's Oak' till it was cut down in 1796. A replacement was planted in 1906.

There is no other early information about Herne/Horne, but in 1792 Samuel Ireland added that he had been a gamekeeper who hanged himself on the oak; this would be a good reason for him to haunt it, and the rattling chain is a standard feature too. Other details are unusual; Herne's powers of blasting trees, 'taking' (i.e. bewitching) cattle, and making cows' milk bloody is more like witches or malevolent fairies than ghosts. Nor do ghosts usually appear as semi-stags, even in forest areas. Shakespeare could have invented the antlers just to make Falstaff look ridiculous; planning to cuckold others, he is tricked into wearing *horns himself.

Attempts have been made to link Herne with other folkloric figures. Jacob *Grimm suggested he was a leader of the *Wild Hunt, an interpretation followed by many; however, the essence of the Wild Hunt is that it rushes wildly from one place to another, often in mid-air, which does not match Shakespeare's account. Others have associated Herne's antlers with those carried by dancers at *Abbots

Bromley, speculating that he was a character in some midwinter custom involving animal disguise. Others have connected his name with the ancient Celtic horned god Cernunnos, even though it is a quite common medieval surname. Shakespeare's text gives no warrant for any of these ideas.

In the 20th century, a tradition has grown up that Herne is seen before national disasters or the deaths of kings, and a fair number of people have reported personal experiences of hearing his horn or hounds (Harte, 1996: 31–2).

Westwood, 1985: 72–6; Petry, 1972; Jeremy Harte, *At The Edge* 3 (1996), 27–33.

Herrick, Robert (1591–1674). Robert Herrick was granted the living of Dean Prior in Devon in 1629, a move which he regarded as a form of exile, 'in this dull Devon-shire' he wrote. He was removed from the living in 1648 by the incoming Puritans, and lived in London for a while, only to be reinstalled in Devon in 1662 at the restoration of the monarchy. Herrick published one great collection of poems in his lifetime, entitled *Hesperides* (1648), and many of his poems include everyday folkloric references which are valuable evidence of custom and belief in his day. In some cases, such as *The Hock Cart* and *The Country Life*, the whole poem describes an event or a season, but in others it is the occasional line which sheds light on an otherwise obscure topic.

> In the morning when ye rise
> Wash your hands, and cleanse your eyes,
> Next be sure ye have a care,
> To disperse the water farre.
> For as farre as that doth light,
> So farre keepes the evill spright.
>
> *(Another [Charme])*

Several of his poems are concerned with *fairies, but in this area he was clearly drawing on the literary tradition of Spenser and Shakespeare rather than the folk traditions of his Devonshire parishioners.

W. Carew Hazlitt (ed.), *Hesperides: The Poems and Other Remains of Robert Herrick Now First Collected* (1869); L. C. Martin (ed.), *The Poems of Robert Herrick* (1965).

Hey Diddle Diddle. The popular *nursery rhyme, of which the Opies wrote 'Probably the best-known nonsense verse in the language, a considerable amount of nonsense has been written about it'. The earliest known text dates from *c.*1765, and it has been regularly printed with little textual variation ever since. Some

of the components of the rhyme, however, appeared much earlier, such as 'a new dance called hey-diddle' mentioned in 1569 and a poem by Alexander Montgomerie ('The Cherry and the Slae', 1597) which includes a cow, a fiddle, and the moon, but which cannot be shown to be the nursery rhyme's precursor. The Opies also list most of the origin theories which have been mooted, none of which has anything to offer beyond speculation. At present we must be content with the fact that the verse is a very effective nonsense rhyme.

Opie and Opie, 1997: 240–1.

hiccoughs. Four remedies for hiccups are generally quoted. One is to breathe into a paper bag (in and out, as long as it takes), another is to hold one's breath. The third is to drink a cup of water *backwards*, that is out of the opposite side of the cup than normal, which can be done by bending over and tilting the cup slightly away from you (with your chin inside the cup). The fourth is to be startled out of them by someone making you jump. Earlier remedies tend to be more complex. 'Take a cup of water, and say: Hiccups, Jiccups, Rise up Jacob, Seven gullups in the cup, Cure Hiccups' (Jones-Baker, 1977: 99). A correspondent in *N&Q* (5s:3 (1865), 465) writes that you must cross the front of the left shoe with the forefinger of the right hand, while you repeat the Lord's Prayer backwards. In the 1820s, Edward Moor recommended holding the breath and saying, three times, 'Hiccup—sniccup—look up—right up—three drops in a cup—is good for the hiccup' (Moor, 1823: 167); long before that, in 1584, Reginald *Scot commented, 'Some will hold fast their thombe in their right hand when they hickot; or else will hold their chinne with their right hand whiles a gospell is soong.'

Opie and Tatem, 1989: 198–9.

Hickathrift, Tom. A local hero in the Wisbech area of Cambridgeshire and Norfolk, amazingly strong, and almost a giant in size. As a lad, he had seemed lazy and stupid, but his huge strength enabled him to walk off with two whole waggonloads of straw on his back, win a wager by draining a hogshead of beer at one gulp, and kill a giant with the axle-tree of his cart. A stone in Tilney churchyard (Norfolk) is supposed to mark his grave (it is almost eight feet long); he threw it from a spot three miles away, demanding to be buried where it fell. Two tall stones in Tilney, originally the uprights of old crosses, are called his 'candlesticks'; one has grooves across the top, said to be the mark of his fingers. Tom's chief exploits were printed in a *chapbook in the 18th century, and were well known in oral tradition too. He was also, until recent times, used as a *bogeyman to frighten children into good behaviour (Porter, 1969: 188–92; 1974: 96–101).

Hickory Dickery Dock. One of our best-known *nursery rhymes, but in former times it was used more as a *counting-out rhyme. First printed about 1744, and reported regularly in children's rhyme books and folklore collections ever since, the rhyme appears to have been particularly popular in Scotland, and the Opies demonstrate the similarity of the first line with the old *'shepherds' counting' method, particularly popular in the northern counties, which includes the numerals Hevera (8), Devera (9), Dick (10).

Opie and Opie, 1997: 244.

hide and seek. The most basic of children's games where somebody or something is hidden and then sought, hide and seek exists in a multitude of versions of which there are two basic forms. In the first form, an item is hidden and the seeker has to find it, while the other players indicate how far he/she is from the item by shouting 'warm' (for close), 'cold' (for far away), and so on. This version is normally named after the item being sought—Hunt the Thimble, for example. Nowadays played almost exclusively by small children, or by adults with small children to amuse, it was one of the most popular Victorian parlour games, especially at *Christmas time.

The second basic form is where all the players except one (the seeker) go and hide. After an agreed interval—enforced by the seeker counting to a hundred, or something similar—he/she has to find the others, and the first one found becomes the new seeker and the last found is the winner. Again, in this simple form Hide and Seek is mainly played by small children, but played outdoors with additions, such as allowing the players to change their hiding places, it is still the basis for many popular games. A number of characteristic calls have developed, such as 'All hid! All hid!' when the players are ready, or 'Ready or not, here I come!' when the seeker has finished

counting, and these have become proverbial in their own right. What appear to be the earliest documentary references to the game are in fact allusions to these sayings, and cannot therefore be counted as definite. Nevertheless, if these prove to be true indications, the game has a long history, as Biron says in Shakespeare's *Love's Labours Lost* (*IV.* iii) 'All hid, all hid—an old infant play' and Dekker 'Our unhansome-fac'd poet does play bo-peepes with your Grace, and cryes all-hidde as boyes doe' (*Satiro-mastix* (1602), v. iii).

Gomme, 1894: i. 211–14; Opie and Opie, 1969: 151–75.

Highgate horns. A custom which used to take place at Highgate, north London, was the 'swearing on the horns'. Anyone passing through the village for the first time was requested to submit to a ceremony in one of the local public houses conducted by the landlord. By the time detailed accounts are available, the ceremony was highly facetious, and carried out with an eye to the tourist trade. The description in Hone's *Every-Day Book* is the fullest. All nineteen pubs in the village offered the ceremony, and all had a similar outline in which the publican claims the newcomers as sons or daughters and insists they call him father. He lays down various rules, such as: 'you must not kiss the maid while you can kiss the mistress, except you like the maid the best, but sooner than lose a good chance you may kiss them both', and 'if at any time you are going through Highgate and want to rest yourself, and you see a pig lying in a ditch you have liberty to kick her out and take her place; but if you see three lying together you must only kick out the middle one and lie between the other two'. At the end of the ceremony, the newcomers have to kiss the horns.

Swearing on the Highgate horns was known far and wide, and people came specially to the village to be sworn, often in convivial parties. The earliest known reference is to 1737 (quoted by Thorne), but it was clearly in full swing already at that date, and other 18th-century references abound. By the mid-19th century, however, the custom was virtually defunct. It is not known whether the custom had always been jocular, or had previously been serious. However, Wright's *English Dialect Dictionary* (iii. 159) glosses 'He has been sworn in at Highgate' as meaning 'he is very sharp or clever'.

Several theories of origin have been put

forward. The simplest is that Highgate was part of the manor of *Hornsey*. The most logical is that Highgate was formerly one of the most important routes into London for cattle drovers, and the custom arose as some sort of occupational initiation ceremony. Hone also prints an anecdote about a horn custom for new waggoners in Hoddesdon, Hertfordshire. Compare also other *initiation ceremonies such as at *Hungerford Hocktide and *Sturbridge Fair, and other symbolism under *horns.

Hone, 1827: ii. 40–4, 188–9; W. Carew Hazlitt, *English Proverbs and Proverbial Phrases* (1905), 184; James Thorne, *Handbook to the Environs of London* (1876; 1983 edn.), 346–7.

highwaymen. Presumably at the time they were active, highwaymen were as much dreaded and loathed by potential victims as street muggers are now, but time has softened and glamorized their image. The fame of Dick Turpin did not wholly eclipse various local figures, especially since the nature of their crime ensured that if caught they would be hanged at the roadside, not in a prison, and usually gibbetted, so their skeletons remained on view for many years. Various nameless roadside *graves are said to be those of highwaymen, buried beside the *gallows.

High Wycombe mayor-making. A unique *civic custom, of unknown origin, which is recorded only from Victorian times in late May. The incoming Mayor of High Wycombe, Buckinghamshire, is weighed, in front of the Town Hall, on peculiar-looking scales which have a seat suspended from a tall metal tripod. The new Mayor's weight is announced and recorded. The outgoing Mayor is then weighed and his/her weight compared to last year's. If the Mayor has lost weight it is counted as a sign that he or she has been busy and worked hard, but if the weight has increased then he/she is accused of attending too many civic luncheons. The Deputy Mayors, Mayoresses, and chief officers are also weighed if they wish.

Kightly, 1986: 230–31; Sykes, 1977: 82–3; Shuel, 1985: 104.

hill figures. Certain steep chalk hills in southern England carry figures made by cutting away turf and topsoil, visible for miles. They can be either outline drawings, or figures solidly blocked out; they need regular maintenance to prevent the return of grass, which was often undertaken communally, and accompanied by festivity.

The oldest are the White Horse of *Uffington, the *Cerne Abbas Giant, and the Long Man of *Wilmington, the first being definitely pre-Christian, and the others arguably so (see individual entries). From the later medieval, Tudor, and Stuart periods there are references to four more giants, now lost (see *Gogmagog); a medieval date is also possible for the lost Red Horse of Tysoe (Warwickshire) and a cross at Whiteleaf (Buckinghamshire). In the 18th and 19th centuries new figures were cut on the orders of landowners and clergy, intent on embellishing the landscape, or as pranks by young men of the same class; the majority were horses, of which sixteen survived when Morris Marples wrote in 1949, and the rest crosses. Twentieth-century designs are varied: there are regimental badges in Wiltshire dating from the First World War; a crown was cut near Wye in Kent in 1902, and an aeroplane near Dover in 1909, to mark Bleriot's cross-Channel flight.

See *UFFINGTON, *CERNE ABBAS, *WILMINGTON, *GOGMAGOG.

For descriptions and documentary evidence, see Marples, 1949, though its archaeology needs updating. Paul Newman's *Lost Gods of Albion* (1997), has up-to-date archaeology, but includes far-fetched theories, and inaccurate assertions about mythology and folklore.

hiring fairs. Also called statute, or mop fairs, the ultimate origin of the hiring fair dates from the time of Edward III, with his attempt to regulate the labour market at a time of acute national shortage. Successive legislation (in particular the Statute of Apprentices of 1563) provided for a particular day when the high constables of the shire would proclaim the stipulated rates of pay and conditions of employment for the coming year. As so many people, employers and employees alike, gathered at this event, it quickly turned into the major place for matching workers and bosses. Even when rates and conditions were no longer officially set, the hiring fair was too useful an institution to be allowed to lapse, especially as much employment in rural areas was by the year. Prospective employees would gather in the street or square, often with some sort of badge or tool to denote their speciality—and employers would look them over and, if all was well, strike a bargain for the coming year, handing over a shilling (variously called earnest money, fest, *God's penny, arles) to seal it.

Obviously, such gatherings attracted all the other trappings and attractions of a real fair, and they turned into major festivals in their own right, and also attracted condemnation for the drunkenness and immorality involved. In some places, a few weeks after the hiring fair, there would be a smaller gathering or 'runaway mop' to sort out any anomalies. Hiring fairs continued in some places well into the 20th century, and even up to the Second World War (Murfin, 1990: 47–8).

Hone, 1827: 86–9, 102; Stone, 1906: 10–11.

hob. In the north of England and some Midlands counties, hob was the most common name for rough, hairy creatures of the *brownie type, whose work brought prosperity to farms; like brownies, they might become mischievous nuisances if annoyed, and would leave for ever if given new clothes. On the other hand, it might prove impossible to get rid of a troublesome hob (Henderson, 1866: 228; Atkinson, 1891: 54–5). There were also outdoor hobs, notably one living in a cave called the Hobhole in Runswick Bay, supposed able to cure whooping cough (Wright, 1913: 202).

There is no special significance to the name; it is a common medieval shortening of 'Robert' or 'Robin', often implying 'country bumpkin, stupid peasant'. The first record of it being used of a supernatural being is from 1460; the compounds *hobgoblin and *hobthrush appear in the following century.

For discussion of this and related words, see Briggs, 1976: 222–3; and Gillian Edwards, *Hobgoblin and Sweet Puck* (1974), 123–42.

hobbit. This name, made famous by J. R. R. Tolkien, does occur once, but only once, in traditional lore. *Denham compiled a list of 202 fairies and spectres with which at one time 'the whole earth was so overrun . . . that there was not a village in England that had not its own peculiar ghost'—or bogle, or fairy. About three-quarters of the way through come: '. . . redmen, portunes, giants, hobbits, hobgoblins, brown-men, cowies . . .' (*Denham Tracts*, 1895: ii. 77–80).

hobby horses. The literature on the hobby horse has been expertly collected and analysed by Dr E. C. Cawte, and this entry relies heavily on his findings. Cawte discusses the various meanings of the term 'hobby horse', which need not concern us here but which

caution researchers to be careful in interpretation of early records. He opts for an ultimate derivation from Scandinavian or Germanic sources, although by an odd accident two of the earliest references are in a 14th-century Welsh poem by Gruffud Gryg, and in the Cornish play Beunas Meriasek (1504). In both cases, however, the actual term is in English. The earliest reference to England comes between these two in time, in the churchwardens' accounts for St Andrew Hubbard, in London, for 1460/1: 'To Mayers child for dawnsyng wt ye hobye hors'.

There are several types of hobby horse, with differences in construction, use, and historical development. Tourney Horses: the 'rider' wears a roughly oval-shaped wooden or basketwork frame around his waist or chest, usually suspended by straps from his shoulders. The frame has some sort of horse's head at one end and a tail at the other, and a piece of cloth is fixed all the way round, hanging like a skirt to the ground and hiding the legs of the rider. Stuffed dummy legs can be attached to the side to look like the rider's legs, but this seems to be a much later embellishment. Mast Horses: a horse's head (made either of wood or from a real horse skull) is fixed to a pole about four or five feet tall. The bearer bends over and grasps the pole in front of him with two hands, and a cloth or sack is attached to the pole and completely covers and hides the bearer. Sieve Horses: the bearer stands inside a large circular wooden frame (such as a farm sieve) hung from his shoulders. A cloth hangs all the way round to hide him, with a horse's head and tail attached. Stick horses: an imitation horse's head is attached to a stick, which the rider bestrides and pretends to ride. The latter has been familiar as a children's toy for centuries, but as far as is known does not play any part in traditional customs. It is worth noting that with the stick horse, the person rides the horse. With the mast and sieve horses, the person is the horse. In the case of the tourney, the person both rides and is the horse, but the effect is predominantly the former.

Historical records concerning hobby horses are almost exclusively concerned with tourney horses; although many of the early records do not stipulate the type of horse concerned, the cumulative evidence is overwhelmingly in the tourney horse's favour. In its long history, the tourney horse turns up in a number of different contexts: ecclesiastical, municipal, court, theatrical, and with the morris dance.

In addition to the 1460 London reference, records show that the hobby horse was one of the major ways of raising money for the church in several parishes—either for special purposes, such as candles, or for general upkeep—from 1529 until well into the 17th century. Accounts include numerous entries for money collected, and also for expenditure on making and repairing the horse, for painting and decorating it, and for people to take the hobby horse role, and show that the performances took place mainly in the *New Year. Municipal horses were more often summer beasts, appearing in *Midsummer Watch and other *civic processions, often in conjunction with *giants and other processional figures, while in civic pageants there could be troupes of horses and mock jousts. Another context for hobby horse performance was at the court, where they are mentioned on several occasions between 1551 and 1575, often as an element in the Christmas/New Year celebrations organized by the official Lord of Misrule. In addition to church, town, and court horses, there are also a few references in this period to travelling players and/or entertainments at the homes of the well-off or in the presence of local dignitaries, such as the two records of performances 'before the mayor' at Newcastle in June 1567 and August 1600.

From the end of the 16th century, literary sources and, particularly, theatrical productions, include numerous references to hobby horses and indeed regularly introduce them on to the stage. Cawte (1978: 48–53) provides a list of plays in which hobby horses are mentioned or appear, commencing with *Paris and Vienna*, performed at court in 1572, and including pieces by Shakespeare, Dekker, Jonson, and Beaumont. In the playwright's mind, the hobby horse is inextricably bound up with the *morris dance, and the horse is rarely mentioned on its own. Descriptions in the plays and pictorial illustrations of the period (e.g. the anonymous painting *The Thames at Richmond*, *c.*1620) confirm that the horse here was a tourney horse. Apart from various revival morris teams, the only surviving traditional tourney horses are those which accompany the *Abbots Bromley Horn Dancers, and Christopher the *Salisbury Giant.

The sieve horse only appears in Lincolnshire, as part of the local *mumming or wooing plays, which are recorded from the 1820s onwards. Cawte suggests that this type of hobby horse is either a modified tourney horse or, conceivably, vice versa.

The mast horses, although apparently much rougher and cruder than the tourney horses, appear much later in the historical record, from the mid-19th century onwards. In many cases they appear on their own, as a *visiting custom, but they are more likely to be found as part of, or accompanying, other groups such as *mummers, *wassailers, and so on. In the category of mast horse, it is convenient to include other animals constructed on the same lines. Examples of the genre are *Old Tup, *Old Horse, the Broad, the Wild Horse, Old Ball, and *Hooden Horse. Even if the very important custom of the Mari Lwyd, found only in South Wales, is included, the earliest record is still only 1798 (see Cawte, 1978: 94–109). The two unique horses, from *Padstow (Cornwall) and *Minehead (Somerset), are also described under their own headings. The Padstow horse in particular has the feeling of an archaic custom, but even this is only recorded from 1803, and Minehead from about 1830.

The idea, proposed by Violet *Alford and others, that these hobby-horse customs are a direct survival of primitive humans' ritual behaviour is not borne out by the available evidence. Certainly the early Church fathers fulminate against people dressing in animal skins, but, as has been shown, the hobby horses and other animals of the 15th to 17th centuries are a very far cry from these skin-clad characters. Our hobby horses are sufficiently respectable to be not merely tolerated but actually organized and owned by church, guild, and corporation. Admittedly, the Puritans of the 17th century argued against these horses, but then they forbade virtually everything which was fun, and their displeasure can hardly be used as evidence of real pagan origins.

The more rough and ready mast horses, which are apparently more akin to what primitives might be expected to construct, are nearly all reported from the 19th century onwards, and so there is the paradox that the apparently rough and primitive comes after the relatively respectable. As is so often the case with English seasonal customs, writers have recourse to foreign analogues to attempt to bridge the historical lacunae, and in this case there are unusually close analogues which can perhaps be taken into account. The most important foreign evidence is found in

Scandinavia, in the form of the Julebukk or Julegeit, 'Christmas goat', although it appears under various other names as well. This goat was widespread across Norway, Sweden, and Denmark, up to the 19th century, as a visiting custom across the whole midwinter period, sometimes on its own and sometimes with other semi-dramatic customs and/or songs detailing its exploits and death. The goat's construction is almost exactly the same as our mast horse, except that the animal's species gave the opportunity for fearsome horns, and the bearer was more likely to be covered in furs than in the English examples. Its behaviour was also very similar. The earliest references predate our mast horses by a considerable margin, although not that of the English tourney horses. The earliest Danish record occurs in 1543, when farmers were warned against 'all-night drinking and unsuitable night-time entertainments' such as the Hvegehors ('Rocking-horse') and Julebuk, but the first definite description of the goat dates from 1646. The origin and development of this goat figure is still open to debate, but should be closely monitored by English researchers, and further comparative research into animal disguise in Germanic countries should also be encouraged. There are glimpses of more primitive behaviour, even in England, as in this from Northumberland:

New Year's Day—On this day of festivity mirth is excited by a rustic masquerading and playing tricks in disguise; the hide of the ox slain for the winter cheer is often put on, and the person thus attired attempts to show the character of the Devil by every horrible device in his power. (W. Hutchinson, *A View of Northumberland* (1778), ii. Appendix 19; quoted by Balfour, 1904: 63).

Cawte, 1978; Alford, 1978; Violet Alford, *JEFDSS* 3:4 (1939), 221–40; Terry Gunnell, *The Origins of Drama in Scandinavia* (1995), 107–28.

hobgoblin. This common Elizabethan variant on the name *hob could be used for helpful household fairies, as when Robert Burton writes of 'Hobgoblins and Robin Goodfellows that would, in these superstitious times, grinde corne for a mess of milk, cut wood, or do any maner of drudgery work' (*Anatomy of Melancholy* (1621), part 1, section 2, subsection 2). However, 'goblin' on its own generally implies a frightening or even demonic creature, and 'hobgoblin' sometimes shared these associations. In more modern use, 'hobgoblin' often carries humorous overtones.

hobhurst, hobthrust, hobthrush. A variant name for a *hob, whether in his capacity as domestic helper or out-of-doors trickster, found in Yorkshire, Westmorland, and Lancashire. It is uncertain whether the second syllable comes from Old English *thurs*, 'giant, demon', or Middle English *hurst*, 'grove, clump of trees'.

A note in *The Lonsdale Magazine or Kendal Repository for the Year 1822* (iii. 254) defines him well:

Hobthrust, or as he was more generally called, Throb-Thrush, was a being distinct from fairies. He was a solitary being who resided in Millom and had his regular range of farm houses. He seems to have been a kind spirit, and willing to do anything he was required to do. His only reward was a quart of milk porridge, in a snipped (chipped) pot. The servant girls would regularly put the cream in the churn, and say, 'I wish Throb would churn that', and they regularly found it done. . . . He left the country at last, through the kindness of a tailor, who made him a coat and a hood to keep him warm during the winter. He was heard singing at night in his favourite haunts,

'Throb-Thrush has got a new coat and a new hood,
And he'll never do more good.'

Hocktide. The second Monday and Tuesday after *Easter were termed Hocktide. In the Middle Ages these were days marked with festivities and rejoicing, although the only place that remembers them now is *Hungerford in Berkshire. The most widespread custom was for the women of the village to capture any men they met, bind them with ropes, and refuse to set them free until they had paid a small ransom. This happened on one of the Hock days, while on the other it was the men who captured the women. It appears that originally the participants kept the money collected themselves, but later it went to the church, and is therefore often recorded in the churchwardens' account books in the 15th and 16th centuries. It is noticeable that the women gathered far more money than the men:

1499 It. rec. of hok money gaderyd of women 20s
      It. rec. of hok money gaderyd of men 4s

(St Leonard's church, Reading)

Other account books show that the collectors expected a feast for their troubles. The earliest references are to attempts to tame or suppress the custom, in London in 1406 and 1409. In many places, the binding with ropes was replaced by a rope stretched across the road, but as late as 1540 a writer could still refer to the binding:

Women for the noble acte that they did in the distruction of the Danes, whych so cruelly reigned in this realme have a daie of memorye therof called hoptide, wherin it is leaful for them to take men, bynde, wasshe them, if they will give them nothing to bankett ... (Quoted in *Journal of the Warburg and Courtauld Institutes* 20 (1957), 178)

This account also contains the popular explanation for the custom, that it commemorates a time when a group of Saxon women outwitted and captured some invading Danes.

It is clear that there is a connection between Hocktide capturing customs and the Easter custom of *Lifting, or Heaving, which took place on the Monday and Tuesday following Easter, with the same sex division on the two days. The distribution map presented by Hutton shows that the two customs were found in different areas of the country, with hardly any overlap. Lifting was confined to western counties (but not the south-west) and north Wales, whereas the Hocktide capture was found in a strip up the central south of England and to the east (but not East Anglia). They would seem, therefore, to be regional variations of the same custom.

The *mock mayor ceremony at *Randwick, Gloucestershire, also took place at Hocktide.

Wright and Lones, 1936: i. 124–9; Hutton, 1996: 206–13; *N&Q* 10s:11 (1909), 488; 10s:12 (1909), 71–3, 139, 214, 253–4, 514–15.

hoglers. A puzzle for scholars for years, and their exact nature and role is only now becoming clear. In many surviving parish records, particularly churchwardens' accounts, from the 15th, to early 17th centuries, hoglers (sometimes hogglers, hognelers, or hoggeners) are listed as contributing substantial amounts to parish coffers, on a regular basis, year after year. By comparing all these entries it has become clear that these people would go round the parish collecting money (and/or corn) for the church, at a period before organized church rates existed (compare also *church ales). In most cases, their activities were concentrated in the *Christmas–*New Year period, and there are hints that they went in procession and some of them at least entertained potential donors with songs. The records indicate that the hoglers were usually drawn from the ranks of the respectable and respected parishioners—

the same sort of people who served as churchwardens—and that some places had several groups, organized on guild lines. Other references indicate the men going hogling at Christmas, while the women went at Easter. As further references come to light, the exact nature of hogling will, it is hoped, become clearer. What needs to be investigated, however, is why hoglers are mentioned in certain southern counties—Somerset, Devon, Sussex, Surrey, Kent, Gloucestershire—but not in the Midlands or north of England. The name also opens up areas of investigation. What is the relationship between hoglers and Hogmanay, the name for New Year in Scotland and the north of England? The first reference to the latter only dates from *c*.1680 (*OED*), 200 years after the first southern occurrence. Derivations of 'Hogmanay' usually cite the medieval French word *aguillanneuf* (meaning 'New Year' or 'New Year's Gift') as possible source. A cognate (and perhaps earlier) term in the south of England would help explain the connection, but more work needs to be done.

James Stokes, 'The Hoglers: Evidences of an Entertainment Tradition in Eleven Somerset Parishes, *Somerset N&Q* 32 (1990), 807–17; Uvedale Lambert, 'Hognel Money and Hogglers', *Surrey Archaeological Collections* 30 (1917), 54–60; Hutton, 1996: 12–13.

Hole, Christina (1896–1985). Her books were written for a 'general public' assumed to have no prior expertise, but without ever stooping to sensationalism or inaccuracy. Her first book on folklore, *Traditions and Customs of Cheshire* (1937), drew on close personal knowledge of that area; her later ones ranged further, but she always tried to observe as many festivals and seasonal customs as possible at first hand. She was always more concerned to describe clearly what was currently done than to speculate on remote origins and lost meanings; her books therefore remain reliable introductions to this aspect of folklore, the most important being *English Custom and Usage* (1941–2), *English Traditional Customs* (1975), and *British Folk Customs* (1976). She also wrote introductory surveys of ghost-lore in *Haunted England* (1940) and of witch beliefs in *Witchcraft In England* (1945; more accurately renamed *Witchcraft in Britain* in the 1977 edition), good for their time but now outdated. The full list of her publications is considerable.

From 1956 to 1978 she devoted much time and care to editing *Folklore*, thus contributing to the post-war revival of the Folklore Society as a focus for scholarship.

For tributes, bibliography, and obituaries, see *Folklore* 90 (1979), 665–6; 97 (1986), 109–10; *The Times* (29 Nov. 1985); Jacqueline Simpson, 'Christina Hole', in *Women and Tradition*, ed. Hilda Davidson and Carmen Blacker, 2001: 175–86.

holed stones. One of the most widespread magic devices to protect both man and beast was a pebble with a natural hole in it, also called 'hagstone', 'witch-stone', or (in the north-east) 'adder-stones'. They were believed to repel *witchcraft, and consequently any disease caused by spells or the *evil eye; in particular, they prevented *hag-riding. The earliest allusion is in a 15th-century charm against *nightmares (Opie and Tatem, 1989: 199, 378–9).

Small ones could be carried in the pocket or hung up over the bed; larger ones were used in stables, as described by Aubrey: 'in the West of England (& I beleeve, almost everywhere in this nation), the Carters, & Groomes, & Hostlers doe hang a flint (that has a hole in it) over Horses that are hagge-ridden for a Preservative against it' (Aubrey, 1686/1880: 28). A variation, still known in the mid-20th century, was to hang the stone on the stable door; usually the doorkey or a bit of old chain would be attached to it, reinforcing its power with that of *iron. The cowshed could be protected in the same way. A correspondent to *N&Q* in July 1894 said that in Whitby (Yorkshire) small stones were tied to front-door keys 'to ensure prosperity to the house and its inmates', and in August another said boatmen in Weymouth fastened them to the bows as charms to keep their boats safe. Small fossil sponges of the species *Porosphaera* are commonly found with natural holes in them; in Victorian times, necklaces of them were sold 'for luck' in Brighton (Sussex), and were much worn by women of fishing families.

One megalithic monument, Mên-an-Tol at Madron in Cornwall, consists of a disk-like holed stone about four feet in diameter, set up on edge between two standing stones, which has long been credited with healing powers. W. C. Borlase wrote:

When I was last at this Monument, in the year 1749, a very intelligent farmer of the neighbourhood assur'd me, that he had known many persons who had crept through this holed Stone for pains in their back and limbs, and that fanciful parents, at certain times of the year, do customarily draw their young Children thro', in order to cure them of the Rickets. (Borlase, 1754: 178–9)

Later Cornish writers add further details current in their own times, e.g. that the stone cured scrofula and a crick in the neck or back (and hence was called the Crick Stone), that those using it must pass through it three or nine times, that the children must be naked.

Such beliefs were more often linked to natural features, there being no other megaliths with suitable holes in:

In various parts of (Cornwall) there are, amongst the granitic masses, rocks which have fallen across each other, leaving small openings, or there are holes, low and narrow, extending under a pile of rocks. In nearly every case of this kind we find it popularly stated, that anyone suffering from rheumatism or lumbago would be cured if he crawled through the openings. (Hunt, 1865: 177)

This phrasing opens the possibility that, at any rate in some cases and from some speakers, the statement was a poker-faced joke—for is it not plain that anybody who managed to crawl through such a hole could not possibly be suffering from lumbago?

holly. Without doubt the most popular plant for *Christmas decorations, the holly has several associated traditions, most of which are positive. It is sometimes stated, however, that it is unlucky to bring holly into the house at times other than Christmas, and Vickery reports some households which will not allow the plant indoors at any time. Nevertheless, in Worcestershire and Herefordshire, a small piece of holly which had adorned a church at Christmas time was regarded as very lucky to hang up in your house, even though the domestic decorations had to be burnt as usual (*N&Q* 5s:11 (1879), 206). The two types—prickly and smooth—have been the focus for a minor domestic battle of the sexes—if the prickly holly was brought in first, the man would rule, but if smooth holly preceded it, the wife would be master (*N&Q* 11s:6 (1912), 486, also 11s:4 (1911), 526).

Holly trees were believed to be generally protective against witches and other evils, and were thus planted near churches and houses, as noticed by John Aubrey (1686: 189). In particular they were a good place to shelter in a storm because they were never struck by lightning. It is still considered unlucky by many to cut down a holly bush or tree, a belief which dates back at least to the 15th century. A good crop of berries on the holly is still said to betoken a hard winter on the way. Because of its connection with Christmas, 'green holly' has long been the emblem of mirth and jollity for poets and playwrights (see *N&Q* 12s:5 (1919), 319; 12s:6 (1920), 21–2, 52 for examples). A practical use for holly, so far recorded only in the 19th and 20th centuries, is for curing chilblains by thrashing them with the spiked leaves or, in some cases, rubbing them with powdered holly berries or their ashes. Holly could also be used in *love divination.

Opie and Tatem, 1989: 199–201; Vickery, 1995: 179–82; Henderson, 1879: 99–100.

Holy Innocents' Day (28 December). This feast honours the babies massacred at Bethlehem on Herod's orders (Matthew 2: 1–18); also formerly called Childermas. Although falling within the joyful Christmas season, it was thought an extremely unlucky day on which one must avoid beginning any important work. It was particularly feared by *fishermen, and by Cornish housewives, who would not wash clothes or do any scrubbing and cleaning. Numerous communities marked the day with muffled peals on the church bells. The ill luck was often felt to extend all through the year to whichever day of the week the feast had fallen on (Opie and Tatem, 1989: 70).

The only lighter side of the day was the notion that children should be indulged more than usual. In the early years of the 19th century, for instance, children were allowed to play in the church at Exton (Rutland) on Innocents' Day (*Leicestershire N&Q* 1: 293; quoted in Billson, 1895: 96), and William Henderson reports it an appropriate day for children's treats and parties (Henderson, 1879: 72). In places where there was a *boy bishop in pre-Reformation times, this date marked the climax and conclusion of his term of office by a procession and a church service at which he preached.

Holy Rood, Cross Day (14 September). This medieval feast, celebrating the supposed discovery of Christ's cross by St Helena, remained traditionally a day on which to abandon one's normal work and go *nutting.

Holy Thorn. There is a variety of *hawthorn which blooms twice a year, at midwinter as well as in May. A poem about the miracles of *Glastonbury, written in 1502, mentions two 'great marvels' to be seen there. One is a walnut tree near *Arthur's grave in the cemetery, which never bears leaves before St Barnabas's Day (11 June), but then suddenly becomes fully leaved. The other is a group of three hawthorns growing 'in Werrall' which produce buds and green leaves at Christmas 'as fresh as others in May'.

'Werrall' is a hill south of the town, now called Weary-All Hill; the poem says nothing about how the trees came to be there. By the time of Elizabeth I there was apparently only one, but it had two trunks. Its Christmas blossoms were treasured as holy; it is said that an Elizabethan Puritan took offence at this and chopped one trunk down, but was miraculously punished when he cut his own leg, and a chip from the tree blinded him in one eye. In 1639 Peter Mundy found it 'standing Neglected by the highe waies side, Now ready to Fall downe for age'; he was willing to believe that it bloomed at midwinter, 'Butt that, as some say, it should have No appearance off anything att all on Christmas Eave and thatt on Christmas day in the Morning itt shall bee Full off leaves and blossomes requires to bee prooved' (*Travels*, iv, p. xxxi).

A Roundhead destroyed what was left of this tree, but many cuttings had been taken; in 1645 people were still visiting a Glastonbury Thorn and taking twigs as souvenirs, believing that it was from a tree of this type that Christ's crown of thorns was made—or even that this particular tree had grown from a single thorn from Christ's crown, planted by *Joseph of Arimathea.

What is now the best-known legend first appeared in 1722; it had been recently collected orally from a Glastonbury innkeeper. He used to tell how Joseph and his travelling companions halted on the hill. 'Friends, we are weary all!' cried Joseph, driving his staff into the ground, where it took root and became the first Holy Thorn. Thus the hill got its name, in a clever but rather frivolous pun, typical of *placename legends. Other versions say Joseph's staff blossomed in answer to prayer, as a miracle to convert local heathens.

On Christmas Eve in 1752 hundreds of people gathered at Glastonbury, and in other places where descendants of the original thorn were growing, to see if they would bloom as usual; they did not, but on the night of 5/6 January 1753 they did. This was held to prove that the calendar change of 1752 was invalid, and 25 December no longer the 'real' Christmas Day (*The Gentleman's Magazine* (1753), 49, 578–9).

Every Christmas sprigs from a holy thorn in the churchyard of St John's Church, Glastonbury, are sent to the Queen and the Queen Mother; this custom began in 1929, when the then vicar sent one to Queen Mary. He was recalling an incident in Stuart times, when the Bishop of Bath and Wells sent twigs from both the walnut and the hawthorn to Queen Anne, wife of James I.

Vickery, 1995: 182–7.

Holy Thursday. Formerly, a name for *Ascension Day; not to be confused with *Maundy Thursday.

holy wells, see *WELLS.

Hone, William (1780–1842), Best remembered by historians as an energetic and enthusiastic champion of liberty and equality and a trenchant critic of the political establishment of the day. As journalist, printer, publisher, book, and print-seller, he was involved in numerous campaigns, and was well known for his pamphlets and political squibs. Folklorists, however, remember him for his later works, the four thick volumes of miscellaneous material, commencing with *The Every-Day Book*. This was a weekly miscellany, launched in January 1825 and continuing to December 1827, which was then bound up into a two-volume set. It included a wide range of material, some of it linked to the calendar but much of it apparently stuck in where there was room, and it included a great deal of folklore in the form of calendar customs, saints' legends, superstitions, and general folk life. The serial publication allowed readers to become contributors, and Hone repeatedly urged his readers to collect information and send it in. Many of the most useful pieces are eyewitness accounts of local customs which would not otherwise have seen the light of day, and they save the books from being mere regurgitations of previous writers' material. Hone also had relatively high editorial standards for his time and insisted that his contributors give proper bibliographic references. The *Every-Day Book* became sufficiently popular for Hone to publish two sequels—*The Table Book* (1827) and *The Year Book* (1831–2). Again, the excellent engravings added to their charm. Hone's works thus joined those of *Brand and *Strutt as essential reading for the 19th-century antiquarian-folklorist, and are still

very much in demand today. Other books written by Hone of particular interest to folklorists are *Ancient Mysteries Described* (1823), which was an examination of the Coventry *mystery plays; and an edition of *Strutt's *Sports and Pastimes of the People of England* (1830).

DNB; Dorson, 1968: 35–43.

honeysuckle. The strong scent of honeysuckle and the way it twines round the stems of other plants are the likely reasons why it symbolizes erotic love. When it coils tightly round a growing plant, the latter develops spiralling grooves and swellings; hazel rods distorted in this way were prized for walking sticks, called 'honeysuckle sticks' or 'twisty sticks'. In Sussex, these were thought to bring luck, especially to young men who were courting.

Honiton Fair. Honiton's charter fair, dating from 1221, lasts for three days, and is one of the few which preserve the ancient 'Glove is up' custom. In former times, while a fair was in progress special rules applied as regards who was allowed to trade in the town and what rights and privileges they had. It was thus important that it was clear to all when the fair officially started and finished, and the normal way to do this was to exhibit a large hand or glove. At Honiton in Devon, the Town Crier appears at midday on the first Tuesday after 19 July, St Margaret's Eve, carrying a twelve-foot pole, covered with flowers, and on top a gilded leather glove. He calls out:

Oyez, Oyez, Oyez
The glove is up
The Fair has begun
No man shall be arrested until the glove is taken down
God save the Queen

All the children in the audience echo his words as he speaks. Next, hot coppers are thrown from an upstairs window of the Angel Hotel, to be *scrambled for. The whole process is repeated outside the King's Arms, and later in the week at the White Lion. The glove is taken down to signify the official end to the fair.

Kightly, 1986: 123–4; Hogg, 1971: 36–7; Sykes, 1977: 109.

Hood, Robin see *ROBIN HOOD.

Hooden Horse. One of a range of animal-disguise customs, Hoodening can be regarded as a regional variant of the *hobby horse, being recorded in about 30 places in east Kent and nowhere else. The custom took place at Christmas, and the team of between four to eight farmworkers visited the neighbourhood houses and pubs performing, singing, and collecting money. The central character was the horse which was made up of a wooden head on a pole, carried by a man who was bent double, leaning on the pole, under a dark cloth covering. The head was decorated with horse brasses, rosettes, ribbons, and so on, and had snapping jaws operated by a string from inside. The horse had a Groom (or Waggoner or Driver) who led him around and who carried a whip. There was also a Jockey, who tried to ride the horse, a man-woman (Mollie), and musicians. The earliest mention is in 1736, which refers to 'Hooding' and is so brief as to be inconclusive, and a better description appeared in the *European Magazine* in May 1807. The custom seems to have died out about 1908. Various suggestions have been made regarding the name of the custom. The most convincing are that 'hooden' may be from 'wooden' or perhaps 'hooded'.

Percy Maylam, *The Hooden Horse: An East Kent Christmas Custom* (1909); Cawte, 1978: 85–93.

Hopkins, Matthew (d. 1647). Notorious for having instigated England's only large-scale witch-hunt, in East Anglia in 1645/6, in which nearly 250 people were tried or investigated; court records being incomplete, the actual number executed is unknown, but 100 seems a reasonable minimum. Hopkins belonged to the minor Puritan gentry, being the son of a Suffolk minister and himself a lawyer; he called himself the 'Witch-Finder General', and at first was well supported by the local communities. He and his associate John Stearne claimed expertise in identifying witches; suspects were stripped and their bodies examined for marks where *familiars sucked, and then kept awake, still naked and tied in uncomfortable positions, till they confessed. This came close to torture, which was illegal; when circuit judges from London next visited Essex, the activities of Hopkins and Stearne were terminated. After a blistering attack from a clergyman, John Gaule, both men wrote booklets defending their work: Hopkins, *The Discovery of Witches* (1647), and Stearne, *A Confirmation and Discovery of Witchcraft* (1648). Hopkins died in 1647, probably of tuberculosis; legend alleged that he had himself been suspected of witchcraft and made to undergo the swim-

ming test, but there is no evidence to support this.

His reputation was maintained in popular memory. In the 1930s, Gerald *Gardner was given a rod topped with a cross, carved with the name 'Matthew Hopkins', and labelled 'Matthew Hopkins's sceptre or tutti-stick, used by him in his travels in the South of England finding and exposing witches. Circa 1790'. Likewise, a box containing various dried leaves, twigs, scraps of skin and bone with magical signs on, a doll's head pierced with a pin, a human finger bone, a lead six-pointed star, and a parchment reading: 'Matthew Hopkins's talisman against alle witches craft.' A label on the box itself reads: 'This talisman, made and sold by Matthew Hopkins about 1790, was given to me by my father, Joseph Carter, of Home Farm, Hill Top, near Marlborough, and contains the finger etc. of Mary Holt, a notorious Wiltshire witch. Signed S. Carter' (G. B. Gardner, *Folk-Lore* 50 (1939), 188–90, with illustrations). The date is obviously wrong; perhaps these objects were bought in 1790 from a Wiltshire *cunning man, who was claiming either to have inherited them from Hopkins or to be following a Hopkins recipe.

There are references to Hopkins in all books on English *witchcraft, the fullest analysis being in Sharpe, 1996: 128–47; see also Deacon, 1976.

hop-picking customs. The customs and beliefs of the hop field have not received much attention, but it is clear that there were a number of traditional practices associated with the hop farm. In pre-mechanical days, hops were harvested by groups of visiting workers who descended on the hop farm for the brief intensive effort needed to harvest the crop. In addition to local workers, there were strong traditions of urban working-class women and children using the hop fields as a paid holiday, and the hop fields of Kent and Sussex were thus picked by Londoners, while the Hereford and Worcester farms were visited by families from the industrial Black Country. Two customs reported by Leather (1912:105–6) both have close analogies in the grain *harvest field. It was customary for any stranger who entered the hop field to be 'cribbed', that is, seized by the pickers and thrown into one of the cribs into which the hops are gathered, and 'one or two of the oldest and fattest women would be thrown in too' whom he had to kiss before he was released (Leather, 1912: 105). The only way to avoid this treatment was for the stranger to pay his 'footing' (compare *occupational customs) by giving money to the pickers. At the end of the picking season, the pickers chose a King and Queen from among their own number, who were dressed up in flowers and ribbons, and these two led the procession, which included hop-poles also decorated with ribbons, to a nearby barn, where they spent the evening in merrymaking. A feature which distinguishes this from usual harvest custom is that the man dressed as the Queen and the woman as the King.

There were variations, however, in both these practices. The *Herne Bay Gazette* (13 Dec. 1985), for example, shows a Hop Queen of the 1960s who was a real woman, and an engraving in the *Penny Magazine* of 21 November 1835 shows that this was not a recent alteration. In the version of 'cribbing' described by Faulkner, it was the foreman or overseer who was thrown in the crib, when the end of the season approached.

Leather also reports a superstition of the Herefordshire hoppers that they believed it was lucky to burn old boots before starting a journey, and they would do this before going home.

Leather, 1912: 105–6, 258; Christine Faulkner, *Folk Life* 30 (1991/2), 7–16; Richard Filmer, *Hops and Hop Picking* (1982).

Hopscotch. The well-known children's game which involves a pattern of squares (beds) marked on the ground, into which players throw a stone and travel across them in a series of hops and jumps, sometimes kicking the stone as they go. The pattern varies considerably within the basic oblong shape, as do the instructions as to which squares need to be avoided, the sequence of hops, and so on. As with all children's games, the terminology also varies. The general name 'Hopscotch' or, almost as frequent in earlier times, 'Scotchhoppers', refers to hopping over the scotches, or marks scored in the ground, rather than containing any reference to Scotland. The earliest definite illustration of the game is found in Jacques Stella, *Les Jeux et plaisirs de l'enfance* (1657), although it is usually presumed to be much older. It is not mentioned in English until William King, *Useful Transactions in Philosophy* (1709), but there are numerous references from that time onwards.

The Opies identify the basic 'ladder' shape, with a number of equal-sized and same-shaped beds, as the earliest form, which was developed in two main ways. One was to add a semicircular bed at the top (usually used for turning round and/or resting in), the other was to divide alternate beds in half. This provides for the basic movement of hop (into a whole bed), split (one foot in each half-bed), hop, split, and so on. A further variation is to divide some beds with diagonal lines, thus quartering them. Other major variants are Spiral Hopscotch, and ball Hopscotch.

Opie and Opie, 1997: 95–109; Gomme, 1894: i. 223–7.

Horn Fair, see *CHARLTON HORN FAIR, *EBERNOE HORN FAIR.

horns. In popular culture for centuries past, the phrase 'he wears the horns' was used to designate a cuckold, and rather than bringing forth sympathy it has been treated as a joke of which people never seem to tire. The metaphor of the horns was so well understood that it could be referred to obliquely by writers—'Let him dub her husband knight of the forked order' (1592) and also in Shakespeare's *Titus Andronicus* ((1594) II. iii). An appropriate gesture, with index and little finger extended, thumb and other fingers curled into the palm, was available for insulting people: one story which attempts to account for this explains that the knights who were away on the Crusades used the symbol of the horn as a device on their shields, and a horn therefore came to mean someone who had been away from his wife for a long time. See also *Charlton Horn Fair for another alleged cuckoldry connection.

A different kind of symbolism is sketched out by William Andrews (*Old Church Lore* (1891), 65–79) in the form of 'charter horns'. He identifies several existing horns which are taken as evidence of ancient land grants or charters, and links these with customs which still have hornblowing elements such as *Hungerford Hocktide, and the *Ripon hornblower.

See also: *ABBOTS BROMLEY HORN DANCE; *CHARLTON FAIR; *EBERNOE HORN FAIR; *HIGHGATE HORNS; *RIPON HORNBLOWER; *BAINBRIDGE HORNBLOWER; *HUNGERFORD HOCKTIDE, *WEYHILL FAIR.

Hazlitt, 1905: 327–8.

horse brasses. Brass plaques as ornaments for the harness of cart-horses were first made in the late 18th century; they became very popular in the 1850s, replacing an older style of adornment with ribbons, woollen fringes, and tooled leather. In some areas brasses were still in normal use in the 1920s, and can still be seen at horse-shows and parades (Brears, 1981).

The oldest examples are also the simplest, and seem to be rural imitations of the silver heraldic badges worn by the carriage-horses of the gentry. A wide range of designs soon appeared, some figurative and some geometric; they included crescents and suns, which might be interpreted as lucky symbols, and the *horseshoe, an undoubted *charm. It is doubtful whether there was deliberate magical intent, since there was apparently no previous English tradition of metal charms on horses. In a general sense, however, anything shiny and eye-catching can protect against the *evil eye and *witchcraft. Popular writers have latched on to this possibility, creating a feedback which confuses the issue. Nowadays, some country people say horse brasses are merely ornaments, while others say: 'The reason that metal was put onto the horse's straps was to protect the horse from bad influences; iron was thought to be a good metal for the job'; or, 'you put . . . the head piece to protect their head and the breast piece to keep away evil spirits from their heart'; or, 'horses wore metal on their head and heart to stop witches putting a spell on them' (Sutton, 1997: 36).

horseman's word. In the days when experienced horsemen were skilled and valued agricultural workers, many believed in their ability to control horses in mysterious and magical ways, reputedly by whispering a secret word into the animal's ear. In particular, they claimed they could handle any horse and make it come to them ('drawing' the horse) or more spectacularly could reduce a horse to immobility ('jading' it) which no power on earth could shift until the horseman himself released it. In Scotland, there is evidence of these horse-workers being inducted into a sort of secret society, but although there is similar evidence of the belief in individuals possessing such powers in England, right into the 20th century, they were apparently less formally organised than their Scottish brethren (Hutton, 1999: 61–4). Descriptions of the horseman's powers are particularly prevalent in East Anglia, although there are scattered references to other parts of the country, but the material is often deliberately vague and 'mysterious', and usually couched in terms of traditional tales rather than hard evidence. George Ewart Evans's work sheds the most light on the subject. He maintains the horseman's real power was based on a knowledge of certain preparations of herbs and oils which acted powerfully on the horse's sense of smell. His informants, however, believed that the power came with possession of a particular toad or frog's bone, gathered in a certain way, and then treated in a special secret manner, which gave the name 'Toadmen' to the individuals with the power.

A particular breed of *toad was sought (the natterjack, or *bufo calamita*, according to one of Evans's informants). It was killed and hung on a whitethorn bush for 24 hours to dry, and then buried for a month in an ant-hill to remove the flesh. At the next full moon, the skeleton was placed in a running stream, where one particular bone should float *upstream*. The participant must watch it carefully, and ignore the terrible noises which will occur just behind him—on no account must he look round or he will lose to the power. The special bone is taken home, treated with particular oils, baked, and powdered, and this gives the bearer power over horses (and, in some versions, pigs and women). Evans also describes an alternative preparation based on the 'milt', which is an oval-shaped lump of fibrous matter found in a foal's mouth immediately after it is born. The ritual convinced the horsemen, and was used by them to impress others, that they were dealing with evil powers or the Devil himself, and thus the power they gained was both mysterious and dangerous, and their own reputation as horse-handlers was enhanced.

Evans's theories on the horseman's word as a relic of an ancient horse fertility cult are unconvincing, partly because the sources he quotes such as Margaret *Murray and Robert Graves are themselves highly suspect, but there is little doubt that the horse knowledge concerned dates back a long way. It is possible to separate the outward form (the business with the toad) from the essence (the use of herbs and oils to gain power over horses), and, paradoxically, we know much more about the former than the latter. The use of *toads and *frogs in ways similar to those described here are found in other old cures, and indeed its essence is paralleled in a passage in Pliny (*Natural History* (AD 77), XXXII. xviii) who writes of a particular frog's bone which cools boiling water and another which makes oil appear to boil and is effective, amongst other things, in keeping dogs at bay. Reginald Scot (1584) shows that the idea of a bone with special powers, and its connection with water, was known in England at that time. Nevertheless, the earliest notices of horsemen possessing such powers are given by Davidson—in 1648 in Sussex and in Renfrewshire in 1664. It is clear that still further work needs to be done on this subject.

Evans, 1960: 238–71; Evans, 1966: 204–39; Evans, 1979: *passim*; Thomas Davidson, *Gwerin* 1:2 (1956), 67–74; G. W. Pattison, *Folk-Lore* 64 (1953), 424–6; Charles Thomas, *Folk-Lore* 65 (1954), 54; Peter Bayliss, *Fortean Times* 83 (1995), 39–40; Porter, 1969: 55–9 (Hutton, 1999: 61–4).

horses. In folk tradition, horses were regarded as very vulnerable to supernatural attack; in particular, their night sweats and exhaustion were interpreted as due to *hag-riding by witches or fairies, from whom they must be protected by *holed stones. Their tendency to shy or refuse to move on, for no visible reason, was (and still often is) attributed to a psychic awareness of the presence of evil, for example in haunted spots and those where blood has been shed. It was also thought that they could be immobilized, tamed, or rendered restive by people with magical power; one of the recurrent tales about *witches and *cunning men was that they would keep a horse spellbound by a word. In some regions, notably East Anglia, men particularly skilled in working farm horses had secret ways of controlling them, apparently by a mixture of magical ritual and material means such as substances whose smell attracted or repelled them (see *Horseman's word, and *toadmen).

Horse *skulls are occasionally found under floorboards in old buildings, for instance at Thrimby Hall (Bedfordshire) in 1860, and in Bungay (Suffolk) in 1933. It is tempting to see this as magical *house protection, but the explanation given by the householders was that they improved the acoustics for home music-making, and this is supported by Irish and Scandinavian instances where the resonance of a horse skull was thought desirable in churches and threshing barns (Merrifield, 1987: 123–6). On the other hand, the purpose of a horse skull with two boar's tusks embedded in its jaw, found in the wall of an 18th-century house at Ballaugh (Isle of Man) can only have been protective (*Folklore* 100 (1989), 105–9). Several horse bones were found

between two courses of brick of a 16th-century cottage in Histon, and a leg-bone under the foundations of stables of a 16th-century inn in Cambridge (Porter, 1969: 180–1).

The Norfolk writer W. H. Barrett remembered seeing a skull laid down in 1897, when he was six. He and his brother were sent to a knacker's yard to buy a horse's head for their uncle, who was building a Methodist chapel in Littleport:

When the two boys returned with it they watched the workmen dig the trench for the foundations and then saw their uncle carefully mark the centre of the site by driving into the ground a wooden stake. The men gathered round while the uncle uncorked a bottle of beer, then the horse's head was placed in the bottom of the trench, the first glass of liquor from the bottle was thrown on it, and, when the rest of the beer had been drunk, the men shovelled bricks and mortar on top of the head. It was explained to W. H. Barrett that this was an old heathen custom to drive evil and witchcraft away. (Porter, 1969: 181).

See also *HAIR (ANIMAL), *HOBBY HORSE, *HORSE BRASSES, *HORSESHOES.

Opie and Tatem, 1989: 201–2, 305–6; Radford, Radford, and Hole, 1961: 193–8.

horseshoes. Nowadays the horseshoe is a generalized symbol of good luck, used, for instance, on greeting cards and wedding cakes; already in the late 14th century it was believed that to find a horseshoe by chance is a lucky thing. Later references are numerous, and give more details: one should pick it up, spit on it, and toss it over the left shoulder, making a wish. The luck is increased if some nails are still in it.

Earlier, horseshoes specifically counteracted *witchcraft. They were set at the door 'so that no witch shall have power to enter' (Scot, 1584: book 12, chapter 18), and 'to afflict the Witch, causing the evil to return back upon them' (J. Blagrave, *Astrological Practice* (1671) 138). The early references (16th to mid-19th centuries) usually talk of horseshoes nailed to the *threshold or the steps leading to the door; this arrangement can still occasionally be seen, for instance at an old smithy at Burpham (Sussex), where several are set into a concrete threshold. It was also common to nail them behind the door, as hidden protectors; nowadays, it is more usual to display them openly, on or above the door. Horseshoes were also much used on ships, being nailed to the main mast and elsewhere.

In Lincolnshire in the 1850s, some people

would nail them to a bed to prevent ague and alcoholic delirium; one woman, reportedly, tapped them with a hammer, saying:

Father, Son and Holy Ghost,
Nail the devil to this post.
With this mell I thrice do knock,
One for God, and one for Wod, and one for Lok.

The clergyman recording this assumed it referred to the Germanic gods Woden and Loki, and capitalized accordingly, but he may have misheard some phrase ending in the more commonplace 'one for luck' (Heanley, *Folk-Lore* i (1898), 186).

In London in the early 20th century, a horseshoe wrapped in *red flannel was hung over the bed to prevent *nightmares. As storms, diseases, and nightmares were often blamed on witches, the underlying idea is still that of protection from evil magic. In Somerset, they were used in stables to stop *pixies riding' the horses. In Yorkshire belief, if a maiden found three horseshoes in one year, threw each over her left shoulder, walked three times round it, and kept it, she and all her children (though not her possessions) would be immune to witchcraft (Blakeborough, 1898: 158–9).

Using astrological shorthand, *Aubrey comments that 'Mars/iron is hostile to Saturn/lead, and therefore to witches', meaning that it is *iron which gives horseshoes their power Aubrey, 1686/1880: 27). As regards positioning, many accounts from the 16th century till now agree that a horseshoe fixed vertically should have its 'heel', i.e. the points, pointing upwards to catch and hold the good luck, though this rule was not always followed—blacksmiths themselves often preferred them to be pointing down. According to Aubrey, horseshoes laid flat on a threshold had 'the hollow' pointing into the house.

Opie and Tatem, 1989: 202–4.

Hot Cockles. An extremely popular game at Victorian *Christmas parties. One player sits down, another player is blindfolded, kneels, and places his/her head in the sitter's lap. The kneeler places an open hand on his/her back, with palm uppermost, which other players take it in turns to strike, and the kneeler must guess who has struck the blow. Hot Cockles was thus one of several traditional games in which someone has to guess who has hit or touched them, and it also existed as a street and playground game, no doubt played more

robustly there than in the Victorian drawing-room. Certainly, in mixed company, it allowed some mild flirtation. The game can claim some considerable antiquity, being referred to by name as early as 1549 and 1590, and an illustration from a 14th-century manuscript, printed by Strutt, appears to take the game back even further in time.

Gomme, 1894: i. 229–31; Opie and Opie, 1969: 292–4; Strutt, 1801/1876: 501–2.

hot cross buns, see *GOOD FRIDAY and *WIDOW'S SON.

houses. The most substantial body of folk practice and belief concerning houses focuses on protecting them from *witchcraft, evil spirits, *fire, *thunder, and lightning; this involved placing protective objects, generally near a point of possible entry—door, hearth and chimney, window. There are ample records showing that certain items (e.g. *holed stones, *horseshoes, *houseleeks, *rowans, *thunderstones, *witch posts, a piece of *Yule Log) were believed to ward off danger; in other cases this interpretation is more conjectural, though plausible (e.g. putting dried *cats, *horse bones, and *shoes inside walls, and stone *heads on the façade). It has recently been suggested (Lloyd, 1999) that certain patterns cut into timbers of East Anglian houses were protective. Some of these features, such as witch posts, must be the work of the builders, presumably by agreement with the owners; others could be added by anyone at any time. It is not always clear where magic ends and decoration begins; traditional features such as the finials on tiled roofs and plaited bird figures on thatches were probably regarded as lucky by some craftsmen and some customers, but as simply ornamental by others. Some trees and shrubs also protected against fire, witchcraft, or both; these include *bay, *elder, *holly, and *rowan.

The only belief about houses themselves appears to be one mentioned by Charles Dickens in *Dombey and Son* ((1848) chapter 51): 'Mr Towlinson ... frequently begs to know whether he didn't say that no good would come of living in a corner house'. This prejudice was 'common in Herefordshire' (*N&Q* 5s:4 (1875), 216), and Opie and Tatem give a further reference from 1947.

Also from the mid-19th century, and more regularly reported, is the idea that to enter a house with a spade (or axe, mattock, etc.) on your shoulder presages death, because these tools are used to dig graves. Standard collections mention this for several regions, including Shropshire, Herefordshire, and Dorset (Burne, 1883: 280; Leather, 1912: 119; Udal, 1922: 286); the first known reference is in *N&Q* 1s:12 (1855), 488. The somewhat similar taboo on opening an *umbrella indoors is less easily explicable.

See also *BUILDING TRADE, *FOUNDATION SACRIFICES. For beliefs about house furnishings, see *BEDS, *FIRES, *MIRRORS, etc.

Opie and Tatem, 1989: 97, 331, 367.

houseleek. Herbalists of the 16th and 17th centuries claimed that no *thunderstorm could harm a house where this plant grows, and the belief persisted among country people in many parts of England, especially as regards houseleeks which had seeded themselves on the roof. To remove these was very unlucky, and people would transplant them if moving to a new house (Latham, 1878: 13; Porter, 1969: 69).

howling, see *WASSAILING.

Humpty Dumpty. One of the best-known *nursery rhymes in English tradition, which has excited much misguided speculation and theory. What has been obscured by centuries of illustrated children's books is that the rhyme is simply a *riddle, and the hearer has to guess the answer as 'egg', but nowadays we all know the answer before we say the rhyme. The first known text only dates from 1797, although the term 'Humpty Dumpty' (meaning an ale-and-brandy drink) is recorded about a century before. Numerous close analogues from continental Europe do not help to date the rhyme, as they are all from 19th-century sources.

Opie and Opie, 1997: 252–5.

hunchback. For the first half of the 20th century, at least, it was considered lucky to touch the hump of a humpbacked person. The first known reference is in *The People* (11 June 1899, quoted in *N&Q* 9s:3 (1899), 486), but here it is implied that the belief is much older. Two other 20th-century references in Opie and Tatem make it clear that people disabled in this way could play on the superstition by charging money for the service at race-meetings and the like.

Opie and Tatem, 1989: 206.

Hungerford Hocktide. Hungerford, Berkshire, preserves a complex of *civic/*manorial customs at *Hocktide, the second Tuesday after Easter, which were concerned with the administration of the town's common land and local fishing rights, but which previously had much more serious duties. Hock Tuesday in Hungerford starts with three blasts of a horn from the Town Hall window, which summons all 'commoners' (residents of particular properties in the town to which grazing and fishing rights are attached) to attend a meeting of the Court. The town bellman also walks the streets crying a summons, and he can still exact a penny fine from any non attenders. At the Court are elected a Constable, Portreeve, Bailiff, Water Bailiff, Ale tasters, Commons overseers, Keeper of the Keys, and the four Tithingmen or Tutti Men. The latter previously had duties of keeping watch, and could therefore expect a penny payment from every household. By long tradition, however, they claim a penny from the men and a kiss from the women, and they carry a ladder to ensure that they can reach any window to exact appropriate payment. They also carry, as staffs of office, Tutti poles which are of wood and adorned with ribbons a-topped with a posy of flowers and an orange. They are accompanied by an Orange Man who carries a bag of oranges and gives one to each child in the house, and one to each female in return for the kiss. A civic luncheon is held, usually at the Three Swans Hotel. Outside, the Tutti Men and Orange Man throw oranges to the waiting children, to be *scrambled for, while inside the ceremony of 'shoeing the colt' takes place. Any newcomer or visitor is liable to undergo this ordeal. The newcomer is lifted bodily from the floor and a man in a blacksmith's apron pretends to hammer nails into the sole of his/her shoe, until he/she cries 'punch' and thereby agrees to buy a round of drinks. The new officers, who are now merely ceremonial, are sworn in later in the week. According to local tradition, the Hungerford rights go back to the time of John of Gaunt (1340–99).

Sykes, 1977: 47–9; Kightly, 1986: 139–40; Shuel 1985:113–14; Hole, 1975: 52–4; Stone, 1906: 94–6.

Hunting the Earl of Rone. This *Ascension Day custom which formerly took place at Combe Martin in Devon, appears to be unique although it includes echoes of other customs such as the *mummers play and the *hobby horse. The performers are: The Earl of Rone wearing mask, frock smock padded with straw, string of twelve hard sea-biscuits round his neck), The Fool (gaudily dressed, carrying besom), a gaily painted Hobby Horse with openable jaws (called the Mapper), a real donkey decorated with flowers and more sea-biscuits, and some Grenadiers (coloured paper hats with ribbons, carrying guns). At 3 p.m. on Ascension Day the Grenadiers march to nearby Lady's Wood to search for, and find, the Earl who has hidden there. They fire a volley, set him on the donkey, facing its tail, and return to the village, accompanied by Fool, Hobby Horse, and crowd of spectators. *En route*, the Grenadiers fire off other volleys and each time the Earl falls as if wounded. The Fool and Horse exhibit signs of grief, and revive him each time. They visit public houses on the way, and try to solicit contributions from the crowd. The performances ceased about 1837, but were revived in the village in 1970 and have continued since. The local legend cited as the basis for the custom explains that a real Earl of Tyrone had, in Queen Elizabeth I's time, taken refuge in the wood, with only a few ship's biscuits to keep him alive and he was captured by soldiers.

Wright and Lones, 1936: i. 144–5; E. L. Radford, 'A Quaint Ascension-Day Festival', *Trans. Of the Devonshire Assoc.* 49 (1917), 71–5; Tom Brown, *The Hunting of the Earl of Rone* (rev. edn., 1997).

Hunt the Slipper. A very popular parlour game, particularly at Victorian family Christmas parties. Oliver Goldsmith's *Vicar of Wakefield* ((1766), chapter 11) provides a lively description:

The company at this play plant themselves in a ring upon the ground, all except one, whose business it is to catch a shoe, which the company shove about under their hams from one to another, something like a weaver's shuttle. As it is impossible, in this case, for the lady who is up to face all the company at once, the great beauty of the play lies in hitting her a thump with the heel of the shoe on that side least capable of making a defence.

Versions included in Gomme, played by children, involve some play-acting by the seated cobblers pretending to mend shoes and a dialogue between them and the chaser, including a rhyme on the lines of: 'Cobbler, cobbler, mend my shoe, Get it done by half-past two'.

Gomme, 1894: i. 241–2; Strutt, 1801/1876: 387.

Hurlers, The. A group of three *stone circles on the moors near Likinhorne (Cornwall) is

collectively known as The Hurlers; a tale first alluded to in William Camden's *Britannia* (1586) claims they were once men, transformed as punishment for 'profaning the Lord's Day with hurling'—*hurling being one of the most popular sports in Cornwall. In 1675 Dr James Yonge of Plymouth recorded a further tradition about them: 'They are now easily numbered, but the people have a story that they never could, till a man took many penny loaffes, and laying one upon each hurler, did compute by the remainder what number they were' (Westwood, 1985: 22).

hurling. Once popular throughout Cornwall, hurling now survives traditionally in only two places—St Columb Major and St Ives. It is a street ball game, similar to the mass *football customs described elsewhere, but in hurling the ball is thrown or carried, but never kicked. The ball is also smaller, about the size of a cricket ball, and although made of wood is coated with silver. At St Columb, the game is still played in the streets, between two sides—the 'town' and the 'country', with the latter coming from the outlying districts. The ball is thrown up in the Market Square and the idea is to get the ball back to your side's base, which is about a mile away. This takes place on *Shrove Tuesday and again on the second Saturday following. The game at St Ives has been tamed somewhat and takes place on the first Monday after 3 February (Quinquagesima Sunday), and play takes place mainly on the beach. References to hurling in Cornwall date back at least to 1602, when Richard Carew wrote of it in some detail. He described two versions of the game, one relatively polite and controlled by strict rules, and the other the mass sport which took place 'over hills, dales, hedges, ditches, yea, and through bushes, briars, mires, plashes, and rivers . . . '. Daniel Defoe called it 'rude violent play', and 'brutish and furious', but virtually the same thing was said about all the mass sports.

Carew, 1602/1953 edn.: 147–50; Daniel Defoe, *A Tour Through the whole Island of Great Britain* (1724–6; Everyman edn., 257); A. Ivan Rabey, *Hurling at St Columb and in Cornwall* (1972).

Husset, see *WOOSET.

hytersprites. These are Norfolk *fairies (also called 'highty sprites' or 'hikey sprites'), first recorded in print in 1872 and still remembered in a few areas of the county

in the 1980s. The earliest source calls them
'rather beneficient than otherwise', but in
most accounts they are used to scare children: 'If you go out in the dark on your own,
the hytersprites will get you', 'If you bain't
quiet, I'll hull you to the hytersprites', etc.
They were supposed to be active in the
woods at dusk. One informant said that as
children she and her friends had imagined
them as man-sized black bats 'hovering
silently in the twilight, waiting to snatch
away disobedient children'; another has
heard birdlike twitterings in the dusk, which
she thought fun; a third said, 'They are the
malign spirits who enter a house if the
Christmas decorations are left up after
Twelfth Night, to cause destructive mischief
and general ill-luck about the house for the
rest of the year'.

Daniel Rabuzzi, *Folklore* 95 (1984), 74–89.

Ickwell May Day. A *May celebration which has survived, probably because it has been adapted by successive generations to fit the current ideas of what May is all about. Local churchwardens' records show that celebrations at Ickwell Green, Bedfordshire, go back at least to 1561, when food, drink, minstrels, and morris dancers are specifically mentioned. In 1872, the village acquired a permanent maypole, donated by local squire John Audley. Also in Victorian times, villagers went gathering may blossom and left garlands on people's doorsteps early in the morning. There was a procession of mayers through the village, carrying *garlands, led by a Lord and Lady and including two Moggies (two men with blackened faces, one dressed as a woman), who would sing a song at people's doors. Nowadays, there are all the elements one would expect to find at a May Day fête, including a *May Queen, *morris dancers, *maypole dancing, and the Moggies themselves have also been revived.

Shuel, 1985: 32–3; Sykes, 1977: 80–1.

image magic. In magic, injuring a model injures the person it represents, especially if it incorporates his hair or fingernails, or is given his *name. In 963 a woman was executed by drowning for driving *nails into an effigy; in 1578 a plot against the Queen was feared when three wax figures were found in a dunghill, transfixed with pig's bristles, one with 'Elizabeth' written on the forehead. Clay images could be burnt, or laid in water to disintegrate. Alternatively, images could be buried or hidden, causing lingering sickness to the victim; this may be the purpose of the 18th-century doll hidden in a house in Hereford, with a written *curse pinned to its skirt.

A Yorkshire farmer in the 1850s, suspecting that a certain man with the *evil eye had bewitched him, made an image from a mix-ture of 'pitch, beeswax, hog's lard, bullock's blood, and a small portion of fat from a bullock's heart'; this was heated over a fire of wickenwood (= *rowan) at midnight, and a pin driven into its eye. Next morning, the suspect was blind in one eye (Blakeborough, 1898: 199–200).

In the 1960s, two of Ruth Tongue's Somerset informants told her:

There was a bad woman in our village—a witch who could do things. She didn't like my mother, so she made a wax doll and stuck thorns into its legs, and my mother had the screws (rheumatism) in her legs ever since.

I know a woman who lives near me, and she said: 'I don't like that there Mrs ——, so I be going back home to make a mommet of she and stick pins in it.' I never dared ask if she did, but the woman was took ill after that. (*Folklore* 74 (1963), 323)

infection. Anxiety about Aids has generated a spate of rumours, gruesome jokes, and a *contemporary legend based on the notion that those infected deliberately infect others, in revenge or despair. The story has often appeared in press reports in the USA, Britain, and Europe. One version, which was 'all over the city' of Sheffield in February 1987, told how a young man picked up an unknown girl at a nightclub and took her home for sex; when he woke she had left, after writing in lipstick on the bathroom mirror, 'Welcome to the world of Aids!' (Bennett and Smith, 1990: 113). In other variants the victim is a girl who, returning from a holiday abroad, unwraps a 'parting gift' from a casual partner, and finds a miniature coffin with the same message. Currently (1998), there is a third version:

Worthing nightclubbers are being asked to be on their guard against sick pranksters who fool them into thinking they have contracted the deadly HIV virus. Rumours have been spreading throughout Worthing that groups of people have been stabbing late-night revellers with needles containing blood contaminated with the virus. Small notes are then left in the revellers' coats or handbags with the sick message, 'Welcome to the Aids club.' ... [Police commented]: 'There is no evidence whatsoever to suggest this is really happening ... if people do find one of these notes it is likely to be no more than a very sick joke.' (*Worthing Herald* (5 Feb. 1998), 25)

Despite the rational police warning, six months later another local paper reported as factual a 'cruel and vicious attack' on a girl in a nightclub, who allegedly felt a sharp jab in the back, and found a card in her pocket with the usual message. Neither the girl's name nor that of the 'family friend' who told the press is given (*Worthing Guardian* (17 Sept. 1998), 1).

In an article on this story-type, Paul Smith pointed to a precedent in Daniel Defoe's *Journal of the Plague Year* (1722):

A poor, unhappy gentlewoman, a substantial citizen's wife, was (if the story be true) murdered by one of these creatures [plague victims] in Aldergate Street, or that way. He was going along the street, raving mad to be sure, and singing ... and meeting this gentlewoman, he would kiss her .... [He] mastered her, and kissed her; and, which was worst of all, when he had done, told her he had the plague, and why should not she have it as well as he? (Defoe, 1722; Penguin edn., 1986: 173)

Similarly, Pepys's *Diary* for 12 February 1666 records that his son's lutemaster had just told him how 'in spite to well people [those already sick] would breathe (out of their windows) into the faces of well people going by'.

There was an old principle that one could cure oneself of a disease by deliberately transferring it to another, which survives in *wart cures and the casual expression about 'giving' someone one's cold. To rid a child of whooping cough or fever, according to various 19th-century sources, one should wrap a few of his hairs in bread and butter and throw it to a dog, which would eat it and die, and the child recover (Opie and Tatem, 1989: 63). The most cruel application concerned venereal diseases; it is discreetly mentioned by Mabel Peacock (*Folk-Lore* 7 (1896), 272), when she says it is widely thought by 'the ignorant and debased' that 'certain cures are only to be effected by doing violence to a girl yet in her childhood'.

Paul Smith, in Bennett and Smith, 1990: 113–41.

initiation, see *OCCUPATIONAL LORE, *PRINTING TRADE.

Institute for Folklore Studies in Britain and Canada, see *NATIONAL CENTRE FOR ENGLISH CULTURAL TRADITION.

Institute of Dialect and Folklife Studies. This first sustained attempt to provide university-level teaching of folklore in England grew out of the *English Dialect Survey, on foundations laid by Harold Orton (1898–1975), and benefited from the expansion in higher education occurring in Britain at the time. It opened at Leeds University in October 1964 under the directorship of Stewart Sanderson, who remained in charge until he retired in 1984. For twenty years, the Institute provided folklorists and dialectologists with an opportunity to undertake serious research and study, and many of the current leading scholars in the field owe their initial training to its existence. The Institute closed in 1984, a victim of the major cuts in higher education funding of that decade, leaving the *Centre for English Cultural Tradition and Language, at Sheffield University, as the only place in England with a commitment to the study of the subject at post-graduate level.

Craig Fees, *The Imperilled Inheritance: Dialect and Folklife Studies at the University of Leeds 1946–1962*, part 1 (1991).

Irish charms. In north-eastern counties, it was thought that stones or sticks brought over from Ireland would cure snake-bites and bee-stings, provided they had never been allowed to touch English soil; such a stick was still kept, and occasionally used, in Farndale (Yorkshire) in 1970. The belief is obviously based on the well-known story of St Patrick driving all snakes out of Ireland; it was already known to Bede, who noted that almost anything coming from Ireland was reckoned effective against snake-bites, and that he himself had seen people drinking water into which scrapings from Irish manuscripts had been dropped, with good results (Davies, 1998: 48–9).

iron. The power of iron to repel evil is very well attested in English folklore, and throughout Europe—all sorts of domestic objects, and even lumps of scrap iron, were placed in homes, stables, and cowsheds as defences against *witchcraft and harmful *fairies, or used in *counterspells. Sharp ones were even more effective, and *Herrick mentions 'hooks and shears' in stables, and knives in babies' cradles (*Hesperides* (1648), nos. 890, 892). Red-hot iron was a potent *counterspell when *milk was bewitched.

*Touching iron, or merely saying 'Touch iron!' or 'Cold iron!', cancels the bad luck of breaking a *taboo or seeing something ill-omened; it is not as widespread as touching wood, but some groups, such as *fishermen, practise it keenly.

A picturesque 19th-century theory was that iron was first reputed magical in prehistoric times, because men using bronze or stone weapons feared those using iron swords; obviously, this is flimsy guesswork, there being no possible evidence for or against the idea.

itching, see *EARS, *ELBOWS, *FEET, *HANDS, *KNEES, *MOUTHS, *NOSES; and Lean, 1903: ii. 283–8; Opie and Tatem, 1989: 479.

ivy. Used in *Christmas decorations, though apparently considered inferior to holly, judging by a rather obscure 15th-century carol:

Holly stond in the hall, fayre to behold;
Ivy stond without the dore, she ys ful sore a-cold.
Holly and hys mery men, they dawnsyn and they
  syng;
Ivy and hur maydenys, they wepen and they wryng.

That ivy is 'female' is also implied by the custom of the *Holly Boy and Ivy Girl. Victorians saw it as an emblem of the ever-faithful, but dependent, love of wife for the husband to whom she clings as the ivy to the oak.

However, ivy also has gloomy associations with graveyards and old ruins; some people think it unlucky to have it indoors at any time other than Christmas. Its leaves were used in a *divination on *Twelfth Night (in Cornwall in the 1880s) or *Halloween (in Herefordshire around 1910); they were left overnight in water, and if next morning black spots or coffin-shaped markings had appeared, someone in the household would die that year (Opie and Tatem, 1989: 214; Leather, 1912: 65).

Jack. In Britain, and also in Canada, the USA, and Australia, 'Jack' is the name routinely used in *fairytales for a resourceful, lucky hero, who may also sometimes be unscrupulous or a trickster. Henry Mayhew in his *London Labour and the London Poor* ((1861), iii. 189–90) describes how a 16-year-old boy in a London workhouse told him a story he called 'Clever Jack', about the exploits of a daring and witty young robber who outwitted various rich gentlemen and a parson. The boy said men in the casual ward of the workhouse sometimes took turns telling stories: 'romantic tales, some; others blackguard kind of tales, about thieving and roguery; not so much about what they'd done themselves, as about some big thief that was very clever at stealing, and could trick anybody. Not stories such as Dick Turpin or Jack Sheppard or things that's in history, but inventions.' The boy added that 'the best man in the story is always called Jack'.

The name has long been used with the implication 'typical (young) man', from nursery-rhyme characters to 'Jack Tar' for a sailor, and modern slang phrases like 'I'm all right, Jack' and 'Jack-the-lad'. The murderer who called himself 'Jack the Ripper' had a sinister sense of humour.

Several English tales with a 'Jack' as hero were collected in the 19th century, and others in the 20th century from Gypsies (Briggs, 1970–1: A. i. 322–5; Philip, 1992: 18–42, 54, 127–32). For Canadian examples, derived from British and Irish tradition, see Herbert Halpert and J. D. A. Widdowson, *The Folktales of Newfoundland* (1996).

Jack and Jill. One of the many popular *nursery rhymes which have suffered the indignity of being subjected to implausible origin theories. The earliest known text dates from *c*.1765, starting life as 'Jack and Gill', two boys, and only one verse long until added to in the early 19th century. The rhyme was popular on *chapbooks and also as the theme for panto-mimes. The phrase 'Jack and Jill' is older than the rhyme, meaning simply 'boy and girl' or 'lad and lass', as in Shakespeare's 'Jack shall have Jill, Nought shall go ill' (*Midsummer Night's Dream*, III. ii).

Opie and Opie, 1997: 265–7.

Jack and the Beanstalk. In this simple but ever popular tale, the hero Jack, a poor widow's feckless son, sells their cow for five magic beans, which his mother angrily throws away. By next day, their stems reach up to the sky; climbing up, Jack finds the castle of a man-eating giant, whose wife befriends and hides him. Three times he steals magic golden treasures; the third time he is discovered and the giant chases him, but he chops down the beanstalk and the giant dies.

There are allusions showing the story was well known by the early 18th century, but the first surviving texts are in two *chapbooks, one in verse and one in prose, both published in 1807; they differ in several details. The former is summarized and the latter reprinted in Opie and Opie, 1974: 162–74. In 1890 Joseph *Jacobs printed a far livelier version based on the way his nurse used to tell it to him as a child in Australia around 1860 (Jacobs, 1890: 57–67; also in Briggs, 1970–1: A. i. 316–21; Philip, 1992: 1–10).

Jack-in-the-Green. An urban street *calendar custom enacted on May Day by chimney sweeps. The sweeps dressed up in their finery if they had any, with added ribbons; one dressed as the Lord, another as a Lady, and one or two as clowns. They had musicians and carried a brush and shovel which they clashed together rhythmically, and a regular feature was a donkey for one of them to ride. The character that really got the audience's attention was the Jack-in-the-Green, a man inside a wood or basketwork frame, from well above his head to his ankles, on which was fixed an abundance of greenery and flowers. The visual effect was a conical-shaped bush on feet, which danced. In the earlier period, the sweeps would be accompanied by their boys, whose capering and antics were popular with the crowds, but the boys disappeared from the scene after public opinion turned against the use of children in the trade. References become fewer and fewer after the 1850s, and descriptions tend to stress the drunkenness, tawdriness, and vulgarity of the proceedings rather than its quaintness. The Victorian drive towards the invented *Merrie England May Day was in full swing, and, as with so many other customs, the real Jack-in-the-Green had to be abolished before it could be reinvented, cleaned up, and made safe, to take its place in the pageants of the late Victorians and Edwardians, and the fêtes, fayres, and processions of the 20th century.

Even in its heyday, the Jack was far from being a national phenomenon. Roy Judge's distribution map shows a highly regionalized custom, including only 81 places, and some of these are of dubious traditional standing. Sightings cluster most thickly in London, Oxfordshire and Buckinghamshire. The earliest references to the Jack are from the late 18th century, but this has not prevented writers extrapolating backwards and claiming him as a true survivor of a wood-spirit, nature worshipper, *Robin Hood, medieval *Wild Man, Gawain and the Green Knight, and so forth, for which there is no evidence but plenty of wishful thinking. Perhaps the most audacious argument-without-evidence was the confident identification of the Jack-in-the-Green with the so-called 'Green Man' (see *foliate heads) to be found on many churches. This was a mere speculation by Lady Raglan in 1939, which has since been quoted as fact countless times.

Judge, 1979/2000; Judge, 1987; Hone, 1827: i. 292–6; George L. Phillips, 'May-Day is Sweeps' Day', *Folk-Lore* 60 (1949), 217–27; Charles Phythian-Adams, 'Milk and Soot: The Changing Vocabulary of a Popular Ritual in Stuart and Hanoverian London', in D. Fraser and A. Sutcliffe, *The Pursuit of Urban History* (1983), 83–104.

Jack o' Kent. A legendary *wizard, hero of a cycle of humorous anecdotes in Herefordshire and Gwent. Some concern the rivalry between Jack and the Devil, each trying to outwit the other or to set the other a task he could not perform; Jack is invariably the winner. Many

common international tales appear here, for example the mowing contest won by cheating, and the trick 'sharing' in which the dupe gets only straw when he chooses 'bottoms' of a wheat crop, and only leaves when he chooses 'tops' of turnips. Jack is also said to have hurled various standing stones in the Wye Valley, and kicked a cleft in the side of the Skirrid mountain; he is credited with magical powers of flight, and over animals. He sold his soul to the Devil 'whether he was buried inside or outside the church', but cheated him by having his tomb set in the thickness of the church wall.

These tales were collected in the 19th century, but an allusion in a play of 1597 shows Jack o' Kent was already famous then. Various historical identifications have been proposed, the likeliest being John Kent, vicar of Kentchurch in the early 15th century, who was a poet and theological writer.

Leather, 1912: 163–6; B. A. Wherry, *Folk-Lore* 15 (1904), 75–86; and R. T. Davies, *Folk-Lore* 48 (1937), 41–59. Leather's tales are reprinted in Briggs, 1970–1: B. i. 106–8, 145; and in Philip, 1992: 288–92. See also J. W. Ashton, *Journal of American Folklore* 47 (1934), 362–8.

Jack o' Lantern. A local name for a *Will-o'-the-Wisp, mainly in East Anglia and in southwest England; also spelled Jack-a-Lantern and Jacky Lantern, according to the whim of the collectors. T. Quiller Couch found that around Polperro (Cornwall) it was regarded as a pixy, and was invoked in the rhyme:

Jack o' the lantern! Joan the wad,
Who tickled the maid and made her mad!
Light me home, the weather's bad.

In the 1970s, little figures representing these two were being sold in Cornwall as lucky charms, for 5s. each, and proved very popular.

In the south-west, the name is also used for the turnip lanterns children carry at *Halloween.

Jack o' Legs. This Jack was a legendary *robber near Weston (Hertfordshire); he was tall enough to look in at the upstairs windows of large houses. Like *Robin Hood, he robbed the rich but fed the poor; according to the earliest account, in Nathaniel Salmon's *History of Hertfordshire* (1728), certain bakers, furious that he had stolen their bread, caught him unawares, blinded him, and hanged him. Again like Robin Hood, his last request was to be handed his bow and buried wherever the arrow fell; two stones in Weston churchyard, fourteen and a half feet apart, are said to mark the grave in which he lies—doubled up!

A massive thighbone used to be displayed as his, but was bought from the parish clerk by the 17th-century antiquary John Tradescant. It passed to the Ashmolean Museum, Oxford, where in the early 19th century it was still labelled 'Thigh-bone of a Giant', until identified as an elephant's leg-bone and discarded. A signboard recently erected in the village illustrates Jack's story (*Hertfordshire Countryside* (June 1998), 28).

Jones-Baker, 1977: 47–9; E. P. Emslie, *Folk-Lore* 26 (1915), 156; Westwood, 1985: 139–40.

Jack o' Lent. In Tudor and Jacobean London, this was the name for gaunt puppets made of straw, rags, and herring skins, personifying the Lenten fast, which boys set up on Ash Wednesday and pelted with heavy sticks, and finally burnt before Easter. He could also be impersonated by living actors; a London pageant just before Easter 1553 showed a richly dressed Lord of Misrule, symbol of the coming feast, contrasted with Jack on his deathbed, with a 'priest' shriving him and a 'wife' begging doctors to save his life for £1,000.

In Oxfordshire in the 17th century, schoolchildren breaking up for the Easter holidays went from house to house rattling wooden clappers and singing:

> Harings harings white and red
> Ten a penny Lent's dead
> Rise dame and give an egg
> Or else a piece of bacon
> One for Peter two for Paul
> Three for Jack a Lents all
> Away Lent away

If they got none, they would 'commonly cut the latch of ye door, or stop the keyhole wth dirt, or leave some more nasty token of displeasure' (White Kennett's note in Aubrey, 1686/1880: 161–2).

Effigies were made, paraded, and burnt at Polperro (Cornwall) early in the 19th century; the image was called 'Jack-o-Lent', but popularly supposed to represent *Judas. So was the effigy which used to be set up at Boston (Lincolnshire) in the 1920s, and pelted with muck from Ash Wednesday till the end of Lent (Sutton, 1997: 55). In some country districts, a jackalent is a scarecrow.

Wright and Lones, 1936: i. 39–40; Hutton, 1996: 172–3.

Jack's Land. In Scotland, there is a relatively well-known custom of 'Cloutie's Croft', the name given to a portion of the best land of a farm which is always left untilled and uncultivated as it belongs to the Devil. In many areas of England, similar patches of untouched land were found, although the dedication to the Devil was rarely so explicit or clear-cut, and they bore local names such as 'Jack's Land' or 'No Man's Land'. In addition to being uncultivated, this land usually had some sort of sinister reputation, or at least was believed to be unusually infertile (see a Devon example in Henderson, 1879: 278). References in *N&Q* attest to the Scottish custom and a similar one in Ireland, and mention another sinister piece of land at Hickling, Nottinghamshire, known as 'Jack Craft'. There is a tendency nowadays—well known to local historians, but usually totally unfounded—for people to explain any patch of apparently unused land, in urban as well as rural areas, as old 'plague-pits'.

Evans, 1966: 136–7; *N&Q* 1s:3 (1851), 477; 8s:10 (1896), 74, 219, 324; 9s:4 (1899), 68, 118.

Jacks (game), see *FIVESTONES.

Jack the Giant-Killer. This story—or rather, this string of episodes attached to one hero—is known to have existed in a *chapbook of 1711, now lost, and is mentioned by several 18th-century writers as having pleased them greatly when young; the earliest surviving text, entitled *The History of Jack and the Giants*, is from the 1750s or 1760s. Several of the giants Jack kills are localized in Cornwall. He defeats them by traditional tricks— he lures one into a pit and beheads him; foils an ogre's murderous plan by substituting a log for himself in bed, thus seeming invulnerable; and convinces the ogre that he has just slit his own stomach open, so that the latter kills himself in trying to do the same. He gains various treasures and rewards, and rescues princesses. The central section has a more sustained plot, in which Jack becomes servant to King Arthur's son and breaks the spell on a princess whom Arthur's son wants to marry. The final sections are again episodic, and mainly humorous, though one ogre does utter the famous rhyme known already in Shakespeare's time (see *King Lear*, III. iv):

> Fee, fau, fum,
> I smell the blood of an English man,
> Be he alive, or be he dead,
> I'll grind his bones to make my bread.

The popularity of these chapbooks is shown by frequent casual allusions in 18th- and 19th-century literature. They formed the basis for many retellings, the first being in J. O. Halliwell, *Popular Rhymes and Nursery Tales of England* (1849); the full chapbook text is in Opie and Opie, 1974: 47–65, and a summary will be found in Briggs, 1970–1: A. i. 329–31. An oral version was collected in Herefordshire in 1909 (Leather, 1912: 174–6; Philip, 1992: 11–17).

Jacobs, Joseph (1854–1916). Born in Australia of Jewish parents, Jacobs wrote chiefly on Jewish history and culture, but between 1889 and 1900 he was actively involved on the Council of the Folklore Society. At his suggestion, the Society renamed its journal *Folk-Lore* in 1890; he was its first Editor under the new title (1890–3), and remained on the editorial board till 1900. He studied narrative genres, especially those involving both oral and written transmission, such as *fables. As regards folklore theory, he held that when similar items are found in separate cultures they have spread from a single place and time of origin, by contact between social groups (diffusionism), rather than developing independently (polygenesis); also, that folklore items such as tales or proverbs are created by a single 'author', not by a whole community.

Jacobs produced several collections of fairy-tales for young readers; they include *English Fairy Tales* (1890, revised 1898) and *More English Fairy Tales* (1894), which did much to spread awareness of our own oral tradition. Two, *'Jack and the Beanstalk' and 'Henny-Penny', are personal memories of tales told him in childhood; the rest are texts previously collected and published by others, some being modified for easier reading. But the lengthy notes accompanying these popularized tales are thoroughly scholarly.

Other important works are his editions of *The Fables of Aesop as First Printed by William Caxton* (1889), of *The Most Delectable History of Reynard the Fox* (1895), and of *Barlam and Josaphat* (1896), and his substantial introduction to E. W. Lane's translation of *The One Thousand and One Nights* (1895).

Obituary: *Folk-Lore* 65 (1954), 126–7. Gary Alan Fine, *Folklore* 98 (1987), 183–93.

Jenny Greenteeth. In Lancashire, Cheshire, and Shropshire, from the 19th century to within living memory, children were threatened that if they went near pools the *water-spirit Jenny (or Ginny) Greenteeth would catch them; some said she also lurked in the tree-tops, where she could be heard moaning at night (Wright, 1913: 198–9). According to Charlotte Burne, this *bogey was 'an old woman who lurks beneath the green weeds that cover stagnant ponds; Ellesmere children were warned that if they venture too near such places, she will stretch out her long arms and drag them to her' (Burne 1883: 79). A Lancashire contributor to *N&Q* recalled: 'Further, I have often been told by my mother and nurse that if I did not keep my teeth clean I should some day be dragged into one of these ponds by Jenny Greenteeth, and I have met many elderly people who have had the same threat applied to them' (*N&Q* 10s:2 (1904), 365).

As recently as 1980 a Merseyside woman aged 68 recalled what she had heard about her as a child: 'pale green skin, green teeth, very long green locks of hair, long green fingers with long nails, and she was very thin with a pointed chin and very big eyes.' Another informant, however, said Ginny 'had no known form, due to the fact that she never appeared above the surface of the pond.' She was especially associated with stagnant water deceptively covered with thick algae or duck-weed; in fact, to some, 'Jenny Greenteeth' was simply a name for duckweed itself, and the horror consisted in the way this weed would close over anything that fell in.

Roy Vickery, *Folklore* 94 (1983), 247–50; Vickery, 1995: 113–14.

Jews. England shared the assumption (general until the later 20th century) that Jews lost their homeland as punishment for murdering Jesus, and have ever since been accursed. Symbolically, this was expressed through the medieval legend of the Wandering Jew, doomed to roam the earth till Christ's Second Coming because he had shouted at him to move faster on the way to Calvary. The story first appeared in Matthew Paris's *Chronicle of the Abbey of St Albans* (begun in 1235), which declares that an Armenian Bishop who visited the Abbey in 1228 had often seen this Jew, now a devoutly penitent Christian hoping for forgiveness on Doomsday. It remained popular all over Europe till late in the 19th century, publicized through ballads and *chapbooks, many of which claimed the wanderer had actually been sighted in one town or another. There is a circumstantial English account of his passing through Stamford on Whitsunday

1658, and curing a consumptive by advising him to drink daily a brew of 'two leaves of red sage and one of bloodworte'. A related notion is that of Jews present during the Crucifixion whose punishment is to become restless night birds, the *Seven Whistlers, or mine-haunting *knockers.

Another important medieval theme was the accusation that Jews kidnapped Christian children and crucified them on Good Friday or Easter Sunday; two child saints, William of Norwich and Hugh of Lincoln, are alleged to have been 'martyred' in this way, and to have miraculously revealed the whereabouts of their corpses by singing prayers after death. Hugh's story was told in ballads, and also by Chaucer as 'The Prioress's Tale'.

Jewish religion was assumed to consist of sorcery and devil-worship, leading Christians to apply the terms 'synagogue' and 'sabbath' to gatherings of *witches. Yet, paradoxically, Hebrew was seen as the most sacred of all languages, outranking even Latin and Greek; hence the widespread use of Hebrew words, letters, and symbols in ritual *magic, and in healing *charms.

Venetia Newall, in *The Witch Figure*, ed. V. Newall (1973), 95–124; George K. Anderson, *The Legend of the Wandering Jew* (1967); S. Baring-Gould, *Curious Myths of the Middle Ages* (1877), 1–31.

Joan the Wad. A Cornish name for a *Will-o'-the-Wisp, originally limited to the area round Polperro, where it was noted by Jonathan Crouch in his history of the town; 'wad' is a dialect word for a torch. Besides leading people astray with her light, she sometimes tickled and pinched them, so Crouch classified her as a *pixy. A rhyme invoked her aid:

> Jack o' the lantern! Joan the wad,
> Who tickled the maid and made her mad!
> Light me home, the weather's bad.

Joseph of Arimathea. A minor figure in the Gospels, who entered folklore when *Glastonbury claimed he founded a church there in AD 63; this story first appears in 1247, as a forged chapter inserted into William of Malmesbury's treatise *On The Antiquity of Glastonbury Church* (written c.1130). Such an early founder conferred great prestige; in the 14th and 15th centuries the Abbots of Glastonbury began calling Joseph 'Saint', dedicating a chapel to him, and claiming miracles. At first, no relics were mentioned, but in the late 15th century came the story that he had brought two flasks

containing the blood and the sweat of Jesus, which were buried in his grave. This seems to be a religious adaptation of a theme long popular in romances of knightly adventure, where Joseph is regarded as the first custodian of the *Grail. The flasks and drops of blood were shown on the Abbey arms.

Traditions about Joseph continued to grow after the Reformation, presumably because the idea of a mission to Britain predating that of Augustine suited Protestants. The story that the *Holy Thorn sprang from Joseph's staff was first printed in 1722, from a local innkeeper's account (Vickery, 1995: 182–7). Currently, there is a legend that Joseph was a tin merchant and the great-uncle of Jesus, and that he brought Jesus to Cornwall and/or to Somerset in the course of a trading journey. How old this legend is is disputed; those who believe it assume it to be medieval, but it is nowhere mentioned before the 1890s, unless William Blake is alluding to it in his poem of 1804 beginning, 'And did those feet in ancient times / Walk upon England's mountains green?' However, these lines could be merely symbolical. The story appeared in Sabine Baring-Gould's *Book of Cornwall* (1899) and subsequent guidebooks, and was widely publicized by three vicars in the 1920s and 1930s—the Revd L. S. Lewis of St John's, Glastonbury, the Revd H. A. Lewis of Talland (Cornwall), and the Revd C. C. Dobson of St Mary's, Hastings (Sussex).

R. F. Treharne, *The Glastonbury Legends* (1967) E. M. R. Ditmas, *Traditions of Glastonbury* (1983) A. W. Smith, *Folklore* 100 (1989), 63–83; Rahtz, 1993.

Journal of the English Folk Dance and Song Society. Launched in 1932, when the *English Folk Dance and Song Society was formed, by the amalgamation of the *Folk-Song Society and the *English Folk Dance Society, and thus replacing the journals of these two societies. It ran until December 1964 (vol. 9 no. 5), when it in turn was replaced by the *Folk Music Journal. Its content was mainly descriptive, comparative, and historical, rather than theoretical, but many of its articles are still required reading. Editors: Frank Howes (1932–45), Margaret *Dean-Smith (1946–51), Sara Jackson (1952–60), Russell Wortley (1961–4).

Journal of the English Folk Dance Society. Although the *English Folk Dance Society existed from 1911 to 1932, it only published a handful of issues of its journal. Volume 1 (parts 1 and 2, 1914–15) was hit by the First World War, and the second series achieved four annual numbers (1927–32) before the Society amalgamated with the *Folk-Song Society. Nevertheless, in its short existence, it included a number of important pieces on the *morris, *sword, and country *dance, *mumming plays, and other matters. The first series was edited by Perceval Lucas, but the editorials in the second series are unsigned. It was replaced in 1932 by the *Journal of the English Folk Dance and Song Society.

Journal of the Folk-Song Society. Launched in 1899, the *JFSS* served as the primary medium for the publication of accurate folk *song material for members of the *Folk-Song Society, running until 1931 (vol. 8, part 35), when the Society amalgamated with the *English Folk Dance Society to form the *English Folk Dance and Song Society, and it was thus replaced by the latter's *Journal*. Although the *JFSS* included some important articles, the bulk of its content comprised songs collected by members and submitted for publication, with annotations provided by members of the journal's Board, including such experts as Cecil *Sharp, Lucy *Broadwood, Frank *Kidson, and Anne *Gilchrist, but there was little sustained argument or overall analysis. The tunes of the songs are printed 'as collected', but often in the earlier volumes only sample verses of the texts were given. The bulk of the songs published were English, but important contributions on Irish, Manx, and Scottish songs also appeared.

E. A. White, *An Index of English Songs Contributed to the JFSS* (1951); Frederick Keel, *JEFDSS* 5:3 (1948), 111–26.

Judas. In folk religion, Judas the traitor and suicide is the ultimate hate-figure, and various supposedly evil or unlucky things are explained by reference to him: he was *red-haired, he spilt the *salt at the Last Supper, he was the *thirteenth person present there and the first to leave the table, he hanged himself on an *elder tree. In the north of England, c.1850, it was said that anyone with black hair and a red beard was 'false by nature', for that had been Judas's colouring (*Denham Tracts*, 1895: ii. 24). In such cases, the beliefs are generally on record earlier than their 'explanations' and/or often to be found without them; the appeal to (pseudo-) Scriptural authority seems likely to be a *post facto* rationalization.

The earliest surviving fragment of an English ballad concerns Judas (F. J. Child, *English and Scottish Ballads*, no. 23). Jesus sends Judas into Jerusalem with 30 pieces of silver to buy food; there he meets his sister 'the treacherous woman', who tells him he deserves to be stoned for believing a false prophet; he warns her to be silent, for Jesus would take revenge if he knew what she had said. At this point the poem becomes confused, but it seems likely that (with typical medieval chauvinism) a woman will be blamed for a man's crime.

Some Lenten customs were validated as being aimed against Judas. The *Jack-o'-Lent effigy burnt on the beach at Polperro (Cornwall) in the early 19th century was explained thus, as was a more recent Ash Wednesday custom from Lincolnshire:

When I was about 15 years old, 70 years ago (= 1920s), they used to make an effigy of Judas from straw and hang it up on Boston market place near the old stocks. The idea was for folks to throw a clod of muck at it for betraying Jesus. If any of it was left at the end of Lent it was torn down or set fire to; that was to make sure it got finished properly. (Sutton, 1997: 55)

In Brighton (Sussex), where fishermen and their families enjoyed long-rope skipping in the fish-market on Good Fridays earlier in the 20th century, it was sometimes said to be instituted in memory of the rope with which Judas hanged himself (Simpson, 1973: 111). Devon people thought it lucky to break a piece of crockery on Good Friday, as its sharp edges would pierce the body of Judas (Wright and Lones, 1936: i. 81–2); no explanation is reported, but it may not be coincidental that in Elizabethan times the corpses of *suicides were pelted with pottery shards.

The most recent and dramatic Judas custom was peculiar to the south end of Liverpool Docks in the 1950s. At daybreak on Good Friday crowds of children congregated round dummies made from old clothes, paper, straw, and a comic mask; the leader of each group hoisted this 'Judas' on a pole, and they went from house to house knocking against bedroom windows and shouting, 'Judas is a penny short of his breakfast' till a few coins were thrown down. By mid-morning the collecting ended, and bonfires were built in the streets to burn the Judases before 11 a.m., but police would often scatter the fires and carry off the Judases, to destroy them at the police station—at which the pursuing children would yell 'Judas!' at the police themselves. In any case, the fun had to be over by noon (Frank Turner, *Folk-Lore* 65 (1954), 47).

Liverpool people believed their custom arose from watching what was done on Spanish ships docking there in Holy Week (Opie and Opie, 1959: 259–60). Certainly it is very similar to customs common in Spain, Portugal, and Latin America. An illustration in the *Graphic* (15 Apr. 1876), 36), shows Portuguese sailors 'flogging Judas Iscariot' in London Docks on Good Friday, and the Opies give other references to the overseas custom being observed on foreign ships in English docks. The *Guardian* (18 Sept. 1996), 17, gives further foreign examples of Judas customs. However, now that the Polperro record has been reinforced by one from Lincolnshire, there is a case for thinking English precedents contributed something to the Liverpool effigies.

judgements and Providence. Belief in God's 'judgements'—dramatic calamities sent to punish sinful individuals or communities, and to warn others—which was prominent from medieval till Victorian times, has shaped much folklore (Thomas, 1971: 79–112, 472–3). It is obvious in many landscape legends (e.g.

*Long Meg, *Semerwater, *Stanton Drew), in some accounts of *monstrous births, in beliefs about *Gabriel Ratchets and the *Wild Hunt, in cautionary pamphlets about the *Black Dog of Bungay or the *Mowing Devil, and even in the tale of the *Lambton Worm. The role of the Devil in many such tales corresponds to an old belief that he was the agent for God's judgements. The sins thus punished include *Sabbath-breaking, blasphemy, rash mention of the Devil, lack of charity, theft, murder, and injustice towards a labourer. According to a plaque on the market cross at Devizes (Devon), in 1753 a woman who said 'she wished she might drop down dead' if she had cheated on a purchase, 'instantly fell down and expired, having the money in her hand'.

Providential deliverances and blessings did not stimulate popular imagination so much. However, Providence may be implied by the astonishing good fortune of Dick *Whittington and the Pedlar of *Swaffham; it underlies the widespread tale of a lost traveller saved by a curfew bell, who then donates land for its upkeep. It is also manifestly the point of the *Angels of Mons rumour.

jump rope, see *SKIPPING.

Karpeles, Maud Pauline (1885–1976).
Together with her sister Helen (who late married Douglas *Kennedy) Maud Karpeles met Cecil *Sharp in 1911 and fell under the spell of his enthusiasm for English folk *dance and *song. The Karpeles sisters were soon included in Sharp's demonstration teams and were closely involved with the *English Folk Dance Society (EFDS) formed later that year. When Sharp developed neuritis, Maud became his amanuensis and thus became directly involved in the collecting, lecturing, and publishing with which Sharp was busy spreading the gospel. She accompanied him on his seminal song-collecting trips to the Appalachians from 1916 to 1918. When Sharp died in 1924 Karpeles dedicated herself to continuing his work, through the editing of his collections for publication, and also through the EFDS and its successor the *English Folk Dance and Song Society. One major contribution of her own was greatly to increase the Societies' overseas contacts, and the successful interchange of dance teams from Britain and Europe before the Second World War was largely due to her enthusiasm and organizational abilities. After the war, she almost single-handedly formed the International Folk Music Council in 1947. She also undertook her own collecting projects—dances in northern England and songs in Newfoundland in 1929 and 1930. After the war, as the folk-song and dance revival underwent rapid change and a series of reassessments, some felt that Karpeles perhaps stuck too rigidly to her role as guardian of Sharp's work and vision. Nevertheless, her first-hand knowledge of the tradition, and her long experience of the revival movement gave her opinions weight and ensured that she remained an important presence throughout her life. She was awarded an OBE in 1961.

Her own books include *Cecil Sharp: His Life and Work* (1967), *Folk Songs from Newfoundland* (1971), *An Introduction to English Folk Song* (1973); and the major ones edited from Sharp's MSS are: *English Folk Songs from the Southern Appalachians* (2 vols., 1932), and *Cecil Sharp's Collection of English Folk Songs* (2 vols., 1974).

Obituaries and tributes: *ED&S* 28:2 (1966), 44–5; 39:1 (1977), 30; *FMJ* 3:3 (1977) 292–4; *Yearbook of the International Folk Music Council* 8 (1977), 9–11; *The Times* (2 Oct. 1976).

Kennedy, Douglas Neil (1893–1988). By profession a biologist, but his life's work turned out to be the *revival and encouragement of folk *dance through the auspices of the *English Folk Dance Society (EFDS) and its successor *English Folk Dance and Song Society (EFDSS). Kennedy was introduced to dancing by his sister in 1911, just at the moment when Cecil *Sharp was planning to found the EFDS, and was immediately brought under the spell of Sharp's enthusiasm and sense of mission. He became a regular in Sharp's demonstration team which he used to illustrate his lectures and spread the gospel, and as one of the few of Sharp's young men to survive the First World War (he was awarded an MBE for his service), Kennedy (and his wife Helen, sister of Maud *Karpeles) became leading lights in the burgeoning revival of interest in both country and morris dancing. On Sharp's death in 1924, Kennedy became Organizing Director of the EFDS and remained Director of the EFDSS until 1961. In that time he was the major organizing force in the dance revival and guided the Societies through many crises brought about by changing circumstances and attitudes, in particular over 'standards' of performance and the scrapping of Society examinations, broadening the repertoire of social dance from an over-reliance on the courtly Playford dances to more vigorous traditional dances being collected in English villages and later to include American square dancing, and the need for such a society to adapt, or die. He taught, demonstrated, edited, lectured, organized festivals, led delegations abroad, and remained the official public face of folk dance for decades. Kennedy was awarded an OBE in 1952. When he died, in 1988, the last direct link with Sharp was severed, and it is probably true to say that, after Sharp, Douglas Kennedy was the most influential person in the 20th-century folk dance revival movement.

Kennedy also served as President of the Folklore Society 1964-7, and his three Presidential Addresses are concerned with the concept of 'Human Ecology' and show his continued interest, as a biologist, in the physical world of dance and song, and on the expression of 'feeling' in traditional cultural activities (*Folklore* 76 (1965), 81-9; 77 (1966), 81-90; 78 (1966) 81-9. His only major book was *England's Dances: Folk Dancing To-Day and Yesterday* (1949), revised as *English Folk Dancing Today and Yesterday* (1964).

Roy Judge and Derek Schofield, 'A Tribute to Douglas Kennedy', *FMJ* 5:4 (1988), 520-36; Obituary *ED&S* 50:1 (1988), 2-4; Douglas Kennedy, 'Folk Dance Revival', *FMJ* (1971), 80-90.

keys. According to a character in Thomas *Hardy's novel *Far From the Madding Crowd* (1874, chapter 33), breaking a key was a bad sign: 'I went to unlock the door and dropped the key, and it fell upon the stone floor and broke into two pieces. Breaking a key is a dreadful bodement.' Keys were also used for divination, in conjunction with a *Bible, and are still commonly recommended to stop a *nosebleed (put the key down the sufferer's back). A report from Norfolk, in the 1890s, described how seamen's wives and girlfriends would gather on the quay, watching for the arrival or departure of a ship, each carrying in her hand a key—presumably their house door-key—turning it in the direction of a departing or expected ship (*Folk-Lore* 4 (1893), 391-2).

Kidson, Frank (1855-1926). Born and living for most of his life in Leeds, he was proud of his home town and Yorkshire roots, and made a modest living as a journalist and author. Along with Lucy *Broadwood and Sabine *Baring-Gould he formed part of an important generation of pre-*Folk Song Society *song enthusiasts whose early collecting activities were undertaken more or less in isolation but whose individual efforts, and first publications, became both standard works and catalysts for the movement which included the

formation of the Society in 1898, and the widespread increase in interest in the subject in the early 20th century. Kidson's first book was *Old English Country Dances* (1890) which made available dance-tunes of previous eras, but his second work, *Traditional Tunes* (1891), had much more effect, despite being published in a limited edition. On the formation of the Society, Kidson was immediately elected to its Executive Committee, and he remained supportive of the Society's work all his life. Kidson became the acknowledged successor to William *Chappell as the leading musical antiquary of his generation, and he built up both a remarkable collection of early printed and manuscript material, and also an unrivalled knowledge of the history of popular song and music. His enthusiasm for folk-song, experience of the oral tradition, and his interest in and knowledge of *broadside and *chapbook material were elements which Chappell lacked. Many tributes from other folk-song collectors, writers, and editors, remark how this tremendous knowledge was always readily available to others, and Kidson served the *Journal of the Folk-Song Society* for many years as advisor, selector, and annotator.

Among Kidson's other publications were his seminal reference work, *British Music Publishers, Printers and Engravers: Provincial, Scottish and Irish, from Queen Elizabeth's Reign to George the Fourth's* (1900), *The Beggars Opera*, and over 400 entries for the *Grove Dictionary of Music and Musicians*. His only other book of folk songs was *A Garland of English Folk-Songs* (1926), but after his death, his niece, Ethel Kidson, edited and published some of the songs from his collection, as *Folk Songs of the North Countrie* (1927) and *English Peasant Songs* (1929).

John Graham and R. Vaughan Williams, *JEFDS* 2s:1 (1927), 48-51; 'Frank Kidson 1855-1927 by Some of His Friends', *JEFDSS* 5:3 (1948), 127-35; Roy Palmer, *FMJ* 5:2 (1986), 150-75; Ray Cowell, *FMJ* 5:4 (1988), 482-8.

kingfisher. A piece of erroneous 'natural history' once common was that if a dried kingfisher is hung up indoors, it swings round till the beak points towards the quarter from which the wind is blowing. 'The belief still survives among the credulous,' remarked one observer (*N&Q* 7s:12 (1891), 218), and Edward Lovett saw one in use in Arundel (Sussex) in the 1920s which supposedly turned one way in fine weather, and the other way during rain (Lovett, 1928: 26).

King of the Bean, see *TWELFTH NIGHT.

king's evil. An old term for scrofula. Kings of England and France claimed to heal it by their touch—a gift conferred by God through the oil used at their coronation. The first English ruler to 'touch for the evil' was Edward the Confessor; several Plantagenets did so, and especially the Tudors and Stuarts, including the Queens Regnant—Mary, Elizabeth, and Anne. In a religious ceremony devised by Henry VII, the sovereign would stroke the sufferer's neck, first with the hand and then with a gold coin; this coin was to be worn as a pendant till the cure was complete. To prevent abuse, those asking to be healed had to bring certificates from their parishes that they really were sick and had not been previously touched by the monarch.

The Stuarts regarded the power as intrinsic to their sacred kingship; Charles II is known to have touched 90,798 sufferers. The Hanoverians refused to do any touching, but the ritual remained in the Book of Common Prayer till 1744; the exiled Stuarts continued to do so on the Continent. Until late in the 18th century scrofulaics visited the bloodstained shirt worn by Charles I on the scaffold and preserved at Ashburnham (Sussex), in hope of a cure.

Alternative popular cures were the touch of a *seventh son or a *blacksmith, or a *toad's leg in a silk bag round one's neck. Reginald Scot said one might also touch the place with the hand of someone that died an untimely death, or get a naked virgin to lay her hand on it, fasting, and spit on it three times ((1584): book 12, chapter 14).

Thomas, 1971: 192–8; Raymond Crawfurd, *The King's Evil* (1911); Marcel Bloch, *Les Rois Thaumaturges* (1925), reprinted 1961.

knives. The most commonly known and practised belief about knives is that giving any sharp instrument as a present will 'cut the friendship' unless a small coin is given in return. Opie and Tatem record examples of the fear that the knife severs love from 1507 onwards, although the earliest reference to mention the payment to avoid it appears in Grose's *Provincial Glossary* (1787) (but see also *scissors). Correspondence in *N&Q* in 1912 (11s:5 (1912), 91, 157) shows that even sharp objects such as brooch pins could be susceptible to this belief, and that lasses had been known to give an unwanted beau a knife, and refuse to accept anything in return, to

get rid of him. Common at least up to the 19th century was the belief that when a knife has caused a wound, the knife is treated with the same ointment as the wound, to ensure effective healing (*N&Q* 9s:10 (1902), 509). This cure was apparently taken seriously by many in the 17th century, with Sir Kenelm Digby advertising his special 'weapon salve' which included as an ingredient moss from the skull of an unburied man (Picard, 1997: 78, 288), but declared magical and thus unlawful by William Foster in 1631 (Hazlitt, 1905: 621). Alternatively, the weapon should simply be kept clean and brightly polished, as any speck of rust would betoken death for the wounded person (*Folk-Lore Record* 1 (1878), 43–4). Others advise against stirring anything with a knife: stir with a knife, stir up strife. A knife and fork or two knives laid across each other on the plate is unlucky or will cause a quarrel in the house (see also *spoon), which was still reported in our *Superstitions Survey 1998/9. Some try to avoid allowing a knife to spin while on the table, while others deliberately do so in *love divination.

knockers. Cornish tin-miners believed there were helpful spirits in the mines, who could be heard hammering at places where there was a good lode of ore; they might also knock as a warning of danger, for instance before a rock-fall. There were several names for them, the two most usual being 'knockers' and 'buccas' (the latter is a common Celtic term for various *fairies and *goblins). Certain *taboos had to be obeyed so as not to annoy them: there must be no *whistling and swearing, nor should anything be marked with a *cross. Workers eating underground should leave a few crumbs for them, for luck. An old man told Bottrell that he had once seen three, 'no bigger than a good sixpenny doll, yet in their faces, dress and movements, they had the look of hearty old tinners'. One was sitting at a little anvil, 'no more than an inch square', sharpening tools for the others.

Knockers were sometimes thought of as fairies, but more often as ghosts of *Jews who could never rest because they were guilty of Christ's death. It was said Jews had worked in the tin-mines, either as slaves in Roman times, or as serfs of an Earl of Cornwall; neither account seems to have any factual basis. Among Shropshire lead miners, similar beliefs were held; there, the helpful spirits were simply called 'the Old Men', and sometimes identified with Wild *Edric's followers (Briggs, 1976: 254–6).

knots. Have long figured in *magic. It was widely held that by tying *three (or *nine) knots on a lace or thread, witches could render a man impotent; according to the astrologer Simon Forman early in the 17th century, this was done during the wedding ceremony itself, with the words 'Whom God hath joined together let the Devil separate; sara till these knots be undone'. Similarly, as told in the *ballad 'Willie's Lady', a witch might prevent a woman in labour from giving birth by secretly knotting her hair ribbons (Opie and Tatem, 1989: 220–1; F. J. Child, The English and Scottish Popular Ballads, no. 6). It was believed witches would 'sell the wind' to sailors in a cord with three knots; untying the first would bring a fine breeze, the second a high wind, the third a destructive storm; this is usually told of witches abroad—in Scandinavia, Scotland, the Isle of Man, or Ireland—rather than in home ports (Opie and Tatem, 1989: 446–7).

Knotting one's garter was a relatively simple form of *divination, which unlike most could be practised on any night of the year, to reveal one's destined partner in a dream. *Aubrey's recipe is to tie one's left garter to one's right stocking and recite the following verses, making a further knot at each comma: 'This knot I knit, To know the thing, I know not yet, That I may see, The man (woman) that shall my husband (wife) be, How he goes, And what he wears, And what he does, all days, and years' (Aubrey, 1696: 131–2). Knotted threads were also used as cures for whooping cough, sprains, *nosebleed, and *warts; in the first three cases they were worn by the patient, but for the last they were touched to each wart and then thrown away to decay (Opie and Tatem, 1989: 221–4).

Knutsford Royal May Day Festival. The annual *May celebrations in Knutsford, Cheshire, on the first Saturday in May comprise a spectacular procession led by the Town Crier and including bands, the May Queen and her attendants, *morris dancers, *Jack-in-the-Green, entertainers, and hundreds of local people in costume. They parade from the old Town Hall out to Knutsford Heath, where the Queen is crowned and the rest of the day is spent with dancing and displays. The custom began in 1864, although it is said that this was a revival rather than an inauguration. A further aspect to the May Day celebrations is the decoration of pavements (especially outside the May Queen's house) with coloured sand (see *sanding).

Revd W. Dallow, 'May Queens', Strand Magazine (May 1892), 484–8; Shuel, 1985: 34–9; Roy Kerridge, Bizarre Britain (1985), 60–6.

ladder. The idea that it is unlucky to walk under a ladder is one of the most widely known and practised *superstitions of modern times, being by far the most often mentioned in replies to our 1998/9 *Superstitions Survey. In most cases now it is simply said to be 'unlucky', but in previous times to walk under a ladder might result in you never marrying, or dying on the gallows. The first known reference to this belief is little more than 200 years old, in Grose's *Provincial Glossary* (1787: 63). For those unfortunate enough to have walked under a ladder, a number of traditional remedies are prescribed—spit through the ladder, spit over your left shoulder, or keep your fingers crossed till you see a dog, do not speak till you see a four-legged animal, make the sign of the cross, and so on. There have also been a number of attempts to explain the belief: the Devil lurked under the ladder at the Crucifixion, the ladder/wall/floor make a triangle which is symbolical of the Trinity, and the ladder stands for the gallows. Needless to say, none of these has a shred of evidence to support them. Unlike many superstitions, however, this one does have a pragmatic element, and many argue that their avoidance is ruled merely by considerations of safety and common sense.

Opie and Tatem, 1989: 225–6; *N&Q* 155 (1928), 172, 209–10, 247; 156 (1929), 177; Harland and Wilkinson, 1882: 229.

ladybird. This bright little insect (also called lady-cow or Bishop Barnaby) is said to bring luck if it alights on someone, and should never be harmed. Children encourage it to fly away with some variant of the rhyme:

Ladybird, ladybird, fly away home,
Your house is on fire, and your children all gone,

or:

Bishy-bishy-barnabee,
Tell me when your wedding be:

If it be tomorrow day,
Take your wings and fly away.

This can also be a divination, as in 19th-century Shropshire:

Lady-cow, lady-cow, fly away, flee!
Tell me which way my wedding's to be,
Uphill, or downhill, or towards the brown Clee!

(Burne, 1883: 237)

A ladybird affected the whole course of modern English folklore studies by settling on Peter *Opie's finger one day in 1944, causing him to quote this rhyme and rouse his wife Iona's curiosity; within a few days they had started the exploration of nursery-lore and child-lore which became their life's work.

Opie and Opie, 1951: 263–4; Opie and Tatem, 1989: 326.

Lady Godiva, see *Godiva.

Lambton Worm, the. Lambton Castle (Co. Durham) is the setting for a lively tale of dragon-slaying which exists in two main forms: in a jocular folk-song probably dating from the 19th century, and in a pamphlet of about 1875 which gives a more detailed but heavily moralized account. How much older the legend itself may be is impossible to tell. Both versions agree that at some vaguely medieval period the Lord of Lambton's young heir was fishing in the river Weir on a Sunday, and caught a strange, ugly, worm-like fish which in disgust he tossed into a nearby well, remarking, 'I think I've catched the Devil'. Soon after this, he went abroad to the Crusades. Meanwhile, the worm grew to a full-sized *dragon; it was impossible to kill it, for if cut to pieces it merely reunited its body.

At length, Young Lambton returned home. On the advice of a local witch, he studded his armour with spear-blades and stood on a rock in the middle of the river; thus, when the dragon coiled itself round him, it impaled itself on the blades, and when he cut it in two the strong current swept the pieces away, preventing them from rejoining.

The witch had demanded as her reward the life of whoever first came from the Castle to greet Young Lambton. He had planned to trick her by arranging that his favourite hound would be loosed first, but it was his father who appeared. Rather than murder his own father, he defied the witch; consequently, she cursed the family, declaring that for nine generations no Lord Lambton would ever die in his bed.

In the folk-song, the story is simpler; there is no studded armour, no witch, and no curse—merely cheerful praise:

> Of bold Sir John and what he done
> Wi' the awful Lambton Worm.

Anon, *The Wonderful Legend of the Lambton Worm* (c.1875); Simpson, 1980: 124–9.

Lancashire Dialect Society. Founded in January 1951 by George Brook, Professor of English Language at Manchester University, the Lancashire Dialect Society was one of several societies dedicated to the study and use of local dialect (see also *Yorkshire Dialect Society). It held meetings, lectures, and other events, and published an annual *Journal*, which included dialect poems and prose in addition to articles on local terminology and grammar. The Society was dissolved in 1992, and the last issue of the *Journal* was no. 41, August 1992 (see the 'Valediction' in that issue, pp. 2–5).

Land lease and tenure auctions. There are a number of surviving customs pertaining to the letting of land, each designed to maximize fairness within the constraints of local conditions, but each has accrued its own methods and traditions which seem quaint and odd to modern eyes. The most common is by *candle auction, but the following are examples of other methods. At Congresbury (Somerset), after four acres were let 'by inch of candle' on the Saturday before Old Midsummer Day, two pieces of common land, called East and West Dolemoors, were divided into acres and each one was marked with a spade in a distinctive way. A number of apples were marked in a similar way, placed in a bag, and pulled out to decide which commoner received which acre for the coming year (Collinson, *History of the County of Somerset* (1791); Keith Gardner, 'Apples in the Landscape: The Puxton Dol-

moors', *Bristol & Avon Archaeology* 4 (1985), 13–20).

At Wishford (Wiltshire) on Rogation Monday, the 'foreshare' or summer grazing on two water meadows is auctioned in the churchyard. At five minutes to sunset, the Parish Clerk starts pacing up and down between church porch and gate, and the people start bidding. As soon as the sun dips beneath the horizon he strikes the church key against the gate and the bidding stops (Kightly, 1986: 66). At Bourne, Surrey, 'White Bread Meadow' used to be let by special auction. At each bid, a boy was sent to run to a particular point and back, and any bid unchallenged when the last boy returned was accepted (*Surrey Magazine* 4 (1902), 150, reprinting from the *Daily Mail*). At Yarnton, Oxfordshire, on the first Monday following St Peter's Day, a complicated process is undergone to determine the rights to the tenancy to Yarnton West Mead. Several local farmers have common ownership of this meadow, and mowing and grazing rights are auctioned in lots. As each 'lot' is actually split up over different sections of the meadow, a further process of drawing lots (using special balls of cherry wood) has to take place, under the auspices of the Meadsman, who organizes the whole affair (Sykes, 1977: 104–7).

Porter, 1969: 348–59.

Lang, Andrew (1844–1912). Born in Scotland, and passionately interested in Scottish topics all his life, Lang also had an immense impact on the development of general British folklore studies in the late 19th century. His publications range very widely, but his interest in folklore was inspired by *Tylor's anthropological writings—particularly *Primitive Culture* (1871). Lang sprang into the public limelight with what proved to be the first of many public controversies in which he engaged, when an article in the *Fortnightly Review* (May 1873) took on Max Müller and the other leading figures of the 'philological school' of solar mythologists, who believed that the study of language was the primary key to the understanding of myths. Lang propounded instead a comparative anthropological approach which brought in evidence from 'savage' cultures on a worldwide basis rather than the relatively narrow Indo-European base of Müller. Lang's timing was excellent, as the philologists' arguments were already somewhat outmoded, and he not only won the day but gave a popular face to the new folklore, and himself, at a stroke. He continued to develop his comparative method, and he joined the *Folklore Society on its formation in 1878, serving as its President in 1889–91. Lang described his comparative method in several of his books, such as:

Our method, then, is to compare the seemingly meaningless customs or manners of civilised races with the similar customs and manners which exist among the uncivilised and still retain their meaning. It is not necessary for comparison of this sort that the uncivilised and the civilised race should be of the same stock, nor need we prove that they were ever in contact with each other. Similar conditions of mind produce similar practices, apart from identity of race or borrowing of ideas and manners. (*Custom and Magic*, new edn., 1904: 21–2)

This *survivals theory is predicated on the belief that all human cultures or civilizations pass through the same evolutionary stages, but that at any given time some are more advanced than others. Unfortunately, this willingness—even eagerness on Lang's part—to pile example upon example from different periods and different places was precisely the element of 'folklore method' which got the discipline such a bad name in academic circles from the early 20th century onwards.

One of Lang's most popular projects—for which he is still remembered—was a series of twelve annual volumes of fairytale books, starting with the *Blue Fairy Book* (1889) and the *Red Fairy Book* (1890). For these, Lang and his wife (and other helpers) drew on a wide range of sources, including the *Arabian Nights* and various mythologies, and retold them in a style suitable for Victorian children. They are thus of little use to the scholar, but they were tremendously popular and introduced several generations to myths and folktales. 'The readers who looked to Andrew Lang for entertainment far outnumbered those who sought instruction from him' (obituary, 359).

Apart from the tendency to speak his mind, another reason for Lang's often strained relationships with his fellow folklorists was that he clearly believed in some psychic phenomena such as ghosts and even fairies, and was involved also in the Society for Psychical Research, which he joined in 1904 and later served as their President. He called for a 'scientific approach to the supernatural', and coined the term 'psycho-folklorist', but his evident belief and 'open-mindedness' on such topics was hardly calculated to appeal to those who were working so hard to convince the

world of folklore's serious scientific credentials and to distance themselves from the immensely popular spiritualism and occultism. There were many times when the poet and romantic in Lang overcame the scholar.

Other books by Lang include *Cock Lane and Common-Sense* (1894); *The Book of Dreams and Ghosts* (1897); *The Making of Religion* (1898); *Magic and Religion* (1901). See also the long-running column 'At the Sign of the Ship' in *Longman's Magazine* (1885–1905).

Obituaries in *Folk-Lore* 23 (1912), 358–75; Roger Lancelyn Green, *Andrew Lang* (1946); Dorson, 1968: 206–20.

lantern man. An East Anglian name for a fierce *Will-o'-the-Wisp. One must never *whistle at night, or he will come; the only protection then is to lie flat with one's face buried in the mud, so that he passes over one's body.

Latham, Charlotte. The first issue of *Folk-Lore Record* (1878) contains an article entitled 'Some West Sussex Superstitions Lingering in 1868' (1–67). Unfortunately, nothing is known about the author, Mrs Charlotte Latham, except that her husband had been rector of the village of Fittleworth, but her paper is a model of its kind, and her methods exemplary; she used to write down 'the scraps of homely conversation' in which she got her information, so that others could 'form a truer judgement than they could otherwise arrive at of the degree of faith existing in the original narrator'. She writes with clarity and immediacy, giving short but vivid sketches of the circumstances of her fieldwork, for example how she once allowed a Sunday School class to 'quite overwhelm' her with 'a torrent of narrative' about their relatives' encounters with *ghosts and the Devil (19); she also draws on her own childhood memories; she even dares (after due apology to readers) to include two traditional cures for bed-wetting.

laying ghosts. Many traditions about hauntings imply that there is nothing the living can do to lay the *ghost to rest. Others, however, describe ghosts which depart once whatever is troubling them has been dealt with; it may be that their bones need burial, or that some unfulfilled duty has to be carried out on their behalf, or some message delivered.. There is a third group of traditions from Oxfordshire, south-west England and English counties bordering on Wales, where ghost-laying is a conflict of wills between an exorcist and a stubborn, malevolent spectre.

These stories are set in the 18th or early 19th century; the ghosts are of local evil-doers (often gentry) and have been disturbing the whole community, until a parson, or more often a group of seven or twelve parsons, succeeds in laying them by fierce and unceasing prayer. The ghost-layers usually hold lighted *candles, and occasionally bring a newly *baptized baby with them. In many of the stories, the ghost, having first appeared as a threatening monster, is 'read down' into smaller and smaller forms; eventually it is imprisoned in a bottle, box, snuff-box, or boot, which is then thrown into a pool or river, or buried, preferably under a heavy stone (Burne, 1883: 107–11, 122–8; Leather, 1912: 29–35; Briggs, 1974: 143–5; Simpson, 1976: 90–6). Alternatively, it may be set endless tasks, for example making ropes of sand, or banished to the Red Sea for a set term of years.

Brown, 1979.

Lazy Lawrence. This imaginary personage is a symbol of laziness in various proverbial sayings. He is also the hero of a humorous *chapbook entitled *The History of Lawrence Lazy*, possibly first printed in 1670. He has a magic ring which can send everyone around him to sleep; this enables him to play various tricks on people, for which he is eventually put on trial. He is acquitted, after earnest pleading from apprentices, who say that if it were not for him they would be worked to death. The story was very popular in the 18th century, and related colloquial sayings ('to have a touch of the Lawrence', 'as lazy as Lawrence', 'as lazy as Lawrence's dog', 'Lazy Lawrence, let me go', etc.) were still in use in the 19th and early 20th centuries.

J. B. Smith, *Folklore* 107 (1996), 101–5.

lead. This has many sinister associations. Heavy and dull in colour, it was linked with Saturn, most ill-omened of the planets; until recent times, it often lined the coffins of the rich, to keep them watertight. Being soft enough to write on, it was widely used by the Romans for inscribing *curses, which would then be placed in a temple or cemetery (Merrifield, 1987: 137–42).

Lead continued to be seen as sinister or 'impure' in the learned systems of alchemy, astrology, and 'high' magic. Lead tablets bearing curses and astrological symbols were still being made in the 16th and 17th centuries; one was found buried in Lincoln's Inn, two more in a barrow on the Yorkshire moors, and one in a cupboard at Wilton Place near Dymock (Gloucestershire). They express the wish that the victim should be ruined and/or forced to leave the district (Hole, 1973: 92–3).

leap year. The dominant belief about leap year is that it is the only time that a woman may propose marriage to a man, rather than what was considered to be the natural order of things: the other way round. This was often called 'The Ladies' Privilege'. At the time of writing, it is probably true to say that younger English people would not be aware of the belief if the media did not run features on the subject every fourth February. In previous times, when relationships between the sexes were more rigid and formal, there were a number of subsidiary beliefs surrounding the Ladies' Privilege. Some said that it was only on Leap Year day, that is 29 February, that it was valid, while others believed that a man proposed to in this way could not refuse, except on substantial payment—a silk gown, or £100, and so on. Indeed, it was widely reported (erroneously) that there had been a Scottish Act of Parliament in the 13th century making this legally binding (see *N&Q* 7s:10 (1890), 188), or that it had passed into English Common Law (*Courtship, Love and Matrimony* (1606), quoted in *N&Q* 4s:8 (1871), 505). One story about the origin of the Ladies' Privilege is set in Ireland: St Bridget met St Patrick one day and complained that women did not have the right to propose. He offered the opportunity once in every seven years, but she bargained him down to one in four (quoted in *Word-Lore* 3 (1928), 51–2).

Leather, Ella Mary (1876–1928). Born in Herefordshire as Ella Mary Smith, Mrs Leather was a prime example of what have been termed the 'County Collectors', who were active in late Victorian and Edwardian times conducting fieldwork in their native area which they knew well, and whose collections have added greatly to our store of folklore knowledge, but who did not otherwise play a large part in the greater world of folklore studies. Mrs Leather's first foray in folklore was a chapter published in *Memorials of Old Herefordshire* (1904), which stimulated her to more collecting work resulting in one of our best books based on personal fieldwork, *The Folk-Lore of Herefordshire* (1912). Leather was an indefatigable worker and her informants included local Gypsies, hop-pickers, and workhouse residents. She became particularly well-known for the carols she discovered, a number of which were published in their raw state in *Folk-Lore of Herefordshire* and the *JFSS*, and tidied up and arranged in *Twelve Traditional Carols from Herefordshire*, while *Vaughan Williams used several in his compositions and carol books. Leather continued to contribute notes to *Folk-Lore* on a wide variety of items collected in Herefordshire and neighbouring counties. After the First World War, in which she lost her eldest son, her folklore output almost ceased, although she remained active in her local community in various spheres.

Mrs F. H. Leather, 'Folk-Lore of the Shire', in Compton Reade (ed.), *Memorials of Old Herefordshire* (1904), 148–66; Ella M. Leather, *The Folk-Lore of Herefordshire* (1912); Ella M. Leather, 'Carols from Herefordshire', *JFSS* 4:14 (1910), 3–51; *Twelve Traditional Carols from Herefordshire*, collected and arranged by E. M. Leather and R. Vaughan Williams (1920); Notes in *Folk-Lore* 23 (1912) to 27 (1916) inclusive, and 37 (1926).

Lavender Jones, *A Nest of Singing Birds: The Life and Work of Ella Mary Leather* (1976); Lavender M. Jones, *ED&S* 27:1 (Dec. 1964), 4–6; 27:2 (Feb. 1965), 38–40; Dorson, 1968: 317–27.

leaves. A number of beliefs centre on plant leaves. The simplest, which is still practised, is that it is lucky to catch a falling leaf before it reaches the ground. The first known mention is from Sussex—'If you catch a falling leaf, you will have twelve months of continued happiness' (*Folk-Lore Record* 1 (1878), 9), although others say a happy day or month for each leaf caught. More serious forms of divination involve particular types of leaf. For example, leaves of *holly are stipulated for a form of divination reported from Northumberland: She-holly leaves must be picked, in absolute silence, late on a Friday and collected in a three-cornered handkerchief. Nine leaves should be tied into the handkerchief, with nine knots, and placed under the pillow, and any dreams will come true (Henderson, 1866: 79). A somewhat different method is recommended by Flora Thompson (*Over to Candleford* (1941), chapter 23) using an *ash leaf with nine leaflets. Another place to put a leaf was in the shoe, after scratching the proposed lover's name or initials on it, and this has much older

roots. Opie and Tatem quote a description from 1507.

Opie and Tatem, 1989: 230.

left. Contempt for the left hand as compared with the *right is found in most cultures, past and present, and may have arisen simply because most people let its strength and skill remain relatively undeveloped; the English word comes from a root whose primary meaning is 'weak, worthless'. To this basic concept further meanings were added; already in the classical world the left was unlucky, ominous, and less honourable than the right, while Christianity associated it with moral evil through its description of a Last Judgement where the damned ('goats') are sent to the left, and the saved ('sheep') to the right (Matthew 25: 33).

English traditions reflect all these ideas. It is presumably because girls are weaker than boys and (formerly) less valued in a family that pseudo-medical lore about *conception and *pregnancy links female foetuses to the left side of the mother's body. Though it is not said here that the left hand is 'unclean' (as it is in many non-European cultures), nevertheless it is never used in situations involving honour and respect, for example shaking hands, saluting, taking an oath, etc.

The connection with bad luck is found, for instance, in the belief that a baby who grips with the left hand before the right will grow up unlucky; that if the first *cuckoo calls on one's left this is ominous; that *first footing is only effective if done with the right foot; and many others. The association of left-handed gestures with black magic is found in some *witchcraft trials, and more consistently among learned occultists of the 19th and 20th centuries, who commonly speak of 'the left-hand path' to mean the use of magic for evil purposes; it is now well known through popular writers and film-makers.

There is nevertheless one very striking exception to this trend: it is upon the left hand that, in Britain, engagement and wedding rings must be worn.

leftward movement. Since *rightward movement is regarded in all European traditions as corresponding to that of the sun, and hence beneficial and joyous, circling to the left is necessarily 'backwards', reversing the norm. Folklore links leftward *circling with bad luck, *cursing, *witchcraft, and raising the *Devil. Until the 19th century, this was purely a Scottish and Irish belief, though one which intrigued English observers, as shown by quotations in the *OED* (under 'sunways' and 'withershins') and in Opie and Tatem (1989: 383–6). The few English references in Victorian times concerned the bad luck involved if a funeral or bridal procession moved anticlockwise. Nowadays, popular writers have built up a conventional picture of black magic rituals, in which turning withershins causes evil, and the belief has become more widespread.

legends. In folklore theory, a 'legend' is a short traditional oral narrative about a person, place, or object that really exists, existed, or is believed to have existed; even when it recounts a supernatural or highly unusual event, this is claimed to have occurred in real life. Unlike a *fairytale or joke, it is presented (and generally accepted) as true; it offers information, moral judgements, or warnings which reflect the preoccupations of the hearers. In practice, the status of legends is more complex, both as regards orality and perceived truthfulness. Many which were once purely oral have repeatedly appeared in books, local newspapers, and TV, from where they feed back into oral tellings; some are commercially exploited (e.g. by *tourist guides) but not believed; in some cases, the truth of the tradition is a matter for heated dispute (e.g. *Robin Hood, Lady *Godiva), while in others what was once regarded as true and important is now mere entertainment.

Legends are extremely common in English folklore, and indeed throughout Europe. Various classifications have been proposed, some based on content, some on function, and some on range of dissemination. Legends about past heroes were the first type to be identified. Many, such as those about King Alfred burning the cakes and King Canute defying the tide, are plausible, and very widely known; others have supernatural content, but are told of real people, such as *St Dunstan or *Drake; in others, the historical identity of the hero has vanished under legendary motifs, and rediscovering it becomes a contentious issue, as with attempts to identify the 'real' Arthur or Robin Hood. The categories of 'historical' and 'local' legend are not mutually exclusive, since there are tales about national figures such as *Cromwell which are only locally known, while others relate to people only important in local history.

*Local legends are found throughout England, and are extremely varied, the one common factor being their association with landmarks or buildings in the locality; yet, far from being unique to one place, they generally fit story-patterns known elsewhere in England or abroad, thus being *migratory as well as local. As regards claims to credibility, they range from amusing fantasies, through stories such as those about *treasures and *tunnels which may (or may not) contain the proverbial 'grain of truth', to religious and supernatural tales embodying firm beliefs and moral principles. Where the belief is actively held, personal experience stories (*memorates) often develop alongside the supernatural legend, and reinforce it; in present-day England this often occurs as regards haunted sites.

Another major category is the *contemporary legend; this type is notorious for its rapid international diffusion, yet each individual telling presents itself as a local story; some tellers, obviously, must be hoaxing their hearers, while others are saying what they honestly believe.

Briggs 1970–1 B, and Westwood 1985 contain numerous examples.

Lent. In the Christian calendar, this is a 40-day period of penitence and self-discipline beginning on *Ash Wednesday and ending with the service on Holy Saturday which marks the start of *Easter. Sundays falling within this period are not counted as part of Lent but as days of normality, or even celebration, notably *Mothering Sunday. In medieval times, the rules of fasting were severe: on weekdays, meat, milk products, and eggs were all forbidden, and only one meal a day could be eaten; marriages could not be celebrated, and couples were expected to refrain from intercourse; dancing and entertainment were forbidden too.

After the Reformation observing Lent as a matter of personal piety persisted, in milder forms, in the High Church sections of Anglicanism. The Victorian growth of Anglo-Catholicism, and the influx of Irish immigrants, made the concept very familiar; most people now are aware that 'giving something up for Lent' is appropriate, even if they do not do it themselves.

See also *SHROVE TUESDAY, *JACK O' LENT.

Lent crocking, see *SHROVETIDE.

lettuce. English lore seems a little confused about the lettuce. On the one hand we are assured that lettuce brings about sterility in men (Dodoens, *Herball* (1578), and Folkard, *Plant Lore* (1884), both quoted in Opie and Tatem), or that 'o'ermuch lettuce in the garden will stop a young wife's bearing' (*N&Q* 1s:7 (1853), 152). On the other hand, the Radfords and Hole assure us that lettuces 'were also said to promote child-bearing if eaten in salads by young women, or taken in the form of decoctions made from the juice or seeds'. They quote a letter from a woman published in the *Daily Mirror* (26 July 1951) saying she was advised by a specialist to eat lettuce to help remedy her childlessness, and that the remedy worked.

Opie and Tatem, 1989: 232; Radford, Radford, and Hole, 1961: 217.

Lewes (East Sussex) Bonfire Night. Lewes is the last place in England to celebrate *November the Fifth (Guy Fawkes or Bonfire Night) in the old spectacular mass public way, and although surrounding towns and villages hold smaller events, Lewes's Fifth is acknowledged as the climax of the season. There are five separate bonfire societies in the town, and each holds its own procession, bonfire, and firework displays, but they come together for a Grand United Procession, over a mile long, through Lewes High Street with bands, banners, effigies, tableaux, flaming torches, and over 2000 participants in fancy dress. There are also huge effigies of unpopular national figures which are filled with fireworks and exploded to much cheering and jubilation. Each of the societies also throws a blazing tar barrel into the river Ouse, and visits the town's war memorial. It remains a mystery why Lewes has retained so many of the features of past celebrations. Admittedly, seventeen Protestant martyrs died in Lewes in the reign of Queen Mary (1553–8), but other places could say the same. Although the 'no popery' theme, so strong in the past, is nowadays played down, some costumes still ridicule popes and priests.

Jim Etherington, *Lewes Bonfire Night* (1993); Jim Etherington, *Bonfire: The Lewes Bonfire Societies in Photographs* (1997); Shuel, 1985: 186–7.

Lichfield Court of Array, Sherriff's Ride, and Greenhill Bower. Lichfield, Stafford-shire, preserves several unique customs which are now linked. The Court of Array is a genuine survival of a previous serious and practical event: by the Assize of Arms, an Act passed in 1176 and restated in 1285 (Statute of Winchester) every freeman aged between 15 and 60 was required to keep arms and armour and be able to handle them properly in times of military need. The Court of Array was set up to enforce these regulations, and to inspect the said arms and armour on a regular basis, and although the Acts were repealed in the reign of James I, Lichfield still keeps its Court in operation, and part of the custom is to inspect some medieval suits of armour which the city possesses.

The Commissioners of Array, or 'dozeners' are appointed at the Court Leet, held every St George's Day. This Court's officers also include an ale tester, constables, pinlock keepers, and pinners and is nowadays conducted in good humour rather than in solemn dignity.

One other *civic survival in Lichfield which is treated with more respect is the Sherriff's Ride in early September. By a charter of Queen Mary (1552), confirmed by Charles II (1664) and apparently still in force, the Bailiffs and Brethren of the city were obliged to elect a Sherriff, one of whose duties was to perambulate the city boundaries once a year. And so he still does, on horseback, accompanied nowadays by anything up to 200 other riders.

Lichfield's other claim to folkloric fame comes in the shape of its Greenhill Bower, which also takes place on Spring Bank Holiday but was previously a *Whit Monday custom. The custom is nowadays a carnival with lorries carrying tableaux, decorated carts, and bands, but previously it was the day when the City Guilds used to meet at Greenhill, where a temporary bower had been erected, carrying emblems of their trades along with flower garlands. Celia Fiennes recorded in her diary in the late 18th century the ceremony of dressing up 'baby's with garlands of flowers' and carrying it through the streets before proceeding to the hill and the large bower made with 'greens' in which they have their feast. A contributor to Hone's *Every-Day Book* in 1826 describes the mechanics of the town carrying small working models symbolizing their trade, fixed on top of six-foot poles, again decorated with flowers and greenery, but even at that time the Greenhill was 'nearly surrounded by houses'.

Stone, 1906: 39–42; *Illustrated London News* (25 May 1850), 364; Crawford, 1938: 54–5; Hone, 1827: ii. 334; Wright and Lones, 1936: i. 166–7; Shuel, 1985: 111–12.

life-cycle customs. Customs which take place at key points in an individual's life are termed life-cycle customs, or rites of passage, and can thus be distinguished from *calendar customs which take place at set points in the year. Examples are *childbirth, coming of age, leaving school, qualification at work, marriage (see *weddings), retirement, and *death.

Lifting (or Heaving). An *Easter *calendar custom found all over the Midlands and the North, but not reported further south than Worcestershire. The custom involved men, on Easter Monday, claiming the privilege of physically lifting off the ground any females they might meet, and on Easter Tuesday the females lifting the men, and only by payment of a fine, or in some cases a kiss, could one escape. In some places a chair decorated with ribbons was carried about for the purpose. Published descriptions vary from the deferential and good-humoured to the rough-and-ready horseplay of labouring men and women, and the latter caused the custom to be viewed with disfavour by magistrates and other local dignitaries. The earliest known reference is in *Gentleman's Magazine* (1784, part I: 96) but the custom does not seem to have survived past the middle of the 19th century. Most writers assert that the lifting represents the resurrection of Jesus Christ, but apart from the time of year there seems to be no reason to believe this. Illustrations of the custom appear in Hone, 1827: i. 212 and *L&L* 3:2B (1980) 81; W. Crooke, 'The Lifting of the Bride', *Folk-Lore* 13 (1902), 226–51, describes this and other lifting, carrying, bumping customs.

lilac. This is one of the flowers reputed to 'bring death into the house' if cut and brought indoors. A Norfolk informant believed lilac 'was used for lining either coffins or graves' (Vickery, 1995: 220), though as its flowering season is short this cannot have been a frequent occurrence.

lions. It was thought in medieval times that the lion, as king of the beasts, was not only noble and virtuous himself but could recognize these qualities in others. It is presumably by extension of this idea that there arose

a belief expressed by a servant-girl in Tobias Smollett's novel *Humphry Clinker* (1771):

Last week I went with mistress to the Tower, to see the crowns and wild beastis; and there was a monstracious lion, with teeth half a quarter long; and a gentleman bid me not go near him, if I wasn't a maid; being as how he would roar, and tear, and play the dickens. (Smollett, Penguin edn., 140)

There was a 19th-century belief that lions in zoos and circuses only bred once in seven years, and that when this 'Lion Year' came round, if either a lioness or a cub died, many women would die in *childbirth. Correspondents in *N&Q* in 1890 and 1895 reported it from Yorkshire, Cheshire, Sussex, Surrey, Newcastle, and Derbyshire, and it was known in Somerset too; in some cases, deaths of piglets were similarly explained (*N&Q* 7s:9 (1890), 385–6; 7s: 10 (1890), 13; 8s:7 (1895), 366; Elworthy, 1895: 76; Opie and Tatem, 1989: 232). In Cheshire, the same belief applied to the she-bears of travelling showmen. It is now rare, but not extinct; it was mentioned in Sussex in 1940 (JS), and in Northamptonshire in 1985 (Opie and Tatem, 1989: 232).

Little Bo-Peep. The first verse of Little Bo-Peep is still a well-known *nursery rhyme, although the Opies print a text with five. The first known texts date only from the early years of the 19th century, but a version of the song 'Yankee Doodle', printed in 1777, has a close analogy commencing 'Our Jemima's lost her mare', and the term 'Bo-Peep' (usually referring to a nursery game) is considerably older. As for the nursery rhyme, however, nothing more can be said about its origins or early development, until further evidence is discovered.

Opie and Opie, 1997: 107–8.

Little Jack Horner. A popular *nursery rhyme, still in circulation after 200 years. The first known printing dates from 1725, but the rhyme was taken up by the *chapbook publishers and incorporated into a much longer rhyming tale entitled 'The History of Jack Horner' printed a number of times later in the 18th century. A 19th-century explanation of the story claims that it celebrates one Tom Horner who was steward to Richard Whiting, Abbot of Glastonbury, at the time of the Dissolution. Whiting entrusted Horner with a pie in which title deeds had been secreted to be delivered to Henry VIII. As in the rhyme,

Horner opened the pie and thus became a major landowner. The story has little to connect it to the rhyme beyond the surname Horner, and is unlikely to be worth pursuing.

Opie and Opie, 1997: 275–9.

Little John. In most versions of the *Robin Hood story, a leading part is allotted to his follower 'Little John', so called because he was a huge man; he is first mentioned in 1420. In the 17th century it was claimed that he had lived in Hathersage (Derbyshire), where his alleged grave, over four metres long, is still shown in the churchyard; a 30-inch thighbone is said to have been unearthed there in 1784. A longbow marked with the name 'Naylor' used to hang in the church, which some claimed had been his.

Lloyd, Albert Lancaster (1908–82). Orphaned in his teens, he emigrated to Australia and spent nine years working on farms and outback sheep stations. By the mid-1930s he was back in England, and after spending some months on a whaling factory ship, settled down to making a living as a journalist, scriptwriter, broadcaster, and, later, folklorist and folk-singer. He worked for the influential *Picture Post* from 1940 to 1950, and for BBC radio and television from 1938 till just before his death, specializing in drama-documentary programmes. Lloyd was a confirmed Marxist, and this is strongly in evidence in all his work, which did not endear him to the broadcasting establishment of the day, but he was well known and respected in left-wing intellectual circles.

Lloyd had encountered traditional songs in his travels, particularly in Australia, and even before the Second World War he had begun to research into the history and morphology of the genre. Each of his four major books in the field was extremely influential in setting the agenda for the post-war folk-song *revival in which he and others like Ewan *MacColl played a crucial founding role. *The Singing Englishman* (1944) was a much-needed introduction to the genre; *Come All Ye Bold Miners* (1952; revised edn. 1978) was the first to recognize the existence and importance of industrial songs; *The Penguin Book of English Folk Songs* (1959, with Ralph *Vaughan Williams) became the staple songbook for the new folk club movement; and *Folk Song in England* (1967) was

the first real attempt at an overall synthesis of traditional song since Cecil *Sharp's *English Folk Song: Some Conclusions* (1907), and far surpassed that work in its historical and social perspective. Coupled with Lloyd's numerous articles, lectures, programmes, song performances, recordings, and the sleeve notes which he wrote for Topic Records (for whom he was Artistic Director for many years), these books were a major inspiration for the new generation of song researchers and academics which emerged in the 1960s. He also undertook major fieldwork expeditions to Eastern Europe, where his political beliefs and generally acknowledged skill with languages made him ideally suited for the task, and he became an internationally known expert in this field.

In retrospect, Lloyd's work has many of the faults of the pioneer, and his work is now treated with caution by most serious researchers. His early editorial methods were often unscholarly, as the poet and singer in his nature often overshadowed the scholar, and his view of history proved essentially romantic. Most authorities comment on how his undoubted talents and the many roles he tried to play, were often incompatible—journalist, communist party activist, scholar-folklorist, singer/entertainer, teacher, and poet—but there is little doubt that the post-war revival could hardly have managed without him. Nevertheless, it could be argued that his most important and longest-lasting contribution to folklore was his work in the Balkans, and he was working on a study of Albanian instruments at the time of his death.

Ian Russell, *Singer, Song and Scholar* (1986) (includes bibliography); obituary by Dave Arthur, *FMJ* 4:4 (1983), 436–9; Michael Grosvenor Myer, *Folk Review* (Sept. 1974), 4–6.

local legends. The most common folk narratives in England (apart from jokes) are stories about remarkable events in the history of a particular locality, the supposed origins of its landmarks and place-names, curious features of its buildings, etc. Their contents range across the whole spectrum of traditional themes, from the realistic, through the amazing-but-not-impossible (e.g. the *Hangman's Stone), to supernatural beliefs now outmoded (the *Devil, *fairies), or still current (*ghosts, *curses). Some are so plausible that only experience can show whether they are, as the tellers assert, memories of a real event, or whether they follow a standard folktale pattern. In general, tellers take for granted that the story is unique to their own district, and factually reliable, unless its content is blatantly fantastic, in which case it is told 'for fun'. However, even where marvels are involved, some will claim there is 'a grain of truth in it'—for instance, that killing a *dragon is 'really' about sinking a Viking ship or killing a wicked nobleman (JS).

Many such stories have featured repeatedly in folklore collections and popular books; however, there are plenty more that are known only in a restricted area. Moreover, local legends do not have just one 'correct' form; there are always slight differences of detail from one teller to the next. Current oral versions are well worth seeking out.

Printed sources include not only all books explicitly dealing with regional folklore, but also references in guidebooks, local papers, local histories, etc. A generous selection is in Briggs, 1970–1: B; a smaller sample, with very informative commentary, in Westwood, 1985. For discussion of the genre, see Simpson, 1983, 1985, 1987, 1991.

London Bridge. 'London Bridge is falling down' or 'broken down' is one of the widest-known children's songs in the English-speaking world and has existed both as a *nursery rhyme and as a *singing game for a very long time. As a singing game, it exists in a wider range of forms than is usual in the genre—the most common is that two players make an arch while the others file through in single file; the arch is lowered at a certain point to 'catch' a player. As is usual for such rhymes, the earliest known text dates from the 18th century (*Tommy Thumb's Pretty Song Book c.*1744) although there are some indications that it may have existed in Britain in the 17th century. Nevertheless, there are many close continental parallels which are much older, with the game or rhyme being reported from France, Germany, Denmark, Italy, Hungary, Holland, and many more countries. Some English versions agree with the European ones that the only way to ensure the success of the bridge is to set a 'watchman' to look after it, and it has been argued that this refers to well-attested long-standing traditions about new bridges needing to have a human being immured in their foundations to counter evil influences. The wide geographical and temporal spread for the rhyme was sufficient to convince even the usually-sceptic Iona and Peter Opie that this is one of the few nursery rhymes which may have a genuine antique ritual basis.

Opie and Opie, 1997: 318–25; Opie, and Opie, 1985: 61–8; Gomme, 1894: i. 333–50.

London Lore. *London Lore* was a newsletter published by the London Folklore Group, edited by Monica and Roy Vickery. It ran for ten issues, from March 1978 to October 1983, and included numerous notes and short articles on customs and other lore of London, past and present.

Long Man of Wilmington, see *Wilmington.

Long Meg. A large *stone circle near Hunsonby (Cumberland/Cumbria) was variously known in the 17th century as 'Long Meg and her Daughters' or 'Great Meg and her Sisters'; Meg, twelve foot high, stands outside the ring formed by the rest—77 of them, according to one source of that period, 66 or 67 according to Victorian sightseers, 59 by a modern count. Tradition says that when counting the stones it is impossible to reach the same total twice, and that men who once tried to uproot them were scared off by a fierce storm. They are said to be women turned to stone for witchcraft, or because Meg's sisters 'solicited her to an unlawful love'. A treasure is buried under Meg, and she is said to bleed if a piece is chipped off her. The name is unlikely to refer to a particular individual, since 'Long Meg' was a proverbial nickname for any tall, thin woman (Westwood, 1985: 310–11).

Lore and Language. Launched in July 1969 as the journal of the *Survey of Language and Folklore at the University of Sheffield (renamed the *Centre for English Cultural Tradition and Language (CECTAL) in 1976), *Lore and Language* is still published, edited throughout its time by Professor J. D. A. Widdowson. As befits its genesis in the Department of English at Sheffield, the journal has always had a strong interest in linguistics, as seen in numerous articles on dialect studies and verbal genres such as proverbs, jokes, and riddles. Its volumes thus represent a particularly important contribution in these areas as well as more general folklore topics including custom, narrative, belief. The early volumes were heavily influenced by the Survey ideal, the urgently felt need to collect material which had been previously neglected, and the articles closely mirror the activities of the students and volunteers involved. This must be counted as a major strength, as its pages present a wealth of raw data which would otherwise have remained unavailable to later scholarship, and the collectors also helped to break down the idea that folklore was solely concerned with the past and the rural. This collecting zeal gradually fades after the first volume, to be replaced by more polished pieces, although the Centre's students have continued to contribute a high proportion of the articles.

love divination. Of all the varieties of *divination in English folklore, by far the most common is concerned with love, courtship, and marriage, and most *regional collections include several examples. Love divinations take a wide variety of forms but the basic principles are clear enough, and the underlying premiss is as follows: If you (1) do something (2) in a certain way (3) at a certain time (4) you will discover or influence the future of your love-life. For any particular instance of divination, the instructions for elements 1–3 can be plotted on a continuum from simple to complex ingredients and actions, and these correlate closely with a scale from easy to do to difficult to do. More striking, however, is the scale subsumed in element 4—ranging from *information* to *compulsion*. The desired result can at the simplest end be to find out something about one's future spouse (the first letter of his name, his occupation, etc.), while at the other end the actions can be designed to *force* the man of your choice to take notice of you, which is where divination shades off into *magic. At a point between these extremes are actions designed to make him *appear* to you— either safely in a dream or less safely in a mirror or even as a sort of spirit or *wraith who is drawn to your presence.

In older records, love divinations cluster around certain days of the year (*Halloween, *Midsummer, *St Agnes's Eve, St *Valentine's Day, *New Year), and the symbolic power of the particular date is thus added to the potency of the time of day (usually midnight), as well as the prescribed ingredients and actions.

At the simplest end of the spectrum are the cherry-stones, buttons, petals on a daisy, and so on, chanting 'He loves me, loves me not

. . .', or the ubiquitous 'Tinker, tailor, soldier, sailor . . .'. The first recorded version of this type of procedure only dates from the 1820s, but it is commonly reported from then on.

A little more complex are those which use everyday objects:

To meet your future wife or husband count seven stars in the sky on seven successive nights, and on the eighth day the first person with whom you shake hands will be your wife or husband. (Addy, 1895: 76)

To find out whether your husband will have light or dark hair, take a table-knife with a white haft and spin it round on a table. If it stops with the blade towards you your husband will be a dark-haired man; if with the haft, he will be a light-haired man. (Addy, 1895: 82)

More complicated:

If a girl wishes to dream of her future husband let her go upstairs backwards on a Tuesday or a Friday night with a garter in her hands, saying these words as she ties it:

> I tie my garter in two knots
> That I my beloved may see
> Not in his best apparel
> But in the clothes he wears every day

(Addy, 1895: 78)

The following charm is practised on Midsummer Day—A bucket of spring-water is set in the middle of a yard at midnight. If a girl looks therein at the hour of twelve she will see the face of the young man whom she is to marry. If she does not see it she will die an old maid. (Addy, 1895: 78)

If you eat an apple at midnight on All Halloween, and, without looking behind you, gaze into a mirror, you will see the face of your future husband or wife. (Addy, 1895: 84)

Those designed to conjure the man's wraith or spirit are understandably more complicated still:

The following charm is to be practised at midnight on St Anne's Eve (July 26). A stool is set in the middle of a room and a bowl of water put thereon. A string or piece of rope is then hung across the room. Seven unmarried girls, who must not speak till the ceremony is over, come in, and each hangs a smock on the line. Then each of the girls in turn drops a bayleaf into the bowl of water, and sits down immediately opposite to the smock which she has hung up. Soon afterwards a young man will enter the room, take a bay-leaf from the bowl, and sprinkle the smock of the girl whom he intends to marry. He will marry her that year. (Addy, 1895: 78)

On All-Halloween or New Year's Eve a Border maiden may wash her sark, and hang it over a chair to dry, taking care to tell no one what she is about. If she lie awake long enough, she will see the form of her future spouse enter the room and turn the sark. We are told of one young girl who, after fulfilling this rite, looked out of bed and saw a coffin behind the sark; it remained visible for some time and then disappeared. The girl rose up in agony and told her family what had occurred, and the next morning she heard of her lover's death. (Henderson, 1866: 79)

Alternatively, the procedure could be designed to compel the man in real life. These are often told in narrative form, as they had happened to someone, and invariably with an unhappy ending as a warning:

In another instance related in East Yorkshire the girl took a live frog, stuck it all over with pins, put it in a box, kept it shut up for a week, after which she looked in and found that the frog was dead. She kept it until it was consumed away to bones. Then she took out of the frog a small key-shaped bone, got into the company of the young man she wanted, fastened the bone to his coat, and said:

> I do not want to hurt this frog
> But my true lover's heart to turn
> Wishing that he no rest may find
> Till he come to me and speak his mind.

After this he had a week's torture, as the frog had, and then he went to her and said he had had a queer sensation for a week, but he didn't know what it meant. 'However', he said, 'I will marry thee, but I know we shall never be happy'. They were married and lived very uncomfortably together'. (Addy, 1895: 79)

(Compare this frog-bone procedure with that listed under *horseman's word).

Worst of all, the divinatory actions of the girl might cause rather than predict a real-life tragedy. Henderson (1866: 79–81) gives an example from the Scottish borders which describes a complex procedure involving *holly leaves and three pails of water, designed to summon up the future husband. In one reported case, however, the lover who had thus been summoned 'let fall a rope with a noose at the end, which the young woman took up the next morning and laid in her press'. They were soon married, but within a fortnight the husband hung himself with the rope she had hidden away. Henderson gives one or two similar tales from European sources.

*Weddings are an obvious time for love divination, but the ones that cluster around this event have less of the complicated rigmarole and few of the frightening elements. The simplest is the throwing of the bouquet or stocking, or putting a piece of wedding cake under your pillow to dream of your future spouse, but several demand the use of a wedding ring (Addy, 1895: 78).

Amidst the wide variety of items used and actions prescribed, recurrent motifs can be discerned. Doing things *backwards, staying silent, washing things, placing items under the pillow, the rhyme commencing 'It is not this —— I mean to hurt', or the promise that 'The first person you meet . . .', are all regular ingredients, as are pails of water, *pins, apples and apple pips, seeds and *leaves of various sorts, and, common enough to warrant their own entries, *dumb cake, and *dragon's blood. In sum, most of the recipes combine everyday objects in unusual ways or places. Those which are not designed to conjure the form of the man, usually result in symbols which need to be interpreted—shapes of molten *lead (or *tea leaves) to denote a trade, a letter of the alphabet to indicate his name, and so on.

Young women have certainly not stopped wanting to learn about their future love-life, but the complex and frightening procedures detailed above are no longer reported, although some may be practised in private. What does exist is a series of formulas by which schoolgirls use numbers and letters of the alphabet to compare boys' and girls' names to calculate their chances with each other, and diagrams on which answers to questions are plotted and their future revealed, and these are regularly printed in girls' magazines, as well as being passed on informally at schools (see *Folklore Society Children's Folklore Newsletter* 2 (1988), 17; 3 (1989), 10–12; 4 (1990), 20–2). Younger girls also have a range of *skipping rhymes which appear to be divinatory. It is difficult for the outsider to know where the line between game and seriousness lies in these matters, but it is ever the privilege of the young both to believe and not believe at the same time.

Opie and Tatem, 1989: 472–3.

luck. Whether good or bad, 'luck' is an idea basic to folk belief, ancient, and widespread; it is best understood by contrast with other abstract concepts which purport to explain life's events. Unlike mere chance or accident, it is thought to work through regular cause-and-effect—all *horseshoes are lucky, all *Fridays unlucky, and their influence is exerted automatically. Yet, unlike *fate, luck can change; sometimes it 'turns' spontaneously, sometimes it can be manipulated (you can attract good luck by carrying a *mascot, cancel an unlucky action by turning round *three times, etc.). Unlike providence and *judgements, it has no connection with benevolence, wisdom, or justice, no purposeful plan; there is no meaning behind it.

It is usually futile to enquire why a particular object or action is thought to be lucky or unlucky. 'Pagan survival' is a popular suggestion, but few of the symbols, animals, plants, etc., sacred in Celtic, Germanic, or Roman religion are identical with those now considered lucky or unlucky. A handful of items can be explained as Christian; a good many are based on symbolism, being akin to *magic rituals, or *omens. But the majority resist any logical explanation, and seem trivial and meaningless. Serious or semi-serious belief in luck is still vigorous in modern society.

See also *SUPERSTITIONS.

luck money, see *GOD'S PENNY.

lucky beans. A number of types of beans and large seeds are regularly washed up on the western shores of Britain, having been carried by the Gulf Stream from the Caribbean or South America, and there is a long tradition of these being found and treasured as amulets, under a variety of names—Lucky beans, Molucca beans, Sea beans, Virgin Mary's nuts, and so on. The tradition seems to have been particularly strong in Western Scotland, although the first known reference is in Richard Carew's *Survey of Cornwall* (1602), 27, who mentions their use 'for women travailling in child-birth'. These beans were often worn on a string around the neck to avert *witchcraft and the *evil eye. Their use as commercial generic 'lucky charms' has persisted into the present day, and Vickery gives several instances of them being offered for sale at seaside resorts and elsewhere.

Vickery, 1995: 337–40; Opie and Tatem, 1989: 258.

lucky bit, see *TONGUE.

lucky bone. This a T-shaped bone found in a sheep's head which was worn round the neck or carried in a pocket to bring luck, or as a protection against witches. First mentioned under that name in Northamptonshire in 1851 (Sternberg, 1851: 154), nearly all the

other 19th-century references to the bone are from the northern counties, although elsewhere a pig's bone seems to have had a similar use. Letters in *N&Q* (3s:9 (1866), 59, 146) mention a pig's head bone carried as a charm in Cornwall, and a newspaper advertisement from a quack doctor in July 1764: 'I do give twopence for the little round bone in a pig's skull; it lies inside between the eye and ear'. The sheep bone's shape has led some folklorists to speculate that its similarity to the cross explains its presumed efficacy.

Compare *BONES, *CRAMP.

Opie and Tatem, 1989: 234.

lullabies. England does not have a large stock of traditional lullabies, or at least they have not been documented as such. It has probably always been the case that many parents simply use any sufficiently soothing tune which they happen to know. Nevertheless, two which are still generally known are 'Hush-a-bye baby' (or 'Rock-a-bye baby') and 'Cry Baby Bunting', both of which first appear in print in the late 18th century. Two less well-known lullabies are:

> Sleep like a lady (or gentleman)
> You shall have milk
> When the cows come home
> Father is the butcher
> Mother cooks the meat
> Johnnie rocks the cradle
> While baby goes to sleep
>
> (Newmarket, Cambridgeshire;
> *Folk-Lore* 25 (1914), 364).

> Sleep bonnie bairnie, behind the castle
> By! By! By! By!
> Thou shalt have a golden apple
> By! By! By! By!
>
> (Newcastle; *JFSS* 5 (1915), 121)

The nurse who sang the latter 'used to sing the By! By! With the greatest energy, accenting each By! By clapping her hand vigorously on her knee and beating her foot on the floor, in a way that any one but an infant would have considered the reverse of soothing'. See Opie for a general discussion of lullabies and some further variants.

Opie and Opie, 1997: 17–18, 69–73; Evelyn Carrington, 'Folk Lullabies', *Fraser's Magazine* 103 (1881), 87–99; Leslie Daiken, *The Lullaby Book* (1959); 'Three Northern Lullabies', *JFSS* 5 (1915), 117–21.

lying tales, see *TALL STORIES.

Lyke-Wake Dirge, The. This song is quoted

by *Aubrey (1686/1880: 31–2) as having been sung at *wakes in Yorkshire up to 1616, by women who came specially for the purpose. It is both a prayer for the dead, with the refrain 'Christ receive thy soul', and an account of the soul's journey to Purgatory across Whinney-moor, a heath covered in gorse, and the Bridge of Dread. Only those who in life have given shoes or drink to the poor can pass through unhurt.

Mab, Queen. Several Elizabethan and Jacobean poets name 'Mab' or 'Queen Mab' as a mischievous *fairy. Shakespeare describes her as tiny, but he also says she can blister women's faces and tangle horses' manes (*Romeo and Juliet*, I. iv). Ben Jonson says she can help or spoil the churning, steals babies, and makes midwives lose their way and fall in ponds and ditches by night. According to John Brand (Brand, 1849: iii. 397), to be 'Mab-led' was a Warwickshire term for being led astray by a Will-o'-the-wisp. Robert *Herrick warns slovenly housewives that Mab will pinch them (*Hesperides* (1648), no. 557).

Macbeth. Nowadays it is often said that Shakespeare's *Macbeth* brings bad luck and must never be named, nor should one quote from it; one should call it 'the Scottish play' and refer to its main characters as 'M' and 'Lady M'—except, of course, when actually rehearsing and performing. It is also said to cause accidents to the cast, because the song of the Three Witches is an authentic evil spell, especially when sung to Matthew Locke's setting. However, the belief itself seems relatively recent; the first reference is from 1910 and alludes to 'old' actors, implying currency in the later 19th century (Opie and Tatem, 1989: 396).

MacColl, Ewan (1915–89). Born as Jimmy Miller in Salford, of Scottish parents, Ewan MacColl was one of the key architects of the post-war folk-song *revival, and a dominant but controversial figure in its development for decades. A lifelong communist, his initial passion was workers' theatre, and in a series of influential groups throughout the 1930s and 1940s, culminating with the Theatre Workshop, he became well known in left-wing drama circles as actor, producer, writer, and propagandist. MacColl moved away from the theatre after the Second World War, although

his expertise in dramatic production never left him and imbued much of his subsequent work. In the early 1950s, at the suggestion of American folklorist and collector Alan Lomax, MacColl teamed up with A. L. *Lloyd and others to found the new British folk-song revival movement. The timing was perfect. By means of the Ballads and Blues club (which later became the Singers' Club), radio programmes for the BBC (including drama-documentaries in which MacColl's theatrical experience was evident), articles, innumerable concerts, talks, LP records, appearances at Trade Union meetings, clubs, and other venues, they laid the foundations for a highly successful national movement. MacColl's hard-line political agenda had its devotees but also alienated many in the new movement, and his subsequent actions brought equal amounts of praise and vehement criticism. MacColl's partnership with his third wife, American-born Peggy Seeger, added an expert musical dimension to his career. In addition to researching British folk traditions, with particular emphasis on the songs and language of industrial and urban workers, MacColl also wrote hundreds of songs—political and otherwise—including one, 'The First Time Ever I saw Your Face', which was recorded by various pop singers including Elvis Presley and Roberta Flack, who topped the US charts with it in 1972. One particular triumph was the series of *Radio Ballads (1958–64) programmes made with Seeger and Charles Parker, which broke new ground by their use of tape-recordings of ordinary people talking about their lives in a range of topics, including coal-mining, boxing, Gypsies, teenagers, and herring fishing. MacColl's entire career can be explained in terms of his fascination with language and attempts to understand, record, replicate, and utilize it.

Main folklore publications: *Scotland Sings: A Collection of Folk Songs and Ballads* (1953); *The Shuttle and the Cage: Industrial Folk-Ballads* (1954).

The following with Peggy Seeger: *The Singing Island* (1960); *Travellers' Songs from England and Scotland* (1977); *Till Doomsday in the Afternoon: The Folklore of a Family of Scots Travellers, the Stewarts of Blairgowrie* (1986).

Ewan MacColl, *Journeyman: An Autobiography* (1990); Ewan MacColl, in Raphael Samuel *et al.* (eds.), *Theatres of the Left 1880–1935* (1985), 205–55; Karl Dallas, *ED&S* 51:4 (1989), 11–14; Obituary by Pat Mackenzie and Jim Carroll, *FMJ* 6:1 (1990), 121–4; Interviews by Fred Woods, *Folk Review* (May 1973), 4–7; (June 1973), 4–7; (July 1973), 4–8; (Aug. 1973), 6–8.

Magdalen College May Day singing. At six o'clock on May Day morning, the choir of Magdalen College, Oxford, ascend to the top of the College tower and there sing a Latin hymn, 'Te Deum patrem colimus'. Meanwhile, in the streets below, thousands of onlookers have gathered for the event, including, nowadays, teams of *morris dancers, jugglers, and other entertainers, and once the singing is over the church bells are rung, and a general street party ensues. The singing is documented since the late 18th century, but the other events have gradually developed since the 1920s. There are two main theories on the origin of the singing—one that it commemorates the building of the College tower (completed in 1509), the other that the custom started as an obit, or requiem mass for Henry VII (died 21 Apr. 1509).

Roy Judge, *Folklore* 97:1 (1986), 15–40; Shuel, 1985: 30–1.

magic. This can be defined as the use of symbolic actions, words, or objects to produce results in the real world, either mechanically through their intrinsic nature (e.g. displaying *horseshoes, *touching wood for luck), or by the personal willpower of the user, or because he or she has authority over supernatural beings. But formulas which rely on help from God, saints, or angels (e.g. many healing *charms) should not be classified as magic but as folk Christianity. This distinction, theoretically clear, becomes blurred in practice, where magical actions are often accompanied by religious words such as 'in the name of the Father, Son and Holy Ghost'. The boundary between magic and science is also blurred, because an apparently non-rational procedure may simply reflect mistaken ideas about the natural properties of some object, so that the person performing it never thinks of it as 'magic'. Indeed, scientific fact and symbolic appropriateness sometimes coincide—

*dandelions really are diuretic, but not because their flowers are yellow like urine.

Magic assumes there are non-material connections between material objects; *Frazer usefully divided it into 'sympathetic' or 'imitative' magic, where the action performed or object used resembles the result desired ('like causes like'), and 'contagious' magic, where something once in contact with a person provides a link through which he or she can be helped or harmed. It can also be divided into 'low' and 'high' magic, according to the degree of sophistication in the procedures involved. The most elaborate and intellectual system, also called 'ritual' or 'ceremonial' magic, flourished in late medieval and Renaissance times, and was revived by occultists at the close of the 19th century. Its aim was to summon and control angels or demons, by incantations and *pentacles; the practitioner needed special robes, perfumes, and other equipment. It was far too expensive and time-consuming ever to be part of folk practice, but some of the simpler aspects could be adapted for popular use (see *astrology, *pentacles).

The difference between 'black' and 'white' magic depends on morality, not techniques: is the magic being used for a good purpose or a harmful one? This of course depends on the point of view of the observer; aggressive *counterspells against witches are meant to inflict pain, but since the witch is seen as evil, the counterspell is 'white' magic.

See also *CUNNING MEN, *CHARMS, *COUNTERSPELLS, *DIVINATIONS, *IMAGE MAGIC, and *WITCHCRAFT.

The best descriptions of English popular magic are in Thomas, 1971, especially pp. 177–252, and Davies, 1999a. Studies of witchcraft also contain relevant material, e.g. Thomas, 1971: 435–69, and Sharpe, 1996. Almost all regional collections contain examples of charms, the best of which are conveniently brought together in Opie and Tatem, 1989. For the early phase of 'ritual' or 'high' magic, see Richard Kiekhefer, *Magic in the Middle Ages* (1989) and *Forbidden Rites* (1997).

magpies. A rhyme about magpies is well known all over the country, although presumably not believed. The divination depends on the number of birds seen; there are naturally numerous variations, although nearly all agree that *one* magpie is bad, but *two* are good. The earliest record, *c*.1780, from Lincolnshire, runs:

> One for sorrow,
> Two for mirth,
> Three for a wedding,
> And four for a death.

Common variations are 'Four for a birth', and:

> One for sorrow,
> Two for joy,
> Three for a girl,
> And four for a boy.

There are many variations for the higher numbers. The grimmest, first noted from Northumberland (*Denham Tracts*, 1895: ii. 20–2), runs:

> Five for silver, six for gold,
> Seven for a secret not to be told,
> Eight for heaven, nine for hell,
> And ten is for the Devil's own sel'.

Other possibilities are:

> Five for rich, six for poor,
> Seven for a witch, I can tell you no more.

> Five for rich, six for poor,
> Seven for a bitch, eight for a whore,
> Nine for a burying, ten for a dance,
> Eleven for England, twelve for France.

Denham says the bad luck of a single bird can be averted by drawing a cross on the ground or by saying:

> Magpie, magpie, chatter and flee,
> Turn up thy tail and good luck fall me.

Other ways of averting the evil are to take off one's hat on seeing the bird, bow, wish it 'Good day', or blow a kiss to it; or spit over the left shoulder; or turn round three times; or cross one's fingers and say:

> I cross the magpie,
>   The magpie crosses me;
> Bad luck to the magpie,
>   And good luck to me.

Though the magpie rhyme has not been traced earlier than *c.*1780, magpie omens go back to medieval times. Sometimes they are favourable, for example that the chattering means that guests or strangers are coming (1159 and onwards); more often not: '. . . when pyes chatter vpon a house it is a sygne of ryghte euyll tydynges' (1507). This is especially so if the bird is flying around, or perching on, a house where someone is ill. In Sheffield, it was disliked because it refused to enter Noah's ark, preferring to sit on its roof 'and jabber over the drowning world' (*N&Q* 4s:7 (1871), 299); in Sussex, because 'it was a bad bird, and knew more than it should do, and was always looking about and prying into other people's affairs' (Latham, 1878: 9).

Swainson, 1885: 76–81; Opie and Tatem, 1989: 235–6.

Maid Marian. From about 1500, Marian appears among *Robin Hood's companions; she is said to be his sweetheart who joins him in outlawry. She is chiefly important in *May Day celebrations, court entertainments, and stage and literary tradition; the ballads rarely mention her. She may have been imported from French literature, where 'Robin et Marion' had been stock names for country lovers since the 13th century. But there was also an English 'Marian', a comic figure played by a man in drag, who accompanied Elizabethan morris dancers; he is usually linked to the Fool who, according to a tract of 1589, 'dances round him in a cotton coat, to court him with a leathern pudding' (i.e. a mock sausage, no doubt bawdily used). It is unclear which type of Marian came first, and whether either influenced the other.

See also *FRIAR TUCK, *ABBOTS BROMLEY.

Maidens' Garlands (Virgins' Garlands, Virgins' Crowns). These were formerly constructed to mark the death of a local person, usually but not exclusively female, who had led an unblemished life and had died unmarried. The *garland was carried over the coffin at the funeral and then hung in the church, where it stayed until it rotted away. Methods of construction and exact details of the custom varied from place to place, but the following description is a reasonable synopsis:

They are made of variegated coloured paper, representing flowers, fastened to small sticks crossing each other at the top, and fixed at the bottom by a circular hoop. From the centre is suspended the form of a woman's glove cut in white paper, on which the name and age of the deceased are sometimes written. (Brockett, 1825: 225)

Earlier references mention fresh flowers and real gloves, but in later examples paper rosettes and glove shapes were more common. The custom was clearly very widespread in England, but changing fashions in religion and local church life gradually wiped it out. Old garlands were often swept away when a local church was rebuilt or 'renovated'. Examples can still be seen in churches and museums (listed by Spriggs), and the church of St Mary the Virgin, Abbotts Ann, Hampshire, is the one parish which still continues the custom.

Aubrey, 1686: 109; Gareth M. Spriggs, *Folk Life* 21 (1982/3) 21–35; Chambers, 1878: i. 271–4; Brears, 1989: 178–203;

N&Q 172 (1937), 30, 156, 231, 302–3; 181 (1941), 91, 123–4, 148, 166, 223, 277.

mandrake. The true mandrake is a poisonous plant with a forked root, related to nightshade; classical writers and the Bible mention it as an aphrodisiac and as making barren women fertile, while in medieval times it was used as a powerful soporific and pain-killer. However, as it does not grow easily in Britain, dried roots of white or black bryony were sold as 'mandrakes'; sliced or grated, they were used medicinally on horses and humans. In Sussex in the 1920s mandrake was being sold by a village herbalist as 'the finest cure in all the world for indigestion and malaria . . . rheumatism, pains in the chest, headaches and so on' (*Sussex County Magazine* 1 (1927), 453). Bryony roots were classed as males or females; in Lincolnshire, 'mandrakes' would be used on women and mares, and 'womandrakes' on men and stallions (Rudkin, 1936: 28–9).

However, the reputation of the mandrake is due to sinister legends from medieval Europe, which reached England in Tudor times. It was said to grow under *gallows and gibbets, springing from the sperm ejaculated by hanged men; it shrieked so horribly when uprooted that anyone hearing it would go mad, so a dog would be tricked into pulling it from the ground. According to the manuals of *magic, anyone who keeps a mandrake wrapped in silk in a small chest will never lack money, for if one coin is laid beside it at night, there will be two by morning.

The making of mandrake puppets is described by several Elizabethan and Jacobean writers; the bryony roots were trimmed to look as human as possible, and given hair and a beard by pricking small holes into them and inserting sprouting millet or barley seeds. The craft was still practised in East Anglia early in the 20th century, but partly in fun; countrymen would display 'female' mandrakes in the pub, and the most realistically carved would win a prize—after which the figures would be hung in a sow's sty to make her prolific, or put among money under the mattress (Porter, 1969: 46–7). In London street-markets in the 1920s the mannikins were sold to be fixed to the bedhead 'for good luck' (Lovett, 1925: 74).

Vickery, 1995: 393–4; Opie and Tatem, 1989: 237–8; H. F. Clark, *Folklore* 73 (1962), 257–69.

Man in the Moon. Several medieval and Elizabethan writers refer jokingly to the Man in the Moon, who carries a bundle of thorntwigs and is accompanied by a dog; legend says he was set there as punishment for stealing the sticks, or for gathering them on a Sunday, or for strewing thorny branches on a church path. He is also mentioned in nursery rhymes and shown on inn signs.

manorial customs. In folklore writing, the term 'manorial custom' is used to refer to customs which originated, or are thought to have originated, in the practices of the medieval manor or manor courts. The origins of the system of manors in England are unclear, but they were firmly established by the time of the Domesday Survey in 1086, and it is difficult to generalize as differences between them were legion, and much depended on local practice. The manor involved a hierarchy of loyalty and duty which each level owed to those above, sometimes payable in services, sometimes in money, and also a complex of economically important rights enjoyed by tenants and other occupants, such as taking wood from the Lord's forest, grazing-rights for cattle, or acorns for pigs. Over the years numerous local customary practices evolved, a handful of which survived in isolation after the manorial system became replaced by other forms of local organization. The day-to-day business of the manor was ruled by courts—court leet and court baron—which also developed their own ways of proceeding, and again some of these lived on into modern times, particularly where administration of common land was necessary. Examples of customs which have, or probably have, manorial connections are: *Hungerford Hocktide; *Wroth Silver; *Wishford Magna; Whitby *Penny Hedge.

David Hey, *The Oxford Companion to Local and Family History* (1996), 118–19, 296–7; William Figg, 'Manorial Customs of Southese-with-Heighton, Near Lewes', *Sussex Archaeological Collections* 3 (1850), 249–52; Harland and Wilkinson, 1882: 277–302.

Map, Walter (*c.*1140–*c.*1209). A clerk in the household of Henry II, who made him an itinerant judge; he also had a good career in the Church, rising to be Archdeacon of Oxford. Around 1190 he wrote a light-hearted miscellany called *De Nugis Curialium* ('Courtiers' Trifles') including various tales of marvels he had heard, for example the story of *Herla and the dwarf, that of *Edric the Wild and his fairy wife, and two accounts of the laying of dangerous *undead.

marbles. The early history of marbles is still obscure. Certainly, in the ancient world children played games rolling nuts, and coloured clay balls have been found in Egyptian tombs, but it is not known for sure what they were used for. It seems unlikely that such a simple and obvious game did not occur to people before the first definite references (as *tribekugeln*) in 13th century Germany, and in Bruegel's picture of children's games in 1560. The first mention in English calls the game 'bowling-stones', but this is a translation by Charles Hoole of Comenius's *Orbis Pictus* (1659). There are numerous variants of marbles play, and usually a local specialist terminology to go with each.

The marbles available in England in the late 17th century were probably made of actual marble, or at least alabaster, but later materials include earthenware, painted porcelain (imported from Germany), stone, and clay. The modern glass marbles, with the intriguing coloured swirl in the middle, emerged in the 1840s, made possible by developments in glass manufacture. Once these appeared they rapidly became more prized than the drab clay marbles prevalent at the time, and gradually superseded them as mass production (latterly usually abroad) brought the price down. Some players used metal ball-bearings, but others refused to play with anyone using such things as they could too easily destroy the glass or clay marbles. Another source of supply was the round stopper used in early fizzy-drink bottles. Local names include: Taws, Alleys (Blood-alleys had a streak of red through them), Cat's eyes, and Marvels.

Marbles has been a children's game for a very long time, but there are a few instances of its survival in the adult sphere, particularly in Sussex, where a well-known annual Good Friday championship match takes place at Tinsley Green, and another is held at Battle.

Opie and Opie, 1997: 17–55; Gomme, 1894: i. 364 (and other pages); Wales, 1990: 52–3.

Marshfield Paper Boys. The Paper Boys of Marshfield (Gloucestershire) are one of the few extant *mumming play teams which can be regarded as traditional, although they cannot claim an unbroken tradition. The play was revived in 1932 at the instigation of folklorist Violet *Alford, but with the active participation of men who had taken part in the custom in their youth in the 1880s. The Marshfield

play text is a fairly typical Gloucestershire Hero-Combat version. The Marshfield costume follows the general southern pattern of strips sewn on to everyday clothes, covering the whole head and body, but the use of newspapers instead of wallpaper or rag is unusual. The team comes out every Boxing Day, with performances taking place outdoors at set points around the village.

Simon Lichman, 'The Gardener's Story and What Came Next' (Ph.D. thesis, University of Pennsylvania, 1981), and *Folklore* 93:1 (1982), 105–11.

Martinmas, Martlemas. This date, 11 November, is the feast of St Martin of Tours. In medieval and Elizabethan times it was an occasion for an ample feast of meat, because livestock which could not be fed through the winter was being slaughtered. Other joints were hung in the chimney to dry, like bacon, and were called Martlemas beef (or mutton). It was regarded as the end of the farming year, and in many places hiring fairs were held for farm-workers who wished to change jobs.

In some areas, it was said that the weather on this date foretold that of the coming winter. In others, this could be deduced from markings on the breast-bone of a goose eaten on Matinmas Eve; white marks meant snow and dark ones hard frost, while the front part of the bone meant before Christmas and the back part afterwards.

M. Walsh, 'Medieval English Martinmesse', *Folklore* 111 (2000), 231–54.

martins. It is very lucky to have a martin's nest on a house; to destroy it or take the eggs brings disaster, that one's cows will give bloody milk, for example (Opie and Tatem, 1989: 386–8). Cf. *swallows.

Martlemas, see *MARTINMAS.

Mary Had a Little Lamb. There have been many claimants to the authorship of what has been claimed to be the best-known four lines of verse in the English language, and also a number of pretenders to the honour of being the original Mary. One Mary Hughes, of Worthing, Sussex, even has a tombstone pronouncing her fame, but unfortunately in error (*FLS News* 19 (June 1994), 13). The facts, as laid out by Iona and Peter Opie, are that the original four-verse poem was written by Mrs Sarah Josepha Hale (1788–1879), of Boston, in early 1830, and first published in September of that year in the *Juvenile Miscellany*. The poem's other claim to fame, however, is that it is probably the most parodied of verses in the English tradition. As soon as children get too old and wise to appreciate the real thing, they get devilish delight in debunking it, and as they grow older the parodies get ruder or cleverer, and adults are not above using them in comedy routines and satire. All that is needed is the formula 'Mary had a little . . . ' and the audience understands perfectly what is going on.

Opie and Opie, 1997: 353–5.

mascot. The word 'mascot' often implies a strong personal link between the luck-bringing object (which may be quite insignificant in itself) and its owner. Edward Lovett noted mascots carried by soldiers in the First World War: 'left-handed' whelk shells; wool gollywogs; a carved amber bead; a farthing with a hole in it, sewn to one's left brace over one's heart; a little gold Oriental figure; a Chinese coin; a metal button; a domino with ten dots; a cornelian pendant. Mascots from the same war in the Horniman Museum (London) and the Imperial War Museum include figures of *pigs, *cats, and monkeys, *holed stones, a *mandrake, and an amber heart. Strong trust was placed in these objects (Lovett, 1925: 10–15, 18, 30, 34, 41–3, 70–2; Ettlinger, 1939: 152–62).

Mass-produced lucky charms are hung on cars or worn as jewellery. Some draw on foreign traditions, such as the New Zealand tikis and greenstone brooches, Italian horns and hunchbacks, and African copper bangles already being used in London in 1908, alongside British symbols such as miniature horseshoes and pigs, and natural objects such as coal, fossils, and sheep's or rabbit's bones (*Folklore* 19 (1908), 288–303). In 1939, a London clergyman noted sadly that a 'almost every' woman at a church Mothers' Tea had a charm in her handbag, among them 'a tiny green pig, a black cat, a black metal boot, a silver slipper, several hideous imps and idols, and the pentacle of the medieval sorcerers . . . one had preserved a bag-wash ticket, because it had on it the number 666!' He had also read in the press that actors, boxers, airmen, jockeys, and others had mascots, which included 'an ivory hunchback, a hare's foot, an uncut amethyst, a coffin nail, a double walnut, a small jade pig, a meteorite, the knuckle-bone of a pig, a

penny that had closed the eye of a corpse' (Balleine, 1939: 6–7).

See also *COINS, *LUCKY BEAN, *LUCKY BONE.

Maundy Thursday. The ceremonial custom of Royal Maundy, on the Thursday before Easter, is the last secular example of a once widespread ritual whereby figures of authority washed the feet of the poor and gave alms, in memory of Christ's actions before the Last Supper.

May Day, Bringing in the May. Many of the earliest references to May Day are ambiguous, but those which give any detail nearly always refer to the practice of going out into the countryside to gather flowers and greenery—'going a-maying' or 'bringing in the may'. This greenery was used to decorate houses and public buildings to welcome the season, and for the early period this was the archetypal activity of the day (but see also *May Dew and *Maypoles). Robert Grosseteste, Bishop of Lincoln, provides one of the first written references to May Day customs by complaining, *c.*1240, about priests joining in 'games which they call the bringing-in of May' (Hutton: 226). Although this early reference is an ecclesiastical grumble, medieval May celebrations were often officially sponsored and both churchwardens' and municipal account books regularly include money paid out to support the custom. Similarly, the gatherings could include all levels of society including nobility and even royalty.

Against May, Whitsonday, or other time, all the yung men and maides, olde men and wives, run gadding overnight to the woods, groves, hils and mountains, where they spend all the night in pleasant pastimes; and in the morning, they return, bringing with them birch and branches of trees, to deck their assemblies withall . . . (Stubbes, 1583: 149).

Stubbes was campaigning against the May gathering, but the same custom could be used by writers on the other side as an archetypal joyous community event and a ready-made metaphor for the innocent rural idyll:

And furth goth all the Court, both most and lest
To feche the floures fressh, and braunch and blome
And namely, hawthorn brought both page and
   grome
With fressh garlandes, partie blewe and whyte . . .

(*The Court of Love, first printed 1561,
previously attributed to Chaucer*)

The bringing in of the May remained a

staple of the traditional calendar throughout the fifteenth and sixteenth centuries, but voices of opposition began to be raised from reforming Protestant quarters from the time of Edward VI (1547–1553) onwards, gathering pace almost year by year. The assault on May Day took many forms, religious, moral, and legal (public order), but the focus of disapproval of the Bringing-in custom was primarily the concern about what unchaperoned young people would be doing in the woods. Stubbes' reformist zeal may have lead him to overstate his case on the moral dangers of May Day:

I have heard it credibly reported (and that viva voce) by men of great gravitie and reputation, that of fortie, threescore, or a hundred maides going to the wood over night, there have scarecely the thirde parte of them returned home againe undefiled (Stubbes, 1583: 149).

Robert *Herrick, supporter of rural sports and customs, was happy to admit the amorous possilities involved in 'going a-maying':

And some have wept, and woo'd, and plighted troth
And chose their priest, ere we can cast off sloth
Many a green-gown has been given
Many a kisse, both odde and even
Many a glance too has been sent
From out the eye, loves firmament . . .

('Corinna's Going A-Maying', *Hesperides*, 1648).

The 'green gown' was a well-known metaphor for what girls received from lying on the grass with their lovers.

Bringing in the May was banned, along with most other traditional customs, in the Commonwealth period, but returned after the Restoration and survived, in gradually dwindling form, until the early 19th century:

May-day is still observed at Great Gransden [Cambridgeshire], where the young men, farmers' servants, on their return from going a-Maying, leave a hawthorn branch at every house in the village, singing what they call the Night song. On the evenings of May-day and the 2nd of May, they go round to every house where they had left a branch and sing the May Song . . .

(*Time's Telescope* for 1816 p. 130, quoted by Wright and Lones)

Its spirit lived on in the children's May garlanding customs of the nineteenth and twentieth centuries.

See also *MAY: CHILDREN'S GARLANDS AND CUSTOMS, *MAY DEW, *MAYPOLES.

Hazlitt, 1905: 397–9; Wright and Lones, 1938: ii. 200–7, Hutton, 1996: 226–43.

May Day, children's garlands and customs. The most widespread and best known May Day activity in the 19th and early 20th centuries was the children's *garland custom. In essence, this involved groups of children *visiting houses in their community showing a garland, singing a song, and collecting money. The custom appears to have grown directly from the earlier adult activities of 'bringing in the May' (see *May, bringing in), and to have proliferated during the 19th century. Children's garlanding was exactly right for the new romantic rural consciousness which was a growing force in the nation's literary circles, and was just the sort of thing the early folklorists liked to find. However, the practice was not found all over the country, being strongest in the south and Midlands and parts of the west country and almost completely absent in the north and most of East Anglia—a distribution which is puzzling.

Within the same time-frame there was a steady move away from self-organization amongst the children towards increased adult involvement in planning and organization. Adult intervention brought a trend away from small bands of children towards larger, better organized and controlled groups. Nearly all the *regional folklore collections in the right areas include examples of children's May garland customs, but Flora Thompson's fictionalized autobiography *Lark Rise* (1939: chapter 13) is often singled out as the archetypal evocation of the custom. Garlands could be large or small, but always designed to be portable and relatively robust. Naturally, the larger groups tended to present larger more intricate structures. Many were spherical or bell-shaped, with wooden or wire hoops forming the basic structure which was covered in flowers, greenery, ribbons, coloured paper, and so on. These would normally be carried on a pole, between two people. Hand-held garlands tended to be more like decorated poles, and were obviously less elaborate (*N&Q* 6s:3 (1881), 386). Even without overt adult organizational interference, the children usually had set roles to play in the garlanding party—the Queen (elected or self-appointed) being the most important, sometimes a King, sometimes maids of honour, footmen, coat-holder, and so on. In almost all recorded cases, the mayers had a traditional song to sing or at least a rhyme to recite. A number of these rhymes fit into the general pattern of visiting custom songs, having direct parallels in *mumming.

*souling, *wassailing, and so on. The songs were often collected and published independently, and many early folk song collections include them. See Ruddock, Gerish, and Hamer for a number of versions from Leicestershire/Rutland, Hertfordshire, and Bedfordshire respectively, Judge for an overall systematic analysis.

A regular, but not ubiquitous, feature was to place a dressed and decorated doll (sometimes more than one) in the centre of the garland, or in front of it. She was usually called something like Her Lady, or The Queen, and treated with great respect. Commentators assume she represented the Virgin Mary. In some places, it was the doll which was given precedence, rather than the garland, transported in a decorated box or basket:

May Day 1881: . . . at Teignmouth, in Devon, the May babies came round as usual. Parties of girls and children go from house to house, each party carrying a dressed doll laid in a box, and decked with flowers. They cry 'Will you look at my May baby?' and of course they expect you to pay for that privilege . . . (N&Q 6s:3 (1881), 386)

The doll was often covered by a cloth or veil, which could be dramatically drawn aside to 'show' the splendours within, or could be left in place if the visited householder refused to offer a contribution.

Garlands and dolls were not the only May Day activity for children, and there are several customs which appear to be unique to particular areas. In Burnley in the 1920s and 1930s, for example, the boys and girls had different things to do, The girls went round with their 'maypole', a garland made from two hoops nailed to a broom handle to form a bell shape, covered in crepe paper and with long ribbons attached for the girls to hold as they danced round. The boys would enact a performance of a dancing-bear. One would put a sack over his head, tied at the corners to make ears, and with eye and mouth holes cut out, to be the bear. The other would lead him on a rope, carrying a broom handle for a pole, and reciting traditional gibberish on the lines of 'addy addy ompompay' in imitation of the real bearminders (Burnley Express and News (6 May 1922, 1 Feb. 1980, 1 Feb. 1983).

A journalistic piece in the Evening Standard (1 May 1928) details the writer's unsuccessful search for the 'spirit of May Day' in the London of the time until he finally found it:

wandering gloomily through Bermondsey, I found what I had been seeking. From a patch of waste ground came the sound of young laughter and the wheezing of a mouth-organ. A dozen small children were moving solemnly in a circle, each grasping in a grubby hand a piece of string about four feet long, the other end of which was tied to the top of a broomstick, the latter embedded a few inches in the earth.The broomstick was crowned with a piece of faded ribbon. I approached the children, asked them what they were doing. They stared at me in silence for a moment, then one little girl, pointing to the broomstick, said 'Why, this is our maypole. It's May Day today. Didn't you know?'.

In the 1950s, collecting material for their Lore and Language of Schoolchildren (1959: 255–62), Iona and Peter Opie discovered a number of May Day customs still current, such as garlanding in isolated villages, including Bampton, Wheatley, and Lower Heyford in Oxfordshire, and *Abbotsbury in Dorset, home-made maypoles in Shrewsbury (a pram wheel, set on a pole, covered with crepe paper and streamers), and even, at Blackburn, the boys' dancing-bear as described above. They also reported the *May dew belief (and practice) still current in many parts.

See also *MAY, BRINGING IN, *MAYPOLES, *ABBOTSBURY GARLAND DAY, *GARLANDS, *CASTLETON GARLAND DAY, *MAIDENS' GARLANDS.

Flora Thompson, Lark Rise (1939), chapter 13; Wright and Lones, 1938: ii. 200–45; Anne Elizabeth Baker, Glossary of Northamptonshire Words and Phrases (1854): ii. 421–9; Elizabeth Ruddock, 'May Day Songs and Celebrations in Leicestershire and Rutland', Trans. of the Leicestershire Archaeological & Historical Society 40 (1964/5), 69–84; W. B. Gerish, 'The Mayers and Their Song', Trans. of the East Hertfordshire Archaeological Society 2 (1904), 214–28; F. B. Hamer, 'May Songs of Bedfordshire', JEFDSS 9 (1961), 81–90.

May Day Horse Parades. A regular May Day tradition, in town as well as country was for farm-workers, waggoners, and anyone working with horses to decorate them profusely on May Day with rosettes, ribbons, flowers, braid, and shining brass. On a grander scale, many towns held formal May Day horse parades, and companies which had large numbers of horses might have their own annual procession. In each case the horses would be groomed to perfection and decorated to the hilt. These processions were common in the north of England from the mid-19th century, spreading southwards from the 1880s onwards, and lasting well into the 20th century.

Judge, 1987.

May dew. There is a widespread belief, in Britain and abroad, that dew gathered on May Day morning is particularly good for the complexion, and countless people have acted on this knowledge over the last 500 years. Samuel Pepys's wife Elizabeth clearly believed that any time in May would do, as he records her going out on 28 May 1667, and 10 May 1669. In some areas there were extra stipulations: dew gathered under oak trees or off hawthorn bushes being specially good. May dew was also believed to be particularly effective for certain complaints, first mentioned in 1602 for sore eyes and in Launceston, 'poor people say that a swelling in the neck may be cured by the patient, if a woman, going before sunrise on the first of May, to the grave of the young man last buried in the churchyard, collecting therefrom the dew by passing the hand three times from the head to the foot of the grave, and applying the dew to the part affected. If the patient be a man, the grave chosen must be that of the last young woman buried in the churchyard' (N&Q 1s:2 (1850), 474–5). Other ailments such as consumption and weak joints and muscles could also be treated with May dew, or even with May rain.

See also *MAY, BRINGING IN.

Wright and Lones, 1938: ii. 205–7; Opie and Tatem, 1989: 245–6.

May goslings. In Cumberland, Westmorland, and the northern parts of Lancashire and Yorkshire, 'May Goslings' are the equivalent of *April Fools elsewhere, the day for the hoaxing being 1 May. The custom, first reported in 1791, was still flourishing in the 1950s. The tricks must stop by midday; anyone forgetting this is taunted:

May Gosling's dead and gone,
You're the fool for thinking on

(Opie and Opie, 1959: 256–7)

Mayor of Ock Street. One of the few remaining *mock mayor ceremonies in the country, the Ock Street Mayor is said to date from about 1700, although this is probably wishful thinking, as the first recorded reference only occurs in the 1860s (see Chandler, 1993). Legend says that in 1700 the men of Ock Street, Abingdon, Oxfordshire, fought a pitched battle against the men from the Vineyards, for possession of the horns of an ox which had been roasted at the town's fair. Having won the horns, the Ock Street men

paraded them in triumph, and they are still carried before the annually elected Mayor on the Saturday nearest 19 June. The Mayor is always a member of the Abingdon Morris Men, and is elected by the inhabitants of the street and the Morris Men. He is then borne aloft, in a chair decorated with flowers, by his fellow dancers, bearing his ceremonial sword, bowl, and sash.

Keith Chandler, 'The Abingdon Morris and the Election of the Mayor of Ock Street', in Buckland and Wood, 1993: 119–36; Kightly, 1986: 166–7; Shuel, 1985: 43–4.

maypoles. For many people the maypole is the very symbol of the traditional May Day, but its history is not a simple one. The earliest references to maypoles are literary; a mid-14th century Welsh poem and a late 14th-century poem *Chance of the Dice* (Hammond, 1925: 6) which refers to 'the grete shafte of Corneylle', in London. Two earlier references which had often been quoted have now been brought under suspicion as probably referring to pools or even maples rather than maypoles. However, there is no reason to believe that the maypole was a new thing in the 14th century, but neither is there any evidence to show that it existed much before then. Certainly, the limited distribution of poles in Wales and Scotland, and the paucity of references there, argue strongly against the existence of maypoles before the Anglo-Saxon settlement of England.

From the 15th century onwards, references to maypoles proliferate, sometimes in municipal or parish accounts, and often in the writings of the new moralists who were keen to reform the ungodly celebrations surrounding such traditional events as May Day and Christmas. The finding, decorating, and erecting of the maypole emerges as an important part of community life, becoming the focal point for dancing and other celebrations of the season (see also *May, bringing in). Some places had permanent maypoles, such as probably the best known in the country at Cornhill (as referred to by the *Chance* poet) in London, which was reputedly taller than the church to which it gave its name, St Andrew Undershaft, while others started from scratch every year. It is clear that maypoles were as popular in urban as in rural communities.

If the maypole was the clear symbol of traditional May merrymaking, it was equally the clear target for those opposed to the festivities. John Stow (1598) relates how the Cornhill pole was taken down after 'evil May Day' (1517) when rioting apprentices had to be suppressed by the authorities. The pole was laid on iron brackets above the doors of the houses in Shaft Alley, and stayed there for another 32 years. However, in 1549, a reforming curate of St Katherine's took strong exception to this 'idol' and caused it to be chopped up and the wood shared among the inhabitants. As is often the case for this period, our most detailed descriptions are provided by those who opposed the traditions, and Philip Stubbes's *Anatomie of Abuses* (1583) is a case in point:

But their cheefest jewell they bring home from thence [the woods] is their Maie poole, whiche they bring home with great veneration ... this Maie poole (this stynckyng idoll rather) which is covered all over with flowers and hearbes, bounde rounde aboute with stringes, from the top to the bottome, and sometyme painted with variable colours ...

Nevertheless, maypoles had their supporters. They were specifically mentioned in King James I's *Book of Sports* (1618), reissued by Charles I (1633), as a lawful pastime for the people on Sundays, after evening service, and poets and playwrights used the pole as a metaphorical rallying point for the old tolerant days of England. All over the country, however, maypoles were being suppressed or obstructed by a combination of local justices and clergy, and they were one of the first things to be banned once the Puritans gained control in the 1640s. After the Restoration, in 1660, maypoles rapidly came back into favour, again as the symbol of the return to the good old days. And so they continued to stand, taken for granted as a local landmark, but entering a slow but definite decline from around the turn of the 19th century, suffering this time from neglect rather than opposition. By the time the Victorians began reinventing May Day there were few old maypoles left, leaving the field conveniently clear for their reintroduction in modified form.

Leaving aside the theories of maypoles as remnants of tree-worship, phallic symbols, and the like, for which there is no evidence, the pole seems to have had two essential qualities—first, it was a focal point for the celebrations, and second, it was a useful place to hang garlands and greenery. This greenery, flowers, flags, and gay striped paint are often mentioned as the main feature of the pole. People danced round it, but not plaiting rib-

bons as in the modern revival. In the earlier form, they either held hands in a ring, danced solo in the circle, or wove in and out of each other round the circle, and there are reports of people kissing each other as they met. The introduction and spread of the plaited maypole in England is detailed by Roy Judge (1987: 175–94). The earliest examples, from the 1830s, are included in stage performances, but the really influential development came when successive dancing-masters and choreographers deliberately introduced the form into other revived or invented customs such as *well-dressing, usually performed by young girls and boys—but usually girls—dressed in white. By the late 19th century, the plaited maypole had become accepted as the 'traditional' English form; a clear example of the *Merrie England process at work.

A few places, such as *Padstow (Cornwall), and *Barwick in Elmet (West Yorkshire) still have the older style ribbonless pole. Some children's customs had hand-held 'maypoles', which may be a remnant of, or at least a reference to, the full-size ones (see *May, children's garlands and customs).

See also *MERRIE ENGLAND, *CHURCH ALES, *WHITSUN ALES.

Hutton, 1996: 233–7, 301–2; Hutton, 1994: 30, 56–7, 114–16, 223–6; Judge, 1987; Roy Judge, 'Tradition and the Plaited Maypole', *Traditional Dance* 2 (1983), 1–21; Wright and Lones, 1938: ii. 217–28; Hazlitt, 1905: 402–6; Eleanor Prescott Hammond, 'The Chance of the Dice', *Englishe Studien* 59 (1925), 1–16.

May Queens. An accepted part of the modern May celebrations in many towns and villages; the usual pattern being a procession, crowning ceremony, and some sort of parade, as one constituent part of the sports, displays, and stalls of a local fête. While not entirely invented from scratch, the modern May Queen is an example of the Victorian *Merrie England style of reinvented tradition which completely transformed the custom while keeping only a tenuous link with previous practice. Many earlier customs had had a man and woman who, with their entourage of officers, were elected to preside over the celebrations, and were treated with some degree of respect, although often in a jocular way. The more common title for this couple was 'Lord and Lady', although occasionally they are reported as 'King and Queen'. They appear regularly at *Whitsun ales and in children's garlanding customs (see *May Day, children's garlanding). In earlier versions of the latter, the Lord and Lady were chosen by the children themselves, but as the school and vicarage took over control of the custom, the choice also passed increasingly into adult hands. In the new May Day constructed by Victorian reformers, the figure of the May Queen was given more prominence, and finally raised to be the central character. The process was helped by Tennyson's immensely popular poem 'The May Queen', published in 1832, which, although it gave no details of the custom, focused attention on the female character, and by the 1870s and 1880s new May Queen festivals were becoming well established and being described as the 'old traditional' way of celebrating May. Well-known examples were at Knutsford (Cheshire) and, following the ideas of John Ruskin, at Whitelands College, Chelsea.

See also *MAY DAY, CHILDREN'S GARLANDING.

Roy Judge, 'Fact and Fancy in Tennyson's "May Queen" and in Flora Thompson's "May Day", in Buckland and Wood, 1993: 167–83; Judge, 1987; Malcolm Cole, *Whitelands College May Queen Festival* (1981); Revd W. Dallow, 'May Queens', *Strand Magazine* (May 1892), 484–8.

May (the month). Oddly, though the literary associations of this month are with blossoming love, and its customs are all joyous, several widespread superstitions count it unlucky. *Cats born in May are useless and should be drowned at birth; 'May-babies, like May kittens, are said to be weakly and unlikely to thrive' (*Folk-Lore* 68 (1957), 413; cf. *N&Q* 1s:7 (1853) 152); the *broom brings death; boys born in May are particularly cruel to animals (*N&Q* 12s:4 (1918) 133, 172, 257–8).

Most often mentioned is the idea that May marriages will prove unhappy. The belief is undoubtedly ancient, as Ovid mentions it (*Fasti:* V v. ii. 487–90); its first known airing in English, in *Poor Robin's Almanack* for 1675, treats it as already proverbial. Yet, however well-known, it does not seem to have been translated into action; George Monger's research (*Folklore* 105 (1994), 104–8) presents figures showing that despite fluctuations at different periods May has never been the least popular month for weddings, and sometimes was one of the most favoured.

See also *May Day, *May Dew.

Opie and Tatem, 1989: 240–6; Lean, 1902–1904; N&Q 1s:3 (1851)20; 1s:7 (1853) 152.

may (the plant), see *HAWTHORN.

mazes. The mazes of folk tradition are not intended as puzzles; they are single-track coiling patterns cut in turf and used for communal sport, the point being to run round them without stumbling or touching the banks even at the sharp bends. Having reached the centre, the runner retraces his steps along the same path to emerge. *Aubrey noted that one in Dorset had been 'much used by the young people on Holydaies and by ye School-boies', and that 'There is a Maze at this day in Tuthill fields, Westminster, & much frequented in summer-time on fair afternoons' (Aubrey, 1686/1880: 71).

Eight such labyrinths survive, including those at Alkborough (Humberside), Saffron Walden (Essex), and Winchester (Hampshire). At least a hundred more have disappeared for lack of maintenance. On the island of St Agnes in the Scillies there is one marked out with small boulders; it was clumsily 'restored' in 1989, so now neither the site nor the design is accurate.

Several English mazes are named 'Troy Town' or 'Walls of Troy', terms probably derived from a passage in Virgil (*Aeneid,* v. 545–603) describing the 'Troy Game', a test of skill in which young riders manœuvered along a mazy track. Since medieval and Elizabethan English believed themselves to be descended from the Trojans, the appeal is obvious.

There is no way of dating these mazes, nor are they likely to be all equally old; a range of dates from the late Middle Ages to the 18th century is plausible. On the Continent, mazes can symbolize penance or pilgrimage, and some scholars have proposed this interpretation for English ones too. However, surviving English traditions are non-religious: the Winchester maze is said to have been cut by a schoolboy, that on the Scillies by a lighthouse keeper, a lost one at Shrewsbury was called 'The Shoemaker's Race' and was maintained throughout the 17th century by the city's shoemakers' guild for their annual Whitsun feast.

Pennick, 1990. Matthews, 1922, is accurate up to that date, but more mazes have since been discovered.

medicine. 'Folk' medicine is an accumulation of very diverse techniques and beliefs, on which many layers of cultural history have left a mark; it could never have been known in its entirety to any one community, let alone one individual. The two primary aspects, predating any written records, are a practical knowledge of the effects of *herbs and plants, and the principles of *magic by contact or similarity. An important principle was that disease could be transferred from one person to another, or to an animal or object. This is obvious in *wart cures, and in the notion that *onions 'draw' infection; it is probably one factor in more complex rituals such as passing a child with hernia through a split *ash. Perhaps the widespread belief in the curative touch of a *dead hand implied that the ailment would go with the dead man to his grave; however, contact with death seems to have been effective in itself, judging by the healing power attributed to *skulls, *coffin nails, *churchyard earth, and similar grim objects.

Christianity had a strong impact on folk medicine. From Anglo-Saxon times onwards, instructions for gathering or administering medicinal herbs routinely involved making the sign of the cross, and repeating formulas of prayer. Many traditional verbal charms, such as those for *toothache, *nightmare, and *burns, invoke the power of Jesus, or of saints and angels. The medicinal efficacy of *cramp rings, *Good Friday buns, rain falling on *Ascension Day, and much else, rested ultimately on religious associations.

Other traditional cures seem arbitrary: keep a potato in your pocket against rheumatism; give a child cooked *mice for bed-wetting or whooping cough; eat a live *spider for ague; take powdered cockroaches, or woodlice in wine, for dropsy—and very many more. It would be wrong to call such things 'magic', for there was nothing supernatural about them; they were taken for granted as natural properties of everyday items.

When the sickness was itself attributed to *witchcraft, magical *counterspells would be set in motion, often under the guidance of a *cunning man or woman. Others gifted with healing powers were *charmers, *seventh sons or daughters, and (in the case of *king's evil) the anointed monarch. Certain personal peculiarities also made one a healer for certain ailments; thus, a 'left twin' (survivor of a pair where the other had died) could cure thrush by blowing three times in the sufferer's mouth (Latham, 1878: 38); bread and butter made by a couple named Joseph and Mary would cure *whooping cough (Hole, 1937: 10–11); so would anything recommended by any man riding a piebald horse (Opie and Tatem, 1989: 305–6). How long such ideas have existed, or

how they began, is beyond conjecture; one must simply accept that traditional medicine ranges from sound pragmatic advice, through symbolism, to downright silliness.

See also *HERBS and *CHARMS (verbal).

For an assessment of the effectiveness of herbal treatments, see Hatfield, 1994. Books on regional folklore almost always include cures, and there is a good selection from all over England in Wright, 1913: 239–56.

megaliths, see *STANDING STONES.

mell supper. 'Mell' was the dialect word for the last sheaf cut in the *harvest field across the northern counties of England, and the Mell Supper was the Harvest Home gathering to celebrate. In addition to the general feasting and dancing, there was a tradition in some areas for certain 'acts' to be performed—one given in full by Gutch comprises a sung dialogue between Polly and, in succession, an old man, an old lady, and a squire, and the latter she decides to marry. Another feature was a visit from the *Guisers, and it was customary to make a show of resistance to their entry (Blakeborough, 1898: 85–6).

Wright, *EDD*, 1903: iv. 82–3; Gutch, 1901: 257–66

Melton, John (d. 1640). Author and politician, Sir John Melton is of particular interest to folklorists because of his work, *Astrologaster, or, The Figure-Caster,* published in London in 1620. John Melton lived at a time when judicial or prognostic astrology played a high-profile political role, with warring factions regularly using predictions against each other, while Puritans raged against its ungodliness and sceptics such as Melton poured scorn on people's gullibility and the crooks and swindlers who profited by it. Lower down the social scale, there was widespread faith in fortune-telling of all kinds, and thus numerous professional fortune-tellers, a trade which is also satirized in Ben Jonson's *The Alchemist* (1610). *The Astrologaster* is a highly readable attack on these fortune-tellers, prognosticators, astrologers, and purveyors of omens, and Melton's description provides a wealth of detail about their methods. But the most important section for our present purposes is his list of 33 *superstitions, which is one of the earliest attempt at a systematic listing. He blames the cunning-men and figure-casters for their invention and dissemination. He also includes the detail that some of these fortune-tellers pretended to be Gypsies to further impress the country-folk. The list is reprinted in *FLS News* 32 (2000).

DNB: Facsimile reprint of *Astrologaster*, introduced by Hugh G. Dick, Augustan Reprint Society (William Andrews Clark Memorial Library, Los Angeles), 1975.

memorates. A technical term for narratives describing how the speaker personally encountered a supernatural being or experienced a paranormal event, which he/she interpreted in terms of traditional beliefs. Some scholars, but not all, extend the term to cover those where it is a close relative or friend of the speaker who had the experience. Such accounts are excellent evidence for the currency of a belief and its emotional and social implications, but they have been less collected than *legends.

For discussion of English examples see Bennett, 1985: 87–97; 1989: 167–83; 1987.

memorials at death sites. During the late 1980s and 1990s, it became increasingly common to lay flowers at the scene of a murder or some dramatic accident, for instance a train derailment or the crash of a coach carrying children; other tokens, such as toys or football club scarves, are added if appropriate, and the chosen site may not be the actual scene of death but some other relevant place accessible to the public, for example at the gates of a school or club. These signs of communal grief can be on a very large scale; it is said that more than a million people visited Hillsborough football stadium in one week in 1989 to leave flowers and scarves in honour of those who died there. An early instance of this form of mourning was at Aberfan in 1966, when a landslide from a coal-tip destroyed a school, and wreaths sent from all over the world were laid out in a cross a hundred feet long (Vickery, 1995: 146).

A highly dramatic development occurred after the death of Diana Princess of Wales on 31 August 1997. Bouquets bearing personal messages were laid in huge numbers not only in London but in virtually every town and village in Britain—on the steps of churches and town halls, at war memorials, at market crosses, in parks, or at any other central site. Photographs, candles, balloons, and teddy bears were added; the tributes were left in place for about two weeks.

It is also becoming popular for small groups of friends and family to lay or hang flowers at the site of fatal road accidents and suicides as a private tribute to the victim. A photograph may be added, and the memorials may be tended for months or years. Less conspicuous forerunners of this custom in the late 19th and early 20th centuries were crosses scraped on the dust at the roadside, cut into turf, or painted on a wall to mark the scene of a fatality, and maintained over a period of time.

Vickery, 1995: 146–7; *FLS News* 19–21 (1994–5); Tony Walter, *Folklore* 107 (1996), 106–7; George Monger, *Folklore* 108 (1997), 113–14. For the older customs, see Barbara Freire-Marreco, *Folk-Lore* 21 (1910), 387–8; Barbara Aitken, *Folk-Lore* 37 (1926), 80; *The Antiquary* 32 (1896), 94–5.

menstruation. The Bible taught (Leviticus 15: 19–24) that a menstruating woman was not only 'unclean' in herself but polluted others. The scientific authority of Pliny's *Natural History* (AD 77), and many later medical writers, added that she could shrivel plants, kill bees, taint food, and cloud mirrors by her touch, her glance, her breath, or her mere presence—let alone her actual blood. Though many folklore collections avoid this topic, those that do mention it record beliefs and *taboos which seem similar everywhere, some of which were still current in the mid-20th century. During her period, a woman must not handle raw meat or go near ham that is being cured, for she will taint it; she must not enter the dairy, or milk will sour and butter-making will fail.

Theologians disagreed on how rigorously to apply to women the Leviticus rule that anyone 'unclean' must not approach 'the tabernacle or any holy thing'; some said they must not even enter a church, but in 579 Pope *Gregory instructed missionaries working in England to let them do so, and even receive Communion, since what was natural was not sinful (Bede, *Ecclesiastical History*, book I, chapter 27). In the 20th century, the debate was still not over; among Primitive Methodists, no menstruating woman could attend a church service (Porter, 1969: 22), and some Catholic girls thought (wrongly) that to take Communion then was a sin [JS].

Other folkloric warnings, current until recently, protected the woman herself from supposed risks. The best known was never to wash your hair or put your feet in cold water, or 'the blood will fly to your head and send you daft'; this echoes an outdated medical theory about misdirected menstrual blood reaching the brain and causing melancholia. It was also bad to have a bath or go swimming, either because 'the water will get inside' or because 'the water will turn black'. More unusual was the Lincolnshire rule, 'Don't walk in long grass, the snakes will smell you' (Sutton, 1992: 31).

The sudden surge of oestrogen which signals the onset of menstruation affects the sebacious glands, making *hair greasy, lanky, and unmanageable. Hairdressers avoid styling or tinting a woman's hair at this time, since the results will probably be poor. The current phrase 'a bad hair day' for a day when everything goes wrong may be based on the experience that pre-menstrual irritability, clumsiness, and greasy hair coincide [JS].

Sexual intercourse during menstruation was taboo; according to the Bible, it was a crime incurring the death penalty for both parties (Leviticus 20: 18), though secular law has never enforced this. Scripture also warned that 'menstruous women bring forth monsters' (II Esdras 5: 8), and medical writers agreed; a popular handbook, *Aristotle's Masterpiece* (1684, but often reprinted up to 1890), taught that it would probably result in abnormalities such as hairy infants or those with extra limbs (book I, chapter 5). Nowadays, it is occasionally said babies so conceived are *red-haired.

Porter, 1969: 21–3; Opie and Tatem, 1989: 247; Sutton, 1992: 16–32; Patricia Crawford, *Past and Present* 91 (May 1981), 47–73.

Merlin. A figure from Welsh legend, who entered English literature via *Geoffrey of Monmouth's *History of the Kings of Britain* (1136). There, he is a 'fatherless' youth, conceived by an incubus and gifted with prophecy, who becomes counsellor first to the British king Aurelius (for whom he transports and builds *Stonehenge) and later to Aurelius's brother Uther Pendragon, whom he magically helps in an illicit love-affair which results in the birth of *Arthur. In Geoffrey's *History* he plays no further part, but a Burgundian poem *c*.1200 has him continue as young Arthur's protector and adviser, a role later made familiar by Malory. Another strand of tradition, Welsh and Scottish rather than English but reflected in Geoffrey's poem *The Life of Merlin* (*c*.1150), shows Merlin as a tragic figure unconnected with Arthur, a crazed forest-dwelling recluse uttering mysterious verses and foretelling his own death. Medieval, Elizabethan, Victorian, and modern writers further elaborate Merlin's story.

Folk tradition stressed Merlin's prophecies. Geoffrey had previously composed the *Prophecia Merlini*, a series of obscure symbolic utterances, some alluding to political events of his own times, which he incorporated into his *History*; they were so vague that later generations easily found new applications for them. A later anonymous text in the same style, *The Last Kings of the English*, was also alleged to be Merlin's prophecy. Both were widely known, adapted, and used as propaganda in many medieval wars and rebellions, and in Reformation controversies (Thomas, 1971: 389–422). Compilers of almanacs, astrologers, and pamphleteers continued to exploit Merlin's name till the end of the 18th century.

Surprisingly, Merlin rarely features in English local lore, apart from his link with *Stonehenge. The town of Marlborough (Wiltshire) claims that its name means 'Merlin's Barrow' and that he rests under a mound in the grounds of the public school there; James I granted the town the motto *Ubi nunc sapientis ossa Merlini*.

mermaids. To judge from parallel beliefs elsewhere in northern Europe, the sea-dwellers of English folklore were probably originally tailless, but the concept of the fish-tailed mermaid (and merman), long established in Mediterranean lands as a development from the classical siren, arrived here early in the Middle Ages. The mermaid was regarded as a natural if freakish creature, not a supernatural being; according to classical writers, she lulled sailors to sleep by her singing and then drowned them or ate them. She made an excellent moral symbol for preachers, who identified her with the fatal attractions of wealth, sex, drink, etc. For this reason, mermaids are common in minor church sculpture; it is presumably as symbols of vanity that they acquired their comb and mirror, not known in classical art. The belief that they really existed persisted for centuries, reinforced by travellers' tales of sightings and captures, and also by fakes made up from monkeys and fish, which were common from the 16th to the 19th centuries.

Legends about mermaids are found in Cornwall and along the Welsh Border. At Zennor, a mermaid fell in love with a lad and lured him into the sea. Near the Lizard, a man named Lutey helped a stranded mermaid back into the water; she gave him her comb, and said he and his descendants would be able to break witches' spells and control demons, but nine years later she came for him and drew him under the waves. In the 1840s the folklorist Robert Hunt was told that several Cornish families claimed to have uncanny powers because of being descended from a mermaid or merman. On the other hand, a mermaid ruined Padstow harbour with sandbars, because someone there had shot at her.

The mermaids of the Welsh Border area do not live in the sea but in lakes and rivers. At Marden (Herefordshire) a church bell once fell into a deep pool in the river, where a mermaid seized it (Leather, 1912: 168-9). At Child's Ercall (Shropshire) a mermaid from a pool was about to give some men 'a lump of gold, big as a man's head, very near', but one swore in amazement, and she shrieked and vanished (Burne, 1883: 78).

Benwell and Waugh, 1961: 140-50.

mermen. Far rarer than *mermaids in English tradition, but the Suffolk chronicler Ralph of Coggeshall, about c.1210, tells how some fishermen netted a naked, bearded, hairy-chested 'wild man' who looked human 'in all his parts'—i.e. he had no tail. He could not speak; he ate most things, but liked raw fish best. He escaped into the sea once, but returned of his own accord; later he escaped again, this time for good. Ralph comments: 'Whether he was a mortal man, or a kind of fish bearing a resemblance to humanity, or an evil spirit lurking in the body of a drowned man . . . it is difficult to decide.'

Merrie England. The phrase is used to describe a particular arcadian attitude to the past, prevalent in Victorian and Edwardian times but with roots stretching back to the turn of the 19th century and with continuing power to the present day. As such it is an imprecise and unscientific concept, but is none the less useful for describing certain historical attitudes and processes which constituted an important part of the Victorian world-view, and had a profound effect on many traditional festivals and customs. It was particularly popular with writers like Walter Scott who specialized in conjuring a past which was contrasted to the present:

> England was merry England, when
> Old Christmas brought his sports again

(Walter Scott, *Marmion* (1808), introd. Canto VI)

Merrie Englandism is essentially nostalgic. It takes it as given that however much society has progressed materially it has lost something important on the way, and this loss is primarily in terms of 'community'. In Merrie England the social classes were held together in an interlocking web of duties and obligations. The peasants were poor but honest, strong, and happy, their children were well fed and also happy, and the squire or lord of the manor cared for his people as a father would his family, while a benign parson looked after their spiritual needs. At certain points in the year, the people sang, danced, and made merry—in spring, summer, and autumn on the village green or in the fields, while at Christmas the squire threw open his hall, as dictated by his 'old English hospitality'. The adherents of the Merrie England school sought to recreate this golden age, and one of their key tools was to reform the pastimes of the poor which had, quite clearly in their eyes, lost both their innocence and their traditional values.

I value every custom that tends to infuse poetical feeling into the common people, and to sweeten and soften the rudeness of rustic manners, without destroying their simplicity . . . (Washington Irving, *Bracebridge Hall* (1822))

This was the problem. Before customs could be reinvented, they had to be shorn of the undesirable features which they had gathered from being in the hands of the working classes for too long. Sometimes it could be blamed on urban influences:

The people of this neighbourhood are much attached to the celebration of wakes; and on the annual return of these festivals, the cousins assemble from all quarters, fill the church on Sunday, and celebrate Monday with feasting, with musick, and with dancing. The spirit of old English hospitality is conspicuous among the farmers on these occasions; but with the lower sort of people, especially in the manufacturing villages, the return of the wake never fails to produce a week, at least, of idleness, intoxication and riot . . . (Revd A. Macaulay, *The History of Claybrook* [Leicestershire], (1791); quoted in Golby and Purdue, 1984: 17).

The transformation of both the myth and the reality of the major festivals was only possible because of other changes brought about by a sustained attack on traditional working-class merrymaking and leisure pursuits. Customs involving animals, such as *bull-running, bull-baiting, *cock-fighting, throwing at *cocks (but not grouse-shooting or fox-hunting), all came under pressure by the mid-19th century, and were suppressed. Violent sports like street *football and potentially dangerous crowd-based celebrations such as *November the Fifth were similarly suppressed or brought under increased control, and customs where people got drunk or where the sexes met in unsupervised merrymaking were reformed or removed.

Some of this reform took place as a result of national campaigns by such bodies as the Royal Society for the Prevention of Cruelty to Animals, and various Temperance Societies, but in most cases pressure was brought to bear at local level. The combined power of the squire, magistrate, parson, schoolteacher, doctor, solicitor, and the respectable trade and business people of the area was increasingly focused on the recreations of the people, in a combination of outright opposition, accommodation, and diversion of energies. Thus, the mob could be prosecuted under new by-laws against lighting bonfires and fireworks in the street, but would be encouraged to attend a communal bonfire in a field provided by a local farmer or the town council. May Day could be shorn of its hard-drinking and fighting *morris dancers, while the schoolteacher devised a 'morris dance' for children.

Merrie Englandism generally came after these battles had been won, and its ways were more subtle. Countless novelists, magazine journalists, poets, and pageant-masters extolled the virtues of past May Days, and old-time Christmases. Rural life portrayed on the stage could be counted on for a maypole or invented morris dance, the newly transformed village fête could be specially designed and, later on, historical pageants could lend the final gloss of 'historical accuracy'. The two main focuses for Merrie Englandism were *Christmas and *May Day, and both these festivals were completely transformed, in their own way, during the 19th century, but other customs, such as *well-dressing and *rushbearing, received similar treatment on a smaller scale.

The process was still in full force up to the First World War. The Merrie England Society, for example, founded by Joseph Deedy in 1911, and still in operation, included in its objects:

The propagation of May festivals, the encouragement of national songs and dances, the brightening of outdoor life, the fostering of local pageants and festivities, and the preservation of desirable old customs (*Kentish Mercury* (9 May 1913), 3, quoted by Judge, 1987: 411)

One remarkable thing about the whole process was the fact that these new features could be presented as 'traditional' and immediately accepted as being the real thing. Thus, ballet-masters who had devised a dance for representation on stage, or for a pageant, could quite seriously bill their creations as 'the age-old morris dance', or an 'Elizabethan May Day'. Not only did they invent new forms of festival but they invented a history to legitimate them, based loosely on the early antiquaries such as *Strutt and *Brand but with a great deal of embroidering and imagination.

By mid-Victorian times, the past invoked by the demure revivals of maypoles and rush-bearing was too vague to be capable of any precise chronological location. But the attributes of Merry England were constant: a contented, revelling peasantry and a hierarchical order in which each one happily accepted his place and where the feast in the baronial hall symbolised the ideal social relationship (Keith Thomas, *The Perception of the Past in Early Modern England* (1983), 22)

The features of many of the festivals which we now take for granted, and which we believe to be 'old', have been shaped by the Merrie England process.

Roy Judge, 'Merrie England and the Morris', *Folklore* 104 (1993), 124–43; Roy Judge, 'May Day and Merrie England', *Folklore* 102 (1991), 131–48; Judge, 1979: 58–65; Malcolmson, 1973; J. M. Golby and A. W. Purdue, *The Civilisation of the Crowd* (1984).

Merry Maidens, see *NINE MAIDENS.

mice. Used in folk *medicine for a wide range of ailments—most commonly for bed-wetting, but also for *whooping cough, sore throats, and various fevers. They might be boiled, roasted, fried, or reduced to powder and 'given in some pleasant or delightsome drinke', as Edward Topsell advised (*The Historie of Foure-Footed Beastes* (1607), 515), or mixed with jam and served as a sandwich. Cures of this kind were still occasionally used in rural areas in the 1930s.

In some places where belief in *witchcraft persisted into the 20th century, it was thought that the witch's *familiars were white mice, which she would keep in a box; she could not die till she passed them on to a relative. Stories about this were well remembered in Canewdon (Essex) in 1960, with reference to women who had lived there around 1900 (Maple, 1960: 246–7); the belief is also recorded in Sussex in the 1930s (Simpson, 1973: 76).

Mice are considered an *omen of bad luck, sickness, or death if they arrive in large numbers in a house previously free of them, enter a bedroom, gnaw someone's clothes, or run across someone's body. To get rid of them, one should speak to them politely, explaining that their presence is inconvenient, and suggesting some other house they might prefer.

Michaelmas. The feast of St Michael the Archangel, 29 September, is one of the *Quarter Days, a date for the payment of rents and the beginning or ending of hiring engagements (see *hiring fairs). It was also a day for feasting, the traditional fare being a roast goose, fattened on the stubble fields; such geese were sometimes presented by tenant farmers to their landlords. It was said that 'if you eat goose on Michaelmas Day you will never lack money all year'.

Michaelmas goose. In past centuries, the traditional connection between Michaelmas and the goose was as strong as it is today between Christmas and the turkey. Everybody who could afford to ate a goose on St Michael's Day (29 September), and had probably been doing so since at least the 15th century:

1471 A certain John de la Hay was bound to give William Barnaby, Lord of Lastres, Herefordshire, for a parcel of demesne lands, one goose fit for the lord's dinner on the feast of St Michael. (N&Q 3s:4 (1863), 400)

It was not uncommon for such stipulated gifts of seasonal food to be included in *manorial tenancy agreements and as Michaelmas was a Quarter Day when rents were normally paid, and geese were in their prime at that season, this would have helped to perpetuate the custom.

A historical legend seeks to explain the connection between bird and day: Queen Elizabeth I was eating a goose on Michaelmas Day 1588 when she heard of the defeat of the Armada. She therefore declared that everyone should do so every year to commemorate the great victory. Unfortunately for the legend, it can be seen that the connection antedates the Armada by at least 100 years, and anyway that victory was in August.

Wright and Lones, 1940: iii. 81–4; Brand, 1849: i. 367–71.

midday. Theoretically, midday should be as important as *midnight in the daily cycle of *time, but this is not so in English lore—probably because the noonday sun is very rarely uncomfortable, let alone dangerous, in the English climate. Interestingly, one of the few magical rituals prescribed for noon was done on *Midsummer Day; this coinciding of the midpoint of the summer and the daylight hours presumably redoubled its efficacy. It is only in childlore that midday is regularly significant: for schoolchildren, customary periods of permitted tricking or tormenting generally stop at noon, for example *April Fool jokes.

Midgley Pace-Eggers. Midgley, West Yorkshire, has the best-known team of Pace-Eggers, who perform their version of the *mumming play every *Good Friday in the village and surrounding areas. The custom had died out in Midgley around the time of the First World War, but was revived in 1932 by the local schoolmaster with a team of boys, and the play has been performed every year since, still under the auspices of the school.

H. W. Harwood and F. H. Marsden, *The Pace Egg: The Midgley Version* (1935); Sydney Moorhouse, *Country Life* (16 Apr. 1938), 398; John Brennan, *ED&S* (Summer 1976), 50–1.

Mid-Lent Sunday, see *FIG SUNDAY, *MOTHER'S DAY, *MOTHERING SUNDAY.

midnight. In the daily cycle of *time, midnight represents the deepest point of negativity, when *ghosts, *demons, and all uncanny beings are most active. It is prescribed for many *magic rituals and *divinations. In modern times it is mathematically defined, so one is told that such-and-such will happen 'when the clock strikes twelve'; regarded thus, it derives much of its significance from its ambiguous status—does it belong to the day that has just ended or to that which is beginning? However, in earlier centuries the term was more loosely applied, to a period rather than a point of time; it is not clear how long this was considered to be, but all supernatural evil forces were supposed to vanish when the *cocks first crowed.

Confusingly, midnight is also a time for certain celebratory rites, such as *first footing and seeing the *New Year in. This is because by modern reckoning a day begins at midnight (not at sunset, as in ancient cultures), so the day which inaugurates a new cycle must be launched with joyful and luck-bringing rituals at the earliest opportunity.

For powers attributed to those born at midnight, see *CHIME HOURS.

midsummer (23/4 June). Astronomically, the summer solstice is 21 June, but tradition throughout Europe reckons 24 June as Midsummer Day, and calls the night of 23/4 Midsummer Eve, Midsummer Night, or *St John's Eve, since 24 June is the feast of St John the Baptist. In England, the main folkloric features of the season were *bonfires, processions, and *divinations; it was the date for seeking the magical *fernseed, or the 'coal' under the roots of mugwort.

The earliest description of midsummer celebrations, by the 14th century monk John Mirk, of Lilleshall, Shropshire, turns out on examination to be quoting from a continental writer but is often cited as describing his own experience and has thus influenced subsequent ideas on the nature of midsummer celebrations and the etymology of the word *bonfire. John Stow provides a more useful and vivid description of midsummer festivities in London in the 1590s, which gives details of local street bonfires, domestic decorating customs, and also spectacular processions:

In the months of June and July, on the vigils of festival days, and on the same festival days in the evenings after the sun setting, there were usually made bonfires in the streets, every man bestowing wood or labour towards them; the wealthier sort also before their doors near to the said bonfires would set out tables on the vigils furnished with sweet bread and good drink . . . These were called bonfires [i.e. 'boon' or 'good' fires] as well of good amity amongst neighbours that being before at controversy, were there, by the labour of others, reconciled . . . and also for the virtue that a great fire hath to purge the infection of the air . . . (Stow, 1598: 125–9)

Stow continues to describe people's doors bedecked with 'green birch, long fennel, St John's Wort, orpin, white lillies, and such like, garnished upon with garlands of beautiful flowers' and oil-burning lamps. He then writes at length about the marching processions, with 'whifflers, drummers and fifes, standard and ensign bearers, sword players, trumpeters on horseback, demilances on great horses, gunners with hand guns, or half hakes, archers in coats of white fustian . . .' and *giants, *morris dancers, torch-bearers, and many more.

Midsummer processions in London first enter the documentary record as an outgrowth of the system of policing the city called the Watch; men who patrolled the streets at night to prevent wrongdoing and keep the peace. These Watchmen also provided the authorities with a ready-made bodyguard and they were thus ordered by the Corporation, in 1378, to accompany the aldermen in procession on Midsummer and St Peter's Eve. Over the next two centuries the Midsummer Watch processions grew ever more spectacular and sumptuous, as each Lord Mayor attempted to make his mark. Outside London, midsummer was similarly a popular time for municipal processions, especially once these had been divorced from their religious guild origins by the Reformation and taken over by civic authorities. In Norwich and Chester, among other towns, the Mayor and other dignitaries would ride in splendour, without the saints and candles of pre-Reformation times, but still with a dragon, a giant, or other secular effigies. At some places, the effigies could come out on their own: 'At Burford (Oxfordshire), annually, and still within memory, on Midsummer Eve, the men used to carry a figure of a dragon up and down the town. A giant was also added, for what reason I do not know . . .' (Robert Plot, *The Natural History of Oxfordshire* (1677), chapter 10).

Like many popular pastimes, midsummer bonfires came under increasing pressure from Puritan reformers in the 16th and 17th centuries, and were all but extinguished in most of the country during that time. Some, however, survived (or were revived) and lasted long enough for the 19th-century folklorists to find traces of them, particularly, it seems, in the west country and the extreme north of the country. In rural areas, communal fires were lit and people danced and generally ate, drank, and made merry around them, and young men made a point of leaping through the flames when they had died down somewhat, which some commentators like to see as ritual purification but is just as likely to be simple male showing off. Nevertheless, a continuing thread throughout the history of traditional bonfire customs, which has not been totally manufactured by early folklorists, is the notion that the fire and its smoke is beneficial and purifying, keeping at bay disease and misfortune—from crops, cattle, and people. But there is no mention of anything like this in many later reports, which stress the good clean fun of outdoor summer evening festivities. One such is the description of midsummer celebrations in Penzance (Cornwall) in 1801, which describes the fire itself, *tar barrels on poles, fireworks frightening the ladies, and a long game of *Thread the Needle through the streets of the town. The following day was mainly taken up with a fair and boat trips (R. Polwhele, *History of Cornwall* (1816), i. 49–51, quoted in Wright and Lones, 1940: iii. 7–8).

Midsummer Eve was one of the key nights for *love divinations, some of which are unique to the season, while others also turn up at other times, such as *St Mark's and *St Agnes's Eves. A belief reported several times under the title of the 'Midsummer Rose'— from Cornwall, Devon, Worcestershire, and elsewhere—concerns the plucking of a rose on Midsummer's Day, although further details then vary. In the longest form (noted in 1833):

if a young woman, blind-folded, plucks a full-blown rose, on Midsummer day, while the chimes are playing twelve, folds the rose up in a sheet of white paper and does not take out the rose until Christmas day, it will be found fresh as when gathered. Then, if she places the rose on her bosom, the young man to whom she is to be married will come and snatch it away. (A. E. Bray, *Borders of the Tamar and the Tavy* (1879), ii. 120)

In another version she must walk *backwards into the garden. Further examples of divination out of many possible: (Hertfordshire) maidens can pluck St John's Wort on Midsummer Eve and judge their matrimonial chances by seeing if the plant is still fresh in the morning; (Somerset) during the night of Midsummer Eve, a girl must go to the churchyard and wait for the stroke of twelve. She must have rose leaves, and a herb such as rosemary in her hand. At the first stroke of midnight she must start to run round the church, scattering the leaves and singing softly: 'Rose leaves, rose leaves, Rose leaves I strew, He that will love me, Come after me now' (Wright and Lones, 1940: iii. 16). At noon on Midsummer Day, in the 17th century, girls would dig up *plantains, seeking a 'coal' under the roots; they put it under their pillows to dream of future husbands (Aubrey, 1696: 131).

Shakespeare's *Midsummer Night's Dream* cleverly exploits the association of this date with love, sleep, dreams, and magic; it also implies that encounters between humans and fairies were likely at this season. Such an idea would have good parallels in European folklore, but references to it in England are surprisingly scarce. It may be that in Elizabethan times, when fairy-lore was more vigorous, the notion was common, or perhaps Shakespeare was drawing more on foreign parallels than has hitherto been realized.

See also *FERNSEED, *HEMPSEED, *ORPINE.

Wright and Lones, 1940: iii. 6–23; Brand, 1849: i. 298–337; Hutton, 1996: 311–21; Lean, 1902–5; Dyer, 1876: 311–31.

midwinter. Although the astronomical solstice is 21 December, 'midwinter' is a looser concept. Anglo-Saxons used the term *Yule to cover a period of some weeks on either side of the solstice, and in medieval times there were links running from the feast of *St Nicholas (6 December) to Christmas Day, and from Christmas to *Epiphany, or even *Candlemas, which have left traces on the folk customs of these dates. Nowadays, most people would probably see midwinter as centred on 25 December, but extending to cover New Year's Day and the Twelve Days of Christmas.

migratory legends. A legend which is found repeatedly at different places, having the same plot in every case but with place names and/or topographical details tailored to fit the individual site, is called 'migratory' (e.g. *Devil's Dyke, *Hangman's Stone). Owing to the wide distribution of these story-patterns, both in Britain and on the Continent, it is assumed they have circulated for several centuries; some can be proved to have medieval or classical forerunners.

To facilitate identification, a numbering system was devised by Reidar Th. Christiansen on the basis of Norwegian examples (*The Migratory Legends* (1958)). It is used in Briggs, 1970–1, and in most professional collections since the 1960s, but needs further expansion.

milk. The care of cows, milking, and buttermaking were surrounded by multiple magical precautions and fears, presumably because they were subject to difficulties which were poorly understood. Various diseases could cause cows to yield bloody milk, or none, and poor-quality milk or poor hygiene in the dairy could make churning futile, but these failures were often blamed upon *witchcraft. To guard against this, protective charms and plants were placed in or beside cattle-sheds, the cows were blessed and *wassailed, and if need be *countercharms would be used. An alternative explanation for bloody milk was that it was a punishment for the wickedness of stealing a *robin's or *swallow's eggs.

Cattle diseases might also be blamed on witches, as is seen from accounts of *counterspells involving *hearts and pins or burning one of the dead beasts. Whenever a cow miscarried, the custom in Yorkshire was to dig a deep hole under the threshold of the byre and bury the dead calf there, feet up; this would prevent further trouble for many years, but would eventually have to be repeated (Atkinson, 1891: 62).

Dairy work also had its problems, for which magical remedies are reported from many districts. As milk sours easily in thundery weather, it was wise to put *thunderstones on the windowsill, and plant *bay, *elder, or *holly nearby. Witches might steal the goodness of the milk by spells, making it impossible to churn it into butter; the standard countercharm was to plunge a red-hot poker into the churn. The dairy could of course be protected by a *horseshoe or *hagstone, by a *rowan growing nearby; there was also a verbal *charm to be recited while churning:

> Come, butter, come!
> Come, butter, come!
> Peter stands at the gate,
> Waiting for a buttered cake.
> Come, butter, come!

milkmaids' garlands. A regular custom for *May Day and following days in English towns from the 17th to early 19th centuries. The young women who served the townsfolk with milk would dress up in their finest clothes (borrowed or hired if necessary), dance in front of their customers' houses, and collect money from them and passers-by. Several milkmaids would often band together, and their entourage would include a musician and the emblem of the custom, the garland. In most illustrations, the 'garland' was a pyramid-shaped structure of polished metal utensils and vessels such as tankards and plate, the shinier the better (again borrowed or hired for the occasion), topped off with flowers and ribbons. The maid would carry the garland on her head, as she carried her milk-pail the rest of the year, and at least some of them danced with the garland *in situ*. However, many sources show garlands grown too large and either carried on the head of an attendant male or even carried on poles between two men like a sedan chair. The milkmaids were also sometimes found in the company of the *chimney sweeps, who had a similar May Day street custom, with a *Jack-in-the-Green.

It is likely that in the earliest stages, the garland would simply have been the everyday milk-pail decorated with flowers and greenery to welcome the May. The milkmaids are first mentioned in the mid-17th century, although the references are brief and therefore ambiguous, such as Samuel Pepys in his *Diary* for 1 May 1667: 'Thence to Westminster in the way meeting many milk-maids with their garlands upon their pails, dancing with a fiddler before them', which may easily refer simply to flowers, but the earliest illustration, from Tempest's *Cryes of London* (1685–8, reprinted in Judge, 1979: 4) shows the fancy plate and tankard construction already in being. The custom was sufficiently respectable to take place in the highest company: 'On May-Day the Milk-Maids who serve the Court, danced Minuets and Rigadoons before the Royal Family, at St James's House, with great applause' (Read's *Weekly Journal*, 5 May 1733, quoted in *N&Q* 1s:3 (1851), 367).

The milkmaids' garland was still going strong in 1776, when Samuel Curwen, an American visitor, described meeting them in the street on May Day. But the custom had faded out by the early 19th century, leaving the May Day streets to the chimney sweeps. Hone also describes a different milkmaids' procession, seen in Westminster probably around the turn of the 19th century, or just before. The maid in question led a cow around the streets, both of them adorned with ribbons and flowers.

Judge, 1979; Hone, 1827: i. cols. 569–72; George L. Phillips, *Folk-Lore* 62 (1951), 383–7; Charles Phythian-Adams, in D. Fraser and A. Sutcliffe (eds.), *The Pursuit of Urban History* (1983), 83–104.

Minehead Hobby Horse. One of England's two surviving traditional *hobby horses, although less spectacular, and less well known, than the *Padstow Hobby Horse. He makes his appearance in the streets of Minehead, Somerset, briefly on the eve of May Day, on the Day itself, and the following two days, accompanied by musicians and attendants called Gullivers. These attendants had ceased to appear in the late 19th century, but were re-introduced in 1967. A description of the horse, from 1895, shows that it has not changed significantly to the present day:

a wooden framework about 6 feet long of this [boat] shape and narrow enough to rest on a man's shoulders; his head, covered by a hideous mask, appearing in the middle. All round the framework was nailed a drapery of sacking, reaching the ground, very rudely painted with circles, principally blue and white and a long hempen tail at one end was used to swish the boys and passers-by . . . The upper part of the framework was covered with odds and ends of ribbon hanging on both sides . . . (L. Chaworth Musters: MS note in Gomme papers, Folklore Society Archives, dated June 1895).

The earliest known account dates from 1830 and describes a 'grotesque figure' made by fishermen and sailors (James Savage, *History of the Hundred of Carhampton in the County of Somerset* (1830), 583–4).

Cawte, 1978: 168–74; Patten, 1974.

mirrors. The looking-glass is one of the handful of domestic items which have attracted more than their fair share of beliefs. Opie and Tatem identify fourteen different superstitions, and unlike those associated with the *fire, many of them can be shown to date back a long time. One of the best-known and often-quoted superstitions of the late 20th century is that breaking a mirror brings seven years bad luck, and this was the third most often reported item in our *Superstitions Survey 1998/9. The earliest known reference to this being unlucky comes from 1777, and it has been regularly reported ever since, but the 'seven years' is not mentioned until the mid-19th century (Sternberg, 1851: 172). Previous to that time, it was said to mean a death, or simply to be very unlucky. Sternberg is also the first to advise against letting a baby see itself in a mirror, which is subsequently reported from all over England—the result varying from bad luck, contracting rickets, or becoming cross-eyed. Young women especially have traditionally been warned against spending too much time looking at themselves in the mirror by stories that they will see the Devil if they do: 'Some years since I knew a very proud maid in Cambridge, an Alderman's daughter, who running to the looking-glass to view her self, as soon as ever she came home from hearing a sermon upon a Sabbath-Day she thought with her self that she saw the devil in the looking-glass, and thereupon fell distracted . . . ' (1691, quoted Opie and Tatem, 1989: 252).

The danger of seeing something you would rather not appears to be at the root of the cus-

tom of covering mirrors in a house when someone dies. The first known reference to this is in Orkney in 1786, and most of the recorded instances in England are to the northern counties. There are also one or two references to covering mirrors in the rooms of sick people. More common is the practice of covering mirrors in a *thunderstorm, although this is not reported before 1900. In another context, however, gazing into the mirror will reveal your future spouse, if you do it correctly. First mentioned by Burton, *Anatomy of Abuses* (1660), this form of *love divination has been reported up into the 20th century in various versions (Burne, 1883: 381).

More serious divination with a mirror, or other reflective surface, dates back to classical and biblical times, is mentioned in Britain since at least the 14th century, and is the basis for the modern cliché of the crystal-ball gazer. Reginald Scot (1584: book 13, chapter 19) pours scorn on the practices and illusions of those who purport to tell the future with a glass: 'But the woonderous devises, and miraculous sights and conceipts made and conteined in glasse, do farre exceed all other.' Similarly, John *Aubrey recorded the trial and execution of a witch at Salisbury, about 1649, who 'shewed people visions in a glasse, and that a maid saw the devill with her, with whom she made a contract and that she knew 'twas the devill by his cloven foot . . . ' (Aubrey, 1686: 261).

See also *GLASSES, DRINKING.

Opie and Tatem, 1989: 249–53.

Mischief Night. In the traditional calendar of the 19th and 20th centuries, Mischief Night was the evening on which children across the northern counties thought they had the right to cause havoc with tricks and other misbehaviour. Their antics included tying people's door knobs together, removing their gates, dustbin lids, or anything else left lying about, ringing doorbells and running away, or, in some accounts, throwing bricks through bus windows, putting fireworks through letterboxes, and smashing bus shelters. There is clearly a fine line, not always recognized by modern children, between naughty tricks and real vandalism. The accepted date of Mischief Night varies. In the 1950s the Opies reported 4 November as the key night across the counties of Lancashire, Cheshire, Yorkshire, Derbyshire, Nottinghamshire, and north Lincolnshire, but, according to Wright and Lones, reporting mainly 19th century accounts in more or less the same geographical area, it was 30 April. On the available evidence, the April date seems to have been the earlier one, but this is not yet proven. Both dates are on the eve of important children's festivals—*November the fifth and *May Day—and in the former case much of the pilfering was specifically aimed at gathering material for the next night's bonfire. In Yorkshire, *Halloween too was sometimes Mischief Night, and this is the regular time in parts of Scotland and Ireland. Most of the known references date from the 1850s onwards, and they are all from the counties listed above, except for the earliest, from the Scilly Isles in 1822, which is completely outside the area (quoted in Wright and Lones, 1938: ii. 196–7). Nevertheless, children in other areas played similar tricks at different times, such as *Shrovetide, under different names (see Hole, 1976: 210–11). Although not as widespread as formerly, Mischief Night has continued into the 1990s.

Wright and Lones, 1938: ii. 196–8; 1940: iii. 109; Opie and Opie, 1959: 255, 276–80; Hole, 1976: 210–11.

mistletoe. The reputation of mistletoe was created by Pliny in his *Natural History* (AD 77). He wrote that in Gaul the *Druids thought it sacred if it grew on an oak (which it rarely does); they believed it protected against injury by fire or water, made farm animals and women fertile, was an antidote to poison, and cured epilepsy. Virtually every herbalist and folklorist to mention mistletoe, from the 16th century to the present, has repeated this information, assuming it to be equally true of Ancient Britons. Many also claim it as the 'origin' of the very different English custom of using mistletoe as *Christmas decoration.

Yet it is not till 1648 that mistletoe is first listed (by *Herrick, in *Hesperides*, no. 893) among the many *evergreens decking churches and homes at Christmas, whereas *holly and *ivy are well attested in the Middle Ages. In 1656 William Coles noted in *The Art of Simpling* (p. 41) that it was 'carried many miles to set up in houses about Christmas time'. It became important in the late 18th century as part—soon, the most valued part—of the elaborate kissing boughs/bushes hung up in farmhouses and kitchens. There were rules as to when it must be taken down, which varied regionally; in some districts (e.g. Staffordshire and Warwickshire) it was given exceptional

treatment, being kept till the following year to protect the house from lightning and fire (Drury, 1987: 195–6).

Early antiquaries thought all types of Christmas foliage came from that used by ancient Romans at the Saturnalia; however, once mistletoe became especially popular, the more picturesque theory of Druidic origin gained ground. The very influential John *Brand claimed it was never used to decorate churches (Brand, 1849: i. 523–4), but recent research has shown he was wrong, at any rate for some regions such as Staffordshire, where churchwardens' accounts record repeated purchases of mistletoe (Hutton, 1996: 37; Drury, 1987: 195).

Susan Drury, *Folklore* 98 (1987), 194–9; Opie and Tatem, 1989: 253–6; Vickery, 1995: 240–3.

mock mayors. The annual election of a mock mayor was previously a common custom and while the details vary from place to place, the broad picture is similar. As the name suggests, the point of a mock mayor is to parody the real thing, to make fun of *civic pomp and ceremony and corporate complacency, or the pretensions of politicians and parliamentary candidates. Thus, regular features of the mock mayor ceremony are ridiculous rules for who can vote, the speeches before and after the election promising impossible or silly things, and grotesque clothing or regalia (a cabbage stalk as a mace was common). The new mayor is almost always paraded on a chair carried on the shoulders of his supporters amidst noisy scenes of celebration and joy. He naturally hands out favours and punishments as he sees fit. The whole affair, could, and often did, degenerate into a loud, drunken brawl, and it is this aspect which prompted local authorities to take steps to suppress the custom, although the pride-pricking parody may have been just as strong an incentive in many cases. The sarcasm was made more pointed by the fact that the mock elections often took place at the same time as the real ones, in periods when most of the population were denied a vote.

The most famous mock mayor celebration was the Mayor of *Garratt at Wandsworth, and other places which had the custom include Newbury (Berkshire) the 'Mayor of the City', Bideford (Devon) 'Mayor of Shamickshire', Oswaldkirk (Yorkshire), and Lostwithiel (Cornwall). Two surviving examples are the *Mayor of Ock Street and the Lord Mayor of

Kilburn, and a revived version at *Randwick, Gloucestershire. Other places also had analogous mock corporations and courts, such as the Court of Halgavor reported by Richard Carew's *Survey of Cornwall* (1602).

Wright and Lones, 1936–1940: numerous references; Gutch, 1901: 325–31.

moles (on the body). The significance of moles featured in *fortune-telling booklets from the 17th to the 19th centuries. They were thought to be signs of character or fate. One over the heart meant wickedness; over the spleen, a passionate nature, and poor health; on the right armpit or ear, wealth and honour, but on the left, the reverse (Hone, 1832: 739–40).

moles (the animal). Much used in folk cures, all of which involved trapping and mutilating the living animal. One or more of its paws would be cut off, sewn up in a bag, and worn round the neck (for *toothache, epilepsy, or *king's evil), or kept in the pocket (for rheumatism); it would then be released to die slowly, taking the disease with it. Its body cut in half, or the skin flayed off alive, would be bound to the neck till it rotted (for wens on the throat and goitre); its blood drunk in white wine cured epilepsy (Opie and Tatem, 1989: 256–7). According to Francis Grose (*A Provincial Glossary* (1790), 45), if you hold a mole in your hand till it dies your hands will acquire healing power.

Lincolnshire farm-workers used to rid their fields of moles by the same method as was more commonly used for *mice in a house:

Moles were a damn nuisance for eating what you'd planted, especially turnips and swedes, they seemed to love them. They were difficult to get shut of; we tried a number of ways but often we wrote them a note telling them to go away. You wrote on a bit of paper, 'I'm sick of you eating my stuff, bugger off to the next field', you put the note under a stone. It worked, but don't ask me why. (Sutton, 1997: 36)

Molly dancing. A customary dance tradition performed by men at the *Christmas/*New Year/*Plough Monday season in East Anglia in the 19th century and up to about the Second World War. It therefore comes under the classification of ceremonial *dance, but Molly dancing was not as well developed or complex as other dance forms such as *Morris or *Sword dancing and has therefore received much less attention. The performance was sometimes dismissed as 'just jigging about', but was loosely based on 19th-century social dances. Molly dancers wore ordinary clothes, decorated with ribbons and rosettes, and usually had blackened faces, and had at least one man dressed in women's clothes, while in some teams they all wore female clothes. They danced in the village street and collected money door to door and from passers-by, who sometimes joined in.

The earliest references so far discovered are found in local newspaper accounts for the 1820s, although the word 'Molly' in this context does not appear before 1866. There are definite affinities with *Plough Monday plough customs, and it is probable that Molly dancing developed from these, and like the ploughboys, Molly dancers had a reputation for being rough and ready, and even somewhat threatening. There has been renewed interest in recent years, and there are now many revival Molly dance teams. There are several possible derivations for the word 'Molly'. It could well be simply a form of 'Morris', as many customary dance or drama customs were locally termed 'morris dances'. However, 'Molly' is also common as a dialect word for a man dressed as a woman.

Elaine Bradtke, *Truculent Rustics: Molly Dancing in East Anglia before 1940* (1999); Joseph Needham and Arthur L. Peck, *JEFDSS* 1:2 (1933), 79–85.

Monkey Puzzle Tree. The *Araucaria araucana* was introduced from Chile in the late 18th century, and has since gathered a few traditions, although these are not very widely reported: 'It was an old Fenland belief that if a Monkey Puzzle tree was planted on the edge of a graveyard it would prove an obstacle to the Devil when he tried to hide in the branches to watch a burial. Many elderly Cambridgeshire people believe the tree is an unlucky one' (Porter, 1969: 63). Some children have also believed that you must stay silent as you passed one, or bad luck would surely follow.

Vickery, 1995: 245–6; Opie and Tatem, 1989: 260.

monstrous births. Minor defects in a newborn baby were generally explained as due to some shock or unpleasant sight at the moment of *conception, or during the mother's *pregnancy, but major malformations were regarded as God's *judgement on serious sin, especially lack of charity, blasphemy, or breaching a sexual taboo. These ideas were especially prevalent in the 16th and 17th centuries, and continued to appear in popular reprints of old works. Thus, an 1890 reprint of the pseudo-medical *Aristotle's Masterpiece* (1684) explained that 'some monsters are begotten by a woman's unnatural lying with beasts', as happened in 1603 when a child was born that was half-human, half-dog (p. 35); others because the parents made love while the woman was *menstruating (pp. 40–1).

monty. Until about 1914 children in Monmouthshire, Chepstow, and villages of the Wye Valley used to go from house to house early on *New Year's Day carrying 'a monty', which was an apple or orange standing on three sticks and decorated with holly or box leaves, nuts, tinsel, raisins, etc. In return for a few pence they would *display this 'for luck', chanting:

> Monty, Monty, Happy New Year,
> A pocket full of money and a cellar full of beer!

Round St Briavels (Gloucestershire), they were still seen in 1950.

Wright and Lones, 1938: ii. 30–1; I. Waters, *Folklore and Dialect of the Wye Valley* (1973), 11–13.

moon. The waxing moon was long thought to promote healthy growth; this was the time to plant seeds, cut one's hair (so that it would grow back thickly), or undertake new business; animals and children begotten or born with the waxing or full moon would thrive. Conversely, cutting corns and charming *warts should be done with the waning moon, to make them disappear; so should bloodletting, as too strong a flow would be dangerous. The interval between old and new moon is ill omened; a baby born then will die young, or grow up foolish, for 'No moon, no man'.

Equally common was the idea that the full moon affects the mad, worsening their symptoms; it was long considered medically sound, and still survives at the popular level. A related idea, current within living memory, was that it was dangerous to sleep in moonlight, either indoors or out of doors, especially when the moon was full; it could make one blind, or mad.

Customs observed on first seeing a new moon have been recorded from the 16th century to the present day; one should bow, curtsy, or kiss one's hand to it; one should turn over or count the money in one's pocket or purse, and/or spit on it, so that it may increase as the moon waxes; one should make a wish. But it is essential to have a clear view; to see the new moon through glass (or through a tree) brings bad luck. A *love divination known to Aubrey (1686/1880: 36) and still practised in the 19th century was for a girl to sit on a gate or stile to greet the new moon, and wish to see her destined husband in her dreams.

Opie and Tatem, 1989: 260–6, 279–83; also most regional collections.

moonrakers. One of the stock jokes about *fools is that they mistake the reflection of the full moon in a pond for a round cheese, and try to rake it out. The nickname 'moonrakers' is traditionally given to Wiltshire people, especially those from Bishops Cannings. It can be a jeer by outsiders; or, more often, it is proudly used by Wiltshire men themselves, with this explanation: once, some smugglers from Bishops Cannings had hidden barrels of brandy in a pond, and were spotted by Excise men while trying to retrieve them. Challenged, they replied that they were 'only raking for that big cheese down there', pointing at the moon's reflection. The Excise men believed them—more fools they! Exactly the same story is told in Hampshire, while 'moonraker' as a term for a very foolish person occurs also in Herefordshire, West Yorkshire, and Oxfordshire (Wright, 1913: 181–2).

Wiltshire Archaeological and Natural History Magazine 50 (1943), 278–86, 411–16, 481–5.

moonwort. The fern *Botrychium Lunaria*, or Moonwort, was held to have a strong effect on metal. Its popular name was 'Unshoe the horse' as it was believed to draw the nails out of the shoes of any horse that trod on it, and a story is told by Culpeper and others to back it up: 'I have heard commanders say, that on the White Down in Devonshire, near Tiverton, there were found thirty horse shoes, pulled off from the feet of the Earl of Essex's horses, being there drawn up in a body, many of them being but newly shod, and no reason known, which caused much admiration . . .' (*Culpeper's Complete Herbal and English Physician* (1653), 163; 1826 edn., 98–9). Moonwort's other, more useful, attribute is that if put into a keyhole it will open the lock. Opie and Tatem given references to these beliefs back to 1591.

Opie and Tatem, 1989: 266; *N&Q* 11s:7 (1913), 108, 177.

mop fairs, see *hiring fairs.

Mordiford. In the 17th century, the village church at Mordiford, Herefordshire, had on its exterior wall a large picture of a *dragon with four pairs of wings, which was repainted several times before being finally erased when the church was repaired in 1810–12. It was locally taken to be proof that a monster had once lived there, and been killed—though as to how, and by whom, stories varied. The hero was usually said to have been a criminal who volunteered to fight the dragon instead of being hanged; he hid in a cider barrel, and either shot it dead through the bunghole or tricked it into attacking the barrel, which was studded with knives, so that it wounded itself mortally. But the dragon's deadly breath poisoned him, so he never enjoyed his victory.

J. Dacres Devlin, *The Dragon of Mordiford* (1848/1978); Simpson, 1980.

morris dance. The most widely known ceremonial *dance form in England, although the name includes a range of types and styles. The common features are that the dancers were almost invariably male, wore a special costume, and they danced for display on particular occasions and not normally at other times. Morris dancing is also one of the few *calendar customs that are popularly seen as archetypically English and is also one of the few with a demonstrable history back to the early modern period. There are a number of brief references in 15th century sources, the first known being in 1458, and by 1494 at least morris dancers were performing at the king's court:

2 Jan 1494 Privy purse expenses of Henry VII: For playing of the Mourice daunce £2 (and another on 4 Feb 1502) (quoted Hazlitt, 1905: 422)

By all accounts, morris dancing was hardly a rare occurrence in the 16th century, and could be included in a range of spectacular events at various times of year. In 1552–3, for example, Henry Machyn of London recorded four encounters with 'mores dansyng'; twice as part of the king's Lord of Misrule retinue (3 January 1552 and 4 January 1553), once accompanying a 'goodly may-pole' (26 May 1552), and once in the Sherriff of London's procession. These early references give little substantive information, but by the end of that century descriptions start to offer more detail. Philip Stubbes, complaining vociferously in 1583, writes of them bedecking themselves with 'scarfs, ribbons and laces', wearing

bells on their legs, waving handkerchiefs over their heads, and accompanied by hobby horses (Stubbes, 1583). For Shakespeare, a 'Whitsun Morris Dance' was proverbial (*Henry V*, II. iv). In Thomas Dekker's play *The Shoemaker's Holiday* (1599/1600), the shoemakers perform a morris dance to entertain the Lord Mayor, and in his *The Witch of Edmonton* (*c*.1623), one of the main characters plays the hobby horse, and the morris men are shown planning their performances and paraphernalia. Morris dancers are also featured, or at least mentioned, in many other 17th century plays, and early pictorial evidence is presented in the anonymous painting, *The Thames at Richmond, with the Old Royal Palace* (*c*.1620). Morris dancing thus existed in a number of social spheres, and in the absence of detailed information about the activity itself, scholars classify early references by their context, 'court', 'literary', and so on.

When more detailed information became available in the 19th and 20th centuries, scholars identified several types of morris dance, concentrated in different geographical areas, and featuring different styles of dancing, costume, and social organization. The labels assigned to these different types are a rough guide, but are not watertight categories. *Cotswold*: what most people think of as 'morris dancing', found in the area now referred to as the South Midlands; Chandler delineates the area as within an arc with a radius of 40 miles, with the heart of the Wychwood Forest as its centre and the Thames as the southern boundary (p. 23). The normal team has six dancers, plus a spare dancer or two, fool, musician, collector; dances are either handkerchief or stick dances; dancers wear bells on their legs. *North-west*: found only in the Lancashire/Cheshire area, with dances primarily designed for processional performance, such as accompanying rush-carts (see *rushbearing), and participation in carnivals and *wakes. Teams are much larger than in Cotswold, and costume more elaborate (*JEFDSS* 9:1 (1960), 42–55). *Border*: a group of dances collected in villages along the Welsh border, at one time dismissed as 'degenerate' Cotswold, but which could equally be regarded as ancestors of Cotswold (Burne, 1883: 477–82; Leather, 1912: 129–32; *JEFDSS* 9 (1963), 197–212). *Bedlam*: in recent years a group of references have been identified, which indicate a set of dances—labelled 'Bedlam' morris—which can be distinguished from other 'Cotswold' dances, characterized by stick and hand-clapping rather than handkerchiefs, the absence of bells, ribboned costume rather than baldricks, and often by blackened faces. Bedlam and Border morris also share a number of features, and Bedlam characteristics are found in certain Cotswold traditions. Further research is necessary to ascertain their true position in morris development. *Molly dancing:* a relatively simple type of dance, found only in East Anglia from the 19th century, but sufficiently distinct to warrant its own entry. *Carnival morris* developed from North-west during the 20th century, almost exclusively danced by young girls at fêtes and carnivals (JEFDSS 9:1 (1960), 42–55).

The key figure in the revival of interest in morris dancing was Cecil *Sharp, who had encountered the Headington Quarry dancers in 1899 and set about collecting more after being approached by Mary *Neal (in 1907) for dances to teach her *Espérance Club girls. At first working with Neal, but later in opposition after a very public disagreement over artistic standards, Sharp and others set about forging a national revival movement based on his collecting and library researches. The *English Folk Dance Society (EFDS) was formed in 1911/12, and its members sought to encourage morris, and other traditional dances, across the country. Numerous clubs were formed, and a nationwide revival was soon under way. Tensions in the revival rapidly surfaced, however, focusing on questions of style, artistic standards, and the role of women in teaching and dancing a 'masculine' dance form, and these tensions have never been fully resolved. The *Morris Ring was founded in 1934, as an umbrella organization for morris clubs, followed by the *Morris Federation in 1975. There are still hundreds of clubs up and down the country, who dance in a variety of styles.

Sharp's findings were first published in his *The Morris Book* (1907–13) although subsequent experience prompted him to publish heavily revised editions in 1912–13, and it is these second editions which are used today. Further collecting work after Sharp's time identified more village traditions, but also demonstrated that the neat static picture, implied by Sharp, with each village possessing a relatively discrete unbroken tradition stretching back into a remote past was not tenable. None of the places which had active teams in the late 19th century could prove a morris tradition back further than 200 years, and most could not

even approach this figure. As noted above, earlier references showed that morris had been found in a wider variety of contexts in previous years, and it is still not clear how it was transformed into the regionalized *calendar custom which the Edwardian collectors found.

See also *BAMPTON MORRIS DANCERS, *BETLEY WINDOW, *DANCE, *MOLLY DANCING, *BACUP COCONUT DANCERS, *SWORD DANCE.

Keith Chandler, *Ribbons, Bells and Squeaking Fiddles: The Social History of Morris Dancing in the English South Midlands 1660–1900* (1993); Keith Chandler, *Morris Dancing in the English South Midlands, 1660–1900: A Chronological Gazetteer* (1993); Mike Heaney, *An Introductory Bibliography on Morris Dancing* (1985); Cecil J. Sharp, *The Morris Book* (1907–13; 2nd edn., 1912–24); Michael Heaney, *Bedlam Morris* (1985); Roy Judge, 'The Old English Morris Dance: Theatrical Morris 1801–1880', *FMJ* 7:3 (1997), 311–50; John Forrest and Michael Heaney, 'Charting Early Morris', *FMJ* 6:2 (1991), 169–86.

Morris Federation. In the early 1970s, a dramatic rise in the number of women actively involved in *morris dancing gave rise to a bitter debate about females practising what had previously been considered an all-male dance form. Membership of the *Morris Ring, the older organization devoted to morris dancing, has always been restricted to men-only clubs. The Women's Morris Federation was thus formed in 1975 as an umbrella organization for women's morris dance teams. Since that time, much of the heat has gone out of the debate, although there are still men dancers who will have nothing to do with women's morris at all. The Federation changed its name to the Morris Federation in 1983 on the agreement to accept membership of all teams, whether male, female, or mixed, who agree with its aims, which include the clause '. . . encourage and maintain the practice of morris dancing by women and men of all ages'. The Federation has a membership of about 400 clubs, and coexists with the Morris Ring, and a third morris organization, Open Morris, in a spirit of co-operation and mutual assistance.

Morris Ring. An association of *morris dance clubs, founded in 1934 by six of the clubs then in existence. The *English Folk Dance Society (EFDS), founded by Cecil *Sharp in 1911, had been concerned with the teaching of morris dancing since its inception, but by the early 1930s there was a growing feeling amongst many dancers that the EFDS had moved too far from the traditional forms of morris dance, and that there was 'too much of the classroom and the examination hall' and what was lacking was 'the essential unit of the ceremonial dance, a coherent group of performers, learning, practising, and dancing together' (Abson, 1984: 11). Moves to break away from EFDS control had already been made ten years before by the Travelling Morrice founded in 1924 by Rolf Gardiner and Arthur Heffer, which made a point of dancing in the villages, and deliberately seeking out old dancers and other informants. Nevertheless close links between the two organizations were maintained, especially through key individuals such as Douglas *Kennedy.

The Ring remains an umbrella organization for morris clubs, with about 170 clubs as full members, plus about 70 associates, and it publishes *The Morris Dancer* and the *Morris Circular*. It holds an annual spring meeting at Thaxted, Essex (where it was founded), in addition to other meetings organized by member clubs up and down the country. One of the major areas of contention in the inter-war years had been the heavy involvement of women in the EFDS-led revival, and Gardiner was one of the many dancers who sought to return the morris dance to its full masculine glory. The Morris Ring still holds to its original rule that member clubs are for men only, and in the 1970s and 1980s the question of women and the morris dance became an openly contentious issue causing much bitter debate and the formation of rival organizations, the *Morris Federation and Open Morris. The question is no longer a major problem, and the three organisations now coexist in a spirit of co-operation and mutual assistance.

Walter Abson, *ED&S* 46:2 (1984), 11–12; Boyes, 1993: esp. 159–79.

Mother Bunch. Several Elizabethan writers allude jokingly to a notorious Mother Bunch who sold strong ale, kept a brothel, and seems to have been proverbial for coarse humour; various traditional jests and bawdy anecdotes were ascribed to her, for instance in a booklet of 1604, *Pasquil's Jests Mixed with Mother Bunches Merriments*. Later, her name was put to different uses; from the 17th century onwards there were *chapbooks where she figures as a wise old countrywoman, teaching a medley of *charms and magical recipes. *Mother Bunch's Fairy Tales* (1777) is a collection of elegant mor-

alistic *fairytales translated from French, where she is the supposed teller.

Mother Carey's chickens. This is a nickname among late 18th-century sailors for storm petrels, or for snowflakes. Mother Carey is never mentioned in any other connection; she was probably imagined as a crone who controlled bad weather. There is no evidence for the fanciful idea that the name is a corruption of *Mater Cara*, 'Dear Mother', supposedly a title of the Virgin Mary.

Mother Goose. In mid-17th-century France, the phrase *contes de ma mère l'oye* meant 'fairy-tales', and in 1697 it appeared on the frontispiece of Charles *Perrault's *Contes du Temps Passé*; when these were printed in English from 1729 onwards, they were entitled *Mother Goose's Tales*. Later (probably in 1765) the publisher John Newbery produced a collection of traditional *nursery rhymes, *Mother Goose's Melody*, which became so popular that for the next two generations all such rhymes were called 'Mother Goose songs', as they still are in the USA.

A pantomime of 1806 created a tale in which Old Mother Goose is a kindly witch, owning a gander on which she can fly, and a goose that lays golden eggs; soon chapbooks elaborated the story, adding a stupid son named Jack, who unwittingly buys the magic goose. This became popular in Victorian children's books, especially in a rhymed version of 1820.

Opie and Opie, 1951: 30–42, and 1955: 88–90; Ryoji Tsurumi, *Folklore* 101 (1990), 28–35.

Mother Goose rhymes, see *NURSERY RHYMES.

Mothering Sunday. On Mothering Sunday, or Mid-Lent Sunday (fourth Sunday in Lent), children and young people living away from their parents would make a point of going home for the day, taking presents, usually including a cake for their mother, and sharing a meal with their family before returning. This day was particularly important for apprentices, live-in farmworkers, and girls in service, and it was generally accepted that they had a right to the day off. The earliest two references to the custom come hard on the heels of each other in the mid-17th century:

Every Midlent Sunday is a great day at Worcester,

when all the children and god-children meet at the head and cheife of the family and have a feast. They call it the Mothering-day'. (Diary of Richard Symonds, 1644)

and, in Robert Herrick's oft-quoted poem *A Ceremonie in Glocester*: 'I'le to thee a Simnell bring, 'Gainst thou go'st a mothering' (*Hesperides*, 1648).

The first two references are thus from the same western side of the country and support the idea that this was a regional custom which later spread to other parts of western and midland England (and Wales) but was never universal. Several writers make a point of saying that they had never heard of it before, for example in *N&Q* (4s:5 (1870), 399–400) and *Gentleman's Magazine* (1784: 343), but it persisted into the early 20th century in some areas. The visiting gradually died out as living-in with employers became a rarity. The elements that are almost always mentioned are the foodstuffs; either the items taken by the returning youngsters, or the traditional dishes eaten at the home, and variant names for the day were often derived from the food involved.

Several authorities maintain that the ultimate origin of the day is to be found in a previous Church custom in which parishioners went in procession at mid-Lent to visit their Mother Church—hence the name Mothering Sunday. There is no proof either way, but given the regional nature of the family-visit Mothering Sunday it seems unlikely that there is a connection between the two customs.

During the later 20th century, a subsidiary custom developed, based on the local church, with clergy handing out little posies of flowers, and sometimes pieces of cake, to children to give to their mothers. But a much stronger influence came from the USA, from where the invented *Mother's Day was introduced soon after the Second World War, although it was placed on Mid-Lent Sunday rather than the fixed American date. Most British people now use the term Mother's Day, although churchgoing families still tend to call the day Mothering Sunday. It is likely that the latter term will continue to lose ground to the more widely used Mother's Day.

Charles Edward Long (ed.), *Diary of the Marches of the Royal Army During the Great Civil War Kept by Richard Symonds* (Camden Society, 1859), 27; Wright and Lones, 1936: i. 42–51; Hutton, 1996: 174–7.

Mother's Day. Created almost single-handedly by Miss Anna Jarvis of Philadelphia who persuaded Congress, in 1913, that the second Sunday in May would be dedicated to honouring mothers and motherhood. This was brought to Britain by American soldiers during the Second World War, and was later taken up by commercial interests, becoming extremely popular from the 1950s onwards. In Britain, however, the day chosen for Mother's Day was Mid-Lent Sunday, which had previously been the traditional day for *Mothering Sunday, which it in effect replaced. On the modern Mother's Day, children (and husbands) send cards, chocolates, flowers, etc., to their mothers, and many families make the mother breakfast in bed, or take over the housework for the day.

Mother Shipton. According to popular belief, Mother Shipton lived in Tudor times and foretold many major events in English history. A *chapbook of 1641 alleges she was born at Knaresborough (Yorkshire) in 1488 and died in her seventies; however, these details may be inaccurate. A later one (1684) is frankly fabulous, making her a devil's child and a witch. *Prophecies attributed to her were exploited in the Civil War.

In 1862 Charles Hindley, a hack writer and publisher, reprinted one of the old chapbooks, adding some rhyming 'prophecies' of his own invention, concluding dramatically:

> The world then to an end shall come
> In eighteen hundred and eighty-one.

These verses caused considerable alarm among the lower classes. Hindley later confessed he had written them himself (*N&Q* 4s:11 (1873), 355). Even so, there was panic when the Doomsday year arrived, especially around Brighton (Sussex), where Hindley's pamphlet had been printed; people deserted their homes and spent the nights praying in the fields. A few years earlier there had been a brief local panic in Somerset, because Mother Shipton was said to have prophesied that at midday on Good Friday 1879 Ham Hill would be swallowed by an earthquake and Yeovil destroyed by a flood (*Pall Mall Gazette* (Apr. 1879)).

Mother Shipton is still a tourist attraction at Knaresborough, where pamphlets about her are available; during most of the 20th century the Doomsday prediction appeared, but altered to read 'In nineteen hundred and ninety-one'.

William H. Harrison, *Mother Shipton Investigated* (1881);

Richard Head, *The Life, Prophecies and Death of the Famous Mother Shipton* (1684); the same, with additions by Charles Hindley (1862); Anon. *The Life and Prophecies of Ursula Southeil, Better Known as Mother Shipton* (Knaresborough, Yorkshire, no date, frequently reissued).

mountain ash, see *ROWAN.

mourning. The etiquette of mourning in the upper classes is well documented from medieval times onwards; it gradually spread into the middle classes, reaching a peak in Victorian times, particularly for women. Black clothing in matt fabrics was the essential feature, with crape hatbands and armbands for men, and veils for women. Women wore mourning for two and a half years for the death of a husband, but men only three months for a wife; both sexes wore it for a year for a parent, and for varying periods for other relatives. This was followed (for women) by grey, violet, or mauve 'half-mourning'. Very young children could wear white with black trimmings. Servants wore mourning whenever their employers did. The poor copied these customs as best they could; they dyed existing clothes when they could not afford new ones. Friendly Societies and Trade Unions sometimes kept a few plain black dresses to lend out to widows at members' funerals.

In the first half of the 20th century mourning etiquette was greatly reduced, though as late as the 1940s it was common to see people wearing black armbands or black diamond-shaped patches sewn to their sleeves for some while after a death, and a black outfit was still necessary for everyone attending a funeral. Nowadays, no outward marks of bereavement are displayed except on the day of the funeral, for which only close relatives dress entirely in black; for others, any quiet, dark colour will do, though men usually still wear black ties, and women black hats and gloves.

mouse, see *MICE.

mouths. On the analogy that an itch on particular parts of the body is significant of some future event, two early writers refer to an itching mouth or lips:

> My mouth has itched all this long day
> That is a sign of kissing at least

(Chaucer, 'Miller's Tale' (*c*.1387), lines 3683–4)

and John *Melton (1620: 47) similarly maintains that itching lips foretells a kiss. This meaning is so obvious that it seems odd that

these are apparently not confirmed by later authorities in England, although there are one or two in Scotland.

See also *TONGUES.

'Mowing Devil, The'. The *chapbook of this title, printed in 1678, sets out to prove the reality of the Devil by a cautionary tale of an amazing occurrence in Hertfordshire that August. A rich farmer, too mean to pay the wages which a labourer wanted for mowing his oats, angrily said 'that the Devil himself should Mow his Oats before he [the labourer] should have anything to do with them'. But God punished his greed and heartlessness. That night, the oatfield seemed to be on fire, yet next morning, when the farmer went to look at his oats:

he found the Crop was cut down ready to his hands; and as if the Devil had a mind to show his Skill in Husbandry, and scorned to mow them after the usual manner, he cut them in round circles, and plac't every straw with that exactness that it would have taken up above an Age for any Man to perform what he did that one night: and the man that owns them is as yet afraid to remove them.

The text is accompanied by a woodcut showing a small demon crouching over the oats, which lie in rings around him, the whole being surrounded by flames.

The chapbook was reprinted as a pamphlet by W. Gerish in 1913, and in his *Hertfordshire Folklore* (1970); it is mentioned in several books of local folklore (e.g. Jones-Baker 1977). In 1990 it was drawn into the controversy over crop circles.

Mr Fox. This tale (published in 1790) is the English equivalent to 'The Robber Bridegroom' in the *Grimms' collection and, more remotely, to *Perrault's 'Bluebeard'. A certain Lady Mary was wooed by a Mr Fox, and one day went alone to visit his house. It was empty, but she went in and passed through several doorways, over which was written: 'Be bold, but not too bold'. But she opened the doors, and found a room full of blood and bones. At that moment Mr Fox returned home, dragging a girl with him; as she gripped the bannisters he cut off her hand, and then killed her. Lady Mary, who had been hiding, managed to escape unnoticed, taking the fallen hand with her. Next time Mr Fox came to dine with her family, she said she wanted to tell a dream she had had, and began describing her visit to his house. At each stage, Mr Fox tried to stop her, saying:

It is not so, nor it was not so,
And God forbid it should be so!

But she went on telling her 'dream', and when she spoke of the hand, and he denied it in the same words, she produced it in front of everyone, saying:

But it is so, and it was so,
And here's the hand I have to show!

Whereupon the guests drew their swords, and instantly cut Mr Fox into a thousand pieces.

A Gypsy named Eva Gray told a leisurely, carefully detailed version of 'Mr Fox' to the collector W. H. Thompson at Grimsby in 1914, calling the villain 'Dr Forster'. A related story, recorded in some 19th-century collections of local folklore, tells how a girl agrees to meet her lover in some lonely place but arrives early and hides by climbing a tree; to her horror, when he does come he has a spade, and starts digging a grave. So she stays hidden, and later denounces him for planning to murder her.

'Mr Fox' is in Jacobs, 1894/1968: 92–4; Briggs, 1970–1: A. ii. 446–50; Philip, 1992: 158–62. 'The Cellar of Blood'/'Dr Forster' is in Briggs, 1970–1: A. i. 214–16 and ii. 390 (abridged); and in Philip, 1992: 166–86 (full text).

Mulberry Bush. There can be few English people who do not know at least the chorus and tune of the children's *singing game, 'Here we go round the mulberry bush'. The children hold hands in a ring and dance or walk round to this chorus, then stand still, drop hands, and carry out the actions prescribed by the verses: 'This is the way we wash our hands . . .', or 'This is the way we iron our clothes . . .', each describing an element of everyday domestic life. It is presumably the catchy tune (also known as 'Nuts in May' and 'Nancy Dawson') and simple repetitive form, which explain its widespread popularity in the 19th and earlier 20th centuries, but it is played nowadays almost exclusively by young children taught by adults. The game was first mentioned in the 1820s (in Scotland), and turns up regularly in collections of children's games, and some earlier versions have 'gooseberry', 'ivy', or 'holly' bush.

Gomme, 1894: i. 404–7; Opie and Opie, 1985: 286–92.

mumming. The word 'mumming' causes confusion, as it can refer to a number of relatively distinct customs, and many *visiting custom have borne the name, but by far the most widespread is the *mumming play (see below). In late medieval times, it was the fash-

ion amongst the nobility to stage elaborate 'mummings' which involved dressing up or disguising, such as wearing dragon, peacock, and swan heads, or dressing as angels. Other reports show that it was not only at court that people liked to disguise themselves at *Christmas, and there were several occasions when attempts were made to ban mummings and disguisings to prevent masked young men roaming the streets getting up to mischief. A *New Year custom, apparently confined to the Yorkshire area, involved parties of disguised people entering people's houses on New Year's Eve, without knocking as the doors had generally been left unlocked. The residents had to guess their identity, and once they did so offered food and drink to the visitors before they moved on to another house. The custom was almost exactly the same as that which is still going strong (also called mumming or mummering) in Newfoundland. 'At Wakefield and Stanby (Yorkshire) the mummers enter a house, and if it be in a foul state they proceed to sweep the hearth, and clean the kitchen range, humming all the time "Mum-m-m"' (Henderson, 1866: 54). In Barton, Cambridgeshire, up to about 1914, boys with blackened faces, calling themselves 'mummers', paraded the village singing a verse which has echoes from the mumming play (Porter, 1974: 72); and, in addition, some Christmas Eve carolsingers in the West Riding of Yorkshire were also called mummers, as were those who carried the *wassail cup around in the Cleveland area.

Eric Sunderland, 'The New Year Mummers', *Dalesman* (Jan. 1995), 61; Wright and Lones, 1940: iii. 224; Hutton, 1996: 11–12.

mumming plays. The most widespread of English *calendar customs in the 19th century. The mummers would tour their chosen area, at the specified season, enacting their 'play' in houses, pubs, or in the open, collecting money and moving on after each performance. 'Mumming' is the generic term, but the custom and performers went by different names in different areas—Tipteerers (Sussex/Surrey), Seven Champions (Kent), Johnny Jacks (Hampshire), Soulers/Soulcakers (Cheshire), Pace-Eggers (Lancashire), White Boys, Paper boys, *Guisers, and so on. Hundreds of versions of the play are known, from all over England (except, oddly, Norfolk and Suffolk), lowland Scotland, Ireland (north and west), and south Wales, and a few in countries settled by British emigrants. Versions differ in many respects, including text, characters, and costume, but the variations are markedly *regional, and the similarities across the country are more remarkable than the differences. For the majority of teams the customary time for performance was over the Christmas/New Year season, but in the Cheshire area it was Halloween, in the north-west it was Easter, while in the East Midlands *Plough Monday (first after 6 January) was the favoured time. In the majority of cases it was adult, working-class males who made up a mummers team, sometimes specifically the 'young men' of the village, at others the leading lights were older men who had been mummers for years. In some areas, particularly in the north of England, the custom was perpetuated almost entirely by children's teams, but this may have been a relatively recent development after the adults ceased taking part.

Researchers have identified three basic types of play: the Hero-Combat or St George Play; the *Sword Dance play; and the *Plough or Wooing play. The first was by far the most common, and the others have their own entries elsewhere in this dictionary. Within the Hero-Combat division, there are four subdivisions: (1) Standard Hero-Combat; (2) Souling play—characterized by appearance at Halloween and a 'wild horse' character; (3) Pace-Egging play—characterized by appearance at Easter and some different characters; (4) Robin Hood play—relatively rare, but while the basic action is the same as the standard Hero-Combat, the characters and much of the dialogue are taken from traditional Robin Hood ballads. The basic plot, or 'action' of the Hero-Combat play is simple enough: someone introduces the team, calls for 'room', and announces that a performance is about to take place; a character boasts of his prowess and challenges another to fight; another accepts the challenge; they have a sword fight, one is killed or wounded; in some versions the victor fights and vanquishes one or more other characters; a character laments the death and calls for a doctor who arrives, boasting of his skills and his travels; often there is bartering over his fee; in some versions the doctor has an assistant with whom he has some verbal crosstalk; the dead/wounded character is brought back to life; one or more extra characters appear, each with a short speech, one of whom asks the audience for money or food, which ends the play; many teams would then

entertain the company with songs, tunes, and so on.

The play texts have in turn baffled and intrigued most commentators. They are mostly couched in rough rhymed couplets, although parts of the Doctor's speeches are in prose. Local words crop up here and there but in general they are not in dialect. They contain numerous bits and pieces from other genres, including echoes of stage plays, anachronistic references, and topsy-turvy imagery, but cannot be traced to any specific known source. Broadly speaking, the costumes worn by the mummers can be separated into two distinct types. In the older style, the participants dressed all the same, often covered from head to foot in strips of rag or wallpaper of various colours with tall hats covered in rosettes, tinsel, and so on. Even where the whole body was not covered, ribbons, patches, or tufts of material were often sewn at random on to ordinary clothes. Where the face was not covered by fringes, a common feature was to blacken it with burnt cork or soot. In later years, participants attempted to dress appropriately for the character they were portraying. Props were minimal. The combatants' 'swords' were often merely sticks, or walking sticks; the Doctor normally had a bottle or box of pills, and the men needed little else apart from something to collect the money in. Character names varied from place to place, and again showed marked regionalization, and it is often better to talk in terms of character roles—Presenter, Combatants, Doctor, Doctor's helper, and so on. The presenter was often Father Christmas, or a character whose name denotes his role, such as Roomer, Letter-in, etc. By far the most common first combatant is King or St George, while his opponent is most commonly a Turkish Knight or Bold Slasher. The character who laments the death often claims to be the victim's father, and the Presenter often fills this role. The Doctor is the only character who appears in every version, sometimes with a name (Doctor Brown, Doctor Dodd) but more often than not he is just 'The Doctor'. In some areas the doctor has an assistant—Jack Finney or Winney. The most widespread of the characters at the end of the play is Beelzebub (or a variation of his name), but others are Devil Doubt, Twing Twang, Johnny (Jolly) Jack, Billy Sweep, and Souling plays included a Wild Horse character, whose antics closed the performance (see *hobby horses, *Antrobus Soul-Cakers).

A feature of a number of plays was a 'female' character called Molly, Bessie, etc., played by a man. Contrary to popular opinion, the Dragon hardly ever appears as a character in traditional plays—in perhaps twenty of the more than 1,000 versions known—and in most of these there is evidence of literary borrowing to explain its presence.

Describing the custom as a 'play' is misleading in that the word raises expectations which the mummers could not, and did not try, to fulfill. There was little space in many venues, and no theatrical trappings. The men would normally stand in a line or shallow semi-circle against a wall, facing the audience, thus defining a performance space in front of them. Each performer's 'entrance' would simply entail him stepping forward into the performance space, and for his 'exit' he would simply step back into line. There was much pacing up and down, especially during the boast and challenge section, but there was little attempt at characterization or real 'acting', even in the sword fight. Indeed, many writers comment on the stiff upright postures and toneless singsong voices adopted by the men, which is dismissed as inability to act, but it is clear that this was the traditional style in which the play was meant to be performed. As time passed, however, the pressures of the real stage and other expectations gradually killed the older style and more conventional acting styles were adopted, but modern-day revivalists appear to base their performances on the model of either pantomime or melodrama. The presence of St George also leads some writers to presume a overtly nationalistic tone to the custom, but, apart from a few versions collected in the West Country, this is another misinterpretation. Most written accounts are completely silent on why the mummers performed, usually because the writers' own confirmed ideas made it unnecessary to ask. Ex-mummers interviewed in the 20th century almost always stressed the economic benefits of participation. Men could earn the equivalent of several weeks' wages over one season, which they would either spend on drink or on their families. In conversation, however, a second motive was often voiced—'you took pride in it', 'you were the Mummers and you had to get it right'.

The history of mummers scholarship is littered with unfortunate accident and unfulfilled promise. Thomas Fairman *Ordish amassed the first important collection in the 1880s and 1890s, but failed to produce his promised book. R. J. E. Tiddy commenced another collection, but was killed in the First World War, and his *The Mummers Play* (1923) was edited from his notes. E. K. Chambers, the well-known drama historian, was the first to write a book-length study, *The English Folk Play*, published in 1933. Chambers relied entirely on literary sources and does not seem to have bothered to witness any performances or interview any performers even though there were several teams still active within 20 miles of his home in Oxfordshire. His book is thus only useful for tracing early textual connections between mummers and the legitimate stage. At the same time as Chambers was finishing his book, a visiting American ballad scholar, James Madison *Carpenter, collected several hundred texts from ex-performers, but his collection remained completely unknown to British scholars until the late 1970s. In the mid-1950s, Alex *Helm, while researching morris dances and other calendar customs, became interested in the mummers when asked to sort out the Ordish collection. Along with colleagues Dr E. C. Cawte and Norman Peacock, he commenced a systematic programme to gather information, and by 1967 they were able to publish the seminal *English Ritual Drama: A Geographical Index* which listed over 800 versions, demonstrated the distribution of the custom, and gave researchers access to a vast wealth of previously unsuspected material. The introductory chapters also provided the first conceptual framework in which to view the custom. Helm and team also published a series of booklets, providing texts, photographs, and commentary on a scale previously unknown, but, again, Alex Helm died before he could publish his major book on the subject. Helm's manuscript was finally published as *The English Mummers' Play* in 1980, and although some would now question his emphasis on ritual, this book is far and away the best on the subject. Helm's work brought the subject to the attention of a new generation of collectors and a number of valuable collections were amassed in the 1960s to 1980s. These later researchers more than doubled the number of places known to have had a play, but at the time of writing, this material remains largely in private hands and has not yet been processed into major publications. The emphasis of these later collectors has been less to do with the supposed ritual basis of the custom and more to do with the mechanics and the social context of traditions.

The mumming play has been the most consistently misrepresented and misunderstood of English calendar customs. The assumption that the mumming play is a relic of pre-Christian fertility ritual has bedevilled writing on the subject at least since the Second World War, but many writers before that time were more modest in their claims. The presence of St George and the Turkish Knight led many to assume an origin in the period of the Crusades, but as the 20th century advanced, the supposed starting-point of the custom was moved sharply backwards and writers begin to use phrases such as 'pre-Christian', 'pagan', and 'fertility ritual', on a routine basis. The central problem for all these theories is the stunning lack of evidence to support them. The plain unromantic fact is that the first clearly identifiable references to the mumming play as we know it are in the middle to late 18th century—500 years after the Crusades, and a thousand years after the English were converted to Christianity. The play is notable by its absence in the written and pictorial record for all that time, despite the fact that, if later distribution is anything to go by, it would have been performed every year in thousands of places throughout the kingdom, and early antiquarians such as *Aubrey, *Strutt, and *Brand fail to mention it. The question of origins is still unsolved, but the way that references suddenly start appearing in the 18th century would strongly argue for an origin around that time, and, as that period is not noted for its fertility rituals or pagan customs, a 'literary' origin is most likely.

See also *ANTROBUS SOUL-CAKERS, *MARSHFIELD PAPER BOYS, *MIDGLEY PACE-EGGERS.

murder. In earlier centuries, *chapbooks and *broadsides catered for public curiosity about crimes; many were based on murder trials and (real or alleged) confessions of murderers before they were hanged, garnished with sensational details and moralizing comments, and often with folkloric details. For instance, the murder of Maria Marten by her lover at Polstead (Suffolk) in 1827 was supposedly discovered because her mother dreamt three times of the 'Red Barn' where her corpse was hidden; the case became so famous that models of the barn were sold as souvenirs.

A tradition frequently found is that a spot where murder has been committed is marked for ever—if indoors, by an indelible bloodstain; if out of doors, by the fact that no grass will grow there. Evelyn's *Diary* for 8 July 1656 records an example at Colchester, and Robert Southey describes a field near London called 'The Brothers' Steps', where two brothers killed one another in a duel over a woman, and their tracks remain visible (*Common-Place Book*, 2nd series (1849), 20–1). The belief is still with us; the latest reference in Opie and Tatem (1989: 271) is from 1978.

'Murder will out' was a maxim widely believed, which might prove true in strange ways. The victim's ghost might haunt the murderer until he confessed, or the corpse bleed at its murderer's touch. At Kockin (Shropshire) in 1590 a man named Thomas Elks drowned his little nephew to get an inheritance, fled, and was caught; the story told some hundred years later was that his hiding-place was revealed by the cry of ravens, which had followed him ever since his crime (Richard Gough, *The History of Myddle* (1701; 1981 edn.) 122).

A *ballad known both in England and Scotland (Child, no. 10, 'The Twa Sisters') tells how one sister drowned another through jealousy, but when the corpse was found a musician made a harp or a fiddle from the bones which sang by itself to denounce the crime. The same plot also existed as a folktale, versions of which have recently been collected from teenagers (Wilson, 1997: 119–34). Nowadays the girl is killed by her boyfriend, brother, or husband, and it is he who makes the instrument, a piano, which later reveals the crime. The tale includes rhymes and, eventually, a shriek:

Mother, mother, you're playing on my bones,
Someone killed me and stole my precious stones . . .

Davey, Davey, you're playing on my bones,
Someone killed me—YOU KILLED ME!

(Wilson, 1997: 123)

Murray, Margaret (1863–1963). An Egyptologist at University College London, who in middle life became curious about the origins of European *witchcraft. She evolved a theory that witches were members of a highly organized secret society whose purpose was to maintain a pre-Christian—indeed, prehistoric—fertility cult practising human sacrifice and worshipping a horned god. She imposed rationalistic interpretations on the material wherever possible; thus, references to flying were either about dancing or due to hallucinations, while the 'Devil' whom the witches revered was merely their human leader, wearing a horned mask.

She set out her ideas in three books: *The Witch-Cult in Western Europe* (1921), *The God of the Witches* (1933), *The Divine King in England* (1954). Although they did not convince most historians or folklorists, they had great popular success, especially after they were reprinted in the 1960s, and have deeply affected the public perception of witchcraft. It was she who invented the ideas that witches were organized into *covens of thirteen, observed fixed annual festivals, were concerned with nature and *fertility, and wor-

shipped archaic gods. None of these ideas can stand up to historical investigation.

Jacqueline Simpson, *Folklore* 105 (1994); Hutton, 1991: 301–6, 331–4; Hutton, 1999: 194–201, 377–8; Simpson, in Davidson and Blacker, 2001: 103–17.

myths. Stories about divine beings, generally arranged in a coherent system; they are revered as true and sacred; they are endorsed by rulers and priests, and closely linked to religion. Once this link is broken, and the actors in the story are not regarded as gods but as human heroes, giants or fairies, it is no longer a myth but a folktale. Where the central actor is divine but the story is trivial, as in the tale of Jesus and the *owl, the result is religious legend, not myth.

nails (1), see *FINGERNAILS.

nails (2). Various powers were ascribed to nails, especially large 'tenpenny nails', and those taken from *coffins. Reforged into a finger-ring, they were a cure for *cramp; driven into a witch's footprint, they broke her power; rubbed against one's gum and then driven into a tree, they took away *toothache; driven into the road, or into a stile, they were a medium through which one's ague or *warts could be transferred to the next person passing over them.

names. Socially, legally, and emotionally, 'name', 'identity', and 'status' are closely linked. The Christian naming ceremony (christening or *baptism), has both a religious and an identifying social function: the baby is admitted into the Church, but it is given a name considered attractive in its family's social circle, or is 'named after' a relative or friend. As practising genealogists know, inherited forenames are a regular feature of English families, often over many generations—the idea that naming a baby after a living parent is unlucky, mentioned in Camden's *Britannia* (1586) and occasionally in the 19th century, can never have been widespread. More common in the 19th and 20th centuries has been the belief (still current) that a child should not be given the same name as a dead sibling (Opie and Tatem, 1989: 277–8).

From the mid-19th century onwards, there was a fairly widespread disinclination to mention the baby's name before the christening; it might even be kept secret. Most references imply that it would be tempting fate to pre-empt the ceremony, but some are explicit that it could give ill-wishers a chance to harm the baby magically (Opie and Tatem, 1989: 278). Most folklorists have taken for granted that the latter notion is rooted in prehistory, since

'Many savages at the present day regard their names as vital parts of themselves, and take great pains to conceal their real names, lest these should give to evil-disposed persons a handle by which to injure their owners' (Frazer, 1922: 244). One clear illustration is the fairytale * Tom Tit Tot, and further instances can be found among *magic practices in England. A written *curse or a malevolent *image may have the victim's name on it; magically summoning or banishing supernatural beings usually involves uttering their name(s); some verbal *charms aggressively address the sickness or injury they are meant to cure ('Ague, ague, I thee defy!'). Nevertheless, the analogies must not be pressed too far; in particular, whatever 'primitive man' may have done, there is no sign that within historic times in England people tried to hide their names from witches, as they did their *hair or *fingernail clippings.

There has been a strong tradition, especially among male workers and in communities such as the armed forces and schools, of substituting nicknames for proper Christian names. Many of these are conventionally linked to particular surnames, for example 'Nobby' Clark, and 'Dusty' Miller.

Opie and Tatem, 1989: 276–8.

National Centre for English Cultural Tradition (NATCECT). The Sheffield Survey of Language and Folklore was founded at the University of Sheffield in 1964, to collect material and provide an academic resource centre, and its journal *Lore and Language* was launched in 1969. The Survey formed the basis of the Centre for English Cultural Tradition and Language (CECTAL), inaugurated in 1975 within the University's Department of English to bring the folklore teaching into a unified programme. CECTAL thus joined the *Institute of Dialect and Folklife Studies (Leeds

University) as the two institutions which offered courses in folklore, but the latter closed in 1984. CECTAL was renamed the National Centre for English Cultural Tradition (NATCECT) in 1997. Throughout its history, the Centre has been organized by its Director, Professor J. D. A. Widdowson. The combined resources of its library, archive, and Traditional Heritage Museum represent one of the best collections of folklore and dialect material in the country, and it is still the only place in England where folklore can be studied at university level, at present offering M.Phil., Ph.D., and undergraduate courses. Numerous other projects have emanated from the Centre, including the Institute of Folklore Studies in Britain and Canada, founded in 1986 in conjunction with the Folklore Department at Memorial University of Newfoundland, the English Dialect Lexicon Database, and the Names Project.

Neal, Mary (1860–1944). Clara Sophia Neal (she became known as 'Mary' in 1888) began her philanthropic work in 1888 with the Wesleyan Methodist Mission in West London, and in 1895 formed, with co-worker Emmeline Pethick, her own Espérance Girls' Club for working girls. In 1906, in search of activities to interest the Espérance girls, Neal approached Cecil *Sharp, who put her in touch with William Kimber, *morris dancer from Headington Quarry, Oxford, who visited the Club to teach the girls morris dances. Neal and her associates were captivated by the songs and dances, and almost immediately embarked upon a crusade with a view to founding a national *revival movement. Sharp and Neal were kept busy collecting, lecturing, writing, and organizing events, and the Espérance girls were soon travelling the country as teachers of morris dancing. For a while, Sharp and Neal worked together, but from 1908 rising tensions over artistic standards and the way the morris dance was taught and presented, resulted in a very public parting and the formation of two opposing camps which vied for control of the new movement. Sharp's side stressed the need for high artistic standards and for experts to collect and interpret the dances, while Neal was concerned with the good that the dances could do to raise the spirits and artistic sensibilities of the poor and was less concerned with standards. Several years of argument and manœuvre followed, but by 1914 Sharp was beginning to win the day,

partly because Neal had other interests to claim her attention, and after the First World War Neal did not return to the fray, leaving Sharp's *English Folk Dance Society firmly in control of the future of the dance revival. As history is written by the victors, Neal's contribution to the early revival has, until recently, been consistently underplayed, but her point of view has been echoed many times since by people in dance clubs and societies who react against the idea of rigid artistic control. After the First World War Mary Neal continued to devote her life to philanthropic causes, but took no further active part in the folk revival.

Mary Neal, *The Espérance Morris Book* (1910); Roy Judge, 'Mary Neal and the Espérance Morris', *FMJ* 5:5 (1989), 545–91.

need fires, see *BONFIRES.

nettles. It is still generally accepted that nettle stings can be cured by the application of a dock leaf, but in the past it seems that the accompanying words were as important a part of the procedure as the physical process: 'Nettle in—dock out, dock in—nettle out' (Northumberland, 1851); or 'Dock, go in, nettle, go out, Dock shall have a white smock, And nettle shall go without' (Addy, 1895: 92). Even Chaucer knew the charm: as Troilus is protesting that he cannot suddenly stop loving Criseyde, 'But kanstow playen racket, to and fro, Nettle in, dok out, now this, now that' (*Troilus and Criseyde* (c.1374), IV, lines 460–1). Nettles also featured strongly in the calendar customs associated with *Royal Oak Day. The traditional punishment for children not wearing an oak leaf on that day was that their legs could be attacked with nettles wielded by other children. The plant also features regularly in folk medicine (see Vickery).

Vickery, 1995: 253–8; Opie and Tatem, 1989: 279; Roy Vickery, *Folk Life* 31 (1992–3), 88–93.

New Year. In England this has lost nearly all of its traditional customs and beliefs. For most English people, New Year's Eve is either spent quietly at home, or at a party, which lasts till after midnight to 'see the New Year in'. Such gatherings differ little from other parties, apart from the ubiquitous singing of 'Auld Lang Syne'. For some, the proper way to celebrate is to gather at a public place appropriated for such use. In all cases the stroke of midnight is immediately followed by much cheering, shouting, hooting of horns, and again 'Auld Lang Syne'. A piece in the *Illustrated London News* (2 Jan. 1897, 1, 3) described how masses of people had started to accumulate every year on the steps of St Paul's in London after new bells were installed in 1878. Church authorities stopped the New Year bell-ringing because they were worried about public disorder, but the meeting-place had become traditional and the crowds continued to gather each year. In the 1930s, the church again took notice of the New Year crowds and arranged community singing, which was even broadcast to 'listeners-in' to the new wireless (reports in *The Times*, 18, 19 Nov. 1935, 1 Jan. 1936, 1 Jan. 1937). After the Second World War, the focus of London celebration shifted to Trafalgar Square, where it has remained. The only other regular features of the season are the ubiquitous saluations of 'Happy New Year' and the tendency to make personal 'New Year resolutions'. Nevertheless, there is a general awareness in England that New Year is really the Scottish celebration *par excellence*.

In earlier times, the season was taken more seriously. Many of the following superstitions and customs can be seen in the light of the principle that the beginning of any enterprise or period is vitally important, and largely determines its relative success or failure. The literature on New Year in the past is dominated by the custom of 'first footing' or 'letting in the New Year'. Again this custom is nowadays associated mainly with Scotland, but in the 19th century it was known and practised over most of England as well, although clearly taken more seriously in the northern counties. In broad outline it was very similar everywhere—the first person to come into the house after midnight on New Year's Eve had to have certain personal characteristics and to conform to certain rules in order to bring luck to the house for the coming year. The details of the custom, however, vary considerably from place to place, and there seems to be no discernible pattern. In most places the first-footer must be dark haired, or dark skinned, but some insisted on a fair haired or light complexion. Almost invariably, a male first-footer was required, and some stipulated a married man while others required a bachelor, while some say flat-footed or cross-eyed people must be avoided. It was common for the first-footer to carry symbolic gifts—bread and coal being the most common commodities, but whiskey, and 'something green' (i.e. alive) were also popular. In some areas, the first-footer was called the 'Lucky Bird'. On entering, the first-footer would sometimes remain silent until he had poked the fire, or had placed coal on it, and several references maintain that he should enter by the front and leave by the back door. A simpler way of ensuring luck was to open the front and back doors to let the old year out and the new one in (*N&Q* 4s:1 (1868), 193). In almost all cases the first-footer was rewarded with food, drink, and/or money, and people who fitted the local ideal for first-footer often made a substantial sum by going from house to house (by arrangement) early on New Year's Day. The seriousness with which some people took the first-foot rules is evidenced in various sources, such as the following reported in *N&Q* (7s:10 (1890), 5): reporting on a trial in Mansfield (Nottinghamshire), and explaining why a young woman was walking the streets at one o'clock in the morning, it was stated that she had returned from the midnight service at her local church but her mother would not let her into the house until her father or brother came in first, which was some hours later. The same journal (4s:5 (1870), 89) reports a farmer who could not get into his own house on New Year morning until someone with darker hair came hours later.

New Year's Eve or Day was also one of the key times for divination. Particularly popular was 'dipping' into the Bible and reading aloud a passage to predict how the coming year would be (see under *book (divination with)). Another widespread method involved inspecting the ashes of the domestic fire for shapes (Aubrey, 1686/1880: 95), while many put their faith in whom they met first on New Year's Day, preferring certain types of people for luck (as in the first footing), but a variation was the idea that the Christian name of the first person of the opposite sex you see on that day will be that of your future partner (Henderson, 1866: 55). Even before the day was declared a *Bank Holiday in England (in 1974), there were strong traditions that no work should be done, and it was one of the days when *washing was particularly unlucky, and when new clothes should be worn (see *clothes), but it was essential to ensure you had money in your pocket or you would be poor all year.

On the principle of setting a precedent, there was a widespread belief that nothing should be taken out of the house before something had been brought in. Adherence to this tenet would ensure that the net flow of luck, prosperity, food, and so on, over the next year would be inward and positive rather than outward. 'Never throw any ashes, dirty water, or anything, however worthless, out of your house on this day . . .' (*Denham Tracts*, 1895: ii. 24; Henderson, 1866: 57). There was a particularly strong aversion to taking fire, in any form, out of the house, and woe betide anyone who let their *fire go out on New Year's Eve or Day (Harland and Wilkinson, 1882: 214).

Another important element of New Year celebrations was visiting. This could take the form of neighbours visiting each other, when an essential ingredient was, of course, the food and drink provided. A form of *visiting custom involved children going from door to door, singing traditional verses and hoping for money or food in return.

> I wish you a merry Christmas
> And a happy New Year
> A pocket full of money
> And a cellar full of beer
> A good fat pig
> That will last you all the year
> I wish you a merry Christmas
> And a happy New Year
>
> (Herefordshire: Leather, 1912: 90)

At Driffield (Yorkshire), Hastings (Sussex), and Pudsey (Yorkshire), and probably elsewhere, there was a *scrambling custom, where boys assembled in the street, outside shops, calling on the shopkeepers to throw items out to them (Nicholson, 1890: 21; *Sussex Archaeological Collections* 33 (1883), 238; *N&Q* 5s:8 (1877), 504).

Most of the customs already discussed cannot be shown to be very old, and the picture of New Year before the 19th century was very different indeed. Despite its ubiquity, neither the phrase nor the custom of first footing can be traced before the turn of the 19th century—even in Scotland—and most of the other beliefs detailed above are not found before the 1850s. As is well known, the name for the New Year in Scotland is Hogmanay, and this, in various spellings such as Hagmena, was also the regular term in northern England and the earliest use of the word so far discovered is in Yorkshire. An entry in the household accounts of Sir Robert Waterton, of Methley, in 1444, records payments for a big 'hogmanayse' and a little 'hogmanayse'. The entry is all in Latin apart from that word (see *Folklore* 95:2 (1984), 252–4). The *OED*, after admitting that the word

is 'of obscure history', proffers an Old French word, *aguillanneuf*, as a probable source, meaning 'the last day of the year, new year's gift, the festival at which new year's gifts were given and asked with the shout of *aguillanneuf*', which almost exactly fits the descriptions of New Year between the 15th and 17th centuries, where the emphasis is on gifts and visiting. The oldest references to gift-giving at New Year refer to royalty and nobility exchanging expensive presents, as far back as the time of Henry III (see Brand, 1849: i. 15) and up to Elizabeth I. In later periods the custom certainly existed within families as well as between friends and those with social obligations up or down the social scale. More modest traditional gifts were oranges stuck with cloves, gilded nutmegs, capons (from tenant farmers to landlords), various other foodstuffs, and papers of pins. The earlier visiting custom is again mostly reported from Scotland, but again it is clear that it was also common in northern England. It consisted of bands of young men (later children) going from door to door on New Year's Eve, singing and expecting gifts. A version from Richmond, Yorkshire, commences:

> To-night it is the New Year's night, to-morrow is the day
> And we have come for our right and for our ray
> As we used to do in King Henry's day
> Sing, fellows, sing Hagmen heigh!
>
> (Ingledew, *Ballads and Songs of Yorkshire* (1860))

The fact that Scotland and England have different views of the relative importance of Christmas and New Year is the result of the divergence of religion during the Puritan revolutions of the 17th century. As is well known, the gradual increase in influence and power of 'Puritan' Protestant sects across much of Europe in the 16th and 17th centuries brought increasing pressure on saints' days and other festivals which were branded as Catholic inventions. Christmas was thus increasingly discouraged and finally banned altogether in England in 1645. At a popular level, there was thus a tendency for people to transfer their celebrations from the dangerous Christmas to the secular New Year. At the Restoration, Christmas was reinstated, only to be removed again in Scotland, by the Kirk, in 1688–90. The stage was thus set for the two countries to go their own way, and Scottish people made New Year their main midwinter festival.

Details of New Year celebrations up to medieval times are sketchy, although if the Church condemnations are to be believed the people certainly indulged in some sort of behaviour which offended ecclesiastical sensibilities. The upper echelons of society had New Year feasts, although, as noticed in the entry for *Christmas, there was a strong tradition of the 'Twelve Days of Christmas' and it is thus not always easy to separate Christmas and New Year. Reading between the lines, the main thrust of the Church's disquiet was concerned with *divination (see Hutton, 1996: 7–8) which, as already stated, would be a logical thing to be doing at the start of a New Year. Beyond this the picture is even more speculative, but ' . . . there is sufficient to argue strongly for the existence of a major pre-Christian festival marking the opening of the new year, at the moment at which the sun had reached the winter solstice, and its strength was being renewed. There is testimony to this in the Anglo-Saxon, Viking and Welsh components of the British heritage' (Hutton, 1996: 8), but what they did is still open to debate.

For other customs which took place at New Year, see *ALLENDALE TAR BARRELS, *BOOK (DIVINATION WITH), *HOBBY HORSES, *LIFTING, *MUMMING, *MUMMING PLAYS, *RIDING THE STANG, *SWORD DANCES, *WASSAILING.

Wright and Lones, 1938: ii. 1–49; Opie and Tatem,1989: 283–7; *Folk-Lore* 3 (1892), 253–64; M. E. Ringwood, *Folklore* 71 (1960), 252–5. Brand, 1849: i. 10–20.

nightjars. Because of their silent flight, large eyes, and weird purring cry, nightjars were regarded as uncanny. In Yorkshire they were said to be the souls of *unbaptized infants, wandering for ever, and/or to be the sinister *Gabriel Ratchets. In Shropshire and Cheshire they were called 'lich fowl', i.e. 'corpse birds', and in several counties the 'night hawk', 'night raven', or 'night crow', a term taken from a biblical list of birds which are 'an abomination' and should never be eaten (Leviticus 11: 16). They were also commonly called 'goatsuckers', being thought to suck the udders of goats and cows, infecting them with disease (Swainson, 1885/1969: 97–8).

nightmares. In folklore, a 'mare' or 'nightmare' is not a distressing dream, but a supernatural being who crushes a sleeper's body by sitting on it (see *hag-riding; the word is sometimes mistakenly associated with 'mare' = 'female horse'. Around Durham, it was thought that the experience was 'caused by some witch turning the unlucky sleeper into a horse or mare' and riding him or her through the air to a sabbath (Brockie, 1886: 32).

The usual charm to prevent nightmares was hanging a *holed stone over the bed, but *horseshoes wrapped in red flannel were used in the same way, for example in early 20th-century London (Lovett, 1925: 12). The earliest account is from a 15th-century manuscript, where the stone is combined with a rhymed prayer to *St George:

Take a flynt stone that hath an hole thorow it of hys owen growynge, & hange it ouer the stabill dore, or ell ouer ye horse, and writhe this charme: In nomine Patris &c. Seynt Iorge, our ladys knyght, he walked day, he walked nyght, till that he fownde that fowle wyght [foul creature]; & when he her fownde, he her beat and her bownde, till trewly ther her trowthe sche plyght that sche sholde not come be nyght withinne vij rode [seven rods] of londe space ther as Seynt Ieorge i-namyd was. In nomine Patri &c. And wryte this in a bille and hange it in the hors' mane. (MS Bod. Rawlinson C 506 fo. 297)

Shakespeare gives a similar verse in *King Lear* (III. iv), invoking St Withold:

Swithold footed thrice the old (wold, moor),
He met the night-mare, and her nine fold (foals?),
 Bid her alight,
 And her troth plight,
And aroint thee, witch, aroint thee!

night raven. A name given in some early translations of the Bible for one of the birds of abomination (Leviticus 11: 16). It was applied in country speech either to the nightjar, the night heron, or the bittern. The deep booming call of the male bittern was regarded as a fearful *omen; Oliver Goldsmith remembered from his boyhood 'with what terror the bird's note affected the whole village; they considered it to be the presage of some sad event . . . if any person in the neighbourhood died, they supposed it could not be otherwise, for the Night Raven had foretold it' (*An History of the Earth and Animated Nature* (1774)).

nine. A very powerful odd *number for luck and magic; being 3×3 it multiplies the force of *three, and it is the number of months of pregnancy. Many curative *charms, *divinations, and other magical procedures require words or actions to be repeated nine times, nine objects gathered, etc.

Nine Maidens. Several groups of *standing

stones in Cornwall and Devon are called 'The Nine Maidens', or 'The Merry Maidens'. Supposedly, these were girls who were turned to stone for dancing on a Sunday; at Belstone (Devon) the piper was petrified too and the stones are said to dance every day at noon. Such tales are pan-European; they date from the Middle Ages to warn of *judgements on sinners who disregard holy times or places.

S. P. Menefee, *Folklore* 85 (1974), 23–42; Westwood, 1985: 201–2.

Nixon the Cheshire Prophet. During the rivalry of Jacobites and Hanoverians in the early 18th century, both parties interpreted *prophecies attributed to 'Robert Nixon of Cheshire' to their own advantage. Nixon is supposed to have been an imbecile living in the days of Henry VII (or James I, in other versions) but it is unlikely that he really existed; sayings ascribed to him were circulating in Cheshire from the 1520s. The only early manuscript surviving is of the late 16th or early 17th century. It is full of local allusions, mingled with political sayings drawn from late medieval and oral folk tradition; they are vague, but picturesque, for example:

> When a raven shall build in a stone lion's mouth
> On a church top beside the Grey Forest,
> Then shall a king of England be drove from his crown,
> And return no more.

The first known printed text appeared in 1713, and has a Jacobite bias, corresponding to the views of several Cheshire aristocrats at that time, notably the Cholmondeleys of Vale Royal (who secretly held the manuscript until 1943). Hanoverian pamphlets appeared in 1714 and 1719, and were frequently reprinted, especially in the 1740s. They were reissued in the 1790s in collections of *Doomsday predictions.

Jacqueline Simpson, *Folklore* 86 (1975), 201–7; Ian Sellers, *Folklore* 92 (1981), 30–42; T. Thornton, in *Prophecy*, ed. Bertrand Taithe and Tim Thornton (1997), 51–67.

noodles, see *FOOLS.

north. According to Scripture, Satan set up his throne on a mountain in the north (Isaiah 14: 13), and demonic attacks are to be expected from that quarter (Jeremiah 1: 14, 6: 1). The symbolism of church architecture reflects this; the medieval clerestory windows at Fairford (Gloucestershire) show evil tyrants with attendant demons on the north side, saints and angels on the south. The main entrance of old churches is rarely on the north, but many have a smaller door there which was opened only during baptism, for the fiend to escape by (Charlotte Burne, *Folk-Lore* 19 (1908), 458–9).

For the same reason, many were unwilling to accept burial on the north side of a churchyard, this being regarded as unhallowed ground; the prejudice persisted from the 16th to the early 20th centuries. Gilbert White, writing of Selborne (Hampshire) in the 1780s, complained that:

the churchyard is very scanty, especially as all wish to be buried in the south-side, which is become such a mass of mortality that no person can be there interred without disturbing or displacing the bones of his ancestors. . . . At the east end are a few graves, yet none, till very lately, on the north-side; but as two or three families of the best repute have begun to bury in that quarter, prejudice may wear out by degrees, and their example be followed by the rest of the neighbourhood. (*The Natural History and Antiquities of Selborne* (1788), 322)

nosebleed. General *charms to staunch blood are dealt with under *bleeding, but there are also some specific methods aimed at stopping nosebleeds. It could certainly be argued that few people in modern England would rely on verbal charms and sympathetic magic to stop bleeding from real wounds, but the realm of the nosebleed is still susceptible to 'folk medicine' and belief. The most-quoted cure in modern tradition is to put a key down the back of the sufferer, but it has been difficult to find out how old this belief is, being recorded only since the 19th century (*N&Q* 4s:7 (1871), 91; Black, 1883). A ribbon or thread tied round the neck was another regular cure, and a detailed note in *Folk-Lore* (23 (1912), 349) records the use of a special 'bloodstone', worn round the neck on a knotted red silk thread. In earlier times, others preferred to wear a *toad round the neck (Gutch, 1901: 170, quoting a manuscript of *c*.1600) but this is claimed as a remedy for many ailments. Cobwebs placed in the nostril were recommended by some, while one man at least claimed that moss which had grown on a human skull was particularly effective (Black, 1883: 96–7).

A sudden nosebleed has long been taken as a sign of bad luck to come, especially if it takes the form of two or three drops of blood only. Opie and Tatem list examples from 1180 through into the late 19th century, and Samuel Pepys recorded in his *Diary* (6 June 1667): '. . . But it was an ominous thing methought, just as he was bidding me his last adieu, his nose fell a-bleeding, which run in my mind a pretty while after'. Occasional sources distinguish between the left (bad luck) and right (good luck) nostrils (see Lean, 1903: ii. 289).

Porter, 1969: 83–4; Black, 1883: 62, 76, 96–7, 111, 183, 190–1; Opie and Tatem, 1989: 287–8; Lean, 1903: ii. 52, 288–90; Forbes, 1971: 293–316.

noses. One of the many parts of the body which is significant if it itches, but a range of meanings have been reported since the 17th century. In Thomas Dekker's play *The Honest Whore* ((1604), II. i): 'We shall ha' guests to day, I lay my little maidenhead; my nose itches so', while John *Melton (1620: 47) declares: 'When a man's nose itcheth, it is a signe he shall drink wine'. Multiple reasons, with satisfying rhythm, are often given: 'You will shake hands with or kiss a fool, drink a glass of wine, run against a cuckold's door, or miss them all four' (*Connoisseur* (13 Mar. 1755); compare *Folk-Lore* 24 (1913), 90). A similar confusion pertains to a blue vein which can appear across the top of the nose: you will drown, be hanged, die young, and so on (*The Shepherd's Kalendar* (1503); Lean, 1903: ii. 291; *Folk-Lore* 68 (1957), 413). According to Addy (1895: 144) a turned-up nose indicates deceit.

See also *NOSEBLEED.

Lean, 1903: ii. 142, 283–8, 291; Opie and Tatem, 1989: 288; Hazlitt, 1905: 441–2.

Notes & Queries. Launched in November 1849, as a weekly miscellany, *Notes & Queries* (*N&Q*) was the brainchild of William J. *Thoms. He had previously organized a column in the *Athenaeum* as a medium for the exchange of information between folklorists, antiquarians, literary researchers, and the like, and *N&Q* was an extension of the same idea. *N&Q* became an indispensable part of the scholar's library, and folklorists in particular are grateful for the mass of information its pages contain; as evidenced by the number of citations included in this *Dictionary*. Thoms edited *N&Q* himself until 1872, and he compiled a selection of the folklore material contained in the first twelve volumes, which was published as *Choice Notes* (1859). He also described the circumstances of its foundation in a series of articles in: 5s:6 (1876), 1–2, 41–2, 101–2, 221–2; 5s:7 (1877), 1–2, 222–3, 303–5. The publication still con-

tinues, but the amount of folklore included in its pages decreased sharply around the First World War.

November the Fifth. Variously called Bonfire Night, Guy Fawkes Night, Firework Night, Plot Night, Squib Night, November the Fifth was officially declared a day of national celebration and commemoration in response to the failed attempt by Guy Fawkes and other Catholic sympathizers to blow up both King James I and Parliament in 1605. As originally decreed, a special thanksgiving service was to be offered on the day, church bells were to be rung, and the people allowed to celebrate with bonfires and merrymaking. This was nothing unusual at the time, as *bonfires and *bells were the normal means used to mark national celebrations, and this encouragement by the authorities continued for many years. A custom which legitimized the position of those in power and which combined religious polemic with political mobilization would clearly have continued and powerful support, and it is no coincidence that November the Fifth was one of the few public customs which was not suppressed during the rule of the Puritans in the 17th century.

Nevertheless, the custom changed considerably over the years as the people gradually appropriated it for their own purposes. *Effigies were burnt as early as the 1670s, although until the 19th century these were more likely to be of the Pope or some domestic political enemy rather than Guy Fawkes himself. Orderly processions and controlled bonfires soon gave way to the carrying and rolling of blazing tar barrels, letting off of guns or fireworks and general noisy, drunken, and dangerous mayhem became the norm. When these activities took place in the confines of city streets rather than more spacious rural areas, serious questions of public order and the safety of property were raised, which was not helped by a generally held notion that November the Fifth was a day on which extra licence was permitted.

By the 19th century respectable people in many towns were beginning first to withdraw their support from such crowd-based customs and then actively to oppose them. As these people also held power as vestrymen, councillors, and magistrates, they were able to use the full authority of police and even, when necessary, local militia, to suppress the more boisterous and dangerous aspects of the custom. Lighting fires and setting off fireworks within towns were forbidden and perpetrators increasingly harassed by the police. Many towns in England were the scenes of protracted and often bitter struggles between those who wanted to keep their old customs intact and those dedicated to suppress, or at least reform, them. Straightforward suppression was sometimes ameliorated by the suggestion of different ways of carrying out the celebration, such as encouraging celebrators to move to a nearby public open space where the custom could be better controlled. A less overtly manipulatory development was the tendency to privatize the custom by encouraging people to hold their Guy Fawkes celebrations in family groups within the privacy of their own gardens and yards, and many of the better-off families had already withdrawn to the safety of their own property some time before mass celebrations were finally suppressed. These private celebrations had become the norm by the early 20th century, and continued to be the basic pattern until fears over safety and other societal changes in the 1960s and 1970s brought about another, again partly orchestrated, move towards controlled public displays. At the time of writing (1997), the private back-garden celebration is still on the decline and the organized set-piece display, provided again by local council or local group or charity, has become the commonest way to enjoy fireworks and bonfires. A few places in England still preserve some of the older traditions associated with the Fifth:*Lewes (Sussex) where impressive torch-lit processions and giant effigies are the main feature, while *Ottery St Mary (Devon) and *Hatherleigh (Devon) maintain the spectacular, but dangerous, blazing *tar barrels.

It was also during the 19th-century suppression of the mass celebrations that the custom became increasingly associated with children. During the late 19th century and most of the 20th century, the sight of children displaying their effigies and accosting passers-by with a plaintive or aggressive 'Penny for the Guy?' was commonplace, and there were numerous regional variations. In Lancashire children would go Cob-Coaling to collect material for their bonfire, while in Yorkshire it was common for children to go *Guising, or acting a cut-down version of the *Pace Egg play. There were also rhymes accompanying Guy Fawkes customs, usually on the lines of:

Please to remember the Fifth of November
Gunpowder treason and plot
I see no reason why gunpowder treason
Should ever be forgot

See also *QUEEN ELIZABETH I'S ANNIVERSARY.

Cressy, 1989; Roger Swift, *History Today* (Nov. 1981), 5–9; Gavin Morgan, 'The Guildford Guy Riots 1842–1865', *Surrey Archaeological Collections* 76 (1985), 61–8; Ervin Beck, *Folklore* 95:2 (1984), 191–203; D. G. Paz, *Historical Research* 63 (1990), 316–28. Folklore Society Cuttings Files.

number 666. Among the prophecies in the Book of Revelations (Apocalypse) is one about a 'Great Beast' who will rule the earth and mark his followers on the brow or hand with the 'number of his name', which is 666. Commentators soon dubbed this figure 'the Antichrist', and tried to identify him. Clearly, the original allusion was to the pagan Roman empire, its statues, and its coinage; with some forcing, 666 can be matched to the numerical value of 'Nero Caesar' written in Hebrew letters. Over the centuries new interpretations arose—to English Protestants, 'Antichrist' was usually the Pope, but Napoleon, the Kaiser, and Hitler have also been given the title. In the 17th century, some feared Doomsday would come in 1666. This was the theme of Francis Potter's *An Interpretation of the Number 666* (1642), which Pepys read during the fateful year: 'His close is most excellent, and whether it be right or wrong, is mighty ingenious' (Pepys, *Diary*, 16 Feb. 1665/6 and 10 Nov. 1666).

In current popular imagination, 666 is regarded as Satanic. There have been many press reports of 'unlucky' cars with 666 as the licence number, and no such licences have been issued since 1991. Similarly, in 1993 Croydon Council renumbered a grave-plot in its cemetery from 666 to 665a (*FLS News* 19 (1994), 10). Phone numbers with 666 in them may be rejected, or regarded as a joke. Some marginal Christian sects have further fears: that bar-codes on retail goods secretly include 666 as Satan's device to enslave the world, and that hospitals brand this number invisibly on the hands of newborn babies (*FLS News* 20 (1994), 4).

numbers. There is no systematic numerology in English folklore; the only numbers widely regarded as significant are *three, *seven, *nine, *thirteen. The latter only acquired importance over the last two or three centuries, but the good luck ascribed to odd numbers below ten is a regular feature of European folklore. Curiously, five has little role in folklore, except as the *pentacle. Twelve is the only even number occasionally regarded as significant; it presumably stands for completeness, by association with the twelve hours on a clock-face, the twelve months of the year, and the old way of reckoning by dozens.

Occasionally, it is said there are 365 windows in a very large house (or trees in a copse, or steps in a long flight), 'one for each day of the year'. *Number 666 is regarded as Satanic and unlucky.

numskulls, see *FOOLS.

nursery rhymes. Traditional rhymes which are passed on to children while they are still of nursery age. The key point here is that the transmission is normally from adult to child, which can be distinguished from *children's lore, which is mainly transmitted between children. Most adults have a basic repertoire of nursery rhymes at their disposal—there can be few adults in England who cannot recite *Baa Baa Black Sheep, *Little Jack Horner, or *Jack and Jill—but many buy books of rhymes when they become parents, which have the added advantage of illustrations, from which they read to their children. The rhymes themselves provide a fascinating array of imagery, rhythm, and simple structure, which have pleased generations of children and adults, and, despite their apparent inconsequentiality, far outstrip any other verse form in terms of distribution and popularity, and their place in the national consciousness is proved by the frequency with which advertisers and parodists use them.

A surprising number of nursery rhyme collections, usually in the form of *chapbooks, were published from the mid-18th century onwards, with titles such as *Tommy Thumb's Pretty Song Book* (c.1744), *The Top Book of All, for Little Masters and Mistresses* (c.1760), and *Gammer Gurton's Garland* (1784); but no scholar thought the rhymes worth their notice until James Orchard *Halliwell published his two collections of *The Nursery Rhymes of England* (1842) and *Popular Rhymes and Nursery Tales of England* (1849), on which virtually all subsequent collections relied for material, until the researches of Iona and Peter *Opie's seminal

work, *The Oxford Dictionary of Nursery Rhymes* (1951; 2nd edn., 1997).

Nursery rhymes have suffered the indignity of having more nonsense written about them than any other folklore genre. Commentators have sought to explain nursery rhymes in terms of political satire, ancient mythology, Freudian psychology, fertility ritual, sun-worship, and any other intellectual fad of the time, and the game of spotting hidden meanings is likely to continue for the foreseeable future. The truth is that few of the rhymes can shown to be older than the 18th century, many of them have identifiable authors, and are easily understood as nonsense rhymes for children or the flotsam and jetsam of adult songs, poems, customs, plays, and so on. This is not to underestimate the problems of evidence of this field, and the possibility that many rhymes could be much older than their first known printings, but inventing origins from stray internal clues is hardly likely to produce real knowledge.

The normal term for nursery rhymes in the USA is *Mother Goose Rhymes.

See also *BAA BAA BLACK SHEEP, *GOOSEY GOOSEY GANDER, *HEY DIDDLE DIDDLE, *HICKORY DICKORY DOCK, *HUMPTY DUMPTY, *JACK AND JILL, *LITTLE BO PEEP, *LITTLE JACK HORNER, *MARY HAD A LITTLE LAMB, *OLD KING COLE, *OLD MOTHER HUBBARD, *ORANGES AND LEMONS.

nutting. In areas where wild hazels grew freely, large groups of villagers (particularly women) would go into the woods to gather them as food, or to sell to dyers. These expeditions were lively affairs, where a good deal of love-making went on; this sexual aspect, combined with the traditional use of 'nuts' to mean 'testicles', accounts for the jokes in folksongs and nursery rhymes about girls 'gathering nuts in May'.

It was also said that if you go nutting on a holy day you'll meet the *Devil; the first record (in 1670) refers to *Holy Rood Day (14 September), but it was more commonly applied to Sundays. The present writer heard it seriously said in Sussex in the 1940s [JS]. On the other hand, a vicar of Hailsham (Sussex) wrote flippantly in 1884 that the Devil who helped a girl who went nutting commonly appeared in the form of her sweetheart (Simpson, 1973: 65).

Vickery, 1995: 172–4; Opie and Tatem, 1989: 290.

oak. The oak symbolizes steadfast courage, royalty, and England. There are specific associations with the Royal Navy, and with the Restoration of the monarchy in 1660, celebrated on *Royal Oak Day.

Individual oaks can be locally famous. Many are called 'Gospel Oaks', because they mark a spot on the parish boundary where *Rogation processions used to pause while a Gospel passage was read. One in Sherwood Forest is said to have been a meeting-place for *Robin Hood and his men. Another, at Clipstone (Nottinghamshire) is the Parliament Oak, so called because either King John or Edward I convened a Parliament there. Another, in the grounds of Boscobel House (Shropshire) is said to be the one in which Charles II hid after the Battle of Worcester, while all along the route of his escape there are trees (not necessarily oaks) in which, it is claimed, he also hid from pursuers—for example an oak near Melksham Court (Gloucestershire), and a hollow elm in Brighton (Sussex). Wesley several times held open-air services at the tree now called Wesley's Oak near Altrincham (Cheshire).

Cords of window-blinds had a toggle shaped like an acorn, which was said to prevent lightning from entering through the window, since it was believed (mistakenly) that oak trees are never struck by lightning. Such blinds are now rare, so the belief must be dying out. Grated oak bark or acorns were a country remedy for diarrhoea, and an infusion of oak bark was drunk for rheumatism (Hatfield, 1994: 36, 46).

Oak Apple Day, see *ROYAL OAK DAY.

Oberon. Shakespeare found this name for a fairy king in literature, not folklore—in a late medieval French romance, *Huon of Bordeaux*, translated into English in 1548. Several later poets copied him, but the name did not enter folk tradition.

occupational customs. There are few places of work which have no customs or lore attached to them at all, even if it is only the buying of cakes on one's birthday or the office Christmas party. Some occupations, however, have a much wider range of traditional practices and beliefs. Outsiders often dismiss the older customs as barbaric or 'anything for an excuse to get drunk', but insiders argue that such events are only a bit of fun and help to promote camaraderie and loyalty to workmates which helps in the daily grind of work, and anyway they survived it all right in their time. Such customs, indeed, range from the mild, low key, and friendly to the boisterous and wild horseplay which can clearly be used as a guise for cruelty and victimization. Customs usually cluster around particular identifiable points in an individual's working life: entering a trade or a new firm (footing/initiation), qualifying as a fully-fledged worker (banging out, for example), leaving a firm or retiring. Some trades have particular points in the work cycle to celebrate, such as completing a building (*topping out) or crossing the line at sea. Other times for celebration are key events in the worker's life outside the workplace, in particular his/her impending wedding, birth of a baby, and so on.

The first key point is starting at a new workplace, and various customs exist to 'welcome' or initiate a newcomer. A key variable is the age and status of the worker—new youngsters are more likely to be greeted with practical jokes and horseplay, while older people changing jobs would normally get away with buying a round of drinks. The latter was formalized in the past in many trades as 'footing', which the *English Dialect Dictionary* defines as 'the entrance upon a new position or occupation: the fine levied upon a new workman, &c., generally spent in drink. Usually in phrase To pay one's footing'. Thomas Gent, later famous as a printer in York, described a custom enacted when he joined a London printing firm about 1713 is his *The Life of Mr. Thomas Gent, Printer, of York* ((1832), 15–17).

At the darker end of the spectrum is the 'initiation rite' with which newcomers are greeted, which can be the disguise for bullying and racial or sexual harassment. Practices in the British army were heavily criticized during the 1980s for allowing degrading and barbaric rites, and the Fire Service was similarly attacked for customs apparently aimed at keeping women out of the occupation (Folklore Society Cuttings File). A less vindictive way of greeting novices existed in many trades and businesses, and involved sending the youngster to fetch some non-existent item— striped paint, sky-hooks, the burglars' address book, elbow grease, pigeon's milk, and so on. All the seasoned workers are party to the joke and contrive to send the dupe on to someone else, in some versions giving him/her something to carry on the way (traditional examples in *N&Q* 186 (1944), 24, 78–9, 120–1, 124, 278).

The most tenacious of occupational customs, now mainly associated with the printing trade but previously practised more widely, is the 'banging-out' of apprentices as they reach the end of their training, which still (1998) takes place despite being frowned on by many employers and Trade Unions. In modern guise, the ceremony usually involves the victim being tied up, covered in anything sticky and nasty and left outside in some public place, but previous examples also stress the noise involved (see *printing trade). A similar custom existed in other trades, such as *coopering, where it was called Trussing the Cooper. Most apprentices are relatively willing, but things can go very wrong, and there are occasional reports of accidents and even the death of the victim (e.g. *Guardian* (22 Dec. 1989)).

It is not just the men who enjoy the licence permitted by customary activity: 'It's my 23rd birthday next month and I'm dreading it. I've just started working in a factory where there are only a dozen men and about 20 women, and every time a man has a birthday they gang up and strip him . . .' (*Woman* (19 June 1989), 62). Another occupational custom which seems set to persist into the twenty-first century is the marking of a colleague's upcoming wedding by female printing office and factory workers. Details vary from place to place, but the central themes are the decorating of the desk or workstation with ribbons, pictures, paper

flowers, and so on, and similarly the dressing up of the girl herself. In many cases she has to wear the decorations all day and all the way home (accompanied by a workmate to ensure that she follows the rules). If appropriate her car may also be decorated. This type of celebration is normally carried out by women, but there are some reports of practices in male workplaces, involving the filling of jacket linings with confetti. Again, the procedure can be unwelcome, as detailed in the *Daily Express* (31 Jan. 1996, reprinted *FLS News* 24 (1996), 14) where workers at a Yorkshire factory were sacked for subjecting a girl soon to be married to being sellotaped to a chair, drenched with water, covered with scraps of plastic, and whiskers painted on her face. Earlier examples of wedding occupational customs are described under *printing trade.

An earlier form of occupational custom, largely forgotten now, was the annual procession on the day of the trade's patron saint (e.g. the woolcombers on *St Blaize's Day) or as part of the general trade guild involvement in local *civic customs.

See also *BLACKSMITHS, *BUILDING TRADE, *COOPERING TRADE, *HARVEST CUSTOMS, *FISHING INDUSTRY, *PRINTING TRADE, *SAINT BLAIZE, *SAINT CRISPIN'S DAY, *ST MONDAY.

Smith, 1969; George Monger, *Folklore* 82 (1971), 314–16, and *Folklore* 86 (1975), 50–61; David White, *New Society* (13 May 1971), 805–7: Folklore Society Cuttings File.

ogres. A term adopted from the French, and more literary than colloquial, for a man-eating giant like the ones in Jack and the Beanstalk and Jack the Giant-Killer.

Old Horse. In a similar situation to the *Old Tup, the Old Horse is both a song and a custom. As a song, it is found in different versions all over England, and it details how the horse used to be so proud and fine but is now old and decayed:

> But now that he's grown old
> And scarcely can he crawl
> He's forced to eat the coarsest grass
> That grows against the wall
> Poor old horse.

The Old Horse was also an animal disguise custom, performed at *Christmas/*New Year and found in and around the area where the counties of Yorkshire, Derbyshire, and Nottinghamshire meet. The Horse was constructed by mounting a horse's skull, or wooden horse's head, on a pole. The mouth could open and close, operated by a string. The team consisted of the Horse and an unspecified number of men who would sing the song while the animal pranced or otherwise acted up. In some versions they pretended to shoe the horse during the song. The earliest references to the custom only date to the 1840s.

See also *HOBBY HORSES, *SEAFARING CUSTOMS.

Cawte, 1978: 117–24.

Old King Cole. One of the most popular of the *nursery rhyme canon, which also exists as an adults' cumulative song and in many parodies, obscene and otherwise. The song is first mentioned in 1708/9, but only appears regularly in print from the late 18th century onwards. Numerous attempts to identify a real 'Old King Cole' have been unconvincing and unnecessary.

Opie and Opie, 1997: 156–8.

Old Mother Hubbard. One of the first superstars of the *nursery rhyme field, Mother Hubbard featured in the *Comic Adventures of Old Mother Hubbard and her Dog* printed by J. Harris in 1805, which was an immediate success, sold tens of thousands of copies, and spawned pirate editions, parodies, and sequels, and the rhyme itself was reprinted in countless other collections. Almost overnight Old Mother Hubbard became a stock figure in early 19th-century popular culture. The fourteen-verse rhyme was written by Sarah Catherine Martin (1768–1826) in 1804, and the first verse at least is still very well known. Nothing is simple in the nursery rhyme field, however. It appears that Miss Martin did not compose the whole piece, but took an already known three-verse rhyme and extended it with new stanzas, possibly modelled on another rhyme concerning *Old Dame Trot and her Comical Cat*. These three verses had appeared in print in the 1790s and were probably even older still, but we have no evidence to prove it.

Opie and Opie, 1997: 374–80.

Old Nick. This humorous nickname for the Devil is first recorded in the 17th century. Its origins are uncertain, but it may be related to certain German and Scandinavian words beginning in *nik-*, used for various dangerous supernatural creatures.

old style (dates), see *CALENDAR.

Old Tup, Derby Ram. 'The Derby Ram' or 'Old Tup' is a widely collected traditional song, found all over the English-speaking world. As with all traditional songs, it exists in numerous versions, including bawdy ones, but it always describes, in hyperbolic terms, a wondrous ram or tup:

> This ram it had two horns, sir
> That reached right up to the moon
> A man went up in January
> And he didn't come down till June.

The song also describes how the ram was butchered and how the parts of his body were used.

In the vicinity of Sheffield, however, the Old Tup was more than just a song, as there they had a *Christmas *visiting custom which included someone impersonating the Tup and a dramatic performance. The Tup's construction varied according to the age and abilities of the performers. At the most sophisticated end of the spectrum, a wooden head (or sometimes a real sheep's head) was fixed to a pole which was carried by a man hidden by a sack or a cloth. The head could have real ram's horns and boast other attributes such as a red tongue. But at the most amateur end the animal could simply be made by a boy wearing a sack which had its corners tied to resemble ears, over his head. The Tup was accompanied by a group of four to six, who sang the song and in the simplest versions he merely jigged about in time with the music. In the more developed versions they enacted the killing of the Tup, and added characters such as Little Devil Doubt and Beelzebub, borrowed from local versions of the *mummers play. The earliest references to the custom are from the mid-19th century, although the song is much older, and the custom is still not quite extinct.

Compare *OLD HORSE. See also *hobby horses.

Cawte, 1978: 110–17; P. S. Smith, *L&L* 1 (1969), 6–8.

omens. Occurrences outside human control, interpreted by communal tradition as foretelling future events (e.g. seeing *magpies, hearing an *owl hoot); they differ from *taboo actions which cause bad luck but can and should be avoided, and also from deliberate attempts to discover the future by *divinations and *fortune-telling. Some foretell something pleasant: to see a small *spider on your hand means money, to find nine peas in one pod means (for a girl) a happy marriage. Others foretell misfortunes, especially death. Such beliefs are extremely widespread in European folk culture, where many English examples can find parallels.

Many omens are drawn from things natural in themselves; they become significant either because the observer is currently in some stressful situation, or retrospectively, once something has happened to 'fulfil' them. Others are perceived as supernatural phenomena which only ever appear as warnings—*corpse candles, *wraiths, the *Gabriel Ratchets. Some items straddle the categories: *comets were supernatural to some, natural but sinister to others; *dreams are, to most people, a natural phenomenon, but some think they can be sent from God, while others regard the ability to 'dream true' as a personal psychic power. Underlying the whole concept is a belief in *fate (or Providence) rather than mere chance: the future is already fixed, and omens offer glimpses of its pattern.

Most folklore collections and all books on superstitions mix together the things said to *cause* good or bad luck and the true omens, which merely *foretell* it; their bald listings give no clue to the emotional importance omens can have in helping people to see a pattern in their lives, come to terms with loss, and so forth.

onions. Long prized for medicinal purposes. Popular tradition lays particular stress on the efficacy of raw onion rubbed on wasp and bee stings, and on warm onion juice dropped into the ear for earache; they are also mentioned for kidney troubles, coughs and colds, chilblains, baldness, aching wrists and ankles, and as a general antiseptic ointment. They are also believed to dissolve hardened substances in the stomach—especially useful after eating hard-boiled eggs, regarded as indigestible— and to take away the smell of new paint.

There was, and is, a widespread belief that onions attract and absorb impurities from the air. Many sources claim that peeled or cut onions kept in a room will destroy germs, thus preventing or curing any fevers or colds; their shrivelling and gradual blackening is held to prove this, and once they have done their work they should be burnt. This is supported by stories about particular epidemics such as the cholera outbreak in London in 1849 and

the Great *Plague of the 1660s, when it was widely believed that tobacconists and onion sellers were largely immune. The same belief leads some people to think it unlucky or dangerous to keep a cut, raw onion, for fear it might attract illness into the house from the outside air; any unused part, and even the peelings, must be thrown out at once.

An idea common among schoolchildren in the 19th and 20th centuries was that if you rubbed raw onion on to your palm, the pain of being caned on the hand would be much lessened, or, even better, the cane would split in half (cf. *hair, animal).

*Love divinations involving onions were practised on *St Thomas's Eve.

Opie and Tatem, 1989: 292–4; Vickery, 1995: 265–8; N&Q 11s:11 (1915), 68, 117–18, 409, 477; 11s:12 (1915), 101, 149–50, 167–8, 209, 245–6, 286, 367–8, 406; Culpeper's Complete Herbal and English Physician (1653; 1862 edn.), 109.

Ooser. The so-called Dorset Ooser has excited and puzzled folklorists since it was first brought to public attention in 1891. It was a large carved wooden head with staring eyes, flattened nose, hair, beard, and, most notably, sweeping curved bull's horns. Its lower jaw was hinged so that the mouth could be opened and shut by a string, in the same way as many *hobby horses and the *Salisbury Giant. The Ooser was apparently unique and was in the possession of a Crewkerne family until it disappeared, or fell to pieces, before the 1930s. The devilish nature of the face, and its usual description as a 'mask', led many people to presume its use in some diabolic rite, but this is unlikely. Although it was large enough to be worn on the head, the wood was solid and there was no provision for the wearer to see through it. It is much more likely that this was the head of a processional figure, designed to be carried like the *Salisbury Giant, or perhaps in a *rough music procession such as the *Wooset in nearby Wiltshire/Berkshire. The similarity in name supports the latter interpretation. The situation is confused, however, by two earlier references to the word 'Ooser'. In Thomas Hardy's novel The Return of the Native (1878, book 4, chapter 6), a character says 'What have made you so down? Have you seen a ooser?', and in W. Barnes's Glossary of the Dorset Dialect (1886, 85) the word is glossed as 'A mask with grim jaws, put on with a cow's skin to frighten folk'. If no other information comes to light, the exact nature of the Ooser will remain a mystery. The only reliable description, with photograph, is in *Somerset N&Q* 2 (1891), frontispiece and 289–90.

opals. In the 20th century, opals have been considered by many to be unlucky, especially as engagement rings, because they symbolize widowhood and tears. Those who know their astrology maintain, however, that the stone is lucky for those born under Libra. This modern prejudice against the opal is curious, as in the past it was a treasured and lucky stone, and it seems to have undergone a reversal of fortune as regards popular belief. Correspondence in *N&Q* in 1869 and 1875 states clearly that opals were regarded as unlucky stones by some people at the time, and other references (e.g. *Fortnightly Review* (July 1884), 85, and Addy, 1895: 93) add confirmation, but there are some dissenting voices which maintain that the colour of the opal makes the difference between good and bad luck. In classical times the opal was certainly treasured, and Pliny (*Natural History* (AD 77), XXXVII. xxi–xxii) devotes much space to it. It is not clear when or why the reversal occurred, although one or two theories have been advanced. Sir Walter Scott's novel *Anne of Geierstein* (1829), which features an unlucky opal, may perhaps take some of the blame for its bad reputation, but this remains speculation. Opals were also considered to be connected with eyesight, and there are hints that they conferred invisibility on the wearer (e.g. Ben Jonson, *The New Inne* (1631), I. vi).

Opie and Tatem, 1989: 294; *N&Q* 4s:3 (1869), 59, 154; 5s:3 (1875), 429, 475; 5s:4 (1875), 56, 97; 167 (1934), 458; 168 (1935), 30, 86.

Opie, Peter Mason. (1918–1982). Apart from a brief army career in his early twenties, Peter Opie's life was devoted to collecting and studying folklore, especially children's lore, on which he and his wofe Iona became worldfamous authorities. Using both library research and fieldwork, and drawing on information from many correspondents, they assembled materials from which were built a series of scholarly and elegantly written books, which are recognized as essential reference works in their respective fields: *The Oxford Dictionary of Nursery Rhymes* (1951), *The Lore and Language of Schoolchildren* (1959), *Children's Games in Street and Playground* (1969), *The Classic Fairy Tales* (1974), and the posthumously published *The Singing Game* (1985) and *Children's Games with Things* (1997). The card-indexes

kept by Peter and Iona also formed the basis for the latter's *Dictionary of Superstitions* (1989, with Moira Tatem).

Peter and Iona's work began at a time when folklore studies in England were at a low ebb, and made a startling impact, both in its meticulous pursuit of historical accuracy and its painstaking recording of contemporary material from children of school age. Never had the systematic gathering of material on such a large scale been attempted in England, and the results were an impressive testimony to the vigour and constant development of tradition. Their use of printed sources was also exemplary in its precision.

Peter Opie was President of the Anthropology Section of the British Association for 1962–3, and President of the Folklore Society for 1963–4. Poor health, however, forced him to husband his strength; he lectured rarely, and concentrated on research, writing, and his superb collection of early children's books and toys, part of which is now in the Bodleian in Oxford.

Oranges and Lemons. The traditional rhyme which details some of the church-bells of London is known all over the English-speaking world, and exists in numerous versions. Its first known printing was *c.*1744, in a version that starts with

> Two sticks and an apple
> Ring ye bells at Whitechapple
> Old Father Bald Pate
> Ring ye bells at Aldgate . . .

and it appeared regularly in 18th- and 19thcentury printed sources. It was not unusual for rhymes to be made on local bell-chimes, and it was presumably its regular appearance in print which made the London rhyme become the standard. Traditionally, the rhyme also accompanied a game (see *Gomme). There is some doubt about which St Clement's the rhyme refers to, although the congregation of St Clement Danes are sure it is their church which is mentioned, as they have a custom which began in 1920 on the occasion of the restoration and re-hanging of the church's bells. Every year, on or near 31 March, the church is decorated with oranges and lemons, and children from the nearest school attend for a special service. They are given fruit as they leave, which is traditionally provided by the London Danish community.

Opie and Opie, 1997: 398–401; Gomme, 1898: ii. 25–35; Hole, 1975: 151–2; Howard, 1964: 65–6.

Ordish, Thomas Fairman (1855–1924). All his working life was spent in the Civil Service, but he is remembered for his research into early theatre (particularly Shakespeare) and the history of London. He joined the Folklore Society in 1886/7 and served on its Council from 1888 to 1909 (with gaps), with traditional drama as his main interest. Ordish made the first real attempt to make a systematic collection of material on *mumming plays and *sword dances, primarily by published appeals for assistance, but also by his own collecting. He published three influential articles: 'Morris Dance at Revesby', *Folk-Lore Journal* 7 (1889), 331–56; 'Folk Drama', *Folk-Lore* 2 (1891), 314–35; 'English Folk-Drama II', *Folk-Lore* 4 (1893), 149–75, and a third in this series is to be found in his unpublished papers. Ordish tried to convince the theatre history establishment that their literary bias had led them to err in commencing their account of the development of drama with the medieval miracle and mystery plays. He maintained that the traditional drama which was collected in the 19th century was a direct survival of Anglo-Saxon and Danish custom which, along with the *May games, *hobby horses, pageants, and processions, were the true origins of the flowering of the dramatic impulse in post-medieval England.

As early as 1896, his projected book on the mumming play was announced as forthcoming, and it was still being advertised as such in 1905, but it never materialized, and there is evidence that its imminent arrival discouraged others from embarking on such a project. On his death, his extensive collection disappeared from view until it was resurrected, sorted, and transcribed by Alex *Helm and Margaret *Dean-Smith in the early 1950s, and is now lodged in the Folklore Society Archives. It was this exposure to a mass of mumming material which resulted in Helm's continued interest and influential writing on the subject, which put traditional drama back on the folklore agenda in England in the 1960s.

Alex Helm, *Folklore* 66 (1955), 360–2; Margaret Dean-Smith, *Folk-lore* 66 (1955), 432–4. Obituaries: *Folk-Lore* 35 (1924), 379.

'Orfeo, Sir'. This narrative poem, written in southern England in the late 13th or early 14th century and probably based on a lost French original, retells the myth of Orpheus and Euridice as the story of an abduction to, and rescue from, *fairyland—here described as a land inside a mountain, with a rich castle standing among fertile fields; there Orfeo sees people who on earth had seemed to die by sickness or violence, but had really been taken by fairies. As a reward for his music, he is allowed to take Heurodis home (there is no taboo on looking in this version).

Text in Kenneth Sisam (ed.), *14th Century Verse and Prose* (1921), 13–31; modern translation in J. R. R. Tolkien, *Sir Gawain and the Green Knight, Pearl, and Sir Orfeo* (1975).

origin stories. For centuries, there have been folktales which set out to explain how a custom began, why a *place-name was given, how some feature of the landscape was formed, why an animal, bird, or plant has certain characteristics. They not only explain, but, in many cases, supply a justification by reference to a prestigious authority or a notable past event, the more impressive the better. Examples from the religious sphere include legends claiming topographical features resulted from a saint's act or a *judgement on sinners (see *wells, *trees, *standing stones, *Semerwater); pious stories linking animals or birds with Jesus (see *donkey, *owl, *robin); customs validated by a link with the Christian calendar (see burning *Judas, *catterning, *souling).

Secular stories to account for local customs are fascinatingly varied, some containing a fair degree of historical accuracy, while others are colourful pseudo-history, or even jokes. Several events were allegedly founded by a noble medieval benefactress (see *bread and cheese dole, *Haxey Hood Game, *Tichborne dole); some supposedly celebrated a victory, for example catching a traitor (*Hunting the Earl of Rone), foiling French invaders (*Padstow), or simply outwitting a rival village (*Painswick). Street *football in several places was said to have originated in kicking an enemy's head—a Scotsman's at Alnwick (Northumberland), a Dane's at Chester. People giving money to a *Jack-in-the-Green were following the precedent of 'a lady who found her long-lost son as a sweep, and then she gave a celebration each year' (Judge, 1979: 45–51). Tinsley Green claims its *marbles championship began when two Elizabethan gentlemen, rivals in love, staked the lady's hand on a marbles match.

Besides these tales, which arise from within folk tradition, there are origin theories which were initially proposed by intellectual observers, but now permeate popular culture. One type claims a 'historical core of fact' underlying a fantastic or nonsensical item: for example, a dragon legend is 'really' a memory of Viking attacks, a nursery rhyme is 'really' about the Plague. The other is *Frazer's theory that folk customs are survivals of *fertility cults. Performers, press, and public now largely ignore individual origin tales in favour of a single all-purpose explanation: it is prehistoric and *pagan (preferably *Celtic), and whatever it may look like now, it was 'really, originally' a fertility ritual. Thus origin tales, like other aspects of folklore, evolve to reflect current tastes.

orpine. One of the orpine's nicknames is 'Midsummer Men', after a *love divination custom carried out on *Midsummer's Eve and reported all over the country since at least the 18th century. To test the potential relationship between two people, take slips of orpine, stick them upright, and place them side by side in pairs. The mutual attraction or aversion is judged by whether the slips inclined towards or away from each other. John Aubrey (1686: 25–6) claims that in his day it was particularly 'cooke mayds and dayrymaids' who were partial to this procedure, but the method and meaning remained remarkably stable until well into the 20th century.

Opie and Tatem, 1989: 295; Vickery, 1995: 270–1.

Otherworld. There is no clearly defined Otherworld for the dead in English folk tradition. Most stories and practices imply Christian beliefs, plus, in some cases, a vague, half-formulated idea that the dead are present in their graves. Traditions about *ghosts indicate that their presence on earth is an anomaly, but usually do not explicitly address the question of where they come from and where they should rightly be; one exception is the type of tale where an exorcist forces a ghost into a lake or under a boulder (see *laying) and binds it there; this might imply an Otherworld in the depths of the earth.

*Fairyland, too, is a form of Otherworld; it

was thought to be close alongside the human world, but underground or under water. Belief in this was strong in the Middle Ages, but diminished in later centuries.

Ottery St Mary (Devon). Here there are two, apparently unrelated, customs for Bonfire Night, or *November the Fifth. The most spectacular is the *tar barrel rolling in the evening, in which blazing tar-barrels are carried on the shoulders of local men as they run around the village streets. The other is the firing of the 'rock cannons', which are ten partly hollowed metal bars filled with gunpowder and exploded at three points during the day, allegedly to commemorate the landing of William III in 1688 (Kightly, 1986: 131). Compare *Fenny Poppers.

Shuel, 1985: 187

overlooking, see *EVIL EYE.

owls. That an owl's cry means death or disaster is an old and widespread motif, both in folk belief and as a literary convention; it applies most strongly to the screech of the barn owl. To see an owl by daylight, or to have one knock against the window, is especially ominous (Opie and Tatem, 1989: 295–6).

Ophelia in her madness remarks 'They say the owl was a baker's daughter' (*Hamlet*, IV. v), a reference to a medieval legend of the widespread type which offers an 'explanation' based on some imaginary incident in Jesus's life. Jesus, passing a baker's shop, asked for bread; the baker's wife was about to put a good slab of dough into her oven for him, when her daughter snatched most of it back, saying it was far too much for a beggar. But at once it swelled up enormously. 'Oo, ooo, oooo!' she cried, and turned into an owl (Howard Staunton (ed.), *The Plays of Shakespeare* (1858)).

oysters, see *GROTTOES.

pace eggs, see *EASTER EGGS. Where *Mumming Plays are performed at Easter they are called Pace-Egg Plays; see Eddie Cass, *The Lancashire Pace-Egg Play: A Social History*, 2001.

padfoot. A shape-changing Yorkshire *bogey, particularly belonging to the district round Leeds. Henderson (1866: 237–8) says one old woman saw it rolling ahead of her like a bale of wool; others said it was invisible, though one could hear the soft padding of its feet, followed by an ear-splitting roar.

Padstow Hobby Horse. This north Cornwall village has a day-long custom to celebrate the coming of May, with a *hobby horse who dances in the streets while its attendants sing:

> Unite and unite and let us all unite
> For summer is acome unto day
> And whither we are going we will all unite
> In the merry morning of May.

The narrow streets of the town are decorated with flags, flowers, branches, and bunting, half the locals are dressed all in white with a dash of blue or red as a wrist-band, sash, head-scarf, or neckerchief, there is a huge *maypole in the middle of the town, and the 'Obby 'Oss cavorts through the narrow streets to the sound of massed accordions, drums, and singing. This goes on all day, and there is nothing else like it in the English calendar. At present there are two Osses and therefore two teams, blue and red, and there have been others in the past. Both Osses are constructed in the same way: a circular wooden framework with a man inside with his head poking out through a hole in the top. A skirt of black material hangs all the way round the frame, and a tall pointed head, with mask, is placed on the man's head. The Oss also has a small head in front and a tail behind, but by no stretch of imagination does it look like a horse. The Oss can be made to dance, it can

swing from side to side, up and down, swirling and swaying. The musicians walk slowly in front or behind, and there is one who acts as Teaser, dancing in front of the Oss, holding a painted club. Others in the party dance as well. The whole party sings the song, over and over again, the first verse of which is quoted above, and other verses make little sense but work remarkably well. Every now and then the music slows, the rhythm of the song changes, the Oss sinks to the ground, the dancers crouch down, those nearest stroke it gently:

> O where is St George
> O where is he O
> He is out on his long boat on the salt sea O
> Up flies the kite
> And down falls the lark O
> Aunt Ursula Broadwood she had an old ewe
> And she died in her own park

and to the triumphant shout of 'Oss! Oss! Wee Oss!', it springs back to life with renewed vigour.

Earlier in the day, children's horses can be seen around the town, smaller versions of the real thing, learning their trade. The night before, starting as the church clock strikes midnight, the night-singers perambulate the town, singing to the inhabitants. Padstow Obby Oss has fascinated folklorists and other commentators for years, and many are the theories of origin which are presented, normally on some variation of the fertility ritual. It is true that women caught under the skirts of the Oss will be married (or pregnant) within a year, and there are numerous other little details which can be used to 'prove' anything one likes. One local story relates that once, when Padstow was about to be invaded by the French, and the menfolk were away at sea fishing, the women of the town constructed the Oss and its antics frightened the cowardly invaders away.

Donald R. Rawe, *Padstow's Obby Oss and May Day Festivities* (1971); Doc Rowe, *We'll Call Once More Unto Your House* (1982).

paganism. The term (with its synonym 'heathenism') for any religion where several gods and goddesses are worshipped; its relationship to folklore has long been debated, and is central to most *origin theories.

In England, the first people to discuss folklore from the outside (as opposed to participating in it) were Elizabethan Protestants, who used it as a weapon in their campaign to identify Catholicism with paganism. They sought out every possible similarity between medieval customs and rituals and those of the only two pagan cultures they knew about: Old Testament Gentiles, and classical Greeks and Romans. This was the argument of Philip Stubbes's *The Anatomie of Abuses* (1583), with its famous diatribe against the *maypole as a 'stinking idol'; it was taken up by antiquarians such as the Revd Henry *Bourne, whose *Antiquitates Vulgares* (1725) attacks popular customs and beliefs as coming from Pagan Rome via Papist Rome. Even *Aubrey, who liked old ways, held the same theory. In his significantly titled *Remaines of Gentilisme and Judaisme* (1686) he argues that ceremonies and beliefs were 'imbibed' by the ancient Britons from the Romans, and survived wherever 'the Inundation of the Goths' (i.e. Anglo-Saxons) did not penetrate (Aubrey, 1686/1880: 55).

Several generations of writers referred back to Flora, Ceres, or the Saturnalia, to explain English festivals. Then 19th-century scholars showed that early Germanic and Celtic peoples had had myths and rituals of their own, independent from Rome, supplying closer precedents for English traditions. Claims for pre-Christian origins have always had great appeal among the general public, if only for the glamour antiquity confers; currently they are more popular than ever, for pagan beliefs (especially *Celtic ones) are seen by many as admirable, and Christian tradition as repressive and dull.

However, there is an important distinction between showing that a custom or belief is older than Christianity, and arguing that when it is found among Christians it means paganism is still alive. Some aspects of the supernatural (e.g. fear of *ghosts and *witchcraft, belief in *dreams) are so commonplace that they can occur in virtually any period, including our own, and do not correlate with

one religion rather than another. The same is true of large categories of non-rational thought and action, e.g. those involving *fate, *luck, *omens, and minor practices such as *touching wood; Christians who think or act in this way rarely see it as inconsistent with faith. *Calendar and *life-cycle customs usually involve celebratory activities (e.g. dancing, special foods, drinking, disguise, bonfires) distinct from the religious side of the event (if any), but not felt to be in conflict with it. The appropriate word for these is 'secular', not 'pagan'.

In England, a fair amount is known about Roman, Celtic, and Anglo-Saxon religions before the arrival of Christianity, but little about the conversion process itself, which has led modern advocates of paganism to claim that tolerance and continuity was the norm. For the first wave of Christianization, that which reached the Celtic Britons of the 4th century, the only evidence points the other way: when Celtic Christians reused pagan sites, they mutilated and dumped the statues of the gods (Merrifield, 1987: 96–106). The final conversion, that of the Anglo-Saxons, is described by Bede as a peaceful process, but evidence of continuity is again scanty. Despite the interpretation sometimes put on *Pope Gregory's letter, no Saxon pagan shrine has yet been found underlying a church; though (very exceptionally) some Roman sacred sites were reused (Merrifield, 1987: 93–5). Coincidence of dates is even less significant. The dates of *Christmas and *Easter had been fixed long before Christianity reached Britain, and reflected Roman paganism and the Jewish Passover respectively, not the festivals of northern Europe; since every day in the Christian year celebrated at least one saint, every pagan festival necessarily coincided with a saint's day, for reasons quite unconnected with local cults.

The only significant documents are some law-codes of the 7th and 8th centuries forbidding sacrifices to Germanic deities, and some more in the early 11th century applying to the diocese of York, where Viking settlers had reintroduced them. The names of some gods appear in place-names, royal genealogies, and one or two *charms, but their myths vanish; surviving hero-legends (*Beowulf, *Wayland) have no religious content.

There is thus no general framework to support claims that individual folklore items are pagan survivals, and each must be assessed on its own merits. For discussion of the main candidates, see *ABBOTS BROMLEY, *ANIMAL DISGUISE, *CERNE ABBAS, *FOLIATE HEADS, *GREEN MAN, *HALLOWEEN, *HEADS, *JACK-IN-THE-GREEN, *MAY DAY, *MAYPOLES, *MUMMING, *SHEILA-NA-GIGS, *SKULLS, *SWORD DANCES, *UFFINGTON, *WELLS, *WILMINGTON, *YULE.

For discussion of British religions in relation to later folklore, see Hutton, 1991. For the religions individually, see Martin Henig, *Religion in Roman Britain* (1984); G. A. Waite, *Ritual and Religion in Iron Age Britain* (1985); Miranda Green, *The Gods of the Celts* (1986); Proinsas Mac-Cana, *Celtic Mythology* (1983); Gale Owen, *Rites and Religions of the Anglo-Saxons* (1981); David Wilson, *Anglo-Saxon Paganism* (1992).

Painswick Feast and Church Clipping. This Gloucestershire town is noted for several traditions, which cluster around the old *Feast day. The church is dedicated to the Virgin Mary, and on the first Sunday after her Nativity on 19 September (Old Style), the parishioners, and many visitors, gather at the church for the *Clipping ceremony. This involves a procession of local children, led by church banner, clergy, band, and choir, around the churchyard. For the 'clipping', the children join hands and encircle the church, and while a special hymn is sung they walk forwards and backwards three times. Everyone then processes to the stone steps of the tower where the vicar delivers a sermon.The children wear their best clothes and flowers—the boys as buttonholes, the girls in their hair or carrying baskets—and they receive a bun and a token payment.

One element of the Painswick custom which has fallen by the wayside, and for which no one can offer a satisfactory account, was the behaviour of the children after the clipping was over. They used to run, pell-mell, along the road to the vicarage, shouting 'Highgates'. It is conceivable that the bun and/or payment is a remnant of a *scrambling custom, previously carried out at the vicarage, but this is guesswork. The word 'clipping' means 'embracing', but at Painswick it has been confused with the physical clipping of the 99 *yew trees in the churchyard. It used to be believed that only 99 yews would grow in the churchyard, and that all attempts at planting more would be unsuccessful.

The other tradition for which Painswick is known is the baking of Puppy-Dog Pies. Writers differ quite sharply in describing these delicacies and it is as hard to get an authoritative description as it is to pin down

the custom's origin. Most agree that the pies had small china dogs inside, but they are referred to variously as plum pies, apple pies, meat pies, or even cakes topped with almond paste. Explanations of the pies also vary. The one most often quoted by journalists links the custom with the Roman festival of Lupercalia, which, it is said, involved the sacrifice of dogs. As usual this can be dismissed completely. The local legends are far more interesting—one is that the local landlord, despairing as to how to feed all the people flocking to Painswick Feast actually resorted to cooking puppy-dogs. People from neighbouring villages use the dog-filled pies as a way of deriding Painswick people as barbarians, but the Painswickians turn this round. They maintain that they once invited the young men from neighbouring villages to a feast, and afterwards informed them they had been eating dog-pies especially cooked for them.

Shuel, 1985: 84–5; Sykes, 1977: 124; Hole, 1975: 94–5; Stone, 1906: 19–21; Briggs, 1974: 35–6.

Palm Sunday. In the late Middle Ages, this was one of the most vivid festivals of the year. Before Mass, the priests blessed 'palms' (twigs of sallow, box or yew) which the congregation carried in procession and later took home. During Mass people made crosses, either from their 'palms' or from sticks and string they had brought to the church; these too were blessed, and taken home to ward off evil (Duffy, 1992: 23–7).

Echoes remained in the secular folk custom of 'going a-palming', common from the 18th century until the mid-19th century. Groups of young people went into the woods to collect the catkin-bearing hazel and sallow, to decorate their homes and bring luck for the year, and to wear in their buttonholes. In northern counties, sallow was still made into crosses and hung on walls; William Henderson recalled making them himself as a boy in the 1820s, 'like a St Andrew's Cross, with a tuft of catkins at each point, bound with knots and bows of ribbon'. In some places those gathering 'palms' then headed for a prominent hill, to dance and hold sports, eat figs and cakes, and drink sugared water. This caused annoyance to landowners whose hedges and woods were invaded, and was held to encourage drunkenness, brawling, and immorality; it was discouraged by the later Victorian gentry.

See also *FIG SUNDAY, *PAX CAKES.

pancake races. The custom of eating pancakes on *Shrove Tuesday is well attested from the 16th century onwards; in the 19th century there are many references to the custom of tolling a church bell at 11. a.m. or midday to show the day's work was over and jollifications could begin, including cooking the pancakes. This was variously known as the Pancake Bell, Fritter Bell, or Pan-Burn Bell, and is thought to have evolved from a medieval custom of ringing to call people to church for 'shriving'.

Nowadays, all over the country, there are races in which women must toss pancakes in a pan while running; they are now generally accepted as an integral part of the season, and some have been held sufficiently regularly to be regarded as established local customs. The most famous, at Olney (Buckinghamshire) claims as its *origin legend that back in 1445 a woman rushed off to church on hearing the shriving bell, still holding her frying pan. Its real age is hard to establish. It is not mentioned in Wright and Lones, which must mean not only that it was not held in the 1930s but that there were no references to it in older works. What is certain is that soon after the Second World War the vicar 'revived' it (is it significant that the alleged origin date is exactly 500 years before 1945?), and that in 1949 'the Junior Chamber of Commerce of Liberal, Kansas, USA ... challenged the women of Olney as to who could win a race over the same distance' (Ingram, 1954: 90). The races have been twinned ever since; the times of the American and English winner are then compared, and an overall prize awarded. Any female resident over 16 can take part, provided she is wearing an apron, has her head covered, and is carrying a frying pan complete with pancake, which must be tossed three times on the way. The publicity inspired a host of imitators from the 1960s onwards, and today pancake races multiply yearly.

Wright and Lones, 1936: i. 8–16; Tom Ingram, *Bells in England* (1954), 89–92.

parsley. There are various sayings about sowing parsley, which is notoriously slow to germinate. It must be sown on *Good Friday before noon; its roots go seven (or nine) times down to Hell and back before any shoots appear; it will only grow where the wife is boss of the household. Transplanting it is thought to bring death or disaster, and some also say it should never be given away.

It also has sexual connotations; 'parsley bed' is a euphemism for female genitals and 'parsley' for pubic hair—hence a traditional put-off used since the early 17th century when children ask where babies come from; they are told 'from the parsley bed' (variants: 'from the nettle bed' or 'under the gooseberry bush'). Its role in gynaecological lore seems inconsistent: some sources say sowing, picking, or eating parsley will make a woman conceive easily; others say crushed parsley placed in the vagina, or eaten three times daily for three weeks, will bring on a period and cause miscarriage; others recommend eating large quantities to recover from childbirth (Opie and Tatem, 1989: 298–9; Vickery, 1995: 273–5).

pavement. A well-known game or superstition of 20th-century children is to avoid stepping on the cracks between the paving stones (or even on cracked stones) of the pavement. There is a wide variety of predicted consequences. Treading on a crack could bring general bad luck, predict how many pieces of china you would break, or even mean that you would have a black baby. Alternatively, bears or snakes will chase you. Opie and Tatem give the first known reference as *c*.1890. Several responses to our 1998/9 *Superstitions Survey related a current children's belief that stepping on a 'three-drain' (a drain or manhole cover in three sections) is particularly unlucky.

Opie and Opie, 1959: 220–2; Opie and Tatem, 1989: 300.

pax cakes. The churches of King's Caple, Hentland, Sellack, and Hoarwithy—all now in Hereford and Worcester—have a tradition of distributing small buns on *Palm Sunday after the morning service; they are called pax cakes, signifying reconciliation and goodwill. It was established in 1570 by a local landowner, Lady Scudamore; in the 19th century, local farmers provided cider and ale (Leather, 1912: 97–8). After lapsing in the early 20th century, the Hentland custom has been revived, and is now well kept up both there and at Sellack, where cider too is given. The distribution is made as the parishioners leave church, the vicars saying to each, 'God and good neighbourhood', or 'Peace and goodwill'.

peacocks. In medieval symbolism, peacocks represented vanity and pride. Nowadays, some think they bring bad luck; more commonly, it is only their tail-feathers that are feared, and should not be worn, used in fans, or brought indoors as decorations. This belief is first noted around the mid-19th century, and has been widespread since; it is generally explained by the green eye-like markings, emblem of jealousy and the evil eye. The bird's screech is also said to foretell rain.

Pearly King, Queen. London costermongers (street vendors) are the only English occupational group to have evolved a festive costume. Men of their leading families wear black velveteen suits to which hundreds of mother-of-pearl buttons are sewn in decorative patterns; the women's black velveteen dresses are similarly adorned, and they wear huge hats with ostrich feathers. This showy style dates from the late 19th century, and probably developed out of a single row of buttons stitched to the trouser-seam by coster lads; the first to wear it is said to have been Henry Croft (1863–1930). In each borough, the eldest couple in the most respected family holds the title of Pearly King and Queen. Pearlies are much in demand as tourist attractions, and at charity fund-raising events (Binder, 1975).

Peeping Tom, see *GODIVA.

Peg o' Nell. The *water-spirit of the *river Ribble in Lancashire. She was said to be the ghost of a servant at Waddow Hall, Clitheroe, who broke her neck when she slipped on the ice, having been sent to fetch water on a frosty night. Every seven years she would claim a life in revenge, but this would not necessarily be human—she could be tricked by deliberately drowning a cat, bird, or dog. A local story tells how a young man once insisted on fording the river, even though he was warned that it was the seventh year and no animal had yet been sacrificed; he and his horse were swept away by a sudden gush of water (Henderson, 1866: 229).

In other versions, she was said to live in 'Peggy Nell's Well', in a meadow on the edge of the river, where a headless stone statue beside the well is supposed to represent her, the head having been chopped off as punishment after she caused a Puritan preacher to fall in the river.

Peg Powler. A green-haired *water-spirit in the *river Tees, used by adults as a *bogey; children were told that if they played on the

banks, especially on Sundays, she would drag them in and eat them (Henderson, 1866: 229).

Penny Hedge. At 9 o'clock in the morning of the day before *Ascension Day a small group of Whitby residents in north Yorkshire gather on the foreshore of the harbour to construct what looks like a small fence, but is called a 'hedge', out of willow sticks and interwoven strips of hazel. This hedge has to be strong enough to withstand three tides, and always is. When the hedge is complete, the Bailiff of the Court Leet of Fyling blows a horn and shouts 'Out upon ye! Out upon ye!', meaning 'shame on you'. As usual, there is a legend to explain this odd event. In 1159, two lords, William de Bruce and Ralph de Piercie were out boar-hunting on the Abbot of Whitby's land. One particular boar took refuge in a local hermitage, and the hermit refused (or neglected, as he was praying) to open the door. They were so angry that they attacked, and mortally wounded, the poor hermit. Before he finally died, the hermit begged the Abbot to spare the lives of the lords if they agreed to an annual penance. He left precise instructions that they should build this hedge, on the foreshore, having carried the sticks on their backs, supervised by the Officer of Eskdale-Side. Failure to do so would result in forfeiture of their lands. There is no doubt that this legend is completely untrue. All authorities agree that the custom goes back well beyond the 12th century and is a relic of Horngarth, which was a *manorial obligation by which tenants had to build and maintain particular hedges or fences on the Lord of the Manor's land. These same authorities all disagree on this particular hedge, and whether it was to keep animals in or out, and whether the horn refers to the horned animal or a hunting horn, and so on.

Smith, 1989: 29–32; Kightly, 1986: 187–8; Jeffrey, 1923: 38–45; Gutch, 1901: 344–8.

pentacle, pentangle, pentagram. A five-pointed star made by drawing a single line as interlocked triangles, also sometimes called Solomon's Seal, or the Endless Knot, used as a powerful protective symbol; now often regarded as the essential mark of a magician.

It is first found in ancient Greece and the Near East as a decorative pattern on coins and buildings, and was a symbol of the perfect universe (four elements plus spirit) among Gnostics and Neoplatonists in the early centuries AD. It reached medieval Europe via

Jewish and Arab culture, and was reinterpreted in Christian terms as an emblem of the Five Wounds of Jesus, guaranteed to put demons to flight. In the 1660s, Aubrey had a clergyman friend who always headed his letters with it; this custom had once been widespread, 'for good-luck's sake' (Aubrey, 1686/1880: 51).

Medieval legend said that either this design or the six-pointed star had been engraved on a seal-ring used by Solomon to control demons. The author of *Gawain and the Green Knight* calls the 'pentangle' on Gawain's shield 'Solomon's Sign', but interprets it in terms of the Five Wounds, five senses, five virtues, and the Five Joys of Mary. A pentagram within a circle was the basis for most of the complex protective patterns drawn on the ground by ritual magicians of the Renaissance (and later) when summoning or banishing spirits; modern magicians sometimes extend the term 'pentacle' to cover any disc engraved with magic symbols, reserving 'pentagram' for the five-pointed star itself. When it is displayed vertically (e.g. when worn as a medallion), it has one point upwards if the intention is protective; since the late 19th century occultists have regarded a pentagram with two points upwards as sinister, even Satanic, though this distinction does not appear in older writings.

Percy, Thomas (1729–1811). Bishop of Dromore from 1782 to 1798, he also had a lifelong interest in literary matters, wrote poetry, and edited a number of publications, including translations from the Chinese and Icelandic. His major claim to fame, however, came with a manuscript which he discovered (probably about 1753) 'lying dirty on the floor under a bureau in ye parlour' of his friend Humphrey Pitt's house in Shifnal (Shropshire), which the maids were using to light the fire. The manuscript contained, amongst other poetical items, versions of traditional *ballads, and had probably been compiled in the mid-17th century. Percy was finally persuaded to publish his find, in February 1765, as *Reliques of Ancient English Poetry: Consisting of Old Heroic Ballads, Songs and Other Pieces of Our Earlier Poets (Chiefly of the Lyric Kind) Together with Some Few of Later Date*. This was the first real collection of ballads, and was an immediate success, with a new edition required a month later, a third in 1775, and a fourth in 1794. *Reliques* laid the foundations for ballad collection and study in Britain, but also changed the face of poetry, being cited as a source of inspiration on all

sides—including Wordsworth, Scott, and Coleridge. It caught the mood of the time, which was for an unsophisticated, relatively natural style of verse, and the wildness of the ballads, even in the attenuated form printed by Percy, proved irresistible to the stirring romantic notions of the literary world. Nevertheless, while poets welcomed the book wholeheartedly, scholars such as *Ritson attacked Percy's editorial methods which by modern standards were extremely poor, but which were unexceptional for the time. Percy had certainly interfered with the ballads he published, editing, conflating, softening, rewriting, and all but faking. He attempted, in later editions, to remove at least the most glaring editorial faults, and was also forced to rewrite the incorporated essays on origins—in particular as regards the history of the professional minstrel class. By the time the fourth edition was needed, in 1794, Percy himself was reluctant to have his name still connected with such trivial matter, and it was thus ostensibly edited by his nephew, also called Thomas (1768–1808). The scholarly world had to wait until 1867–8 to see the manuscript in its entirety and be able to judge for themselves the full nature of Percy's handling of the ballads, when it was finally edited and published in full by J. W. Hales and F. J. Furnivall as *Percy's Folio MS*, as a result of the perseverance of Professor F. J. *Child. Despite his editorial shortcomings, Percy has retained his fame as a pioneer, and one of the Victorian societies founded to reprint early ballad and poetical material was fittingly called the Percy Society.

Bertram H. Davis, *A Scholar—Critic in the Age of Johnson* (1989); Albert B. Friedman, *The Ballad Revival: Studies in the Influence of Popular on Sophisticated Poetry* (1961); DNB.

Perrault, Charles (1628–1703). In 1697 this French writer published *Histoires et Contes du Temps Passé*, eight fairytales with traditional plots, rendered in a polished and witty style; they were translated into English in 1729 as *Mother Goose Tales*, a term taken from Perrault's subtitle. Five are now among the basic tales all English children know: 'Cinderella', 'Sleeping Beauty', 'Puss in Boots', 'Bluebeard', and 'Red Riding Hood'.

phantom carriages. A fairly common motif in legends of the 19th century or earlier is that the *ghost of some local aristocrat or landowner rides about the countryside at night in a spectral black carriage; its horses may be headless, or fire-breathing, or luminous, and similarly monstrous *black dogs may precede it. Recorded versions show considerable relish for these macabre details. A famous instance is the carriage of Lady Howard of Tavistock (Devon), who died in 1671 after marrying, and allegedly murdering, four husbands in turn; it is made of bones, with a skull at each corner, and runs nightly from Tavistock to Okehampton Castle (Brown, 1979: 32).

Besides these elaborate but fanciful tales, there were sober personal anecdotes about sightings of phantom funerals which were dreaded as death *omens, foreshadowing real funerals.

phantom ships. Several 19th-century folklorists noted traditions in Cornwall about phantom ships. Some were to be seen sailing straight ashore, skimming over dry land as if it were sea; the sight was an *omen of storms and wrecks. Sometimes dramatic explanations were offered: that the ship bore the *ghosts of two pirates, one of whom had murdered the other, or the *Devil coming to carry off the soul of an old wrecker (Bottrell, 1873: 247–9).

Tales about spectral ships generally involve re-enactment of tragedy, the vessel appearing near the place where it sank on an anniversary of the disaster. There are two such legends about wrecks on the Goodwin Sands (off Kent). The first concerns the warship *Northumberland*, one among several driven on to the Sands during a gale in November 1703; 50 years later she allegedly reappeared, with her ghostly crew leaping into the sea. The second concerns the *Lady Lovibund*, said to have been deliberately wrecked on the Sands on 13 February 1748 (or 1724) by the mate, because the woman he loved had married the captain, who had brought her aboard for their wedding voyage. This ship too supposedly returned every 50 years, in 1798, 1848, and 1898; to the bitter disappointment of journalists, she was not seen in 1998. These tales are often included in modern books on sea-lore, but it is unclear how old they are; the *Lady Lovibund*, for instance, seems first to have been mentioned in 1924.

The first known reference to that most famous of all phantom vessels, *The Flying Dutchman*, is in *The Life of a Sea Officer*, by Jeffrey, Baron de Reigersfeld (Maidstone, c.1830). His account is yet another 're-enactment' story—one of two ships rounding the Cape of Good Hope on the way to the East Indies foundered in a storm and was callously abandoned by the other; in this version, when the ghostly ship is sighted, it is sinking below the waves (A. W. Smith, forthcoming). However, during the 19th century a more dramatic legend evolved in Europe, and became widely known, in England as elsewhere; in this, the *Dutchman* is not a wrecked vessel, but one that is doomed to sail for ever, because her captain blasphemously swore God could not prevent him rounding the Cape.

pharisees, see *farisees.

photocopylore. When the photocopier became readily available in offices in the 1960s, people seized on the new medium for their own unofficial purposes and a new folklore genre was born. Photocopylore exploits the machinery to create multiple copies of items, which are then circulated from person to person. Much of the content of photocopylore is traditional, including jokes and cartoons, while other pieces are new, such as spoof memos, and satirical comments on office procedures. As the item gets repeatedly copied, and gradually fades, somebody redraws or retypes it, and slightly different versions are created, in the same way as oral tradition creates subtly different versions. Many of the items circulated are bawdy, or downright obscene, while others perpetuate racist and sexist stereotypes, and the ease and privacy of the copying process are ideal for this sort of material. The use of headed notepaper adds a spurious authority.

Also called 'Xerox-lore'.

Smith, 1984; Dundes and Pagter, 1975; Dundes and Pagter, 1991.

pictures. The idea that a picture suddenly falling off the wall betokens a death—especially if it is a portrait—has been current since at least the late 17th century, and is still not obsolete. The belief is quite understandable if one accepts that sudden unexplained happenings can be literally ominous and the fact that a portrait can symbolically represent the real person. In some circles, it was regarded as unlucky to hang pictures over a door or a bed. The first mention of this belief is in Igglesden (c.1932: 234) who reports it as a superstition of the *theatre.

See also *'CRYING BOY' PAINTING.

Opie and Tatem, 1989: 304–5.

pigeons. Often connected with illness and

death in English folklore. Beliefs regarded a pigeon alighting on a bed, or even on a house, as a sign of at least sickness, and sometimes death, and there is a tradition that a sick person asking for a pigeon must be near death as 'that is almost the last thing they want'. Numerous references from the 17th century onwards concern the use of pigeons in medical, often near-death, contexts. It was commonly believed that a live pigeon, cut in half, and applied to a sick person's body, would draw out a fever or sickness. Samuel Pepys' *Diary*, for example, twice mentions this procedure: 'they did lay pigeons to his feet while I was in the house; and all despair of him ...' (21 Jan. 1668). Similarly, application of a pigeon would draw out adder poison. A saying that 'He who is sprinkled with pigeon's blood will never die a natural death' has a legend to support it. When Charles I was receiving a new bust of himself, sculpted by Bernini, a pigeon flying overhead was attacked by a hawk, and the pigeon's blood fell on the bust, staining it red round the neck—a stain that could never be removed. In other versions (such as Aubrey, 1696) it is a different or unnamed bird (*N&Q* 7s:8 (1889), 468; 7s:9 (1890), 13–14, 77). See also *adders, *feathers.

Black, 1883: 163–4; Opie and Tatem, 1989: 308–9; *N&Q* 151 (1926), 136.

pigs. Sailors and *fishermen commonly regard pigs as very unlucky; they will not say the word 'pig' at sea ('grunter' or 'porker' is used instead); those who meet a pig on the way to their boat will not sail that day; some will not allow pork or bacon on board (Clark, 1982: 151–60; Gill, 1993: 78–81). This fear is presumably based on the 'uncleanness' of pigs in the Bible, and perhaps more specifically on the Gadarene swine (Mark 5: 11–15; Luke 8: 22–3), who drowned. Some said marks on pigs' legs were caused by the pressure of the Devil's fingers, when he entered that herd.

It is said that pigs can see the wind, and also (inaccurately) that they cannot swim, because they cut their throats with their own trotters. In Sussex, pigs are respected for their independent spirit and associated with the county's informal motto, 'We wun't be druv'. Perhaps because of 'piggy bank' money boxes, pig figures are lucky *charms.

pilgrimage. Medieval England had many pilgrimage centres, including those of Thomas à Becket at Canterbury, the Virgin Mary at Wals-

ingham (Norfolk), the Holy Rood at Broomholm (Norfolk), the Holy Blood at Hailes Abbey (Gloucestershire), and *Glastonbury. People went on pilgrimage as a penance for sin, or to fulfil a vow, or seeking a cure for sickness. The usual procedure was to spend several days praying near the saint's tomb or the altar where the holy relic was kept, and if possible to touch it; at Canterbury, pilgrims drank water which allegedly contained a trace of Becket's blood. Flasks of water and pouches of dust scraped from the shrine were taken home for future use.

It was normal to make offerings at shrines. A common custom was to bend a silver *coin when vowing to make a pilgrimage, and give it on arrival. Another was to measure the height of a sick person (or the length of an injured limb) with thread, and then use this as the wick of a *candle to be burned at the shrine. Those who had experienced a miraculous recovery or escape might leave miniature wax, silver, or gilded images of bodies, heads, limbs, eyes, teeth, hearts, animals, boats, anchors, or carts, each representing an injury healed or an accident averted. Votive offerings hung in hundreds round the shrines; periodically wax ones would be melted down into candles and silver ones into coins, but plenty always remained.

Finucane, 1977; Ben Nilson, *Cathedral Shrines of Medieval England* (1998).

pin-a-sight. A *display custom of little girls in an Oxfordshire village in the 1880s. In *Lark Rise To Candleford* (1945, chapter 9), Flora Thompson describes making 'a kind of floral sandwich' by stripping as many brightly coloured petals as possible from flowers, and laying them on a small sheet of glass, with another sheet placed over it. The whole thing would be wrapped in brown paper, 'in which a little square window was cut, with a flap left hanging to act as a drop-scene'. The device was called a 'pin-a-sight'; if the girls showed them to adults, they expected to be rewarded with a pin, and recited:

> A pin to see a pin-a-sight,
> All the ladies dressed in white.
> A pin behind and a pin before,
> And a pin to knock at the lady's door.

See also *POPPY SHOW.

pins. One important folkloric function of pins is to symbolize attack. Witches were regularly suspected of using them in their destructive *image magic, and of mysteriously introducing them into the bodies of their victims, who would then vomit them. The crew of a fishing smack, in the 1880s, were dismayed when a pinned-up parcel was brought aboard; the captain dropped the pins overboard one by one, at arm's length, explaining they were 'spiteful witches', and all subsequent misfortunes in that trip were blamed on the pins (N&Q 7s:4 (1887), 165–6).

Pins were also much used in aggressive *counterspells by those who thought themselves bewitched (see *hearts and pins, *witch bottles). In the fiercely worded love charm involving an animal *blade-bone, pins were sometimes used instead of a knife to prick the bone, and there are tales from East Yorkshire and from Derbyshire of girls driving pins into a live frog as part of a charm to force a man to marry them (Hole, 1973: 90). They also serve as a medium of magical transference, for example when rubbed over a *wart and then stuck in the ground, so that someone may tread on them and 'catch' the wart.

Pins were popular offerings in holy *wells and *wishing wells, though now *coins are more usual; when so used, they were generally bent.

The best-known belief about finding pins is expressed in the rhyme (first recorded in 1842 and still current):

> See a pin and pick it up,
> All the day you'll have good luck;
> See a pin and let it lay,
> You'll have bad luck all the day.

Opie and Tatem, 1989: 309–12.

pixy, pisky. This is the standard term in Devon, Cornwall, and Somerset for a *fairy, though many writers from the early 19th century onwards have insisted that the two races are quite distinct; the word is probably related to *Puck. One distinctive feature is the belief in Devon and Cornwall that pixies are the ghosts of babies who died unbaptized, an explanation often given for the *Will-o'-the-Wisp, but not for other English fairies. However, stories told elsewhere about fairies are told of pixies in the south-west, for example that they ask a human midwife to assist at their births, abduct babies and leave changelings, steal from human homes, etc.

Their best-known characteristic is causing people to lose their way, even in a familiar neighbourhood; victims can escape by turning some item of clothing inside out. They may do this by appearing as a flickering light, or by turning into what seems to be a horse (a 'colt-pixy') and luring the traveller's own horse into a bog. They may operate either singly or in groups; the latter may be seen dancing in circles. They invade stables at night, tangling the horses' manes and making them sweat; they cause strange noises and play tricks, like poltergeists.

However, single pixies are sometimes credited with being helpful, like *brownies, and like them will cease working if spied on, thanked, mocked, or given clothes. In the latter case, proud and delighted, the pixy disappears, crying:

> Pixy fine, pixy gay,
> Pixy now will run away.

Pixy tales will be found in Bray, 1836; Bottrell, 1870–90; Hunt, 1865; Courtney, 1890; Tongue, 1965.

place-names. To find the true origin and meaning of place-names requires access to early documents and familiarity with Old and Middle English dialects, but lack of these resources never stopped people devising explanations by relating names to real or imagined history, legend, or fanciful wordplay. There are hundreds such in every county, not only for towns and villages but for fields, woods, rocks, lakes, etc. Some draw on established story-patterns; others are mere puns and jokes.

Village rivalry has led to many place-name rhymes which recur in various parts of England with differing but appropriate names. Thus:

> —— for riches, —— for poor,
> —— for a pretty girl, and —— for a whore.

Taunts rhyming 'people' and 'steeple' are widespread, for example:

> Dirty Tredington, wooden steeple,
> Funny parson, wicked people.
>
> (Gloucestershire)

> Berwick is a dirty town,
> A church without a steeple,
> A dunghill before every door,
> And very deceitful people.
>
> (Northumberland)

So are lists with insulting epithets:

> Beggarly Bisley, strutting Stroud,
> Mincing Hampton, Painswick proud.
>
> (Gloucestershire)

Mary Williams, *Folklore* 74 (1963), 361–76; W. F. H. Nicolaisen, *Folklore* 87 (1976), 146–59. The latter uses Scottish examples, but sets out principles equally applicable to English material.

placenta. The information on popular *childbirth practices is too inadequate to allow us to judge whether the placenta was always formally disposed of (not just thrown away), but this seems likely. In 20th-century midwifery, the official rule was to burn it—on the fire in the living-room or bedroom for home deliveries, in an incinerator at hospital. Some said one could tell how many more children the woman would have by counting the pops it made while burning; *Aubrey said midwives predicted how long a baby would live by burning the afterbirth (Aubrey, 1686/1880: 73).

Nowadays, women who give birth at home sometimes choose to have the placenta buried in the garden, with a shrub planted over it. This is a revival of an older custom, with continental parallels (Gélis, 1991: 167–71); some informants recall the practice from before the Second World War, and add that a placenta was the best possible fertilizer for rose bushes [JS]. Others eat the placenta as a natural medicine to avoid post-natal depression, and this too may have a traditional basis, since French evidence suggests that it was sometimes eaten to encourage lactation (Gélis, 1991: 167–71). The National Childbirth Trust recently published a book, *Placenta Special: Eat It or Plant It?*, since it is 'a frequent topic among young mothers' (*Independent* (27 Nov. 1998), 3). A placenta can also serve as a dressing to promote healing of pressure sores and deep ulcers, and be rubbed on the mother's breasts to prevent chapping when breast-feeding [JS].

In 19th-century Cheshire, some men believed they 'could gain the affections of a woman almost against her will by burying a placenta at the threshold of her house. This was actually done within living memory at Gatley (Cheshire) by a man named Gatley, he having procured one for two guineas. The charm failed in this instance, the woman being very self-willed' (Moss, 1898: 169).

Some farmers disposed of a cow's or mare's placenta by hanging it in a hawthorn tree. In Hampshire in the 1930s this was done 'as a preventative of fever in the cow' (Vickery, 1995: 170); on a farm in Bilsdale (Yorkshire) it is still being done, to bring luck to newborn foals (*FLS News* 28 (1998), 8–9). They may also have wanted to thwart the animal's instinct to eat her afterbirth if (as in France) they feared she would then eat her offspring too (Gélis, 1991: 166).

Plague. The Great Plague ravaged London, and other places, in 1665/6, and as with all major events generated its own set of beliefs and customs at the time, and also reverberating ever since. We are fortunate to have in Daniel Defoe's *A Journal of the Plague Year* (1722), a 'fictionalized' account of life in London in 1665, numerous examples of the folklore of the time. Indeed, Defoe proves to be an excellent observer of the folkloric, including, amongst other things, portents, preventative charms, herbal remedies, and omens. In the early stages of the plague, people's fears drove them to 'running about to fortune-tellers, cunning-men and astrologers to know their fortune' (p. 47), and he gives details of some of the charms used—'papers tied up with so many knots, and certain words or figures written on them, as particularly the word Abracadabra, formed in a triangle or pyramid . . .' (pp. 51–3). Other preventatives were herbal, including garlic, rue, tobacco, and vinegar. Defoe was also one of the first writers to identify what we now term *contemporary legends (p. 102).

The Great Plague lives on, in various ways, in English folklore. At Eyam, Derbyshire, since 1905, the last Sunday in August has been Plague Sunday. This commemorates the heroic part played by the village people when the disease broke out in their midst. By maintaining a self-imposed quarantine neighbouring communities were spared, but 259 of Eyam's 350 inhabitants died (Kightly, 1986: 189; Palmer, 1991: 122). In addition, several places in England claim to have a Plague Stone, the distinguishing mark of which is an indentation which served as a receptacle for vinegar in which money could be placed by non-locals doing business with a quarantined village. Correspondence in *N&Q* 159 (1930) identifies existing examples and gives numerous references. In modern times, the plague is often cited as the origin of saying 'bless you' when someone *sneezes, and also as the basis for the children's game *Ring-a-Ring-a-Roses. Neither has any evidence to support it. In local lore, the presence of a 'plague-pit' is often postulated as the possible cause for hauntings or to explain unused pieces of land.

plantain. Bruised plantain leaves applied to a cut are said to stop it bleeding; more dubiously, an infusion of bucks horn plantain and honey or treacle was said in East Anglia to cure rabies; its flowers are among those which should not be brought indoors, on pain of causing one's mother to die (Vickery, 1995: 52, 161, 285). For the magic 'coal' allegedly found under its roots, see *Midsummer.

plants. The most recent and most authoritative work on the folklore of plants in the British Isles is Roy Vickery's *A Dictionary of Plant Lore* (1995), drawing on information gathered between 1981 and 1994, as well as on previous books and journals. It covers beliefs, customs, and traditional uses, and is supplemented by his booklet on *Unlucky Plants* (1985). Among older works, the most important are T. F. Thistleton Dyer's *The Folk-Lore of Plants* (1889), and Geoffrey Grigson's *The Englishman's Flora* (1955; 2nd edn., 1987).

See *FLOWERS, *HERBS, *TREES, and the names of individual plants.

Plough Monday. The first Monday after *Twelfth Day (6 January) and in rural communities this was traditionally the day on which farmworkers prepared to go back to work after the Christmas break, and to start the all-important task of ploughing the fields ready for sowing later in the year. The day itself had its own customs, including one in which one of the farm lads had to get into the kitchen and place one of the tools of his trade at the screen, or fireplace, before the maid had put the early morning water on to boil (see Tusser, 1580/1878 edn.: 180). More common, however, was some form of ceremony involving a plough. In many areas there was a 'common plough', housed in the church, which could be used by any smallholder too poor to own one himself. At New Year or Plough Monday the plough would be blessed by the parish priest and then decorated and paraded around the neighbourhood by the ploughboys of the local farms. Money collected by these men went to maintain the 'plough lights' which were candles kept burning in the church to ensure continued divine blessing on this essential operation in the farming cycle. The Reformation of the church in the 16th century abolished both the lights and the plough blessing, and also removed the ecclesiastical sanction for the plough procession, but the latter continued, or was revived, by the farmworkers now collecting money on their own behalf—to be spent on drink and merrymaking. The pro-

cession and plough were the main focus, but the custom took on divergent forms, with some teams performing versions of *plough plays, others simply dancing and singing or reciting rhymes. The first known reference to the plough procession dates from January 1413, in Durham, but it is not until the 18th century that informative descriptions of the custom become available.

See also *MOLLY DANCING, *MUMMING PLAYS.

Hutton, 1996: 124–33; Wright and Lones, 1938: ii. 93–103; E. C. Cawte, 'It's an Ancient Custom—but How Ancient?', in Buckland and Wood, 1993: 37-56.

plough plays. One of the three main types of *mumming play, found only in the East Midlands, and first reported in the 1820s. Performances were concentrated on *Plough Monday, but could take place at any time over the *Christmas/*New Year period, and were typically by teams of male farmworkers who, in addition to performing the play around the neighbourhood, dragged a plough with them, and were thus often called by local names such as Plough Jags, Plough Bullocks, and so on. Plough plays invariably include the combat/cure sequence of the more widespread Hero-Combat type of play, but their main feature, which distinguishes them, is a 'wooing' section. Either a 'Lady' (played by a man) is wooed by a series of suitors or, more commonly, a Recruiting Sergeant entices the Lady's farmworker lover away and she then accepts the Fool's advances. Much of the wooing is expressed in sung dialogue.

Peter Millington, *FMJ* 7:1 (1995), 71–2; Helm, 1981: 11–19; M. W. Barley, *JEFDSS* 7:2 (1953), 68–95; C. R. Baskervill, *Modern Philology* 21 (1923), 225–72.

poldies. In the Wirral and along the Cheshire/Lancashire border, poldies are a type of *fairy said to live in woodland. One of the present authors [JS] was told by a friend who often visited that area as a child in the 1950s, how children going to the woods would be told by their parents to come home in good time—'You take care of the poldies. As soon as it starts to get dark the poldies come out.' They were also thought of as guardian spirits of the woods, who would punish anyone who did damage there by causing them to have some accident. The informant recalls a cousin of hers deliberately twisting small branches off a tree and tossing them away, despite her protests; a few minutes later he sprained his ankle badly, which she thought might well be the poldies' doing. Some years later, she heard of a building contractor abandoning plans to grub up a wood in the Wirral because of constant delays from flooding, machinery breakdowns, etc.; local people said it was due to poldies defending their homes.

poltergeists. Although the name is a Victorian borrowing from German, the phenomenon has been repeatedly described in English sources from Elizabethan times onwards; sometimes a *boggart or similar household goblin was blamed, sometimes *witchcraft, sometimes a demon or a ghost. Famous examples, much discussed by learned writers at the time, were the 'devil' haunting the royal palace at Woodstock in 1649; the 'Tedworth Drummer' which caused innumerable disturbances in a Wiltshire house from 1661 to 1663, and was thought to be a demon magically sent by an aggrieved ex-soldier whose drum had been confiscated by the magistrate living there; and the 'Cock Lane Ghost' of 1760–2 (Bennett, 1987: 184–8; Finucane, 1982: 140–3, 157; D. Grant, *The Cock Lane Ghost* (1965)).

Pope Gregory's Letter (AD 601). Very often quoted, but rarely in full, is a letter sent by Pope Gregory to Abbot Mellitus, who was about to join Augustine in England, in the year 601; we know of it only through Bede's *Ecclesiastical History of the English Nation*, written in 731 (book 1, chapter 30). Those who wish to demonstrate the origins of traditional customs and lore in pagan times use it as a much-needed bridge across the societal chasm of Christianization; they take it to mean that the Church in England adopted a general policy of appropriation rather than confrontation, and from this basis argue for a large-scale survival of non-Christian elements within the Church and/or within society. It has become a key element in many modern interpretations of folklore.

This is thus a crucial text, requiring close scrutiny. The numerous translations agree in substance but differ a little in emphasis; the one quoted here was first published by Dent in 1910. Gregory asks Mellitus to tell Augustine:

what I have, upon mature deliberation of the affair of the English, determined upon, viz., that the temples of the idols in those nations ought not to be destroyed; but let the idols that are in them be destroyed; let holy water be made and sprinkled in the said temples, let altars be erected, and relics placed.

For if those temples are well built, it is requisite that they be converted from the worship of devils to the service of the true God; that the nation, seeing that their temples are not destroyed ... may the more familiarly resort to the places to which they are accustomed.

So far, the letter is permissive rather than prescriptive: well-built temples can be reused, once properly consecrated. It does not say that every temple must be so used—far less that the siting of purpose-built churches should be determined by proximity to pagan shrines and landmarks. Gregory then turns to festivals:

And because they have been used to slaughter many oxen in the sacrifices to devils, some solemnity must be exchanged for them on this account, as that on the day of the dedication, or the nativities of the holy martyrs whose relics are there deposited, they may build themselves huts of the boughs of trees, about those churches that have been turned to that use from temples, and celebrate the solemnity with religious feasting, and no more offer beasts to the Devil, but kill cattle to the praise of God in their eating, and return thanks to the Giver of all things ...

To schedule the new feasts to coincide with the anniversary of the church's dedication, or the feast-day of its patron saint, would almost inevitably break any previous links with the agricultural cycle or seasonal turning-points—the letter does not advise picking saints whose days match pagan festivals. His advice that people should build huts (*tabernacula*) of tree branches does not imply that this was already an English custom; it is more likely that he had in mind the Old Testament Feast of Tabernacles (Leviticus 23: 39–43) as a suitable model for converts to adopt. There is no reason to think the English had such huts, and far likelier that they feasted comfortably indoors in the halls of local leaders, or possibly in the temples themselves, if these were large. That Gregory was thinking of the Old Testament is borne out by the rest of the letter, which discusses how 'the Lord made Himself known to the people of Israel in Egypt' by gradual degrees, allowing them to go on killing beasts, but 'in his own worship', not as an offering to the Devil. This raises the question of how much Gregory actually knew about English paganism; did he have detailed information, or was he making generalized assumptions about how pagans behaved?

It is in any case doubtful that the policy outlined in this letter was widely adopted. In the same year, Pope Gregory wrote to King Ethelbert, urging him to 'abolish the worship of idols and destroy their shrines' (Bede; book 1, chapter 32). The few other relevant documents include no other reference to any policy of accommodation, but on the contrary mention several temples deliberately destroyed; archaeology has so far found no traces of pagan Saxon shrines under any churches. David Wilson concludes: 'There is no intimation from the literature that any attempt was made to convert these sites into Christian churches on the lines suggested by Gregory' (Wilson, 1992: 29–43).

Vida D. Scudder (ed.), Bede's *The Ecclesiastical History of the English Nation* (1910).

poppet, poppy shows. A *display custom of children in the 19th and early 20th centuries, where they arranged flowers, small dolls, dolls' house furnishings, etc., inside a shoe-box or similar container; adults or other children would be asked to pay a penny, or sometimes only a pin, for the privilege of looking in through a slit in the side. Poppies were not necessarily used; the name may be a misunderstanding of 'peepshow'. As children carried their boxes through the street, they would chant such rhymes as:

> A pin to see the poppet show
> All manners of colours oh!
> See the ladies all below!

A recent informant recalls how, as a little girl living in Hove (Sussex) in the 1920s, she would put ferns and beach pebbles on the bottom of a shoe-box, and then flowers and 'little bits and pieces of coloured glass, feathers, shells—anything to make a pretty pattern', especially, if possible, 'coloured paper from a sweet wrapping'. Boys in Norwood (London) at the same period made peepshows in cereal boxes, depicting scenes from stories or nursery rhymes.

Gomme, 1894: 41–2; Irene Saxby, *London Lore* 1:2 (1978), 19–20.

poppies. Besides symbolizing sleep and unconsciousness, poppies were also associated with death, and already at the time of Waterloo it was said that those growing on the battlefield had sprung from the blood of soldiers (Dyer, 1889: 115). This symbolism was taken up during and after the First World War; in the period leading up to Armistice Day and Remembrance Sunday (11 November, and the Sunday nearest to it) they are widely worn as lapel badges, and wreaths of them laid at memorials for the dead of all recent wars.

Country beliefs about poppies were chiefly warnings: to pick or sniff them supposedly caused headaches, earache, blindness, warts, or a strong possibility of being struck by lightning. The purpose may have been to stop children trampling the corn in order to pick flowers (Vickery, 1995: 286–90).

Porter, Enid (1909–84). Curator of the Cambridge and Country Folk Museum, Cambridge, from 1947 to 1976, and a leading authority on that region's material culture, dialect, place-names, local history, cures, customs, tales, and beliefs. During her fieldwork she discovered two excellent Fenland informants, W. H. Barrett and Arthur Randall, from whom she collected enough tales and reminiscences to edit into five books (published under their names, not hers), important sources for the region's life and storytelling. Her own major work is *Cambridgeshire Customs and Folklore* (1969), a *regional study equal to the finest in earlier generations, covering University and civic customs as well as rural lore. Her *Folklore of East Anglia* (1974) is a smaller book, but equally well researched; she contributed numerous articles to local journals. Both her museum work and her writings are major achievements.

Carmen Blacker, in *Women and Tradition*, ed. Hilda Davidson and Carmen Blacker, 2001: 233–44.

potatoes. Carried in one's pocket, potatoes were widely thought to cure or prevent rheumatism, especially if they had been stolen; as they dry and harden, they supposedly are drawing from the sufferer's body the uric acid (or, according to other informants, the iron) which causes the pain. The idea was common in the 1950s (Radford, Radford, and Hole, 1961: 272), and is probably still to be found. A common cure for *warts was to rub them with a slice of potato, and bury it; as it shrivelled, so would the warts.

prams, see *CRADLES.

precious stones. Lapidaries, i.e. treatises on the 'virtues' of precious and semi-precious stones, circulated throughout medieval and Renaissance Europe. Some writers dealt only with their supposed curative properties; others said they had a moral influence too, for example that amethyst prevents drunkenness, and sapphire cures anger and stupidity; the majority also listed magical powers, for example detecting poison, driving demons away, ensuring the favour of princes, etc. The power of the jewel could be enhanced by engraving it with planetary or zodiacal symbols, or with religious formulas such as Hebrew titles for God, names of angels, acronyms representing Scriptural phrases, etc. Many surviving medieval and Elizabethan rings and pendants prove that these principles were put into practice by those who could afford to do so. Those who could not, nevertheless knew about them at second hand, through popular manuals of magic such as *The Secrets of Albertus Magnus, of the Vertues of Herbes, Stones, and certaine Beasts* (1637). Unrelated but analogous beliefs have arisen in the 20th century, first as regards the luck of birthstones, and more recently as regards the healing properties and spiritual symbolism of crystals.

pregnancy. The folklore of pregnancy, like that of *childbirth, is inadequately recorded in England. The process was jokingly compared with baking bread; a pregnant woman is still said to 'have a bun in the oven', and a mentally impaired child to be 'half-baked'. Various signs were thought to indicate the baby's sex. Ancient Greek authorities had taught that a male foetus lay to the *right of the mother's womb and affected the right side of her body, and this notion can be found as late as 1724 in Jane Sharp's *The Compleat Midwife's Companion*: 'If it be a Boy, she is better Coloured, her Right Breast will swell more, for Males lie most on the right side and her Belly especially on that side lieth rounder and more tumefied and the Child will be first felt to move on that side, the Woman is more cheerful and in better Health, her Pains are not so often or so great' (cited in Chamberlain, 1981: 190).

Women still pass on such tips to one another, though often with amusement rather than belief. Some say one can tell the baby's sex by whether it is carried high or low, and whether it kicks to the right or to the left; others, that 'boy baby bumps are all out at the front, while girl baby bumps are spread round the side as well'. Many say boy babies kick harder ('He'll be a footballer!'), but the reverse is recorded too: 'If you don't feel much movement from the baby it is a boy' (Chamberlain, 1981: 241).

A divination frequently mentioned is to suspend a wedding ring or a key over the pregnant woman's womb on a thread, or one of her own hairs, to see if it spins clockwise or anti-clockwise, or straight; however, informants disagree on which movement means which sex (Opie and Tatem, 1989: 302–3; Chamberlain, 1981: 241; Sutton, 1992: 57).

Blemishes in a newborn infant were blamed on the circumstances of its *conception, or events during the mother's pregnancy. The best known is the harelip, caused by a *hare crossing the mother's path, but virtually any troubles could be explained this way. If, for instance, a child had an ugly birthmark, it would be said to resemble something the mother had stared too hard at, or been frightened by, or longed in vain to eat. Examples of this belief can be found from the 16th century to the present. A woman from Hackthorn (Lincolnshire) recalled in the 1980s:

I knew of a child who was born with a perfect mouse on his wrist. His mother had gone into the pantry and had seen a mouse (it's the truth I'm telling you) and she grabbed her wrist like *this* and the child was born with the shape of a mouse on his wrist. My husband used to say it was balderdash, but it's true. Anyway, he had to go into hospital to have it taken off, so there. (Sutton, 1992: 56)

Deformities were also sometimes seen as God's *judgement on a sin of the mother (not the father), typically a blasphemous remark, or a refusal of charity. The belief was exploited for propaganda by both sides during the Civil War. A royalist pamphleteer claimed a Puritan woman had declared while pregnant that she would rather bear a headless baby than let her baby be baptized, and that this had duly happened; a Puritan pamphleteer matched this with the story that a royalist woman had said it would be better her child had no head than become a Roundhead, with the same result. In 1871, the Revd Francis Kilvert learnt of a crippled woman then living in Presteigne, who was said to have the face and feet of a frog:

The story about this unfortunate being is as follows. Shortly before she was born, a woman came begging to her mother's door with two or three little children. Her mother was angry and ordered the woman away. 'Get away with your young frogs,' she said. And the child she was expecting was born partly in the form of a frog, as a punishment and a curse upon her. (*Kilvert's Diary*, ed. W. Plomer (1960), i. 380–1)

See also *CHILDBIRTH, *CONCEPTION, *CRADLE, *LIONS, *MONSTROUS BIRTHS.

prehistoric sites. Visible landscape features

which seemed artificial, yet had no practical function and no known history, frequently feature in *local legends. They are associated with the *Devil, *giants, *fairies, and legendary heroes or wizards. Many are said to conceal *treasures, or to be places where ritual actions (such as running round them) can raise *ghosts. How much of all this was seriously believed, and how much merely repeated for fun, is hard to assess.

See also *BARROWS, *STANDING STONES, *CADBURY CASTLE, *LONG MEG, *MERRY MAIDENS, *ROLLRIGHT STONES, *STONEHENGE, *WAYLAND'S SMITHY, *WILLY HOWE.

Grinsell, 1976, is a systematic listing; more detail for individual sites will be found in regional collections, and in some cases also in Westwood, 1985.

primroses. These flowers were believed to affect luck in poultry rearing, presumably because primroses and chicks are both bright yellow ('like affects like'). From the mid-19th century to within living memory, children were warned never to bring fewer than thirteen primroses into the house, for this was the optimum number for a clutch of chicks, and fewer primroses meant fewer eggs would hatch. It was sometimes further believed that giving someone a single primrose, or bringing one indoors, would cause death (Vickery, 1995: 293–7).

printing trade. At least until recently, the printing trade has had many of the characteristics which encourage the development of *occupational lore and customs, being a particularly well-organized, long-standing trade where skilled workers and trainees are employed in close co-operative conditions. As with other trades, most customs were associated with key events in an individual's domestic or work life: birthday, wedding, birth of first child, first day at work, completion of training, promotion, retirement, and so on. The custom of 'banging out' workers at the end of their apprenticeship is still carried out, and it usually involves covering the victim in anything sticky and messy (printing ink, flour, feathers, and so on), tying him up and leaving him thus in a public place. The custom gets its name from another part of the custom, in which the whole workforce mark the event by making a tremendous noise: 'each seized one of the heavy metal frames in which the type is arranged and a small bar of iron. They hammered on the frames with such force that

it was as if a dozen blacksmiths had gone suddenly crazy' (Drake-Carnell, 1938: 111–12).

In previous times the trade had also many other customs to mark key points in the worker's life. Charles Manby Smith describes a mock wedding custom at the firm of Hansard's, about 1836, to celebrate a colleague's forthcoming marriage. First of all his workstation was decorated with branches, ribbons, and so on. The workers then commenced making the fearful banging noise, and then came a procession around the workshop with a man dressed as the bride, a surrogate groom (the real one being a little frail), elaborately attired master of ceremonies, fiddler, and others. A none-too-decent oration was delivered and the whole party decamped to the pub (Charles Manby Smith, *The Working Man's Way in the World* (1853)). This is all a far cry from the elaborate and dignified May Day ceremonies at Stationers' Hall, described by Hone in 1827 (*Every-Day Book*, ii. 314–15).

See also *OCCUPATIONAL LORE.

Prisoners' Base. One of the most popular chasing games on record, although only played nowadays in watered down form. It requires a fair degree of organization, and also needs more concentration and strategy than most chasing games and it was played in earlier times as much by adults as children. Two teams are chosen, each has a home-base and a prison at opposite ends of the playing area. Players chase each other and if caught are placed in the opposing prison, but can be freed again by their own side. The essence of the game is that a player chases one opponent at a time, but can also be chased him/herself at the same time, and play is directed by two captains. Full instructions are printed in Gomme and Opie. The latter also gives early references back to the 14th century, and there are numerous literary mentions, including Shakespeare (as 'Country Base' in *Cymbeline*, v. iii) and Spenser's *Faerie Queene* (1590–96: v. viii. 5): 'as they had been at bace, They being chased that did others chase'. The earliest references are French, and the game may have originated there. Certainly it was as popular on the Continent as in Britain. Also called Prison Base, Prison Bars, Chevy Chase, Chivy, Country Base, Fast and Loose, or simply, Bars, Base, etc.

Gomme, 1898: ii. 79–83; Opie and Opie, 1969: 143–6.

prophecies. For English popular 'prophetic'

writings, see *Merlin, *Nixon, *Mother Shipton. Foreign texts, notably the verses of Nostradamus, have also been frequently translated and reinterpreted to fit the pre-occupations of each generation.

See also *DOOMSDAY, *NUMBER 666.

proverbs. Short, crisply structured sayings widely known in a community, which convey traditional observations on human nature and natural phenomena, moral judgements, mockery, warnings, etc. Though circulating orally, their wording is fairly stable; they generally display formal devices including alliteration, rhyme and assonance, rhythmic phrasing, balanced opposition, and parallelism, which govern the formation of such modern examples as 'garbage in, garbage out' and 'the family that prays together, stays together'. These features, however, may be absent, especially in those which started life as literary quotations, for example 'Hell hath no fury like a woman scorned'. Familiar proverbs are often alluded to rather than given in full, and may also be deliberately distorted for humorous effect (see *Wellerisms); they influence the language of slogans and advertising.

Collections of English proverbs first appear in the 16th and 17th centuries, where they are usually set alongside parallels in other European languages and the classics, reflecting the educated collectors' awareness of international cultural tradition; a high proportion of English proverbs are of foreign origin.

See the *Oxford Dictionary of English Proverbs* (3rd edn., ed. F. P. Wilson, 1970); Simpson and Speake, 1992.

Puck. Although 'Puck' is now mainly thought of as the personal name of one character in Shakespeare's *Midsummer Night's Dream*, it is in fact an ancient word, found both in Germanic and in Celtic languages, for a demon, *goblin, or troublesome *fairy. In medieval and Elizabethan English, the connections can be quite sinister; Langland calls Hell 'the poukes poundfold', and Spenser, calling down blessings on a newly married couple, prays that they may be safe from fires, lightning, witches, 'the Pouke and other evill sprights'. But Shakespeare's Puck is only a mischievous trickster who boasts of shape-changing and leading travellers astray; like a helpful domestic *brownie he arrives at the end of the play, broom in hand, to sweep the house so that the fairies may bless it.

The name 'Puck' appears in two Sussex variants of the story of the man who spies on his fairy helpers, one published in 1854 and the other in 1875. A farmer (or a carter) who realizes someone has been secretly threshing his corn (or feeding his horses) watches two small fairies toiling at these tasks until one says to the other, 'I say, Puck, I sweats, do you sweat?' The man bursts out laughing (or cursing), and the fairies rush off; he falls sick and pines away (or his horses do) (Simpson, 1973: 55–7). Also in the mid-19th century, being 'poake led' was a dialect term in the Midlands and west of England for having lost one's way at night or feeling bewildered and confused.

Briggs, 1959.

Punch and Judy. Puppet shows were well established in Elizabethan and Stuart times, especially as a popular fairground entertainment. The subjects were very various: Bible stories, the legends of Faustus, *St George or Dick *Whittington, historical episodes such as the Gunpowder Plot, and so forth. In 1662 Pepys noted the arrival of a new character from Italy, called Pollicinella or Punchinello, but soon to be renamed 'Punch'—a fat hunchback with a shrill voice who would disrupt the more serious plays by bawdy remarks, fighting, and farting.

Soon, Punch developed a mini-drama of his own (first mentioned in 1682), centred on the battles between him and the shrewish 'Mrs Punch', whose name at this period was Joan. Another of its standard features was an encounter with the Devil; a writer in *The London Spy* on 10 May 1699 says that at a May Day fair he heard 'a senseless Dialogue between *Punchinello* and the *Devil* . . . conveyed to the Ears of a Listening Rabble thro' a Tin Squeaker'. The ending varied; most evidence from the 18th century supports Strutt's comment in 1802 that 'Punch is constantly taken away from the stage by the Devil at the end of the puppet show', but some writers say that it was always Punch who beat the Devil.

In 1828 John Payne Collier, a journalist, interviewed a puppeteer called Giovanni Piccini and took down the text of 'Punch and Judy' from his dictation, while the illustrator George Cruikshank drew scenes of the puppets in action. The basic plot is the one used ever since: Punch loses his temper with his own baby and kills it, fights his wife and kills her, kills a succession of characters, beats a policeman, tricks Jack Ketch the hangman into hanging himself rather than Punch, and finally kills the Devil. Later showmen added further characters and episodes, notably a clown, a ghost, a beadle or constable, and a crocodile, and developed the role of Dog Toby (a real dog, not a puppet); to this day, no two shows are alike in every detail.

Towards the end of the 19th century Punch changed from an itinerant fairground and street show appealing primarily to adults to a children's treat associated with seaside holidays and Christmas parties. Since 1962, the 300th anniversary of the arrival of Punch in England, the show has been enjoying a strong revival, but is increasingly geared to children's tastes, with much audience participation and topicality, as in pantomimes, to mask the unwelcome violence of the basic plot.

Traditionally, the showmen carved their own puppets and jealously guarded their personal method of making a 'swazzle', the metal device which, held in the mouth, transforms the human voice into Punch's screech. Some families performed Punch for several generations. The 'script' was always open to variation and improvisation around a central structure; this interplay of fluidity and stability, individuality and anonymity, marks Punch and Judy as folk art.

Speaight, 1955/1990, and 1970; Leach, 1985. J. P. Collier's 1828 text, *The Tragical Comedy or Comical Tragedy of Punch and Judy* was reprinted several times, for example in a booklet from Routledge & Kegan Paul in 1976, which, however, omits the important introduction and notes. For an analysis of one present-day performer's art, see Robert Leach, *Folklore* 94 (1983), 75–85.

Punkie Night. A punkie is a hollowed out mangold-wurzel, with shapes cut through the sides, and a lighted candle inside. The children of Hinton St George, Somerset, parade the village streets on the last Thursday in October, with their lighted punkies, calling at different houses in the hope of receiving money or sweets, singing:

> It's punkie night tonight
> It's punkie night tonight
> Give us a candle, give us a light
> It's punkie night tonight

There is nowadays a competition for the best punkie designs. A local legend purports to explain the custom's origin. The village menfolk went to Chiselborough Fair, and got too drunk to find their way home. Their wives fashioned lanterns out of mangoldwurzels and went to fetch them. The problem with this explanation is that it implies that the men only got drunk at Chiselborough once. The neighbouring village of Lopen claims the custom (and legend) as their own, and other villages have started punkie nights.

K. Palmer, *Folklore* 83 (1972), 240–4; Kightly, 1986: 191; Hole, 1975: 96–7.

Quarter Days, see *CALENDAR.

Queen Elizabeth I anniversary (17 November). The anniversary of Queen Elizabeth I's accession to the throne in 1558 was previously an important date in the Protestant festival calendar, and was used well into the 18th century as a way of propagating the Protestant faith and denigrating the Roman Catholic Church. Parades and processions took place on the day, anti-popery sermons were preached, and bonfires and effigies, similar to those of *November the Fifth, were much in evidence.

Brand, 1849: i. 404–8; Cressy 1989.

rabbits. The idea that rabbits are unlucky is mainly limited to *fishermen, who insist that the word 'rabbit' must never be uttered at sea, nor the actual animal brought on board; they should be called 'long-ears', 'furry things', or 'bob-tailed bastards' (Gill, 1993: 84–6). There was a similar fear among Dorset quarrymen in the 1950s (Opie and Tatem, 1989: 191). Wild white rabbits might be witches, or death *omens (Tongue, 1965: 51; Maple, 1960: 243; Folk-Lore 4 (1893), 258).

Nevertheless, a rabbit's foot carried in the pocket was a lucky *charm in the 20th century; examples mounted in silver made in America but sold in England were advertised as 'the left hind foot of a rabbit killed in a country churchyard at midnight, during the dark of the moon, on Friday the 13th of the month, by a cross-eyed, left-handed, red-headed bow-legged Negro riding a white horse—this we do not guarantee' (Folk-Lore 19 (1908), 296).

A fairly widespread modern custom among children was first recorded in 1909:

My two daughters are in the habit of saying 'Rabbits!' on the first day of each month. The word must be spoken aloud, and be the first word said in the month. It brings luck for that month. Other children, I find, use the same formula. (N&Q 10s:11 (1909), 208)

Other versions, common between the wars, use the formulas 'White rabbits!' or 'Rabbits, rabbits, rabbits!', and some add that one must say 'Hares!' or 'Black rabbits!' last thing the previous night.

Radio Ballads. A highly influential series of radio programmes devised by Ewan *MacColl and Peggy Seeger and produced by Charles Parker for the BBC, between 1958 and 1964. The programmes covered a wide range of topics and broke new ground in the extensive use of tape recordings of ordinary people talking and singing, interwoven with songs and music specially written by MacColl and Seeger. The full list of Radio Ballad programmes, with first broadcast dates, is as follows: The Ballad of John Axon (railwayman) (July 1958), Song of the Road (the building of the M1) (Nov. 1959), Singing the Fishing (the herring industry) (Aug. 1960; winner of the Prix d'Italia that year), The Big Hewer (mining) (Aug. 1961), The Body Blow (polio sufferers) (Mar. 1962), On the Edge (teenagers) (Feb. 1963), The Fight Game (boxing) (July 1963), and The Travelling People (Gypsies) (Apr. 1964). Three of these were turned into television programmes by Philip Donellan: Shoals of Herring (1972), The Fight Game (1973), and The Big Hewer (1973). The programmes were re-issued on compact disc in 1999.

Ewan MacColl, Journeyman: An Autobiography (1990), 311–36.

rag trees, see *WELLS.

rainbows. A rainbow is now regarded as lucky, a symbol of peace, and an occasion for making a wish; it is sometimes said to mean good news coming. In older lore, however, there was some fear of rainbows; in the 19th century, children tried to drive them away by 'crossing them out', i.e. laying crossed twigs or straws on the ground (Opie and Tatem, 1989: 322). To point at one brought 'dreadful bad luck' (Leather, 1912: 16).

Ram Roasting. Every *Whitsun, a live and suitably decorated ram was driven in a cart in procession around Kingsteignton, Devon, and then publicly roasted. Nowadays, the ram is already dead before being paraded, and the custom has moved to the nearest bank holiday, but the principle is the same. While the ram is being roasted, there are games and other celebrations, and everyone present should have a piece of the ram's meat, but there are now so many visitors that only those with special programmes get a piece of the animal itself. Animal-roasting customs were relatively common in the past, but Kingsteignton is the only one to survive in this area, and even this one was radically altered around 1885. Phyllis Crawford records that, about 1937, an aged woman had explained that her husband, the vicar, had started the procession, eradicated the drunkenness, and transformed the custom into a 'fine old ceremony'. This is an excellent example of how *calendar customs can change, on *Merrie England lines, virtually overnight. The accompanying origin legend is noteworthy in that, uniquely among calendar customs, it approximates the pagan-origins view of the early folklorists, and it would not be at all surprising to learn that a wandering amateur folklorist had planted it. The story is that, long long ago, the Fairwater stream, on which the village relied for water, unaccountably dried up. The people sacrificed a ram in the dry river bed and that started it flowing again, and it has continued to flow ever since, because the custom has been kept up.

Crawford,1938: 131–3; Wright and Lones, 1936: i. 169–70; Kightly, 1986: 193; *N&Q* 6s:7 (1883), 345.

Randwick Cheese-Rolling and Wap. Randwick, Gloucestershire, had two, probably unrelated, *calendar customs of note. The cheese-rolling was described in a letter, dated April 1827, published in William Hone's *Table Book*, which related that every May Day three large Gloucester cheeses were decked with flowers and carried on litters in procession through the town, and were then rolled around the church before being cut up and distributed. This custom has been revived, following closely the old description, but with only one cheese being distributed and the other two set aside for rolling at the start of Randwick Wap. The term 'Wap' has not been satisfactorily explained, but it is the name for the local revel or feast, which was held on the second Monday after *Easter, and it perhaps pertains to the weaving trade which was the mainstay of the village economy. The celebrations included a *mock mayor ceremony, first mentioned in 1703, and suppressed about 1892 because of the drunkenness it encouraged. It was revived in 1972, along with other celebrations of the new Randwick Wap (see Briggs).

Hone, 1827: i. 277; Hartland, 1895: 33–7; Wright and Lones, 1936: i. 128–9; Gomme, 1883: 228–30 (reprinting pieces from 1794); Kightly, 1986: 71, 166–7; Briggs, 1974: 184–6.

rapper dances, see *sword dances.

rats. Regarded as uncannily intelligent, hostile to humanity, dirty, and destructive. They are supposed to foresee the destruction of any house or ship they are living in, and to abandon it; hence the proverbial saying that 'rats leave a sinking ship'. *Fishermen think they must not be named on board, and say 'longtails' instead (Gill, 1993: 86); an East Anglian girl told the Opies in 1953 that one should only speak of a rat as 'Joseph', to avoid bad luck (Opie and Tatem, 1989: 322–3).

Plagues of rats were regarded as sinister. Charlotte Latham was told of a Sussex man whose cottage was said to be full of evil spirits in the form of rats; every night one would hear him cursing them and begging them to leave him in peace, and his neighbours thought they would eventually carry him off to Hell (Latham, 1878: 23). Charles Dickens recalled a terrifying tale his nurse used to tell him, about a carpenter who 'sold himself to the Devil for an iron pot and a bushel of tenpenny nails and half a ton of copper and a rat that could speak', and thereafter is so tormented by this rat that he tries to kill it, only to find himself haunted by dozens of them. He is pressed for a sailor, and finds rats on board, led by the speaking rat, gnawing the ship to pieces; nobody believes his warnings, and all are drowned (Dickens, *The Uncommercial Traveller*, chapter 15).

Similar horror surrounds sewer rats. An elderly eccentric man in Worthing (Sussex) in the 1970s firmly believed that armies of them would emerge and overrun the town if he did not regularly scare them away by noisily thrashing lamp-posts and railings [JS]. In Manchester in 1981, a woman told how, when her father-in-law was young, he once saw a horde moving from one part of the town to another, led by a King Rat, 'the biggest rat of the whole shebang' (Bennett, 1988: 17–18).

A very different tradition is remembered in the families of 'toshers' who worked in London sewers in the late 19th century. They believed in a character called the Queen Rat, who could turn into an attractive girl and seduce any tosher she fancied; if he satisfied her, she would see to it that he had good luck and found money and other valuables lost down the gratings—provided he never boasted of meeting her, for if he did he might get drowned. Usually the man did not guess who she was, for she looked quite human, except that her eyes caught the light like an animal's, and she had claws instead of toenails; however, she might give him a rat-like love-bite on the shoulder or neck. The children a man had with his human wife after having been with the Queen Rat would have one blue eye and one grey one, grey being the colour of the river (Liz Thompson, *FLS News* 21 (1995), 5; 22 (1995), 4–6).

Most people, however, wanted to get rid of rats. Like *mice, they were believed to respond to magic; a Cornish rat-charmer of the 1950s worked by whistling, which 'seems to have a hypnotic effect on rats, causing them to crawl to him, or, if fleeing, to stop: whereupon the rat-charmer is able to pick them up and subsequently to dispose of them' (*Folk-Lore* 64 (1953), 304).

ravens. In general, ravens are unlucky birds, and their croaking an *omen of death. However, the tame ones at the Tower of London are England's *mascots; if ever they die out, or fly away, the Crown and the country will be destroyed. It was Charles II who gave the first ravens to the Tower, and the belief may only date from his time. On the other hand, *Arthur himself, the archetypal protector of Britain, was linked with these birds. Cervantes wrote in *Don Quixote* (1605, book II, chapter 5) that no Englishman will kill a raven because 'there is an ancient tradition common all over that kingdom of Great Britain that this king did not die, but by arts of enchantment was transformed into a raven'. Similarly, a contributor to *N&Q* (1s:8 (1853), 618) told how his father, some sixty years earlier, aimed a shot at a raven on Marazion Green (Cornwall), and was rebuked by an old man who said King Arthur was still alive in the form of that bird.

Raw-Head and Bloody-Bones. A traditional *bogeyman; also used allusively for robbers, etc., whose rumoured activities created panic. The earliest citation in the *OED*, from 1550, lists 'Hobgoblin, Rawhed, and Bloody-bone', with punctuation implying that the latter are two distinct beings; other early quotations seem to support this, but in the 19th century the whole phrase is generally a hyphenated unit. In East Anglia, Lincolnshire, Warwickshire, Lancashire and Yorkshire, children were told there was an ogre lurking in deep ponds

and marlpits to drown them, known as Tommy Rawhead, or Bloody-bones (Wright, 1913: 199).

red. In most contexts, red is associated with good luck, health, and joy, presumably because it is the colour of blood, and hence of the living body as opposed to the corpse. There are numerous references in folklore collections to the use of red threads, ribbons, wool, or pieces of flannel to prevent or cure a wide variety of ailments; also to red thread as protection against *witchcraft—a selection of examples can be found in Opie and Tatem, 1989: 326. Trees and shrubs with red berries are powerful, either for good or ill (*hawthorn, *holly, *rowan, *yew).

However, a few beliefs link red with foreboding, notably a widespread current taboo on giving a mixed bunch of red and white *flowers to a sick person, and another, less common, that petals dropping from a red rose or a poppy are an evil omen for the person holding it (Opie and Tatem, 1989: 325). The association with blood can turn sinister, as when the heraldic emblem of a red hand is taken to mean that the family founder was a murderer, or when legend claims that after some battle a local river ran red with blood. In popular art and stage tradition, the Devil may be red, though *black is more usual. The symbolism whereby red means 'danger' or 'halt' is modern, and does not seem to have folkloric roots.

redemption rumours. Redemption rumours are a subgroup of *contemporary legend. The core of the story is that a person, usually young or vulnerable, is in trouble or need but can be saved or cured if we all do some relatively minor but cumulatively useful thing. The earliest known example was reported in the *Illustrated London News* (18 May 1850), 349:

EXTRAORDINARY POSTAGE STAMPS CONTRIBUTION: Some time since, there appeared in the public journals a statement to the effect that a certain young lady, under age, was to be placed in a convent, by her father, if she did not procure, before the 30th of April last, one million of used postage stamps. This caused numerous persons to forward stamps for the purpose of securing her liberty . . .'

Modern versions of the story often involve the collection of particular branded products—crisp packets of a certain brand, the pull-out tabs of cigarette packets, the bar-codes off other packets, ring-pulls from soft-drink cans, and so on, and if we collect a million . . . One favourite promised outcome is that they will supply a kidney machine to a local hospital. These are regularly reported in local and national newspapers when the disappointed dedicated collectors find they have been deluded.

Another force comes into play here in the form of ostension, which is the term used for when 'folklore' becomes 'reality' by someone pursuing an idea and making it real. In Britain, the classic case was young Craig Shergold, of Surrey. There have been numerous examples of rumoured sick children wanting our help in cheering up or cure, and when Craig, aged 10 in 1989, was diagnosed as having a terminal brain tumour a friend suggested an appeal for get-well cards to get him into the *Guinness Book of Records* and cheer him up. From a slow local start, Craig started receiving cards from all over the world. By 1991, over 33 million cards had been received (*Sun* (7 Mar. 1991)), and they still arrive. As countless people copied the details and passed them on, the name and address and age became garbled ('Craig John' is how it appears most often), and someone somewhere changed it to 'business cards' and 'compliments slips'. The invention of the fax and E-mail has speeded up the distribution process. Craig's family has appealed, on numerous occasions, for the deluge to cease (they stopped counting at 100 million), but there seems to be no way to stop it. Craig underwent a successful operation in America in 1991.

Marion Shergold, *Craig Shergold: A Mother's Story* (1993); Folklore Society Cuttings Collection.

red hair. Traditional ideas about red-haired people are not complimentary. Physically, they are said to sweat easily, bleed copiously, have a strong foxy smell, and such bad breath that they can raise blisters on other people simply by breathing over them. Morally, they are expected to be 'bad children' who cause nothing but trouble; they will be hot-tempered, treacherous, and highly sexed. The medieval notion that *Judas, Cain, and Mary Magdalene were red-heads arose from these beliefs, and helped to perpetuate them. They carried over into conventions for stage villains; Shylock was regularly given a red wig, as was Mephistopheles in Grattan's *Faust* at Sadler's Wells in 1842.

It is held that meeting a red-head brings bad luck; when *first footing is done at New Year, they are unwelcome (Harland and Wilkinson, 1873: 225; Opie and Tatem, 1989: 325–6). On the other hand, their fighting spirit is admired.

Families where red hair is frequent are often said to be descended from the Danes, from the Scots, or from Spanish sailors of the Armada— all formerly enemies of England. If only one child has this colouring, it might be vaguely ascribed to 'bad blood', or, more specifically, to the mother's adultery—nowadays, it is usually jokingly said, 'with the milkman'. Another 'explanation' is that the parents had made love during the woman's period, thus breaking a powerful taboo. This does not appear in standard English folklore collections, presumably because of its unseemly nature, but was known, and used as a taunt, in Kent and London in the 1950s and 1960s, and is remembered by some elderly nurses [JS]; French parallels prove its authenticity (Gélis, 1991: 14–15). More frivolously, it is said that if two women pour tea from the same teapot, one will have ginger-haired twins.

N&Q 12s:2 (1916), 128, 196–7, 239, 379; 12s:5 (1918), 194, 218.

regional folklore. The collection and publication of folklore on regional lines has such a long and respectable history in England that many would not even think of questioning it, but it is not the only, or necessarily the best, way of organizing folklore material. The regional impulse has a number of strong roots, both practical and theoretical. Collecting folklore is time consuming and arduous even today, and in Victorian and Edwardian times a local emphasis was often a practical necessity, but a stronger impulse came from local pride. It was not only the Scots, Irish, and Welsh who felt the need to celebrate their traditions and demonstrate their unique qualities to bolster feelings of nationhood, but inhabitants of, say, Yorkshire, or the West Country could be equally proud of their local traditions.

Earlier antiquarians such as *Aubrey, *Brand, and *Hone published compendia on a national scale, but from Victorian times most of the major fieldwork collections have been undertaken on a regional or county basis, including Henderson's *Notes on the Folklore of the Northern Counties of England* (1866), Burne's *Shropshire Folklore* (1883), Udal's *Dorset Folklore* (1922), while the Folklore Society's project to reprint earlier printed material, the *County Folk-Lore* series, was organized on similar lines. In post-war Britain, the major *Folklore of the British Isles* series published by Batsford (1973–7) and individual items such as Tongue's *Somerset Folklore* (1965) and Sutton's *Lincolnshire Calendar* (1997) show that the impulse is still as strong as ever. The general public also take a strongly local view of the subject, and, in publishing terms, it is clear that the existence of an identifiable local 'market' is a major factor in determining whether or not a folklore book is published.

Some traditional genres are indeed regional. Dialect is one obvious example, and *calendar customs are another. With customs, the term 'regional' can have two distinct meanings—one being that certain customs are only found in one area (e.g. *souling), the other that versions of customs found over a wide area (such as *mumming plays) display regional or local characteristics which distinguish them from those of another area. Similarly, Iona and Peter *Opie were able to show that many aspects of children's lore in the 1950s (e.g. *truce terms and the names of certain games) could usefully be plotted on distribution maps. Mumming plays are a good example of a genre in which much collecting and publishing has been on a regional basis, but the conclusions of some leading authorities have delayed further enquiry based on geographical distribution. Margaret *Dean-Smith and Alex *Helm declared that the core of the action of the play, the death and resurrection, was what mattered, and that the texts were simply 'local accretions' which did not need to be studied. Later researchers, however, have realized that a close analysis of a large number of texts would give an opportunity for understanding how traditional transmission from place to place has functioned, and may also give clues about the earlier stages of development, if not actual origins of the custom. Some experiments have been carried out in this direction, using computers to map distribution, but a major study remains to be undertaken, and other customs could potentially benefit from a similar approach.

Several other major genres, including narrative, superstition, and song, display little or no sign of regional aspects, although it is certainly possible that the apparent homogeneity here is only a reflection of collecting activity. There has been little systematic collecting of superstitions or narrative, but there has been sufficient song collecting, over many decades, to reach overall conclusions, and it is clear that, apart from a handful of local songs, the folk-song repertoire is very similar all over the country.

At its best, intensive localized fieldwork can result in the development of detailed expert knowledge of a more holistic kind than genre-based collecting over a wider area usually allows, but the time constraints on research often make the intensive approach impractical. For the genre-based researcher, a broad sweep is necessary. The major problem with the regional material which we have inherited is its unsystematic nature, and comparisons are fraught with difficulty. The collectors had their own particular definitions and agendas from which to work, and many areas, such as Surrey and Essex, remained largely unresearched. To complicate comparison further, the major collections were compiled decades apart. The evidence is thus too patchy for an overall picture of many genres to be easily discerned. In a multi-genre work such as the present *Dictionary*, this presents problems for the reader. An entry on calendar custom, for example, may read, 'in a Hampshire version . . .', or 'in the West Country . . .', and thereby indicate an important distinction, whereas in an entry on a superstition which reads 'A Yorkshire farmer reported . . . ' the place-name is provided for contextual purposes, but may not have any geographical significance.

All the major regional books are listed in the Bibliography.

revels, see *WAKES.

revival. A deceptively simple term which has excited protracted debate in the folklore world, primarily because its meaning shifts with the perspective of each onlooker. In the folk *song and *dance world, 'the Revival' usually refers to one of the two major upsurges of popular interest in those topics, which became national movements.

In other spheres, the term is used to cover both the restarting of a custom after a temporary lapse, and the deliberate introduction of a custom into a different community or social context. Clearly, few if any local customs can prove an unbroken record of performance throughout their history, and folklorists normally accept any revival in this sense as part of the traditional nature of things. Problems of definition start to occur when others *start* a new series of performances which they have copied from elsewhere, and this is particularly noticeable in genres which have strong regional or local characteristics. The morris dancers of *Bampton stopping and restarting, for example, is a different matter from the people of Burnley or Bridgwater starting to perform the Bampton dances. It is clear that the dissemination of traditions in the past must have included precisely this kind of 'copying' of others' existing traditions, by communities or individuals, and new performers may thus be seen to be starting a tradition of their own, in time-honoured fashion. This debate brings into the open the further notion of 'authenticity', and the question of who 'owns' folklore. A common-sense argument that folkloric traditions, as part of our common heritage, belong to everybody and therefore to nobody, often fails to appease those who see their own local customs or traditions appropriated by others, whether for pleasure or for profit. As noted under *regional folklore, fierce local pride is often attached to a community's customs and traditions.

It is not only in the geographic sense that the appropriation of others' traditional lore can be seen as contentious. Songs collected from working-class singers by middle-class collectors turn up in different guise in the latter's compositions, on the concert stage sung by professional singers, or on commercial recordings by folk or pop groups, very often with no acknowledgement of their original source, or payment of any sort of 'royalty'. Even without the moral/legal questions involved, the relationship of these performances to 'folklore' is at best ambiguous and open to further debate.

Victorian and Edwardian reformers were expert in the art of 'revivals' which, while claiming to be genuinely traditional, were either invented or changed so radically as to retain only a tenuous connection with the original source (see *Merrie England), but which helped to create a generalized notion of a 'national' traditional culture belonging to all. At the end of the 20th century, the same processes appeared to be still in force.

See also *DANCE, *FAKELORE, *REGIONAL FOLKLORE, *SONG REVIVAL, *TOURIST LORE.

ribbons. In the 1990s, a fashion arose for wearing a small loop of coloured ribbon on one's lapel to declare support for some suffer-

ing or victimized group. The first and best known is the red Aids Awareness ribbon launched in New York in 1991, and almost immediately adopted in Britain. It was quickly followed by pink or blue ones for cancer victims, and then by others for various political causes: yellow ones to demand the release of hostages or those unjustly imprisoned, again on an American model; green in support of Irish political prisoners; purple for animal rights campaigners; 'rainbow' for racial tolerance, and also for homosexual equality; dark blue or black in mourning for public disasters. In 1995, Lewisham Town Council gave out free blue lapel ribbons to express awareness of the dangers of drinking and driving (*FLS News* 22 (1995), 8–9; 23 (1996), 10).

Although so new, the custom draws on an older 'language' of distinctively coloured markers worn on the lapel or stitched to the clothing—examples would include the rosettes of political parties, the Blue Ribbon badge of the Victorian temperance movement, black arm-bands or patches sown on to men's jackets in *mourning, fabric *poppies and *Alexandra Day roses tucked in the lapel buttonhole. A more remote precursor would be the coloured 'favours' which Phillip Stubbes in his *Anatomie of Abuses* (1583) says were worn at *Midsummer revels. After several decades in which metal badges and stick-on labels predominated, ribbon, the oldest medium for such displays, is enjoying a resurgence.

rice. Although mentioned rarely in the standard folklore works, there are several traditions concerning rice. It was a common fallacy amongst sailors that regular use of rice is conducive to blindness, and a slang term for rice on board ship was 'Strike-me-blind' (Hazlitt, 1905: 510). Many young women in the 19th century ate quantities of raw rice to improve their complexions (*N&Q* 11s:3 (1911) 189, 258), while others believed that rice 'prevents the increase of the population' and that it was thus given deliberately to Poor Relief claimants (Chambers, 1878: ii. 39).

See also *WEDDINGS.

riddles. A word game or joke, comprising a question or statement couched in deliberately puzzling terms, propounded for solving by the hearer/reader using clues embedded within that wording. Closely related to other forms including the conundrum (which relies more on puns) and the catch (joking questions which pretend to be riddles), the riddle's distinguishing mark is its use of metaphor. Riddles have a very long and respectable history, and there is hardly a literature, oral or written, in which riddles do not occur, often in the form of riddle contests. Six of the *ballads included in *Child's collection include riddle motifs, and they occur in numerous other songs and tales.

In England, the riddle was popular with adults for centuries, at both a domestic level and in literary circles, existing as a party or parlour game well into the 19th century, but from that time it gradually lost favour until it reached its present condition, surviving only in children's humour, and in certain well-defined genres such as in the *Christmas cracker. In children's hands riddles are alive and well, and they are very popular with all ages. Riddles are usually the first form of joke mastered by the child, partly because of their satisfying formula which, once mastered, can serve as vehicle for a range of ideas, in which the child can test the boundaries of humour, and the formula is readily understood by everyone. The riddle repertoire is constantly replenished with new items on old lines, but includes a core which has been around a long time. The Opies showed that several of the riddles they collected in the 1950s had been current since the 16th century in English, and even further back abroad—'How deep is the ocean?—A stone's throw'; 'How many balls of string would it take to reach the moon?—One if it was long enough'.

Mark Bryant, *Dictionary of Riddles* (1990); McCosh, 1979; Opie and Opie, 1959: 73–86; Susan Edmunds, 'The Riddle Ballad and the Riddle', *L&L* 5:2 (1986), 35–46.

Riding the Stang. A *New Year's Day custom, apparently unique to the Cumberland, Westmorland, Yorkshire area. A band of people, armed with stangs (poles) and baskets took to the streets and accosted any stranger they met and subjected him to be mounted across the pole, or, if a women, in a basket, and thus carried, shoulder height, to the nearest pub where he/she was expected to buy a drink. The only way to avoid this treatment was to pay a fine straightaway (*Gentleman's Magazine* (1791), quoted in Gomme, 1884: 14–15). This is one of a range of customs in which the working classes claim the right to 'manhandle' their superiors (compare *Lifting). Riding the Stang is also the name for a local form of *rough music in many other parts of the country, and,

in other contexts, a form of 'riding the stang' could be used as a punishment at any time of year. Compare also *Corby Pole Fair.

right. Most past and present cultures (perhaps all) contrast the right and *left hand to the advantage of the former, presumably because in most people it is stronger and more skilled; in English, there is also a strong verbal connection with 'right' in the senses 'correct, good'. The right hand symbolizes power, authority, benevolence, honour, and loyalty; it is used in gestures of greeting or blessing, in shaking hands, taking oaths, etc. In the ancient Roman system of augury, omens to the right of the enquirer were favourable. Whatever the origins of these semi-conscious meanings, Christianity strengthened them by some vivid imagery: the risen Christ sits 'at the right hand of the Father', and at the Last Judgement the 'sheep' will be on the right, the 'goats' on the left (Matthew 25: 33).

In folk beliefs, good luck is regularly associated with the right side: it is lucky to see the new moon to one's right, to put the right stocking or shoe on first, to cross a threshold with the right foot, and so on, while in each case the *left is unlucky.

See also *LEFT.

rightward movement. A *circling movement made by turning to the *right is described as a 'right-handed', 'clockwise', or 'sunwise' turn, and is regarded as bringing good luck. Though the belief is strongest in Scotland and Ireland, it was customary in parts of England in 19th-century country *funerals to carry the coffin sunwise round the churchyard (*Hereford Times* (20 Mar. 1838), cited in Opie and Tatem, 1989: 384). Recent instances of the idea in England are that when making sauces, puddings, or cakes the stirring must always be done clockwise, or the cooking will go wrong; that ropes should be coiled clockwise; even, that in stirring tea and laying a table one must never go 'against the sun' (Opie and Tatem, 1989: 385–6).

The primary reason why this direction of movement is said to be 'sunwise' appears to be that in order to remain facing the sun as it moves from east through south to west, one has to pivot round constantly to one's right.

See also *LEFTWARD MOVEMENT.

Ring-a-Ring-a-Roses. Children's singing game, known throughout the English-speaking world, and with many continental analogues. Nowadays, the game tends to be one of the first taught to children by adults, rather than being learnt from other children, and is therefore considered babyish by school-age children. The first known published versions are from the 1880s, although an American forerunner (Ring a ring a rosie A bottle full of posie All the girls in our town Ring for little Josie) is reported from 1790.

The belief that the rhyme originated with the Great *Plague is now almost universal, but has no evidence to support it and is almost certainly nonsense. Early writers on the Plague do not mention the rhyme or, indeed, sneezing as a symptom of the disease, and the rhyme only appears 200 years later. The earlier folklore collectors do not make the connection between the rhyme and the Plague, and the idea appears to date only from the 1960s, but is now so widely believed as to be unshakable.

See also *SNEEZING.

Opie and Opie, 1985: 220–7; Gomme, 1898: ii. 108–11.

Ringing the Devil's Knell. About ten o'clock on *Christmas Eve, ringers gather at All Saints church, Dewsbury, Yorkshire, to Ring the Devil's Knell. The church's tenor bell, called Black Tom of Southill, is rung once for every year since Christ's birth. It is called the Devil's Knell, or more colourfully, The Old Lad's Passing Bell, because of the belief that the Devil died when Christ was born. The tolling is carefully timed to finish on the stroke of midnight. A local legend explains the custom as established by one Thomas de Soothill, in penance for murdering one of his servants five or six hundred years ago.

Sykes, 1977: 149; Hole, 1975: 12–13.

rings. Rings make excellent symbols of identity, authority, and obligations, being worn on the hand (itself a symbol of power), and visible both to the wearer and others. Hence they can indicate married status, personal pledges of love, legal identity, and family affiliations (the seal-ring), and royal or episcopal authority. For a woman to lose or break her wedding ring was a terrible *omen, probably foreshadowing the husband's death, and even removing it for a few moments was thought wrong, or unlucky. It was and is common to be buried with one's wedding ring. With the growing prosperity of the past two centuries, engage-

ment rings and eternity rings have become widespread, and in the latter part of the 20th century men took to wearing wedding rings too.

Rings showing a true-love-knot and those showing a heart held by clasped hands have long been favoured as love tokens, as has the gimbal ring, also spelled 'gimmal' or 'jimmal' ring, which is one that can be split in two (the name derives ultimately from Latin *geminus*, 'twin'), and joined up again at will. It is possible that the many traditional songs of the 18th and 19th centuries in which a sailor breaks a ring in two and leaves half with his sweetheart are referring to gimbal rings, as it would be quite difficult to break an ordinary ring.

Rings can also be imagined as conferring benefits on the wearer; examples set with gemstones engraved with occult letters and designs were common till Elizabethan times (Evans, 1922: 110–39; Ettlinger, 1939: 167–9), but grew rare with the general decline of magic in the later 17th century. Copper rings and bracelets are now commonly worn to prevent rheumatic pain, but this seems to be a fairly recent development; silver *cramp rings, on the other hand, are attested from the 14th to the 19th centuries. The current semi-playful revival of interest in astrology and magic has created a market for a wide variety of 'lucky' and symbolic rings.

Ripon hornblower. A *civic custom in which the official Hornblower for Ripon, North Yorkshire, blows blasts on his horn at 9 p.m. every night of the year in four different directions from the four corners of the obelisk in the main square of the town, and also three blasts outside the home of the Mayor. The present horn dates from 1865 and when not in use is displayed in a glass case, along with a 17th-century predecessor, and an even more ancient horn which are only taken out on special days (called 'horn days'). The Hornblower is the direct descendant of the Wakeman whose job it was, up to the 16th century, to keep nightly watch for burglars and thieves, and the blowing of the horn signified the start of the watch. The custom is said to date from Anglo-Saxon times, which is feasible, but the earliest evidence dates only from the 15th century. *Bainbridge (North Yorkshire) also has a hornblowing custom.

Kightly, 1986: 141; Smith, 1989: 142–5.

rites of passage, see *LIFE-CYCLE CUSTOMS.

Ritson, Joseph (1752–1803). Although he scraped a living as a conveyancer, Ritson's real preoccupations were with his antiquarian researches and writing, and he quickly amassed an unparalleled knowledge and collection of early British poetry and song, which at the time had been neglected by other scholars. His undoubted strengths as gatherer and annotator resulted in a number of valuable publications on his chosen subjects, often issued at his own expense. On a personal level, however, Ritson had definite problems, and he publicly attacked a number of other authorities—particularly Warton (*History of English Poetry*), Pinkerton, and *Percy—for their errors and what he saw as their slapdash and dishonest editorial methods. These attacks were so vehemently worded and so personally abusive that, despite often being right in point of fact, he made few friends and many enemies. Combined with his other personal peculiarities—vegetarianism and atheism included—Ritson's pedantry and obsessive behaviour meant that when he died after a brief spell of 'madness' he was not much mourned. In hindsight, there is no doubt that his public strictures on the likes of Pinkerton and Percy forced editors of the time and later to be more careful in the way they handled and presented their sources, and he thus contributed a fair amount in the development of scholarly method which is now taken for granted. His main publications in folklore-related fields are: *A Select Collection of English Songs* (1783), *Gammer Gurton's Garland* (c.1783), *Ancient Songs from the Time of King Henry III to the Revolution* (1792), *The English Anthology* (1793), *Scotish Songs* (1794), *Robin Hood* (1795).

Bertrand H. Bronson, *Joseph Ritson, Scholar-at-Arms* (1938); Henry A. Burd, *Joseph Ritson: A Critical Biography* (1916).

rivers. There are a few traces in 19th-century local traditions of a belief that certain rivers are malevolent, and will periodically take a human life. The best known is the Dart (Devon), about which there is a rhyme:

> River of Dart, River of Dart,
> Every year thou claimest a heart.

The contributor who reported this to *N&Q* (1s:2 (1850), 511) explained that 'it is said that a year never passes without the drowning of one person, at least, in the Dart', and that 'it is liable to sudden risings, when the water comes down with great strength and violence'; Dartmoor men call the river 'he', not 'it'. There was a similar attitude towards the Derwent (Derbyshire); in 1903, discussing a recent drowning, a local woman talked of the river as if it were a living being, blaming the victim for his arrogance:

'He didna know Darrant, he said it were nought but a brook. But Darrant got 'im. They never saw his head, he threw his arms up, but Darrant wouldna let him go. Aye, it's a sad pity, seven children! But he shouldna ha' made so light o' Darrant. He knows now! Naught but a brook! He knows now!' (*Folk-Lore* 15 (1904), 99)

See also *PEG O' NELL, *PEG POWLER, *WATER-SPIRITS.

robbers. Local oral history often preserved reasonably accurate memories of the crimes of robbers, *smugglers, and *highwaymen for several generations, especially if the inns they frequented and the *gallows and gibbets where they died were still standing. Yet there was always a tendency for tales to grow in the telling. Sometimes the rogue is recalled as a hero for his physical strength, sometimes for his clever tricks to outwit the law: stolen sheep hidden in a cider barrel, horses shod backwards, smuggled goods carried in coffins, etc. The opposite tendency was to see the robber as a villain who met an appropriate fate, as in the story of the *Hangman's Stone.

There are several tales from Victorian times, presented as true, in which a robber gains entry to a house in disguise, or hidden in a box or bundle left there by an accomplice, or by using a *Hand of Glory; a young servant-girl, alone in the house, contrives to wound him, put him to flight, or even kill him by pouring boiling fat down his throat as he sleeps, or applying a red-hot poker (Briggs, 1970–1: A. i. 307; B. i. 171–2, 183–4; Charles Dickens, 'The Holly Tree' (1855)).

Robin Goodfellow. This was the best-known name for an individual *fairy in late medieval and Tudor England. He was a mocking shape-changer, with a characteristic guffawing laugh of 'Ho, ho, hoh!'. He could turn into a horse, tempting weary travellers to mount him, and then dumping them in a river; or lead them astray as a Will-o'-the-Wisp; or appear in some terrifying shape. Yet he also took on the helpful *brownie role in homes and farms. Elizabethan and Stuart writers often alluded to his tricks; a blackletter pamphlet which appeared in 1628, entitled *Robin Good-Fellow, his Mad*

Prankes and Merry Jests, asserts that he was the son of *Oberon by a human girl, was granted his powers by his father, and eventually joined the fairy dance and was carried off to fairyland. It includes the standard brownie motif that when a grateful girl gives him a waistcoat instead of a bowl of creamy milk, he disappears for ever. His name reflects this ambiguity; 'Goodfellow' might be either a tribute to his merry nature and helpfulness, or an evasive term based on fear, since his pranks could be troublesome.

Some Elizabethans regarded all fairies as demons. Robert Burton included Robin in his list of 'terrestrial devils ... which as they are most conversant with men, so they do them most harm' (*The Anatomy of Melancholy* (1621), part I, section 2, 'A Digression of Spirits'). The *Mad Prankes* pamphlet has a curious woodcut showing him (identified by the initials G F) as a phallic, goat-footed, horned figure like Pan or Satan, but carrying a lighted candle and a broom, presumably to show he does housework by night; there are bats and birds overhead, and small figures, fully clad, are dancing round him. The image does not fit anything in the text; the artist may have been adapting an illustration of a witches' sabbath.

For a collection of literary texts mentioning Robin Goodfellow, see W. Carew Hazlitt, *Fairy Tales, Legends and Romances Illustrating Shakespeare* (1875); for discussion, Briggs, 1959 and 1976.

Robin Hood. The merry outlaw Robin Hood, skilled in archery and singlestick fighting and a master of tricks and disguise, has been popular from the 14th century till today; in early sources he is localized (if at all) in Barnsdale (probably Yorkshire, possibly Rutland), and in later ones in Sherwood Forest. Various companions are named, notably *Little John, and in one ballad a 'King Edward' appears.

None of the many attempts to provide a historical identity for him is wholly convincing; the clues are too slight and contradictory, and 'Robert' and 'Hood' were both common medieval names. The opposite approach, which, relying on his green clothes, sees him as a woodland spirit, is untenable; throughout the tradition Robin is merely a human being whose adventures, unlike Arthurian material, contain no magic or marvels (Keen, 1977: 219–22). The third possibility is that 'Robin Hood' was simply a fictional figure typifying banditry, just as 'Jack Straw' and later 'Captain

Swing' typified revolt; there are medieval instances of the name being applied to rioters and robbers, and of criminals using it and *Friar Tuck's as aliases (Knight, 1994: 25, 105, 108–9).

Rhymes about Robin Hood are mentioned in the 1370s; the 38 extant ballads date from the 15th to the 17th centuries, most dealing with a single adventure, with much similarity in situations. They do not explain Robin's past, nor why he was outlawed; only two mention his death, murdered by the Prioress of Kirklees. They show him robbing the rich, but only once giving the proceeds to a poor man—though in 1500 a Scottish chronicler says this was his usual practice, and it is now seen as the defining trait of his character. In the ballads, Robin gleefully defies middle-ranking authority figures such as sheriffs and abbots, though he honours King Edward; the chief emphasis is on the loyalty between him and his companions, their exciting adventures, and the freedom of forest life. In some, he acts with a ruthlessness which modern presentations conveniently ignore.

Acting was as important as verse in transmitting the tradition. In Tudor times, throughout southern and midland counties, Robin and his followers appeared in local pageants organized by churches as fundraising events, often at *Whitsun; men in costume would parade through the village or town, or visit neighbouring ones, to collect money. Bishop Latimer was once furious to find a church where he intended to preach closed for this reason. Associated amusements included archery, wrestling, mock combats, and folk-plays about Robin's fights and disguises (three short scripts survive), and the whole event could form part of the *May games.

The idea that Robin was no ordinary outlaw but an impoverished Earl appears first in Richard Grafton's *Chronicle at Large* (1569) and was elaborated in plays by Anthony Munday (1598–9) and Martin Parker's ballad, 'A True Tale of Robin Hood' (1632). These sources shift the period to that of Richard I, and Munday invents a love-triangle between Robin, *Maid Marian, and Prince John. Variations on these ideas appear from the early 19th century onwards in plays, novels, children's books, and films; Robin becomes a symbol of gallantry, patriotism, freedom, and justice.

Various barrows and huge rocks are named after him in many parts of England besides those where tradition says he lived; like other heroes, he was popularly endowed with gigantic strength. There is a tomb in Kirklees Park (Yorkshire) alleged to be his; 16th- and 17th-century antiquarians mention an inscribed gravestone there, but their acounts are inconsistent with one another and with the existing monument (Keen, 1977: 179–82). There is no reason to suppose it is authentic.

See also *FRIAR TUCK, *LITTLE JOHN, *MAID MARIAN.

The ballad texts can be found in Child, 1882–98/1965, and in Dobson and Taylor, 1976. For the May plays, see Wiles, 1981, and Hutton, 1996: 270–4. Keen, 1977, argues for a fictional hero embodying a popular longing for social justice. Knight, 1994, stresses the multiplicity of the legend; Knight 1999 reprints all the main sources. John C. Bellamy's *Robin Hood: A Historical Inquiry* (1985), and J. C. Holt's *Robin Hood* (1982;, rev. edn., 1990), seek a real-life original.

robins. Folk traditions about the robin are contradictory; some link it with death, others see it as a sacred bird, cheerful and friendly to humans. The idea that a robin pecking on a window or entering the house brings death has been recorded in many areas from the early 19th century onwards, and is still sometimes found; a Gloucestershire girl in the 1950s said it was a death-sign to receive a *Christmas card with a robin on it (*Folklore* 66 (1955), 324), and a woman in Hull in the 1990s always threw away such cards from mixed packs (Gill, 1993: 67). However, the great popularity of robins on Christmas cards from Victorian times onwards shows this fear must be rare.

A belief first recorded in the late 16th century may explain the link with death. It was thought that if a robin found someone lying dead, it would cover the face (or even the whole corpse) with moss, leaves, or flowers, being a 'charitable' bird, 'that loves mankind both alive and dead'. There are many literary allusions to this idea, and it forms the climax of the ballad of 'The Babes in the Wood'.

The robin, and his alleged 'wife' the *wren, were sacred, according to well-known rhymes:

> The robin redbreast and the wren
> Are God Almighty's cock and hen.

and:

> Hurt a robin or a wran,
> Never prosper, boy or man.

A pious legend, probably from medieval times, says the bird got its red breast when it injured itself in trying to pluck out a thorn

from Christ's crown of thorns; alternatively, that its feathers got singed as it carried water to souls in the fire of Purgatory. Either way, it was blessed by God for its kindness.

To kill or injure a robin, or steal its eggs, was regarded as wicked, and sure to bring bad luck; 19th-century sources speak of cows giving bloody milk, piglets dying, or buildings catching fire, while the *Farmer's Weekly* in 1974 quotes a warning that 'you'll end up with a broken leg or arm'. In Yorkshire in the 1880s, a boy who took a robin's eggs would be surrounded by other boys, pointing, hissing and slapping at him, and chanting

> Robin takker, robbin takker,
> Sin, sin, sin!

Swainson, 1885: 12–18; Radford, Radford, and Hole, 1961: 282–4; Opie and Tatem, 1989: 328–30.

Rogation Days. These are the Monday, Tuesday, and Wednesday before *Ascension Day, on which, before the Reformation, priests led processions round the fields, blessing crops and praying for good harvests. A secondary purpose was to bless the main boundary markers of each parish, in towns as well as rural areas. A cross, relics, hand-bells, and banners were carried; those taking part were sometimes given a communal meal supplied from church funds, or received food at the houses they passed. The event was also known as Cross Days or, in northern districts, Gang Days (from *gang* = 'walk').

Inevitably, some early Protestants attacked the processions as superstitious; how far they succeeded is debated (Thomas, 1971: 62–5; Hutton, 1994: 175–7). However, there were financial reasons why parishes wished to establish exact boundaries publicly, so a modified form of the custom, minus its blessings and other Catholic features, was established under Elizabeth I and became widespread in the 17th century, especially after the Restoration. It was known as *beating the bounds.

Wright and Lones, 1936: i. 129–38; Hutton, 1996: 277–87.

rolling pins (glass). Decorative glass rolling pins, hung in cottages in the late 18th and 19th centuries, are generally love tokens from sailors to their wives and sweethearts, or vice versa, as their designs and inscriptions often show. They were also linked to luck; if one was broken, it was a sign that the ship carrying the giver had been wrecked, or that some great misfortune was about to strike the family. The pins are hollow, the knob at one end being a stoppered opening; it is said they could hold gifts of tea or rum, but when used as household charms were generally filled with *salt, or sometimes with coloured beads, seeds, or threads. They, and the similarly decorative glass rods and 'walking sticks', were sometimes called *charm wands.

Rollright Stones. A lively story is told about this prehistoric monument in Oxfordshire, which consists of a circle of stones plus a single taller stone, some 50 yards off, called the King Stone. An invading king had encamped his army on the hill, encouraged by a witch's promise that if he could reach the crest in seven strides and see the village of Long Compton in the valley, he would be king of all England. It seemed easy, but the witch cheated him, raising a mound to block the view. He and his men became stones, and she an elder.

It is said that the King Stone goes down to the stream to drink 'when he hears the church clock strike midnight'; the stones of the circle sometimes dance in the air. The elder tree bleeds if cut on *Midsummer Eve, at which the King Stone nods approval. Anyone trying to remove the stones meets bad luck, and it is impossible to count them—a baker who tried to do so by putting a loaf on each stone found one always disappeared. In the 19th century, some said *fairies lived underground near the King Stone; others thought chips from the King Stone brought good luck.

Descriptions of the Rollright Stones begin with Camden in the 16th century, and the legends grow more detailed as time passes; the fullest account is by L. V. Grinsell, *The Rollright Stones and Their Folklore* (1977).

Romanies, see *GYPSIES.

rosemary. According to traditional lore, rosemary is a versatile little plant, and in general its uses are positive. Lines in *A Nosegaie Alwaies Sweet, for Lovers to Send for Tokens of Love* ... (c.1582), provide the famous definition of rosemary for remembrance, as quoted by Ophelia in *Hamlet*, IV. v: 'Rosemarie is for remembrance, betweene us daie and night'. Rosemary was essential at both *weddings and *funerals, and its use at the latter is partly explained by its reputation for practical rather than symbolic protection. A writer in *The Monthly Packet* (23, (1862), 88) describes meet-

ing a funeral party in a West Sussex village and asking about the nosegays many of them carried, and being told that the rosemary and rue in them were 'fine things against infection'.

Rosemary was also popular as a *Christmas decoration, an all-purpose disinfectant, and even as a hair rinse. As late as the 1990s people were still calling it the 'friendship bush': 'You always had to plant rosemary in your garden so that you wouldn't be short of friends' (Vickery, 1995: 318). Nevertheless, a parallel belief states that rosemary only thrives where the woman of the house is dominant. A much older tradition, reported by Nuttall, holds that rosemary plants never grow taller than the height of Christ when he was on earth, and that when they are 33 years old their upward growth stops.

Opie and Tatem, 1989: 332–3; Vickery, 1995: 318–19; Hazlitt, 1905: 524–6; Hone, 1832: 19–21; G. Clarke Nuttall, 'Rosemary at Christmas', *The 19th Century* 98 (1925), 797–804.

roses. Medieval and later poets constantly used the red rose to symbolize sexual love, pleasure, and woman's beauty; these meanings are still well understood, e.g. red roses are given to a woman, paper rose petals are thrown as confetti. It was also a medieval custom to wear coronets of roses (or other blossoms) as festive adornments; this survives as the bridal wreath. However, this flower rarely figures in folk customs, presumably because its period of blooming is so short; the only magical belief about it was that if a girl picks a rose on *Midsummer Eve, wraps it up, and finds it unfaded on Christmas Eve, her lover is true (Opie and Tatem, 1989: 332). Nowadays, roses are thought appropriate to all forms of love; they may be laid on a coffin, a rose bush planted as a memorial to the dead, etc.

Rose Tree, the. This gruesome *fairytale (analogous to the *Grimms' 'The Juniper Tree') was collected in Devonshire by *Baring-Gould in the 1860s. A pretty little girl is murdered by her stepmother, who cooks her heart and liver and serves them to the child's father; she is then buried by a rose tree, where her little brother weeps for her daily. In the spring a white bird appears among the roses, sweetly singing:

> My wicked mother slew me,
> My dear father ate me,
> My little brother whom I love

> Sits below, and I sing above,
> Stick, stock, stone dead.

The bird's song so charms various craftsmen that she gets from them a fine pair of shoes, a gold watch and chain, and a millstone. Carrying these, she lures the family out of the house one by one and drops the watch and chain on her father, the shoes on her brother—and the millstone on her stepmother.

Text in Henderson, 1866: 314–17; Jacobs, 1894/1968: 13–16; and Philip, 1992: 143–6, who adds references for some Yorkshire variants.

rough music. Under a variety of local names and differing methods, rough music was the main customary way in which members of a community expressed displeasure at transgressions of societal norms, usually, but not exclusively, concerned with sexual and marital matters such as wife- or husband-beating, adultery, co-habitation, and so on. The term 'rough music' and other local names such as 'ran-tanning', reflect the almost universal element of *noise*—participants would bang on old kettles, saucepans, or shovels, blow on whistles, cow-horns, wave rattles, shout and bawl—anything to make a loud and discordant noise. Other names, such as '*Riding the Stang' and 'Skimmington Riding' encapsulate the other regular feature—the parading of *effigies of the guilty parties, or sometimes neighbours impersonating them. The effigies would be mounted on a pole, a cart, or a donkey—often with the man placed backwards facing the tail. After processing the neighbourhood, these effigies would usually be burnt in front of the victims' house.

Examples are recorded regularly from the 16th century onwards, including Henry Machyn's *Diary* (22 Feb. 1562/3), Stow (1598/1994: 200), Samuel Pepys, *Diary* (10 June 1667), the engraving by William Hogarth entitled *Hudibras Encounters the Skimmington* (1726), and a well-known literary example is in Thomas *Hardy's *The Mayor of Casterbridge* (1884), chapters 36, 39. The proceedings were 'regulated' by locally understood rules and expectations. In earlier examples, it seems to be accepted that the next-door neighbour of the offending party should take the place of the effigy, and the occasion would provide the opportunity for much ribald humour. As with all such vigilante behaviour, these proceedings could be seen as great fun or highly frightening mob behaviour, depending on whether you were on the performing side or receiving end. It is

clear that the authorities, such as the local police, whilst not condoning such behaviour, would often make sure to be 'out of the way' while it was going on and nobody would be willing to testify even if charges were brought. The victims would usually move away, or at least keep a low profile and appear to mend their ways, but in extreme cases the stress or shame could lead to suicide. Rough music is clearly related to continental customs, of which the French Charivari is probably the best known.

E. P. Thompson, *Customs in Common* (1991), 467–538.

Round Table. A large oak table-top, six metres wide, is displayed in the Great Hall of Winchester Castle (Hampshire) as being *Arthur's Round Table. It was made in the 14th century, possibly for Edward III, who in 1344 planned to found an 'Order of the Round Table'. A design was painted on it on the orders of Henry VIII in 1522; at the centre is the Tudor rose, and at the top a 'portrait' of Arthur modelled on Henry himself. A central inscription reads: 'This is the rownde table of kynge Arthur w[ith] xxiiii of hys namyde knyttes'; the names are written round the edge, with Galahad's and Mordred's on either side of the king.

At Mayburgh (Cumbria), a Bronze Age earthwork, a flat round platform within a ditch is called the Round Table; on the beach near Cresswell Point (Northumberland) there was a large circular rock called King Arthur's table, destroyed by the 1870s (*N&Q* 4s:7 (1871), 281).

rowan. Also known as mountain ash, wittern, whitty, wiggen, and quickbeam, rowan was the tree most often credited with protective magical powers against all effects of *witchcraft, not merely in Celtic areas but throughout Britain (Opie and Tatem, 1989: 333–4; Vickery, 1995: 319–22). A correspondent from Westmorland in Hone's *Table Book* (1827: ii, cols. 674–5) says 'its anti-witching properties are held in very high esteem' in northern counties, where, to prevent spells on farm animals and butter-making, the churn-staff and the shafts of forks used in the cowhouse and stable must be made of its wood. The same was true in many other areas, as was the use of rowan wood for carters' whips, the pegs of cattle tethers, and cradles. In Lancashire, rowan twigs over the bed ensured peaceful sleep, i.e.

repelled the *nightmare; in Yorkshire, looped twigs were hung on gateposts; in both counties, rowan wood was used to make *witch posts. In some North Yorkshire farms, the protective twigs over every door and bed, known as 'witch-wood', were annually renewed; one must cut them from a tree one had never seen before, and bring them home by a different route (Atkinson, 1891: 97–9).

Oddly, some Lancashire people thought it an unlucky tree and would not have one in the garden, transplant one, or bring cuttings into the house; in such cases, its ominous white *flowers were more important than its *red berries.

Royal Maundy, see *MAUNDY THURSDAY.

Royal Oak Day, Oak Apple Day (29 May). One of the few customary days which have an identifiable historical starting-point:

This was the first anniversary appointed by Act of Parliament to be observ'd as a day of general Thanksgiving for the miraculous Restauration of his Majestie: our Vicar preaching on 118 Psalm 24. Requiring us to be Thankfull & rejoice, as indeede we had Cause. (John Evelyn's *Diary*, 29 May 1661)

When Charles II arrived in London on his birthday in 1660, it signified not only the restoration of the monarchy itself, but also, it was hoped, the return of the pre-Puritan tolerance of popular sports, customs, and celebrations. The story of how Charles had hidden in an oak tree to avoid capture after the Battle of Worcester had become part of the nation's popular memory, and the oak leaf quickly became the symbol of the day. Until well into the 20th century, anyone caught not wearing an oak leaf or oak apple on 29 May could be pinched, kicked, or otherwise abused. Whipping with nettles was a favourite punishment, hence the name 'Nettle Day' in some areas. In its heyday, Oak Apple Day appears to have absorbed some of the customs we would normally associate with May Day. Certainly, some places kept their maypole celebrations up for the whole month. William Hone's *Every-Day Book* (1827: 356–61) details some of the customs extant in the 1820s. Some relatively low-key loyal customs still take place: at Worcester the Guildhall gates are festooned with oak branches (Shuel, 1985: 60) while at Northampton a previous procession of Mayor, Corporation, and children, carrying oak apples, has now been replaced by the simple placing of an

oak-leaf wreath around the neck of a statue of Charles in All Saints' Church. Other localized names include 'Shick Shack Day' and 'Yak Bob Day'.

See also *ARBOR DAY, *CASTLETON GARLAND, *WISHFORD MAGNA.

Opie and Opie, 1959: 263–6; Wright and Lones, 1936: i. 254–70.

Rudkin, Ethel (1893–1985). Born Ethel Hutchinson in Willoughton, Lincolnshire, Mrs Rudkin spent little of her long life away from her native Lincolnshire. She was a dedicated collector of Lincolnshire material, and was active in a number of fields including local history, archaeology, folk-life, and dialect, as well as folklore, working for many years with little recognition or encouragement but eventually becoming an acknowledged expert in all these subjects. Her home, which was packed with artefacts, farm implements, and memorabilia, as well as books and manuscripts, became a place of pilgrimage for researchers. Her main folklore collecting, in the 1920s and 1930s, was made directly from the people of the villages up and down the county and covered the broadest range of topics. A string of articles published in the *Folklore Society's journal, detailed below, included her careful descriptions of *calendar customs, beliefs in witches and devils, stone-lore, and an important contribution on *Black Dogs. Her one book, *Lincolnshire Folklore* was published at her own expense in 1936, reprinted in 1973 by EP Publishing of East Ardsley, and is still in demand.

Major articles: 'An Account of the Haxey Hood Game', *Folk-Lore* 43 (1932), 294–301; 'Lincolnshire Folklore', *Folk-Lore* 44 (1933), 189–214, 279–95; 45 (1934), 144–57, 248–67; 66 (1955), 385–400; 'The Black Dog', *Folk-Lore* 49 (1938), 111–31; 'Lincolnshire Plough Plays', *Folk-Lore* 50 (1939), 88–97; 'The Plough Jack's Play', *Folk-Lore* 50 (1939), 291–4.

Foreword by J. D. A. Widdowson, to the 1973 reprint of her *Lincolnshire Folklore*; Obituary by Theo Brown, *Folklore* 97:2 (1986), 222–3.

rue. By coincidence, the name of this plant (from Greek, via French) is identical with an English word meaning 'to regret bitterly', and so the plant symbolized grief or repentance. Discussing Herefordshire wedding customs, Ella M. Leather records an incident where a jilted girl waited in the porch at her ex-lover's wedding and, as the couple emerged, threw a handful of rue at them, in a parody of the throwing of flower petals, saying, 'May you rue this day as long as you live!' This curse was thought particularly effective because the rue 'was taken direct from the plant to the churchyard, and thrown "between holy and unholy ground", that is, between church and churchyard'. Other jilted girls had put a bunch of rue enclosing a half-eaten slice of bread and butter in the church porch (Leather, 1912: 115).

Medicinally, rue tea was used in East Anglia for stomach ache and as a spring tonic (Hatfield, 1994: 54, 56), but also to cause abortions (Chamberlain, 1981: 122, 128).

rushbearing. A prime example of a custom which originally had a logical practical purpose but which was turned into an elaborate occasion by tradition and which continues in isolated places long after the original *raison d'être* is gone. When churches had earth floors, or even cold stone floors, it was the custom to make the building more habitable by laying a thick layer of rushes (or hay or straw) on the floor. It was not only rural parishes that had rushes, as the churchwarden's accounts for St Mary-at-Hill, London, for example, includes a payment of 3d. in 1493 'For three burdens of rushes for new pews'. These rushes were renewed periodically, and the process of bringing in the new supply was what became expanded in many places into the elaborate rushbearing custom, particularly in the north-western counties of England. The date for rushbearing varied, but was often during the local *wakes week if in the right season.

Rushbearing was one of the pastimes specifically permitted on Sundays by order of King James I's *Book of Sports* (1618), in terms which indicate that it was already more than simply a practical exercise to keep the feet warm in church: '. . . and that women shall have leave to carry rushes to the church for the decoring of it, according to their old custom'.

The usual method of bringing in the rushes involved them being piled high on a waggon highly decorated with flowers and ribbons. Illustrations of the custom often show the rushes built into elaborate shapes. The waggon was accompanied by *morris dancers, and people carrying garlands (which could be hung in the church afterwards); the procession would often go round the whole parish before ending up at the church. As wooden floors became more common, rushbearing lost its purpose, and in most places gradually faded away. A few have proved more tenacious and have the custom still, while others have revived it in recent years (see *Grasmere, *Ambleside).

Alfred Burton, *Rushbearing* (1891); Hole, 1975: 85–8; Kightly, 1986: 199–201; E. F. Rawnsley, *The Rushbearing in Grasmere and Ambleside* (1953); Brears, 1989: 178–203; Linda Fletcher, *Folk Life* 36 (1997/98), 66–71.

Rye hot pennies. A *scrambling custom which still takes place on 23 May, as part of the annual mayor-making ceremony in Rye (East Sussex). Immediately after the new Mayor's election, he/she appears at a window of the Town Hall and throws hot new pennies to the waiting crowd of children and adults. Rye is not unique in including a scrambling element in a *civic custom and the two local stories which seek to explain it are also found elsewhere. One is that at one time the Mayor of Rye was also a Member of Parliament and sought to bribe voters, while the other explains that when Rye had the privilege of its own mint, the town ran out of pennies and that they were brought so fast that they were still hot.

Simpson, 1973: 119; Howard, 1964: 112.

sabbat(h), witches'. In many parts of Europe from about 1400 onwards it was thought that on certain nights witches gathered to worship Satan, with feasting and obscene orgies, and to plan their evil deeds. Such assemblies were called 'synagogues' or 'sabbaths', since Jews supposedly worshipped the Devil. These ideas barely touched England; only half a dozen references have been found—three in Lancashire (two in 1612, one in 1633), and one each in Yorkshire (1622), Devon (1638), and Northumberland (1673) (Sharpe, 1996: 76–8, 278–80). Two of the Lancashire sabbaths were said to have been held on a *Good Friday, 'one constant day for a yearly generall meeting of witches'—a dramatic reversal of Christian ritual, by feasting on a fast-day. The Devon sabbath was set on *Midsummer Eve; for the others no date is given.

These English accounts mention no sexual orgies, but the *Devil is usually said to be present, and in the Devon account he licks the witches, leaving a black mark; one Lancashire teenager said she had seen witches dig up and eat a dead baby. However, there are also fantasies drawn from folk traditions, especially in the statements from the boy Edmund Robinson in Lancashire in 1633 and from Anne Armstrong in Northumberland in 1673. Both claimed to have been turned into horses and ridden to a house where witches pulled on ropes hanging from the rafters, whereupon roast meat, milk, butter, cheese, and wine fell from the air for their feast.

Sabbath-breaking. English folklore is full of warnings against Sabbath-breaking. The theme occurs in local legends, in the stories of the *Seven Whistlers and of the *Man in the Moon. Children were told the Devil would get them for *nutting, sewing, or playing ball on Sunday; whoever celebrates a birthday on Sunday, will die before the next; work done on Sunday never prospers; cheques dated on a Sunday are invalid, etc. (Opie and Tatem, 1989: 382–3). The underlying religious rules were relaxed during the 20th century, and the beliefs have now faded out.

sage. Features in a *love divination procedure, reported only occasionally, such as:

On All Saints' Eve a young woman must go out into the garden alone at midnight, and while the clock strikes twelve she must pluck nine sage leaves, one at every stroke up to the ninth. Then, if she is destined to be married, she will see the face of her husband; if not, she will see a coffin. (Burne, 1883: 177).

A similar description, from Lincolnshire, calls for twelve leaves at midday on St Mark's Eve (quoted in Opie and Tatem). Like *parsley, sage is said to grow best where the wife is dominant, while others claim a link between the plant and the prosperity of the family. Sage has also had its medicinal uses; to keep teeth clean, relieve sore gums, and boiled in water to make a drink to alleviate arthritis.

Opie and Tatem, 1989: 335; Vickery, 1995: 328.

sailor, touching. A generally reported belief is that it is lucky to touch a sailor, or at least a sailor's collar. In most cases it appears to be females, or children, who are actually willing to carry out the action, which may say more about the gender-based societal norms of interpersonal contact than about who holds the belief itself. The earliest known references, however, date only to 1916, and it is possible that it originated during the First World War. See also other beliefs involving touching under *hunchback, *touching iron/wood, *statues.

N&Q 12s: 1 (1916) 430, 491; Opie and Tatem, 1989: 335.

St Agnes's Eve (20/1 January). Martyred in AD 303, St Agnes was the patron saint of young girls, so this was a favourite date for *love divinations—a tradition which became widely known through Keats's poem 'The Eve of St Agnes', though his idea of the ritual is heavily romanticized. Reality was much simpler. In Derbyshire, girls fasted for 24 hours before going to bed at midnight of the 20/1 January, and lying on the left side said three times:

> St Agnes be a friend to me,
> In the gift I ask of thee,
> Let me this night my husband see.

They then dreamed of their future husbands (*Long Ago* 2 (1874), 80). John Aubrey gives another: 'Upon St Agnes night, you take a row of pins, and pull out every one, one after another, saying a paternoster, sticking a pin in your sleeve, and you will dream of him or her you will marry' (Aubrey, 1696: 136).

Other methods included making the *dumb cake, and scattering barley seeds. The latter was practised in Lincolnshire up to the Second World War:

Two or three lasses at a time would go out into the orchard or garden and one or two kept guard while the other sowed the barley. They didn't like being out in the dark on their own so they went out a few at a time. If an apple tree was not at hand an oak tree would do. A ditty was said while the seeds were sown, I never got to know what that was. A secret, I was told. The seeds did grow quite quickly in many cases. (Sutton, 1997: 27–8).

Wright and Lones, 1938: ii. 106–10.

St Andrew's Day (30 November). In some areas, such as Bedfordshire, Buckinghamshire, Hertfordshire, and Northamptonshire, St Andrew was regarded as the patron saint of lace-makers (but see also *St Catherine) and his day was thus kept as a holiday, or 'tandering feast', by many in that trade. Thomas Sternberg, describing customs in mid-19th-century Northamptonshire, claims that St Andrew's Day Old Style (11 December) was a major festival day 'in many out of the way villages' of the county: '. . . the day is one of unbridled license—a kind of carnival; village scholars *bar out the master, the lace schools are deserted, and drinking and feasting prevail to a riotous extent. Towards evening the villagers walk about and masquerade, the women wearing men's dress and the men wearing female attire, visiting one another's cottages and drinking hot elderberry wine, the chief beverage of the season . . .' (Sternberg, 1851: 183–5). In Leighton Buzzard, Bedfordshire, a feature of the day was the making and eating of Tandry Wigs (a wig in this case being a cake or bun) (*N&Q* 5s:2 (1874), 138). A strange

belief reported by Wright and Lones is that wherever lillies of the valley grow wild the parish church is usually dedicated to St Andrew.

See also *SQUIRREL HUNTING.

Wright and Lones, 1940: iii. 186–91.

St Anne's Day (26 July). Sidney Oldall Addy describes the following *love divination procedure for St Anne's Eve, probably as collected in Derbyshire or Yorkshire, although similar ones are reported elsewhere for Midsummer and other times.

A stool is set in the middle of a room, and a bowl of water put thereon. A string or piece of rope is then hung across the room. Seven unmarried girls, who must not speak till the ceremony is over, come in, and each hangs a smock on the line. Then each of the girls in turn drops a bay-leaf into the water, and sits down immediately opposite to the smock which she has hung up. Soon afterwards a young man will enter the room, take a bay-leaf from the bowl, and sprinkle the smock of the girl whom he intends to marry. He will marry her that year.

Ben Jonson includes a reference to divinatory dreams in his masque 'The Satyr', but John *Aubrey (1686/1880: 54) challenges this and says he must mean *St Agnes. It is certainly true that St Agnes's Eve/Day is a far more common time for love divinations, but as Thomas Killigrew (*Thomaso*, (1663), II. iv) includes the term 'St Ann's Vision' in a list of failed love charms, it seems that Jonson was correct.

St Bartholomew's Day (24 August). Every 24 August, the Mayor of Sandwich visits St Bartholomew's Hospital (Almshouses) at Sandwich, Kent, and attends a memorial service for the Hospital's founders, and one of the sixteen residents is chosen as 'Master' by sticking a pin in a list of names. Then the local children race round the building and are rewarded with a bun each. The ceremony's date of origin is not known, but there was once a dole of bread, cheese, and beer and the bun race is probably a modified version of this.

Kightly, 1986: 202–3; Wright and Lones, 1940: iii. 49–50.

St Blaise, see *BLESSING THE THROATS.

St Briavels (Gloucestershire), see *BREAD AND CHEESE THROWING.

St Bride's Day (1 February). St Bride or Bridget

is much more popular in Ireland and the Isle of Man than in England, but one belief reported from the Midlands maintains that dew collected from plants on this day is particularly good for the complexion (compare *May dew).

Wright and Lones, 1938: ii. 117.

St Catherine's Day (25 November). This (probably fictional) martyr, very popular in the Middle Ages, was said to have been broken on a wheel—hence the 'Catherine wheel' firework. She was patron saint of lace-makers, spinners, rope-makers, wheelwrights, carpenters, young women, and female students, and some of these had customs particular to her day, although some of them seem to have confused the Saint with Queen Catherine of Aragon. In Buckinghamshire and Hertfordshire, lace-makers and children attending lace-making school, took Catterns Day as a holiday. They called at neighbours' houses requesting refreshment, and some of them dressed up as men to do so. Cakes called wiggs (oblong-shaped and flavoured with caraway seeds) and 'hot pot' (warm beer containing beaten eggs and rum) were traditional fare on the day. In the evening, catherine wheels were ignited and a game of jumping the candlestick was played—if the candle went out as a woman jumped over it she would have bad luck for the coming year (compare a similar game under *buckets). These customs had largely died out by the 1890s. A tradition which explains the connection between lace-making and St Catherine's Day relates that Queen Catherine of Aragon first taught the trade to English women and that once, when trade was very poor, she burnt her lace and ordered new to be made, encouraging other ladies at the court to follow suit (*N&Q* 3s:1 (1862), 387) (see also *St Andrew).

In the mid-19th century, the rope-makers of Kent also celebrated the day in style. There they had torchlight processions on 25 November, with drums and fifes, and six men carrying a female wearing muslin and a gilt crown, to represent Queen Catherine (*N&Q* 2s:5 (1858), 47). In the earlier 19th century, the female children of the workhouse of Peterborough also went in procession on this day, dressed in white, with coloured ribbons. The tallest girl represented the Queen and had a crown and sceptre, and they visited houses and sang:

Here comes Queen Catherine, as fine as any queen
With a coach and six horses a-coming to be seen
And a spinning we will go, will go, will go
And a spinning we will go

(Baker, 1854: ii. 436–7)

At Melton Abbey, Dorset, there is a St Catherine's Chapel where, according to a local tradition recorded in 1865, spinsters used to pray: 'A husband, St Catherine; a handsome one, St Catherine; a rich one, St Catherine; a nice one, St Catherine; and *soon*, St Catherine!'. Another version of the alleged prayer ends: 'But arn-a-one's better than narn-a-one, St Catherine!' (*The Family Herald* (16 Sept. 1865), 319; quoted in Opie and Tatem, 1989: 336). Brand also gives detailed instructions for a *love divination for St Catherine's Day, taken from a chapbook called *Mother Bunch's Golden Fortune-Teller*. For the *visiting custom called 'Catterning', see *souling.

Wright and Lones, 1940: iii. 177–86; Brand, 1849: i. 410–14.

St Christopher. All that is known historically of Christopher is that he was a martyr in Asia Minor (3rd century?); his name means 'Christ-carrier'. According to medieval legend, he was a giant who became Christian and used to serve travellers by carrying them across a river. One day he was almost crushed by the weight of a young boy, for the boy was Jesus, who carries the weight of the world. Many English churches had wall paintings and windows depicting Christopher, usually facing the main entrance, as it was said that anyone who saw an image of him would not die that day. He was also patron of travellers, and protected people from plague and storm. Processional *giants were sometimes named after him, he being a rare example of a virtuous giant; one survives, at *Salisbury (Wiltshire). St Christopher medals were already known in the Middle Ages; one of Chaucer's pilgrims, the Yeoman, wears a silver one. They are very popular charms in the 20th century, especially among motorists and those travelling by air.

St Clement's Day (23 November). Claimed as the patron saint of blacksmiths, who celebrated his Day in various ways. Earlier references, however, indicate that other trades had an interest in the day, and that it was previously an important festival: 'Itm. geuen to the bakers of the Prince house on saynt Clementes Even comyng wt theyre Bolle vs (November 1537)' (Hazlitt, 1905: 131), and similarly at

Newcastle in 1637 (J. J. Anderson, *Records of Early English Drama: Newcastle Upon Tyne* (1982), 157–8). Proclamations of 1540 and 1541 to suppress *boy bishop ceremonies also include St Clement's as one of the times that children should not be dressed up and taken in procession (Ian Lancashire, *Dramatic Texts and Records of Britain* (1984), 66).

See also *SOULING, for the *VISITING CUSTOM called 'Clementing'.

St Crispin's Day (25 October). Crispin and Crispian, martyred in AD 285, were said to be brothers of noble birth who learnt the humble trade of shoemaking rather than be a burden on the persecuted Christian community; they were therefore patron saints of cobblers and of the Shoemakers' Guild. One legend claimed they lived for a while at Faversham (Kent), but the popularity of their cult in England may also reflect patriotic pride in the victory at Agincourt, fought on their feast day, 25 October.

The Shoemakers' Guild celebrated this day in style. In early Stuart times they were responsible for staging plays, presumably about the life of these saints, one of which was for the Queen at Wells (Somerset) in 1613 (Ian Lancashire, *Dramatic Texts and Records of Britain* (1984), 280). Their power and confidence, and their love of pageantry and dramatic impersonation, was still obvious in Suffolk in 1777, when a parade of Shoemakers and their 'Prince' rode through the town, with trumpets, fifes, and drums:

The Prince was mounted on a fine grey horse and most magnificently habited. He was attended by his nobles, superbly dressed in green and white, and his guards in blue and white, which made a very good appearance. His noble and warlike Br. Crispianus appeared in a coat of mail, attended by his troops, in two divisions, one in red and white, the other in purple and white. They all rode in half boots, made of morocco, in different colours adapted to the uniforms; their jackets and caps were extremely neat in elegant taste, made all of leather.... The prince, attended by his guard, with his torch bearers and a grand band of musick playing before him, went to the Play, and was received with every mark of respect. (Quoted in Glyde, 1866/1976: 280–1)

St Crispin's day seems to have been particularly well celebrated in Sussex, with bonfires, fireworks, tar barrels, and behaviour more usually associated with *November the Fifth, at least in the 19th century, by which time heavy drinking and some rowdyism had replaced solemn pageantry. Boys copied the customs of Guy Fawkes Night by asking for money 'in the name of St Crispin'. At Horsham (Sussex) a further custom had developed by the 1830s: every year an effigy was made of someone 'who had misconducted himself or herself, or had become particularly notorious during the year'. This was hung up outside a pub near the offender's home and left there till 5 November, when it would be taken down and burnt. It was called 'the Crispin', by analogy with 'the Guy', and for weeks people would be wondering 'Who is to be the Crispin?' (Henry Burstow, *Reminiscences of Horsham* (1911), 76–7).

Wright and Lones, 1940: iii. 102–4; Simpson, 1973: 131–3.

St David's Day (1 March). As the patron saint of Wales, St David is obviously more honoured there than in England. According to *Times Telescope* for 1823 (p. 56): 'Early on the first of March, girls of Steben Hethe, now called Stepney, used to go to Goodman's Fields in search of a blade of grass of a reddish tint'. Whoever found one would be sure to secure the husband of her dreams within a month. All over England it was believed necessary to keep your windows closed on 1 March to keep the fleas out: 'If from fleas you would be free, On 1st of March, let your windows closed be' (Sussex) or 'The Devil shakes a bag of fleas at everybody's door on 1st of March' (Shropshire).

St David's Day was, however, the time for the English to make anti-Welsh gestures, although it is not clear why, unless it was in retaliation against the wearing of leeks which was taken to recall a famous Welsh victory over the 'Saxons'. The protest often took the form of processions carrying and burning *effigies of stereotypical Welshmen, such as that recorded by Samuel Pepys in his *Diary* for 1 March 1667:

in the street in Mark-lane do observe (it being St David's day) the picture of a man dressed like a Welchman, hanging by the neck on one of the poles that stand out at the top of one of the merchants' houses, in full proportion and very handsomely done—which is one of the oddest sights I have seen in a good while, for it was so like a man that one would have thought it was endeed a man.

Welshmen were often portrayed as riding goats, and a correspondent to William Hone's *Year Book* (1832: 796) described the sale of edible 'taffies' on St David's Day, which were made of white 'parlement' in the shape of 'a Welshman riding on a goat' provided by the gingerbread sellers, but these had recently disappeared.

Wright and Lones, 1938: ii. 158-9; Brand, 1849: i. 105-7.

St Dunstan (909-88). Dunstan, Abbot of *Glastonbury Abbey and later Archbishop of Canterbury, played a major role in both Church and State matters, and when young was a fine craftsman in painting, embroidery, and metal-working. Within ten years of his death he was regarded as a national saint. In folklore, he is remembered for his conflict with the *Devil (a 12th-century story); this is sometimes said to have happened at Glastonbury, sometimes at Mayfield (Sussex). The tale goes that one day when Dunstan was working at his forge making a chalice, a lovely girl arrived and began tempting him, whereupon he gripped her nose with red-hot tongs, and she turned back into a demon, whom the saint dragged round the smithy by his nose. A convent school at Mayfield still shows medieval tongs, alleged to be the very ones. Various modern elaborations include the idea that the Devil cooled his burnt nose in the springs at Tunbridge Wells (Kent) or the Roaring Spring near Mayfield; that he flew off with the tongs still in place, till they dropped off at Tongdean (Sussex); and that he tried to destroy Mayfield, but was foiled by Dunstan's inventive new use for *horseshoes—i.e. fixing them to doors. Hilaire Belloc's *The Four Men* (1911) makes Dunstan the hero of the *Devil's Dyke legend.

See Farmer, 1978: 136-9 for the facts; Westwood, 1985: 96-7, and Simpson, 1973: 63-4, for the legends.

St George (d. *c*.300). This early martyr was probably a soldier. He is credited with enduring astounding tortures and performing equally astounding miracles, but it was the tale of his combat against a *dragon to save a princess's life which really ensured his popularity. This first appears in the *Legenda Aurea* (*The Golden Legend*) in the 13th century.

His importance in Western Europe increased after a reported vision of him during the siege of Antioch in the First Crusade was taken as a sign of victory. A military and aristocratic cult rapidly developed. His feast day (23 April) was made a holiday in England in 1222; Edward III chose him as patron of the Order of the Garter in 1343; Henry V invoked him at Agincourt; by the close of the Middle Ages he was regarded as the patron saint of England, and a model of chivalry. His feast was celebrated by civic and guild processions, which gave much scope for horse-riding knights and effigy dragons, such as *Snap at Norwich. Parades were held at Leicester, Chester, Coventry, Reading, and King's Lynn, as well as many smaller places, but they did not long survive the Reformation; popular customs were then transferred to warmer dates such as *May Day and *Midsummer, and 23 April is not now marked by any traditional customs.

George's persona was remodelled in a remarkably popular work, *The Famous History of the Seven Champions of Christendom* (1596-7) by Richard Johnson, which strips away the Christian elements, replacing them with chivalric and magical adventures imitated from medieval romances. Here, George is born in Coventry, son of the Lord Steward of England, but stolen soon after birth by an enchantress whose power he eventually outwits; he saves Sabra, the King of Egypt's daughter, by killing a dragon; after further adventures he dies from the poison of another (English) dragon, and is buried in Windsor Chapel. Johnson's book was often reprinted, and formed the basis for *chapbook abridgements, plays, and children's versions; it is thanks to this that George appears in many texts of the *mumming play.

There have been repeated attempts to persuade English people to celebrate St George's Day by flying flags or wearing a rose, and frequent newspaper complaints of the lack of a national holiday. Local celebrations were fairly common in the 1930s, but faded out again after the Second World War. Currently (1996-9) appropriate greeting cards are commercially available, and a civic pageant was once again held at Salisbury in 1997. The St George flag (red cross on white ground) has recently been enthusiatically adopted by English football fans as a national symbol.

Wright and Lones, 1938: ii. 178-83; Christina Hole, *English Folk Heroes* (1948), 103-20; Simons, 1998: 80-94.

St John's Eve (23/4 June). This is the night of 23/4 June, now more generally called *Midsummer Night or Midsummer Eve, and an important date for *bonfires and *divinations.

St Mark's Eve (24/5 April). This was the night for keeping watch to see the *wraiths of those who would die during the year. The practice has been recorded throughout England from the 17th century till late in the 19th century, especially in northern and western counties. The first reference to it is in 1608, when a woman in Walesbie (Nottinghamshire) was charged before a church court 'for watching upon Saint Markes even at Nighte laste in the Church porche to presage by divelishe demonstracion the deathe of somme neighbours within this yeere' (*Transactions of the Thoroton Society* 30: 12, cited in Opie and Tatem, 1989: 80). In 1673, a Yorkshire vicar said it 'was frequently practised by those poor ignorant souls' who waited in pairs in the churchyard to see the wraiths pass into the church, in the order in which they will dye, 'and when they are all in they hear a murmuring noise in church for a while' (Gutch, 1912: 44).

There are variations of detail; some sources say the watcher must be fasting, others that he must circle the church before taking up his position; some say he will see headless or rotting corpses approaching, or coffins, but most describe identifiable wraiths. 'Those who are to die soon, enter the first, and those who will almost survive the year do not approach until nearly one o'clock. ... If the person is to be drowned, his representative will come as if struggling and splashing in water, and so on for other cases of premature death,' wrote a Yorkshire correspondent to Hone's *Every-Day Book* in 1827 (cols. 548–9). Those who would become gravely but not fatally ill, he added, would approach the church and peep in, but not enter. There are several tales of watchers who saw their own wraith, and died not long after.

This date was also, though less often, chosen for *love divinations; in a lawsuit in 1827, a woman was reported as saying: 'I'll tell you what I did to know if I could have Mr Barker. On St Mark's night I ran round a haystack nine times, with a ring in my hand, calling out, "Here's the sheath, but where's the knife?", and when I was running round the ninth time, I thought I saw Mr Barker coming home' (Hone, 1827: ii. 159).

One Lincolnshire writer says a girl who picks twelve leaves of *sage while the clock strikes midnight will see her future husband, and anyone can become 'as wise as the devil' by catching *fernseed (J. A. Penny, *Lincolnshire N&Q* 3 (1892–3), 209). Another was told that every year witches and others who have sold themselves to the Devil must go round the church backwards three times, look in at the keyhole, and say certain words, or lose their power (Rudkin, 1936: 73).

S. P. Menefee, in *The Seer*, ed. Hilda Ellis Davidson (1989), 80–99.

Saint Monday. Not a saint at all, but 'keeping Saint Monday' was formerly used to describe the regular practice of staying off work on Mondays, particularly in the shoemaking trade. The custom was already well known in the 17th century, as evidenced by the line in the play: 'They say Monday's Shooemaker's holliday, I'le fall to that trade' (Dekker, *If It Be Not Good, The Diuel Is In It* (1612)). This gives the lie to a legend, involving a Perth shoemaker and Oliver Cromwell, which seeks to explain its origin (*Folk-Lore Record* 1 (1878), 245–6). The custom fell into disuse following the gradual spread of more regulated working hours and the introduction of half-day working on Saturdays. There is a French phrase, reported from the 16th century, *faire le lundi des savetiers*, or 'to keep the cobbler's Monday'.

N&Q 8s:1 (1892), 88, 212, 232–3, 252, 441, 523.

St Nicholas (4th century). Little is known of the real life of this Bishop of Myra in Turkey, but he was very popular in the Middle Ages. Legend says he once resuscitated three little boys whom an innkeeper had murdered and salted down to make into pies, and on another occasion secretly threw three bags of gold through the window of a poor man's house, as dowries for his three daughters, who would otherwise have been sold into prostitution. He is therefore regarded as a patron saint of children, who, in many Catholic countries, get presents during the night of his feast (6 December).

His feast was once linked to children in England too; merrymaking and unruliness were allowed in some schools. Aubrey wrote in the 1680s:

And the Schoole-boies in the west still religiously observe St Nicholas day (Decemb. 6th), he was the Patron of the Schoole-boies. At Currey-Yeoville in Somersetshire, where there is a Howschole (or schole) in the Church, they have annually at that time a Barrell of good Ale brought into the church; and that night they have the priviledge to breake open their Masters Cellar-dore. (Aubrey, 1686/1880: 40–1).

It was the date for choosing *boy bishops, who were actually called 'St Nicholas'; the church historian John Strype noted that in

1554, in London, 'the Nicholases' were going about the streets as usual, though this had been forbidden, since the citizens liked the show so much (*Annals of the Reformation* (1709–31)). So they did two years later, according to Henry Machyn's *Diary*, 'and had mych good cheer as ever they had, in mony places'. These customs died out in England but their continental equivalents are important in the development of *Santa Claus. St Nicholas and his gifts reached America through German and Dutch settlers, and became famous there in a poem by Clement Clark Moore, 'The Visit of Saint Nicholas' (1822). In Moore's account he is no longer a bishop but a chubby, pipe-smoking, cheerful old man 'dressed all in fur from his head to his foot', driving a reindeer sledge and carrying a sack of toys—details that have North European parallels. Forty years later, in the 1860s, illustrations to this poem by Thomas Nast were captioned as *Santa Claus, no longer as St Nicholas.

St Peter's Eve (28/9 June). The joint feast of Sts Peter and Paul is on 29 June, and the preceding night is the occasion for a variant form of *love divination, recorded only from Tattershall (Lincolnshire). Girls wishing to dream of their destined husbands must take nine keys to bed with them, knotted with their hair, and say:

> St Peter don't take it amiss
> To gain your favour I've done this.
> You are the holder of the keys
> Favour me I ask you please.

> (Sutton, 1997: 138)

saints. The importance of saints in medieval England has left many traces in folklore. Dates were commonly expressed by reference to saints' feasts, the more important of which (nationally or locally) were holidays. Church *ales, *fairs, and many *calendar customs were originally set on such holidays; well into the 20th century, the date of village *wakes often recalled the saint to whom their church was dedicated, allowing for the eleven-day calendar shift of 1752. Saints' days were the usual markers mentioned in weather lore, and in farmers' rules for the timing of seasonal tasks; rents and hiring agreements were fixed by them, hence the legal importance of Lady Day and *Michaelmas. In popular belief, the eves of certain feasts were appropriate times for divination.

Places as well as times were dedicated to a particular saint—churches, obviously, but also colleges, hospitals, towns, streets, *wells, hills, woods, wayside crosses, and much else—and these names often survive. Saints were also adopted as patrons of social groupings, especially trade and craft guilds; after the Reformation, official celebrations were secularized, but at folk level the links of certain crafts to saints were remembered (see *St Catherine, *St Clement, *St Crispin).

Saints protected those who honoured them, both spiritually and against material misfortunes; many were regarded as defenders against one particular disease or danger. Such specializations were not peculiar to England; throughout the Catholic world people thought of St Christopher as the protector of travellers, St Clare as the healer of eye troubles, St Margaret as a helper in childbirth, etc. There was a vast international corpus of legendary biographies, the most famous being the *Legenda Aurea* (*The Golden Legend*) in the 13th century; an English version printed in 1483 was extremely popular. The stories there standardized were known to everyone, literate or not, for generations; they were taught through sermons and through visual representation in church murals, windows, etc. Most saints also had an identifying symbol which was equally standardized—St Peter carrying keys, St John the Evangelist with an eagle, St Luke with an ox, St Mark with a lion, etc.

Most saints revered in England were those known throughout Europe; others were native to this country. Cornwall remains an area notable for numerous Celtic saints unknown elsewhere, dating from the first period of Christianity (i.e. Romano-British, not Saxon). The Anglo-Saxons venerated some Celtic saints, plus many missionaries and martyrs from their own Conversion period, monks, nuns, bishops, and kings; some were deleted from the calendar after the Conquest, but others remained or were reinstated, e.g. Alban, Chad, Cuthbert, Dunstan, Oswald, Edmund of East Anglia, and Edward the Confessor. The medieval period saw the canonization of Thomas à Becket, who rapidly became England's most famous saint, Bishop Hugh of Lincoln, Bishop William FitzHerbert of York, and Bishop Thomas Cantilupe of Hereford. Others were locally revered, but canonization was a slow process and the Reformation intervened before they were officially declared saints; they include the healer and exorcist

John Schorne of North Marston (Buckingham-shire), and Henry VI.

The Roman Catholic Church continues to adopt new saints. The Forty English Martyrs, i.e. Catholics executed between 1535 and 1679, had received popular veneration from the time of their deaths, and are now officially classed as saints; Thomas More and John Fisher were canonized in 1935 and the others in 1970.

See also the entries for individual saints and their feasts; also *PILGRIMAGES and *WELLS.

Farmer, 1978, describes all English saints and all international saints who are or once were venerated in England; the Introduction outlines the history of the cult of saints here. An influential earlier compilation is Alban Butler's *The Lives of the Fathers, Martyrs, and Other Principal Saints* (4 vols., 1756–9; rev. edn., 1953–4). See also David Rollason, *Saints and Relics in Anglo-Saxon England* (1989); Finucane, 1977; Ben Nilson, *Cathedral Shrines of Medieval England* (1998).

St Stephen's Day (26 December). The day after Christmas Day, or 'Boxing Day' to most of us, St Stephen's Day is nowadays subsumed into the general two-day Christmas period and has little character of its own. Boxing Day derives its name from a previous custom on the day of asking and giving 'Christmas boxes', i.e. presents, either money or in kind. The 'box' was originally the receptacle into which the money was placed, but it gradually came to refer to the gift itself. There are strong historical traditions of gift-giving on *Christmas Day and *New Year's Day, and at different periods each of these days was considered the proper time for presents to family and friends, but the Boxing Day gifts were different again. On this day, there was a definite feeling of a gratuity for services rendered, rather than of a gift between equals. The earliest references, in the 1620s to 1640s refer to apprentices and servants as recipients of money gifts from their employers, and later in the same century there are references to money being given to tradespeople who had served one well during the year, staff at clubs, and so on. But as the custom spread, tradespeople themselves also felt obliged to give Christmas boxes:

It is customary for employees to call upon those who employed their masters and ask for money. Grocers used to make their customers a present of plums for their Christmas puddings and bakers invariably gave a plum cake at this time. The custom extends to certain subordinate officials, e.g. the sexton, clerk, ringers and watchmen. (Baker, 1854: 73)

Already in the 18th century people were complaining loudly of the amount they were expected to pay out to all and sundry—Hutton quotes Jonathan Swift and Joseph Fielding on the subject—and the satirical magazine *Punch* included regular pieces against the custom throughout the mid-19th century, with varying proportions of good humour and bitter complaint, as for example: 'How much longer, we ask with indignant sorrow, is the humbug of Boxing-day to be kept up for the sake of draining the pockets of struggling trades-men . . .' (*Punch* (1848), 271).

Clearly, there was a complex network of social obligations regarding who gave Christmas boxes to whom, and further details are given by Hannah Cullwick, working as a maid-servant in London, in her diary for 1863, when she recieved money from the tradesmen who dealt with her 'Missis' (Liz Stanley (ed.), *The Diaries of Hannah Cullwick: Victorian Maidservant* (1984), 145, 261).

There are a number of references to parties of villagers descending on the local woods on Christmas Day or St Stephen's Day in an orgy of 'hunting' any live animal or bird they could find. In some cases this was under the guise of hunting the *wren' or *squirrel hunting customs, but it was also widely believed, especially in the northern counties, that the game laws did not apply on these days.

It was also generally the custom to bleed horses on this day, often after riding them hard first, as it was believed that it would do them good for the coming year (see Brand for 16th- to 18th-century references). One or two other isolated customs are recorded. An ancient custom existed in the parish of Drayton Beauchamp, Buckinghamshire, called 'Stephening', which probably originated in a charity dole. Inhabitants would visit the Rectory and assert their right to eat as much bread and cheese and drink as much ale as they chose. The rector managed to discontinue the custom in 1808 (*Transactions of the Buckinghamshire Archaeological Soc.* 1 (1858), 577–8). Another curious custom existed at Brighton of bowling or throwing oranges along the high-roads on this day. The one whose orange is hit by that of another forfeits it to the successful hitter (*Sussex Archaeological Collections* 33 (1883), 256).

See also *CHRISTMAS, *MARSHFIELD PAPER BOYS, *MUMMING PLAYS, *SQUIRREL HUNTING, *WASSAILING, *WRENS.

Wright and Lones, 1940: iii. 273–9; Brand, 1849: 532–4; Hutton, 1996: 23–4, 114.

St Swithin (d. 862). Swithin (or, more properly, Swithun) was Bishop of Winchester. As a mark of humility, when he was dying he asked to be buried out of doors, where he would be trodden on and rained on; in the following century he was regarded as a saint, and the then Bishop had his bones reburied in a shrine inside the cathedral on 15 July 971. According to legend there was a heavy rainstorm, either during this ceremony or on its anniversary; one 14th-century chronicler says it caused massive flooding, several drownings, and a famine. Hence the popular saying, known since Elizabethan times, that if it rains on St Swithin's Day (15 July) it will go on raining for forty days (Opie and Tatem, 1989: 337–8).

St Thomas's Day (21 December). In many areas this was the date for *thomasing (or gooding), a ritualized begging for food in readiness for Christmas, and Wright and Lones list a number of doles formerly distributed on this day. There are a few scattered reports of other customs and beliefs: in several parts of the country, including Buckinghamshire, Yorkshire, and Warwickshire, it was the custom up to the 19th century to 'ring Christmas in' by a peal of church bells on St Thomas's Day. In Kent, one should sow broad beans on this day, and *Denham Tracts* (1895: ii. 92) goes further:

The day of St Thomas, blessed divine,
Is good for brewing, baking, and killing fat swine.

Wright and Lones, 1940: iii. 200–9.

St Thomas's Eve (20/21 December). A *love divination designated for this night, involving the use of an *onion, has varied little for 300 years. In *Mother Bunch's Closet* (1685: 7) the instructions are:

Take a St Thomas onion, and peel it, and lay it in a clean handkerchief and lay it under your head . . . and as soon as you be laid down . . . say these words:

Good St Thomas do me right
And bring my love to me tonight
That I may look him in the face
And in my arms may him embrace.

Then in thy first sleep thou shalt dream of him that shall be thy husband.

A Victorian example from Derbyshire says the onion should be stuck with nine *pins, and has a slightly longer verse (*Long Ago* 2 (1874), 21). In modern Lincolnshire, the girl says:

Good Saint Thomas see me right
Let me see my love tonight
In his clothes and his array
That he wears most every day.

(Sutton, 1997: 204)

Wright and Lones, 1940: iii. 198–9.

St Wilfrid's Feast. This *feast celebrates the day that St Wilfrid returned to Ripon, North Yorkshire, from Rome in AD 686, although there is no evidence that it goes anywhere near that far back. The centre of the celebration is the procession on the Saturday before the first Monday in August, led by a man dressed as the saint on a white horse and including bands, morris dancers, and carnival floats. A short service is held at the cathedral, and the saint gives prizes for the best floats. Special Wilfrid pies (cheese and apple) and Wilfra tarts (almonds and lemon) are made and sold in the town.

Smith, 1989: 107–8; Shuel, 1985: 88; Kightly, 1986: 203.

Salisbury Giant and Hob-Nob. St Christopher, the Salisbury *giant, now lives in the Salisbury Museum (Wiltshire) and only comes out on special occasions. He is the twelve-foot (previously fourteen-foot) tall pageant giant originally belonging to the Salisbury Guild of Merchant Tailors, and is the last surviving example of a once popular genre. He is light enough for one man to carry him, and is designed so that the carrier cannot be seen, and, in procession, he can sway, lean, and turn. The giant's costume has been renewed many times in his existence, altering his appearance quite dramatically. In 1982 he acquired a red woollen robe, 15th-century style head-dress, leather gauntlets, and leather baldrick. The head is definitely the oldest part of the figure, although it is not possible to determine whether it is the original one. It is carved from a block of wood, and, in the past, his lips were able to move, presumably worked by the carrier from inside. When in procession, he is accompanied by two men ('whifflers') carrying his regalia, a huge wooden sword and a mace, and a Yeoman to carry his staff of office. The procession also usually includes *morris dancers, first mentioned in 1564. The first mention of the giant is in 1570, but he was already old enough then to need repairs to his costume. It is possible, though not at present provable, that he is as old as the Guild itself, which received its charter in 1447.

His other companion of long standing is

Hob-Nob, the *hobby horse (occasionally referred to as a dragon). In E. C. Cawte's definition, Hob-Nob is a 'tourney' horse, that is, the operator wears a framework around his waist, suspended from his shoulders, which has a horse's head and tail, and a cloth which hangs all round, reaching the ground so that it hides his legs. In Hob-Nob's case, the operator's upper body is covered in netting—perhaps to disguise him, or to protect him from rotten fruit thrown by exuberant onlookers. As usual, Hob-Nob's jaws are designed to open and shut. Hob-Nob is not mentioned specifically in the earliest records, but appears in 1572, when 'Thomas Barker dyd bringe in one Hobby-Horse . . .'. Since 1873, the giant and Hob-Nob have belonged to the Museum.

Hugh Shortt, *The Giant and Hob-Nob* (1972; 2nd edn., revised John Chandler, 1988); Cawte, 1978.

sallow. In early spring, sallow twigs bear fluffy yellow flowers before they have any leaves. These were gathered for use in church decorations and processions on *Palm Sunday, and were widely known as 'palms'; nowadays, real palm is imported instead. Some people believed sallow or willow twigs protect a house from witchcraft and the evil eye, but also that one should never use them to beat an animal or child, for they would stunt its growth (Vickery, 1995: 134–5).

salt. The belief that spilling salt brings bad luck (especially, a quarrel between friends) was first noted in the 16th century, and is widely known today; to avert the evil, one should take a pinch of the spilt salt with the *right hand and throw it over the *left shoulder—into the fire, according to older sources, or 'to blind the Devil', as is now sometimes said. To explain this belief, some people claim that *Judas spilt the salt at the Last Supper, but the symbolic role of salt in folklore is strong enough to account for it.

Just as it keeps food wholesome, so salt was used to repel spiritual and magical evil, both in Catholic ritual and in folk practice, and as a symbol of incorruptibility and virtue (Matthew 5: 13). The use of salt as *magical protection is recorded from various parts of England, though less regularly than in Scotland and Wales. A handful thrown into the fire would torment witches and drive them away; in Lancashire this had to be done for *nine successive mornings, with the words: 'Salt, salt! I put thee into the fire, and may the per-

son who has bewitched me neither eat, drink, nor sleep, till the spell is broken' (Harland and Wilkinson, 1873: 235).

A widespread custom in the days when the dead were laid out at home was to put a plate of salt on the chest of the corpse, and keep it there till the *funeral; in Cumberland in the early 20th century it was 'almost universal among the poorer classes' (*Folk-Lore* 31 (1920), 154), and the same was probably true elsewhere. The reason, it was generally said, was to prevent the body swelling; however, the salt might once have been regarded as a magical defence against evil spirits, or against the possibility of the *ghost walking.

Like *bread and *coal, salt is one of the appropriate token gifts brought when first footing on New Year's Day, or given to a new *baby, or brought into a new house; in these cases it represents prosperity.

Opie and Tatem, 1989: 338–44; Radford, Radford, and Hole, 1961: 297–9.

Samhain. Meaning 'summer's end' and pronounced 'sarwin', this is the Irish name for 1 November, the beginning of winter; in medieval Irish tales, the preceding night is often associated with fairies, ghosts, and supernatural adventures. It has never been an English word, but *Wiccans and other Neo-Pagans use it in preference to *All Saints' Day and *Halloween.

sanding. A custom reported in several locations but surviving only at *Knutsford, Cheshire, is the decoration of pavements with coloured sand on special occasions such as *May Day and for local *weddings. At Knutsford, the sand is dispensed through a funnel, and it is said that it is better when it rains because the colour thus lives on for a while in the paving stones. Henderson (1879: 40–1) also mentions sand strewing for weddings in 19th-century Newcastle.

Shuel, 1985: 34; D. Haworth and W. M. Comber, *Cheshire Village Memories* (1961), plate 23; Roy Kerridge, *Bizarre Britain* (1985), 60–3.

Sandman, the. An imaginary figure who sprinkles sand on your eyes to send you to sleep; if you can feel hard grains on your eyelashes in the morning, you know the Sandman came last night. It is not clear how long this has been part of nursery lore, or where it came from. 'Dustman' with the same meaning is found in 1821, and there was a Lancashire figure called Billy-Winker, 'a mythical sprite that closes the eyes of children at bedtime' (Wright, 1913: 202). However, the first record for 'Sandman' itself is in a translation of Hans *Anderson's tales in 1861 (*OED*), so a continental origin seems possible.

Santa Claus. This American name for the Christmas gift-bringer is increasingly used in England, generally in the shortened form 'Santa'. Early American settlers, being Puritans, rejected the English *Father Christmas, but later Dutch immigrants brought traditions about *St Nicholas, popularized through a poem by Clement Clark Moore, 'The Visit of Saint Nicholas' (1822), now more usually called 'The Night Before Christmas'. Moore describes the saint not as a bishop in a red cope, as in Holland, but as a fat man dressed in fur, driving a reindeer sleigh. He may well have been aware that in many European traditions, notably in Germany, St Nicholas is accompanied by fur-clad or gnome-like servants who carry presents for good children, but a birch for bad ones; such images might seem more appealing than a saint in religious garb. Illustrating Moore's poem in the 1860s, Thomas Nast used the colloquial Dutch 'Santa Claus' rather than the formal 'St Nicholas', and dressed him in a belted jacket and furry cap.

During the rest of the 19th century, Santa was often shown in a red jacket but with blue knickerbockers, as befits a Dutchman; in the 20th century, an all-red outfit with white trimmings became the norm, especially after a Coca-Cola advertising campaign exploited his figure in 1931. The artist, the Swede Haddon Sundblom, also gave him a drooping tassled red cap like those associated with elves and gnomes; he may have been thinking of a Swedish Christmas gnome. Scandinavian influence also accounts for the elfin assistants often mentioned, and the home at the North Pole. Rudolph the Red-Nosed Reindeer dates from 1949, in a song by Johnny Marks.

The name apparently reached England in the 1870s, to the puzzlement of observers, though the hanging-up of stockings was already an 'old' custom, at any rate in the northern counties (Henderson, 1866: 50). The first mention of the gift-bringer's name which we have traced is a letter to *N&Q* (5s:11 (1879), 66), where a Mr Edwin Lees says he has 'only lately been told' of a custom currently observed in Herefordshire, Worcestershire, and Devonshire, which he has not seen recorded anywhere:

On Christmas Eve, when the inmates of a house in the country retire to bed, all those desirous of a present place a stocking outside the door of their bedroom, with the expectation that some mythical being called *Santiclaus* will fill the stocking or place something within it before morning. This is of course well known, and the master of the house does in reality place a Christmas gift secretly in each stocking; but the giggling girls in the morning, when bringing down their presents, affect to say that Santiclaus visited and filled the stockings in the night. From what region of the earth or air this benevolent Santiclaus takes flight I have not been able to ascertain.

William Brockie noticed the same custom round Durham in the 1880s; he too was puzzled by the unfamiliar name and made the ingenious but mistaken guess that it was 'Santa Cruz, the Holy Cross' which brought the presents (Brockie, 1886: 92–3). By what channels this American feature reached Victorian England is at present unknown. One possibility (proposed anonymously in *The Times* of 22 December 1956) is a popular American story, *The Christmas Stocking* by Susan Warner, printed in London in 1854 and several times thereafter.

See also *FATHER CHRISTMAS.

Saturday. Two related beliefs concern working on Saturdays. Firstly, there was a prejudice against starting a new job on a Saturday, or even starting any important work: 'I recollect, when I was a boy in Norfolk, thirty-five years ago, hearing old labourers say that it was bad luck to put in a crop on a Saturday' (*N&Q* 9s:7 (1901), 337–8). The other warns against working at all on this day. These ideas have been reported most frequently from Scotland, and only in scattered instances in England, and they appear to originate in the religious practice of keeping Saturday afternoon clear of regular work to prepare for Sunday, which was observed in medieval and later periods.

Opie and Tatem, 1989: 344–5; Brand, 1849: ii. 37–41.

scissors. As with *knives and other sharp objects, tradition dictates that anyone who receives scissors as a present must give the donor a coin, otherwise the gift will 'cut the love' between them. The earliest known references (1507 and 1611) relate to knives in this context, but the first to refer specifically to scissors is also the first to mention the payment in return:

Dearest brother, I give you a grate many thanks for

the siszers you sent me by Mr. Shokman. I gave him sixpence for fear tha should cute love one your side: but for mine 'tis to well gronded to fear ather siszers ar knifs cutting of it. (Letter from Elizabeth Wentworth, Feb. 1707, quoted in Opie and Tatem)

The belief has been recorded regularly ever since that time, and is still current. There are a number of beliefs about dropping a pair of scissors, reported since the late 19th century, but with little agreement on what it means or what to do if it happens. Some maintain that if you drop a pair of scissors someone else must pick them up for you (also said of other everyday objects, such as *spoons, *umbrellas, etc.), while others say that if the points stick into the ground it is a sign of a wedding, or death, or more work on the way (for dressmakers). Igglesden adds: 'Should a sempstress drop her scissors accidentally it means a mourning order . . .' (c.1932: 209).

Scissors were sometimes used as a defence against *witchcraft. If a pair was hidden under the doormat, no witch could enter the house; if behind a cushion, she would be uneasy in the room, and would soon leave, without harming anyone. Some said that scissors used in this way should be open, thus adding the power of the *cross to that of *iron and cutting edge.

Opie and Tatem, 1989: 345.

Scot, Reginald (?1538–99). Scot's *The Discoverie of Witchcraft* (1584) is the first English book devoted to this topic, and also has valuable sections on *fairies, brownies, demons, and other supernatural beings, and the use of *charms. In its ambiguous title, 'discovery' means 'unmasking, debunking'; Scot regarded all alleged magical acts as mere trickery. From his acid comments, it is clear that he had closely observed both rural witches and their accusers. They are, he writes, poor and ugly women who live by begging, going from house to house 'for a pot full of milke, yeast, drinke, pottage, or some such releefe', and if refused will curse anything from the master of the house to 'the little pig that lieth in the stie'; whatever goes wrong after that is blamed on the witch.

Scot's book was loudly condemned by his contemporaries; James I, outraged, wrote his own *Daemonologie* to refute it. A modern edition by Montague Summers was reprinted in 1972.

scrambling customs. A recurrent feature of customs, all over the country, is a 'scrambling', whereby something is thrown to a crowd and everyone scrambles to get it. In many cases the item thrown is edible—nuts, oranges, apples, or even pieces of pie (at *Hallaton), bread and cheese (at *St Briavels) or pancake (*Westminster School). In other circumstances it is money—usually pennies, and sometimes heated first (e.g. *Rye, Sussex). Scrambling is often part of another custom, particularly *civic customs and doles. In the cold light of day, scrambling can seem somewhat odd behaviour. In a children's custom the point is obviously the fun of the scrambling itself, but in a charity dole such as the Bread and Cheese throwing at St Briavel's the logic is less easy to find. The point here, perhaps, is the element of luck, or random choice in the distribution. In addition, there are traditions of bridegrooms throwing handfuls of coins at *weddings.

See also *HUNGERFORD HOCKTIDE, *PAINSWICK FEAST.

Scrapfaggot Green, the witch of. According to articles in the *Sunday Pictorial* of 8 and 15 October 1944, the village of Great Leighs (Essex) was being plagued by nocturnal accidents to livestock, tools scattered, bells ringing, etc. They said it was because bulldozers widening a lane to a military base had pushed aside a boulder at a crossroads called Scrapfaggot Green—a boulder covering the remains of a witch, together with the fire that burnt her. When the boulder was replaced, trouble stopped.

The 'weird events' have been taken seriously by several writers on the occult (e.g. Valiente, 1973: 352–4), but locals now admit they were tricks played on the London journalist. How much genuine folklore underlay them is now unclear; the name 'Scrapfaggot' invites puns, there are historical records of a witchcraft case at nearby Boreham, and there seems to have been a 'Witch's Stone' around in the 1930s (though not at the crossroads). Since the 1980s, a stone outside a pub in Great Leighs is claimed to be the original, supposedly brought there in 1945.

FLS News 17 (1993), 12–13; 19 (1994), 11; 20 (1994), 11; 24 (1996), 2; 26 (1997) 3–4; Revd W. J. T. Smith, *The Boreham Witch: Fact or Fiction?* (1995).

sea beans, see *LUCKY BEANS.

seafaring customs and beliefs. Two deep-sea customs have been reported on a regular basis and are thus well known. The first is usually called 'burying the dead horse' but in the following account, written by an emigrant on the *Northumberland* in 1874, it is 'burning':

We having been a month at sea, they 'burnt the dead horse' tonight. This is a usual custom, these being the particulars. All the ship's company have a month's salary in advance, that is they get a draft payable three days after the ship has sailed, which they leave at home in old England. Therefore they work the first month on board shop and are earning no money, so when the month is up they 'burn the dead horse' thereby meaning that they have commenced afresh and now are earning money. The ceremony took place about 7.30pm. An effigy as near the form of a horse is made out of sailcloth etc., with a tar barrel full of combustibles for its body, & is mounted on a carriage with a sailor as jockey & hauled around the decks, with songs. Then an auctioneer is appointed & puts it up for auction, giving its pedigree etc. The highest bidder has it or rather has to make his bid good, which money is made up by general collection. This money which amounts to several pounds is divided amongst the sailors. After this they hauled the horse up to the yard arm & set fire to him, & then cut him adrift. On the whole the performance was very amusing & caused considerable excitement. (Simon Braydon and Robert Songhurst (eds.), *The Diary of Joseph Sams* (1982), 34)

A very similar account is given, of a voyage from London to Melbourne about 1897, in *Folk-Lore* 8 (1897), 281–4, with the addition of the text and tune of the song 'Poor Old Horse', sung on the occasion. The idea of doing work already paid for being a 'dead horse' is not simply a seaman's term, being reported with similar meaning from various parts of the country and in several trades (Joseph Wright, *EDD* II, 1900: 38).

The ceremony of 'crossing the line' is carried out on crossing the equator, on anyone in the ship's crew who has not previously done so. One sailor dresses as Neptune and is let over the side so that he may make a grand show of coming on board, where he is greeted with respect and is welcomed by the captain. Various ceremonies and speeches are performed, but the key part of the custom is carried out on any novices. One by one they are brought forward, blindfolded and with hands tied, and seated on a board. Sometimes a doctor examines them, with humorous dialogue, but invariably the main part is the shaving. After being daubed with tar, treacle, or anything else to hand, their face is scraped with a piece of rusty iron, and they are finally dumped into a sail or tub of water. The precise details changed from ship to ship, but the basic outline was very similar, and a great deal of horseplay took place. Modern cruise liner crews still perform the ceremony on passengers, although the rough handling is obviously toned down on these occasions. Good accounts can be found in Simon Braydon and Robert Songhurst (eds.), *The Diary of Joseph Sams* (1982), 30–1; Frederick Pease Harlow, *The Making of a Sailor* (1928), 176–86; Hone, 1827: ii. 697–8. Hone's *Table-Book* (1827: 315–16) contains an interesting parallel from the Greenland whale fishery, enacted on May Day 1824 on board the ship *Neptune*, from London. The seamen had apparently prepared for the event, before sailing, by acquiring coloured ribbons, with which to decorate their garland. The basis of the garland was a cask hoop, covered with ribbons, set on a pole, about four feet high. A model of the ship, prepared by the ship's carpenter was fixed on top like a weather vane. What occurred on May Day was an almost exact replica of the crossing the line ceremony, with Neptune addressing the captain, and the comic shaving of any newcomers in the crew.

There are countless superstitions and beliefs attributed to seamen, but only a sample can be given. In the days of sail, the wind was clearly both a potential ally and feared enemy, and a number of strategies were available for summoning a wind, although few for getting rid of it. *Whistling and the untying of magical *knots are generally known, but other ways include the whipping of the ship's boys, which is reported in 1620 and 1811, cutting a pig's throat, and buying wind with coins (*FLS News* 21 (1995), 15–16). Seamen were amongst those who believed it dangerous to sleep in the light of the *moon, which was still being reported well into the 20th century (*FLS News* 20 (1994), 7). Sailors had a particular antipathy to sharks, and when they caught one they delighted in treating it with more than ordinary savagery, in revenge for colleagues lost at sea. A shark following a ship was regarded as unlucky, perhaps because it was thought that they could 'smell' a sickness on board and thus seemed to be waiting for a death (*FLS News* 20 (1994) 6–7). Many sailors were particularly prone to seeing omens in any occurrence out of the ordinary. The ship's cat being lost overboard, birds alighting on the rigging or following the ship (Opie and Tatem, 1989: 1; *FLS News*

11 (1990), 15–16; 24 (1996), 7–8), and the curious belief reported in *The Times* (2 Dec. 1966) that no bird has ever been known to alight on the deck or rigging of *HMS Victory*.

See also *COINS, *DAVY JONES, *EARS, *FISHING INDUSTRY, *KEYS, *WHISTLING.

See series of articles by A. W. Smith, and others, in *FLS News* 12 (1991), onwards.

seagulls. It is said in coastal areas that the souls of drowned sailors and fishermen may become seagulls, and that therefore these birds should never be killed; the belief is fairly widely known nowadays, but the first record given by Opie and Tatem (1989: 345–6) is only from 1878. Occasionally gulls are linked with death in a more general way; in the 1970s a Sussex woman commented that some had swooped into her garden 'as a warning' on the day her sick mother died [JS].

sea shanties. Sea shanties, a sub-genre of folk *song, were songs sung on board sailing ships to assist with the hard manual work involved by providing rhythmic co-ordination among the team of workers and also enlivening their toil. The basic pattern of a shanty was for a leader (shantyman) to sing some lines, while the others joined in the chorus or refrain. The relative proportion of call and response, the length of lines, and the rhythm would vary according to the type of work being undertaken, which Hugill divides into two main categories: heaving songs for continuous tasks (capstan, windlass, or pumping work), and hauling songs for intermittent tasks (mainly sail-work). A good shanty could prove highly effective in improving the efficiency of a team of sailors, and a good shantyman was in constant demand. Unlike other types of English folk-song, shanties are characterized by being mainly improvised, and a narrative or coherent text was hardly thought necessary. A shantyman could insert 'verses' in any order, could make them up, or retrieve them from memory, and it was only the chorus, in which the others would join, which needed to be in set form, and even here it was only the rhythm that really mattered. Many shanties were adapted from popular songs of the day, and they were also likely to be bawdy, or even obscene, with nearly all authorities who write from personal experience explaining that the published versions are necessarily pale reflections of the real thing.

There is still no agreement on the derivation of the word 'shanty' (usually spelt 'chanty' in earlier works), which only appears from the mid-19th century, although sailors' work songs certainly existed before that time. Hugill (1961: 20–3) summarizes the main theories, which include: from the West Indian huts, called 'shanties' which could be moved by concerted effort of the community, accompanied by hauling songs; drinking dens of the Gulf ports, called 'shanties'; from the French *chanter*, 'to sing', or from the English word 'chant'. None of these is wholly convincing, but Hugill himself inclined towards the first. The earliest clear reference to a sea shanty is found in a manuscript of about 1400, quoted by J. O. *Halliwell (*The Early Naval Ballads of England* (1841)) which includes the lines: 'Y-how! Taylia! The remenaunte cryen, And pull with all theyr myght'.

Stan Hugill, *Shanties from the Seven Seas* (1961); Stan Hugill, *Shanties and Sailors' Songs* (1969); W. B. Whall, *Sea Songs and Shanties* (1910).

seasonal customs, see *CALENDAR CUSTOMS.

Semerwater, Simmerwater. A lake called Semer or Simmer Water near Askrigg (North Yorkshire) is said to cover the site of a lost village, submerged as a *judgement on the wickedness of the inhabitants, according to a tale first recorded in the 19th century. A weary traveller, who was really a disguised angel (or Christ, or St Paul, or *Joseph of Arimathea, or a witch, according to various versions), went from house to house begging food and shelter. All refused, except one poor widow in the last cottage of the village; in one version (Addy, 1895: 61), the kindly widow was a Quaker, and the traveller a witch, who waved an ash twig over the village, saying:

'Simmerdale, Simmerdale, Simmerdale, sink,
Save the house of the woman who gave me to drink.'

Thereupon water filled the valley, drowning all the houses but one; on fine days the ruins can still be glimpsed under the lake.

seven. Powerful and lucky, like other odd *numbers, and also because it corresponds to the seven *days of the week, themselves derived from the moon's phases in its 28-day cycle. In folk belief, it is linked to the idea of cycles of growth: at 7, a child supposedly reaches 'the age of reason'; at 14, puberty; at 21 (formerly), legal adulthood. In astrology and old medical theory, every seventh year of one's life was a time of crisis, the most dangerous being one's sixty-third year (9×7), the 'grand climacteric'. There is still a fairly common idea that in the course of seven years every cell in one's body is renewed.

In folk magic, seven is less often mentioned than *three or *nine, but does occur; it may be said, for example, that running seven times round a particular *grave will raise a *ghost. A *seventh son (or daughter) was widely credited with healing power.

seventh son, daughter. From the 16th century onwards, a seventh son (or, more rarely, seventh daughter) was widely thought to have psychic powers, usually as a healer, but sometimes as a dowser or fortune-teller; even more powerful was one whose father (or mother) was also a seventh son (or daughter) (Opie and Tatem, 1989: 346–7). The first English record is in Thomas Lupton, *A Thousand Notable Things* (1579), and like many others refers to the *king's evil: 'It is manifest by experience that the seuenth Male Chyld by iust order (neuer a Gyrle or Wench being borne betweene) doth heele onely with touching through a naturall gyft, the Kings Euyll' (ii, § 2). Throughout the 18th and 19th centuries there are instances of male and female healers claiming this gift, and extending it to many other types of ailment; the *Post Man* of 6–9 October 1711 announced:

There is lately come to town Martha Sneath, a gentlewoman who is the seventh daughter, who has cured the evil for this twenty years, both in town and country; she useth medicines, but toucheth seven mornings; likewise a diet drink that cures the dropsy; she is to be spoken with any time of the day at Mrs. Smith's, at Black Horse Yard, in Nightingale Lane, East Smithfield. (Quoted in *N&Q* 7s:1 (1886), 6)

A related idea was that a seventh son was destined to become a doctor, for he would have a natural aptitude for the profession; some said he would have a birthmark like seven stars (*Denham Tracts*, 1895: ii, 273).

Seven Whistlers. These were said to be seven birds, flying together by night, whose cries forebode disaster. Belief in them was fairly common among seamen and coal-miners in the 19th century, these being risky occupations where *whistling was thought to be unlucky. Sometimes the Whistlers were said to be the spirits of the dead, especially those

who had themselves been miners or *fishermen, returning to warn comrades of danger; when they were heard, one must at once stop work and go home, otherwise lives would be lost. Even those who knew the cries were in fact those of curlews and similar birds still dreaded the sound, and would not work till the next day (Henderson, 1866: 100; Burne, 1883: 231–2; Billson, 1895: 36–8; Wright, 1913: 197). In Leicestershire, the Whistlers were said to be seven colliers who got drunk on a Sunday and agreed to whistle after dark, for a bet; a whirlwind carried them up into the clouds, where they must fly as swifts for ever (Palmer, 1985: 61, 100–1). In Lancashire, some said they were the souls of wandering *Jews, similarly doomed. In Worcestershire, and occasionally in Shropshire, it was said that 'six of them fly about looking for the seventh, and when they find him the world will end' (Burne, 1883: 232).

Swainson, 1885: 180–1, 200–1; Radford, Radford, and Hole, 1961: 300–1.

sex. Information and misinformation on sex, and jokes about it, must always have circulated informally, yet, paradoxically, it is literary scholars who give most insight into this semi-secret oral tradition. Elizabethan sexual slang and jokes are well documented, since they are central to Shakespeare's humour; so are the innuendoes in Restoration dramatists and 18th-century satirists; there are even anthologies of such minor genres as the bawdy limerick, a form of wit popular among educated men in the late 19th and 20th centuries, and the bawdy songs of all-male groups (students, rugby footballers, army, etc.). Dirty jokes are a flourishing oral genre (sometimes aggregating into joke cycles, e.g. about Viagra, or Essex girls), and are frequently found as graffiti.

Sexual folklore certainly exists, both on a serious and on a jocular level. One widespread notion, seriously taught by doctors and schoolmasters well into the 20th century, was that boys who masturbate go blind, or 'soft in the head'. Girls' taboos about *menstruation were equally unscientific, though less alarming. There was, and still is, a good deal of 'folk wisdom' about sexual characteristics, though it is hard to tell how seriously it is held. Thus, it is said that the size of a man's nose indicates that of his penis; of a woman's mouth, the size and tightness of the entry to her vagina. Big feet could have the same meaning. Baldness in a youngish man is supposed to indicate virility, especially if accompanied by thick bodily hair, so women allegedly find bald men sexy. Oysters, Spanish fly, valerian, and ground-up animal horn are all reputed to be aphrodisiacs.

In older folk beliefs, certain animals which were inherently virtuous, such as *bees and *lions, would respect a virgin, but attack an unchaste girl; hence, a virgin could walk through a swarm of bees unstung. Nowadays it is sometimes said that if a woman forgets to put *salt on the table when setting it for a meal, it is a sign she has lost her virginity.

In the days when public behaviour had to be discreet, various rumours circulated about visual signals indicating sexual status and intentions. In the 1950s, it was said that a girl wearing a Robertson Marmalade golliwog badge meant 'I've lost my virginity', and any woman wearing a thin bracelet round her ankle was sexually available, or even a prostitute. Some said if a woman wore a red hat, or red shoes, or allowed her petticoat to show, it meant she was not wearing knickers. Prostitutes had ways of attracting clients without actually soliciting in the legal sense; some used to walk slowly, accompanied by a poodle, while others might stand in shop doorways jingling a bunch of keys to show they were available, and had a flat to take the client to. A red lamp in the window was the sign of a brothel, hence the phrase 'red light district'.

In recent years, there has been similar talk about homosexual signals based on how one's tie is knotted or one's breast-pocket handkerchief folded, though probably the wisest guide is the folk saying, 'It takes one to know one'. It is often said by 'straight' people that any man wearing one earring is gay, though they disagree as to whether it is the left or the right ear that matters; in any case, male earrings are now so common that they can hardly be significant.

Colloquial speech abounds in references to sexual acts and organs. Until recently they were completely taboo in general society, so for the male subgroups which did use them among themselves they were a powerful mark of 'belonging'. Currently, they are used freely by far more people than at any previous period in England. They still have aggressive and insulting force, but in some contexts are exploited for humorous effect; they are common in minor verbal genres such as riddles, playground rhymes, and limericks, where the wit may consist either in uttering the offensive word or unexpectedly avoiding it.

Few folklorists have yet done research on the topic; Sutton, 1992, is the only book based on English current material, from women informants. The present authors sent out a questionnaire in 1998, on which much of the present entry is based.

See also *CONCEPTION, *MENSTRUATION, *PREGNANCY.

sexism. Taken as a whole, folk tradition firmly reinforces traditional gender roles, and sees women as inferior to men. This view is of course far older and more widespread than Christianity, but in a Christian culture such as England's it would be confirmed both by biblical teaching and by the practical rules of Church life. Until very recently, Catholics and most Protestants forbade active participation by women in ritual, and devised rules to make their presence as unobtrusive as possible; they must keep their heads covered, must not preach, nor serve as acolytes, nor enter the sanctuary, since *menstruation was seen as polluting.

Sexism is implied by many details of custom and belief, and examples will be found throughout this work—for example, *first footing must be done by a man; at *baptism boys must precede girls; in *conception and *pregnancy the favoured *right side is associated with boys, but the *left with girls; the 'females' in traditional customs were men comically dressed up; and so forth. The most serious instance of this stereotyping was that *witchcraft was far more often ascribed to women than to men.

In songs and narratives, the picture is less consistent. There are songs describing strong, active heroines who dress as soldiers to follow their lovers to war, or clever ones who outwit evil men; on the other hand, there are plenty of mocking nagging wives. Folktale heroines are often brave and resourceful in dealing with would-be *robbers, murderers, and dangerous supernatural beings, as in *Mr Fox and related stories. In local legend, one finds a handful of noble ladies honoured as benefactors, or as founders of a tradition; *Godiva is the best known, and others are associated with the *Haxey Hood Game, the *Tichborne Dole, and the St Briavels *bread and cheese throwing.

Powerful supernatural females were fairly common in medieval and Elizabethan literature (e.g. Morgan le Fay, *Mab, Titania), but not in later folklore; those that do occur are almost all sinister *bogeys such as *Black Annis, *Jenny Greenteeth, and *Peg Powler. Only the recently discovered Queen *Rat of Cockney toshers' lore fits the ancient role of the goddess who bestows good luck on her human lovers.

Torborg Lundell, *Folklore* 94 (1983), 240–6; Malcolm Jones, *Folklore* 101 (1990), 69–87; Jacqueline Simpson, *Folklore* 102 (1991), 16–30.

Shaftesbury Byzant. An annual *manorial custom by which the inhabitants of Shaftesbury, Dorset, perpetuated their right to draw water from wells in the neighbouring hamlet of Enmore Green. To preserve this right, the people had to go to Enmore Green on Holy Cross Day (first Sunday after 3 May), perform some sort of a dance, and hand over a penny loaf, a gallon of ale, a calf's head, and a pair of gloves, to the Lord of the Manor's bailiff. These details are given in an account of 1527, but other sources confirm that the custom was already in place as early as 1364. The day of the event was changed to the Monday before Ascension in 1662, to move it off the Sabbath, and the celebrations soon developed into a week-long fair. The 'Byzant' is a three or four foot trophy, made of wood and splendidly decorated with silver and gold medals, necklaces, buckles, and rings, which was formerly carried on a pole at the head of the procession, and is now preserved in the Shaftesbury Museum. The custom lapsed in 1829, ostensibly to save Shaftesbury Corporation some money, but there have been a number of revivals.

George Frampton, *Folklore* 101:2 (1990), 152–61.

shape-changing. A frequent belief about witches was that they would turn into animals. As *Gervase of Tilbury wrote (c.1211), 'Women have been seen and wounded in the shape of cats by persons who were secretly on the watch, and . . . next day the women have shown wounds or loss of limbs.' At witch trials, such anecdotes were sometimes proffered in evidence, for instance at Taunton in 1663; Edward Fairfax wrote in his *Daemonologia* (1622) that 'The changing of witches into hares, cats and the like shapes is so common, as late testimonies and confessions approve unto us, that none but the stupidly incredulous can wrong the credit of the reporters or doubt of the certainty.'

All over rural England in the 19th century, folklorists recorded a semi-humorous story of a hunted *hare which always escaped and disappeared near the cottage of a reputed witch; if the hunters entered, they would find her at home, but panting. Eventually, a dog managed to bite the hare's rump, and when next seen the woman had a wounded leg. Versions of this tale were still current in Sussex in the 1930s (Simpson, 1973: 69–70), while in Warwickshire at the same period there were stories of women wounded while in the form of *cats (Palmer, 1976: 86–7); both types were believed and told in Somerset in the 1960s (*Folklore* 74 (1963), 323–4)).

Shape-changing is also characteristic of certain fairies; see *BOGGART, *GUYTRASH, *PUCK, etc.

Sharp, Cecil James (1859–1924). Born in London, Sharp spent much of his early adulthood in Australia, returning to England in 1892, planning to make a living in music. He served for many years as music master at Ludgrove Preparatory School, and Principal of the Hampstead Conservatoire of Music, and he seemed destined to remain an obscure figure on the fringes of the respectable music establishment, but two chance encounters with traditional music transformed him into the most important figure in the Edwardian *revival of interest in folk *song and *dance. On Boxing Day 1899, Sharp first saw the Headington *morris dancers perform, and noted down the tunes from the young concertina-player, William Kimber. At the time, he did little more than arrange the tunes for piano, but the experience took on greater significance some years later. At that period, Sharp was not alone in contemporary musical circles in feeling that British music had been overshadowed by continental models for too long, and to start thinking about how to forge a new British (in most cases, English) form of musical expression. His first attempt was to edit and publish a *Book of British Song* (1902), which was drawn from previous collections of 'national' songs, but a second chance meeting changed his view, and the direction of his life, completely. On a visit to Hambridge (Somerset) in summer 1903, Sharp overheard a gardener—John England—singing 'The Seeds of Love'. He soon commenced an ambitious programme of collecting, publishing, lecturing, and propagandizing, and constructed the theory that as folk-song had existed in the hands of unspoilt and uneducated rural people, it necessarily embodied the true musical soul of the nation.

The first volume of his *Folk Songs from Somerset* appeared in 1904. He joined the *Folk-Song Society, which he publicly accused of being virtually moribund. After a very public disagreement with the Board of Education over the type of songs taught in schools, he published (with Sabine *Baring-Gould) *English Folk-Songs for Schools* in 1906, and the immensely influential *English Folk Song: Some Conclusions* in 1907.

Sharp was approached, in 1906, by Mary *Neal, organizer of the Espérance Working Girls' Club, in St Pancras, London, which catered mainly for poor young women in the dressmaking trade, for advice on songs and dances to teach the girls. Sharp sent her to see William Kimber, who came to London to give lessons to the girls, who were soon performing morris dances at their own gatherings and increasingly in public as outside interest grew rapidly. Sharp published the first part of his *Morris Book* in 1907 (completely revised in the second edition of 1912), and he used the Espérance girls at his lectures and also as teachers for the growing number of morris devotees. Tensions between Sharp and Neal, however, had begun to surface, focusing on questions of artistic standards and control of the burgeoning folk-dance revival, and these burst into increasingly acrimonious public exchanges. Both sides gathered supporters, but Sharp finally won the day as Neal, who had other concerns than folk-dance, withdrew from the field. Meanwhile, the Board of Education had included morris dance in their recommendations for physical exercise in schools, and Sharp cultivated a close relationship with the South-Western Polytechnic Institute (later the Chelsea Physical Training College), in part to provide himself with a body of teachers to replace the Espérance women, and the *English Folk Dance Society was formed in 1911, firmly under his control. Many leading lights of the folk-dance revival became involved at this time, including George *Butterworth, Douglas *Kennedy, Alice *Gomme, and Maud *Karpeles, and the principles he laid down had a lasting effect on the revival for decades. Sharp was also keen to revive the old social *dances (country dances) which had almost faded from memory, and he undertook research into Playford's *English Dancing Master* (first published in 1651) and other early dance manuals, and also collected what he could from village traditions; publishing the first part of his *Country Dance Book* in

1909. In 1914, Sharp went to America to help with Granville-Barker's New York production of *A Midsummer Night's Dream*, and while there gave lectures and conducted a number of classes in folk-song and dance and established a USA branch of the English Folk Dance Society. He returned there in 1915 and again in 1916 to start an intensive and highly successful song collecting campaign in the Appalachian Mountains, which continued in 1917 and 1918. After the First World War, Sharp's position as leading expert on folk-song and dance was secure, and his principles and aims increasingly accepted by the musical and educational establishments, and his appointment as Occasional Inspector of Training Colleges in Folk Song and Dancing gave him the opportunity to inculcate his views into the future teaching force. He was still active in lecturing, demonstrating, adjudicating, and organizing right up to the time of his death. The building which bears his name, *Cecil Sharp House, was raised as a memorial to him, and opened in 1930.

There was a tendency after his death for Sharp to be regarded as the unquestioned founder of the folk-song and dance revivals in England, and as he had in essence vanquished most dissenters by then, those who carried on his work after his death were necessarily drawn from his associates and disciples. Hardly a word of criticism was raised against him until a new generation of enthusiasts in the 1970s—children of the second revival—began to reassess their own roots in the first revival, and Sharp came under critical scrutiny, verging on vilification (e.g. Harker, 1972). Fortunately, more balanced assessments have also appeared, but the man and his actions still excite strong emotions and interest among researchers and lay people alike. It is all too easy to find evidence to show Sharp in a bad light. He was certainly autocratic and stubborn, and too willing to engage in unseemly public argument, even when he himself was on unsure ground. His criticism of the Board of Education's policy on national songs sits awkwardly with his own *British Songs* publication only four years previously, and his first *Morris Book* volume was almost completely rewritten for its second edition as doubt was cast on the traditional standing of some of the dances, and his own interpretation of the genre. Nevertheless, most of his faults can be explained, if not excused, by reference to his role as a pioneer, a man with a mission, and, importantly, a man in a hurry (he came to his life's work in his mid-forties).

His editorial practices have also been questioned. On the song side, he was far more interested in the music than the texts and while the tunes were noted and published as exactly as possible, the words suffered every possible editorial indignity, being 'softened', amalgamated, tidied up, and, in some early cases, completely rewritten. Sharp was certainly not alone in these attitudes, and he defended his practices by saying that he needed to produce 'singable' versions which would suit the tastes of the Edwardian music-buying public. The early collectors believed that the texts had been corrupted by the *broadside trade anyway. Similarly, comparison of his fieldwork notebooks and his published works show that he was willing to take liberties with dance material to reach a performable result, and his morris and sword dance books must be seen as practical manuals rather than academic studies. Sharp is also criticized on a class basis—portrayed as the middle-class man exploiting working-class culture for his own profit and status—an accusation which can be levelled at most folklorists—but on closer examination the view is simplistic. To maintain that the material 'belonged' to the working class alone is to beg questions of origin and cultural transmission at least. Sharp certainly had many of the characteristics of his class, but there is plenty of evidence that he got on well with his 'informants', and his guiding principle was to return the treasures of traditional song and dance to a people swamped by commercial (e.g. music hall) popular culture. However patronising this sounds today, it was a valid argument at the time. Nevertheless, Mary Neal's assertion that her working girls learning direct from traditional (working-class) dancers was more valid than his model of filtration through trained (middle-class) experts found little sympathy from him, secure in his notion that these important items could only be saved by experts like himself.

Sharp was the only one of his generation to attempt a serious definition of the field of folksong and folk music, as encapsulated in his *English Folk Song: Some Conclusions* (1907). His attempt was ultimately unsuccessful (see *song, and Wilgus, 1959, for further discussion), but he provided a working definition which served as the basis for all in the field until well after the Second World War. The basis of Sharp's definition is that folk-song originated with 'the people', and is therefore distinguished from both the 'art' music of the educated classes and the commercial popular music of the time, and that it has undergone a form of evolution by being 'selected' for perpetuation by the community. Items which do not suit the community's taste fall by the wayside, and those which survive are thus necessarily genuine 'folk' and therefore have intrinsic value. This evolution takes place at both micro (village) and macro (national) levels and is the basis of Sharp's belief that a knowledge of genuine folk music was necessary to revitalize English classical music: '. . . as that (musical) taste is the controlling factor in the evolution of folksong, national peculiarities must ultimately determine the specific characteristics of the folksongs of the different nations' (*Some Conclusions*, 38). The three processes involved in this evolution are, according to Sharp, continuity, variation, and selection. This definition included a number of problems—not least in positing an ancient origin for traditional songs when later research has shown that many of the songs collected originated on the 18th century stage and pleasure gardens. His definition of the 'common people' as 'those whose mental development has been due not to any formal style of training or education but solely to environment, communal association and direct contact with the ups and downs of life' (p. 4) is also untenable, and, in fact, is at odds with the real backgrounds of most of his best informants. Only in the case of the 'modes' in which traditional song tunes are sometimes set, did his early definitional work prove of lasting value.

Cecil Sharp left three lasting positive legacies: a huge body of collected song and dance material, most of which would otherwise have perished unrecorded; the foundations of viable revival movements in song and dance; and greatly enhanced public perception of the existence and inherent value of traditional musical forms. Sharp caught the mood of the time. There was a widespread, but largely incoherent feeling in several intellectual fields that there was something missing in English life; a heady combination of nationalism, xenophobia, rural nostalgia, arts and crafts, and fear of rapid societal change. The apparent simplicity, artlessness, and, above all, pure Englishness of these newly discovered traditional forms were precisely what was needed, and they became widely fashionable for young and old alike. The fact that his immediate successors chose to pursue a relatively passive policy of continuance rather than active reassessment and development, and thus rapidly became out of date, is hardly his fault.

Main publications by Sharp: SONG: *A Book of British Song for Home and School* (1902); *Folk-Songs From Somerset* (5 parts, 1904–9); *English Folk Songs for Schools* (with Sabine Baring-Gould) (1906); *English Folk-Song: Some Conclusions* (1907); *Children's Singing Games* (with Alice Gomme) (5 parts, 1911); *English Folk-Carols* (1911); *English Folk-Chanteys* (1914); *One Hundred English Folk Songs* (1916); *English Folk Songs* (1920); *English Folk Songs from the Southern Appalachians* (edited by Maud Karpeles) (1932); major contributions to the *Journal of the Folk-Song Society* 2 (1905), 5 (1914), 5 (1916), 8 (1927). DANCE: *The Morris Book* (5 parts, 1907–14); *The Country Dance Book* (6 parts, 1909–22); *The Sword Dances of Northern England* (3 parts, 1911–13); *The Dance: An Historical Survey of Dancing in Europe* (with A. P. Oppé) (1924). Sharp's main manuscripts are at Clare College Library, copies (and much other material) at the *Vaughan Williams Memorial Library, London.

Obituary, *Folk-Lore* 35 (1924), 284–7; A. H. Fox Strangways, *Cecil Sharp* (1933); Maud Karpeles, *Cecil Sharp: His Life and Work* (1967); D. Harker, 'Cecil Sharp in Somerset: Some Conclusions', *FMJ* 2:3 (1972), 220–40; Roy Judge, 'Mary Neal and the Espérance Morris', *FMJ* 5:5 (1989), 545–91; Hugh Anderson, 'Virtue in a Wilderness: Cecil Sharp's Sojourn in Australia', *FMJ* 6:5 (1994), 617–52; D. K. Wilgus, *Anglo-American Folksong Scholarship Since 1898* (1959).

sheela-na-gig. This word, or the shorter form 'sheela', has been used since the mid-19th century by antiquarians and folklorists to describe medieval sculptured figures of a hideous naked woman squatting or standing with splayed legs, in such a way as to display her sexual organ, which she is often gripping. The name comes from Ireland, where these carvings were first noticed, but there is doubt whether it was genuinely widespread in common speech (Andersen, 1977: 22–4).

The best-known sheela in England is a dwarfish goggle-eyed carving at Kilpeck (Herefordshire), but there are about two dozen others, some damaged; one found at Egremont Church (Cumbria) in 1880 holds a pair of shears, apparently about to trim her pubic hair (Bailey, 1983). It was long thought that sheelas were mainly an Irish phenomenon, and were charms to make women fertile. English examples were regarded as survivals of Celtic paganism (Sheridan and Ross, 1975: 8). However, a recent study (Weir and Jerman, 1986) has proved that the sheela is neither Irish nor pagan; it originated in medieval France and northern Spain, where it is extremely common as part of a repertoire of grotesque images, often blatantly sexual, found on early 12th century Romanesque churches, especially those along the routes to the great pilgrimage centre of St James of Compostella. The purpose would be to warn pilgrims against sexual sins by rousing disgust, presenting the female body as both voracious and degraded. The fashion for this and other grotesque carvings reached England early in the 11th century, and Ireland slightly later.

Another interpretation which has been proposed several times is that sheelas were meant to drive away the Devil, since there is a belief, known over most of Europe since classical times, that to display the bum or the sexual organs is a powerful apotropaic gesture. Irish peasants gave this explanation when interrogated by antiquarians, saying that men afflicted by the evil eye used to ask prostitutes to perform such displays as a way of turning their luck (Andersen, 1977: 22–4, 103).

Once sheelas began appearing on English churches, the locals must surely have developed stories and beliefs about them, though not along the pious lines which the clergy designing the church had intended. Unfortunately, nothing of the sort appears in folklore collections.

Andersen, 1977; Weir and Jerman, 1986; Sheridan and Ross, 1975; Richard N. Bailey, *Folklore* 94 (1983), 113–17.

Sheffield Survey of Language and Folklore, see *CENTRE FOR ENGLISH CULTURAL TRADITION AND LANGUAGE.

shepherds. The nature of their work kept shepherds somewhat apart from other farmworkers, and they had various traditions of their own: they continued wearing smocks when other labourers had long abandoned them, and they favoured regional differences in the design of crooks and sheep bells. To pass the time while guarding the flock, and to earn extra money, some snared wild birds, and others did elaborate woodcarving. It was customary for a shepherd to be buried with a tuft of wool in his hands, so that at Doomsday he could prove what his calling had been, and so be excused for often missing Sunday church.

The fact that in Sussex fossil sea-urchins found on the Downs were called 'shepherds' crowns' may imply they collected them for sale. They were often displayed on cottage mantlepieces or windowsills, sometimes being blackened with boot polish; the general belief was that they acted as *thunderstones, to keep *thunder away and so prevent milk from turning sour, and some thought they also kept witches away. They were regarded as lucky, and whoever found one must spit on it and toss it over his left shoulder.

See also *SHEEP-SHEARING, *SHEPHERDS' SCORE.

shepherds' score. Across a wide area of northern England and southern Scotland, a curious linguistic feature has been regularly reported in the shape of an unusual method of counting—apparently based on twenty, reputedly used extensively by shepherds, and bearing a distinct similarity to Welsh and other Celtic languages. Individual words vary considerably from place to place, but overall the pattern is remarkably similar:

1	Yan	11	Yan-a-dick
2	Tan	12	Tan-a-dick
3	Tethera	13	Thethera-dick
4	Pethera	14	Pethera-dick
5	Pimp	15	Bumfit
6	Sethera	16	Yan-a-bumfit
7	Lethera	17	Tan-a-bumfit
8	Hovera	18	Tethera-bumfit
9	Dovera	19	Pethera-bumfit
10	Dick	20	Jiggit

(From the Lake District, *N&Q* 180 (1941), 459–60)

In England, the numerals have been collected in the counties of Yorkshire, Cumberland, Westmorland, Lancashire, Northumberland, and Lincolnshire (see Barry for an extensive list of examples). Attention was drawn to these numerals by antiquarians and dialect collectors in the later 19th century, and it has been repeatedly asserted since that time (e.g. by Gay) that they represent a survival of the pre-Anglo-Saxon population of the areas in which they have been collected, and that they are important proof of the theory that pockets of Celtic peoples not only survived in certain areas but kept their own language and traditions well into the Anglo-Saxon era. Unfortunately, the shepherds' score does not support such a hypothesis, on at least two

important counts. Linguists (e.g. Faull) have pointed out that a careful study of the numerals indicates an importation *after* the Saxon settlements. Secondly, the geographical spread of the numerals covers areas which are known to have been settled early and completely by Anglo-Saxons. It is also suspicious that the first known mention of these numerals in Britain is as late as 1745, although a reference to them in the USA, dating from 1717, argues for their earlier existence here. If survival from ancient times is discounted, and later importation surmised, it begs the question of from where, how, and when, and there is, as yet, no definitive answer. For a number of reasons, Barry thinks it unlikely that the numerals were imported to England from Scotland (indeed, he suggests it may have been the other way round), which leaves Wales as the most likely source, in post-medieval times. Drovers bringing sheep to English markets are possible carriers, as are Welsh miners brought to England by mine-owners, but this remains speculation. Barry even casts doubt on the numerals' use, as he failed to gather any first-hand information about sheep-counting. Many of his informants had been told the numbers were for counting sheep, but none had actually used them in that way, while some used the score in knitting, some as a *counting-out rhyme, and others as a *nursery rhyme. There is no doubt that the numerals are traditional and are prized as a genuine part of local dialect (see, for example, correspondence in *The Dalesman*, 1982–3) but their origin is neither as simple, nor as antique as is often supposed.

Michael Barry, *Folk Life* 7 (1969), 75–91; Margaret L. Faull, *Local Historian* 15:1 (1982), 21–3; Tim Gay, *Local Historian* 14:5 (1981), 282–3.

Shergold, Craig, see *REDEMPTION RUMOURS.

shoelaces. Untoward things happening to *clothes, such as apron strings suddenly coming untied, often have beliefs to go with them, and the shoelace is no exception. 'When you discover your shoelace is loose, walk nine paces before tying it, otherwise you will tie ill-luck to you for that day' (Blakeborough, 1898: 150). 'It is very unlucky to give a new bootlace to a friend unless he gives you a broken one in return' (Igglesden, *c.*1932: 221). Much older is the idea that breaking a shoelace can bode ill for a journey. Opie and Tatem quote references in 1652, 1159 (John of Salisbury writing about the apostle Mark), and, indeed, Cicero in 45 BC.

Opie and Tatem, 1989: 350.

shoes. The popular custom of tying an old shoe to the back of the car in which a bride and groom are setting off for their honeymoon is a specialized form of what was once a widespread practice, that of throwing an old shoe at or after someone to wish them luck, especially on a journey. It is mentioned in John Heywood's *Proverbs* (1546).

Another practice, generally interpreted as defensive magic, was more secretive. As Ralph Merrifield writes:

There are few local museums in southern England that do not possess a few shoes, mostly dating from the 17th to the 19th century, that were found hidden in old houses, usually in a wall, roof, or chimney breast, or under a floor ... deposited in places that are normally accessible only at the time of building or structural alteration, or by taking considerable trouble at other times, for example by raising a floorboard .... [A] child saw his father and a workman put an old worn-out boot, that significantly did not belong to the family, in the rubble when laying the kitchen floor, at Wareham St Mary, Norfolk, in 1934–5. He could get no reason for this from his father, who seemed slightly ashamed of what he was doing. (Merrifield, 1987: 131–4).

The only first-hand explanation recorded is this comment from Lincolnshire: 'In the old days, a lot of kids died young, so to keep part of the kid with them, or the spirit of the kid if you like, a shoe was buried in the wall of the house so the kid was still with them' (Sutton, 1992: 135).

Similar finds were made in England's oldest coal mine, at Lounge, near Leicester, in 1990; medieval leather boots, dating from about 1450, had been laid in certain galleries. This must be a forerunner of a custom reported from abandoned lead mines in Yorkshire and Derbyshire, and an old copper mine in Wales, namely placing a single clog at the far end of a passage (i.e. at the last point reached in working it), or in the backfilling of such a passage, or at a spot where a shaft had collapsed.

Explanations as to why shoes should be considered protective can only be conjectural; the two main ones are that they are dirty, especially when old (cf. the saying 'Where there's muck there's luck'), and that they symbolize the female sexual organ. Small model boots or shoes in various materials were used as man-

tlepiece ornaments 'for luck', or as 'lucky charms' in jewellery.

One common *love divination in the 19th century was for a girl to set her shoes at right angles on going to bed, saying:

> I set my shoes in the form of a T,
> Hoping my true-love for to see.

She would then be sure to dream of her destined husband.

Radford, Radford, and Hole, 1961: 305–7; Opie and Tatem, 1989: 350–4. For shoes in buildings, see Merrifield, 1987: 131–6; June Swann, *Journal of the Northampton Museums and Art Gallery* 6 (1969), 8–21, and *Costume* 30 (1996), 56–69; for clogs, *FLS News* 11 (1990), 3–4; 12 (1991), 10. An extensive listing of shoes found in buildings throughout Britain is kept at Northampton Central Museum, and now numbers over 1,500.

shrews. The shrew has a very bad reputation in English folklore. Its bite was believed to be poisonous to domestic animals, and if a shrew crawled over a cow, horse, sheep, or even human, that animal would suffer acute pains and swelling. In Britain, these beliefs go back at least to the 16th century and, indeed, Pliny includes them in his *Natural History* (AD 77). It was one of the superstitions reported by Gilbert White (*The Natural History of Selborne* (1776), letter 28), and see Opie and Tatem for further references. The reported cure and/or prevention was to bore a hole in an ash tree, or split a branch or trunk, catch a live shrew and imprison it in the hole or split and leave it to die and rot away. That tree, henceforth called a 'shrew-ash', would then have healing powers over shrew bites. According to *N&Q* (5s:9 (1878), 65), another method of making an ash effective against shrews was to bury a horseshoe at its roots. A further alternative was to enclose the shrew in clay, and hang it round the neck of the cow to protect it. It was also considered unlucky for a shrew to cross your path, and that shrews themselves could not cross roads or even tracks made by cart wheels without dropping dead on the spot. Some of these beliefs were also held about fieldmice.

Opie and Tatem, 1989: 354–6; H. S. Toms, 'Shrew Folklore', *Sussex N&Q* 2 (1929), 178–9; Lean, 1903: ii. 647–8.

Shrovetide. In the Christian calendar, the three days before Lent were known as Shrovetide, taking their name from 'shrive' or confess. Lent being the longest and strictest fast, however, has given to Shrovetide the character of being the last chance for good food and unrestricted fun before the long period of austerity starting with Ash Wednesday and leading up to Easter. Shrovetide thus became second only to Christmas for its frivolity, or, as William Kethe commented in 1571 'Great gluttony, surfeiting and drunkenness' (*A Sermon Made at Blandford Forum*, quoted by Hutton, 1996: 152).

The three days were generally known as Shrove Sunday, Collop Monday, and Shrove Tuesday. Collop Monday took its name from the habit of eating collops, or cuts of meat fried or boiled. It made sense to eat up any meat still remaining in the house, as it would be banned from the Wednesday. Similarly, on Shrove Tuesday, other perishable foodstuffs were used up, and although there were regional variations, these were usually eaten in the form of pancakes. While Shrovetide now passes unnoticed by any but a dwindling number of religious families, Pancake Day still means something to millions of English people, and to lemon growers and importers. The first known mention of pancakes is by William Warner in *Albions England* (1586), as 'Fast-even pan-puffs' (quoted by Hutton, 1996: 152). The term 'Fast-even' (meaning the evening before the fast) long survived in the north of England as a synonym for Shrove Tuesday.

The pancake-making was not left to chance, but in many areas was signalled by a church bell being rung, at eleven o'clock or twelve o'clock, which obviously became known as the pancake bell. This was the signal for families to start cooking. If John Taylor (1621) is to be believed, some sextons rang the bell as early as nine o'clock. Modern *pancake races are said, completely without foundation, to date from a custom whereby housewives would vie with each other to make the first pancake and race to the sexton to prove it. The pancake bell survived in many places till late in the 19th century (Wright and Lones, 1936: i. 13–15).

A number of other customs and activities also became particularly associated with Shrovetide, especially *football, *cock-fighting, and throwing at *cocks. Even after the Reformation removed much of the importance of Lent, and therefore Shrovetide as a religious observance, Shrove continued to be known for its excesses. In urban areas, it was particularly the day for apprentices to let their hair down, and their behaviour became proverbial—'They presently (like prentices upon Shrove-Tuesday) take the lawe into their owne handes and do what they list' (Dekker, *Seven Deadly Sins of London* (1606), 35). Each of these active cus-

toms was eventually suppressed, although many not until the 19th century.

In many parts of the country, children went Shroving, a standard *visiting custom whereby they sang a song or recited a rhyme and hoped to be rewarded with food or money:

> Knock, knock, the pan's hot
> And we are coming a-shroving
> For a piece of pancake
> Or a piece of bacon
> Or a piece of truckle cheese
> Of your own making

(Hampshire, *Folk-Lore* 22 (1911), 323)

Unlike other such customs, however, if the householder was not forthcoming the children showered his/her front door with stones, or shards of broken pottery—Lent crocking as some called it (see also *JACK O'LENT). Another children's (and adult's) custom on Shrove Tuesday was playing Shuttlecock.

See also *BARRING-OUT, *CHURCH CLIPPING, *COCK-FIGHTING, *COCKS, THROWING AT, *FOOTBALL, *PANCAKE RACES, *THREAD THE NEEDLE, *WESTMINSTER SCHOOL PANCAKE DAY.

Hutton, 1996: 151–68; Wright and Lones, 1936: i. 1–32; Hazlitt, 1905: 545–8. Hone, 1827: i. cols. 241–62.

Shuck, Shock. In Norfolk and Suffolk lore, there are many accounts of an apparition known as 'Old Shuck' or 'Black Shuck' (or 'Shock'), usually described as a phantom dog as big as a calf, shaggy, with fiery eyes, and sometimes dragging a clanking chain. Printed references begin in the 1840s, and memories of personal encounters continue to the present day. In most cases Shuck is said to terrify humans who see him, and their dogs and horses too, and in 19th-century accounts to meet him is often said to mean death, for oneself or another. In other accounts Shuck is harmless, or even benevolent—for instance, by frightening a cyclist into dismounting, and thus saving him from being knocked down by a speeding car. At Overstrand, where Shuck has long been said to run regularly along a coastal path, he is claimed to be the ghost of a faithful dog searching for the bodies of his drowned masters, who were smugglers or fishermen.

Jennifer Westwood, in *Supernatural Enemies*, ed. Hilda R. Davidson and Chaudhri, 2001: 101–16.

shudder. If you suddenly shudder or shiver, for no apparent reason, it is still likely that you will say that 'someone has just walked over your grave', meaning, of course, the site of your future grave. The first known written evidence for this notion is in Jonathan Swift's *Polite Conversation* (1738, i. 4). Occasional variations stipulate what it is that is doing the walking—a donkey or even, as suggested by the pimples associated with a shiver, a goose.

Opie and Tatem, 1989: 356.

sieve and shears. A well-known form of *divination, akin to the *Bible and key method, normally used to name a thief or find something which has been lost. Descriptions vary little, and the following is from Aubrey (1686: 25):

The Sheers are stuck in a Sieve, and two maydens hold up ye sieve with the top of their fingers by the handle of the shiers: then say, By St Peter & St Paule such a one hath stoln (such a thing), the others say, By St Peter and St Paul he hath not stoln it. After many such Adjurations, the Sieve will turne at ye name of ye Thiefe.

The only significant difference is that others maintain that you read out loud 'a certain chapter' from the Bible. This method is mentioned regularly in England from the 16th century onwards, including *Scot (1584: book 12, chapter 17) and *Melton (1620) and many later folklore collections. This antiquity pales into insignificance, however, against the earliest reference given by Opie and Tatem, in Theocritus' *Idylls* (*c*.275 BC).

Opie and Tatem, 1989: 356-7; Henderson, 1879: 233-6.

sillyhow. Literally, 'blessed cap' or 'lucky cap'; a term used in northern England for the *caul.

silver. Silver *coins are mentioned in many different contexts. It is not clear how much intrinsic power ascribed to the metal itself—some, no doubt, since there is evidence that in Suffolk around 1850 people with fits would beg twelve small silver items such as broken spoons or buckles, to melt into a curative *ring, and in some of the stories where a *hare (really a witch) is shot with a silver bullet, this is said to be made from a button. However, silver objects were not regularly thought powerful in the way that domestic *iron objects were.

A silver sixpence is frequently mentioned: as a gift to a new *baby; as a gift left by *fairies for diligent servant girls, or for children shedding a *tooth; as a lucky *charm, especially in a

bride's shoe; as a countercharm against witchcraft when churning *milk. A particular healing power was ascribed to rings made from a silver coin which had been put into the collection in church (so-called 'sacrament money'), usually a shilling or half a crown; to get it, the sufferer had to beg a penny apiece from twelve (or 30) different people, usually with the further condition that they must be unmarried, and of the sex opposite to the sufferer's, and then exchange them for the 'sacrament money'. They were supposed to cure fits. Sometimes, it was thought sufficient to beg five, *seven, or *nine sixpenny or threepenny pieces from persons of the opposite sex, and make the ring of them.

Opie and Tatem, 1989: 327-8, 357-8.

sin-eating. Evidence for this dramatic *funeral custom rests largely on a statement in Aubrey's *Remaines of Gentilisme and Judaisme* (1686/1880), 35:

In the County of Hereford was an old Custome at Funeralls to hire poor people, who were to take upon them all the sinnes of the party deceased. One of them I remember lived in a Cottage on Rosse highway. (He was a long, leane, ugly, lamentable poor raskal.) The manner was that when the Corps was brought out of the house and layd on the Biere, a Loafe of bread was brought out and delivered to the Sinne-eater over the corps, as also a Mazar-bowle ... full of beer, which he was to drinke up, and sixpence in money, in consideration of which he tooke upon him (ipso facto) all the Sinnes of the Defunct, and freed him (or her) from walking after they were dead.

Aubrey adds that he had heard of several Herefordshire examples, and believed the custom had once been common in Wales; in 1714 another antiquarian said he had seen a notebook of Aubrey's giving a second description, from Shropshire. In 1852 a Mr Moggridge of Swansea claimed it had existed at Llanderbie in Wales 'within the last twenty years'; the sin-eater would be given bread and salt which had been laid on the corpse's chest, plus half a crown, after which he quickly left, for he 'was regarded as a mere Pariah, as one irremediably lost' (Sikes, 1881: 322-4).

During the next few decades folklorists hunted for further evidence of the practice. They had no difficulty finding instances of cakes and wine, or bread and ale, being consumed by mourners round the coffin, or distributed to the poor at the house or in the graveyard. This ceremonial eating and drinking in the presence of the corpse was common at 18th- and 19th-century funerals in midland and northern counties, especially in Yorkshire. But there was no further trace of a 'professional' human scapegoat, a sin-eater in Aubrey's and Moggridge's sense.

These customs are best understood as echoes of medieval Requiems, and of the custom of giving alms to the poor (including food) in exchange for their prayers, normally distributed beside the grave or coffin. Scriptural support could be found in the Book of Tobias (or Tobit) which forms part of the Greek and Latin Bible: 'Alms deliver from all sin, and from death, and will not suffer the soul to go into darkness.... Lay your bread and your wine on the grave of a just man' (Tobias 4: 11, 18). Vague memories of this religious context persisted into the late 19th century. One Herefordshire farmer is reported as saying, 'You must drink, sir, it's like the Sacrament, it's to kill the sins of my sister' (Leather, 1912: 121); in Derbyshire a farmer's daughter explained, 'When you drink wine at a funeral every drop that you drink is a sin which the deceased has committed; you thereby take away the dead man's sins and bear them yourself' (Addy, 1895: 123–4; Addy, letter in N&Q 8s:9 (1896), 296).

Some slight hearsay evidence can be added. In 1945 a folklorist said he had heard of a few 19th-century cases in East Anglia where 'some unsuspecting person, usually a tramp' was given bread and *salt which had been laid on a corpse, thus acquiring its sins; he said tramps still avoided houses where there had been a death, for fear of this trick (L. F. Newman, *Folk-Lore* 56 (1945), 291–2). In 1958 came more second-hand information from the Fens: an old lady who had died in 1906 had been told, when young, how a woman who was a sin-eater ('who, incidentally, was shunned by all the villagers') had qualified herself for the task. She had taken so much poppy-tea that she seemed to be dying, and the minister gave her absolution; she recovered, and was told by her friends that now that she was free of her own sins she could take on other people's, which she used to do by eating bread and salt laid on the shrouds of the dead and being paid thirty pennies, whitewashed to look like silver (Enid Porter, *Folklore* 69 (1958), 115).

For an anthropological interpretation, see E. S. Hartland, *Folk-Lore* 3 (1892), 145–57; he thought the custom is derived from cannibalism. Letters debating the issue will be found in *The Times* (18 Sept. 1895), and N&Q 8s:9 (1896), 109–11, 169–70, 296.

singing games. As the name implies, the singing game is a children's activity in which an action is accompanied by sung verses— *Ring-a-Ring-a-Roses, The Farmer's in his Den, *Oranges and Lemons, *Green Gravel are well-known examples, but there are dozens of others. With their roots in adult dances of the distant past and their wonderfully pleasing tunes, singing games have attracted a fair amount of attention from folklorists since the late 19th century and are relatively well documented. But in the playground they have been in slow but steady decline and, although far from dead, the repertoire grows smaller and they are seen less often these days.

Gomme, 1894–8; Opie and Opie, 1985.

skimmington, see *ROUGH MUSIC.

skin, human. There are a number of stories about humans being flayed (alive or dead) and their skin being displayed or used for various purposes and, perhaps surprisingly, there is a factual basis to many of them. The first class of story involves human skin nailed to church doors. At least six places have this tradition, and probably more, as it has the ring of *tour guide lore about it: Hadstock, Copford, and Castle Hedingham (all three in Essex), Rochester Cathedral (Kent), Worcester Cathedral, and Westminster Abbey (London). According to Tyack, Rochester and Castle Hedingham had legends only, while the other four had real fragments of skin still surviving in the 19th century which were analysed and 'proved' to be human. In most cases, the victim is claimed to be a marauding Dane, guilty of the worst crime—sacking a church. Samuel Pepys' diary entry for 10 April 1661 records: 'Then to Rochester and there saw the Cathedrall ... Then away thence observing the great doors of the church, as they say covered with the skins of the Danes'. Few of the doors in question are sufficiently old to be survivors from the time of Danish incursions, but the core of the story is actually the gross sacrilege, and it seems that this barbaric punishment really was used for this particular crime. Nevertheless, many of the reports of the scientific testing of the skin include the phrase 'of a fair-haired person'—sufficiently often for it to appear to be a folkloric motif in itself.

The other class of story is much more recent. From 1752 the bodies of all executed murderers were handed over to surgeons on which to practise their dissection techniques and anatomy lessons. The skins of a surprising number of famous murderers have been preserved, either previously on show in medical museums or used to bind books about them, such as that of William Corder (the murderer of Maria Marten in the infamous Red Barn Murder) at Moyse's Hall Museum, Bury St Edmonds; numerous other examples are listed in Notes & Queries in the 1920s and 1930s. A stray tale reported in N&Q (148 (1925), 424; 149 (1925), 14) concerns a straggler from the Young Pretender's army on their retreat from Derby in 1745 being killed by the Duke of Cumberland's men and his skin used to make a drum.

George S. Tyack, 'Human Skin on Church Doors', in William Andrews (ed.), The Church Treasury of History, Custom, Folk-Lore etc. (1898), 158–67; N&Q 2s:2 (1856), 68, 119, 157, 250–2, 299, 419; 4s:4 (1869), 56–7, 101–2; 4s:5 (1870), 310–11; 4s:10 (1872), 352, 448, 454–5; 4s:11 (1873), 138, 292, 373; 9s:12 (1903), 429, 489–90; 10s:1 (1904), 15, 73–4, 155, 352; 10s:2 (1904), 14–15; 150 (1926), 459; 151 (1926), 68–9; 159 (1930), 303; 163 (1932), 250–1, 302, 356, 394; Ruth Richardson, Death Dissection and the Destitute (1987).

skipping (1): children's game. Nowadays skipping is almost entirely done by girls, but this was not always the case. The earliest references refer to boys, and through most of the 19th century boys regularly took part in the game. This has led some authorities to conclude that skipping was exclusively played by boys until the late 19th century but there are numerous illustrations in chapbooks, books, and magazines of girls skipping, back into the 18th century. Why the boys stopped skipping when they did is not clear. Skipping with a rope cannot be traced further back than the 17th century, to a work by Jacob Cats, Silenus Alcibiadis (1618), and references in England do not appear until the 1730s. As the Opies point out, this may be because in earlier times skipping was normally done with a hoop, or it may simply be an accident of history.

There are several basic variations in skipping, the most important being the distinction between short rope and long rope. Short-rope skipping can be solo, one child with a short skipping rope 'turning' over her head—or duo, with two girls face to face jumping a rope turned by one of them—or skilled practitioners can get three in at the same time. Alternatively, two girls can stand side by side,

holding the rope between them, taking it in turns to jump by angling the rope one side to the other. There are numerous variations in footwork, speed of turning, actions to be performed, and so on. The basic game is static, but skippers can also progress along the street, again either singly or in pairs. The usual learning pathway for beginners is to start with short-rope skipping and, once the basic skills of timing have been mastered, to move on to long rope.

Long-rope skipping involves a person at either end turning a long rope while several others jump, either one at a time or in pairs or groups. A further complication, now called Double Dutch, and much more common in the USA than in England, is where two long ropes are turned simultaneously, in opposite directions. A different form, hardly skipping in the strict sense, is French Skipping or Elastics where a rope, tied in a loop, is placed around the ankles of two girls standing facing each other. Participants take it in turns to jump inside, outside, or on to the rope, in a set sequence of movements and when they have successfully completed them the rope is moved a bit higher up the legs of the end people and the whole procedure is repeated, until the rope is too high for the jumpers to reach. A length of elastic is now often used instead of rope, hence the alternative name.

Numerous skipping rhymes exist to accompany the action, many of which are apparently meaningless but rhythmic chants,

Salt, mustard, vinegar, pepper —

to the initiated, however, these four words indicate different speeds. Some dictate the action:

Teddy bear, teddy bear
Touch the ground
Teddy bear, teddy bear
Turn right round
Teddy bear, teddy bear
Climb upstairs
Teddy bear, teddy bear
Say your prayers
Teddy bear, teddy bear
Turn off the light
Teddy bear, teddy bear
Say goodnight.

Commentators on children's games almost always lament that children no longer play like they used to and that traditions are dead. To the outsider, skipping appears to be one of those areas which is dying, but if so we are witnessing a very long and slow decline, and skipping is certainly not dead yet.

Opie and Opie, 1997: 160–306; Abrahams, 1969; Opie and Opie, 1959.

skipping (2): calendar custom. At noon on *Shrove Tuesday at Scarborough (Yorkshire), hundreds of local people, of all ages, flock to the Foreshore with their ropes and try their hand at skipping, in groups or solo, which goes on until after dark. In the past the ropes were longer, stretching right across the street, turned by local fishermen, and a dozen or fifteen people could skip in one rope, but nowadays it is more common for people to keep to their family group. The custom still seems popular, but many observers have commented that the local people are gradually losing their skipping skills from lack of practice, and that the accompanying rhymes have all but died out. The earliest known reference to the custom is in 1903, and the local theory of origin is that Shrovetide was the time when the local fishing fleet sorted out their ropes, and discarded any which were worn or otherwise past their prime. An associated part of the day is for boys to grab, and 'dump' the girls in the sea—an activity which, from local testimony, goes back at least 30 years, if not before. Similar customs used to take place on *Good Friday, and were particularly popular in coastal areas, such as in Sussex where it was reported at Brighton, Alciston, Hastings, Southwick, and South Heighton, where Good Friday was called Long Rope or Long Line Day. The Brighton custom is mentioned as popular in 1863 (*N&Q* 3s:3 (1863), 444) but it was apparently already on the wane when the closing of the beaches during the Second World War finally killed it. One inland place where Good Friday skipping was popular was Cambridge, where the custom took place on the open space called Parker's Piece, where it seems also to have died out as a regular event during the last war. Other scattered references show that the custom was quite widespread, being reported, for example, at Teignmouth (Devon) in the late 19th century (*N&Q* 172 (1937), 262).

Scarborough: Smith, 1989: 3–8; Shuel, 1985: 152; *Dalesman* (Feb. 1994), 23–4; Sussex: Simpson, 1973: 111; Ralph Merrifield, 'Good Friday Customs in Sussex', *Sussex Archaeological Collections* 89 (1950), 85–97; Wales, 1990: 50–1; Cambridge: Porter, 1969: 107; *N&Q* 172 (1937), 262.

skulls. Several farms and manor houses formerly kept a skull on display, allegedly that of someone who had lived there and had insisted that this be done; the luck of the house and family was said to depend on its presence, and if anyone tried to remove or bury it, it would either return of its own accord, or cause violent and noisy haunting until replaced. There were examples at Wardley Hall, Osbaldeston Hall, and Timberbottom Farm near Bolton (Lancashire), Brougham Hall and Calgarth Hall (Westmorland), and Threlkeld Place (Cumbria); some were explained as relics of Catholic martyrs, but they too took revenge if disturbed. At Warbleton Priory (Sussex), there were two, allegedly a former owner and his murderer, supposed to cause ghastly noises and bring ill luck if moved; they were still there in 1947 (Simpson, 1973: 47–8).

The *origin tales are very varied. At Bettiscombe Manor, near Lyme Regis (Dorset), the skull is said to be that of a Negro slave enraged at not being sent home to Africa for burial; in fact it is female, fossilized, and possibly prehistoric. At Burton Agnes Hall (Yorkshire), it is the youngest of three sisters in Elizabethan times, who on her deathbed made her sisters swear to keep her head on a table so that she could see the Hall completed. The famous 'Dicky' of Tunstead Farm (Derbyshire), already installed in 1790, is said to have been a rightful heir in Elizabethan times, murdered by his cousins (*Folk-Lore* 41 (1930), 98–9); he was buried in the garden in 1985 (Billingsley, 1998: 165–6).

Skulls were used in traditional cures, usually for epilepsy but sometimes also for headaches and plague; either water was drunk from them, or fragments were grated into food. Moss scraped from an old skull was said to staunch bleeding; a tooth from one cured toothache (Opie and Tatem, 1989: 359–60). In Devonshire in the 1880s, a woman whose husband had left her tried to buy from a chemist a substance called 'Oil of Man', made by distilling the skulls of hanged men, believing that by burning it she would call him back; she was disappointed to learn that 'that article cannot be had now' (*Transactions of the Devonshire Association* 21 (1889), 113–14).

See also *BONES.

The fullest listing of protective skulls is by Andy Roberts and David Clarke, *Fortean Studies* 3 (1996), 126–58; the same authors have collected current beliefs and tales about them in their *Twilight of the Celtic Gods* (1996), 138–46; see also Westwood, 1985: 13–4, 327–8.

Small-Tooth Dog, the. A Derbyshire *fairy-tale, an analogue to Beauty and the Beast, with the hero in the form of a dog; he recovers human form when the girl renames him 'sweet-as-honeycomb' (Addy, 1895: 1–4; Philip, 1992: 69–71).

smugglers. There are two levels on which smugglers appear in folk tradition. On the first level, their tricks and exploits are a topic for storytelling; local history recalls routes they followed, places where they fought the Revenue men; local legend alleges they had secret *tunnels. On the second level, people wanting to explain away a supernatural trad-ition often claim it was encouraged, or even invented, by smugglers to frighten people away from churchyards and lonely houses where they hid contraband. While it is poss-ible that 'smugglers' fakelore' did sometimes occur, no references to it have been found in contemporary documents; anecdotes about it only appear much later, and are couched in general terms. They sound like folklore themselves.

snails. A popular divinatory use for the snail, found in Scotland, Wales, and Ireland as well as England, is to place it in the ashes of the hearth, or on a plate of flour, and examine the marks of the creature's random meanderings to see the initial of your future spouse's name. The first known mention of this belief is in Gay's *Shepherd's Week* (1714: 34). Others claimed that it was lucky to throw a snail over your left shoulder (Henderson, 1879: 116). They also had their uses in folk medicine, being recommended for *earache (prick with a needle and drip the juice into the ear), coughs and colds (boil snails in barleywater), to remove *warts, cure the ague (strung on a thread and frizzled over the fire) (Black 1883: 56–7) and for gout (pounded into a plaster) (Aubrey, 1686/1880: 256). The well-known rhyme recited to snails by children:

> Snail, snail, Come out of your hole
> Or else I'll beat you, As black as coal.
> Snail, snail, Put out your horns
> I'll give you bread, And barley corns,

was first printed in the mid-18th century, but the Opies point out its very wide geographical spread, taking in most of Europe and China, which possibly argues for it being consider-ably older.

Opie and Tatem, 1989: 361–2; *N&Q* 5s:5 (1876), 208, 395; 5s:6 (1876), 158; Black, 1883: 56–7, 157–8; Opie and Opie, 1997: 465–7.

snakes, see *ADDERS.

snakestones. Traditions about ring-shaped 'snakestones' are Celtic. Most are Welsh, but there are Cornish references too, the first being in Richard Carew (1602: 21):

The country people retaine a conceite, that the snakes, by their breathing upon a hazel-wand, doe make a stone ring of blew colour, in which there appeareth the yellow figure of a snake, and that beasts which are stung, being given to drink of the water wherein this stone hath bene soaked, will there-through recover.

Such 'rings' were usually small prehistoric beads of striped glass, taken from ancient burials; however, Robert Hunt was told that snakestones were 'about the size of a pigeon's egg', and a friend of his had seen one which was a beautiful ball of coralline limestone, the coral being thought to be entangled young snakes (Hunt, 1865: 418). The oldest tradition, attested by Pliny in AD 77 and ascribed by him to *Druids, was that in summer, at a certain phase of the moon, numerous snakes entwine and form a stony 'egg' from a sticky slime issu-ing from their mouths. He had seen one: 'It was round, and about as large as a smallish apple; the shell was cartilaginous, and pocked like the arms of a polypus' (*Natural History*, XXIX. xii).

In English folklore, fossil ammonites too are called snakestones. Legend claims they are coiled snakes decapitated and turned to stone by St Hilda, Abbess of Whitby, or alternatively by St Cuthbert; trade in ammonites flourished at Whitby (Yorkshire) and Keynsham (Gloucestershire).

Snap, the Norwich Dragon. In the Castle Museum at Norwich there is a *dragon made of painted canvas over a wooden frame, designed to rest on the shoulders of a man walking inside it; its neck can retract, shoot out, and turn, while its iron-clad jaws are opened or snapped shut by a cord. It was made in about 1795, and is the last of a series of effigies recorded since 1408. At first, they fea-tured in a religious procession on *St George's Day, in which both St George and St Margaret were impersonated; after the Reformation, the pageant became a Mayor's Show without saints or religious symbols, but kept the dragon and generally included sword-bearing 'whifflers' to clear the way, and 'Dick Fools' in motley; it was held annually around *Midsummer until 1835.

Two suburbs of Norwich also held dragon parades during the 19th and early 20th centuries, with Snaps of their own; these were burlesque parodies of the main event, with heavy drinking and rough horseplay. Two of their dragons are in the museum too, as is the head of a third.

The 18th-century Snap is still occasionally brought out to celebrate major royal and national events. In the 1980s, a new Snap was made for the local morris side, and assumed the civic role of appearing in the Mayor's parade; costumed whifflers were reintroduced in 1996.

Richard Lane, *Snap the Norwich Dragon* (1976); Simpson, 1980: 95–8, 101–2; Nigel Pennick, *Crossing the Borderline* (1998), 119–24.

sneezing. The belief that a sneeze should be answered by others with a verbal blessing or salutation such as 'Bless you!' is, as far as we can tell, almost universal, and old enough to be quoted by many classical writers. In Britain, the belief has grown up that the custom stems from the Great Plague, but it is clear that it goes back long before that, as for example in Caxton's *The Golden Legend*, printed in 1483, which includes the saying of 'God help you!' or 'Christe help!'. In *Aubrey's time: 'We have a custome, that when one sneezes, every one els putts off his hatt, and bowes, and cries God bless ye Sir' (1686/1880: 103–4). This was only twenty years after the Plague, but he does not make the connection. Nevertheless, groundless as it is, the belief is now so well fixed in the popular mind that it counts as folklore in itself. The equally widespread idea that we say 'bless you' because our ancestors believed we were sneezing our soul out of our body is similarly groundless. See also under *Ring-a-Ring-a-Roses for an allied plague problem.

There are numerous other folklore items connected with sneezing. A widespread rhyme distinguishes the days of the week:

> Sneeze on Monday, sneeze for danger
> Sneeze on Tuesday, kiss a stranger
> Sneeze on Wednesday, get a letter
> Sneeze on Thursday, something better
> Sneeze on Friday, sneeze for sorrow
> Saturday, see your love tomorrow

(Buckinghamshire; Henderson, 1879: 137)

Alternatively, it is the number of sneezes which matter: once a kiss, twice a wish, three times a letter, four times better; or, once is lucky, twice unlucky. Opie and Tatem quote Homer and Theocritus to demonstrate the antiquity of sneeze-counting. A manuscript from the time of Elizabeth I (Lansdowne MS 121, p. 146, quoted in *N&Q* 7s:2 (1886), 165–6) gives a number of current beliefs concerning sneezing, several of which are concerned with the number of sneezes combined with where and when they occur. Other sneeze beliefs are more concerned with the personal situation, of which there seem to be endless variations. Examples include: it was a bad omen if a baby sneezed during its christening (Wiltshire, 1975: 94); if you sneeze on a Saturday night after the candle is lighted, you will next week see a stranger . . . (*N&Q* 1s:4 (1851), 99); if you sneeze before breakfast you will receive news or a present that day (*N&Q* 4s:1 (1880), 42).

Opie and Tatem, 1989: 364–6; Hazlitt, 1905: 553–5; Lean, 1903: ii.i. 24–5, 101, 266–7, 304–5, 327–8, 398–9; *N&Q* 5s:8 (1877), 108, 221–3, 284, 376.

snook, see *COCKING A SNOOK.

snowdrops. Some people feel strongly that if snowdrops are picked and brought indoors they bring bad luck, even death, into the house; to grow them in bowls, however, or in the garden, is safe. One explanation was that they 'look like a corpse in its shroud' and grow so near the ground that they 'seem to belong more to the dead than the living' (Latham, 1878: 52–3); also, like other ill-omened flowers, they are *white (Vickery, 1995: 354–5). Variations mentioned in *N&Q* (8s:7 (1895), 167, 258, 436) are that it is unlucky for a woman to be the first to bring them into the house; that they bring bad luck for the first brood of chickens (cf. *primroses); and that they must only be given by a woman to a man, or vice versa. In 1931, another contributor reported: 'In a London flowershop today—Jan. 29, 1931—I asked for some snowdrops. The assistant replied: "No, sir, we are not allowed to sell them." I expressed surprise, and was told that Mr —— (presumably the proprietor of the shop) thinks them unlucky' (*N&Q* 160 (1931), 100).

soap. Several beliefs cluster around soap. For example, the idea that soap slipping out of one's hand means a forthcoming death (*N&Q* 5s:4 (1875), 9; 5s:6 (1876), 323), or that 'Two persons, more especially if they are sisters, must not pass soap from hand to hand, it should be put down by the first, so that the other can take it up (Leather, 1912: 87). Opie and Tatem also report the notion that it is unlucky to give soap as a present, and a belief from the *theatre that you should not leave soap behind at the end of a run, or you will not return to that venue.

Opie and Tatem, 1989: 366–7.

Society for Folk Life Studies. Founded September 1961, 'The Society aims to further the study of traditional ways of life in Great Britain and Ireland and to provide a common meeting point for the many institutions engaged with the various aspects of the subject'. The movement towards the founding of folk museums and folk life programmes in Britain was already taking shape in the 1930s, heavily influenced by Scandinavian models, and the need for a society and a journal was apparent, but the intervention of the Second World War postponed further development. The relatively short-lived journal *Gwerin*, launched in 1956, proved a useful focal point, and by the early 1960s sufficient interest had been aroused for action to be taken. The Society holds an annual conference, in a different location each year, and its journal *Folk Life* was launched in 1963 and continues its annual publication. Folk life studies in Britain and Ireland have been primarily concerned with the physical aspects of traditional life, and the Society's main membership and audience have been drawn from museum professionals. Past President Trefor Owen, writing in 1981 on its 18th birthday, commented that the Society (as seen through the pages of its journal) had not been particularly argumentative or controversial, but had been more concerned with solid descriptive scholarship rather than with the discussion of theoretical issues. This remains largely true, and many would regard this as one of the field's major strengths.

Iowerth C. Peate, *Folk Life* 1 (1963), 3–4; Alexander Fenton, *Folk Life* 11 (1973), 5–14; Trefor M. Owen, *Folk Life* 19 (1981), 5–16.

song. Until the late 19th century, it was generally agreed within the musical establishment that England, alone amongst the countries which comprise the British Isles, possessed no traditional folk-song or music. The campaign to refute this misconception gathered pace as the turn of the century approached, culminating in the formation of the *Folk-Song Society in 1898, and the great collecting boom of the Edwardian period, led by enthusiasts such as Cecil *Sharp and Ralph *Vaughan Williams (see also *song revival). As the collectors began reporting, and publishing, thousands of finds, music students and composers turned eagerly to them for material and folk-song became an overnight craze, recycled into numerous classical pieces.

The Edwardian collectors had little problem recognizing the genuine article. For them, folk-songs were old and quaint, to be found almost exclusively in the mouths of the elderly rural poor, who were claimed to be the remnants of an unlettered, culturally conservative, and musically uncreative peasantry. They also took it as read that the conditions for the perpetuation of genuine folk-songs had been eroded during the 19th century by railway travel, universal education, urbanization, and the rise of commercial music in the form of the music hall, and that they were involved in a last-ditch rescue operation. Sharp declared in 1907 that 'in less than a decade, English folk singing will be extinct' (Sharp, 1907: 130), and commented: 'I have learned that it is, as a rule, only waste of time to call upon singers under the age of sixty. Their songs are nearly all modern; if, by chance, they happen to sing an old one, it is so infected with the modern spirit that it is hardly worth the gathering' (p. 150).

Sharp attempted the only real definition of the subject for his generation. His collecting and writing perpetuated the rural bias and the idea of 'unlettered peasant' as the prime source, but he also provided a more theoretical framework by identifying key elements fundamental to the genre, which have remained central to later attempts to define folklore. He laid particular stress on Continuity, Selection, and Variation. Continuity ensures that some songs are passed on from singer to singer, generation to generation, and thus exist long enough to become 'traditional'. Selection is the process by which only those items which satisfy the community's criteria for judging a good song survive, while those which do not are forgotten. As songs are passed informally from singer to singer, changes occur, and this variation makes development of the song possible, while selection again ensures that only positive changes will survive. Sharp's debt to evolutionary theories is clear, and his writings underpin his fundamental belief that because folk-songs have resulted from ages of unconscious selection and moulding by English communities, relatively untainted by passing fashion and foreign models, they necessarily embody the musical taste, even the musical soul, of the English nation: '. . . the unconscious output of the human mind, whatever else it may be, is always real and sincere . . . The music of the common people must always, therefore, be genuine and true' (p. 44). Similar sentiments underlay Vaughan Williams's notions of 'National Music'.

By concentrating on the process of transmission rather than the item itself, Sharp side-stepped the problem of origins. By his definition, songs could originate from any source, and only became 'folk-songs' after being submitted to the continuity/selection/variation process, but only if a further condition—the lack of access to an authoritative original—is satisfied. Variation is artificially hampered if singers are able to check their performances against the original form of a song, as happens when they possess a printed score or even a modern sound recording. Thus, the notion of an unbroken 'oral' tradition was mooted as a necessary basis for genuine folk-song. The status of oral transmission, however, was itself controversial. Antiquarians and literary scholars such as William *Chappell and F. J. *Child viewed the variations brought about by oral transmission as 'corruptions', and the process as largely degenerate, while for Sharp's theory to function, the oral tradition needed to be largely beneficial, or at the very least neutral.

It is easy to criticize Sharp's attempts at definition and to challenge his assumptions. His description of 'the folk', for example, as 'Those whose mental development has been due not to any formal system of training or education, but solely to environment, communal association, and direct contact with the ups and downs of life' (p. 4) is condescending and hardly describes the English rural working class of the time, and he systematically downplays the creative role played by successive performers, while overstating the humble status of his informants. The idea that English people have had a purely oral tradition at any time in the last three or four hundred years is clearly wishful thinking, as almost since the invention of printing *broadside and other printed versions of songs have been available. Nevertheless, Sharp and his contemporaries were almost exclusively interested in the tunes as opposed the texts of the songs, pre-

cisely because a much stronger case could be made for the existence of a long-standing 'oral' tradition in the musical sphere, and the tunes were thus deemed to be much 'purer' than the words. Nevertheless, the notion that the rural poor were somehow immune to influence by other forms of music is also untenable.

Sharp's writings were tremendously influential, and, filtered through the work of Maud *Karpeles, formed the basis of the definition which the International Folk Music Council (founded 1947) adopted at their 1955 Congress in São Paulo:

Folk music is the product of a musical tradition that has been evolved through the process of oral transmission. The factors that shape the tradition are: (i) continuity that links the present with the past; (ii) variation which springs from the creative impulse of the individual or the group; and (iii) selection by the community which determines the form or forms in which the music survives. The term can be applied to music that has been evolved from rudimentary beginnings by a community uninfluenced by popular and art music and it can likewise be applied to music which has originated with an individual composer and has subsequently been absorbed into the unwritten living tradition of a community. The term does not cover composed popular music that has been taken over ready-made by a community and remains unchanged, for it is the re-fashioning and re-creation of the music by the community that gives it its folk character. (*Journal of the International Folk Music Council* 7 (1955), 23)

Virtually every element of the Sharp/IFMC definition has been questioned by later writers, although not replaced by any other workable solution, and since the late 1970s it has been common for scholars to doubt the very existence of a separate genre of 'folk-song' (see, for example, Harker, 1985). A further criticism of the earlier collectors is that because of their restricted definition of folk-song they ignored a large part of singers' repertoires, leaving us with only partial knowledge of the singing practices of the time. But as documentation of the full singing picture of the time was not in their brief, and they made no secret of their restricted area of interest, their omissions may be regrettable from our present perspective, but not blameworthy.

The collecting boom had petered out by the First World War, and there was little collecting activity in the 1920s and 1930s, apart from by individuals such as Alfred *Williams and James Madison *Carpenter. By their definition, Sharp's contemporaries were correct about the demise of traditional singing, although they were certainly over-pessimistic on the speed of its decline. Post-Second World War collecting forays by the BBC/EFDSS and other collectors found plenty of songs still known, and many still being sung regularly in homes, pubs, and clubs all over the country, but this was probably the last generation which would be able to provide this sort of material as part of their everyday lives rather than as conscious revival of the past.

As with most folklore genres, the age of folk-song is often overestimated. A small proportion of the folk-song repertoire can be shown to have been current in the 17th century, and most of these are *ballads included in F. J. Child's collection. The bulk of the songs collected at the turn of the 19th century, however, could not claim to be older than 100 years, as they had originated in a variety of popular entertainment sources of the late 18th and 19th centuries: pleasure gardens, song and supper rooms, operas, other stage shows and interludes, music hall, and, most important of all, the printed *broadsides, *chapbooks, and songsters. Nevertheless, despite decades of intensive research, the authors of most songs in the traditional repertoire remain anonymous.

The folk-song repertoire can be categorized in many ways. From the subject point of view, songs about love, or the relationship between the sexes, comprise the vast majority, but range from the wistful to the robust, from the gentle romantic to the comic treatment of adultery. But there were plenty of other topics—battle and adventures at sea, including press-gangs and pirates, poachers, farm life, the pleasures (and occasionally miseries) of drink, highwaymen and other criminals, and, in the older narrative ballads, the exploits of Robin Hood, lords and ladies, kings and queens. They can be narrative, lyrical, humorous, pathetic, sentimental, callous, or coarse. The social mores of Victorian and Edwardian England severely constrained what the collectors noted and even more what they published, and, given their relative lack of concern for the texts, they had few qualms about 'softening' some of the sentiments involved. In addition, many singers censored items which they thought unsuitable for visiting gentlemen or ladies, and this successive filtering process ensured that a further distorted view of the total repertoire was given. There is no doubt that a range of sexually

explicit songs existed, although given the same social mores they would most likely be confined to all-male situations such as army barracks or the sports locker room. Some broadsides overstepped the line between risqué and crude. But England had no collector who made a point of noting everything, including the bawdy. It has been claimed that bawdy song has retained a more purely oral tradition precisely because of this problem of publishing, and this is true to a certain extent. Some books of bawdy songs were actually published, but they tended to be collectors' items, printed abroad, and there is also evidence that bawdy songs circulated in typescript and manuscript form. From the 1960s onwards, however, books and records of 'rugby songs' have been widely available, which have standardized the repertoire. England has not had much of a tradition of work songs (i.e. songs to accompany work as opposed to songs about work), apart from a vigorous tradition of *sea shanties. After the Second World War when politically active enthusiasts such as A. L. *Lloyd and Ewan *MacColl started taking an interest, the song traditions of miners, weavers, and other industrial workers began to be researched. Traditions of song-making and singing were identified in many areas, and a characteristic of these traditions was that many of the songs had been written by identifiable local authors.

It is almost a cliché to claim that people do not sing as they used to, but all the evidence confirms this as an accurate assessment of the decline of vernacular song. Home-grown music of all kinds has been largely swamped by the commercial music industry, and the spread of the radio and gramophone has dramatically changed the way that ordinary people view musical performance. This is not to argue that in the past all singing was 'folk singing', but many popular songs were at least singable by non-professionals, while few modern popular songs are suited to amateur unaccompanied performance, and as performance contexts have dwindled almost to the point of extinction, so has the habit of singing. Ironically, we nowadays have far more day-to-day access to music than any previous generation, but it is now primarily in the role of listener rather than participant. By most definitions, folk-song in England is all but dead, although a case could be made for one or two exceptions, such as children's rhymes and songs, which are still largely passed on informally, bawdy songs, carol-singing, and other informal genres such as football-crowd chants.

As indicated, the Edwardian collectors were primarily interested in tunes rather than texts. Whereas previous antiquarians such as *Chappell had 'corrected' tunes to fit with established musical practice of the time, the folk-song collectors were delighted to find that many traditional tunes used a different tonal basis than the standard major/minor forms of the period; namely, the so-called 'church modes', such as the Dorian, Mixolydian, and Aeolian. To the modern ear, their main characteristic is that certain notes are consistently sharpened or flattened when compared to a conventional major scale. Such modal idioms had not otherwise been in regular use since the religious plain-chants of the 16th century, and were thus held by some to be an important marker of the antiquity of traditional music. Sharp and his successors classified the tunes according to modal theory, but such systematization underestimated the fluidity of traditional tonality and modern scholarship takes a less prescriptive approach. An important exception was Percy *Grainger whose thinking on tonality was well ahead of its time (see *JFSS* 3 (1908), 147–242). It must also be stressed that their interest in modal tunes led the collectors to exaggerate their numerical importance, and a majority of the songs noted were in the standard major.

See also *BALLADS, SABINE *BARING-GOULD, LUCY *BROADWOOD, GEORGE *BUTTERWORTH, F. J. *CHILD, *ENGLISH FOLK DANCE AND SONG SOCIETY, G. B. *GARDINER, ANNE *GILCHRIST, *FOLK SONG SOCIETY, PERCY *GRAINGER, *HAMMOND BROTHERS, FRANK *KIDSON, A. L. LLOYD, EWAN *MacCOLL, THOMAS *PERCY, JOSEPH *RITSON, *SEA SHANTIES, CECIL *SHARP, *SONG REVIVAL, RALPH VAUGHAN *WILLIAMS, ALFRED *WILLIAMS.

Cecil Sharp, *English Folk Song: Some Conclusions* (1907); Dave Harker, *Fakesong: The Manufacture of British Folksong, 1700 to the Present Day* (1985); A. L. Lloyd, *Folk Song in England* (1967); Iolo A. Williams, *English Folk-Song and Dance* (1935). Gammon, 1980; B. H. Bronson, *The Ballad as Song* (1969); Roger D. Abrahams and George Foss, *Anglo-American Folksong Style* (1968).

song revival. There have been two major *song revival movements in England; one lasting from the late Victorian period to the 1920s, the other commencing after the Second World War, and they are conveniently termed the first and second Revivals, although there

was a degree of continuity between them. The starting-point of the first Revival is conveniently placed at 1898, with the formation of the *Folk-Song Society, although it is clear that this was a culmination of a growing interest in traditional song evidenced by the increasing number of publications through the second half of the 19th century. Sabine *Baring-Gould, Frank *Kidson, and Lucy *Broadwood had all published their first volumes of songs before the Society was formed. What distinguished these new folk-song enthusiasts from their primarily antiquarian and literary predecessors was a growing interest in the use of traditional music as raw material for the renaissance of English musical taste, the identification of the 'folk' as carriers of a valuable song tradition, and the willingness to leave the library and undertake fieldwork in villages up and down the country. The motives of these early collectors were a mixture of nostalgia, romanticism, and nationalism, but they were all driven by the idea that here was something essentially 'English' which had all but been destroyed by universal education, railway travel, urban development, industrialization, and the styles of popular music purveyed by the music hall. The movement received a further boost from 1903/4 when major propagandist Cecil *Sharp, and young musicians such as Ralph *Vaughan Williams, Percy *Grainger, and George *Butterworth became enraptured by folk-song tunes and commenced a collecting boom which lasted until the outbreak of the First World War, and which resulted in the major manuscript collections which still exist today.

The first revival movement achieved several positive results. In addition to the large quantity of collected material which would not otherwise have been recorded, the public awareness of a mass of vernacular song was raised, and it became accepted for the first time that England had an interesting and valuable musical heritage. Many English composers made use of folk music in some form or another in their work and certainly enriched the home-grown classical repertoire, and schools taught British 'folk-songs' to children in music lessons. Unlike the parallel *dance revival, however, the first song revival did not result in a major upsurge in the *practice* of folksinging, and it apparently had no appreciable effect on those segments of the population who sang traditional songs. Folk-Song Society members were mainly academics, musicians, or composers, although a few were professional singers who included folk-songs in their recitals. Put simply, the movement made a difference to music in the middle and upper classes, but none in the working classes, and it certainly did nothing to reverse the perceived decline in popular musical taste. On the negative front, the collectors' severely selective definition of folk-song has left us with a hopelessly unbalanced view of the repertoire of traditional song at the time, and the assumption that the rural poor were the only possessors of traditional culture. As they took little interest in the singers themselves, performance venues, or events, we have little knowledge of the social context in which the songs were sung.

After the First World War the collecting boom was over, and only a few newcomers such as Alfred *Williams continued to be active. The Folk-Song Society merged into the *English Folk Dance and Song Society (EFDSS) in 1932, after publicly stating that there remained few folk-songs to collect, only variants. Nevertheless, there were stirrings of interest in other quarters. The newly formed BBC, for example, often used folk music in its early programmes, and developments in other areas were building a new set of enthusiasts which would result in major changes in the 1950s. Pre-war mass unemployment, the trade union movement, popular leisure pursuits such as hiking and cycling, workers' theatre, left-leaning children's organizations like the Woodcraft Folk, and so on, all included elements of vernacular song—either deliberately fostered as a vehicle for protest or political 'education', or as spontaneous 'community singing'—which by one definition or another had connections with folk-song. Wartime propaganda celebrating the achievements of the common people, and further shifts of the political spectrum to the left, encouraged an interest in workers' culture, both rural and urban.

These influences coalesced after the Second World War. In the early 1950s, visiting American folklorist, Alan Lomax, discovered a growing, but largely unorganized, interest in folk-song in Britain, which was fuelled largely from the burgeoning folk revival in his own country. He suggested to Ewan *MacColl, A. L. *Lloyd, and others, that the time was right to found a British Folk Revival movement. These key players were already involved in regular programmes for the BBC, and they thereby introduced folk-song, and the ethos of the new

revival, to a nationwide audience. The adoption of the 'folk club' as the main meeting place/performance venue (borrowed from the jazz scene) rapidly provided new foci for enthusiasts in almost every town in the country. The new movement received a boost from the short-lived 'skiffle' boom of 1957/8, which was largely based on the repertoire of American folk and blues singers such as Leadbelly and Woody Guthrie.

Meanwhile, the EFDSS still survived, dedicated to preserving the legacy of Cecil *Sharp and others of the first revival. By the 1950s the rank-and-file Society membership was more interested in dance than song, and their experience of folk-song would have been at concerts where the songs were 'interpreted' by trained singers and musicians. In contrast, the revival's emphasis was on informality and participation, and the difference between these two performance styles is a key indicator of the way the folk world was changing. A piece in the Society's magazine, in 1953, reported one of the first contacts between the two worlds. After describing a recent concert with its previously announced 'carefully planned menu', the writer contrasts this with an informal Evening of Folk-Song, where the performers sat around and swapped songs: 'It was as though the audience had strayed into some private informal gathering ... What programme there was had been sketched out over coffee beforehand and filled in as the singers' blood warmed. Nothing quite like it had been heard before at Cecil Sharp House ...' (*ED&S* 18:1 (Aug. 1953), 26).

The material for the radio programmes in the early 1950s came largely from an ambitious BBC project (in co-operation with the EFDSS) to tape-record dialect and folk-song across Britain and to preserve the recordings in a permanent archive. Peter Kennedy, Bob Copper, Seamus Ennis, and others, discovered a wealth of material and many previously unknown singers and musicians. Another generation of collectors appeared in the 1960s and 1970s, and again significant numbers of recordings were made for posterity.

For most people, however, the distinguishing feature of the second revival was not the collection and study of materials, but *performance*, and this is the area most fraught with disagreement and debate. There were inevitable disagreements over both repertoire and style, with major divisions between traditionalists and moderns. Even when sticking to a predominantly traditional repertoire, revivalists rapidly developed styles of performance which were radically different from the ones in which the material had been collected and previously performed, and the performance milieu and class context were equally far removed. It could be said that while the first revival was built on the pianoforte and the concert platform, the second was built on the guitar and the folk club; both equally foreign to the traditional music being 'revived'. Other tensions stemmed from the overt left-wing agenda of the movement's founders when faced by later enthusiasts whose interests were less politically motivated. Some argued that all that mattered was that people were making their own music and enjoying themselves; others that the middle classes were playing at being working class and misappropriating their culture as they had done throughout history. Commercial interests moved in as record companies attempted to create a more commercially viable 'folk-song' sound for the mass market by softening, prettifying, and controlling both material and performer. Although the revival supported a number of professional singers and musicians, and many more semi-professionals, there was a widespread determinedly amateur ethos in the movement, against commercialism and impatient with questions of definition and intellectualization. Nevertheless, several of the newly discovered traditional singers became active performers in folk clubs and festivals, and had LP records of their own. The song revival thus contained more than its fair share of paradoxes.

Throughout the 1960s and early 1970s there was a burgeoning nationwide 'folk scene', with sufficient numerical strength to support hundreds of folk clubs, annual festivals, national and local record labels, and a variety of magazines. Although those heady days are gone, 'folk music' is still a definable minority-interest pastime, and appeared, in the late 1990s, to be on the rise again.

The founders of the second revival have mostly passed on or retired, and even the second wave is now giving way to a new generation, and further changes are inevitable.

Georgina Boyes, *The Imagined Village: Culture, Ideology, and the English Folk Revival* (1993); Vic Gammon, 'Folk Song Collecting in Sussex and Surrey 1843–1914', *History Workshop Journal* 10 (1980), 61–89; Niall Mackinnon, *The British Folk Scene: Musical Performance and Social Identity* (1993); Dave Harker, *Fakesong: The Manufacture of British 'Folksong', 1700 to the Present Day* (1985).

souling. A *visiting custom carried out in the 19th and 20th centuries mainly by children, but previously by adults, in the Shropshire, north Staffordshire, Cheshire, and Lancashire area, on *All Saints Day (1 November) and *All Souls Day (2 November). The soulers visited houses, sang a song, and collected money, food, drink, or whatever was given to them. The songs vary somewhat from place to place, but they all follow the same basic pattern:

> Soul, soul for a souling cake
> I pray you, missis, for a souling cake
> Apple or pear, plum or cherry
> Anything good to make us merry
> Up with your kettles and down with your pans
> Give us an answer and we'll be gone
> Little Jack, Jack sat on his gate
> Crying for butter to butter his cake
> One for St. Peter, two for St. Paul
> Three for the man that made us all

> (Shropshire: *Bye-Gones Relating to Wales & the Border Country* (1889–1890), 253)

Begging at All Souls was already proverbial in Shakespeare's time, as Speed comments in *Two Gentlemen of Verona* (II. i)—'to speak puling, like a beggar at Hallowmas'. The soul-cakes mentioned in the song are the remnant of pre-Reformation beliefs concerning the need to help souls out of Purgatory by prayer and alms-giving. John Mirk's *Festial* (14th century) provides an early reference: '... wherefore in olden time good men and women would this day buy bread and deal (give) it for the souls that they loved, hoping with each loaf to get a soul out of purgatory' (p. 269). Denham, writing of the north of England, implies that by the mid-19th century the practice was on its last legs: 'A few thrifty, elderly housewives still practice the old custom of keeping a soul mass-cake for good luck...' (*Denham Tracts*, 1895: ii. 26).

Two other visiting customs took place in roughly the same geographical area, Clementing (23 November), and Catterning (25 November, St Catherine's Day), with the same basic pattern of visiting, singing, and requesting food, although Catterning was apparently regarded as more of a female custom. Charlotte Burne argued persuasively that these three were all aspects of the same custom. Clementing was first mentioned by Plot (1686: 430), and Catterning in 1730 (quoted Wright and Lones, 1940: iii. 168). Of the three customs, Souling was the most widely reported.

Wright and Lones, 1940: iii. 121–45, 167–86; Charlotte Burne, *Folk-Lore* 25 (1914), 285–99.

Spanish Sunday. A local name for *Palm Sunday, after a special drink made on the day by children in the Midlands and parts of Yorkshire until about the 1920s. They took broken pieces of Spanish liquorice, lemon, or peppermint, mixed it with brown sugar and water from a local well (after solemnly walking round it) and shook it vigorously (Hole, 1975: 36–7). Similar customs, with different names, existed elsewhere. 'Sugar Cupping', near Tideswell in Derbyshire, involved mixing sugar and water from a spring at Dropping Tar (reported in 1831). Elsewhere in Derbyshire, 'rinsing' meant mixing well water with broken sweetmeats on Easter Sunday and Monday. At Castleton and Bradwell, Easter Monday was called 'Shakking Monday'. Children filled bottles with well water and pieces of special coloured peppermint (reported 1907) (Wright and Lones, 1936: i. 100–1, 112).

speaking, see *TALKING.

spells. The term 'spell' is generally used for magical procedures which cause harm, or force people to do something against their will—unlike *charms for healing, protection, etc. There is far less available information about spells than about *counterspells; witnesses at *witchcraft trials often alleged that the suspect ill-wished some animal or child, but when actual words are quoted they are not formal spells but commonplace remarks such as 'You'll get no good of that pig'.

spiders. Considering how general is the dislike of spiders, they feature often and have mainly a positive reputation in English lore. The belief that it is unlucky to kill a spider is generally reported: '. . . If you are sweeping, and come on a web, don't destroy it till the spider is safe, when you may sweep away the web; but if you kill the spider it will surely bring poverty to your house', (Isle of Wight: N&Q 12s:3 (1917), 396). It is still considered lucky if a small spider alights on you, and these are thus generally called 'money-spiders' or 'money-spinners'. To ensure good luck, some believe you must throw the spider over your left shoulder, or, more elaborately, hold the thread by which it is hanging, pass it (and spider) three times round your head, and place the spider back where you found it (N&Q 5s:12 (1879), 229, 254, 277, 295, 518).

One legend which seeks to explain our regard for spiders tells that on the flight into Egypt, when the Holy Family took shelter in a cave, a spider quickly spun its web across the mouth, and a dove laid an egg in the web. The pursuing soldiers thus concluded that the cave had been unused for some time and neglected to search it. This tale has numerous international parallels and is also told of King David and of Mahomet. A different story relates how the spider spun a beautiful web over Christ's manger in the stable (N&Q 169 (1935), 460; 170 (1936) 50, 212, 266, 303; Radford, Radford, and Hole, 1961: 317–18; Henderson, 1879: 312).

Spiders do not fare so well in the realm of folk medicine, as the cure usually results in their death one way or another. A long-standing cure for ague or fever was to imprison a spider, often in a nut-shell, which would be worn as an amulet—Pliny (Natural History (AD 77), xxx) includes this cure, and English writers since at least the 16th century have also recommended it. Similar methods were used for whooping cough. Other cures involve eating the spider, for example as a cure for ague, taken with a spoonful of jam (N&Q 151 (1926), 404). Cobwebs were believed to have medicinal value in themselves. Mixed with bread and made into pills, they were another recommended remedy for the ague at least since the 17th century (N&Q 10s:1 (1904), 205, 273–4, 317–18). There are many who still believe that cobwebs slapped on a wound stop the bleeding.

Opie and Tatem, 1989: 368–72; Black, 1883: 58–61; Lean, 1902: ii) (numerous references, the index in vol. iv is incorrect, referring to vol. i instead of vol. ii).

spitting. Though real or pretended spitting 'for luck' or to repel *witchcraft and the *evil eye is an ancient device, concern for hygiene and good manners makes it rare now. However, there are many references to people spitting on a *coin for luck, especially one unexpectedly found or given, or won in a bet; spitting on one's hands before fighting, or when embarking on a tough piece of work, was still done by schoolboys in the 1950s (Radford, Radford, and Hole, 1961: 318–20; Opie and Tatem, 1989: 372–4). Children spit on seeing or doing anything reckoned unlucky (Opie and Opie, 1959: 206–20). They lick a finger before making cross-my-heart or cut-my-throat gestures when swearing to the truth of something, often with the formula:

My finger's wet, my finger's dry,
Cut my throat if I tell a lie.

(Opie and Opie, 1959: 126–8)

Another widespread and ancient belief was that spittle had healing properties, especially if used early in the day, before eating or drinking anything; it was applied to sore eyes, warts, cuts and grazes, babies' rashes, birthmarks, and even deformities in babies (Radford, Radford, and Hole, 1961: 319–20).

spoons. One of the household items (the others include *umbrella, glove, and walking stick) that if accidentally dropped should only be picked up by someone else, or bad luck, or an argument, or a visitor, will follow.

A servant dropped a spoon, and as she made no attempt to pick it up, her mistress told her to do it. Without speaking, the girl left the kitchen, but soon returned with another maid who performed the duty. The one who dropped the spoon explained her subsequent procedure by saying that if she herself had picked it up she would have met with some dire misfortune. (N&Q 11s:10 (1914), 146, 196)

More generally known nowadays is the belief that two teaspoons in one saucer, or one basin, denote a forthcoming wedding, although occasionally it is held to mean twins on the way. In common with many other domestic superstitions, the earliest known reference to this only occurs in the later 19th century (N&Q 4s:10 (1872), 495).

Opie and Tatem, 1989: 374; Radford and Hole, 1961: 320.

spriggans. These are small, ugly, and malicious *fairies found in wild places in Cornwall, where they guard treasures. They steal babies and leave *changelings, and blight crops (Bottrell, 1873: ii. 246). According to Robert Hunt, they are the ghosts of *giants, and therefore able to swell from their usual small size into huge figures (Hunt, 1865: 90). Both Bottrell and Hunt tell local legends in which spriggans are described as merrily playing music and dancing, and attack men who spy on them. Anyone who digs for their *treasures will find himself surrounded by hideous and terrifying figures till he flees in panic; if he is brave enough to return, he will find the pit he dug has closed up again.

Spring-Heel (or Spring-Heeled) Jack. This was a general Victorian nickname for a street *robber who relied on speed in running to escape, and did not necessarily refer to one particular man; in Cheshire, for example, maids who had just been paid their yearly wage would be afraid to go out carrying much money, since 'there are so many of these spring-heeled Jacks about'. There was a panic in the Barnes area of south-west London in the 1830s, culminating in February 1838 when a girl was attacked by a man who then 'soared away into the darkness'. She described him as a demon with fiery eyes and breath, who clawed her with his talons, wearing a tight-fitting white costume and some kind of helmet. Another girl, in Limehouse, said she had been pounced on by a tall cloaked man who spat blue flames at her. The matter was taken seriously, and mounted patrols searched for the mysterious villain, but in vain.

Later, the name was appropriated for the fantastic romanticized hero of a 'Penny Dreadful' called *Spring-Heel Jack, the Terror of London,* printed in the 1870s. This Jack was a seemingly demonic being dressed in a skin-tight glossy crimson suit, with bat's wings, a lion's mane, horns, talons, massive cloven hoofs, and a sulphurous breath; he moved in gigantic leaps, easily jumping over rooftops or rivers, and was extremely strong. But he used his power for good, saving the innocent from the wicked; he was in fact wholly human (a nobleman by birth, cheated of his inheritance), and his amazing leaps were due to compressed springs in the heels of his boots. Various boys' comics and other sensational writings took up the name.

In 1907 contributors to *N&Q* debated whether there had ever been a real Jack. One had heard tell of 'a lively officer' at Aldershot in the 1870s who scared the sentries by vaulting across a canal and pouncing on their shoulders; another, of a prankster in rural Warwickshire in the 1880s using spring-heeled shoes; another, of one in the Midlands in the 1850s; another had been told by his grandmother, as early as the 1840s, that the 'monster' was really a Marquess of Waterford, who used to jump out at people in lonely lanes (preferably women) and pin them to the ground (N&Q 10s:7 (1907), 206, 256, 394–5, 496; 10s:8 (1907), 251, 455). Other local identifications have also been proposed, some seeing him as a joker, others as a bandit.

The figure could also be exploited as a *bogey to control children. In Lewes (Sussex) in the 1890s some children were told that if they were not good he would leap up and peer in at them through their bedroom windows; they imagined him as a weirdly tall figure in white, whose springs rattled as he leapt. At the same period in Worthing (Sussex), boys used this name for a ghostly apparition reputedly haunting a certain alley (JS). Such fears seem to have been fairly widespread among children up to the First World War. Whether or not Spring-Heel Jack was a folklore figure before appearing in popular print, he certainly rapidly became one.

spunky. A name for the *Will-o'-the-Wisp in some areas, for example Lowland Scotland and Somerset, from a dialect word for a spark. In Somerset, spunkies were thought to be the souls of *unbaptized children doomed to wander the earth till Judgement Day (Tongue, 1965: 93–5).

squirrel hunting. In a number of 18th- and 19th-century accounts, squirrel hunting is mentioned as popular on a certain fixed day, in terms which make it sound more like a *calendar custom than an ordinary sport. In only one or two places does it seem that the actual killing or capturing of squirrels was the primary object of the exercise, and most accounts stress the noise and merriment of the party. In many instances the participants are only armed with noise-making implements, and claimed that the noise would frighten the squirrels so much they would fall from the trees. Each area seems to have had its own special day for the sport, including: Derbyshire (first Sunday after 1 November), Kent and East Sussex (*St Andrew's Day, 30 November), Essex (*Good Friday and *Boxing Day), and Suffolk (*Christmas Day). It is possible that these are remnants of excursions to preserve common wood-gathering, hunting, or other forest access rights, and there seems also to have been a general notion that the game laws were not in force over Christmas/Boxing Day. Gerald Lascelles, *Thirty-Five Years in the New Forest* (1915), 242–5, gives details of proper squirrel-hunting techniques using weighted sticks called 'squails' or 'snoggs'.

Wright and Lones, 1940: iii. 136–7, 188, 261, 277.

stag hunt. A form of social disapproval custom noted only in Devon, but akin to the more widespread *rough music ceremony. In the known instances, the hunt was prompted by some form of sexual misconduct or deviancy in the community, usually adultery or homo-

sexuality. It involved one man dressing up as a stag, complete with horns, another dressed as a huntsman, and others as dogs. The huntsman and dogs chased the stag through the streets of the town or village, with much yelping, barking, hallooing, and other noise, finally cornering him on the doorstep of the offender. A very realistic kill was enacted, including the bursting of a bladder full of blood, carried by the stag. It was assumed that the offending parties would leave the area after such a public shaming. In one reported version the custom also included the noisy 'band' of pots and kettles commonly found in rough music ceremonies, and there are also reports that in former times it was the offender himself who was chased and thrown into the local pond or river. Most of the accounts refer to the period from the 1860s to 1880s, but the last known occurrences were just before the First World War. Sabine *Baring-Gould's popular novel *The Red Spider* (1887) includes the stag hunt as a motif.

Theo Brown, *Folk-Lore* 63 (1952), 104–9; Theo Brown, *Folklore* 90:1 (1979), 18–21.

stairs. There are four basic beliefs about stairs—crossing on, stumbling up, stumbling down, and turning round on. The idea that it is unlucky to pass someone on the stairs is still current, being the ninth most often reported belief in our *Superstitions Survey 1998/9, and is reported from the mid-19th century onwards from all over the country, simply given as 'bad luck'. Also first reported in the 19th century is the idea that one should not change direction on the stairs, but continue to top or bottom and then turn. The two stumblings are older; stumbling upstairs means you (or the next person who walks up the stairs) will be married. The first known mention is in the *Connoisseur* for 20 February 1755, and the other references through into the 20th century are unusually unanimous. Stumbling downstairs, however, is bad luck and has been at least since Congreve's time: 'But then I stumbled coming down stairs, and met a weasel; bad omens those' (*Love for Love* (1695), II. i).

See also *STUMBLING.

Opie and Tatem, 1989: 375.

Stamford (Lincolnshire), see *BULL-RUNNING.

standing stones. Erected in prehistoric times, whether solitary or in groups, these frequently attract legends to explain either how they came to be there or what strange powers they have; the same is true of natural boulders and rock formations, if they are sufficiently dramatic. A single stone is often said to have been thrown or dropped by the *Devil, by *giants, or by some mighty hero such as *Robin Hood; occasionally, if the stone is near a church, it is said the Devil was trying to knock it down, but missed. Alternatively, the giant (or Devil) was carrying stones to build something himself, but stupidly dropped one. The very size of the stones inspired some storytellers to claim they were set up with astounding speed and ease. Rudston Stone (Humberside), the tallest standing stone in England, grew up in the churchyard in a single night, by its own power; a group of three large uprights and a capstone at Drewsteignton (Devon) is called the Spinsters' Rock because three old maids set it up one morning before breakfast.

Such stories are clearly frivolous, but there are about a dozen others (*Long Meg and *Stanton Drew are good examples) which tell how evil-doers were turned to stone for dancing, playing sports, or working, instead of respecting the Sabbath, or for witchcraft. The medieval name 'The Giants' Dance' for *Stonehenge hints intriguingly that a tale of this type was once told there.

Another recurrent motif is that megaliths cannot be counted correctly; both at *Stonehenge and at *Stanton Drew anyone who gets the number right will meet misfortune, even death. Nor can they be shifted from their place, or if they are, they return at once by their own power—though they do move voluntarily, at certain times. L. V. Grinsell (1976: 58–60) listed 23 prehistoric megaliths in England which walk, turn round, or go to a river to drink, when they hear the clock strike twelve, or hear the church bells, or hear the cock crow, and then return to their places; there is a further list in Janet and Colin Bord, *The Secret Country* (1978), 144–51, which includes natural boulders such as the impressive Cheesewring on Bodmin Moor (Cornwall). The crucial phrase is 'when they hear', for no stone hears anything; several of the tales contain additional improbabilities, such as a cock crowing in the middle of Bodmin Moor, or a church clock striking thirteen. It is possible that the belief was once seriously held, but it is now merely the basis for a catch to tease children.

Grinsell, 1976; S. P. Menefee, *Folklore* 85 (1974), 23–42; *Folklore* 86 (1975), 146–66.

Stang, Riding the see *RIDING THE STANG.

Stanton Drew (Somerset). The name of the *standing stones near this village is recorded as 'The Wedding' in 1644, and more recently as 'The Fiddler and the Maids'. The account by William Stukeley in 1723 explains: 'This noble monument is . . . a company who assisted a nuptial solemnity, thus petrify'd. In an orchard near the church is a cove consisting of three stones . . . this they call the parson, the bride, and bridegroom. Other circles are said to be the company dancing: and a separate parcel of stones standing a little from the rest, are call'd the fiddlers, or band of music' ('The History of the Temples of the Ancient Celts', unpublished MS).

Other more recent writers explain that the party were dancing late on a Saturday, but at midnight their piper (or harper), a pious man, refused to play on the Sunday, at which the bride angrily swore that 'she would find someone to play if she went to hell to fetch him'. The Devil then appeared, disguised as an old man, and played so wildly that the dancers could not stop; by morning they had all turned to stone. Similar legends are told of various groups of standing stones in Cornwall and Devon. They are of medieval date, reinforced later by Protestant teaching.

S. P. Menefee, *Folklore* 85 (1974), 23–42; L. V. Grinsell, *The Megalithic Monuments of Stanton Drew* (1994).

stars. Even apart from the complexities of *astrology, stars (which, in popular speech, included planets, meteors, and *comets) were thought to affect, or at least to indicate, the character and destiny of individuals and nations. To doubt this seemed almost immoral; in Shakespeare it is villains who deny the power of stars—Cassius (*Julius Caesar*, I. ii), and Edmund (*King Lear*, I. ii). Sirius, the Dog-Star, was thought to have a particularly baleful effect in July and August, when it rose at day-break, causing heat-waves, fevers, and madness. To point at stars or try to count them was reckoned unlucky, or even sinful, in the 19th century; it was said people had been struck dead for doing so.

The Bible included among the signs of *Doomsday that 'the stars shall fall from heaven' (Matthew 24: 29), confirming a widespread fear that shooting stars meant death or disaster. Comets were even more dreaded, and were interpreted in national and political terms; famously, one was seen in 1066, and another shortly before the Great Plague.

statues. It seems to be a widespread instinct for passers-by to touch statues, in greeting or for luck, if they represent a popular personality, as when Tory Members of Parliament rub the toe of Winston Churchill's statue at the entrance to the Chamber, and Liberals that of Lloyd George. Animal images also attract this affectionate gesture; the nose of a lion-faced door-knocker at Durham Cathedral is well polished by the constant touch of visitors, as is the beak of a certain falcon in the Egyptian Gallery of the British Museum. The other recurrent piece of folklore about a statue is the assertion that it gets down from its pedestal and walks about, or sits down for a rest, whenever it hears midnight strike; the lions at the door of the Fitzwilliam Museum, Cambridge, either roar or drink from the gutter. Such statements are a catch, for 'when it hears' is an impossible condition (cf. *standing stones).

Tomb effigies are a striking feature in village churches, and a fruitful inspiration for storytelling, especially if damaged, or if the accompanying heraldry is misunderstood. One example among many is an Elizabethan family memorial at Broad Hinton (Wiltshire) where several figures have their hands broken off; legend says this shows how the hands of Sir Thomas Wroughton and his sons withered away after he wickedly hurled his wife's Bible in the fire.

Stir-Up Sunday. In the Anglican Church, the Collect for the Sunday before Advent, or the twenty-fifth Sunday after Trinity, which occurs some time in late November, commences 'Stir up, we beseech thee, O Lord, the wills of thy faithful people', and all over the country this has given the day the colloquial name of Stir-Up Sunday. Brand reports a verse recited by children: 'Stir up, we beseech thee, The pudding in the pot, And when we get home, We'll eat it all hot'. The day was taken as a marker to advise the housewife to start her Christmas preparations, and the grocer to see to the Christmas stock of his shop (*Sussex Archaeological Collections* 33 (1883), 252–3).

Brand, 1849: i. 414; Simpson, 1973: 141–2; 'Winter and the London Poor', *The Times* (25 Nov. 1863), 12.

Stonehenge. Always this must have seemed a place of mystery. Whatever tales Britons and Romans told about it are lost, but the name itself is a clue to Anglo-Saxon storytelling, for it means 'The Stone Gallows'. Early antiquaries tried to explain the name as 'The Hanging Stones', with reference to the way the lintels balance on the uprights, but this is grammatically impossible, since in Old English adjectives normally come before, not after, their noun; 'stone' is an adjective here, qualifying *hengen*, 'gibbet, gallows'. Clearly, the trilithons reminded the Saxons of the kind of gallows where several men at once are hanged from a crossbar held on two uprights; there must have been some story explaining who hanged whom there, and why—but it is forgotten.

The earliest surviving *origin legend is the Norman one given by *Geoffrey of Monmouth (*c*.1136): the stones were brought by sea from 'Killaraus, a mountain in Ireland', on the advice of *Merlin, to mark the graves of 460 British noblemen murdered by Saxons. In Ireland, the circle had been known as 'the Giants' Dance', having been brought from Africa by giants; its stones had healing powers, as water poured over them cured anyone who bathed in it. This may be one of the few occasions when a legend enshrines an ancient fact, since Stonehenge does contain some stones which are not local, though they come from Wales, not Ireland. Even so, the story need not have been passed on orally for millennia; the difference between the local sarcen stones and the intrusive 'bluestones' is obvious, so an observer at any period could have deduced that the latter were brought from elsewhere. Geoffrey, however, is unaware of the distinction and makes Merlin responsible for the transport and erection of the whole monument.

The name 'Giant's Dance', which he does not explain, implies an alternative legend according to which the stones would themselves have been the giants, turned to stone while dancing (cf. *Stanton Drew), which matches the appearance of Stonehenge very neatly. The belief that the stones could heal persisted; Aubrey (in his unpublished *Monumenta Britannica*, *c*.1690) said local people dropped pieces or powder into their wells to drive toads away, while in the 18th century water in which scrapings had been steeped was used on wounds and sores.

Another folk belief was that the stones could not be counted, since some magic power ensured that the total was never twice the same, and that anyone who happened upon the right total would be sure to die. Daniel Defoe, in his *A Tour through England and Wales* (1724), says he was told how 'a baker carry'd a basket of bread, and laid a loaf upon every stone, and yet could never make out the same number twice'. In 1651, while fleeing to France, Charles II found himself forced to spend a day near Stonehenge, and passed the time by counting and recounting the stones, to his own satisfaction.

The theory that *Druids built Stonehenge was launched by Aubrey (*c*.1690) and elaborated by Stukeley in 1740; at that time the Celts were the only society known to have preceded the Romans in England, so the conjecture was reasonable. Although most people are now aware that Stonehenge is far too old for this to be literally true, it has become a sacred site of prime importance to most groups of Neo-Pagans, including the various modern Druidic Orders dating from the late 18th and 19th centuries, who have worshipped there at the summer solstice (21 June) throughout most of the 20th century. A larger Pagan gathering, the Stonehenge Festival, was held from 1974 until banned in 1985; access to the monument for Midsummer worship was also forbidden in 1985, but was allowed again in 1998 for selected groups.

L. V. Grinsell, *Folklore* 87 (1976), 3–20; Christopher Chippindale, Paul Devereux, *et al.*, *Who Owns Stonehenge?* (1990).

stones. Large boulders and prehistoric *standing stones often attracted folklore; there were also widespread beliefs about the protective powers of small *holed stones, *hagstones, *snakestones, *thunderstones, and geodes called *eaglestones. From antiquity through the Middle Ages and up to the 17th century, much was written on the medicinal and magical powers of *precious stones, though naturally only the wealthy could make use of them.

The only belief concerning ordinary stones in general was that they grew in the soil and then rose to the surface. This was widely held, as correspondents to *N&Q* showed on several occasions in the 19th century; many countrymen insisted it was no use having stones picked off one's fields, because the land produced them, and there would soon be as many as ever. This was still being said in Staffordshire in the 1960s. At Blaxhall (Suffolk) a

five-ton boulder is a famous local marvel, alleged to have grown from the size of a man's two fists in the course of the 19th century; the Leper Stone outside Newport (Cambridgeshire) and the Hoston Stone at Humberstone (Leicestershire) are said to be rising slowly out of the ground; one tale about the huge Rudston standing stone (Yorkshire) is that it grew up in a single night (*FLS News* 26 (1997), 13; 27 (1998), 8; 28 (1998), 6–7). Another theory was that 'pudding-stone', a conglomerate of pebbles, was a 'mother-stone' or 'breeding-stone' from which a number of little pebbles would be born and grow larger.

See also *TURNING THE DEVIL'S STONE, *HANGMAN'S STONE.

storks. The whimsical idea that storks bring babies, universally known in 20th-century England, must have been adopted from northern Europe, where storks nesting on roofs are regarded as a sign of good luck and family happiness.

storms. The notion that great storms accompany the passing of great persons was formerly widespread and generally accepted. The most widely mentioned instance was probably the death of *Cromwell in 1658, still remembered by Samuel Pepys in his *Diary* four years later on 18 February 1662, while the following year he was worried by another storm:

(19 Oct. 1663): Waked with a very highe winde, and said to my wife, 'I pray God I hear not of the death of any great person, this wind is so high', fearing that the Queene might be dead.

It could apparently be the great evil of the deceased or their great fame which caused the disturbance (*Denham Tracts*, 1895: ii. 29–30). On the other side of the coin, several references in Opie and Tatem (1989: 432–3) indicate that good people's deeds are often accompanied by good weather.

storytelling. Until recently, folktales were studied for their content only; scholars did not think to enquire in what circumstances they would normally be told, by whom, to whom, and why. They seemed hardly aware of storytelling as an art form or a social activity. Partly, this was because England had no formal gatherings for story and song like those of Ireland and Scotland, and only one group of professional storytellers, the wandering Cornish 'droll-tellers' of the early 19th century, described by Robert Hunt and William Bottrell. 'Stories were told as the occasion arose, as a natural element of daily life, rather than recited to an audience' (Philip, 1992: p. xiv); clues to the process can be gathered from biographies, memoirs, and novels as well as brief comments by some folklorists.

One major channel of transmission was from nannies and nursemaids to the middle-class children they looked after. Dickens as a child was both horrified and fascinated by grisly tales of *robbers and *murderers told by his nurse, and the Brontë children by tales of the 'wild doings' in old families of the district; many folklore collectors cite old servants as their informants. The stories were sometimes used for moral instruction; a correspondent in *N&Q* describes two tomb-effigies in Wickhampton Church (Norfolk) with oval stones in their hands, and recalls:

When a child, having had an infantile quarrel with my brother, we were taken by our nurse to see these figures, and were informed that they were two brothers named Hampton who had quarrelled, and fought, and torn each other's hearts out. After this Kilkenny cat proceeding, Divine vengeance turned their bodies to stone, and, with their hearts in their hands, they were placed in the church as a monument to their wickedness. (*N&Q* 1s:12 (1855), 486–7)

There are widespread but scrappy references to adults telling one another stories informally, as entertainment in pubs, at *Christmas, at *wakes, as after-dinner anecdotes, in prisons and workhouses; humorous tales, *ghost stories, and *local legends are the types most often mentioned. Only one social group, the *Gypsies, had a repertoire of oral fairytales; these they told among themselves, not as performances for outsiders. William Howitt in *The Rural Life of England* (1837) describes knitting parties then common in the Yorkshire and Lancashire dales; men, women, and children would gather in a neighbour's house, after the day's work was over, for a knitting session, during which:

all the old stories and traditions of the dale come up, and they often get so excited that they say, 'Neighbours, we'll not part tonight', that is, till after twelve o'clock. . . . At Garsdale, the old men sit in companies round the fire, and because they get so intent on knitting and telling stories, they pin cloths on their shins to prevent themselves from getting burnt.

Unfortunately, Howitt was interested in knitting, not folktales, and we learn no more.

Recent interest in *contemporary legends

has led to a better awareness of storytelling as artistic performance, and the interaction of teller and audience. Gillian Bennett has analysed rhetorical strategies and structures used by some individuals when telling personal experiences and contemporary legends (Bennett, 1989). Michael Wilson has collected some 500 stories from young teenagers and analysed their performative techniques, aimed at horrific or humorous effects (Wilson, 1997).

The art of public storytelling is currently enjoying a professional revival, with clubs and festivals flourishing; those taking part use material from many sources worldwide.

See also *CONTEMPORARY LEGENDS, *MEMORATES.

See the introduction and commentaries in Philip, 1992; Doris E. Marrant, *Folklore* 79 (1968), 202–16; Bennett, 1989a; 1989b; Wilson, 1997.

straw bears. A *Plough Monday *visiting custom, confined to the Huntingdonshire and Cambridgeshire area, in which a boy or man was dressed in straw and led from house to house acting like a performing bear. 'It was great fun frightening servant girls and on one occasion a girl strange to the district fainted' (Tebbutt, 1952: 19). The custom was successfully revived in Whittlesey in 1980, and has been performed ever since.

George Frampton, *Whittlesey Straw Bear* (1989); *Folk-Lore* 20 (1909), 202–3; Tebbutt, 1952: 19.

Strutt, Joseph (1749–1802). Apprenticed to an engraver, he later studied at the Royal Academy. He became interested in antiquarian research and used his artistic skills to embellish numerous books on the manners and customs of past ages. His most successful book, published right at the end of his life, was *Glig-Gamena Angel-Deod, or The Sports and Pastimes of the People of England* (1801), subsequently shortened to *The Sports and Pastimes . . .* which went through numerous editions, inspired other antiquary-folklorists such as John *Brand and Henry *Ellis, and is still one of the basic source-books for folklorists and social historians. It brought to light a wealth of material from manuscripts, including a number of invaluable illustrations of games culled from a range of rare sources. At the time of his death, he was writing a work of fiction, which was completed by Walter Scott and published as *Queenhoo Hall* in 1808 and which, although not successful in itself, was a major influence on Scott's developing ideas on the historical novel. Dorson refers to Strutt, and not without justification, as the 'Father of English Antiquaries'.

Dorson, 1968: 30–1; *DNB*.

stumbling. The idea that it is a bad omen to stumble is one of the few superstitions which have sufficient documentary record to indicate a clear lineage in English folk belief back to medieval times and beyond, with a relatively unchanged meaning. The list of citations in England starts in 1180 with Nigel De Longchamps, *Mirror for Fools*, and includes Spenser, *Shepheardes Calendar* (1579), *SCOT (1584), Shakespeare, Webster, *AUBREY, and many more right through to the 20th century. Stumbling on the way out means your journey or mission will go badly, stumbling on the way in (e.g. at the threshold) means that danger or ill luck lurks inside. Opie and Tatem provide all the main references, and two much earlier ones: Plutarch (*c*.110 AD) and Saint Augustine of Hippo (*c*.396 AD). Particularly ill-omened, however, is to stumble in a graveyard (Shakespeare, *Romeo and Juliet* (1592), v. iii).

See also *STAIRS.

Opie and Tatem, 1989: 380–1.

Sturbridge Fair. Generally agreed to have been the greatest of all the fairs in England, Sturbridge was founded by charter *c*.1211 and continued into the 19th century. The last day of the fair was devoted to a horse fair, at which an interesting initiation ceremony took place, at the Robin Hood Inn. A detailed account appears in Hone's *Year Book* (1832), written by someone who underwent the ceremony about 1762.

Hone, 1827: 1299–1307; Hone, 1832: 769–74; William Addison, *English Fairs and Markets* (1953), 42–50; Daniel Defoe, *A Tour Through the Whole of Great Britain* (1724–6).

styes. Two traditional cures for a stye which do not have an obvious scientific basis are to rub the eye with a *gold ring or a *cat's tail, although in many cases there are further stipulations, as some authorities insist on nine strokes of the tail, a black cat, a full moon, and so on. The ring cure at least is of some antiquity, as shown by lines in Beaumont and Fletcher's play *The Mad Lover* (*c*.1622, v. iv): 'I have a sty here, Chilax; I have no gold to cure it, not a penny'. Forbes also quotes a Middle English verbal *charm to accompany the application of a lotion.

Black, 1883: 151; *N&Q* 1s:2 (1850), 37; 9s:5 (1900), 104, 212–13; 9s:6 (1900), 134; 181 (1941), 344; 182 (1942), 23; Forbes, 1971: 293–316; 'Queer West-Country Remedies of To-Day', *Cassell's Saturday Journal* (17 May 1893).

Sugar-and-Water Day, sugar-cupping. Two of the names for a widespread children's custom which entailed visiting a particular well or spring and mixing the water with sugar or sweets to make a special drink, on a particular day of the year. The day, the name, and the other details vary from place to place. See *ASCENSION DAY, *EASTER, *ELECAMPANE, *SPANISH SUNDAY.

suicide. There is some confusion about the burial of suicides, reflecting the fact that legally they were criminals if sane, but not if 'the balance of mind was disturbed'. Up to 1823, those found guilty of the crime given a degrading burial in the roadway, possibly at a *crossroads, and/or staked; after that date, and at all periods for the insane, it was left to the clergy to decide whether churchyard burial could be allowed or not. One solution was to lay the suicide on the *north side (MacDonald and Murphy, 1990).

See *BURIAL, IRREGULAR, *CROSSROADS, *NORTH.

sun. One of the chief *origin theories proposed by 19th-century scholars, especially Max Müller, was that numerous seasonal customs, from *bonfires to *cheese rolling, originally celebrated, encouraged, or mimicked the solar cycle. Arguments for the solar interpretation of fire festivals can be found in *Frazer's *Golden Bough*, though on balance he thinks it likelier that they were designed to ward off evil.

Actual English folk beliefs concerning the sun are few. It was said to be lucky to dance at dawn on *Easter Day, when people would climb hills in the hope of seeing this sight, or try to catch its reflection in pails of water. Occasionally, children were told it was wicked to point at the sun, and you could be struck dead for doing so. More commonly, women maintained that direct sunlight on the hearth would 'put the fire out', and would draw curtains or place screens to prevent this; this may have developed from a medieval idea that if a house was on fire, sunshine could extinguish the blaze (Opie and Tatem, 1989: 381).

See *RIGHTWARD MOVEMENT.

Sunday, see *DAYS OF THE WEEK, *SABBATH-BREAKING.

sunwise, see *RIGHTWARD MOVEMENT.

superstitions. Some recent folklorists shun the term 'superstition' as being too pejorative, preferring the less value-laden 'belief'. This, however, is too broad a term and, for convenience, we have kept the older word, emboldened by the fact that it is universally understood, and that few 'believers' find its normal use offensive. It only becomes so when used by adherents of one religion, or by atheists, to vilify the religious beliefs and practices of others—issues far outside the scope of this work.

Dictionary definitions of the word regularly invoke the ideas of fear, irrationality, ignorance, groundless belief; folklorists can broadly accept this, while giving added emphasis to the communal and traditional nature of the genre. Its Latin etymology is somewhat obscure; numerous writers interpret its root ('standing over') as implying survival from ancient times, but the *OED* declares this unlikely. Victorian evolutionary *survivalists considered them the tattered remnants of archaic religious and scientific beliefs, made obsolete by intellectual progress, though there is little real evidence for this. Nevertheless it is commonly asserted by popular authors and the general public that superstitions date back for thousands of years, and are direct survivals of attempts by primitive humans to explain and control their environment. The fallacy, as so often, arises from a failure to distinguish form from content. Even if it be agreed that the early human worldview was 'superstitious' in modern terms (a point still debatable), it does not follow that particular items of the modern repertoire date from that time. By analogy: we can be pretty sure early humans liked singing, but we know the song 'White Christmas' is not prehistoric. Yet 'explanations' based on this assumption are now so firmly fixed in the public mind as to become traditional themselves (e.g. that *touching wood dates from when people believed in tree spirits).

Even without adequate definition, one can identify some of the patterns, formulas, and basic principles controlling modern superstitions. (*a*) They aim to 'accentuate the positive/eliminate the negative': do this for good luck, avoid that to prevent bad luck. (*b*) Luck can be influenced, but not completely controlled. (*c*) Do not transgress category boundaries, for example wild flowers or open umbrellas (outdoor items) should not be indoors. (*d*) To seem too confident about the future is 'tempting fate' and attracts retribution—'Don't count your chickens before they hatch'. (*e*) Some days or times are lucky or (more usually) unlucky; they vary in frequency (*midnight, *Friday, *Friday the thirteenth, *Holy Innocents Day), and can be individual—'Tuesday is always my lucky day'. (*f*) Something that begins well (or badly) will probably continue that way. (*g*) As in *magic, things once physically linked retain a link even when separated (birds using your hair in their nests will give you a headache). (*h*) Evil forces exist and are actively working to harm you; these may be impersonal, or concentrated in humans (witches, ill-wishers) or other beings (devils, fairies). (*i*) Certain things, words, or actions have powerfully negative effects, and must be avoided or counteracted (*taboo). (*j*) Anything sudden, unexpected, or unusual can be seen as an *omen, usually of misfortune. However, many superstitions do not fit these categories, and individuals can invent their own (e.g. 'Must get back to bed before the toilet stops flushing').

Many have wondered why superstition persists despite improvements in religion, logic, and science. For Gilbert White in 1776, it is because of habits formed when young and imbibed with our mother's milk (White, 1789: letter xxviii). For *Melton (1620) and Igglesden (*c.*1932), it is because astrologers, fortune-tellers, and local cunning men/women deliberately foster credulity for profit; for Puritans of the 16th century onwards, it was due to Roman Catholic priests. Some maintain that rationalism must not be allowed to remove all the romance and mystery of life, and enjoy the idea of 'more things in heaven and earth . . .'. Others point to the distress superstition brings, for example the lifelong guilt felt by a woman who believed she had caused her brother's death at sea by washing clothes on New Year's Day (Gill, 1993: 105–6; cf. Balleine, 1939). At a general level, it is clear that the hold of superstition on people's minds has weakened over the centuries, and that it is increasingly consigned to trivial areas of everyday life.

In autumn 1998, the present authors sent out a questionnaire asking respondents to write down any superstitions they knew, in order to assess the current repertoire; we made clear that we were not asking what they *believed*, only what they knew of. Ten spaces were provided, and respondents were told they could add more items if they wished. Our hypothesis was that most English people nowadays know only a relatively small number of superstitions, which will tend to be the same ones. The first 215 replies received showed this was indeed the case; few of the items reported were uncommon, and many appeared time and again. It seems unlikely that further results will change the basic pattern. The following summary gives the number of times the 'Top Ten' items were mentioned, the percentage (of 215) this represents, and the date of the first known reference to the belief in Britain, taken from Opie and Tatem.

1. 178	83%	Unlucky to walk under a ladder (1787)
2. 144	67%	Lucky/Unlucky to meet black cat (1620) (More respondents said 'lucky' than 'unlucky'; several commented 'don't know which')
3. 117	54%	Unlucky to break a mirror (1777) (Most specified 'seven years' bad luck')
4. 102	47%	Unlucky to see one magpie, lucky to see two, etc. (c.1780)
5. 94	44%	Unlucky to spill salt (1584?) (Most mentioned throwing a pinch over the shoulder to counteract bad luck)
6. 85	39%	Unlucky to open umbrella indoors (1883)
7. 78	36%	Thirteen unlucky/Friday the thirteenth unlucky (1711/1913) (These related items were given in about equal numbers; some gave both)
8. 76	35%	Unlucky to put shoes on table (1869) (Most specified new shoes)
9. 45	21%	Unlucky to pass someone on the stairs (1865)
10. 34	16%	Lucky to touch wood (1877)

These dates suggest a fairly rapid turnover in superstitions. Only one (spilling salt) can be dated to the 16th century, via a vague allusion to those 'that make great divinations upon the spilling of salt' (Scot, 1584: book 11, chapter 15). Another (black cat) can be traced to the 17th century, four to the 18th, four to the 19th; one (Friday the thirteenth) to the 20th only. It is also instructive to compare this list with that given by John *Melton in *Astrologaster* (1620), reprinted in *FLS News* 32 (2000), 9–10. Many of his items are still known, but do not appear among our Top Ten (e.g. cat washing face, cheek/ear burning); conversely, only one of our Top Ten (black cat) was reported by him.

Opie and Tatem, 1989; Igglesden, c.1932.

Surrey Puma, see *ALIEN BIG CATS.

Survey of English Dialects, see *ENGLISH DIALECT SURVEY.

Survey of English Folklore. Founded in 1955 as a new research project directed by Professor A. H. Smith, Head of the English Department at University College London, and Honorary Director of the English Place Name Survey, and funded by donations from Mrs Lake Barnett, stalwart of the *Folklore Society. The Survey's objective was 'To conduct a survey of English folklore', on a systematic basis, 'and to record it in an archive of folklore material'. The Survey was the first of several attempts in post-war England to provide folklore studies with a presence in a higher academic institution, although no teaching programme was planned. However, during its existence, and despite the shared institutional background at University College, and the shared key figure of Mrs Lake Barnett, relations between the Survey and the Folklore Society were strained. In her Presidential Address for 1958 (*Folklore* 69 (1958), 73–92) Sona Rosa Burstein took a clear side-swipe at the Survey, which was answered by Dodgson in his *Museums Journal* piece later in the year, and the points at issue were primarily the fate of the considerable sums of money involved, and the slowness in seeing results. In retrospect, it is clear that the University had no lasting commitment to the project and allowed it to wither as the individuals involved moved on to other interests. By the early 1960s, the Survey had faded away, and no further work was done. It must now be seen as one of the great missed opportunities of post-war folklore studies in England. The Survey's collected material can be accessed via the Folklore Society.

For other academic folklore programmes, see *INSTITUTE OF DIALECT AND FOLKLIFE STUD-IES, *NATIONAL CENTRE FOR ENGLISH CULTURAL TRADITION.

John McNeal Dodgson, *Museums Journal* 58:2 (May 1958), 26–33.

survivals theory. One of the big ideas, proposed by *Tylor and others, which helped 19th-century folklorists aspire to scientific respectability, although it has long been widely discredited. Its ultimate origin lies in attempts to apply the principles and insights of evolution to human cultures and institutions, and is based on the assertion that cultures develop in a series of identifiable stages, from savage to civilized. As each culture evolves, it is argued, certain aspects live on relatively unchanged, gradually losing their original purpose and meaning, and thus become folklore in the care of the uneducated, conservative, and uncreative 'common people'. Thus a serious religious belief may become a superstition, a ritual become a calendar custom, or a burial custom become a children's game. Given this knowledge, a folklorist can examine recent or modern folklore and use it to reconstruct the mind and practices of previous cultural stages, and thus elucidate both the past and the present. Indeed, for many of the early writers such as George Laurence *Gomme and J. G. *Frazer, this elucidation was the main work of the folklorist. The researcher's task was considerably simplified by the idea that the stages of cultural evolution were held to be relatively predictable the world over, although they are not synchronous. Thus, so-called primitive societies of the recent past such as Australian Aborigines or North American Indians can be used as evidence for the study of, say, Celtic Britons.

At its crudest, survival theory takes a particularly cavalier attitude to both history and geography. Argument proceeds by piling up supposedly relevant examples from various cultures and periods until the sheer weight of numbers overwhelms the critical faculties of the reader. Indeed, writers such as Andrew *Lang make a virtue of this 'comparative' method:

Our method, then, is to compare the seemingly meaningless customs or manners of civilised races with the similar customs and manners which exist among the uncivilised and still retain their meaning. It is not necessary for comparison of this sort that the uncivilised and the civilised race should be of the same stock, nor need we prove that they were ever in contact with each other. Similar conditions of mind produce similar practices, apart from identity of race or borrowing of ideas and manners. '(*Custom and Magic* (new edn., 1904), 21–2)

As the 20th century progressed, the theory was gradually rejected by anthropologists and other social scientists, although it held its ground for a considerable time in Folklore Studies, and in watered-down form became accepted by popular writers as the basis of almost all folklore commentary. It promotes the extremely widespread assumption that all our superstitions and customs are thousands of years old, and, as its basis is purely conjectural, it can be used to support any view which is fashionable at the time, whether sun or moon worship, fertility, phallic symbols, female deities, or Freudian or Jungian psychology.

Swaffham Pedlar. When the parish church of Swaffham (Norfolk) was rebuilt in the 1460s, one benefactor contributing to the costs was its churchwarden, a rich local merchant called John Chapman. His family pew showed carvings of a pedlar with his pack, and a man and woman in a shop; these figures, together with memories of John Chapman's wealth, inspired the following story, recorded first in 1653 and again in 1699:

A pedlar living in Swaffham dreamed three times that if he went to London Bridge he would hear very joyful news. So he travelled to London and waited on the Bridge for three days, and nothing happened, till on the third day, a shopkeeper who had noticed him hanging about asked him what he was doing. So he told his story, and the Londoner laughed at him for being such a fool as to believe in dreams. 'I'll tell you, country fellow,' said he, 'I dreamed only last night that I was at Swaffham, a place I don't know, and thought I'd find a vast treasure under an oak tree, in an orchard, behind a pedlar's house. But I'm not such a fool as to make a long journey because of a silly dream. Be like me, good fellow—go home, and see to your business.' So the pedlar went straight home, dug, and found the treasure. In gratitude to God, he paid for the church to be repaired, and had a statue of himself as pedlar put up there.

The plot of this tale is international, and variants were told of Lealholme Hall (Yorkshire), and also in Somerset, Lancashire, and Cornwall (Westwood, 1985: 161–4).

swallows. To have swallows nesting on or near one's house is a sign of good luck. To destroy or rob the nests would bring misfortune; cows would give bloody *milk, or someone would break a leg, or in one case a family was ruined when the bank they owned collapsed (Henderson, 1866: 91).

sweeping. A handful of beliefs centre on the act of sweeping, in addition to those connected with the *broom itself. Sweeping dust out of the house is ill-advised: 'A Lincolnshire maidservant explained to me some years ago that it was wrong "to sweep out at the door, for fear of sweeping luck away"' (N&Q 9s:6 (1900), 393). On a different tack: 'In Suffolk, the people say that if after sweeping a room the broom is accidentally left up in a corner, strangers will visit the house in the course of that day' (Dyer, 1881: 126).

sweeps, see *CHIMNEY-SWEEPS.

swifts. Because of their perpetual rapid flight and shrill cries, swifts were regarded as evil birds, demonic counterparts to the benevolent martin and swallow; in some counties they were called 'Devil birds' or 'screech devils'. In Leicestershire, they were identified with the *Seven Whistlers (Swainson, 1885: 95).

'swimming' ordeal. One way of testing people suspected of *witchcraft was to throw them into water with their hands tied to their feet. Those who sank were thought innocent, and hauled back to land; to float proved guilt, because water, the holy element of baptism, would reject a witch. This form of ordeal originated on the Continent; from the early 17th century it was widely but unofficially used in England, though it had no legal standing and most judges disapproved of it (Davies, 1999a: 86–100).

After 1736, when witchcraft was no longer a crime, 'swimming' persisted as a form of lynching, in which the old ordeal was confused with ducking as punishment, often to the point where life was endangered. Over a dozen cases are recorded from the 18th century, including one at Tring (Hertfordshire) in

1751 where the leader of a mob was hanged for drowning a woman; public sympathy was on his side, and his wife and daughter assured him he was dying in a good cause (Hone, 1827: i. 1045–8; Sharpe, 1996: 1–5). Even in the 19th century there are long reports in *The Times* of 24 September 1863 and 10 March 1864 of a prosecution arising from the death by pneumonia of a *deaf-and-dumb old *fortune-teller at Sible Hedingham (Essex), who was repeatedly ducked in a river after a woman claimed he bewitched her (summarized in FLS News 25 (1997), 15–16; 26 (1997), 4–5).

sword dance. Those found in England are called 'linked' or 'hilt and point' dances to distinguish them from other types of dance using real swords. In the linked sword dance, participants hold the handle of their own 'sword' in one hand, and the point of their neighbour's sword in the other, thus making a linked circle. The 'swords' are either long thin lathes of wood or strips of flexible metal with a swivelling wooden handle at each end. The type of sword also distinguishes the two basic types of dance, respectively: Longsword and Rapper. Longsword is danced with a basic walking step, while Rapper dancers execute a special step which beats a staccato rhythm on the floor, and as the Rappers are shorter than the wooden swords their dance is much tighter and apparently faster.

Examples of linked sword dances have been widely documented over most of Europe since the Middle Ages, with the earliest being found in the Low Countries in the late 14th century. Excellent pictorial evidence exists in the form of paintings such as *The Fair of St George's Day* by Pieter Bruegel the Elder (c.1560) (reproduced in Corrsin, 1997: plate 1). Evidence from England, however, is extremely rare from before the 18th century, and the earliest references are ambiguous. In John Marston's play *The Malcontent* (1604), a character claims he can 'doe the sword dance with any morris-dauncer in Christendom', and the Lancashire gentleman William Blundell recorded a 'Prologue to a sword dance, spoken at Lathom upon Ash Wednesday, 1638'. His grandson, Nicholas Blundell, recorded in his diary for July 1712 the preparations for events to celebrate the completion of a marl-pit on his farm, including garlands, maypole, and sword dance. Blundell records making the costumes and teaching the dance to the men (all quoted in Corrsin, 1997: 93–4). These do not add up to strong evidence for an indigenous custom, and more convincing references do not start appearing until much later in the 18th century. Commenting on the paucity of evidence before that time, Corrsin writes: 'It is as though sword dancing suddenly blossomed in the second half of the 18th century without antecedents' (p. 183). The fact that this could also be said of the *mumming play must at present be put down to coincidence, but may prove more significant after further research.

Sword dance scholarship on the Continent was marred by romanticism and extreme nationalism, and although English commentators avoided the excesses of the latter they had no qualms about the former. Until quite recently, almost without exception, writers have assumed that the dances are a *survival of an ancient custom, concerned with fertility, midwinter sun worship, ritual death and resurrection, and so on. Even on the Continent there is little reason to believe that the sword dance is any older than the Middle Ages, and in England, as has been seen, there is no evidence that it is much more than 200 years old. Attempts to prove a connection between the dances and early trade guilds have also proved unconvincing. The first systematic collection of English sword dances was made by Cecil *Sharp, whose books remain a key source of information on the movements and music of the dances. Sharp was, however, primarily interested in the dances as performance and his publications are thus essential for practitioners but his speculations on history and development are now outmoded. Earlier material was often vague and unsystematic, but it is clear that the tradition was only active in the north of England, in Yorkshire, Northumberland, and County Durham, although some tantalizing references indicate possible dances in Cumberland. In these counties, the dancers are mentioned frequently by 19th-century folklorists and other writers as an essential part of *Christmas or *New Year celebrations, *visiting homes and farms and performing in town and village streets. The 20th century found the traditions in definite decline. Many teams had ceased to function completely, and others performed intermittently. It is certainly true that the interest engendered by the work of Sharp and others enthused by his example resulted in the survival or revival of a number of teams which would have otherwise simply faded away.

There are strong connections between the sword dancers and two other *calendar customs—*plough stots and *mumming plays. In some areas the sword dancers accompanied, or were part of, the groups of farmworkers who carried round a plough at Christmas or *Plough Monday, collecting money to be used for a feast or dance, or simply for drink for themselves. Terminology is also confusing—the sword dancers could be called morris dancers, plough stots, mummers, and so on. Some sword dance traditions included a dramatic element in their performance, and these are normally counted as one of the three distinct types of *mumming play, in which a character is killed by having the swords placed around his neck. Even where there is no developed play, sword dance teams often included extra characters, such as a Fool and Female (a man dressed as a woman) called Bessy or Besty, and many also had 'calling-on songs' in which the dancers were introduced

Corrsin, 1997; Sharp, 1911–13; Helm, 1981; E. C. Cawte, *FMJ* 4:2 (1982), 79–116.

taboos. Rules explicitly forbidding people to do some specific thing, often petty in itself, on pain of serious ill luck, or failure in some enterprise (as opposed to a mere belief that an action is unlucky). Current English examples are the bans on saying 'pig', 'rat', or 'rabbit' at sea, whistling at sea or in the *theatre, and mentioning *Macbeth*. Until recently, there were also taboos on doing seasonal things out of season, for example putting up *Christmas decorations before Christmas Eve or eating festive foods on the wrong dates, but commercial pressures have eroded many of these. Most people, however, still avoid singing carols except during a few weeks either side of Christmas.

A taboo on speaking often features in tales about attempts to recover lost *bells and buried *treasures, in *divination, and in magical procedures such as catching *fernseed, all of which must be performed in silence.

tag, see *TIG.

talking. A sudden lull in the conversation is not random, some believe, but usually occurs at twenty minutes past or to the hour, and is occasioned by angels passing by. Opie and Tatem give several references to this idea, starting with one from Wales in 1909. They also show that the Romans had a belief about sudden silences, quoting Pliny's *Natural History* (AD 77). Some families or communities had little rituals to cover sudden silences, such as one reported from Durham: If silence suddenly fell, someone would break it by saying 'silence in the pork shop', which had an implied response—'and let the old sow speak' (*FLS News* 12 (1991), 7). It is also thought to be significant if two people say the same thing at the same time, or if one just anticipates the other. In the latter case the one who spoke will marry before the other (current since at least 1738), whereas simultaneous speakers should

link little fingers and make a wish. A complex ceremony is reported from a 13-year-old girl from Bath, in 1935:

When two people say the same thing at the same moment without saying anything further, they hook right-hand little fingers, say the name of a poet (not Shakespeare or Burns (which spears or burns your wish) silently make a wish, and then one says, 'I wish, I wish your wish come true', and the other replies, 'I wish, I wish the same to you'. But if you both said the same poet that invalidated the whole thing. (Opie and Tatem, 1989: 368)

Several other isolated beliefs about talking have been recorded. According to Leather (1912: 86) if you accidentally speak in rhyme you can expect a present before the end of the month. Igglesden (*c.*1932: 229) reports that it was unlucky to talk when passing under a railway bridge. To get your words in the wrong order means a stranger on the way (Lean, 1903: ii. 318). In modern times it is common to say that talking to yourself is 'the first sign of madness', but according to *N&Q* it means you will die a violent death (quoted Lean, 1903: ii. 305).

See also *BACKWARDS, *DUMB CAKE, *LOVE DIVINATION.

Opie and Tatem, 1989: 95, 367–8; Lean, 1903: ii. 305, 318–20.

tall stories. These are anecdotes about astonishing exploits and adventures, for example in hunting, or about animals or objects of astounding size—such as a sailing ship with masts so tall that any lad sent up as a midshipman will have grey in his beard by the time he comes back down. Tall stories are usually told by men; the teller knows them to be inventions, but presents them as truth, and sometimes as an alleged personal experience or boast, to test the credulity of the hearers as the realistic opening gradually leads to an impossible (though not supernatural) climax.

A fine example of the genre is a story told,

according to the *Surrey Gazette* of 7 November 1865, by 'a boy who was begging in the streets of Plymouth the other day':

He said he was a cabin boy on board an American liner, and for some of his mischievous pranks was headed up in a water cask, with only the bung-hole to breathe through. On the following night a squall came up, and the ship went down with all on board, except himself, the cask containing him having rolled over into the sea on a sudden lurch of the vessel. Fortunately, it kept bung up, and after thirty hours floating he was cast on the coast, where after he had made desperate eforts to release himself he gave himself up to die. Some cows strolling along the beach were attracted to the cask, and one of them accidentally slipped her tail into the bung-hole, which the boy grasped immediately, and kept fast holding with admirable resolution. The cow started off, and after running about three hundred yards the cask struck against a rock and broke to pieces.

tankerabogus. A Somerset and Devon name for an imaginary *bogey, used for threatening children into good behaviour: 'Now, Polly, yu've abin a bad, naughty maid, and ef yu be sich a wicked cheel again, I'll zend vor tankerabogus tu come and car' yu away tu 'is pittee-awl [pit-hole]' (Wright, 1913: 198).

Tandering, see *ST ANDREW'S DAY.

tansy. In the Cambridgeshire fens people held two oddly contradictory beliefs about the medical effects of this plant. Couples anxious to have children ate tansy leaves as a salad, on the theory that rabbits like the plant and are notorious breeders; but also, women wanting to end a pregnancy chewed tansy leaves to provoke miscarriage (Porter, 1969: 10).

In northern counties, it is regularly mentioned as an ingredient in cakes and puddings, especially at *Easter in remembrance of the 'bitter herbs' of the Passover, and an infusion of tansy could be drunk as tea. There are numerous references to tansy cakes in the *OED*, dating back to the 15th century.

tea, coffee. Samuel Pepys recorded his first cup of tea on 25 September 1660, and also reported that the apothecary told his wife it would be 'good for her, for her cold and defluxions' (28 June 1667). The first known reference to reading coffee or tea grounds for a glimpse of the future appears 60 years later, but if it is to be taken literally, it indicates that this was not a brand-new idea:

Advice is hereby given, that there is lately arrived in this City, the Famous Mrs. Cherry, the only Gentlewoman truly Learned in that Occult Science of Tossing of Coffee Grounds; who has ... for some time past, practiced, to the General Satisfaction of her Female Visitants ... (*Dublin Weekly Journal* (11 June 1726), 4, quoted in Opie and Tatem, 1989).

Several other 18th century writers mention the custom, in terms of familiarity, and as a predominantly female pastime: 'true-love-knots lurked in the bottom of the teacup', as Oliver Goldsmith commented (*Vicar of Wakefield* (1766), chapter 10). Tea-leaf reading became commonplace in the 19th and 20th centuries and books devoted to the art were published, each putting forward a relatively simple but structured approach to reading the signs.

A different tea omen predicts a stranger on the way if a tea-leaf or stalk is found floating on the surface of the tea. This was reported from the mid-19th century right through to the 1980s, in a relatively stable form. Another sign of a stranger coming was to accidentally leave the teapot lid open, which was again reported from the 1850s until the 1980s and is probably not dead yet. A few other items of tea-lore have surfaced over the years: 'To put milk into one's tea before sugar, is to "cross" the love of the party so doing', as an item of north of England folklore (*N&Q* 4s:2 (1868), 553), which is confirmed by a later correspondent (4s:10 (1872), 495). Two people should avoid pouring from the same pot, for varying reasons but usually concerned with pregnancy, for example: 'one of them will have ginger-headed twins within a year' (*Folk-Lore* 51 (1940), 117). Bubbles on the tea denoted money, or kisses.

See also *SPOON.

Opie and Tatem, 1989: 390–3.

Teddy Rowe's Band. In the morning of Old Michaelmas Day (10 October) in Sherborne, Dorset, the coming of Pack Monday Fair was formerly signalled by Teddy Rowe's Band. The Band was composed of young people who paraded the streets making as much discordant noise as possible on horns, bugles, whistles, tin trays, saucepans, and so on. The origin story explains that Teddy Rowe was the master mason employed in the 15th century to build the great fan vault in the nave of the Abbey Church. When the work was completed, the workmen packed their tools and paraded in triumph around the town. This neatly explains the procession and the name 'Pack Monday' for the fair itself. Teddy Rowe's Band was suppressed in the 1960s because of the potential for rowdyism it offered. The signalling of a fair with a discordant band is not unique (see *Tin Can Band), and such a noisy gathering is also a core feature of *rough music ceremonies.

Hole, 1976: 291–2; Wright and Lones, 1940: iii. 95–6.

teeth. Any departure from the normal pattern in the way a baby cuts its first tooth could be significant. Teeth usually show through the lower gums first; 'If a child tooths first in the upper jaw, it is considered ominous of its dying in its infancy' (Brand, 1849: ii. 87). The belief was still remembered in Halifax in 1957, when a man told Iona Opie: 'They used to say that a child who cut the first tooth upward was almost sure to live; if the first tooth was cut downward it was not so sure to live.' To cut teeth unusually early was also thought meaningful, but there were two interpretations. One, recorded in 1659 in the proverb 'Soon todd [toothed], soon with God', was that the baby would soon be dead; the other, expressed in a later proverb 'Soon teeth, soon toes', was that the mother would quickly be pregnant again.

If any teeth were already showing at the child's birth, this was taken to mean that he or she would grow up vicious. Richard III was supposed to have been born thus, according to Shakespeare (3 *Henry the Sixth*, v. vi). In the 1950s, Christina Hole wrote:

To be born with teeth is an extremely bad sign. The usual theory is that it foretells death by violence, but one midwife informed me a few years ago that the true meaning is even worse. 'I never speak of it,' she said, 'and if anyone asks me I deny it, for the sake of the mother; but it means the child will grow up to be a murderer.' It is possible that this is the older form of the superstition. A milder version gives it as a sign of a very bad temper; and in some districts it has been watered down to a vague prophecy of simple bad luck [*Folklore* 68 (1957), 413]. By 1987, a correspondent writing to the *Daily Mirror* [28 August 1987, p. 20] reports being puzzled by two contrasting beliefs—one, that such a child will be extremely clever, the other that he or she is born to be hanged.

If a child was having difficulty cutting its first teeth, a little bag containing animal's teeth or adult human teeth might be hung round its neck as a *charm. In London around 1905 calf's teeth were sold in street markets for this purpose, but it was far more common for girls and young women to keep any of their own teeth which had been extracted, to help their babies later (Lovett, 1925: 25–6). In Herefordshire at about the same period, the bag held woodlice, or a few hairs from the cross on a *donkey's back (Leather, 1912: 70, 81); in Shropshire, a necklace of *rowan twigs was worn (Burne, 1883: 195).

When a milk tooth fell out, it was important to dispose of it correctly. One method, known to Aubrey (1686/1880: 11) and still widely used up to the mid-20th century, was to throw it in the fire at once, often after rubbing salt on it, and sometimes saying a charm:

> Fire, fire, burn a bone,
> God send me another tooth again;
> A straight one,
> A white one,
> And in the same place.

or:

> Black tooth, blue tooth,
> Please God send me a new tooth —

which, as a correspondent from Sheffield noted in the *Guardian* (letters page, 20 Oct. 1988), 'never failed to work'. One traditional explanation was that if the tooth was simply discarded with other rubbish, a dog or pig might gnaw it, in which case the child's new tooth would be misshapen, like the animal's. Throughout the 20th century, an alternative way of treating a milk tooth has become ever more popular: to hide it overnight under the child's pillow, so that fairies, or the *Tooth Fairy, will take it away and leave a coin instead. This playful gift-giving is pleasanter for all concerned.

An idea current to the end of the 19th century, but now obsolete, was that fallen or extracted teeth (whether of child or adult) must either be immediately burned, or eventually buried with their owner, ready for *Doomsday; otherwise, one would have to hunt for them in a bucket of blood in Hell. In Derbyshire, people stored their teeth in jars, to be placed in their coffins eventually, since 'when you go to heaven you will have to account for all the teeth you have had upon earth' (Addy, 1895: 125). Occasionally, malevolent magic was feared; at Westleigh (Devon) in the 19th century, women kept all their extracted teeth carefully hidden 'to prevent enemies or dogs getting hold of them' (Elworthy, 1895: 437).

Radford, Radford, and Hole, 1961: 336–9; Opie and Tatem, 1989: 393–5.

theatre. Actors and theatre-workers appear to be one of the most superstitious of all occupational groups, and indeed many seem to regard being superstitious as a badge of the trade. Many of the superstitions are well known—*whistling anywhere in a theatre being very unlucky, and *Macbeth* being so unlucky as to be referred to as 'The Scottish Play' rather than by its real name. Others are less well known—actors will not say the last lines of a play in rehearsal, to place an umbrella on a table during rehearsals spells disaster, and some unlucky tunes—such as 'Three Blind Mice' and 'I dreamt I dwelt in Marble Halls'—are studiously avoided. Knowlson also devotes some paragraphs to the beliefs of 'front-of-house' staff such as ushers and box-office workers. Few of the reported superstitions can be traced back before 1900, and most are considerably later. Some exceptions are those printed in the *Folk-Lore Record* of 1879 which include a dislike of the colour blue for costumes, unless counteracted by silver, the dread of rehearsals on Sundays, and the belief that if the first customer to enter the auditorium on the first night is a woman the play is doomed.

Folk-Lore Record 2 (1879), 203–5; Opie and Tatem, 1989: 228, 395–7; Knowlson, *The Origins of Popular Superstitions and Customs* (1930), 225–9; J. B. Booth, *Pink Parade* (1933), 95–116; Roy Harley Lewis, *Theatre Ghosts* (1988).

thirteen. In medieval England, thirteen was not ill-omened. It was associated either with the 'extra' item customarily added to the dozen when selling certain produce, for example buns or eggs (hence 'baker's dozen'); or with groups of twelve-plus-a-leader, modelled on Christ and the Apostles. By the end of the 17th century, a belief had developed that if thirteen people sat down to a meal together, this meant one of them would die within a year; the first known reference is in *The Athenian Mercury* for June 1695, in an anecdote about a lady who was warned by the ghost of a friend that she would shortly die in these circumstances (reprinted by the editor of Aubrey's *Miscellanies* in 1857, pp. 207–8). The explanation suggested, both then and now, is that at the Last Supper one of the thirteen present, *Judas Iscariot, was the first to leave the table and killed himself soon afterwards.

From the 1890s onwards, thirteen was con-

sidered unlucky in various other contexts, for example as the number of a hotel room or a house; as the belief grew stronger in the 20th century, such items were often renumbered as '12A' or omitted entirely. *Friday the thirteenth came to be particularly dreaded. Further explanations now sometimes offered are that there are thirteen witches in a *coven, and that the Death card is the thirteenth tarot trump. However, there is a counter-belief that thirteen is 'lucky for some' in bingo and other games of chance.

Opie and Tatem, 1989: 397–9.

thomasing. An annual custom which was found all over England on 21 December (St Thomas's Day) whereby the poor people of a village visited the houses of their better-off neighbours requesting food and/or provisions to help them through the winter. What was given varied considerably from place to place, but was usually governed by local rules and sanctioned by long custom—a measure of wheat, a stone of flour, a candle, some coal, and so on. Unusually for a *visiting custom, nothing was offered in exchange by the callers in most areas, although there are occasional mentions of a rhyme being recited or a piece of mistletoe or holly being given. Under the name 'Gooding', the earliest reference to the custom is in John Stow's *Survey of London* (1560), and it was a regular feature of rural life until it gradually declined through the 19th century as different ways of helping the poor were found, and the well-off turned against 'begging'. In some parishes, the custom was institutionalized into a regular dole organized by parson and squire. Thomasing lasted in a few districts into Edwardian times. Also called Mumping, Corning, and Doleing.

Wright and Lones, 1940: iii. 200–7; Brand, 1849: i. 455–7.

Thoms, William John (1803–85). His working life was spent as a civil servant. He showed early promise as a literary-antiquarian, and, encouraged by established figures such as Francis *Douce, was soon editing neglected literary materials, beginning with a three-volume edition of *Early Prose Romances* (1827–8). Thoms was a key figure in the development of British folklore; he invented the word itself, launched *Notes & Queries* [N&Q], one of the main vehicles for information exchange, and was instrumental in the formation of the *Folklore Society.

By the 1840s, it was clear that a new field of enquiry was emerging from the activities of antiquarians and historians, and a burgeoning interest in what is now called folklore. Various phrases had been suggested or used—'popular antiquities' being a front-runner—but when Thoms wrote to the *Athenaeum* (under the pseudonym 'Ambrose Merton') to suggest a regular column in which enthusiasts could exchange information, he coined the term 'Folk Lore' to cover it. The column soon outgrew the *Athenaeum*, and Thoms launched the weekly *Notes & Queries* on 3 November 1849, which he himself edited until 1872. It was fitting that, in the 1870s, when the need for a society devoted to the collection and publication of folklore was felt, it was a suggestion published in *Notes & Queries* in 1876, and the subsequent correspondence on the subject, which persuaded Thoms to give his backing to the formation of the Folk-Lore Society and to serve as its first Director. Thoms also gave considerable time to other bodies, serving as secretary of the Camden Society from 1838 to 1873, for example. In retrospect, his talents were as an editor and organizer, rather than as a theorist, and he was content to gather the material which he knew to be important and make it available—with annotations—for others to use, and at this level he was indeed successful.

DNB; Obituary, *N&Q* 6s:12 (1885), 141; Dorson, 1968: 75–80; William J. Thoms, 'Gossip of an Old Bookworm', *The 19th Century* 10 (1881), 63–79, 886–900.

Thread the Needle. A game which can exist independently, as a dance movement, or as part of other customs or festivities. The basic movement is a line of people holding hands, two of whom hold their hands up to make an arch, and the leader goes through the arch with everyone following. Often found in conjunction with *clipping the church, at *Easter, and also as part of the *Midsummer celebrations at Penzance, described in 1801 (R. Polwhele, *History of Cornwall* (1816), i. 49–51).

J. B. Partridge, 'The Game of Thread the Needle and Custom of Church Clipping', *Folk-Lore* 23 (1912), 196–203; Gomme, 1898: ii. 228–32; Opie and Opie, 1985: 33–43.

three, third. By far the most widespread of the traditionally significant *numbers. It is a commonplace in folktales that persons and events are triplicated, the third of the set being often 'weighted' (the third brother the best, the third ogre the fiercest, the third cas-

ket the right one, etc.). In folk rhymes there is a fondness for groups of three ('triads'), with the third often lengthened to form a climax:

Rub-a-dub-dub! Three men in a tub,
The butcher, the baker, the candlestick-maker . . .

One flew east, and one flew west,
And one flew over the cuckoo's nest . . .

There is a common saying that 'deaths come in threes', or, less specifically, that 'all good/bad things come in threes'; another is 'third time lucky', or 'third time pays for all'. In rituals of magic, luck, or healing, it is very frequent to find words or actions being repeated three times; the same is often true of prayers and religious gestures. These features appear throughout European tradition, for reasons unknown.

Three Bears, The. When Robert Southey included 'The Story of the Three Bears' in his miscellany entitled *The Doctor* (1837, iv. 327), readers took it for granted that he had invented it himself, even though his narrator claims to have learnt it from an uncle. He tells how a bad-tempered, dirty, thieving old woman gets into the bears' cottage, eats the little bear's porridge, and sleeps in his bed; when discovered, she jumps out of a window and is seen no more, having perhaps broken her neck, or got lost in the woods, or been arrested as a vagrant. The story is delightfully told, with repeated phrases, and imitation of the bears' different voices, and Southey's telling ensured its popularity.

But had he invented it? As early as 1849, Joseph Cundall, retelling it in his *Treasury of Pleasure Books for Young Children*, said it was 'a very old Nursery Tale', better known as 'Silver-Hair', because the intruder was a little girl of that name. For the rest of the century the story was told that way, with the nice little heroine called Silver-Hair or Silverlocks; then, in an anonymous collection of *Old Nursery Stories and Rhymes c.*1904, she was renamed Goldilocks, and this is now standard. Meanwhile, Joseph Jacobs, who had originally regarded the tale as Southey's invention, had come round to agreeing that this was a genuine folktale, since a variant had come to light in which the intruder is neither an old woman nor a child, but a fox called Scrapefoot; there are also partial foreign parallels such as Snow White's arrival at the dwarfs' cottage. Final proof came in 1951, with the discovery of a version written down and illustrated by hand in 1831, as a birthday present for a little boy. This predates Southey; like him, it has an old woman as the villain (Opie and Opie, 1974: 199–205).

Three Blind Mice. Since the 19th century known as a *nursery rhyme, Three Blind Mice was previously an adult round or catch, and the earliest known text, from 1609, is considerably different from the modern version:

> Three blinde mice, three blinde mice
> Dame Iulian, Dame Iulian,
> The miller and his merry olde wife
> She scrapte her tripe licke thou the knife.

See also *THEATRE.

Opie and Opie, 1997: 360–1.

three dishes. A cluster of related divinatory customs, called 'three dishes' after one variant, but better known in Scotland and Ireland (where it often took place at Halloween or at funerals), than in England. In its simplest form, three basins are set out—one with clean water, one with dirty water, and the third empty. Participants are blindfolded and place their hand into one of the bowls, which signifies their future, as, for example, he or she will marry a maiden, a widow, or remain single, respectively. In a version reported from Gloucestershire c.1890 (Folk-Lore 34 (1923), 155), three plates were set out at Halloween, containing gold, a ring, and a thimble, which symbolized a rich marriage, an early marriage, and no marriage. Another variant from Devon (N&Q 3s:2 (1862), 62) had objects placed on the floor of an otherwise empty room, including a turf, basin of water, ring, and so on.

Opie and Tatem, 1989: 120–1.

Three Heads in the Well, The. This is a *fairytale included in a *chapbook of 1764 entitled The History of Four Kings, their Queens and Daughters; it was already popular in Elizabethan times, as is shown by the partial incorporation of its main scene into George Peele's The Old Wives' Tale (1595). According to the chapbook, the King of Colchester's daughter, ill-used by her stepmother, goes off to seek her fortune, shows kindness to a beggar, and comes to a well from which three heads rise one after another, singing 'Wash me, comb me, lay me down softly'; she does so, and they give her such beauty that she marries a king. Her jealous hunchbacked half-sister tries to imitate her, but her meanness and rudeness to the beggar and the heads bring her leprosy, bad

breath, and marriage to a poor cobbler (Opie and Opie, 1974: 156–61; Philip, 1992: 48–52, 55–6).

Three Wise Monkeys. Small statuettes of three monkeys, one covering his eyes, another his ears, and another his mouth, have been popular in Britain since (probably) the 1900s; they are known to have been carried as lucky *charms by soldiers in the First World War. They are identified with a proverbial saying, 'See no evil, hear no evil, speak no evil', first recorded in 1926 and now generally used sarcastically against those who, through selfishness or cowardice, choose to ignore some wrongdoing. A few figurines show the first two monkeys peeping and listening, while the third has a finger on his lips; these may reflect the proverb 'Hear all, see all, say nowt', known since the late Middle Ages.

The Wise Monkeys originated in Japan, where they have been known since the 16th century; statues of them are set at crossroads in honour of Koshin, the God of Roads, whose attendants they are. There, their slogan is Mi-zaru, kika-zaru, iwa-zaru, 'No seeing, no hearing, no speaking', with a pun on saru, Japanese for 'monkey', and it is used seriously to teach prudence and purity.

Wolfgang Mieder, Tradition and Innovation in Folk Literature (1987), 157–77; A. W. Smith, Folklore 104 (1993), 144–50.

threshold. Symbolically, a threshold marks the boundary between a household and the outer world, and hence between belonging and not-belonging, and between safety and danger. Guarding the doorway is an important aspect of magical *house protection, which can involve the threshold. In Tudor and Stuart times this (rather than the door itself) was the usual place to fix *horseshoes, and in some cases the threshold itself was an *iron slab (C. F. Tebbutt, Folklore 91 (1980), 240). Later, there was a custom in some areas of making patterns on well-scrubbed doorsteps, which some people regarded as simply decorative, but others as defensive. Thus, in Herefordshire a pattern of nine *crosses kept witches out (Leather, 1912: 18), and up to about 1900 every Shropshire farmhouse and cottage had its doorstep and hearthstone decorated with patterns made from the pigment produced by squeezing elder or dock leaves, and some still did in the 1930s.

[They] are for the most part very simple—a border of

crosses between two lines; a series of vandykes with or without a circle in the wide part of each vandyke; two large crosses, divided by a vertical line. . . . I can remember that when I was a child, one of our maids used to decorate the back doorstep with a border of loops, and it is an interesting point that these loops had to be done straight round in an unbroken chain. It would have been 'unlucky' to do the top of the step and then break off and do the bottom of it before the sides. . . . These patterns were said to keep the Devil away. . . . Nowadays they say the patterns are 'laid' for luck; or a young woman may say that she does them to 'plaze granny, who dotes on 'em, bein' as they've allus bin laid 'ere'. (L. H. Hayward, *Folk-Lore* 49 (1938), 236–7)

thumbs. A surprising number of gestures and practices of past times involved the thumb. The folding of the thumb into the palm of the hand, with the other fingers closed over it, was believed to be a protection against witches, or general evil:

Some years ago, children in Northumberland were taught to double the thumb within the hand as a preservative from danger, and especially to repel sorcery. It was the custom also to fold the thumbs of dead persons within the hand for the same purpose . . .'. (W. Hutchinson, *View of Northumberland* (1778), quoted in Lean, 1903: ii. 456)

Opie and Tatem give a number of references to this action, commencing with one dated *c*.1350 and running up through the 19th century, although on the strength of the available information it would seem to have been a mainly north country or Scottish practice. The idea that a part of the body itching signifies a future event is well attested in English lore, and this combined with the protective thumb in the hand presumably explains Shakespeare's lines 'By the pricking of my thumbes, Something wicked this way comes' (*Macbeth* IV. i). Nineteenth- and 20th-century references to holding or squeezing thumbs are more akin in meaning to the modern crossing fingers for luck.

Another Shakespeare quotation, 'I will bite my thumb at them, which is disgrace to them if they bear it' (*Romeo and Juliet*, i. i) indicates another gesture, meaning a challenge or insult, which is well attested in Britain from the 16th to 18th centuries. Morris equates this with the 'teeth flick' gesture current in many parts of Europe.

The thumbs-up gesture, to signify assent or 'OK' is so well accepted that few English people would even question its meaning. The popular, but incorrect, explanation is that it

dates from Roman times, when the crowd would signify the fate of a vanquished gladiator by thumbs up or down. What they did in that context was either hide their thumbs in their hand, or extend them, although there are other Latin sources which speak of other thumb gestures. In the absence of the spurious antiquity given the gesture by the Roman connection, all we can be sure of is that it existed in England in the mid-17th century, as the earliest reasonably unambiguous reference to 'thumbs up' in England is found in John Bulwer's *Chirologia* (1644) 'To hold up the thumbe is the gesture . . . of one shewing his assent or approbation. To hold up both thumbs, is an expression imparting a transcendency of praise' (quoted in Morris, 1979: 191). Another thumb gesture may hold the key to further elucidation. In previous times, a regular method for two people to seal a bargain was for them to wet their thumbs and press them together—summed up by the phrase 'Here's my thumb on it'. This certainly signifies agreement, and Hazlitt (1905: 586–7) provides a reference to the custom in a letter in the Close Rolls of King John, dated 1208, and it continues to be reported until at least the late 19th century, although again most of the references are Scottish.

The raised thumb could also be a form of greeting: 'It is still the custom—or was fifty years ago in the North of England—for coachmen whose hands are occupied driving to salute a comrade by raising the thumb' (*N&Q* 160 (1931), 393).

Other thumb lore includes the 17th- and 18th- century custom of widows signifying their status by wearing a thumb-ring (Hazlitt, 1905: 586–7), and in the post-Second World War period, the erect thumb has also become the international sign of the hitch-hiker, although in some parts of southern Europe it is considered an obscene gesture (see Morris, 1979).

See also *FINGERS.

Opie and Tatem, 1989: 404; Morris, 1979: 186–204; Hazlitt, 1905: 586–7; Chambers, 1878: i. 358–60; *N&Q* 160 (1931), 190–1, 231, 286, 393.

thunder and lightning. There are numerous traditional beliefs and significations attached to thunder and lightning, although, according to the available evidence, earlier people were more worried about the effects of thunder than of lightning, although they must have been aware of the real danger of lightning strikes. Certain trees were believed prone to lightning, while others were apparently immune. It was clearly a good idea to plant some of the latter near a building, or to know which to shelter under in a storm:

> Beware of an oak
> It draws the stroke
> Avoid an ash
> It courts the flash
> Creep under the thorn
> It can save you from harm

(from Sussex: *Folk-Lore Record* 1 (1878), 43, similar rhyme in *N&Q* 168 (1935), 457)

A long-standing belief regarded the *bay tree as particularly safe

> . . . reach the bays
> I'll tie a garland here about his head
> 'Twill keep my boy from lightning

(Webster, *White Devil* (1612))

while others swore by the *elder, laurel, or the *holly.

It was believed that a particular problem in storms was that thunder would spoil stored liquor unless prevented. John Aubrey (1686: 22) reported a practice to protect beer 'they lay a piece of iron on the barrell to keepe it from sowring', but according to the more scientifically minded editor of *The Agreeable Companion* (1742), 42, the 'violent motion and unnatural fermentation' could be prevented by any weight.

For some, the day of the week mattered: *A Prognostication Everlasting of Ryght Good Effecte*, of 1556, gives a list of the days and those whose death the thunder prognosticated (quoted by *N&Q* 12s:11 (1922), 24–5, which also gives more elaborate verses from a Yorkshire farmer in 1875).

A widely reported and long-standing protection for a house against lightning was to place some houseleek in the roof, quoted from 1562 and 1962 and often in between (Vickery, 1995; 197–8; Porter, 1969: 69). Porter also reports a number of other widespread items of stormlore, collected in the 1960s: for example, leave the doors open so that any lightning or thunderbolt will 'pass through the house', and cover shiny metal objects and *mirrors in case they attract the lightning. If a thunderstorm occurred during a marriage ceremony the couple would have no children, and nursing mothers should never suckle their babies during a thunderstorm as their milk would be tainted with brimstone and sulphur. Opie and Tatem report three more thunder/lightning

beliefs. It was considered unlucky to point to, or otherwise draw particular attention to thunder or lightning. This is reported as far back as Pliny (*Natural History* (AD 77), ii. 55) and several times in Britain in the 19th and 20th centuries. The interpretation of thunder and lightning as the voice or weapon of God is also quoted from Pliny and Tacitus and in Britain since at least the 16th century.

From at least the 15th to the 17th centuries it was common to ring church bells to make thunderstorms go away. Aubrey (1686: 22) mentions St Anselm's bell at Malmesbury Abbey in this context, and Camp (1988: 87) records a reference to bell-ringers at Sandwich (Kent), in 1464, being paid for ringing at 'the great thuderying'. From Wiltshire and Lincolnshire, and probably elsewhere, the belief is reported that sheet-lightning helps to ripen the corn (*N&Q* 175 (1938), 172, 214). It was also firmly believed at one time that swans' eggs cannot hatch without the help of thunder (*N&Q* 162 (1932), 252–6, quoting a source published in 1583).

Opie and Tatem, 1989: 405–6; Lean, 1903: esp. ii. 415–17; Hazlitt, 1905: 622–6.

thunderstones. When a particularly loud crack of *thunder was heard, it was thought that something more than mere lightning had buried itself in the ground; certain unusual objects found in the earth were popularly called 'thunderbolts' or 'thunderstones', including fossil belemnites, sea-urchins, and, more rarely, ammonites, pointed quartz crystals, lumps of iron pyrites, and Neolithic stone axes. On the principle that lightning never strikes the same place twice, their presence was thought to protect a house. In Sussex in the early 20th century fossil sea-urchins were set on the outside windowsills of kitchens and dairies to stop milk going sour, because thunder was believed to 'turn' milk; ammonites were used in the same way in Wiltshire and Gloucestershire in the 1860s, and it was noticed that mischievous village boys never interfered with them, simply because they were thunderbolts. Examples of all these objects could be found in London street markets in the late 19th and early 20th centuries, on sale under this name (Lovett, 1925: 49–51).

Tichborne Dole. An annual dole of flour distributed to the parishioners of Tichborne, Cheriton, and Lane End, Hampshire, on Lady Day (25 March). The accompanying legend relates that in the 12th century one Lady Mabella, wife of Sir Henry de Tichborne, was much loved by the local people for her charity and kindness. When she was dying, she asked her husband to dedicate some land to support a charity for the poor in her name. His reply was to pull a burning brand from the fire and say that she could have as much land as she could walk round, carrying the torch, before it went out. As ill as she was, she still managed to crawl around 23 acres of land, before the fire petered out—the husband's reaction is not recorded in this version. Her actions not only secured the charity, but also prompted the name 'the Crawls' by which those acres are still known. Lady Mabella was also sufficiently cautious to lay a curse on Sir Henry, and his heirs, if they ever interfered with the charity. The real origin of the charity is not known. Nowadays, flour made from wheat grown on the Crawls is distributed on the steps of the church, after a short open-air service. A gallon of flour is given to adults, and half a gallon to children.

Sykes, 1977: 36; Shuel, 1985: 127–8; Kightly, 1986: 218–19; Nicholas James, *L&L* 6:1 (1987), 59–64.

Tiddy Men, Tiddy People. In north Lincolnshire, *fairies were called Tiddy People because they were no bigger than a newborn baby. Collecting in the 1880s, Mrs *Balfour found one old woman who told a long, poetic story about one particular Tiddy Mun; he lived 'down deep in the green still water', but would come out at dusk, looking like a small, white-bearded, limping old man, and laughing in a shrill voice like a peewit. 'To her, Tiddy Mun was a perfect reality, and one to be loved as well as feared', but she was the last person who remembered him. He controlled the rise and fall of fenland flooding; the story concerns his fury when Dutchmen drained the fens in the 17th century, which provoked him into bringing disease on the fenmen till he was appeased by pails of water poured into the dry dykes.

M. C. Balfour, *Folk-Lore* 2 (1891), 149–56; summarized in Briggs, 1971–1: B. i. 277–8, and also in Briggs, 1976: 395–7.

tide. The belief that people at the coast will only die as the tide goes out is included in Charles Dickens's *David Copperfield* ((1849), chapter 30), and has been around a long time, as shown by Thomas Tusser's *Five Hundred Points of Good Husbandrie* (1557): 'Tyde flowing

is feared for many a thing Great danger to such as be sick it doth bring' (xiv, stanza 4); it is also mentioned by Pliny (*Natural History* (AD 77), i. 128) quoting Aristotle. English references continue well into the second half of the 20th century.

Opie and Tatem, 1989: 406–7.

tig. The basic children's chasing game in which one child tries to touch one of the others, and whoever is touched becomes the chaser and tries to touch another, is known by various local names. The Opies present a map showing that the main names as found in their research in the 1950s and 1960s are markedly *regional, of which 'tig' is the most widespread, but 'he', 'tag', 'tick', and 'touch' all have broad geographical areas in which they are dominant. The game is simplicity itself, and can be used for a range of variants—'chain-tig' in which the chasers have to hold hands, 'French-tig' in which the person 'tigged' has to hold the place he/she was touched while chasing the others, and so on. There are also variant words for the person who is doing the chasing, 'it' or 'he' being common, which children use as unselfconsciously as any dialect word—'We played He and I was had, so I had to be he', or even 'If she hads a person when she is he the person she hads becomes he'. Of all the names noted by the Opies, 'tick' seems to be the oldest, being found in Drayton's *Poly-Olbion* ((1622), p. xxx), whereas 'tag' is found from the 18th century, and 'tig' and 'touch' from the 19th century.

Opie and Opie, 1969: 20–3, 62–123.

time. The basic way of experiencing time is not as a succession of fixed units (e.g. hours), but through three natural cycles: night and day, the moon's phases, and the year. The first is the most immediate, and the most charged with symbolic and emotional meanings; darkness is equated with the unknown, evil, and death, while light is equated with goodness, activity, the familiar world, life, and ultimately God. Nevertheless, in mythic thought darkness precedes light, and night precedes day, as can be seen both in Genesis 1 and in the Germanic and Celtic custom of counting nights rather than days. In modern time-keeping, as in Ancient Rome, a day begins immediately after midnight, not at dawn; in liturgical reckoning, a day begins at sunset (e.g. the Jewish Sabbath includes Friday evening, the first Mass of Easter Sunday is held on the Saturday night).

Within the night/day cycle, special importance was given to *midnight and *midday, and to certain transitional moments or periods—the first *cockcrow, dawn, and sunrise. Night, especially the period around midnight, belongs to ghostly, devilish, and uncanny forces, which humans should not risk meeting; however, this taboo also makes it a time of power, suitable for *divinations and sinister magic, and those born at midnight were thought to have occult abilities (see *chime hours). Dawn (or cockcrow) drives away the evil spirits of night; sunrise is right for healing rituals such as passing a child through a split *ash or a bramble arch, and for various luck-bringing customs such as gathering *May dew. Sunset and twilight, though of course relevant to the routine of daily work, are not associated with customs or serious beliefs, though children were until recently threatened with various *bogeys if they stayed out late (see *poldies, *hytersprites).

The *moon was mainly associated with agricultural and medicinal lore, since its waxing and waning was thought to affect plants, animals, and humans; there are customs linking luck to the new moon, and magic to the full moon.

Theoretically, the natural annual cycle repeats the night/day cycle on a larger scale, with *midwinter and *midsummer corresponding to midnight and midday, and the equinoxes to sunrise and sunset. In practice, this pattern is lacking in English tradition: the equinoxes are ignored and midsummer has lost much of its significance, while the midwinter period of *Christmas and *New Year has become overwhelmingly important. However, its associations are now almost wholly cheerful and benign; eeriness has been transferred to *Halloween, leaving only a vague idea that telling ghost stories is a fitting amusement at Christmas.

See *CALENDAR, *DAYS OF THE WEEK, *FRIDAY, *MOON.

Tin Can Band. Young people in Broughton, Northamptonshire, gather at midnight on the second Sunday in December for an hour's worth of procession round the village making as much raucous noise as possible. To this end they bring tins with stones in, dustbin lids, old metal containers with sticks to bang them, and so on. They do not know why, or for how

long the custom has existed, but the villagers have successfully fought off attempts to suppress it. There are one or two stories to explain the custom—it was done to frighten off Gypsies, or it was done to express disapproval of the birth of an illegitimate baby, and the latter is possible because of the similarity between the Tin Can Band and *rough musicking. However, most writers point to the fact that this is the eve of the town's *feast day (Old St Andrew's Day) and may simply be a way of starting the festivities attached to that celebration. A very similar gathering, *Teddy Rowe's Band, formerly signified the coming of Pack Monday Fair, at Sherborne, Dorset.

Kightly, 1986: 219; Shuel, 1985: 71; Sykes, 1977: 148.

toadman. This is an East Anglian term, current till the mid-20th century, for a man with an uncanny knack of controlling horses, supposedly obtained by possession of a toad's magical bone (see *horseman's word). The term 'toad-doctor', however, as used by working-class Londoners in 1939, meant someone who cures people of aches and pains by selling them dried toad's legs, to be worn in a leather pouch round one's neck (Balleine, 1939: 6).

toads. The toad features widely in English folklore, in beliefs, cures, and customs, but its roles are often contradictory, and in many of the following *frogs and toads are apparently interchangeable. One of the factors which contributed to the toad's evil reputation was its reputed connection with witchcraft, as witches were widely believed to use them as familiars and to turn themselves into toads when they wished. A story reported from Ashburton (Devon) in 1876 relates how a man who had no strength to work found a great toad in his house one evening. He killed it with a pitchfork and threw it on the fire. The following evening he found another, which he dispatched in the same way and his strength returned (quoted in Opie and Tatem, 1989: 408).

On the other hand, beliefs printed in several 19th-century folklore collections stress that should you find a toad in the house you should remove it carefully, precisely because it might be a witch. Toads in the house are generally reported as unlucky or dangerous, but the earliest known reference to this belief only dates from the 1830s. Earlier sources, from the

12th century onwards, refer to meeting a toad in the outdoors, and in most cases this is, paradoxically, regarded as lucky, although there is a hint that if it crosses your path from the left it is not so good. By the 19th and 20th centuries, however, as many reports say it is unlucky as lucky.

For centuries, it was taken for granted that toads were poisonous. Shakespeare refers to this, and the *toadstone:

> Sweet are the uses of adversity
> Which, like the toad, ugly and venomous,
> Wears yet a precious jewel in his head
>
> (*As You Like It* II. I)

Another old notion, based on the belief that both toads and *spiders were venomous, was that they had such an antipathy for each other that they would fight if they met and would both be killed in any encounter.

But it is in the realm of folk-medicine that the toad becomes a valuable commodity. Many of the older folklore collections report remedies in which the toad figures strongly, being used to cure, among many other ailments, cancer, rheumatism, plague, abscesses, nosebleeds, sprains, smallpox, the king's evil, and whooping cough. The methods of preparing the toad vary, but there are two main ways, depending on whether you want the whole toad or only part of it. A number of cures call for the toad to be powdered: 'Put the toads alive into an earthen pot, and dry them in an oven moderately heated, till they become fit to be powdered' (Paris's *Pharmacologia* (1833), 6, quoted in *N&Q* 10s:2 (1904), 325) while others use the live toad whole, or a leg: 'In the neighbourhood of Hartlebury (Worcestershire) they break the legs of a toad, sew it up in a bag alive, and tie it round the neck of a patient' (*Gentleman's Magazine*, part II (1855), 384–6). The wearing of something in a bag around the neck is a common element in folk-medicine.

On occasion, the live toad's back is rubbed on the afflicted part, while other recipes call for particular bones of the animal. The traditional method here is to place a toad in an anthill, and the ants will clean the skeleton off nicely for you. This is certainly no recent idea, as Pliny (*Natural History* (AD 77), XXXII. xviii) recommends the use of such a bone to assuage the fury of dogs and as an aphrodisiac. See under *horseman's word for another, related, use of toad's bones. Following a well-known principle in folk-medicine, the toad is some-

times set free, and the disease or affliction will wither as it does. For the whooping cough, hold a live toad with its head in the mouth of the afflicted person. The toad will thus catch the disease and take it away from the sufferer (*N&Q* 1s:3 (1851), 258).

Another persistent motif, which stretches back at least to the 12th century in England, is that toads can survive even when entombed within rock or other impenetrable substance. Similar stories circulated on the European continent. The earliest known reference is by *William of Newburgh (*Historia Anglia* (c.1186) book 1, chapter 28), but Robert Plot (1686: 247–51) was the first English writer to devote real attention to the phenomenon, and references have continued to appear to the present day.

See also *TOADSTONE.

Opie and Tatem, 1989: 407–10; Black, 1883: 62–3; *N&Q* 4s:7 (1871), 324, 399, 484, 540–2; 8s:8 (1895), 65–6, 217, 312, 438; Bob Skinner, *Toad in the Hole: Source Material on the Entombed Toad Phenomenon* (1986?).

toadstones. A widespread medieval opinion was that a toad has a jewel embedded in its head, which could detect and counteract poisons, heal bites and stings, and help women in childbirth. Various semi-precious stones, and also the teeth of certain fossil fish, were called toadstones and worn as pendants or rings. The traditional way to get one was to bury a toad in a pot in an anthill for the ants to eat, till only the bones and the stone were left. An anonymous treatise of the 1660s explains:

It must bee a Toade that is very greate and old and hath Lived Long in hedges or diches or a fenne of Reeds because it will be many years or ever the stone can come to any bignesse. . . . [It] is off Cullar eyther white or a Littel darkish Browne or Blacke haveing in the middest of the stone Like unto an Eye beeing of a greenish Cullar. Especially if the stone bee taken from the Toade alive and so is off most vertue off operation. . . . Butt myself had one wch was black and spotted with redd spotts wch I did set in a ring off gold off 20/- vallew and I sold it ffor £6. Butt I never since could meete with such another. (BM Sloane 2539, fo. 34; cited in Evans, 1922: 150)

Tom Thumb. This is the English version of an international humorous *fairytale in which a woman's wish to have a son 'even if he is no bigger than my husband's thumb' is literally granted—in this case, by *Merlin. Tom receives magic gifts from his godmother the Fairy Queen, but his tiny size leads to many mishaps, as when he falls into a pudding, is carried off by a raven, is swallowed by a grazing cow, a fish, a giant, and so on. The earliest surviving version appeared in 1621 and is probably by a popular pamphleteer, Richard Johnson (1573–?1659); however, earlier references to the hero by name show that he was already known in the 1570s. Johnson's humour is mildly coarse; Tom makes his exit from the cow via a cowpat, and causes such 'rumbling and tumbling' in the giant's guts that the latter vomits him 'at least three miles into the sea'. Later versions were made more 'suitable' for children; some end with Tom dying heroically in battle with a spider.

His name was used by early publishers of children's verses, for instance *Tommy Thumb's Pretty Song Book* (1744) and *The Famous Tommy Thumb's Little Story-Book* (*c*.1760); at this period 'Tommy Thumb songs' was the usual English term for *nursery rhymes.

The full text of the 1621 pamphlet, with a commentary, is in Opie and Opie, 1974: 30–3; it is also edited by C. F. Buhler, *The History of Tom Thumbe* (1965).

Tom Tit Tot. This, one of the most famous English *fairytales, is an analogue to 'Rumplestiltskin' in the *Grimms' collection. A peasant girl is taken as wife by a king, on the understanding that she will spin five skeins of flax per day for a month, as her mother had boasted she could; a 'small little black thing with a long tail' performs the task for her, on condition that he will carry her off if she cannot guess his *name by the end of the month. By chance he is heard boasting 'Niminy niminy not, My name's Tom Tit Tot', so she is able to 'guess' correctly, and the imp disappears. The story was contributed to the *Ipswich Journal* on 15 January 1878 by Mrs Anna Walter-Thomas, who recreated it in full Suffolk dialect from her memory of how her nurse had told it to her about 25 years before; it has since been many times reprinted, usually with the dialect reduced.

In 1992 Michael Wilson recorded an excellent variant from a 13-year-old girl in Plymouth, based on how her Liverpool grandmother told it; the task is to spin wool into gold, which is done by 'a little green imp', who a year later takes the girl's baby as the forfeit, but has to restore it when she discovers the name (Wilson, 1997: 255–8).

Original text in Briggs, 1970–1: A. i. 535–9; Philip, 1992: 111–17. Modified text in Jacobs, 1894/1968: 5–9.

Tongue, Ruth (1898–1981). A problematic fig-ure. Though belonging to the gentry class and educated in music and drama, she was passionately attached to country life and believed herself to have a special rapport with the craftsmen and labourers of Somerset, her native county, and also with Gypsies. She claimed (incorrectly) that she had been born between midnight on a Friday and cockcrow on a Saturday, that this gave her psychic gifts, and that therefore many people had confided tales, songs, and magical lore to her when she was a very young child. Her family moved to Hertfordshire while she was still a child. Much later, after the Second World War, she returned to Somerset; from about 1950 she began giving talks on folklore to local groups, and also on radio, enriched with vivid performances of tales and songs. She impressed Katharine *Briggs and Theo *Brown, and the former helped her to organize her material and arranged for its publication. The result was four books, *Somerset Folklore* (1965), edited by Briggs; *Folktales of England*, written mainly by Briggs but containing many of Tongue's stories; *The Chime Child, or Somerset Singers* (1968); and *Forgotten Folktales of the English Counties* (1970).

The problem is that Tongue was a performer, and that many years had passed since she had learnt these songs and tales; the uniform style and recurrent themes and phrases make it virtually certain that they had been reshaped, perhaps only half-consciously, to suit her personality. Some look like patchworks, built up round mere scraps of traditional beliefs or sayings. She should be regarded as a creative singer and storyteller reworking fragments of tradition, not as a reliable collector.

The Chime Child contains sketches of her chief informants among country singers, but these are based on very early childhood memories; in *Forgotten Folktales* she gives only the vaguest hints as to where, when, and from whom she had obtained the stories; any notes she may have made at the time were lost in moves and fires. *Somerset Folklore* is the soundest of her books, in which much information about local beliefs and customs is given straightforwardly and reliably. The others must be used with caution.

Obituary, *Folklore* 94 (1983), 890. Robert and Jacqueline Patten, 'Ruth Tongue', in *Women and Tradition*, ed. Hilda R. E. Davidson and Carmen Blacker, 2001: 205–16.

tongues. The common remark to people who complain of having a pimple or spot on their tongue, that they have been lying, is old indeed. In England it goes back at least to the 17th century—Shakespeare alludes to it (*Winter's Tale* (1611), ii. ii): 'If I prove honeymouthed, let my tongue blister', as do John Aubrey (1686/1880: 28) and several other 17th-century writers. But this is nothing compared to Theocritus (*Idylls* (*c.*275 BC), XII) 'Nor midst my song shall tell-tale blisters rise, and gall my tongue'. The same thing about falsehood is said of people who accidentally bite their tongue when eating. The tip of a calf's tongue is regularly reported as a lucky charm, carried in the pocket and called the 'lucky bit', this was first mentioned in Northamptonshire in its mid-19th century (Sternberg, 1851: 172–3). Igglesden (*c.*1932: 127, 146) reports a surgeon who carried a tip of a human tongue, and a Thames bargee who believed in the luck of a cat's tongue.

Opie and Tatem, 1989: 410–11; Igglesden, *c.*1932: 127, 146; Lean, 1903: ii. 296.

toothache. The following *charm was collected by M. A. Denham in the north of England in the 1840s (Denham, 1895: 9–10):

> Peter was sitting on a marble stone
> And Jesus passed by
> Peter said, 'My Lord! My God!
> How my tooth doth ache!'
> Jesus said, 'Peter art whole!
> And whoever keeps these words for my sake,
> Shall never have the toothache!' Amen.

Others report similar stories, adding that to be effective the words should be written on a piece of paper and worn round the neck. Opie and Tatem reprint a Latin version from *c.*1000 AD, and an East Anglian version from 1957. *Aubrey (1686/1880: 164–5) reports a more gruesome cure: 'I remember at Bristow (when I was a boy) it was common fashion for the woemen, to get a Tooth out of a Sckull in ye churchyard, wch they wore as a preservative against the Tooth-ach', and more prosaically, the use of ginger at the same period (he was born in 1626).

See also *TEETH, *TOOTH FAIRY.

Opie and Tatem, 1989: 411–12; Forbes, 1971: 293–316.

Tooth Fairy. When a child loses one of its milk *teeth, this is put in a safe place (usually under the child's pillow, but sometimes in an egg-cup or under a carpet), and the child is told that *fairies will take it in the night, and leave a coin instead—or actually turn it into a coin. Between the wars, this was generally a *silver threepenny piece, and when these were withdrawn in the 1940s, some families still insisted on using them. A contributor to *FLS News* (15 (1992), 11) wrote: 'We kept a small stock of silver threepenny pieces specially for the occasion, always reclaiming them from the children and recompensing them. They always maintained that the silver coin was far superior to their schoolfriends, who maybe received 6d.' Nowadays, the money given has increased to 50p or even £1.

The only folklorists who have mentioned this custom in print are the Opies, who noted it as widespread in the 1950s (Opie and Opie, 1959: 305); however, many people still living can bear witness that it was common in the 1920s, which makes it probable that it was known in the previous century. There is an allusion in Kenneth Graham's *The Golden Age* (1898: 133) to older boys being customarily tipped half a crown when a tooth is extracted by a dentist, which is a related idea.

There is one early source which links fairies and children's teeth, namely Robert *Herrick's poem on 'Oberon's Palace' (1648); he describes this as a grotto adorned with various small and useless objects from the human world, 'brought hither by the elves' —

> . . . and for to pave
> The excellency of this Cave,
> Squirrils and childrens teeth late shed
> Are neatly here enchequerèd
> With brownest Toadstones, and the gum
> That shines upon the blewer Plum,
> The nails faln off by Whit-flaws: Art's
> Wise hand enchasing here those warts
> Which we to others (from ourselves)
> Sell, and brought hither by the Elves.

> (*Hesperides* (1648), no. 444)

Herrick's poem matches half the modern tale, namely that fairies collect shed teeth; the other half, the money left in exchange, may have grown out of the old belief that fairies will reward a hard-working servant by leaving sixpence in her shoe at night, a gift presumably placed there secretly by her employer; the child too is being rewarded, for being brave and not making a fuss.

Up to the 1950s, the tooth-takers were generally referred to as 'fairies', in the plural, but now people more often speak of *the* Tooth Fairy, possibly under American influence. A retired dental nurse in Lincolnshire recalls how 'We kept special tiny envelopes for children to take their teeth home in for the tooth fairy; I used to write on the envelope "For the fairy".' Unfortunately, this memory is not specifically dated; from the context, it could be from the 1940s (Sutton, 1992: 125). The fantasy can become more elaborate; in letters to the *Guardian* in October 1988, parents said that when their children asked why fairies wanted human teeth, they replied that it was to make bricks for their houses, or to carve them into toys and ornaments—much the same notion as Herrick had (*FLS News* 14 (1992), 4; 15 (1992), 11–12).

topping out, see *BUILDING TRADE.

touching iron, wood. The archetypal superstition in modern England, in that even many non-superstitious people will say 'touch wood', even if they do not actually carry out the action of touching wood, after boasting or making some statement which will 'tempt fate'. It is also one of the superstitions which appear in almost all popular articles on the subject, with the confident assertion that the belief goes back to the days when our ancestors worshipped trees and believed in tree-spirits. An alternative explanation is that we invoke the protection of Jesus Christ, because the cross was made of wood.

Needless to say, there is no basis whatsoever for these explanations, beyond guesswork. Despite considerable effort, no earlier reference has been found before 1805, as 'tig-touch-wood' in R. Anderson's *Ballads in Cumberland Dialect* (p. 35) as noted by Opie and Tatem. The 1,200 year silence between the Christianization of England and that reference make it unlikely that the belief existed, let alone was popularly held, in that time. It is interesting to note that this, and the next quotation offered by Opie and Tatem (in 1828), are both to children's chasing games where you are safe while you are touching wood. There are many other similar games where temporary safety relies on being in a particular place or situation, with an accompanying phrase (see also touching iron, below). In the absence of further evidence, we would suggest that 'touch wood', as a phrase and as an action, comes from a popular children's game, of the late 18th century.

'Touching iron' is recorded earlier than 'touching wood', although still not nearly back into pre-Christian times. Opie and Tatem quote from *The Craftsman* of 4 February 1738, 'In Queen Mary's reign, "Tag" was all the play,

where the lad saves himself by touching cold iron'. Note again the children's game context. Touching metal, and saying 'Cold iron' is outwardly similar to 'touch wood' but is used nowadays in different contexts, although it is still protective. In normal use, it is enacted or said when some taboo has been broken, such as superstitious fishermen hearing the forbidden word 'pig' or 'rabbit', or factory girls from the Staffordshire Potteries who would touch metal if they met a clergyman (*Folk-lore* 52 (1941), 237). The picture is potentially much more complex with 'cold iron', however, than with 'touch wood' discussed above. There is a widespread, and ancient, belief that iron is an effective protection against witches, fairies, the Devil, and other sorts of evil or troublesome beings, and a range of other beliefs about iron are recorded in cures, taboos, and luck-bringing where it is not always easy to decide whether it is the object (the horseshoe, the poker) or the material (the metal) which is being invoked or is having the desired effect. See under *Iron for further discussion.

For other beliefs involving touching for luck see *SAILOR, TOUCHING, *STATUES.

Opie and Tatem, 1989: 213, 449–50; *N&Q* 10s:6 (1906), 130, 174, 230–2.

tourist lore. In recent decades, the increase in tourism has provided a major new context for the transmission of folklore. Guides leading conducted tours of ancient buildings and historic towns diversify the historical information with colourful titbits of legend, in which murders, treasures, pirates, and ghosts are likely to figure; in some towns, there are specialist 'ghost tours' where visitors are led, after dark, to look at reputedly haunted sites and hear the tales attached to them. Hotels and pubs may publicize their ghosts as an attraction to visitors, and innumerable booklets offer 'Tales and Traditions of X-shire', where similar material is prominent. Some comes, directly or indirectly, from older books of regional folklore, some from current rumour, speculation, and creative variation on older themes. Naturally, it then feeds back into popular awareness and gets passed on.

There is a lively market for traditional artefacts, especially foods based on local recipes; pubs and restaurants in historic towns often adopt menus and decor exploiting nostalgic links, real or alleged, with past 'heritage'. *Corn dollies are on sale all the year round; *wishing wells raise money for good causes;

*Pearly Kings and Queens appear at events arranged by the Tourist Board. These items or events are generally accompanied by printed hand-outs briefly explaining their traditional basis.

Trash. A sinister Lancashire *black dog, once widely feared in the Burnley area as a sure *omen of the death of a member of one's family (N&Q 1s:2 (1850), 51). It was large and shaggy, with 'eyes as big as saucers', and got its name from the noise made by its feet, like 'that of a heavy shoe in a miry road'. It was also called Skriker, from the sound of its howling voice on occasions when it was invisible.

treacle mines. In many parts of England certain small villages are jokingly said to have a secret treacle mine on their territory. 20th-century examples have been reported from Cumbria, Devon, Essex, Gloucestershire, Hampshire, Kent, Lancashire, Leicestershire, Norfolk, Surrey, Sussex, and Wiltshire; no doubt there are others too. Similar jokes are made about porridge or toothpaste quarries, snuff mills and jam mines, but they are less widespread and far less elaborate.

Basically, the joke is about impossibility—treacle is *not* found in mines, any more than money on trees—but it can work on many levels. Sometimes it is a taunt, implying that the people of X are such fools that they go digging for treacle, or too lazy to do honest work, or so poor they live only on bread and treacle; sometimes it is a hoax, in which a child or a newcomer is gulled or bewildered; sometimes a put-off from mother to child ('Don't bother me now, I'm off to the treacle mine'); sometimes an emblem of local identity, proudly used in the name of a pub or a sports team, or as a tourist attraction.

The treacle mine is a theme on which poker-faced humorists play elaborate variations, the aim being to produce some plausible explanation of what and where it is, weaving in as many local allusions as possible. Perhaps the treacle comes from an abandoned dump of army food dating from the Crimean War (Chobham, Surrey); or by the geological compression of ancient sugar-cane forests (Dunchidock, Devon); or it is waste oil from an American airbase (Tadley, Hampshire). The machinery for extracting it, and the docks from which it is exported, are lovingly described (Corpusty and Fring, Norfolk); one mine employs *boggarts (Sabden, Lancashire).

Simpson, 1982; FLS News 18 (1993), 7–8; 19 (1994), 5–6; 20 (1994), 4–6; 21 (1995), 11–12; 25 (1997), 12–13.

treasure. Buried treasure is a favourite theme in popular lore; many, if not most, ancient earthworks, barrows, standing stones, and similar sites are alleged to contain it (Grinsell, 1976), as are old churches and mansions, ruined castles, crossroads, and the ubiquitous secret *tunnels. Sometimes it is linked to historical persons and events; thus, in Hertfordshire there are tales of a lost Roman 'treasure city', the hidden gold of the Knights Templar, the 'plate and monys' of St Albans Abbey, and the loot of Wicked Lady Ferrers, who lived by highway robbery (Jones-Baker, 1977: 31–45). Legends such as these could be duplicated from every county. Sometimes this wealth takes on fantastic forms—a man buried in gold or silver armour, gold or silver coffins, silver gates, even the Golden Calf of the Bible.

However, it was not thought easy to find the treasure, or to keep it, for spirits were likely to be guarding it. In Lancashire, ghostly black hens, cocks, horses, and dogs are mentioned, and also *boggarts and *bogles. In Sussex, legends tell of two huge snakes preventing access to a pot of gold in a tunnel; the *Devil deterring treasure-seekers with thunder-claps and/or shifting the Golden Calf underground as soon as they approach it; a ghostly calf with fiery eyes; and an evil spirit in the form of a black hen (Simpson, 1973: 23–5). In Cheshire, it is said that demons guard Richard II's gold in a well at Beeston Castle, and ensure that anyone trying to reach it will go mad or be stricken dumb with horror (Hole, 1937: 67). In other tales, seekers fail at the last minute by breaking a *taboo on speaking before the work is complete; they may compound their mistake by boasting, swearing, or blaspheming, as at *Willy Howe. In real life, magical books gave instructions for making 'Mosaical rods' to help in the search, and for invoking other spirits to defeat the guardians; magicians at all levels, from village fortune-tellers to Dr *Dee, claimed the ability to find treasure, and many accounts of such attempts are on record (Thomas, 1971: 236–8).

trees. The characteristics traditionally ascribed to various species of tree differ sharply, and will be found under the name of each species. Certain themes, however, can be applied to any that is locally famous (Thomas, 1983: 216–19). The most widespread is a claim that it is the tallest, largest, or oldest of its species in the country; the great ages mentioned are probably exaggerated, especially for *oaks and *yews. *Origin legends are also common; some claim the tree was planted by some famous personage, others that there was something sinister or miraculous about its growth. It may be supposedly sprung from a seed laid in the mouth of a dead man, as is said of an elm in the graveyard at Kingston-on-Sea in Sussex (JS), and a sycamore growing out of a tomb at Clavering (Essex); or from the stake thrust through the corpse of a murderer or a suicide, as is said of a beech called 'the Amy Tree' at St Mellion (Cornwall), and certain elms in Bedfordshire and Gloucestershire (*Folk-Lore* 56 (1945), 307; Palmer, 1994: 43). Naturally, these are among the many trees said to be haunted. In Hertfordshire, the churchyards of Aldenham, Chesunt, Tewin, and Watford each contain (or formerly contained) an old tomb split apart by one or more trees, said to be that of an unbeliever who declared that if there really was a God, or a life after death, a tree would sprout from his or her tomb (*N&Q* 11s:8 (1913), 425).

Some individual trees had an important social and symbolic role as landmarks, assembly points, or boundary markers, since they 'were older than any of the inhabitants, and they symbolized the community's continued existence' (Thomas, 1983: 216); large *oaks were, and are, particularly cherished, and often served as markers for *beating the bounds. Links with real or imagined history are numerous—the Boscobel Oak where Charles I hid, the New Forest oak from which, allegedly, the arrow glanced off to kill William Rufus, *Herne's Oak in Windsor Great Park, the stump of one in Hatfield Park where Elizabeth I heard news of her accession, the 'Remedy Oak' at Wimborne St Giles (Dorset) where it is said Edward VI used to sit to touch for the *king's evil.

See also *ARBOR DAY, *BAWMING THE THORN, *HOLY THORN.

Tregagle, John. A Cornish lawyer and magistrate, John Tregagle (or Tregeagle), who died in 1655, was remembered in tradition as an utterly dishonest, unscrupulous man who had sold his soul to the Devil. Legend says his ghost was called up from the grave by one of the parties in a lawsuit, since he alone knew the truth of the disputed matter, but that it then proved hard to get rid of him. Various conjur-

ers and parsons tried to *lay him by setting him endless tasks: to empty the 'bottomless' Dozmary Pool with a cracked limpet shell, or weave ropes of sand in Gwenvor Cove, or sweep all sand away from Porthcurno Cove, while demons harassed him. He is still struggling with these tasks, and his howls of fury are heard in every gale.

Hunt, 1865: 131–45; B. C. Spooner, *John Tregagle of Trevorder: Man and Ghost* (1935); A. L. Rowse, *History Today* 15 (1965), 828–34.

trick or treat, see *HALLOWEEN.

truce terms. Words which are accepted amongst a group of children as a valid way of calling a temporary truce during the course of a game or other activity, and thereby claiming immunity from being caught, touched, etc. Iona and Peter Opie were the first to attempt a systematic look at this aspect of what they termed children's 'code of oral legislation', and their fieldwork in the 1950s brought striking results. A range of words were found, but their use was markedly *regional and they were able to present a map showing the dominant words in each area (see Opie and Opie, 1959: 149). The word with the widest distribution was 'barley', which has a very long literary history, and others were 'fainites' (probably from Middle English), 'kings', 'kings and crosses', 'skinch', 'scribs', and 'cree'. The small survey reported by Beckwith and Shirley confirmed and extended the Opies' findings for Lincolnshire in 1974, but an even smaller-scale survey by Kate and Steve Roud in 1988 completely disagreed. Their research focused on the London Borough of Croydon—which in the 1950s was firmly in the 'fainites' area—and they discovered three widely used terms: 'jecs' (previously unrecorded), 'pax' (previously thought to be only used in private schools), and 'fainites' a definitely poor third. Without further research, it is impossible to say whether the geographical pattern reported by the Opies has completely broken down, or whether the Croydon area is anomalous. It is quite conceivable that major changes have taken place in the nearly 30 years between the Opies' and the Rouds' research, as seven or eight generations of schoolchildren have passed through the country's junior schools in that time, which is the equivalent of over 140 years in adult generation terms.

In most historical sources, it is taken for

granted that the truce word is accompanied by crossing the fingers, and in many cases the truce only lasts while the fingers remain crossed. Again the Croydon survey revealed several other gestures, although crossed fingers was by far the most common. At some schools, boys and girls made different gestures. Further work on truce terms is certainly needed.

Opie and Opie, 1959: 141–53; Ian Beckwith and Bob Shirley, 'Truce Terms: A Lincolnshire Survey', *Local Historian* 11:8 (1975), 441–4; Kate and Steve Roud, 'Truce Terms in Croydon, Surrey, 1988', *Talking Folklore* 7 (1989), 15–20.

tunnels. There is nothing more common in local tradition than stories about secret tunnels; to give individual references is impossible, but most books on local history and lore include some. They are said to run from castles, inns, churches, manor houses, or virtually any old and notable building, and to lead to another building, or down to the sea, or occasionally into the depths of a hill. Most people who talk or write about them do so with belief, partly because sometimes short lengths of tunnelling are indeed found leading off from the cellars of old buildings, though so far these have always turned out, on investigation, to be merely ice-houses or drains. But the tunnels of rumour and tradition are far longer, often running for impossible distances, and through impossible terrain—under rivers, through swampy or sandy ground, where they would inevitably soon collapse or become flooded.

Most have some sort of explanation attached, drawing on real or imagined history. The tunnel may be said to have served as a secret passage for smugglers; or to enable priests or monks to leave their buildings unobserved (in order to meet their mistresses, especially if these were nuns); or as a secret entrance to a castle. A modern variation is to allege the existence of deep civil or military shelters, linked by a network of underground passages. Such places do exist (the cliffs of Dover are said to be honeycombed with them), but it strains credulity to be told, 'When the new Public Library was being built at X, they put in a nuclear shelter for the Mayor at the same time.'

Tunnels can also be places where *treasure is hidden, and where *ghosts walk, either in the tunnel or above ground, following its track. A tragic story is told about eight or nine

of them: two men who had seen one end of a tunnel wanted to know where it led to, or whether there was treasure in it. One of them was a musician; at Richmond Castle (Yorkshire) he is said to have been a drummer boy, but at Grantchester (Cambridgeshire) and elsewhere, a fiddler or a piper. This musician entered the tunnel and walked along it, playing as he went, while his friend followed above ground, tracking him by the sound; suddenly the music ceased, and the musician was never seen again. It has been pointed out that in some places where this story is told there is a small wood called Fiddler's Copse midway along the supposed course of the tunnel (*Folk-Lore* 34 (1923), 378–9).

Turning the Devil's Stone. Just outside the churchyard in Shebbear, Devon, lies a large stone, which was apparently accidentally dropped by Satan, or perhaps brought deliberately from nearby Henscott to stop them using it as a foundation for a new church. Every year, on the evening of *November the Fifth, the bell-ringers sound a jangled peal on the church bells and then proceed to turn the Devil's Boulder over, with crowbars. It would be unlucky not to do so.

Hole, 1975:101; Shuel, 1985: 17, 19; Kightly, 1986: 222.

Tutbury Bull-Running, see *BULL-RUNNING.

Twelfth Night (5/6 January). Still regarded by many people as the end of the *Christmas season, and this has a long-standing official sanction, as the Council of Tours of AD 567 ruled that the twelve days from the Nativity to the Epiphany would constitute one religious festival. For most of us nowadays the only practical aspect of the date is that it is said to be the day (or the last day) for taking down the Christmas decorations, or bad luck will follow, but in the past Twelfth Night had its own traditions, which have largely been forgotten.

The overriding feeling of reports of Twelfth Night celebrations in the 18th and 19th centuries is that although substantial in their own right, they were somewhat quieter and more subdued that those at Christmas, but the other recurrent feature is that there is invariably mention of cake and alcohol. The Twelfth Night cake was made the centre of a particular custom, by which a King and Queen were chosen to preside over the festivities. A bean and a pea were baked in the cake, and when slices were handed out to the company, whoever got the piece with the bean in it became King, while whoever got the pea was Queen. The custom was so well known that 'The King of the Bean' was proverbial for someone temporarily in charge of celebratory fun. In some cases, coins were used instead of beans and peas, while others adopted the more prosaic method of drawing names from a hat, which gave scope for widening the play-acting, by giving everybody present characters as well. Samuel Pepys recorded using this method for the first time in his *Diary* for 6 January 1669. *Herrick (*Hesperides*, 1648) also devotes a whole poem to the 'Twelfe Night King and Queene'. Substantially the same bean-King custom existed on the European continent, and Hutton believes that the custom was reintroduced to Britain from the Continent by the late Tudor period.

The drink was often in the form of a ceremonial *wassail bowl—a large receptacle, similar to the modern punch bowl, from which everyone was served. It contained a special drink, often called Lamb's Wool, made from roasted apples, sugar, and nutmeg in ale, or sometimes wine. By extension from the one Twelfth Night cake, the day had become by the 19th century a great one for cakes and pastries in general. Hone reports that every London confectioner made a point of displaying a splendid windowful of cakes in all sorts of shapes and sizes (Hone, 1827: 24–30).

In agricultural areas, two interrelated customs connected to Twelfth Night were *wassailing, and the lighting of fires in the wheat fields, to ensure a good crop for the coming year. The latter was apparently confined to the western side of England as reported from Herefordshire, Worcestershire, and Gloucestershire: '. . . they make twelve fires of straw, in a row. Around one fire, which they make larger than the rest, they drink a glass of cider to their master's health and success to the next harvest. Returning home they receive carraway seed cakes and cider . . .' (Thomas Rudge, *History of the County of Gloucester* (1803), ii. 42).

See also *BADDELEY CAKE, *HOLY THORN, *WASSAILING.

Wright and Lones, 1938: ii. 50–91; Hutton, 1996: 15–16, 110–11; Brand, 1849: i. 21–34; Hone, 1827: i. 24–30.

Tylor, Edward Burnet (1832–1917). His interest in ethnology, which developed while travelling in Cuba and Mexico, led to his three influential books, *Researches into the Early History of Mankind* (1865); *Primitive Culture* (1871); and *Anthropology, an Introduction to the Study of Man and Civilisation* (1881), which established him as an original and important thinker and earned him the title 'Father of Anthropology'. He was appointed Keeper of the University Museum at Oxford in 1883, Reader in Anthropology 1884, and served as the first ever Professor of Anthropology 1896–1909. Tylor was knighted in 1912.

Tylor was also hailed as the 'Father of Folklore', as his theories were eagerly adopted by all the early British folklorists—*Clodd, *Gomme, *Lang, *Hartland, and many others. In his application of Darwin's evolutionary theories to human cultures he constructed the theory of *survivals (the idea that modern folklore is a survival from a previous stage of civilization and can thus be used to reconstruct that stage), which became the cornerstone of folklore thinking for generations. He was also one of the first to use what became the 'comparative method', drawing on material from all over the world in his attempts to correlate customs, and he identified 'animism' as the universal primitive belief in the existence of spiritual beings which he claimed provided the basis for all religions, and so a means of comparing them. The new discipline of anthropology, while grateful for Tylor's organizational as well as theoretical work, soon moved on from his theories, but the folklorists did not. They continued to couch their investigations in terms of survivals well into the 20th century. Nevertheless, as Dorson clearly shows, Tylor's folklore followers were extremely selective in their readings of his books, as there is much that they should have disagreed with. Andrew Lang, for example, who was probably the most effusive in his thanks to Tylor, chose to ignore the latter's obvious debt to Max Müller and the solar mythologists whom Lang himself had lambasted a few years before. Even on the knotty question of whether outwardly similar myths could be explained by transmission or by independent creation, Lang favoured coincident and multiple invention, whereas Tylor leaned more towards the borrowing of myths between peoples.

Dorson, 1968: *passim*; Justin Wintle, *Makers of 19th Century Culture* (1982), 640–1; *DNB*.

Uffington, White Horse of (Oxfordshire, formerly Berkshire). This famous *hill figure certainly existed in the middle of the 12th century, when it is mentioned in a legal document as a landmark, but its true age and purpose have been hotly debated. Aubrey asserted that 'the White Horse was made by Hengist, who bore one on his arms or standard'; in 1738 the Revd Francis Wise said Alfred the Great had it cut to celebrate his victory over the Danes at Ashdown in 871. Archaeologists assigned it to the *Celtic period c.100 BC, because of its style—a disjointed figure composed of single thin lines, with a schematically rendered head (Piggott, 1931). This argument was challenged by supporters of Saxon dating, arguing that traces of a more realistic design remained (Woolner, 1967). In the 1990s, excavation confirmed the Horse's disjointed outline; moreover, luminescent silt dating produced the startlingly early date of c.1000 BC, making stylistic arguments irrelevant (Miles and Palmer, 1995).

The White Horse needed regular scraping, and in 1677 a tourist noted that 'some that dwell herabout have an obligation upon their lands to repair and cleanse this landmark, or else in time it may turn green'. Thomas Cox, in his edition of *Britannia* (1720), said it was weeded annually, the workmen ending the day 'in feasting and merriment'. *The Scouring of the White Horse*, a novel by Thomas Hughes (1857), gives a lively description of the accompanying fair, with stalls, sideshows, and games—including tobogganing down the steep hill on the jawbone of a horse.

Legends and beliefs concerning the White Horse are few. It was sometimes said that *St George killed his dragon on a nearby hill, and that the White Horse is a picture of the saint's horse (according to some), or the dragon itself (according to others). A wish made while standing on the horse's eye would come true. A tradition that it was 'creeping up the hill'

makes sense, as the figure's position did change slightly over the centuries.

Marples, 1949: 28–66; Stuart Piggott, *Antiquity* 5 (1931), 37–46; Diana Woolner, *Folklore* 78 (1967), 90–111; David Miles and S. Palmer, *Current Archaeology* 12: no. 10 (1995), 372–8.

umbrellas. The fact that it is unlucky to open an umbrella indoors is one of the most widely known superstitions in England today, achieving sixth place in our *Superstitions Survey 1998/9 Top Ten. Some go further to say it is particularly bad if you hold it over your head. There are other less well-known beliefs about umbrellas: it is unlucky to place an umbrella on a table, or a bed, and if you drop your umbrella someone else must pick it up for you (this is also said of walking sticks and *spoons). Clearly, these beliefs cannot be particularly old, as the umbrella itself only became widely accepted in England at the end of the 18th century. Indeed, none of them has been found earlier than the 1880s. There seems to be no explanation—rational or otherwise—for these superstitions.

Opie and Tatem, 1989: 415; *N&Q* 8s:10 (1896), 196, 472; 8s:11 (1897), 332, 430.

unbaptized babies. Until recent times, the Church of England and Roman Catholic Church did not allow miscarried or stillborn babies to be buried in consecrated ground, as they had not been *baptized; it was thought (explicitly by Catholics, more vaguely by Anglicans) that they went neither to Heaven nor Hell, but to Limbo, where they could never know God. Yet, being human, they deserved some respect; the professional oath required of midwives in 1649 instructed them:

Item, if any childe bee dead borne, you your selfe shall see it buried in such secret place as neither Hogg nor Dogg, nor any other Beast may come unto it, and in such sort done, as it may not be found or perceived, as much as you may; and that you shall not suffer any such childe to be cast into the Jaques (privy) or any other inconvenient place. (Anon., *The Book of Oaths* (1649), 289)

The lack of a proper *funeral was bitterly felt; in Gosforth (Lancashire) in the 1950s, a village craftsman said 'If tha didn't get kiddy baptised by t'parson, it would have to be put in a box and stuck in t'ground like some sort o' animal ... It wouldn't be right like a proper babby, it would be just like burying a dog or a sheep' (Clark, 1982: 117).

Various compromises were devised to soften the rule. The baby might be laid on the unpopular *north side of the churchyard, or just inside its wall, without ceremony or gravestone, or it might be secretly placed in the coffin of an adult, to share the latter's funeral and grave. In 1859, when an undertaker was caught doing this, the *Daily Telegraph* denounced him as ignorant and ghoulish (10 Oct. 1859), but the practice remained common throughout the 20th century, especially among the poor (Radford, Radford, and Hole, 1961: 346). As a hospital administrator explained in a letter to *The Times* (31 Mar. 1983) after a similar case, it was hard to get permission for burying stillbirths in consecrated ground, and 'tandem disposal' eased the parents' pain. Some Anglican clergy knew and approved the custom; one said it was 'in order that the little ghost may not torment its parents with reproachful lamentation' (Puckle, 1926).

The opposite attitude was expressed by a Devonshire man in 1852: 'When I was a young man it was thought lucky to have a stillborn child put into any open grave, as it was considered a sure passport to heaven for the next person buried there' (*N&Q* 1s:5 (1852), 77). In the last quarter of the 20th century, social and religious attitudes have changed greatly; it is now normal for the bereaved parents, the medical staff, and the hospital chaplain to arrange a funeral (Walter, 1990: 271–80).

In English folklore, ghosts of unbaptized babies appear in various forms; in Devon, they are said to become butterflies or moths; in Devon and Cornwall, *pixies; in Yorkshire, *nightjars; in many districts, *Will-o'-the-Wisps (Radford, Radford, and Hole, 1961: 346). It was sometimes thought they would rest if given a name; a monk in medieval Yorkshire recorded how a man met the ghost of his own infant son and named it in the name of the

Trinity, at which it ran off joyfully (James, 1922: 421).

Socially, an infant was not fully integrated into the community before *baptism; in some Yorkshire fishing villages, it was until recently 'unthinkable' to take it into any house but its parents' (Clark, 1982: 116, 124).

undead, the. This modern term usefully differentiates the reanimated corpse emerging physically from its tomb from the *ghost (a spiritual entity). The former is mentioned by several medieval writers; William of Malmesbury says it is well known that the Devil causes bodies of the evil dead to walk (*Gesta Regum*, ii, chapter 4). *William of Newburgh tells of three cases, at Alnwick and Berwick-on-Tweed and in Buckinghamshire (see *vampires). Walter *Map describes one in Hereford which called people by night, so that they sickened and died; it was laid by decapitation (*De Nugis Curialium*, ii, chapter 27).

Some intriguing local stories about revenants were jotted down in Latin by a monk of Byland Abbey (Yorkshire) around 1400, as undoubted facts (James, 1922); one concerns a certain Robert of Killiburne, who used to come out of his grave at night and roam about, terrifying the townsfolk and their dogs, until some youths caught him in the churchyard and held him there till the priest arrived to hear his confession and absolve him.

Post-medieval English folklore prefers ghosts to wandering corpses, but the older belief is implied when the bodies of suicides, criminals, and witches are said to be staked or buried face down, to prevent them 'walking'; in the case of suicides, staked burial in the roadway was required by law until 1823. In County Durham, it was thought that unless this was done, the Devil would enter the corpse and reanimate it (Brockie, 1886: 151–2).

See also *BURIAL, IRREGULAR.

underground passages, see *TUNNELS.

unicorns. The unicorn's horn was credited with the ability to detect or neutralize poisons, and to cure many diseases, including plague, epilepsy, and the bite of a mad dog. Various objects were sold as such, at very high prices; one kept in the Tower of London was officially valued at £600 in 1649, though one visitor in 1635 had estimated it at £18,000 or £20,000 (*Travels of Peter Mundy*, III, I, p. xx). Most were narwhal tusks; a slice from one, mounted in enamelled gold and dating from about 1560, known as the Campion Pendant, has been partly pared away on the reverse, presumably so that the parings could be taken as medicine. Walrus tusks and rhinoceros horns were also used, for example sliced to make cups and spoons. Less expensive were medical powders and potions supposedly containing scrapings of unicorn horn; these were still being sold by English pharmacists in the mid-18th century (Shepard, 1930/1996).

urban legends, see *CONTEMPORARY LEGENDS.

urine. For centuries, diagnosing illness by observing the patient's urine was standard medical procedure, and folk healers and *cun-ning men continued doing so, especially for suspected *witchcraft. It had an essential role in a common type of *counterspell to cure such illness, based on the idea that the magic link between the witch and her victim could be exploited to cause pain to the former, using the victim's urine as the medium. It could be heated in a *witch bottle, or baked in a cake, as *Herrick describes (*Hesperides* (1648), no. 891). The witch would hurry to her victim's house, begging for mercy, and would agree to lift her spell (Opie and Tatem, 1989: 416–18).

In folk *medicine, a lotion made from urine was thought good for chilblains; in the Fens, it had to be 'the last urine passed by a dying person, mixed with beastlings, the first milk given by a cow after calving' (*Folklore* 69 (1958), 118).

Valentine's Day (14 February). For today's adolescents and young adults, this is a highly popular festival, bolstered by the powerful greetings-card industry and huge media coverage.

The custom of choosing sweethearts on Valentine's Day arose in court circles in France and England in the 14th century, supposedly because birds began mating on this date. Poems were composed for the event, the earliest being Chaucer's *Parliament of Fowls* (c.1381), about rival bird-suitors quarrelling on Valentine's Day. Some 30 years later, the poet John Lydgate used the word 'valentine' both for the person loved and the poem sent, as in modern English ('A Valantine to Her That Excelleth All', and 'A Kalendare'); in 1477, Margery Brews wrote to her fiancé John Paston as her 'right wellbelovyd Voluntyn'. Why this particular date was chosen is uncertain. Most likely, it counted as the first day of spring in whichever French region invented the custom (many medieval calendars reckoned spring began in February, either on the 7th or the 22nd). There is nothing in legends about St Valentine to link him with birds or lovers, nor any evidence supporting an 18th-century theory deriving the festival from the Roman *Lupercalia* (15 February).

Upper-class Valentine customs are well documented, but there is little information about the rest of society before 19th-century folklore collections; it is quite feasible that most people took little notice of the day until quite late on. Emphasis has changed over time, but the main elements have been: (1) choosing someone to be your 'Valentine' by lot, by accident, or deliberately; (2) gifts; (3) letters or cards, signed or anonymous; (4) love *divinations.

Pepys gives excellent descriptions of 17th-century Valentines, rarely failing to mention the day; the details varied from year to year, showing the custom was fluid. His entries for 1666, for example, include references to drawing Valentines by lot, and complaints about the expense of several presents he felt obliged to give the lady who had drawn him, for example 'a dozen pairs of gloves and a pair of silk stockings' as late as 10 March. More modest gifts, sometimes anonymous, are mentioned in 19th-century accounts; thus, at Norwich, people laid packages on doorsteps, banged the knocker, and rushed away (Wright and Lones, 1938: ii. 137–8). Besides genuine presents there was a tradition of sending joky ones, or worthless items grandly wrapped.

Sending special letters probably dates from the mid-18th century, and grew steadily more popular. Special writing paper was available in the 1820s; the commercially produced card appeared around 1840, and by the 1860s was big business. Early examples are exquisite, expensive confections in lace and satin, but more down-market printed cards gradually became the norm—along with joke parodies and spiteful anti-Valentines. These are often held responsible for the decline of the custom around the turn of the century; it began to pick up again in the late 1920s, and mushroomed after the Second World War. Currently Valentine's Day is going from strength to strength; a recent development has been whole pages of messages in newspapers and magazines.

Other customs and beliefs include, naturally, girls' love charms and *divinations, for example putting *yarrow under one's pillow or turning stockings inside out (Porter, 1969: 106). It was widely said that the first person seen would be one's future spouse, and various strategies were adopted to manipulate this omen; in 1662, Mrs Pepys spent the day with her hands over her eyes to avoid seeing some painters working in her house. Children in many areas took occasion to go from door to door in the early morning, singing 'Good morrow, Valentine', and expecting cakes, fruit, or money (Wright and Lones, 1938: ii. 147).

Jack B. Oruch, 'St Valentine, Chaucer, and Spring in February', *Speculum* 56:3 (1981), 534–65; Hutton, 1996: 146–50; Wright and Lones, 1938: ii. 136–57; Folklore Society Cuttings File.

vampires. In East European folklore, a vampire is a a bloated, blood-filled corpse which leaves its tomb, bringing disease and death. It is often assumed that the concept was unknown in England until imported (in glamorized form) by 19th-century novelists. However, *William of Newburgh in the late 12th century recorded several contemporary accounts of active corpses, one of which corresponds perfectly to the folkloric vampire's appearance and behaviour (*Historia Rerum Anglicarum*, book V, chapter 24).

It appeared at Alnwick (Northumberland) in 1196, emerging nightly from its grave to roam the streets, corrupting the air with 'pestiferous breath', so that plague broke out and many died. When two bold men decided to 'dig up this baneful pest and burn it with fire', they found the corpse much closer to the surface than they had expected; it had swollen to a horrifying size, its face was 'turgid and suffused with blood', and its shroud in tatters. They gave it a sharp blow with a spade; from the wound gushed 'such a stream of blood that it might have been taken for a leech (*sanguisuga*) filled with the blood of many people' (trans. Stevenson, 1856/1996: 660–1). So they tore the heart out, dragged the body away, and burned it; this put an end to the plague.

William gives three further accounts of aggressive *undead (chapters 22–4), all recent and vouched for by eyewitnesses. In Buckinghamshire, a dead man returned to his widow's bed, almost crushing her with his weight, and then terrorized kinsmen and neighbours; the body was found uncorrupted, and a written pardon was laid on its breast, though some had advised burning it. At Berwick-on-Tweed, a 'pestiferous corpse' roamed the city, 'pursued by a pack of dogs with loud barkings'; it was cut to pieces by ten brave young men, and burnt. At Melrose (Scotland) a monk who was attacked by a corpse struck it with an axe and chased it back to its grave; next day it was dug up to be burnt, and observers noted its 'huge wound, and a great quantity of gore which had flowed from it in the sepulchre'.

Though blood is only mentioned in two of these tales, all have features regularly associated with vampires in Europe—the link with plague, and the need to destroy the uncorrupted bodies. In later folklore, a tradition persisted that suicides, criminals, or witches should be staked 'to stop them walking'.

Full translations of the texts are in Joseph Stevenson, *The History of William of Newburgh* (1856; reprint 1996), 656–61; and Montague Summers, *The Vampire in Europe* (1929; reprint 1996), 80–8. The latter renders *sanguisuga* (literally 'blood-sucker') as 'vampire', not 'leech'; though tempting, this is too bold. For European vampire lore, see Paul Barber, *Vampires, Burial and Death: Folklore and Reality* (1988).

Vanishing Hitchhiker, the. A common international *contemporary legend, first so named by American scholars in 1942; it became famous as the title-story in Jan Brunvand's *The Vanishing Hitchhiker: American Urban Legends and their Meanings* (1981). It has two basic forms, the first being as well known in England as America. A car driver picks up a girl who is hitching a lift home; she chooses the back seat, but disappears while they are in transit. He goes to her home anyway, where he learns she had died years before, in a car crash; sometimes in the cemetery he finds a jacket he had lent her draped over a grave. In the second form (rare in England), the hitchhiker is male, and supernatural, not ghostly; he foretells some large-scale event such as war, and then adds a minor prophecy before disappearing; the latter soon comes true, and the driver realizes his passenger was an angel, or Jesus.

Both versions are often told with full belief; the first draws on the widespread current belief in *ghosts, while the second circulates in more restricted groups where its religious implications are credible. How old the story is depends on how you define it; if the criterion is not car travel but the sudden appearance and disappearance of a spectral or supernatural fellow traveller, parallels from the 19th century or earlier are easy to find (Bennett, in Bennett and Smith 1984: 45–63). Hitching a lift features in a tale of an allegedly true encounter in Lincolnshire in 1918: two women in a gig take up a weary-looking man, who silently leaves once they reach an inn; it turns out it is the ghost of a drowned man, whose corpse is laid out in that very inn (*N&Q* 12s:5 (1919), 205–6).

Vaughan Williams, Ralph (1872–1958). One

of the most important figures in the British classical musical scene in the 20th century, Vaughan Williams was also the one who made most use of a knowledge of folk-song in his compositions. By 1903, Vaughan Williams was already aware of folk-song, having access to the publications of Frank *Kidson, Sabine *Baring-Gould, and Lucy *Broadwood, and indeed he was already lecturing on the subject. A trip to Essex in December of that year introduced him to Mr Pottipher of Ingrave, who sang him the song 'Bushes and Briars', which immediately fired Vaughan Williams's interest and enthusiasm, and opened his eyes to the real thing. On subsequent trips to Essex, Norfolk, Suffolk, Surrey, Hampshire, Herefordshire, and elsewhere in the country, he had amassed the bulk of his collection of 810 songs by 1913. Vaughan Williams was typical of his generation when it came to collecting procedures. He was primarily interested in the tunes and often failed to note more than the first verse of a text. He did not try to note the whole repertoire of a singer, but concentrated on those he found interesting, and neither did he record any details of the singer's life or attitudes to singing beyond the bare name, age, and occupation. Collecting songs at that time was an arduous business, getting to remote villages (often by bicycle), spending hours searching out singers, noting tunes and words by hand in the open air or pub taprooms.

The fact that Vaughan Williams, more than any of his contemporaries, used the tunes he collected in his own works has been labelled as a form of cultural theft, but there is no doubt that he felt this musical heritage was important for the future health of society and the overwhelming importance of returning these tunes to the people, and this was his way of doing so—as a composer and musician. He felt he was on a rescue mission, and, of course, he was right. That Vaughan Williams was deeply affected, as a composer, by the songs he found is well known. Their tunes turn up directly in over 30 of his pieces, made a direct impact on his work on carols, and their more subtle influence can be seen and felt in many others. He constructed a theory of 'national music' based largely on his experience of folk-song:

Folk-song is not a cause of national music, it is a manifestation of it. The cultivation of folk-songs is only one aspect of the desire to found an art on the fundamental principles which are essential to its well-being. National music is not necessarily folk-song; on the other hand folk-song is, by nature,

necessarily national. (First published in 1934, reprinted in *National Music and Other Essays* (2nd edn., 1986), 63)

Although his collecting days ended in the 1920s, Vaughan Williams maintained an active interest in traditional music for the rest of his life. He played an important part in both the *English Folk Dance Society and the *Folk-Song Society and was instrumental in arranging their amalgamation in 1932. The Library at *Cecil Sharp House, headquarters of the *English Folk Dance and Song Society, is named after him.

Some of the songs he collected were published in the *Journal of the Folk-Song Society, Folk-Songs from the Eastern Counties (1908), Eight Traditional English Carols (1919), Twelve Traditional Carols from Herefordshire (with E. M. Leather, 1920), and see also, Roy Palmer, Folk Songs Collected by Ralph Vaughan Williams (1983); R. Vaughan Williams and A. L. Lloyd, The Penguin Book of English Folk Songs (1959); Percy Dearmer, Ralph Vaughan Williams, and Martin Shaw, The Oxford Book of Carols (1928). Articles about Vaughan Williams appear in Folk Music Journal, 2:3 (1972), English Dance & Song, 34:3 (1972), and 45:1 (1983). His own views are presented in National Music and Other Essays (1963; 2nd edn., 1986).

Vaughan Williams Memorial Library (VWML). The library and archives service of the *English Folk Dance and Song Society. The original nucleus for the library was the collection of books bequeathed by Cecil *Sharp on his death in 1924, and the collection was renamed after Ralph *Vaughan Williams's death in 1958. The collection has continued to grow and by a gradual process of professionalization the VWML has become the most important concentration of material on traditional song, dance, and music in the country. Address: Cecil Sharp House, 2 Regents Parks Road, London NW1 7AY (Tel.: 020 7485 2206).

vervain. Pieces of vervain root, or a sachet of its dried leaves, were hung round the neck to cure scrofula, prevent *nightmares, and make one immune to snakebite; it was also said to staunch blood, because it grew at the foot of Christ's cross. One Jacobean poet says it 'hindreth witches of their will' (Drayton, Nimphidia (1627), line 391); this probably alludes to *hagriding, since it is nowhere mentioned as a *house protection.

Virgins' Garlands, see *MAIDENS' GARLANDS.

visiting customs, see *CALENDAR CUSTOMS.

V-sign. The quintessential British offensive *gesture for most of the 20th century, formed by holding up a hand with the middle and index finger upright in a V shape, the thumb and other two fingers curled into the palm; the palm facing *towards the gesturer*. If asked, most people would gloss the meaning as 'F—— you' or something similar, and it was certainly a very potent offensive gesture until recent years when it seems to be losing its ability to offend. Nevertheless, most British people would still be careful, if they needed to signify the number two in a gesture to someone else, to make the sign with palm *facing the recipient*. The history of the gesture is uncertain, and there is no evidence of its existence before the first decade of the 20th century. In recent years an explanation for the origin of the V-sign dating it from the Battle of Agincourt has appeared. This story maintains that British archers were so effective and so feared by their enemy that when the French captured an archer they chopped off the two fingers he needed to draw a bow-string. Bowmen who had not been thus disfigured took to holding up two fingers to taunt their cowardly foes. Needless to say, there is no shred of evidence to support this unlikely origin, but it is on its way to becoming entrenched in the popular mind and becoming folklore in itself. It is possible that the V-sign developed from the much older *horns symbol, used to imply someone is a cuckold since at least the 16th century, although this gesture was traditionally made with little finger and index finger, and did not have the aggressive force of the V-sign. The American gesture, formed by holding up the middle finger alone, which was roughly equivalent to the V-sign, has been introduced to British culture by American films and other media, since about the 1960s, and is now well understood by most British people. It will be interesting to note whether it replaces the V-sign in the offensive gesture vocabulary.

The V-sign formed with the palm *away from the gesturer* has had a number of meanings. It was used effectively during the Second World War to signify 'Victory', especially by Winston Churchill, and in this sense it can still be seen in news reports from conflicts all round the world. In the 1960s, however, it was annexed by American, and later British, youth as the 'Peace sign', and a further change was signalled when in 1997 the pop group The Spice Girls used it to signify 'Girl power'.

See also: *FINGERS, *GESTURES, *COCKING A SNOOK, *HORNS, *THUMBS.

Morris, 1979: 226–40; *Talking Folklore* 1:2 (1986/7), 25–42.

Wade. In Yorkshire, Wade was a *giant who built Mulgrave Castle, while his wife Bell built Pickering Castle; they also built 'Wade's Causey' to link the two (it is actually a Roman road). Bell owned a huge cow; a whale's jawbone over a metre long was displayed as this cow's rib at Mulgrave Castle in the 18th century. Wade was supposed to have been buried at Barnby, where two *standing stones marked the grave (only one now remains). The name is that of an early Germanic hero, father of *Wayland (Westwood, 1985: 343–6).

waits. Originally bands of musicians employed by city corporations such as Norwich, York, Chester, and Leicester, to parade the streets at night playing music to soothe and reassure the inhabitants, and were thus allied to the Watch who also policed the streets in medieval towns. The waits also played at civic ceremonial occasions and offered their musical services to whoever needed them and were willing to pay. As city employees they were provided with a livery and badge of office and, at least in earlier periods, were granted a near-monopoly on music-making within the city. The earliest references are to the 13th century at York (1272) and Norwich (1288), and they lasted in many places well into the 19th century; at Leicester they were only abolished by the 1836 Reform Act. Even then they did not disappear completely in many places, as each year at *Christmas they were given a licence to play during the festive season, collecting money at houses that they had serenaded on Boxing Day, which explains why many writers after the 1830s define the waits as specifically Christmas visiting musicians. In most cases they played wind instruments, hautboys, clarinets, bassoons, and so on, but there are also mentions of violins and other stringed instruments, and it is clear that the Waits could be accomplished and well-known musicians in their own right; but there are also reports of drunkenness and disorderly conduct.

Jonathan E. O. Wilshere, *Leicester Towne Waytes* (1970); Chambers, 1878: ii. 742–4.

wakes (1). Wakes, feasts, and revels are regional terms for the same type of event. In most parishes in pre-Reformation England, the day dedicated to the patron saint of the local church was set aside for major celebrations, as most 'holidays' were linked to religious observance. The word 'wake' derives from the custom of sitting up and watching (or 'waking') in the church overnight, and then spending the next day in revelry. In medieval times, these celebrations would have included processions led by images of the saint, as well as general sports, games, and feasting. However, the Reformation brought in different ideas and the festivities were gradually toned down, although many places still kept them up as a day of jollification. Many parishes whose patronal festivals occurred in winter moved the celebration to *Whitsun or September, and the change of calendar in 1752 also confused the pattern of feast days. When some industrial towns adopted the system of closing down the factories or mills for a particular week, the term 'wakes' was adopted. Some wakes gradually turned into full-blown fairs, others faded away during the 19th century, while the ones which still had a religious base became attenuated into garden fêtes or small-scale church celebrations.

In the industrial areas, such as the cotton belt of Lancashire, the wakes took on a much higher profile in the festival year, and became the major celebratory occasion for the semi-rural communities and newly urbanized workers. They were often linked with the rushcarts (see *rushbearing), featuring *morris dancers, fairground amusements and stalls, and, by all accounts, a great deal of drinking and fighting. During the 19th century they increasingly became the target of a combination of reforming employers, local middle-class citizens, and respectable working-class leaders, who argued that the workers' spare time should be spent in rational and 'improving' pastimes or healthy sport, rather than the hard-drinking, fighting, and dancing for which wakes had become infamous. Admittedly, this roughness was only the more visible part of the celebrations, and there were plenty of other features which were less objectionable, but their days were numbered and one by one they either faded away, were suppressed, or transformed.

J. K. Walton and Robert Poole, 'The Lancashire Wakes in the 19th Century', in: Storch, 1982: 100–24; Hole,1975: 154–7; Kightly, 1986: 113–14.

wakes (2). Until well into the 20th century, it was usual for the dead to be kept at home until the funeral. Since the body should never be left alone, family members would keep watch beside it, but the organized 'wake' attended by many relatives and neighbours, as in Ireland, virtually vanished from England soon after the Reformation. Only two records of it remain. One comes from Aubrey, who noted the mixture of prayer, drinking, and games so characteristic of wake customs:

At the funeralls in Yorkshire, to this day they continue the custome of watching & sitting-up all night till the body is interred. In the interim some kneel downe and pray (by the corps), some play at cards, some drink & take Tobacco: they have also Mimicall playes and sports, e.g., they choose a simple young fellow to be a Judge, and then the Suppliants (having first blacked their hands by rubbing it under the bottome of the Pott), beseech his Lordship and smutt all his face. They play likewise at Hot-cockles. (Aubrey, 1686/1880: 30–1)

He gives a glimpse of popular ideas about the ordeals awaiting the dead: 'The beliefe in Yorkshire was amongst the vulgar (perhaps is in part still), that after the persons death the soule went over Whinney-moore' (i.e. a moor of gorse). 'Till about 1616', some hired woman would come to the wake to sing the *Lyke-Wake Dirge, about the soul's journey. It must pass Whinney-moor and the Bridge of Dread to reach Purgatory fire; those who have given shoes to the poor can cross the moor unhurt, and those who have given 'milk or drink' can pass through the fire, but the uncharitable will be pricked and burnt 'to the bare bone'. The second reference is a late 16th-century let-

ter cited by Walter Scott in his *Minstrelsy of the Scottish Border*. This too describes women singing round the corpse about the dead coming to 'a great launde full of thornes and furzen', where an old man will meet them with the very shoes they once gave away, so they can cross unhurt (Scott, ed. T. F. Henderson (1902), iii. 163–4).

This type of wake, mixing prayer-vigil, hospitality, and entertainment, left no later trace. Occasionally, however, something similar was reinvented for practical reasons; thus, Victorian London costermongers wanting to raise money for a funeral would visit the widow's house in groups, make donations, and gather round the corpse in a deliberately jolly mood (Binder, 1975: 42–3).

warts. There are more folk cures for warts than for any other ailment, featured in virtually every regional collection. Some simply advise rubbing them with a specified plant product, for example the inner skin of broad-bean pods, sliced potato, the juice of dandelion, spurge, or greater celandine. If the wart is a large, fleshy one, it can be starved of blood by tying a thread or hair tightly round the base, and will soon shrivel and drop off. But very often *magical actions are prescribed; the warts are touched with some object(s) such as pebbles, pins, or knotted cord, or identified with them by counting, after which the object(s) is/are thrown away or buried. Such methods have been recommended since the Middle Ages; recently recorded examples include: 'Rub wart with raw meat and bury meat afterwards' ('at a crossroads at midnight', according to some); 'Tie as many knots as there are warts in a piece of string, throw away the string'; 'Count warts, take the same number of buds from an alder bush, bury them'. Some older sources suggest rubbing the wart with a snail or slug, which is then impaled on a thorn bush and left to die.

The underlying assumption is that the fate of the object(s) determines that of the warts: as it rots or is lost, so will the warts be; as the *snail dies, so does the wart. Sometimes, it is thought they will be transferred to someone else; in 1807 Robert Southey wrote:

Stealing dry peas or beans, and wrapping them up, one for each wart, he carries the parcel to a place where four roads meet, and tosses it over his head, not looking behind to see where it falls; he will lose the warts, and whoever picks it up will find them. (*Letters from England*, no. 50)

Less maliciously, they can be 'given' to the dead:

Wait till you see a funeral then stroke the wart in the direction in which the funeral is going, saying at the same time: 'Corpse, corpse, take my wart with you'.... [I]t never fails, but again secrecy is important, for no one must see or hear what you are doing. (N&Q 11s:3 (1911), 446)

There were, and are, people credited with the ability to charm away warts by 'buying' them, making the sign of the cross over them, touching them, or merely looking at them; they sometimes also murmured a charm, but its words are not recorded. Various rhymes are known for self-administered charms, for instance to stick a pin in an *ash tree and say:

Ashy tree, ashy tree,
Pray buy these warts off me,

or cut a *cross in a potato, throw it away, and say:

One, two, three,
Warts go away from me,
One, two, three, four,
Never come back no more.

(Tongue, 1965: 43)

For samples of cures, see Opie and Tatem, 1989: 422–4; Susan Drury, Folklore 102 (1991), 97–100. For material from the 1960s and 1990s, see Gabrielle Hatfield, *Warts: Summary of the Wart-Cure Survey for the Folklore Society* (1998).

washing. There are a number of beliefs about washing, either the person or clothes, some of which are still current. It was considered unlucky, all over the country, for two people to use the same water to wash their hands. The specific result usually quoted is that they will quarrel, and there are two remedies advised—for one of them to make the sign of the cross with their hand over the water, or for one or both to spit in the water. The belief is at least as old as the 17th century, as John Aubrey (1686: 99) includes it, and Opie and Tatem mention another reference from 1652. For 19th-century examples, see N&Q 4s:8 (1871), 505; 8s:9 (1896), 425. At a much earlier date, washing hands with someone while reciting a particular psalm was published as a cure for the ague (Scot, 1584). Presumably as an extension to the shared washing rule, it was reported from Devonshire that it was unlucky for two persons to wipe themselves upon a towel at the same time (N&Q 10s:12 (1909), 66). Cuthbert Bede, writing in N&Q (1s:12 (1855), 489) reported a Worcestershire servant girl

who was convinced she could not successfully kill anything (e.g. the chicken she was plucking) until she had washed her face, implying that this was a well-known fact. Henderson (1879: 113) reports exactly the same belief from Durham.

Robert *Herrick has another admonition to servant maids on the subject of washing hands:

Unwasht hands, ye Maidens, know
Dead the fire, though ye blow

(Hesperides, 1648)

and also how far to throw the water out of the door, the further the better to keep out the 'evil spright'.

More dangerous was to wash clothes at the wrong time. In fishing communities there was (and still is in some families) a strict taboo against washing clothes on the day a family-member has set sail, or on certain other inauspicious days, because such an action would 'wash him overboard' or even sink his ship (Gill, 1993: 15–20, 105–6). One of the most inauspicious days for washing was *Good Friday. Clothes hung out on that day would be spotted with blood, and a story is told that Jesus cursed a woman who was washing clothes as he passed by on the way to Calvary (Henderson, 1879: 82). Similarly, New Year's Day was another on which no washing should be attempted, and washing blankets in May was also considered unlucky. Good housewifely practice was recommended in a rhyme which was known in various versions all over the country:

They that wash on Monday, have all the week to dry
They that wash on Tuesday, are not so much awry
They that wash on Wednesday, are not so much to blame
They that wash on Thursday, wash for shame
They that wash on Friday, wash in need
They that wash on Saturday, Oh! They're sluts indeed.

(Yorkshire, N&Q 5s:7 (1877), 139)

See also *SOAP.

Opie and Tatem, 1989: 424–6; Henderson, 1879; N&Q 5s:7 (1877), 26, 108, 139, 378; 5s:8 (1877), 77.

wasps. These seem to have been little regarded by English folklore. Kill the first wasp you see and you will have good luck and freedom from enemies all the year is reported from Northamptonshire in N&Q in 1850, and occasionally since then, but this is more commonly said of *butterflies and sometimes of *snakes. Lean records a proverb, 'If you kill one wasp, three will come to his funeral' (Lean, 1902: i. 451), but this is said of other insects, such as *beetles. Cures for wasp-stings naturally occur regularly in traditional medicine, a raw *onion rubbed on the sting being a favourite cure. According to a correspondent from Stourport in N&Q (4s:8 (1874), 547) it is possible to handle wasps without being stung: 'A small boy in this parish takes wasps' nests with impunity, and without the usual armour of gloves and mask, by merely uttering a low whistle, keeping it up while he removes the comb.'

Opie and Tatem, 1989: 426; Lean, 1902: i. 451; ii. 32.

wassailing. Amongst all the calendar customs which popular folklore enthusiasts have claimed as remnants of luck-bringing rituals, wassailing is the only one that has a relatively clear and undisputed claim to this lineage. The very name, wassail, comes from *wæs hæil* meaning 'Be healthy' which in Anglo-Saxon was used as a salutation or toast in its own right. There are two basic forms of this many-faceted custom, and both are probably of some considerable antiquity. The first is a house-*visiting custom, wishing health to neighbours, and the other is what could be termed a 'field-visiting' custom, wishing health to, usually, fruit trees, but also sometimes other farm crops, animals, and so on. The proper day for wassailing varied from place to place, but was always in midwinter, at *Christmas, or *New Year, and the name also varies considerably, including vessel-cup, waysailing, and howling.

In the house-visiting version, young women went about the neighbourhood with a bowl of drink, often spiced ale, dressed up with garlands and ribbons, singing or reciting a set of verses that wished luck to the inhabitants, and naturally they expected money or food in return. The drink could be of any suitably festive sort, but was often described as Lamb's Wool, made from spiced ale or cider and baked apples. Later instances of the custom involve men and women, but most of the earlier references take it for granted that it was a female custom, and although the actual words may vary, the basic structure and import of the verses do not differ a great deal from place to place:

Wassail, wassail all over the town
Our toast it is white, our ale is brown

Our bowl it is made of a maplin tree
We be good fellows all, I drink to thee.

Successive verses salute the horse, the cow, the maids, and the butler (Gloucestershire: *Time's Telescope* (1814), 3).

As an alternative or addition to the drink in the bowl, many wassailers carried a box with one or two dolls inside to represent the baby Jesus and the Virgin Mary, decorated on the outside with flowers, ribbons, evergreens, and so on. Well-made examples had a glass lid for the box, which was covered by a white cloth, so that the contents could be 'shown' on each visit. The song sung by these visitors was more likely to be a *Christmas carol, such as 'The Seven Joys of Mary', and it could be carried out by a single individual or a small group. This custom seems to have become increasingly rare during the second half of the 19th century.

The second form of wassailing was much more of a man's custom. Again, New Year was the favourite time, but groups might be found any time over the Christmas/New Year season. The custom involved visiting the local orchards and wassailing the trees to encourage a good crop in the coming year. Songs would be sung, the trunks beaten with sticks or splashed with cider, cider-soaked toast might be laid at the roots or placed in the branches, there was much cheering, and, usually, guns were fired into the air. The verses were normally on the lines of:

Here stands a good old apple tree, stand fast root
Every little twig bear an apple big
Hats full, caps full, and three score sacks full
Hip! Hip! Hurrah!

(Edward Swanton, *Bygone Haslemere* (1914), 285)

This form of wassailing lasted much longer than the house-visit custom, and can still be seen at Curry Rivel (Somerset) and has been revived elsewhere. Many sources link wassailing with the West Country, but it was widespread all over the country. In Sussex, for example, it was called 'Apple Howling', a name that goes back at least to the 17th century (*Sussex Archaeological Collections* 1 (1848), 110).The earliest references to come to light so far are to c.1486–93 for payments for wassails at New Year at St Mary De Pré Priory, St Albans (*Victoria County History: Hertford*, iv. 431) and to 1585 at Fordwich, in Kent (Hutton, 1996: 46), and it is likely that more will be discovered as research into early sources continues.

Wright and Lones, 1940: iii. 223–4, 284–8; Hutton, 1996: 13–14, 45–63.

water-spirits. Several *rivers were said to be inhabited by beings who dragged people (especially children) into the water to drown them. These include the Ribble and the Tees (both in Lancashire), homes of *Peg o' Nell and *Peg Powler (Henderson, 1866: 265). Several northern and western counties used the name Nelly Long-Arms; there was also *Jenny Greenteeth in pools in Lancashire and Cheshire, and a male figure called Nicky Nye in Somerset (Tongue, 1970: 108–16).

Wayland's Smithy. This megalithic chamber tomb in Oxfordshire (formerly Berkshire) was identified in a charter of AD 855 as *Welandes smiðð e;* the spelling 'Wayland', popularized by Scott and Kipling, is now the usual one. Wayland was a master-craftsman in Germanic legends, sometimes described as an elf or a giant, more often as human; he was lamed and held captive by a king, but avenged himself by killing the king's young sons and raping his daughter, and then escaped by magic flight.

In folklore Wayland lost his individuality and was remembered merely as a fairy blacksmith, of a type known in several European countries. The antiquary Francis Wise wrote in 1738: 'At this place lived formerly an invisible Smith, and if a traveller's Horse had lost a Shoe upon the road, he had no more to do than to bring the Horse to this place with a piece of money, and leaving both there for some little time, he might come again and find the money gone, but the Horse new shod.' In the 19th century, local children used to visit the Smithy and try to hear the clink of his hammer.

Hilda R. E. Davidson, *Folklore* 69 (1958), 145–59.

weapon salve, see *KNIVES.

weather. Lore about the weather consisted mainly of practical information and advice, based on observation of nature, and transmitted orally. Such expertise was essential to farmers and seafarers. For the literate, there were also other channels of transmission, notably almanacs, which gave guidance on the right date for sowing this or that crop, beginning hay-making, and so on. Some scraps of this lore are still remembered: that rooks, gulls, or swifts flying high are a sign of fine weather, or that a good crop of berries foretells a hard winter (which is probably not true). A few rhymed tags are well known:

> Red at night,
> Shepherd's delight;
> Red in the morning,
> Shepherd's warning.

Alluding to high wispy clouds:

> See in the sky the painter's brush,
> The wind around you soon will rush.

For January weather:

> As the day lengthens,
> So the cold strengthens.

A rhyme found in many places uses the way low cloud hides hilltops as a sign of rain, naming whichever hill is nearest:

> When —— wears a cap,
> We in the valley gets a drop.

In some cases, weather lore is parodied in jokes which have themselves become traditional: 'If you can see X from Y, there will be rain soon; if you can't see X from Y, it's raining already.'

Less rational ways of forecasting included the idea that rain on *St Swithin's Day will continue for 40 days, and that the weather on each of the twelve days of Christmas shows what to expect for each month of the coming year. An unusual and dramatic form of weather divination was practised at Adderbury (Oxfordshire) in the latter part of the 19th century; men would go out to the fields towards eleven o'clock on Martinmas Eve (10 November) and keep vigil till midnight, listening to the wind, for they believed that 'the four Angels of the Earth' were flying round and round, stirring up the winds. At midnight this ceased, and the watchers noted which way the wind was then blowing, for that would be its prevailing direction for the next three months (Michael Pickering, *Folklore* 94 (1983), 252). In Derbyshire, people would take a candle to the bottom of the garden on *Halloween to see which way the wind blew, for it would remain in that quarter for three months (Addy, 1895: 118).

Notable storms could be seen as *omens accompanying a great man's death, or as signs either of the wrath of God or of the activity of the Devil. Witches were believed capable of 'selling' winds to sailors in the form of *knotted cords, and of malicious storm-raising; the penalty of various unlucky actions, notably *whistling and drowning a *cat at sea, is that they cause fierce winds.

See also *STORMS, *THUNDER.

weddings. Of all the *life-cycle points, getting married is the most public. The way couples celebrate their wedding has always depended largely on their class, relative affluence or poverty, religion, and the region where they lived, but also on the dictates of fashion, which may vie strongly with those of tradition. The Victorian era was a major watershed in the way weddings were held, and E. M. Wright correctly identifies mobility (both social and geographical) and fashion as the factors involved:

The bridegroom's friends and relations are often complete strangers to the bride's kith and kin, their ways and beliefs are unknown to each other. They cannot join together in some time-honoured ceremonial when the newly-wedded pair enter their new home; instead, they wave hats and handkerchiefs in the wake of a train or a motor which is carrying the couple to a distant dwelling-place. The bride, too, has up-to-date ideas. She wants to make a sensation, like Lady Dunfunkus Macgregor's daughter, a description of whose marriage she has just read in the *Daily Mail* ... Her dress and her doings, and all the wedding festivities, must as far as possible be modelled on a fashionable pattern, till finally modern conventionalities and not ancient customs rule the day. (Wright, 1913: 270)

Weddings necessarily take place under the constraints of legal and ecclesiastical regulations, but these change over time. Medieval rules forbidding marriage during penitential seasons, on high festival days, and after midday, are long gone; civil marriages came in in 1836; the 1994 Marriage Act allowed premises other than churches and registry offices to host marriage ceremonies. By May 1998 there were over 2,000 newly approved venues, mostly hotels and stately homes, but also museums, sports facilities, and halls, and a new industry of what might be called 'genre weddings' sprang up almost overnight. In addition, many couples now choose to go abroad to marry, and members of alternative religions (*Wiccans, *Druids, etc.) hold 'handfasting' rituals at sacred sites which, though not binding in law, are true marriages to the participants. It is too soon to say how these major changes will affect the traditional aspects of weddings, and what compromises between old and new will evolve.

Numerous sources since the early 19th century report that various days of the week were seen as lucky or unlucky for weddings, and virtually all say Fridays and Saturdays are worst. A widespread rhyme sums it up, here in a County Durham version:

> Monday for wealth
> Tuesday for health
> Wednesday the best day of all
> Thursday for losses
> Friday for crosses
> And Saturday no luck at all

(Henderson, 1879: 33)

Nowadays, the convenience of a weekend wedding outweighs any lingering superstition. Saturday is by far the most popular day, with 76 per cent of weddings in 1979 and 68 per cent in 1994; Friday is easily the second choice, with 11 per cent and 14 per cent, nearly three times as many as any midweek day. Similarly with the precepts noted in so many 19th-century sources, but now disregarded:

> If you marry in Lent,
> You will live to repent.

> Marry in May,
> Rue for aye.

The May proscription seems to have been stronger, and more long lasting, in Scotland than in England. Victorian parsons' diaries show Christmas Day as quite a popular day to marry, but a down-to-earth northern farmer's view says:

> He's a fule that marries at Yule
> For when the bairn's to bear
> The corn's to shear

(*Denham Tracts*, 1895: ii. 92)

The custom of throwing things over the bride and groom has a long history, though the items thrown have changed. The earliest reference is from 1486; when Henry VII brought his wife to Bristol 'a baker's wife cast out of a window a great quantity of wheat, crying "Welcome! and Good Luck!"' (S. Seyer, *Memoirs of Bristol*, quoted in *Folk-Lore Record* 3 (1880), 133). Wheat or corn is mentioned regularly until the later 19th century, and occasionally flower petals and sugar plums. In 1874 Francis Kilvert recorded in his *Diary* (11 August) the throwing of rice, and this remained common till paper confetti was introduced around the turn of the 20th century. Almost at once there were complaints that it littered the aisle and spoiled the bridal costume, and was merely 'a refined kind of horseplay' (*Surrey Gazette*, (13 Sept. 1904), 3 reprinting from a Coventry parish magazine) Vicars and registrars regularly ban it, to little effect; a return to rice is often proposed as more environmentally sound.

Writers from the early 17th century onwards often mention the strewing of rushes, herbs, or flowers for the bride to walk on. A malevolent parody, using *rue, occurred in Herefordshire (Leather, 1912: 115). The only remnant of strewing is the custom of having little girls throwing flower petals down the aisle, perhaps reimported to Britain via American films. An unusual variation was reported from Cranbrook (Kent) in the 1850s; there, it was customary to strew the path from the church 'with emblems of the bridegroom's calling; carpenters walk on shavings; butchers on the skins of slaughtered sheep; the followers of St Crispin are honoured with leather parings; paper-hangers with strips of paper; blacksmiths with old iron, rusty nails, etc.' (N&Q 1s:10 (1855), 181). The groom's occupation may be reflected in other ways, for example a 'guard of honour' outside the church with raised swords, police truncheons, or tools of a trade. At a butcher's wedding in Croydon in 1902, other butchers greeted the couple by 'ringing the bells' on marrow-bones and cleavers (Croydon Advertiser (21 June 1902); cf. Chambers, 1878: i. 360).

Other long-standing but boisterous customs which are now obsolete include firing the anvil, and horseplay during the walk to and from church:

a wedding in the Dales of Yorkshire is indeed a thing to see; nothing can be imagined comparable to it in wildness and obstreperous mirth. The bride and bridegroom may be a little subdued, but his friends are like men bereft of reason. They career round the bridal party like Arabs of the desert, galloping over ground on which, in cooler moments, they would hesitate even to walk a horse—shouting all the time, and firing volleys from the guns they carry with them. Next they will dash along the road in advance of the party, carrying the whiskey-bottle, and compelling everyone they meet to pledge the newly-married pair. (Henderson, 1879:37)

In Yorkshire villages, guns were often filled with feathers and fired over the bride's and groom's heads (Blakeborough, 1898: 95–6; Nicholson, 1890: 3). A more dangerous custom is revealed when a man tried for shooting at, and damaging, the door of the bride's mother at Pensham (Worcestershire) pleaded this was customary at weddings (Worcester Herald (22 Mar. 1845)). It was quite common to bar the way of the party returning from church, for example by a locked gate or a rope across the

road; the groom would be expected to pay to be allowed through, often by tossing coins to be *scrambled for (Palmer, 1976: 31–2).

It is now almost universal at formal receptions to have an iced cake, the first cut being made ceremonially by bride and groom together; this is first mentioned in the 1890s. Using pieces of wedding cake in *love divinations is reported regularly since the early 18th century, often with complications such as passing the fragment nine times through a wedding ring (Gentleman's Magazine (1832), 492). Throwing pieces of cake (not usually the cake itself) over the heads of the bride and/or groom was common in Yorkshire and Northumberland; sometimes guests did this, sometimes the bride herself; sometimes a plate was thrown too. In all cases it was lucky for the cake and plate to break, and usually the guests tried to snatch a piece for themselves (N&Q 1s:7 (1853), 545; Blakeborough, 1898: 96).

A widespread modern feature is that all unmarried women (and sometimes men) gather as the bride is about to depart; she throws her bouquet over her shoulder (to avoid favouritism), and whoever catches it will be married next. Opie and Tatem give the first reference for this as 1923, and in 1963 it could still be called 'American'. In past generations, other items were thrown, to similar purpose. The stocking is the missile in numerous literary references of the 17th and 18th centuries: at the end of the day, when the couple are sitting up in bed, young men take the bride's stocking and girls the groom's, and throw it over their shoulders. Whoever hits the bride or groom ('on the nose', many sources say) will marry soon (Brand, 1849: i. 170; Balfour, 1904: 97–8; Evelyn's Diary, 9 Oct. 1671). Another regular custom of the 18th and 19th centuries, which Brand thought 'bordered very closely upon indecency', was for young unmarried men to compete in a race for the privilege of removing and keeping the bride's garter. Earlier references imply an indecent scramble 'before the very altar'(Brand, 1849: ii. 139–40). Later, mere ribbons were raced for, probably as a decorous substitute (Henderson, 1879: 41–2; N&Q 146 (1924), 113–14, 163).

There has been much comment on throwing old *shoes after the departing couple, which has been done for 300 years at least, but little elucidation. It is important to realize that it is merely one application of a practice first mentioned in Heywood's Proverbs (1546) of throwing shoes at people for luck when leaving on a journey, or entering a new house; whatever the underlying symbolism, it cannot be unique to weddings. A playful elaboration reported from Kent in 1894 was for the chief bridesmaid to retrieve one of the shoes and throw it again for the bridesmaids to race for, and then again for the men (*Lippincott's Magazine* 54 (1894), 884). Nowadays shoes are tied to the couple's car, along with tin cans, balloons, and streamers.

There is a wide assortment of beliefs and taboos to ensure a happy marriage, beginning well before the wedding day. Many are still known, though not necessarily taken seriously. Two sayings which are still quoted are 'Change the name and not the letter, Change for the worse and not the better' (reported everywhere from the 1850s onwards), and 'Happy the bride the sun shines on', known already to *Herrick (*Hesperides* (1648)). Some rules seem to be based on 'not tempting fate'. That the couple should not hear their own banns called, lest the firstborn child be deaf and dumb, was reported from all regions from the 1850s onwards. The bride must not make her own dress; some small part—a thread, a bow, whatever—must be left off until the actual moment she leaves for church (*Folk-Lore* 68 (1957), 146); she should not look in a mirror once it is all complete (*N&Q* 2s:12 (1861), 490); and, as everyone knows, the groom must not see her in her wedding dress before she arrives in church.

Before white dresses became virtually universal, colour was important. *Green was shunned as unlucky; *blue was favoured—except, according to Blakeborough, in 19th-century Yorkshire, where it too was unlucky. A well-known rhyme ran:

> Married in green, ashamed to be seen
> Married in grey, will go far away
> Married in red, wish yourself dead
> Married in blue, always be true
> Married in yellow, ashamed of your fellow
> Married in black, wish yourself back
> Married in pink, of you he'll think
> Married in white, sure to go right.

The widest-known rhyme today is 'Something old, something new, something borrowed, something blue', first recorded in Shropshire only in 1883 (Burne, 1883: 290). Many say the item borrowed should be something worn at a previous wedding, provided the marriage turned out happily; the veil is often singled out as the luckiest.

The general belief that meeting a *chimney-sweep is lucky, reported since the late 19th century, became specifically linked to weddings during the 20th century; such meetings are now deliberately arranged. For a bridal party to meet a funeral is very unlucky; one young bride told her vicar, in tears, that it meant all her babies would be born dead (Balleine, 1939: 5). Other bad omens were for the church *clock to strike during the ceremony (Opie and Tatem, 1989: 85–6); a thunderstorm meant the couple would have no children (Porter, 1969: 7). Various signs foretold whether the bride or the groom would die first. In Yorkshire, 'them as speaks loudest dies first' (*N&Q* 6s:1 (1880), 75); in Shropshire, whichever drops the *ring (Burne, 1883: 294–5); in Herefordshire, whichever turns away from the altar first (Leather, 1912: 114); in Lincolnshire, whichever kneels down first (*N&Q* 4s:12 (1873), 44); in Yorkshire again, whichever first falls asleep on the wedding night (*N&Q* 1s:6 (1852), 312). The behaviour of bride and groom could also show which would be 'master' in the new home: whichever stepped out of church first, left the bride's home first after the meal, crossed the threshold first, and so on (Wright, 1913: 273).

Everyone now knows the groom 'should' carry the bride over the threshold of their new home, though it is not always actually performed. The history of this is obscure; Brand calls it 'an ancient custom', but it is not regularly reported in 19th-century sources, though other threshold customs are—for example the widespread 'warming the doorstep' of the bride's *old* home by pouring hot water over it once the bride and groom had left, and the custom at Knutsford (Cheshire) that neighbours made patterns in white sand outside the bride's and groom's doors (*N&Q* 2s:10 (1860), 264; *Folk-Lore Journal* 1 (1883), 227). The interpretation is even more doubtful. Herrick, who does not actually mention lifting, has the line 'Now o'er the threshold force her in' (*Hesperides* (1648)), implying that a show of modest reluctance was expected. Others speculate that it is meant to avert the bad luck of *stumbling, or that it ensures that as neither is first to enter, neither will be 'master'.

Given the nature of the celebration, weddings can involve a fair amount of ribaldry from onlookers and guests, but this is underplayed in published accounts, and difficult to document. One instance is the business with the stocking or garter detailed above, another, a trick of placing a bell under the bridal bed; a writer in 1543 complained that the couple would be serenaded through the chamber door, with 'vicious and naughty ballads' (Brand, 1849: ii. 173). In modern times, much of this has been hived off to the stag and hen nights, but echoes survive in the licence in innuendo allowed to the Best Man in his speech at the wedding breakfast.

weighing. On the same principle that it is tempting fate to *count things too closely, there was previously a prejudice in many people's minds about weighing newborn babies. First noticed by Chambers (1878: ii. 39), from Suffolk, although it was clearly well entrenched already, the belief is reported a number of times into the 20th century, and was not even extinct in the 1950s (*Folk-Lore* 68 (1957), 414). Opie and Tatem also record an earlier reference to the weighing of adults being considered unlucky, published in the *British Apollo* (7 Sept. 1709).

Opie and Tatem, 1989: 437.

well-dressing. The custom of well-dressing takes place nowadays in dozens of villages, including Wirksworth, Belper, Youlgrave, Barlow, Bradwell, Tideswell, Stoney Middleton, Hope, Ashford-in-the-Water, Wormhill, Bonsall, Eyam, and Buxton, but Tissington is the best known and, most probably, the oldest. The well-dressing season runs from May to September with each village having its own regular time. In some cases this is a Bank Holiday, while others are fortunate to have a convenient saint's day associated with their parish church. Tissington is one of the earliest, taking place on *Ascension Day.

Dressing takes a similar form in most villages. A large (up to twelve feet long) shallow wooden tray is constructed, into which a base of smooth soft clay is packed. Elaborate pictures or patterns are made by pressing thousands of flower petals into the clay, plus other natural materials such as moss, stones, or shells. The trays are mounted vertically on scaffolding erected across, behind, or round the well. The pictures are most often biblical scenes, with an appropriate short text or caption, but other subjects can be presented and views of the local church used to be popular. Many have a single panel, others have two or three.

The custom probably arose around the turn of the 19th century, evolving from the more widespread, but less picturesque, decoration of wells with ribbons and garlands. A visitor to Tissington in 1758 commented that 'We saw the spring adorned with garlands; in one of these was a tablet inscribed with rhymes'. One Ebenezer Rhodes, however, writing in 1818, reported 'newly-gathered flowers disposed in various boards . . . cut to the figures intended to be represented, and covered with moist clay into which the stems of the flowers are inserted' which sounds similar to how it is today. Hone's *Every-Day Book* gives further details. Well-dressing is still growing in popularity and more villages are added to the list nearly every year.

Crichton Porteous, *The Well-Dressing Guide* (1970); Stone, 1906: 73–5; Hone, 1827: ii. 318–20; Shuel, 1985: 93–102; Kightly, 1986: 231–3; Charlotte A. Norman, 'Annual Well-Dressing—Another Brilliant Success', in Buckland and Wood, 1993: 137–46.

Wellerisms. A form of verbal joke following the pattern '—— —— ——, as —— said when ——', or 'as —— said to ——'. The first part is a harmless cliché or *proverb, which is then undermined by a mocking or vulgar addition. Some examples of the genre are old, for example 'Every little helps, as the wren said when she pissed in the sea', recorded in 1602. It was popular among 19th-century working-class men, some examples being respectable, and others coarse: 'Neat but not gaudy, as the monkey said when he painted his tail sky-blue'; 'You must draw the line somewhere, as the monkey said, peeing across the carpet'. In the mid-20th there was a vogue for turning innocent phrases into innuendos by adding 'as the bishop said to the actress', or vice versa. The genre is named after Sam Weller in Dickens's *The Pickwick Papers* (1836).

Archer Taylor, *The Proverb* (1962), 200–20; Florence E. Baer, *Folklore* 94 (1983), 173–83.

wells. Healing or holy wells are rarer in England than in Scotland, Wales, or Ireland; even so, almost 200 are extant, and hundreds more once existed, as indicated on old documents. Those that remain are often regarded as *wishing wells. They are the latest phase in a long tradition of ritual activity, traceable archaeologically through Roman and *Celtic culture to prehistoric times; its present form was shaped by medieval Catholicism, where wells were often dedicated to a saint—sometimes a local one. Thus, St Oswald's Well at Winwick

(Cheshire) reputedly marks the place where he was killed; St Withburga's Well at East Dereham (Norfolk), the place where she was buried; St Chad's Well at Lichfield (Staffordshire) was sanctified by the fact that he baptized converts there.

Medieval *pilgrimage centres often had holy wells; the water of one in Canterbury Cathedral (now blocked up) allegedly turned red when dust stained with Thomas à Beckett's blood was thrown into it, and little flasks of it were sold to pilgrims and drunk as medicine. The ailments most often mentioned in connection with medieval wells were sore eyes, skin diseases, epilepsy, and insanity. Some were said to enable barren women to conceive after drinking the water, for example Bore Well near Bingfield (Northumberland), and Child's Well at Oxford. During the vogue for spas in the 18th and 19th centuries, the medicinal value of some ancient water-sources was recognized, notably at Bath (Somerset) and Malvern (Herefordshire).

Medieval ritual usually involved making an offering, while folk customs include dropping *pins or *coins in, and tying strips of cloth to nearby trees. The latter had become rare by the 19th century, though a few 'rag-trees' remained in Yorkshire, Lancashire, and Cornwall. Currently, there seem to be three: one at St Helen's Well at Walton, the second at St Helen's Well at Eshton (both in Yorkshire), the third at a unnamed well at Madron (Cornwall) which is still much visited. The modern pilgrimages to Walsingham (Norfolk) also involve drinking from a holy well, and there is a cult of the 'Chalice Well' at *Glastonbury.

From the 17th century onwards, certain wells were credited with prophetic powers. One at Oundle (Northamptonshire) emitted noises like a drum beating a march. Richard Baxter, in The Certainty of the World of Spirits Fully Evinced (1691), 157, says he heard it himself as a boy when a Scottish invasion was expected, and that it was also heard at the death of Charles II. St Helen's Well at Rushton Spencer (Staffordshire) would dry up, and St Nipperton's Well at Ashill (Somerset) would ebb and flow, before national calamities. Others offered *omens for individuals; if the shirt or shift of a sick person floated when thrown into a certain well dedicated to St Oswald, he or she would recover, but if not, not.

See also *WELL-DRESSING, *WISHING WELLS.

Hope, 1893/1968; A. Lane-Parker, Holy Wells of Cornwall

(1970); J. Meyrick, Holy Wells of Cornwall (1982); Mark Valentine, The Holy Wells of Northamptonshire (1984).

Welsh, see *ST DAVID'S DAY.

werewolves. Although *Gervase of Tilbury wrote in 1211 that werewolves were common in England, the examples he then gave are all French; there are no werewolf tales in English folklore, presumably because wolves have been extinct here for centuries.

Westminster School Pancake Greaze. A unique custom which takes place every *Shrove Tuesday at Westminster School, London. The school cook makes a substantial pancake which he takes in a frying-pan to the school hall, and tosses over an iron bar which runs across the room, about twenty feet above ground. In a mad scramble, representatives from each form in the school try to grab hold of a piece of the pancake, and whoever succeeds in getting the largest piece wins a guinea from the Dean of the school. The custom has been in existence since at least the mid-18th century when Jeremy Bentham mentioned it, and William Hone (1827: 130) quotes a 1790 reference. Fancy dress for participants is now common.

Shuel, 1985: 151–2; H. Barton Baker, The Graphic (3 Feb. 1894), 130; Stone, 1906: 85–8; Thomas Staveley Oldham, Strand Magazine 12 (1896), 186–96.

whistling. Regarded as at least unwise and unlucky in a number of professions, including sailors who maintain that it conjures up a wind, miners, and actors. This latter has been rationalized by some as the fact that in old theatres certain sounds carry so readily that anyone whistling backstage can ruin a performance. However, many less logical reports state that whistling in the dressing-room causes the person nearest the door to be ill or sacked. Anyone guilty of whistling has to go outside and turn round three times and, in some cases, cannot come back into the dressing-room until invited to return (reported since 1910). Whistling after dark, in any situation, has been regarded as unwise since at least the beginning of the 18th century. Often no particular reason is given, but it is probably again based on the idea that whistling summons spirits or draws attention to oneself. Similarly, whistling should be particularly avoided by women; it was typically a skill with which men and boys entertained themselves, so a woman or girl attempting it would be labelled unfeminine. The rhyme quoted to reinforce this has a constant first but varied second line:

A whistling woman and a crowing hen
Is enough to make the Devil come out of his den

Versions of this rhyme have been regularly reported from all over Britain since at least 1721.

See also *SEAFARING CUSTOMS AND BELIEFS.

Opie and Tatem, 1989: 440–2.

white. The primary symbolism of this colour is innocence, beauty, and virtue, for which reason it is favoured for bridal dresses and babies' clothes. However, it also has strong associations with shrouds and the pallor of death, and hence with spectral apparitions and death *omens. A blacksmith's wife at Ashington (Sussex) said in 1868:

I shall hear bad news before the day is over; for late last night, as I was sitting up waiting for my husband, who had gone to Horsham, what should I see, on looking out of the window, lying close under it, but a thing like a duck, yet a great deal whiter than it ought to have been, whiter than any snow. I was all of a tremble and cried out quite loud, and off went the thing, faster than I ever saw anything run before (Latham, 1878: 54).

She could not accept that it might have been a cat in the moonlight, for 'those white things were sent as warnings'.

Most of the *flowers which should not be brought indoors are white ones, though white *heather is lucky. A correspondent in *N&Q* wrote in 1931:

I have heard from a social worker in London that it is most unlucky—almost offensively unlucky, in fact—to give any white flowers, even those not native to England, like white chrysanthemums, to sick people. Apparently some implication that, being white, they would be suitable for the funeral, is involved. The people to whom these particular white chrysanthemums were given were quite young, moderately well educated, typical Londoners, and yet superstitious on this point—which they said was well known to everyone. (*N&Q* 160 (1931), 195)

The strongest current taboo is against having *red and white flowers in the same vase without any of another colour; this portends death, especially if given to a sick person. The colours are said to stand for 'blood and bandages'.

white witch. This term, together with the equivalent 'good witch', or even 'witch' on its own, might be applied in Tudor and Stuart times to people who used healing spells and performed other useful services. Bishop Latimer complains in 1552 that 'A great many of us, when we be in trouble, or sickness, or lose anything, we run hither and thither to witches, or sorcerers, whom we call wise men . . . seeking aid and comfort at their hands'. Reginald *Scot notes in 1584 that 'At this day, it is indifferent to say in the English tongue, "she is a witch" or "she is a wise woman"'. This usage seems rare in later folk-speech, where healers were politely called 'blessers', 'charmers', or 'wise women'. Nevertheless, *Brand and some other folklorists adopted the term 'white witch', so it is now widely known.

It is sometimes suggested that women tried for malevolent witchcraft were in fact healers, but trial records show this was very rarely so (Hester, 1992: 116; Sharpe, 1996: 174–5).

Whitsun. The English name for the Church festival otherwise called Pentecost, held on the seventh Sunday after Easter as the commemoration of the descent of the Holy Spirit and the inspiration of the Apostles. The derivation of the word Whitsun is still unclear, despite a great deal of discussion and argument by experts and others for well over a hundred years. The first mention of the word in English is found in the *Anglo-Saxon Chronicle* for 1067, as 'hwitan sunnan daeg'. Whitsun was one of the festivals in the pre-Reformation Church when the biblical story was dramatized to educate the parishioners.

In English tradition, Whitsun has long been a day of feasting and merrymaking, as befits its time of year as well as its religious origins. Medieval *church ales, *wakes, feasts, and revels survived in the fêtes, sports days, fairs, and other convivial meetings of later periods, for which Whitsun was well known, but, in the secular sphere, Whitsun finally lost all meaning when its *Bank Holiday status was taken away in the 1970s, and the Spring Bank Holiday created to replace it.

Whitsun merrymaking had a long-standing and proverbial connection with the *morris dance, as evidenced in Shakespeare's *Henry V* (II. iv). Another widely reported custom, which apparently died out in the late 19th century, was the decoration of churches with boughs of trees, especially birch, placed in holes at the ends of pews and elsewhere, and another decorating custom, *Well-dressing starts at Whitsun in some villages, and other customs and beliefs have also clustered around the season.

Whitsun was one of those times (the others being *New Year and *Easter) when it was important to wear new *clothes if you could. Opie and Tatem list the earliest reference to this in 1626, and the latest from 1985. This developed into a sort of *visiting custom in south Yorkshire, where children would visit neighbours and relatives to show off their new clothes and hope to get a little money in return (L&L 1:3 (1970), 15). The desire for new clothes was also linked to another strong tradition, particularly popular in, but not exclusive to, the Lancashire/Yorkshire area, the custom of Whit Walks. These were organized primarily by churches (of various denominations) and involved the faithful processing around the neighbourhood, in their best clothes and if possible wearing white, led by a local band. At key points there would be mass open-air hymn singing, and an outdoor tea at the end of the day. In many cases it was the Sunday Schools who organized the walks for children, and they could be large affairs indeed, with thousands taking part on the day:

Whit-Monday, as usual in Manchester, was a great gala day for Sunday scholars. A procession of all the school children in connection with the Established Church, numbering about 16,000, took place in the morning through all the principal streets of the town. Each school was headed by its band of music . . . The remaining days of the week will be given up to processions by the children of other denominational schools . . . ' (Croydon Chronicle (6 June 1868)).

There have been numerous attempts to revive the custom (e.g. Dalesman (Nov. 1982), 616–8), and the massed singing has continued in the form of Whit Sings.

A child born on Whit Sunday is doomed either to kill or be killed. This fate can be averted by going through a ceremony of a mock funeral of the child, or alternatively by squashing an insect in the child's hand.

See also *CHEESE ROLLING, *CORBY POLE FAIR, *LICHFIELD BOWER, *RAM ROASTING, *ST BRIAVELS, *WHITSUN ALES.

Wright and Lones, 1936: i. 148–71; Hutton, 1996: 277–80; N&Q 5s:1 (1874), 401–3; 5s:9 (1878), 441–2; Dyer, 1876: 278–92; Opie and Tatem, 1989: 445; Steve Fielding, 'The Catholic Whit-Walk in Manchester and Salford 1890-1939', Manchester Region History Review 1:1 (1987), 3–10; Olive M. Philpott, 'Whitsuntide in our Village', Dorset Year Book (1961/2), 173–7.

Whitsun ales. The term 'Whitsun ale' is somewhat ambiguous, being used in both a general and specific way. The 'ale' part signifies a festival or celebration; originally one in

which ale was specially brewed and sold by the organizer for profit, and from the 15th and 16th centuries *church ales were regularly held to raise money for repair and upkeep of the parish church. Ales could also be held for other purposes, and could be at any time of year, but Whitsun was a favoured time as being already a holiday and a time when the weather was normally improving. Ales included the whole range of popular activities—food, drink, sports and games, music, and dancing—and as the Church authorities gradually turned against, first, clerical involvement in the celebrations, and later the festivities themselves, there was an inexorable move towards the establishment of church rates as a more reliable and respectable method of ecclesiastical funding, and church ales slowly disappeared from the scene, to be completely suppressed by the Puritans in the 1640s. After the Restoration, the Church was content to leave matters as they stood, but others sought to revive the ales, for a combination of profit and community goodwill, usually with the agreement or support of the local landowners or gentry, and again many of these were held at Whitsun. The post-Reformation ales retained some of the features of their predecessors, in particular the semi-formal ceremonial aspects of electing a Lord and Lady, a Fool, and other office-holders to organize and preside over the event. A greenery bower, and *morris dancers were also prominent features.

The following account summarizes the mock solemnity and humour of a Whitsun ale at Woodstock, Oxfordshire:

The Woodstock Whitsun Ale was held every seven years; it began on Holy Thursday, and was carried on the whole of Whitsun week . . . The day before Holy Thursday the maypole was set up, provided by the Duke of Marlborough, which remained up for the rest of the feast. It was a bare pole ornamented with ribbons and flowers. Near it was a drinking booth, and opposite this a shed some fifty feet long with benches round the sides, decorated with evergreens, also provided by the Duke, known as 'The Bowery'. A 'Lord' and a 'Lady' were chosen, who were attended by a 'waiting-man' and 'waiting-maid'. Both 'Lord' and 'Lady' carried 'maces', which were short sticks stuck into small squares of board; from the four corners of which semicircular hoops crossed diagonally, the whole being covered with ribbons. The lord and lady were also attended by two men carrying a painted wooden horse, to which was fastened two stout poles that stuck out in front and behind. This was followed by a band of morris dancers. The procession would then go round the town, the 'Lord' and 'Lady' carrying in the centre of their maces a small cake like the modern Banbury cake, called the 'Whit cake', and these were offered to people to taste in return for a small payment. A man carrying a basket of these cakes for sale also followed. In front of the 'Bowery' was hung up an owl and a hawk in cages, and two threshing flails, which went by the names of 'The Lady's Parrot' and 'The Lady's Nut-crackers'. Anyone who misnamed them (i.e. called them by their real names) had to forfeit a shilling, or else be carried behind the lady, shoulder high on the wooden horse, round the may pole. If they still refused to pay the forfeit, their hats were taken in lieu of payment. Many University men would come over from Oxford to ride the wooden horse for the fun of the thing, and frequent fights took place between them and the morrice-dancers, when they would not pay forfeit . . . (*Folk-Lore* 14 (1903), 171–5)

This account goes on to describe a young Oxonian and his problems at the ale, quoting from Thomas Little, *Confessions of an Oxonian* (1826: i. 169–73). The punishment of riding the horse has strong echoes in other customs, notably *rough music, and *Riding the Stang.

Church ales had been common all over the southern half of the country, but the later Whitsun ales were concentrated in the south Midlands, and particularly in Oxfordshire. Many lasted into the first half of the 19th century, but the rough-and-ready ways in which the working classes enjoyed themselves inevitably led to withdrawal of support and later downright opposition by local élites across the country, and the ales were suppressed—to be later replaced by more controlled village fêtes or local club feast days.

See also *CHURCH ALES, *WHITSUN.

Chandler, 1993: 59–79; Hutton, 1996: 244–61; Hazlitt, 1905: 631–2; . Wright and Lones, 1936: i. 150–7.

Whittington, Dick. Sir Richard Whittington, who died in 1423 after being three times Lord Mayor of London, was the youngest son of a prosperous Gloucestershire family, who began his career by going to London at thirteen to be apprenticed to a merchant whose daughter he later married. He died childless, leaving money to rebuild various churches and almshouses, Newgate Prison, and St Bartholomew's Hospital.

The traditional account of his life, first recorded in the 17th century, stresses his supposed early poverty and sufferings; his luck changed when he sent a cat which he had bought for a penny as his stake in a trading voyage, and the captain sold it on his behalf

for a huge price to an African king whose palace was overrun with rats. There are similar stories in Europe, often adding that the grateful hero devoted part of his wealth to good works; presumably Whittington's charitable bequests led to the story being told of him.

See Jacobs, 1890/1968: 104–10, for the best-known text, combined out of older chapbooks; it is reprinted in Briggs, 1970–1: B. ii. 139–45.

Wicca. This Old English masculine noun meaning 'male witch, wizard' was curiously misinterpreted by Gerald *Gardner's followers as an abstract noun meaning 'witchcraft', and is now the title of a modern pagan movement which is both religious and magical. It was founded by Gardner in the 1950s, who claimed it was an ancient cult preserved secretly by persecuted but benevolent witches (see *Murray); it combined worship of a horned and phallic god such as Murray described, with that of a universal goddess, who is now the chief deity. There are now many independent groups within the movement; most are polytheistic, revering gods and goddesses from many mythologies as aspects of a sexual pair of deities, but some feminist covens worship the goddess only. Rituals are linked to the seasonal cycle and the phases of the moon; prehistoric sites and places of natural beauty are greatly respected. A wide variety of magical and meditational techniques are learnt; altars, magic circles, consecrated tools, and ritual invocations are used (Hutton, 1999).

The foundation texts for Wicca are Charles Leland, *Aradia or the Gospel of the Witches* (1899); Margaret Murray, *The Witch-Cult in Western Europe* (1921); and Gerald Gardner, *Witchcraft Today* (1954). Accounts from within the movement include Margot Adler, *Drawing Down the Moon* (1981); Doreen Valiente, *The Rebirth of Witchcraft* (1989); Janet and Stewart Farrar, *Eight Sabbats for Witches* (1981); Aidan Kelly, *Crafting the Art of Magic, Book I* (1991).

widdershins, withershins. This word, a Scottish and northern English term meaning 'against the sun, counter-clockwise', is used for *leftward circling movement, especially in the context of magical action, where such movement is thought unlucky, or malevolent.

Widow's Son Bun Ceremony. Hanging from the ceiling of the Widow's Son pub in East London is a bundle of about 200 dust-covered, shrivelling *hot cross buns. Every year, on *Good Friday, a sailor adds another. The story is that a widow's house previously stood on the site. Expecting her sailor son home one Easter, she naturally baked him a hot cross bun but, unfortunately, he did not return. The widow lived in hope and next year made another bun, and so on. The house became famous for its collection of buns, and when the pub was built on the same site it was naturally called the Widow's Son and the custom continued. It was commonly believed that bread or buns baked on Good Friday would never grow mouldy and had a marked medicinal value, and it was also not unknown for such items to be hung up. F. K. Robinson, for example, in his *Glossary of Words Used in the Neighbourhood of Whitby* (1876), writes of seeing Good Friday biscuits with holes in the centre, hanging from the ceiling, and this is likely to be the origin of the custom, to explain which the story was later concocted. The Widow's Son custom still continues, although the official involvement of the Royal Navy in recent years (because it was getting difficult to find a sailor) has brought it more of an air of the conscious publicity stunt than it used to have.

Kightly, 1986: 235; Shuel, 1985: 16; E. B. H., *London Lore* 1:2 (1978), 15–16.

wife-selling. For at least 300 years, according to popular belief, a man could get rid of his wife, and, more importantly, get rid of any responsibility for her future upkeep or actions, by selling her to another man. The sale normally had its formalities—it would take place in the market or at a fair, the woman would be led by a halter, and any tolls or fees usually payable for the sale of animals would be carefully paid and recorded. Most importantly, the sale would take place in front of witnesses. For her part, the wife had normally given her consent and in many cases the deal had already been agreed privately, and the purchaser was someone of her choice. The first definite recorded instances come from the 16th century, with the diary of Henry Machyn being the earliest: 'The xxiiij day of November [1553] dyd ryde in a cart Cheken, parsun of sant Necolas Coldabby, abowt London, for he sold ys wyff to a bowcher'. Wife-selling is reported regularly in early folklore collections and local newspapers until the late 19th century, and is used in Thomas Hardy's novel of *The Mayor of Casterbridge* (1886).

S. P. Menefee, *Wives For Sale: an Ethnographic Study of Popular Divorce* (1981); E. P. Thompson, *Customs in Common* (1991), 404–66.

Wild Edric, see *EDRIC THE WILD.

Wild Hunt. This is the general term for any ghostly or demonic huntsman or group of huntsmen, accompanied by phantom hounds, seen—or, more often, simply heard—galloping across the sky by night. Local terms include *Dando's Dogs in Cornwall, Wish Hounds on Dartmoor, *Gabriel Hounds in northern England, *Seven Whistlers in Worcestershire. They were thought to be either demons pursuing dead sinners, or damned souls themselves. They were an *omen of disaster; Henderson was told in the 1860s that 'Sometimes they appear to hang over a house, and then death or calamity are sure to visit it, 'as had been noted when a child was burned to death in Sheffield' (Henderson, 1879: 97–106). In Cornwall, the leader was sometimes said to be the *Devil himself (Hunt, 1865: i. 247), sometimes a notorious local landowner who had defied God by going hunting on a *Sunday. Stories of this type have been recorded in Cleveland (Atkinson, 1891: 70) and Oxfordshire (Briggs, 1970–1, B. i. 602–3). The earliest description comes from the *Peterborough Chronicle*, telling how after the appointment of a wicked abbot in 1127:

Then soon afterwards many people saw and heard many hunters hunting. The hunters were big and black and loathsome, and their hounds all black and wide-eyed and loathsome, and they rode on black horses and black goats. This was seen in the very deer-park in the town of Peterborough, and in all the woods that there were between this town and Stamford, and the monks heard the horns blow that they were blowing at night.

Such apparitions, however, were not necessarily demons and lost souls. Walter *Map describes King *Herla's phantom riders as under enchantment, while *Gervase of Tilbury had heard of others who were *Arthur's knights. Many keepers in the royal forests of Britain and Brittany, says Gervase, would tell how: '. . . about noon, and in the first part of the following night if there is a full moon, they have frequently seen a host of knights with hunting dogs and heard the sound of horns. To those who challenge them, they answer that they belong to the fellowship and household of Arthur.'

Westwood, 1985: 32–4, 155–7; Petry, 1972.

Wild Man, Woman. Medieval art included Wild Men (and occasionally Women) among, its grotesques. They were a race of primitive sub-humans covered in shaggy hair, immensely strong, and living in forests; the males were usually shown wielding a branch, or even a whole tree, as a club, and sometimes crowned and belted with leaves. Their reality was confirmed by respected classical writers and by references to 'hairy creatures in desert places' in the Latin versions of Isaiah 13: 21 and 34: 14; they were often identified with satyrs and fauns.

In literature, Wild Men could symbolize savagery, lust, and uncontrolled passions, or, alternatively, a natural innocence which could easily be brought to virtue; both aspects can be seen in Spenser's *Faerie Queene* (1596). In Book IV, canto vii, there is a monstrous specimen, grotesquely ugly and hairy, naked except for a girdle of ivy, and carrying a young oak as a club, whose delight is to rape and eat women; in Book VI, however, there is one who acts as a stupid but loyal protector to one of Spenser's heroines.

Wild Men are found among the costumed performers at courtly masques. At a Twelfth Night entertainment for Henry VIII in 1515 'eight wyldemen, all apparayled in green mosse with sleved sylke, with ugly weapons and terrible visages' fought against eight knights; at Kenilworth in 1575 a poet costumed as a Savage Man draped in moss and ivy emerged from a wood to greet Elizabeth I; at Cowdray Park (Sussex) in 1591 the Queen was addressed by a Wild Man 'cladde in ivy'. They also appeared in civic pageants, clearing the way for the main procession, where they were referred to as Savages or *Green Men. They were common in heraldry, and Aubrey notes that a Wild Man or Green Man (he uses the terms interchangeably) was 'not uncommon' as an inn sign in and about London, and was drawn as 'a kind of Hercules with a green club and green leaves about his pudenda and head' (Aubrey, 1686/1880: 134–5, 177).

Richard Bernheimer, *Wild Men in the Middle Ages* (1952).

William of Newburgh (1135/6–?1198). A monk at Newburgh Priory (Yorkshire), William wrote a chronicle covering the period from 1066 to 1197. He was a careful historian, rejecting the 'idle lies' of *Geoffrey of Monmouth concerning *Arthur and *Merlin. He included accounts of some *vampire-like *undead (on the authority of reputable clerics who claimed first-hand knowledge) and the legend of *Willy Howe. *The History of William of Newburgh* translated by Joseph Stevenson (1856) has been reissued in paperback (1996).

Williams, Alfred (1877–1930). As 'the Hammerman Poet', he published a number of books, but his main contribution to English folklore was his *Folk Songs of the Upper Thames* (1923) in which he presented the texts of material collected in Oxfordshire, Wiltshire, and Berkshire from 1914 to 1916. Williams did not develop his interest in folk-song any further, and the book contains no evidence of wider reading on the subject, but, paradoxically, this is what gives the collection its main value, even today. Williams was much closer to his informants, in terms of background, than most other song collectors, and he clearly had less exclusive definitions of the subject. He thus noted a wider range of songs than most of his contemporaries, and gives a more complete picture of the singing tradition of the time. He did not, however, note down the tunes of the songs. His song manuscripts are preserved in Wiltshire Record Office.

Leonard Clark, *Alfred Williams: His Life and Work* (1969); special issue of *FMJ* 1:5 (1969).

Will-o'-the-Wisp. This is the commonest English name for faint, flickering lights seen in marshy areas. It implies a supernatural being, carrying a burning bundle of straw as a torch, to lead travellers astray; there are many other local names (Wright, 1913: 200–1; Briggs, 1976: 231). Tradition varies as to their nature; some informants spoke of them as *ghosts, others as *fairies. If ghosts, they were usually said to be *unbaptized infants, unable to enter Heaven yet not deserving Hell; if fairies, they were usually regarded as a specialized species, but sometimes an individual trickster like *Puck or *Robin Goodfellow, or a local group such as the *pixies, will be credited with this role.

willow. Vickery (1995: 399–401) points out the biblical basis of the sadness and grief associated with the tree in England:

> By the rivers of Babylon we sat down and wept
> when we remembered Zion
> There on the willow trees
> we hung our harps
>
> (Psalm 137)

but continues by saying that these would not actually have been willows at all, but poplars.

It is possible that the original translators of the King James Bible were led to use the word willow by already existing English traditions connecting willows and weeping. Certainly the shape of the tree is sufficient to explain its epithet. Two poems by *Herrick (*Hesperides* (1648)) confirm the willow as a symbol of sadness and lost love. See also Lean (1903: ii. 638) and Hazlitt (1905: 621–2) for numerous similar quotations from 16th- and 17th-century literary sources.

Willow also features in a number of other beliefs, recorded in the 19th and 20th centuries only: it is unlucky to burn its wood, willow blossom must not be brought into the house, except on May Day, and no animal or child should be hit with a willow twig or stick because that would stop them growing afterwards (Opie and Tatem, 1989: 446–7; Leather, 1912: 19). The willow stick is a central feature of a traditional song called 'The Bitter Withy', collected a number of times in England in the early years of the 20th century, in which Jesus as a boy tries to play with other children but they refuse to have anything to do with a carpenter's son. He builds a rainbow and runs across it and when the others try it they fall and are injured or killed. Mary beats Jesus with a willow stick (or 'sally twig') and Jesus curses the twig. The main elements of the story have been traced to the Apocryphal Gospel of Pseudo–Matthew, but the willow motif is a later addition (Leather, 1912: 181–6; *Folk-Lore* 19 (1908), 190–200).

Opie and Tatem, 1989: 446–7; Lean, 1903: ii. 638.

Willy Howe. The fullest English version of the 'stolen fairy cup' legend is localized at Willy Howe, a large round *barrow near Wold Newton in Humberside (formerly East Yorkshire); it was recorded as a real event by *William of Newburgh (died c.1198), who had been born nearby and had known about it since childhood. A village man, riding home late one night and rather drunk, heard singing and laughter coming from the mound; then he saw an open door, and people feasting inside. When a servant came out and offered him a cup, 'he wisely forebore to drink, but, pouring out the contents, and retaining the vessel, he quickly departed,' pursued by the furious guests.

It was a vessel of an unknown material, unusual colour, and strange form. It was offered as a great present to Henry the Elder, King of England, and then handed over to the Queen's brother, David, King of Scotland, and deposited for many years among the treasures of his kingdom; and, a few years since, as we have heard from authentic relation, it was given up by William, king of the Scots, to Henry the Second, on his desiring to see it. (Trans. Joseph Stevenson (1856/1996), 438)

Clearly, the cup was real, even though the tale is an international legend. *Gervase of Tilbury knew a similar story about a mound in the Forest of Dean where thirsty travellers were offered drink in a jewelled horn 'such as was used among the old English', by a silent servant; eventually, a knight stole the horn and gave it to Robert, Earl of Gloucester, who then gave it to Henry I (Westwood, 1985: 25–6, 350–2).

There is yet a third version allegedly attached to Rillaton Barrow in Cornwall, and purporting to explain a prehistoric gold goblet found there (now in the British Museum, after having been used by George V as a shaving mug). However, the goblet was found in 1837 and the story first appeared in 1899 in *A Book of the West: Cornwall* by the Revd Sabine Baring-Gould, who was familiar with medieval material; its authenticity is more than dubious.

Stories of fairy treasure continued to be told about Willy Howe. A man once found a chest of gold there, so heavy that it took a train of horses a quarter of a mile long to drag it out, but lost it at the last minute by blasphemously exclaiming, 'Whether God's will or not, we'll have this ark'. Another man used to find a guinea on the mound every morning, left for him by fairies, but boasted of the gifts, after which they ceased (Hone, 1827: 92).

See also *EDENHALL.

Wilmington, the Long Man of. This *hill figure on the Sussex Downs shows a naked standing man, grasping two poles taller than himself. Originally formed by cutting turf away to expose the white chalk, it became so overgrown as to be almost lost, and was restored in 1874. The earliest record is a sketch made in 1710; this differs from the present figure in the placing of the feet, and in showing vague facial features, and possibly a hat (Farrant, 1993). Its actual age is unknown; one plausible theory compares it to figures of helmeted, spear-carrying warriors (often naked) on Anglo-Saxon and Scandinavian helmets and buckles, implying a link with the cult of a war-god (Hawkes, 1965). In 1874, and again in 1969, splinters of Roman tiles were found under the outline; these could have been used at any post-Roman period.

According to local legend, the Long Man was a *giant who died there on the hillside; some said he was killed by a shepherd boy, others that he just fell down the steep slope and broke his neck, others that he was killed by a rival giant when they were hurling stones at each other, and the figure was drawn around his corpse. There is also said to be *treasure buried nearby.

J. P. Elmslie, *Folk-Lore* 26 (1915), 162–4; C. Hawkes, *Antiquity* 39 (1965), 27–30; J. H. Farrant, *Sussex Archaeological Collections* 131 (1993), 129–38.

wise men, women, see *CUNNING MEN, WOMEN.

wishbone. The forked *furcula* bone which lies between the breast and neck of a chicken, or other fowl, is popularly called the wishbone or Merrythought—the latter being the much older term—named after the custom which has incorporated it since at least the 17th century. Two people take hold of either side of the bone, some insist they must use their little fingers only, and pull until it breaks. Whoever gets the largest piece can make a wish which, if not told to anyone, will come true. Nowadays mainly done by children, the custom is first described by John *Aubrey in 1686, although the word 'Merrythought' appears in earlier 17th-century contexts (see *OED*).

Aubrey, 1686: 92–3; Opie and Tatem, 1989: 448; *N&Q* 5s:11 (1879), 86.

Wishford Magna. A unique *manorial custom takes place in Great Wishford, Wiltshire, every *Oak Apple Day (29 May). Under the terms of a charter of 1603, the inhabitants of Wishford are allowed to take wood from nearby Grovely Wood as well as various other rights and duties as regards access and such things as pawnedge for 'all their hogges and pigges'. The charter states that it is merely confirming rights and privileges existing from 'time out of mynde'. It is further stipulated that to perpetuate these rights the inhabitants should, as they had done in 'auntient tyme', 'go in a daunce to the Cathedral Church of our blessed Ladie in the Cittie of new Sarum on Whit Tuesdaie in the said countie of Wiltes, and there made theire clayme to their custome in the Forrest of Grovely in theis wordes: Groveley Groveley and all Groveley'. And so

they still do. At some point, presumably in the late 17th century, the custom was moved from Whit Tuesday to Oak Apple Day. On that day, the inhabitants of the village rise early, and set out for Grovely Wood to cut branches to decorate their houses and to carry in the procession later in the day, and help themselves to any other wood they need. Later, a party led by the rector proceeds to Salisbury Cathedral where four women in 19th-century costume, carrying bundles of wood, dance on the Green. In the Cathedral, on the steps to the High Altar parts of the charter are read out and those present shout their 'Grovely, Grovely, Grovely and All Groveley' to assert their rights for another year. The custom has quite naturally acquired other trappings such as a procession, *May Queen, fancy dress, and marching band. The whole affair is organized by the Oak Apple Club which was formed in 1892 specifically to ensure the continuance of the local rights and to ward off periodic attempts to remove them. The Club's motto is 'Unity is Strength'. A further part of the day is the hoisting of a large oak bough, decorated with coloured ribbons, to the top of the parish church tower. This is called the Marriage Bough, and brings good luck to those married in the church in the coming year.

The History of Oak Apple Day in Wishford Magna (c.1972); George Frampton, *Grovely! Grovely! Grovely! And All Grovely! The History of Oak Apple Day in Great Wishford* (1992).

wish(t) hounds, wight hounds. Devonshire names for the dogs of the *Wild Hunt, sometimes said to be headless.

wishing wells. A popular custom nowadays is to throw *coins into water, making a wish. It is obviously related to offerings at holy and healing *wells, and may well be equally old, though less fully documented; in 19th-century Shropshire and Herefordshire there were wells into which people dropped pebbles or *pins while making a wish in a ritualistic way—in silence, or at midnight, or drinking water from one's hand and tossing the rest at a particular stone (Burne, 1883: 422–9; Leather, 1912: 13). The *OED*'s first record for the term 'wishing well' is from 1792.

This behaviour is often actively publicized and encouraged, to amuse tourists and/or raise money for charity or for the upkeep of a museum, beauty spot, etc. In most cases, the water is clear and shallow, showing the offerings of previous visitors, and the 'well' is often a man-made fountain or artificial pool. Among innumerable and very varied examples may be mentioned the ancient hot springs at Bath, an old mill at Bibury (Gloucestershire), the cascades at Gatwick Airport, and a former baptismal pool in a church converted to a pub in Worthing (Sussex) [JS]. At Bibury, a notice offers two *origin stories: first, that whenever ancient Romans crossed water, they threw silver coins in; secondly, that 'It is told that a poor mill worker dropped his meagre wages into a millstream. He was unable to find his money, but on looking for his money next day he found a purse of gold sovereigns. Every time he passed the stream again he threw in a coin, and his luck continued to improve.'

witch balls. Large, heavy glass balls coated with glossy reflecting silver, gold, or brightly coloured paint, first made about 1690, and popular in the 19th century; or a smaller type from the late 18th century, with swirling multi-coloured patterns. Both were meant to hang in cottage windows; their purpose was to attract and neutralize the *evil eye of a passing witch, either by reflecting it back upon her or by puzzling her with the pattern. Plain glass balls filled with bright tangled threads were thought to have the same effect. Alternative names are 'wish ball' and 'watch ball'; the latter is sometimes explained by saying that the ball grows dull if there is infection 'in the air', and so should be watched for a warning.

witch bottles. A common *counterspell against illness caused by witchcraft was to put the sick person's *urine (and sometimes also *hair and *fingernail clippings) in a bottle with *nails, *pins, or threads, cork it tightly, and either set it to heat by the hearth or bury it in the ground. This, as Joseph Blagrave wrote in 1671, 'will endanger the witches' life, for ... they will be grievously tormented, making their water with great difficulty, if any at all' (*The Astrological Practice of Physick* (1671), 154–5; cited in Merrifield, 1987: 169). Blagrave's contemporaries Aubrey and Joseph Glanvil record instances of this causing the deaths of those responsible for a horse's bewitchment and for a woman's languishing illness (Aubrey, *Miscellanies*, 1696/1857: 140; Glanvil, *Sadducismus Triumphatus* (1681), part 2, 169–70). The theory was that the witch had created a magical link with her victim, which could be reversed via the victim's body-products; the witch would have to break the link to save herself, and the victim would recover.

The recipe was still known in a Norfolk village in 1939:

Take a stone bottle, make water in it, fill it with your own toe-nails and finger-nails, iron nails and anything which belongs to you. Hang the bottle over the fire and keep stirring it. The room must be in darkness; you must not speak or make a noise. The witch will come to your door and make a lot of noise and beg you to open the door and let her in. If you do not take any notice, but keep silent, the witch will burst. The strain on the mind of the person when the witch is begging to be let in is usually so great that the person often speaks and the witch is set free. (E. G. Bales, *Folk-Lore* 50 (1939), 67)

In London, 17th-century pottery jugs of the kind called 'greybeards' or 'bellarmines' have been found buried in ditches or streams, containing such things as bent nails and felt hearts stuck with pins; in Essex and Suffolk many others have been found, but under the hearths or thresholds of houses. Later, cheap glass bottles were used in the same way; one holding over 200 bent pins was found under the hearth of a Sussex cottage in the 1860s, as was common in the county. A friend of Charlotte Latham actually saw one being heated, to cure a girl of epilepsy supposedly caused by a witch (Latham, 1878: 25–6). An example dating from the early years of the 20th century was found in a shop at Padstow (Cornwall); urine was put in a cod-liver-oil bottle which had its cork pierced with eight pins and one needle, and was bricked up in a chimney. In Cambridgeshire, a three-sided iron bottle held hen's blood and feathers mingled with the usual human urine, salt, hair, and nail-clippings; also (for protection rather than cure) small bottles of greenish or blueish glass filled with coloured silk threads were displayed beside doors or windows, to divert the witch's power by confusing her gaze (Porter, 1969: 169, 180).

According to the *East London Advertiser* on 1 August 1903, a barber in Bishop's Stortford (Herts.) had recently been asked to save some hair-clippings from a customer's neck in order that someone who wanted revenge on the man could put them in a bottle and heat it until it burst at *midnight, to bring sickness on him (*N&Q* 9s:3 (1903), 187). This is no defensive counterspell, but an active magic attack, via the intended victim's hair; sometimes, witch bottles were similarly used (Porter, 1969: 179).

Merrifield, 1987: 163–83; Opie and Tatem, 1989: 416–17.

witchcraft. No topic in folklore has caused more argument than witchcraft. However, the work of historians over the past 30 years has disentangled various levels of meaning within the word itself, and analysed the social context for accusations. The phenomenon is seen as essentially one of belief-systems, stereotyping, rumour, and social pressures; debate now centres on the interaction of upper-class and popular attitudes, and of prejudice against women. There is no longer any scholarly support for theories that witches formed a secret society, whether political, as the French historian Michelet proposed, or pagan, as claimed by Margaret *Murray; the equally simplistic idea that witch-hunts were a cynical establishment plot has also been abandoned.

The Old English word 'witch' meant 'one who casts a spell'. Intrinsically neutral, it could be applied to those using *magic helpfully (see *white witch); in most contexts, however, 'witchcraft' means using magic to harm humans, farm animals, or property. Fear of it permeates folklore of all periods, but it was not until the late 15th century that it was perceived in Europe as a threat grave enough to require systematic prosecution, on the assumption that it implied a pact between the witch and Satan. It was first declared a crime in English law in 1542; the number of English trials peaked in the 1580s and again in the 1640s, but fell off sharply after 1660. The last, in 1717, ended in acquittal, and in 1736 the Witchcraft Act was repealed and the crime officially ceased to exist (though people claiming magic powers could still be prosecuted for fraud). Thereafter, fear and hatred of witches, though still common, was frowned on by the élite as mere 'superstition'.

Witch-trials in England differed from those in Scotland in highlighting charges of material harm, not devil-worship, though religious writers and preachers were naturally preoccupied with the latter issue. The first two Witchcraft Acts (1542, 1563) made hanging the penalty for murder through witchcraft, and the pillory, imprisonment, or loss of goods the punishments for lesser injuries. The Act of James I (1604) added another capital offence, to 'consult, covenant with, employ, feed or reward any evil or wicked spirit', and a handbook for judges published in 1618 stressed the importance of *familiars as evidence; yet in practice trials still centred on the harm allegedly done.

Witchcraft accusations arose occasionally among the ruling classes, but more frequently among minor gentry and lower orders; almost 90 per cent of those charged were women, often elderly ones. The accusations were sparked off by some previous quarrel or vendetta; frequently, conflict arose when the alleged witch and her victim were neighbours, but not equals, the victim being relatively well off, the witch poor, and sometimes having a bad reputation. The latter requested some small gift or friendly service, and showed anger when this was refused. The better-off neighbour, aware of having failed in charity, would later interpret any sickness or misfortune as magical revenge; he or she often consulted a *cunning man, who identified the cause by *divination, confirming the diagnosis. The eventual court-case might involve charges brought by several families, the fruit of years of accumulating suspicions.

Almost all English witch-trials arose in this spontaneous way. There was no pressure from central Church or State to prosecute witches, though locally some justices of the peace were more vigorous than others in rounding up suspects; Matthew *Hopkins is the only individual known to have initiated a systematic campaign. Moreover, since witches were thought to operate singly or in very small family groups (*covens and *sabbaths being rarely mentioned), interrogations were not aimed at forcing the accused to incriminate others. Hence English 'witch-hunts' were small scale, by European standards, with marked variations between one region and another. Full statistics are lacking because court records in many areas are missing or incomplete; those of the Home Assize Circuit between 1559 and 1736 show 513 persons charged, of whom 200 were convicted, 109 of them being hanged. Estimates of the total number executed have recently been revised from 'under 1,000' to 'probably less than 500' (Thomas, 1971: 450; Sharpe, 1996: 125).

Contemporary pamphlets describing the trials occupied a borderline between reportage and fictive narrative; they sought to convince, but also to 'entertain' readers by shocking them. They drew upon traditional stereotypes and anecdotes, reinforced them, and spread them. The beliefs they reveal are more elaborate and dramatic than the actual charges. They include accounts of witches feeding their *familiars with their blood; meeting Satan in the form of a black man (or *black dog), making a covenant with him, or having sexual intercourse with him; changing themselves into *hares; changing others into horses and riding them to a sabbath, to feast there with the Devil. These beliefs seem to have grown steadily more common and more complex over the two centuries of the trials; all except the sabbath continue to appear frequently in later folklore, plus the motif of magic *flying.

Fear of witchcraft was still widespread in the 19th century. Folklore of this period is rich in anecdotes about local witches and stresses the importance of defending oneself against them. There were charms to guard the home and farm against potential witchcraft (e.g. *hagstones, *horseshoes, *rowan), and *counterspells to use if it had already occurred. As law no longer offered redress to people believing themselves bewitched, the help of *cunning men was still in demand; mob violence, including *swimming witches, still occurred.

As late as the 1970s, in Hertfordshire:

Many now living, even in market towns, can remember being told by parents not to cross or trouble certain dangerous men or women and thus invite their displeasure and revenge. Nor can the name of the last witch in many villages be discovered, the truthful reply from those who will talk about this forbidden subject being that 'the time has not yet come'. (Jones-Baker, 1977: 114)

See also *COUNTERSPELLS, *CUNNING MEN, *FAMILIARS, *FLYING, *HAG-RIDING, *IMAGE MAGIC, *SHAPE-CHANGING, *SWIMMING WITCHES, *WHITE WITCHES, *WITCH BOTTLES. For 'witchcraft' in the sense of modern paganism, see *WICCA.

Macfarlane, 1970/1999; Thomas, 1971: 435–585; Sharpe, 1996; Hester, 1992; Gilbert Geis and Ivan Bunn, *A Trial of Witches* (1997). Parallel Scottish material will be found in Christina Larner, *Enemies of God: The Witch-Hunt in Scotland* (1981). Briggs, 1962, discusses witchcraft in Elizabethan and Jacobean literature.
For witchcraft in later English belief, see Davies, 1998 and 1999a and b; Maple, 1960, 1962, 1965. Relevant material occurs in most regional collections and in Briggs, 1970–1: B. ii. 609–761.
Introductory surveys to the European background include Jeffrey B. Russell, *A History of Witchcraft* (1980); and Brian Levack, *The Witch-Hunt in Early Modern Europe* (1987). A brief outline of recent scholarship is Jacqueline Simpson, *Folklore* 107 (1996), 5–18. Two important collections of essays are *Early Modern European Witchcraft: Centres and Peripheries*, ed. Bengt Ankarloo and Gustav Henningsen (1990); and *Witchcraft in Early Modern Europe*, ed. Jonathan Barry, Marianne Hester, and Gareth Roberts (1996).

witch ladder. In 1886, during repairs to an old house in Wellington (Somerset), a blocked-off roof space was found to contain broomsticks and a length of rope interwoven with goose and rook feathers. The workmen who found it called it 'a witches' ladder', but other local informants thought it was used in *cursing, and would have been hidden in the victim's house. Sabine *Baring-Gould describes this procedure in his novel *Curgenven* (1893), but the details are probably his invention. Other informants, in the early 20th century, said the object must have been a 'wishing rope', or that the maker would have hung it outside, either 'to draw the milk from her neighbours' cowsheds' or to summon someone magically (Tongue, 1965: 67–8).

Abraham Colles, *Folk-Lore Journal* 5 (1887), 1–3, and correspondence, 81–4, 257–9, 354–6.

witch of Berkeley, see *BERKELEY.

Witch of Scrapfaggot Green, see *SCRAPFAGGOT GREEN.

witch posts. In North Yorkshire farmhouses of the 17th and 18th centuries, hearths were screened by partitions ending in posts of *rowan wood carved with X-shaped patterns, called 'witch posts'. Lancashire farms had similar rowan posts, but without the decoration. Belief in their protective power continued into the 1920s, when Yorkshire builders made new ones when old houses were being rebuilt. A modern stonemason explained:

The witch, in order to gain power over a dwelling house, must go through the house and past the hearth. The door and chimney were the only means of access, but she could not pass the witch post with its cross. Hence it was a defence at the hearth . . . a crooked sixpence was kept in a hole at the centre of the post. When the butter would not turn you took a knitting needle, which was kept for the purpose in a groove at the top, and with it got out the sixpence and put it in the churn. (Brears, 1989: 31)

wittan, see *ROWAN.

wizards. A late medieval term, derived from 'wise' and always implying arcane knowledge and mysterious authority, generally derived from written symbols and designs, and sacred words in ancient languages. It is used of *Merlin; of local heroes such as *Jack o' Kent, who could outwit the Devil and command his services; but also, in real life, of village *charmers and *cunning men. The latter were also sometimes called *conjurers.

Women's Morris Federation, see *MORRIS FEDERATION.

woodwose. An alternative name for the *Wild Man; from Old English *wudu wasa* = 'woodland being', but with the meaning modified through the influence of Middle English *wood* = 'mad, furious'.

wooset, husset. A form of *rough music, reported from the Berkshire/Wiltshire/Somerset area, under a variety of variant spellings and pronunciations—wooset, husset, housset, hooset, and so on. The main distinguishing feature was the 'Wooset'—a horse's head with snapping jaws and added horns, carried in procession on a pole.

Compare also *HOBBY HORSES, *OOSER.

Wiltshire Archaeological and Natural History Magazine 1 (1854), 88–9; *EDD* (1902), iii, under 'Hooset'; Major B. Lowsley, *A Glossary of Berkshire Words and Phrases* (1888), 92.

Word-Lore. Subtitled *The 'Folk' Magazine* and published by the Folk Press Ltd., edited by Douglas Macmillan. It ran for twelve numbers, January 1926 to December 1927, and included short pieces on many aspects of language and folklore, including dialect poems and stories, song-texts, word-lists, place-names, word-puzzles, and notes and queries. *Word-Lore* had an amateur, home-made feel, and some of its content was of dubious authority, but it is a product of its time, and there is much valuable material to be found in its pages.

wraiths. This can be a synonym for *ghost, but generally means the spectral double of someone still alive. Usually, it appears at or near the time of the person's death, as a sign for close friends or relatives; sometimes it is a more long-term warning; occasionally it means the person is in danger or distress. To see one's own wraith (also called a 'fetch') is a sure sign of death. The apparition of a destined husband summoned by some *love divinations is also a wraith. The belief is old, and still strongly held; a Manchester woman in 1981 said:

Some years ago, it was at the end of the First World War. My husband was quite young, and he was away with his older sister,—on holiday or something. And

the young man his sister was engaged to appeared before them in the bedroom, as plainly as anything, in his uniform. He said it was just as if he was almost there! And he'd been killed just at that time in the War! (Bennett, 1987: 55)

There was a widespread idea that once a year, usually on *St Mark's Eve but sometimes at *All Souls or *Midsummer Night, anyone who watched in the church porch from *midnight till one o'clock would see those fated to die that year entering the church, usually in the order of their deaths. An account of 1634, from Burton in Lincolnshire, describes a procession of figures in winding-sheets led by the curate, and sounds of a burial service.

However, keeping this watch was disapproved of, and could bring its own punishment. It was said of a certain Jonny Joneson, sexton of Middleton (near Manchester) around 1800, that he kept watch on All Souls' Eve, counting the wraiths and gloating to think how many burial fees he would earn, until one appeared which he recognized as himself. He fell ill, and was dead within a year (Samuel Bamford, *Autobiography* (1848–9), i. 160–2). Similarly at Dorstone (Herefordshire) on All Souls' Eve a man saw wraiths gathering in the church, where the Devil, dressed as a monk, called out the names of those fated to die; he heard his own name, and died shortly after (Leather, 1912: 107). For further examples, see *St Mark's Eve.

Opie and Tatem, 1989: 80–1; Bennett, 1987: 55–64; S. P. Menefee, in *The Seer*, ed. Hilda Ellis Davidson (1989), 80–99. Some Victorian accounts of wraiths are in Briggs, 1970–1: B. ii. 489–93, 505–6, 518–19, 525–6, 549, 576, 595.

wrens. In folk tradition, the wren is regarded as always female ('Jenny Wren'), and as wife to the *robin; like the latter she is a sacred bird and must not be harmed, nor should her eggs be taken, otherwise someone close to the taker will die:

> The robin redbreast and the wren
> Are God Almighty's cock and hen.

Nevertheless, there exists a *calendar custom called 'Hunting the Wren' which was widespread in Ireland, Wales, and the Isle of Man, and not unknown in England. The usual time for the custom is St Stephen's Day (26 December), when groups of young men hunted and killed wrens and then paraded them around the neighbourhood with much singing and music. Hunting the Wren is thus normally disregarded in discussions of English customs, but there have been sufficient reports to indicate a reasonably strong presence in this country. In some instances, the custom may well have been performed by Irish or Welsh immigrants, as a writer from Plymouth, Devon, confirms: 'I have often known the Irish boys living in Stonehouse Lane, the St. Giles of Plymouth, go round the town with sticks and garlands, singing the well-known song of the Wren Boys from door to door, on St Stephen's Day, in order to get money, but I am happy to say I never could find either a living or dead wren among them' (*Land and Water* (30 Oct. 1880)). But there are too many references for them all to be explained in this way, as Armstrong, for example, lists fifteen English counties in which he found traces. One description includes the rhyme that is commonly used in Ireland: 'At Christmas-tide, boys are accustomed in Essex to kill wrens and carry them about in furze bushes, from house to house, asking a present in these words:

> The wren, the wren, the king of the birds
> St. Stephen's Day was killed in the furze
> Although he be little his honour is great
> And so, good people, pray give us a treat'

(Henderson, 1879: 125)

The picture is slightly obscured by an occasionally reported custom which may or may not be related. Several reports state that at Christmas time it was customary for villagers to go out into the woods to 'hunt', which often turned into an indiscriminate orgy of killing anything that moved, including wrens and other small birds (see *St Stephen's Day, and *squirrel hunting).

Another strand in our wren lore is a widespread song which has excited folklorists' imagination for many years, 'The Cutty Wren' or 'Richat to Robert', which has been collected all over the British Isles and North America, with a first-known publication date of 1744. In a hypnotic, repetitive chant, the song details how we are to go hunting to kill a wren, in terms of how huge the bird is, how difficult to kill, and the prodigious amount of meat there will be to share out. It has been claimed that it has ancient ritual origins, which may be true, but there is no evidence and it is also possible that it belongs to the genre of hyperbolic comedy songs such as 'The Wonderful Crocodile', 'The Derby Ram', and so on.

Armstrong, 1958: 141–66; Swainson, 1886: 35–43; Opie and Opie, 1997: 437–40.

Wright, Arthur Robinson (1862–1932). His working life was spent as a civil servant in the Patent Office. He was an active member of the *Folklore Society, serving for many years as Editor of the journal *Folk-Lore* (1909–31) and as President (1927–8). Wright was a great gatherer of information. His personal library (donated to the Folklore Society on his death) numbered some 5,000 folklore volumes, and he was an inveterate cutter of items from newspapers. He was unusual in the inter-war generation for being equally interested in the 'modern' as in the ancient, and in numerous letters to *Folk-Lore* he commented on topics such as vehicle mascots (in 1913), confetti, the three lights superstition, the number thirteen, and the burial of amputated limbs, and his small book *English Folklore* (1928) is packed with material on a wide variety of topics and can still be useful as an introduction to folklore. In his second Presidential Address, entitled 'The Unfinished Tasks of the Folk-Lore Society' (*Folk-Lore* 39 (1928), 15–38), he commented:

folklore is very much a thing of life and growth today, and not a mere 'survival' from the smelly and fear-haunted days of 'primitive' man, no more capable of development or growth than a fossil bone or stone axe.

Wright's other lifelong folklore interest was in *calendar customs, and he laboured long to gather material for what he saw as a new version of *Brand's *Popular Antiquities*. He died before it was completed, but his material was edited into shape by T. E. Lones, and published by the Folklore Society under their joint names as *British Calendar Customs: England* (3 vols., 1936–40), which still serves as a standard work on the subject.

Obituary by M. Gaster and A. A. Gomme: *Folk-Lore* 44 (1933), 116–20; *Who Was Who*.

Wright, Elizabeth Mary (b. 1863). Born Elizabeth Mary Lea, eldest daughter of an East London and Herefordshire clergyman; after a conventional schooling, she enrolled at Lady Margaret Hall, Oxford, in 1887, where she attended classes in Old English given by Professor Joseph Wright, under whose supervision she prepared a grammar of the dialect of Northumbria, and whom she later married. She assisted Joseph with his books on grammar and worked closely with him on his monumental *English Dialect Dictionary* (1896–1905). She had, in fact, already encountered this sort of material—'My father was greatly interested in folk-lore and dialect, and would expound to us superstitions he had come across in his pastoral visits'—and she published, in her own right, *Rustic Speech and Folk-Lore* (1913), an excellent book packed full of astute personal observation and knowledge and unusual for its time as not being confined to one particular region. After her husband's death in 1930, she published a two-volume biography, *The Life of Joseph Wright* (1932), which also gives many details of her own life.

Wright, Joseph (1855-1930). Born in poverty in Thackley, Yorkshire, Joseph Wright taught himself to read and write and educated himself to university level. He studied for a Ph.D. at Heidelberg, and served as Deputy Professor (1891-1901) and later Professor of Comparative Philology at Oxford University (1901-25). Wright published numerous standard texts on the grammar of various languages, and an interest in English dialects resulted in his *Windhill Dialect Grammar* (1893), which was, he claimed, 'The first grammar of its kind in England: as scientific study of a living dialect intended to be useful to philologists' (Wright, 1932: 138). In 1887 Wright accepted the position of editor of the long-planned *English Dialect Dictionary*, which was finally published in six volumes between 1896 and 1905, mostly at Wright's own expense. He was also the instigator of the Yorkshire Dialect Society. Joseph Wright married Elizabeth Mary Lea (see E. M. *Wright) in 1896.

Elizabeth Mary Wright, *The Life of Joseph Wright* (1932); F. Austin Hyde, 'Yorkshire Remembers Dr. Joseph Wright', *The Dalesman* (Oct. 1955), 335-7; *DNB*.

Wright, Thomas (1810-77). After showing early promise in the literary-antiquarian field, settling in London in 1836, he served as Secretary of both the Camden and Percy Societies, and for many years worked in collaboration with fellow antiquarian *Halliwell-Phillipps. Most of Wright's prodigious output was concerned with literary or topographical matters, but his interest in early poetry led him to publish collections of songs and ballads which the folklorist can still find useful, including: *Songs and Carols from a Manuscript of the 15th Century in* *the British Museum* (1856), *Political Poems and Songs Relating to English History from Edward III to Richard III* (1859-61), and *Songs and Ballads with other Short Poems Chiefly of the Reign of Philip and Mary* (1860). Other works of his with important folklore elements were: *Narratives of Sorcery and Magic* (1851), and *Essays on Subjects Connected with Literature, Popular Superstitions and History of England in the Middle Ages* (1846). Unfortunately, Wright does not have a very good reputation as far as accuracy of transcription is concerned.

DNB; Dorson, 1968: 61-6.

Wroth Silver. Early in the morning of 11 November (St Martin's Day), representatives of various Warwickshire parishes—along with a large crowd of onlookers—gather on Knightlow Hill to pay money, or Wroth Silver, to the agent of the Duke of Buccleuch, Lord of the Hundred of Knightlow. As each person is called, they step forward and throw their money into a square hollow stone, which was previously the base of a stone cross, saying 'wroth silver'. In much earlier days they were required to walk round the stone first. Having paid their dues, which only takes a few minutes, the company then set off to the Dun Cow where they all sit down to breakfast. Nowadays, the breakfast is by ticket only (the collected Wroth Silver usually amounts to less than 50p), and includes a glass of hot milk and rum which is traditional to the occasion. Defaulters could be fined £1 for every penny owed, or the Duke could demand from them a 'White bull, with red nose and ears of the same colour'. The ceremony is clearly a relic of the payment of dues or rents to the Lord of the *Manor, although the exact nature of the rights or privileges paid for is not known. As several neighbouring parishes are liable for payment, it is likely that the fees were for access or movement by locals and their cattle over the Duke's land. The name Wroth is of unknown meaning, and is not unique to this custom. There was, for example, Wrather Money, paid by New Forest tenants to their Lords of the Manor.

William Waddilove and David Eadon, *Wroth Silver Today: An Ancient Warwickshire Custom* (1983); Stone, 1906: 23-4

Xerox-lore, see *Photocopy-lore.

Yallery Brown. This Lincolnshire tale is a sinister variation on the *brownie theme. The man who told it, a farm labourer, claimed that it had happened to himself in his youth. One day, he had freed a little man with yellow hair and brown skin, trapped under a large flat stone. The creature asked what reward he would like; the man asked for help with his work, and Yallery Brown agreed, on condition he was never thanked. Things turned out badly, for though the man's work was magically done for him the others found theirs spoiled and their tools blunted, so they accused him of being a wizard. So he was sacked, and raged at the fairy: 'I'll thank thee to leave me alone, I want none of thy help!' It screeched with laughter because it had been 'thanked', and told him he would be poor now to his dying day.

M. C. *Balfour (*Folk-Lore* 2 (1891), 264–71) gives the original version in full dialect. *Jacobs (1894/1968: 163–7) turned it into a third-person story in Standard English, and called the workman Tom Tiver; it is this version which is usually reprinted.

yarrow. In Devon and Cornwall, girls wanting to dream of their future husbands would pick this plant at night—some said, from a young man's grave—and put it under their pillows, saying:

> Good night, fair yarrow,
> Thrice good night to thee,
> I hope before tomorrow
> My true love to see.

East Anglian girls pinned yarrow to their dresses to draw the attention of the lads they fancied; or, barefoot and with their eyes shut, they picked a bunch at midnight by the light of the full moon and kept it overnight, for if at dawn it was still wet with dew they would soon be courted (Porter, 1969: 3); to test a

man's love, they would push a yarrow leaf up their nose, saying:

> Yarroway, yarroway, bear a white blow [blossom],
> If my love love me, my nose will bleed now.
>
> (Wright, 1913: 258)

The plant was actually called 'Nosebleed' in some areas; some said this was because to smell its flowers stopped a nosebleed, others because a leaf up the nostril caused bleeding, which relieved headaches. Medicinal uses in East Anglia in the 20th century include yarrow tea for measles and fevers, ointment for cuts and grazes, and an infusion of its roots for rheumatism (Hatfield, 1994: 33, 43, 46). A bunch tied to a cradle was said to calm a baby and make it sweet-tempered; a pillow stuffed with it brought happiness; yarrow strewn on the doorstep kept witches out (Porter, 1969: 17, 49). However, it was unlucky to bring its flowers into the house as decoration.

yell-hounds, yeth-hounds. In Somerset, Devon, and Cornwall, a name for the dogs of the *Wild Hunt (Wright, 1913: 196).

yellow. This colour carries few meanings in English lore, and no beliefs are attached to it. In the Middle Ages it stood for jealousy and treachery, and in the 19th and 20th centuries for cowardice; 'yellow-belly' is a mocking nickname for people of marshy districts, comparing them to frogs. In America a yellow *ribbon indicates loyalty to an absent soldier or prisoner; this symbolism is spreading in Britain.

yew. Yew trees symbolize both death and immortality, being poisonous but long-lived, and able to re-root their branches to produce fresh saplings. Until the 18th century, their foliage was laid in coffins and graves at *funerals. The custom of planting yews in churchyards seems to have come with

Christianity to Ireland and Wales, in imitation of Mediterranean cemeteries with cypress and laurel; it then spread to England, probably as early as the 12th century.

Later generations, however, found churchyard yews puzzling. Two practical explanations are often put forward, namely to provide wood for longbows, and/or to ensure farmers did not let cows graze among the graves. Both lack documentary support, and the slow growth of yews makes the first implausible; naturally, the branches of an already mature tree could be cut for bows, but existing trees show no sign of having been lopped, nor do parish records note sales of yew staves (N&Q 5s:12 (1879), 112–13).

The age of large yews is hard to assess, but 1,000 years is not impossible, suggesting that some were planted soon after their church was built. When a large one at Selborne (Hampshire) collapsed in a gale in January 1990, medieval graves were found beneath its roots, the oldest being from around AD 1200 (Harte, 1996: 6–7). However, some have claimed that large churchyard yews are from 2,000 to 5,000 years old and were sacred to *Druids or earlier peoples, implying that the church was built because the tree was there, not vice versa. This is improbable, both botanically and archaeologically, and lacks supporting evidence.

Round the church at *Painswick (Gloucestershire) are many clipped yews, traditionally said to number 99; it was alleged that every attempt to plant a hundredth would fail—and so it did! At length the mystery was solved, when a lady wrote to The Times (7 July 1963), explaining that her father, a scientist and practical joker who lived beside the churchyard, 'used to pour acid or poison on the roots of the hundredth yew tree whenever they planted a new one. It's highly likely that he started the legend himself.'

Vaughan Cornish, The Churchyard Yew and Immortality (1949); Jennifer Chandler, FLS News 15 (1992), 3–6; Jeremy Harte, At the Edge 4 (1996), 1–9.

Yorkshire Dialect Society. Founded in 1897, although it had its roots in a committee formed in 1894 to assist Joseph *Wright in the compilation of his English Dialect Dictionary. Since its inception, the Society has acted as a focus for dialect studies in the area, prompting research, encouraging the writing of dialect verse and prose, sponsoring lectures and meetings, and publishing. Its annual Transac-

tions was launched in 1898 and is still being published.

W. J. Halliday, The Yorkshire Dialect Society: History and Aims (c.1942); Peter Anderson, Yorkshire at Work: a Selection of Articles Reprinted from the Yorkshire Dialect Society (1980).

Yule. This word, in various spellings, means a loosely defined midwinter period (not a single day) in the early languages of most Germanic and Scandinavian countries. Bede, writing of pagan England, mentions two months, 'early Yule' and 'later Yule', corresponding to Roman December and January; after the Conversion, 'Yule' was narrowed to mean either the Nativity (25 December), or the twelve days of festivity beginning on this date. The word *Christmas replaced 'Yule' in most of England in the 11th century, but not in north-eastern areas of Danish settlement, where it survived strongly till modern times as the normal dialect term for Christmas. Nineteenth-century writers took up the word as a way of denoting the 'Christmas of olden times', with its lavish food and secular jollity, situated in a largely invented *'Merrie England'.

The medieval liking for pageantry and symbolism sometimes led to Yule being impersonated (cf. *Father Christmas). In 1572 the Archbishop of York ordered the Mayor and Aldermen to suppress an annual parade on St Thomas's Day (21 December) called 'The Riding of Yule and his Wife', because it drew 'great concourses of people' away from church-going, and involved disguising. The man representing Yule carried a shoulder of lamb and a large cake of fine bread; he was accompanied by his 'wife', carrying a distaff, and by attendants who threw nuts to the crowd (Duffy, 1992: 581–2).

The Yule Log (or Clog, or Christmas Block) is mentioned in folklore collections from most parts of England, but especially the West Country and the North. It would be the largest piece of wood which could fit on the family hearth, and was usually brought in on Christmas Eve with some ceremony, and put on the fire that evening; many writers, including *Herrick, say it was kindled with a fragment kept from the previous year's log (Hesperides (1648), no. 785; N&Q 11s:1 (1910), 129–30). It was also generally believed that it would be very unlucky for the family if the log was allowed to go out on Christmas Day. It is not clear when the custom arose, since the first definite references are only from the 17th century, for example Aubrey's 'In the West-riding of Yorkshire on Christmas Eve at night they bring in a large Yule-log, or Christmas block, and set it on fire and lap their Christmas ale and sing "Yule, Yule, a pack of new cards and a Christmas stool" ' (Aubrey, 1686/1880: 134). Victorian illustrations of a medieval Christmas often show several men hauling huge trees or stumps in with ropes, but the antiquity of the word 'Yule' cannot prove the custom's age.

Less well known is the custom of lighting a Yule candle on Christmas Eve, first recorded by this name in 1817. These were taller than usual candles ('half a yard in length'), and there was a tradition of chandlers and grocers giving them to their regular customers. The custom is reported chiefly from the north of the country, but its wider range is indicated by Parson Woodeforde's diary entries, in Norfolk, such as: 'I lighted my large wax-candle being Xmas day during tea-time this afternoon for abt. an hour' (25 December 1790). The pre-Reformation Church made a particular feature of candles at Christmas, and strong connections between the season and candles persist to this day. It was thought unlucky to light the Yule candle before dusk on Christmas Eve, and once alight it was not moved. As with the log, a small piece was kept 'for luck' in the coming year (Wright and Lones 1940: iii. 215; Opie and Tatem, 1989: 75).

Bibliography

ABRAHAMS, ROGER D., *Jump-Rope Rhymes: A Dictionary* (Austin: University of Texas Press, 1969).

—— and RANKIN, LOIS, *Counting-Out Rhymes: A Dictionary* (Austin: University of Texas Press, 1980).

ACKERMAN, ROBERT, *J. G. Frazer: His Life and Work* (Cambridge: Cambridge University Press, 1987).

ADAIR, JOHN, *The Pilgrim's Way: Shrines and Saints in Britain and Ireland* (London: Thames & Hudson, 1978).

ADDY, SIDNEY OLDALL, *Folk Tales and Superstitions* (Wakefield: EP, 1973; previously published as *Household Tales with Other Traditional Remains*, 1895).

ALFORD, VIOLET, *Sword Dance and Drama* (London: Merlin, 1962).

—— *The Hobby Horse and Other Animal Masks* (London: Merlin, 1978).

ANDERSEN, JØRGEN, *The Witch on the Wall* (London: Allen and Unwin, 1977).

ANDERSON, WILLIAM, *Green Man: Archetype of our Oneness with the Earth* (London: HarperCollins, 1990).

ANDREWS, WILLIAM, *Old Church Lore* (Hull: Wm. Andrews, 1891).

—— *The Church Treasury of History, Folk-Lore, Custom, etc.* (London: Wm. Andrews, 1898).

—— *Old Church Life* (London: Wm. Andrews, 1909).

ANSON, PETER F., *Fisher Folk-Lore* (London: Faith Press, 1965).

ARMSTRONG, EDWARD M., *The Folklore of Birds* (London: Collins, 1958).

ATKINSON, J. C., *Forty Years in a Moorland Parish: Reminiscences and Researches at Danby in Cleveland* (London: Macmillan, 1891).

AUBREY, JOHN, *Remaines of Gentilisme and Judaisme* (1686–7), ed. James Britten (London: The Folklore Society, 1880).

—— *Miscellanies Upon Various Subjects* (1696; 4th edn., London: Russell Smith, 1857).

—— *Three Prose Works* (i.e. *Miscellanies, Remaines of Gentilisme and Judaisme, Observations*), ed. John Buchanan-Brown (Carbondale, Ill.: Southern Illinois University Press, 1972).

BAER, FLORENCE E., *Folklore and Literature of the British Isles: An Annotated Bibliography* (New York: Garland, 1986).

BAKER, ANNE ELIZABETH, *Glossary of Northamptonshire Words and Phrases* (London: Russell Smith, 1854).

BALFOUR, M. C., 'Legends of the [Lincolnshire] Cars', *Folk-lore* 2 (1891), 145–70, 257–83, 401–18.

—— *County Folklore: Northumberland* (London: Folklore Society, 1904).

BALLEINE, Rev. G. R., *What is Superstition? A Trail of Unhappiness* (London: Press and Publications Board of the Church Assembly, 1939).

BARRETT, W. H., and GARROD, R. P., *East Anglian Folklore and Other Tales* (London: Routledge & Kegan Paul, 1976).

BASFORD, KATHLEEN, *The Green Man* (Ipswich: Boydell & Brewer, 1978; reprint, 1996).

BASKERVILL, CHARLES READ, *The Elizabethan Jig and Related Song Drama* (Chicago: University of Chicago Press, 1929).

BAUGHMAN, ERNEST W., *Type and Motif Index of the Folktales of England and North America* (The Hague: Mouton, 1966).

BEDDINGTON, WINIFRED G., and CHRISTY, ELSA B., *It Happened in Hampshire* (Winchester: Hampshire Fed. of Women's Institutes, 1977).

BENNETT, GILLIAN, 'Heavenly Protection and Family Unity', *Folklore* 96 (1985), 87–97.

—— *Traditions of Belief* (London: Penguin, 1987).

—— 'Legend, Performance and Truth', in *Monsters with Iron Teeth*, ed. Gillian Bennett and Paul Smith, (Sheffield: Sheffield University Press, 1988), 13–36.

—— 'Playful Chaos: Anatomy of a Storytelling Session', in *The Questing Beast*, ed. Gillian Bennett and Paul Smith, (Sheffield: Sheffield University Press, 1989a), 193–212.

—— 'And I Turned Round to Her and Said ... : A Preliminary Analysis of Shape and Structure in Women's Storytelling', *Folklore* 100 (1989b), 167–83.

—— *Alas, Poor Ghost!* (Logan: Utah State University Press, 1999).

——and SMITH, PAUL, *Monsters With Iron Teeth: Perspectives on Contemporary Legend*, iii (Sheffield: Sheffield Academic Press, 1988).

—— and —— *The Questing Beast: Perspectives on Contemporary Legend*, iv (Sheffield: Sheffield Academic Press, 1989).

—— and —— *A Nest of Vipers: Perspectives on Contemporary Legend*, v (Sheffield: Sheffield Academic Press, 1990).

—— and —— *Contemporary Legend: A Folklore Bibliography* (New York: Garland, 1993).

—— and —— *Contemporary Legend: A Reader* (New York: Garland, 1996).

—— —— and WIDDOWSON, J. D. A., *Perspectives on Contemporary Legend*, ii (Sheffield: Sheffield Academic Press, 1987).

BENWELL, GWEN, and WAUGH, ARTHUR, *Sea Enchantress* (London: Hutchinson, 1961).

BERGERON, DAVID M., *English Civic Pageantry 1558–1642* (London: Edward Arnold, 1971).

Berkshire Book (Reading: Berkshire Fed. of WIs, (1939)) (see Gathorne-Hardy for second edition).

BILLINGSLEY, JOHN, *Stony Gaze: Investigating Celtic and Other Stone Heads* (Chieveley: Capall Bann, 1998).

BILLINGTON, SANDRA, *A Social History of the Fool* (Brighton: Harvester, 1984).

BILLSON, C. J., *County Folklore Printed Extracts 3: Leicestershire and Rutland* (London: Folklore Society, 1895; reprint, Llanerch, 1997).

BINDER, PEARL, *The Pearlies: A Social Record* (London: Jupiter Books, 1975).

BLACK, WILLIAM GEORGE, *Folk-Medicine: A Chapter in the History of Culture* (London: Folklore Society, 1883).

BLAKEBOROUGH, RICHARD, *Wit, Character, Folklore and Customs of the North Riding of Yorkshire* (London: Frowde, 1898).

BLOOM, J. HARVEY, *Folk Lore, Old Customs and Superstitions in Shakespeare Land* (London: Mitchell Hughes & Clarke, [1929]).

BOLTON, HENRY CARRINGTON, *The Counting-Out Rhymes of Children* (London: Elliot Stock, 1888).

BONSER, WILFRED, *The Medical Background of Anglo-Saxon England* (London: Wellcome Historical Medical Library, 1963).

BORD, JANET, and BORD, COLIN, *Sacred Waters: Holy Wells and Water Lore in Britain and Ireland* (London and New York: Granada, 1985).

BORLASE, WILLIAM, *Observations . . . on the Antiquities of Cornwall* (1754).

BOSANQUET, ROSALIE E., *In the Troublesome Times* (Northumberland Press, 1929).

BOTTRELL, WILLIAM, *Traditions and Hearthside Stories of West Cornwall* (Penzance: The Author, 1870; 2nd series 1873; 3rd series 1880).

BOULTON, WILLIAM B., *The Amusements of Old London* (London: Nimmo, 1901).

BOURNE, HENRY, *Antiquitates Vulgares, or the Antiquities of the Common People* (Newcastle: The Author, 1725).

BOWKER, JAMES, *Goblin Tales of Lancashire* (London: Swan Sonnenschein, [1883]).

BOYES, GEORGINA, *The Imagined Village: Culture, Ideology and the English Folk Revival* (Manchester: Manchester University Press, 1993).

BRAND, JOHN, *Observations on the Popular Antiquities of Great Britain*, new edn., ed. Henry Ellis (London: Bohn, 1849).

BRAY, Mrs A. E., *The Borders of the Tamar and the Tavy* (London: Murray, 1836; reissued, 1879).

—— *Traditions, Legends, Superstitions, and Sketches of Devonshire* (London: Murray, 1838).

BREARS, PETER, *Horse Brasses* (London: Paul Hamlyn, 1981).

—— *Traditional Food in Yorkshire* (Edinburgh: John Donald, 1987).

—— *North Country Folk Art* (Edinburgh: John Donald, 1989).

BRENTNALL, MARGARET, *Old Customs and Ceremonies of London* (London: Batsford, 1975).

BRIGGS, KATHARINE M., *The Anatomy of Puck* (London: Routledge & Kegan Paul, 1959).

—— *Pale Hecate's Team* (London: Routledge & Kegan Paul, 1962).

—— *Fairies in Tradition and Literature* (London: Routledge & Kegan Paul, 1967).

—— *A Dictionary of British Folk-Tales in the English Language*, Parts A and B, 4 vols. (London: Routledge & Kegan Paul, 1970–1).

—— *The Folklore of the Cotswolds* (London: Batsford, 1974).

—— *A Dictionary of Fairies* (London: Allen Lane, 1976).

—— *The Vanishing People* (London: Batsford, 1978).

—— and TONGUE, RUTH L., *Folktales of England* (London: Routledge & Kegan Paul, 1965).

BROCKETT, JOHN TROTTER, *A Glossary of North Country Words* (Newcastle: Emerson Charnley, 1825).

BROCKIE, WILLIAM, *Legends and Superstitions of the County of Durham* (Sunderland, 1886; reprint, Wakefield: EP, 1974).

BROWN, THEO, *The Fate of the Dead: Folk Eschatology in the West Country after the Reformation* (Ipswich: D. S. Brewer, 1979).

BROWNE, THOMAS, *The Works of Sir Thomas Browne*, ed. Charles Sayle (Edinburgh: John Grant, 1927 (includes reprint of 6th edn. (1672) of *Pseudodoxia Epidemica*)).

BUCKLAND, THERESA, and WOOD, JULIETTE, *Aspects of British Calendar Customs* (Sheffield: Sheffield Academic Press, 1993).

BURNE, CHARLOTTE, *Shropshire Folk-Lore: A Sheaf of Gleanings* (London: Trübner, 1883).

BURTON, ALFRED, *Rush-Bearing* (Manchester: Brooke & Chrystal, 1891).

BUSHAWAY, BOB, *By Rite: Custom, Ceremony and Community in England 1700–1880* (London: Junction Books, 1982).

CAMP, JOHN, *In Praise of Bells: The Folklore and Traditions of British Bells* (London: Robert Hale, 1988).

CAREW, RICHARD, *The Survey of Cornwall* (1602; reprint, London: Adams & Dart, 1969).

CASS, EDDIE, *The Lancashire Pace-Egg Play: A Social History* (London: FLS Books, 2001).

CAWTE, E. C., *Ritual Animal Disguise* (Ipswich: Brewer, 1978).

—— HELM, ALEX, and PEACOCK, N., *English Ritual Drama: A Geographical Index* (London: Folklore Society, 1967).

CHAMBERLAIN, MARY, *Old Wives' Tales* (London: Virago, 1981).

CHAMBERS, EDMUND K., *The English Folk-Play* (Oxford: Oxford University Press, 1933).

CHAMBERS, R., *The Book of Days: A Miscellany of Popular Antiquities* (London: Chambers, 1878).

CHANDLER, KEITH, *Ribbons, Bells and Squeaking Fiddles: The Social History of Morris Dancing in the English South Midlands 1660–1900* (London: Hisarlik, 1993).

CHETWYND-STAPYLTON, MARK, *Discovering Wayside Graves and Memorial Stones* (Tring: Shire, 1968).

CHILD, FRANCIS JAMES, *The English and Scottish Popular Ballads* (Boston: Little Brown, 1882–98; reprint, New York: Dover, 1965).

Choice Notes from 'Notes and Queries': Folk-Lore (London: Bell and Daldy, 1859).

CLARE, JOHN, *The Midsummer Cushion* (Manchester: Carcanet, 1990).

CLARK, DAVID, *Between Pulpit and Pew: Folk Religion in a North Yorkshire Fishing Village* (Cambridge: Cambridge University Press, 1982).

CLOUSTON, W. A., *The Book of Noodles: Stories of Simpletons, or, Fools and their Follies* (London: Elliot Stock, 1888).

COLLS, ROBERT, and DODD, PHILIP, *Englishness: Politics and Culture 1880–1920* (London: Croom Helm, 1986).

COOPER, JOE, *The Case of the Cottingley Fairies* (London: Robert Hale, 1990).

COPPER, BOB, *A Song for Every Season* (London: Heinemann, 1971).

—— *Early to Rise* (London: Heinemann, 1976).

—— *Songs and Southern Breezes: Country Folk and Country Ways* (London: Heinemann, 1973).

CORRSIN, STEPHEN, *Sword Dancing in Europe: A History* (Enfield Lock: Hisarlik, 1997).

COURTNEY, M. A., *Cornish Feasts and Folk-Lore* (Penzance: Beare, 1890).

CRAWFORD, PHYLLIS, *In England Still* (London: Arrowsmith, 1938).

CRESSY, DAVID, *Bonfires and Bells: National Memory and the Protestant Calendar in Elizabethan and Stuart England* (London: Weidenfeld & Nicolson, 1989).

DACOMBE, MARIANNE R., *Dorset Up Down and Along* (Dorchester: Dorset Fed. of WIs, 1935).

DAVIDSON, HILDA R., and BLACKER, CARMEN, *Women and Tradition* (Chapel Hill, NC: University of North Carolina Press, 2001).

—— and CHAUDRI, ANNA, *Supernatural Enemies* (Chapel Hill, NC: University of North Carolina Press, 2001).

DAVIDSON, H. R. ELLIS, *Katharine Briggs: Story-Teller* (Cambridge: Lutterworth Press, 1986).

DAVIES, OWEN, 'Healing Charms in Use in England and Wales 1700–1950', *Folklore* 107 (1996), 19–32.

—— 'Hag-Riding in Nineteenth Century West Country England and Modern Newfoundland', *Folk Life* 35 (1997), 36–53.

—— 'Cunning Folk in England and Wales during the Eighteenth and Nineteenth Centuries', *Rural History* 8 (1997), 91–107.

—— 'Charmers and Charming in England and Wales from the Eighteenth to the Twentieth Century', *Folklore* 109 (1998), 41–52.

—— 'Newspapers and the Popular Belief in Magic in the Modern Period', *Journal of British Studies* 37 (1998), 139–65.

—— *Witchcraft, Magic and Culture 1736–1951* (Manchester: Manchester University Press, 1999[a]).

—— *A People Bewitched* (Bruton, Somerset: The Author, 1999[b]).

DEACON, RICHARD, *Matthew Hopkins: Witch Finder General* (London: Frederick Muller, 1976).

DEANE, TONY, and SHAW, TONY, *The Folklore of Cornwall* (London: Batsford, 1975).

Denham Tracts: A Collection of Folklore by Michael Aislabie Denham, ed. James Hardy, 2 vols. (London: Folklore Society, 1892–5).

Dives and Pauper (c.1405–10; London: Early English Text Society, 1976/80).

DOBSON, R. B., and TAYLOR, JOHN, *Rymes of Robin Hood: An Introduction to the English Outlaw* (London: Heinemann, 1976).

DOEL, FRAN and GEOFF, *Robin Hood: Outlaw or Greenwood Myth* (Stroud: Tempus, 2000).

DORSON, RICHARD M., *The British Folklorists: A History* (Chicago: University of Chicago Press, 1968).

—— *Peasant Myths and Savage Customs: Selections from the British Folklorists*, 2 vols. (London: Routledge & Kegan Paul, 1968).

DRAKE-CARNELL, F. J., *Old English Customs and Ceremonies* (London: Batsford, 1938).

DUFFY, EAMON, *The Stripping of the Altars: Traditional Religion in England 1400–1580* (New Haven: Yale University Press, 1992).

DUNDES, ALAN, and PAGTER, CARL R., *Urban Folklore from the Paperwork Empire* (Austin, Tex.: American Folklore Society, 1975).

—— *Never Try to Teach a Pig to Sing: Still More Urban Folklore from the Paperwork Empire* (Detroit: Wayne State University Press, 1991).

DYER, T. F. THISELTON, *British Popular Customs, Past and Present* (London: George Bell, 1876).

—— *Domestic Folk-Lore* (London: Cassell, 1881).

—— *Folk-Lore of Shakespeare* (London; Griffith & Farran, 1883).

—— *The Folk-Lore of Plants* (London: Chatto & Windus, 1889).

—— *Folk-Lore of Women* (London: Elliot Stock, 1905).

EDWARDS, H., *A Collection of Old English Customs and Curious Bequests and Charities* (London: Nichols, 1842).

ELWORTHY, F. T., *The Evil Eye* (1895; reprint New York: The Julian Press, 1958).

ETTLINGER, ELLEN, 'British Amulets in London Museums', *Folk-Lore* 50 (1939), 148–75.

EVANS, GEORGE EWART, *Ask the Fellows who Cut the Hay* (London: Faber, 1956).

—— *The Horse in the Furrow* (London: Faber, 1960).

—— *The Pattern Under the Plough: Aspects of Folk-Life in East Anglia* (London: Faber, 1966).

—— *The Farm and the Village* (London: Faber, 1969).

—— *Where Beards Wag All: The Relevance of the Oral Tradition* (London: Faber, 1970).

—— *Horse Power and Magic* (London: Faber, 1979).

—— and THOMSON, DAVID, *The Leaping Hare* (London: Faber, 1972).

EVANS, JOAN, *Magical Jewels of the Middle Ages and Renaissance* (Oxford: Clarendon Press, 1922).

FARMER, DAVID, *Oxford Dictionary of Saints* (Oxford: Oxford University Press, 1978).

FERGUSON, ROBERT, *The Dialect of Cumberland* (1873).

FINUCANE, R. C., *Miracles and Pilgrims: Popular Beliefs in Medieval England* (London: Dent, 1977).

—— *Appearances of the Dead: A Cultural History of Ghosts* (London: Junction Books, 1982).

FITZ STEPHEN, WILLIAM, *Norman London* (written c.1180; New York: Italica, 1990).

FORBES, THOMAS R., *The Midwife and the Witch* (New Haven and London: Yale University Press, 1966).

—— 'Verbal Charms in British Folk Medicine', *Proceedings of the American Philological Society* 115:4 (1971), 293–316.

FORBY, ROBERT, *The Vocabulary of East Anglia* (London: Nichols, 1830).

FRAZER, J. G., *The Golden Bough* (abridged edn., London: Macmillan, 1922).

GAMMON, VIC, 'Folk Song Collecting in Sussex and Surrey 1843-1914', *History Workshop Journal* 10 (1980), 61-89.

GATHORNE-HARDY, ROBERT, *The Berkshire Book* (Reading: Berkshire Fed. Of Women's Institutes, 1951) (see under *Berkshire Book* for first edition).

GÉLIS, JACQUES, *History of Childbirth* (Oxford: Polity Press, 1991).

GILL, ALEC, *Superstition: Folk Magic in Hull's Fishing Community* (Beverley: Hutton Press, 1993).

GITTINGS, CLARE, *Death, Burial and the Individual in Early Modern England* (London: Croom Helm, 1984).

GLYDE, JOHN, *Folklore and Customs of Suffolk* (Wakefield: EP, 1976 (reprint of part of *The New Suffolk Garland*, 1866)).

GOLBY, J. M., and PURDUE, A. W., *The Civilisation of the Crowd: Popular Culture in England 1750-1900* (London: Batsford, 1984).

GOMME, ALICE B., *The Traditional Games of England, Scotland, and Ireland*, 2 vols. (London: Nutt, 1894, 1898).

GOMME, G. L. (ed.), *Manners and Customs* (London: Eliot Stock, 1883).

—— *The Gentleman's Magazine Library: Popular Superstitions* (London: Elliot Stock, 1884).

—— *English Traditions and Foreign Customs* (London: Elliot Stock, 1885).

GOODY, JACK, *The Culture of Flowers* (Cambridge: Cambridge University Press, 1993).

GOVETT, L. A., *The King's Book of Sports* (London: Elliot Stock, 1890).

GRIBBEN, ARTHUR, *Holy Wells and Sacred Water Sources in Britain and Ireland: An Annotated Bibliography* (New York: Garland, 1992).

GRINSELL, LESLIE V., *Folklore of Prehistoric Sites in Britain* (Newton Abbot: David & Charles, 1976).

GURDON, E. C., *County Folk-Lore of Suffolk* (London: Folklore Society, 1893).

GUTCH, MRS, *County Folk-Lore*, iv. *The North Riding of Yorkshire, York and the Ainsty* (London: Nutt, 1901).

—— *County Folk-Lore*, vi. *The East Riding of Yorkshire* (London: David Nutt, 1912).

—— and PEACOCK, MABEL, *County Folk-Lore*, v. *Lincolnshire* (London: David Nutt, 1908).

HALLIWELL, JAMES ORCHARD, *The Nursery Rhymes of England* (London: Percy Society, 1842; reprint, London: Bodley Head, 1970).

—— *The Popular Rhymes and Nursery Tales of England* (London: John Russell Smith, 1849; reprint, London: Bodley Head, 1970).

HARDY, JAMES, see *Denham Tracts*.

HARLAND, JOHN, and WILKINSON, T. T., *Lancashire Folk-Lore* (Manchester: Heywood, 1882).

—— and —— *Lancashire Legends, Traditions, Pageants and Sports* (London: Routledge, 1873).

HARRISON, WILLIAM, *The Description of England* (c.1587; reprint, New York: Dover, 1994).

HARTLAND, EDWIN SIDNEY, *County Folklore*, i: *Gloucestershire* (London: Folklore Society, 1892; reprint, Felinfach: Llanerch, 1997).

HATFIELD, GABRIELLE, *Country Remedies* (Woodbridge: Boydell Press, 1994).

HAWORTH, D. and COMBER, W. M., *Cheshire Village Memories* (Malpas: Cheshire Fed. of Women's Institutes, 1952).

HAZLITT, W. C., *A Dictionary of Faiths and Folk-Lore* (London: Reeves & Turner, 1905).

HELM, ALEX, *The English Mummers' Play* (Woodbridge: Brewer, 1981).

HENDERSON, WILLIAM, *Notes on the Folk Lore of the Northern Counties of England and the Border* (London: Longmans Green, 1866; reprint, Wakefield: EP, 1973; 2nd edn., London: Folklore Society, 1879).

HESTER, MARIANNE, *Lewd Women and Wicked Witches* (London: Routledge, 1992).

HOBSBAWM, ERIC, and RANGER, TERENCE, *The Invention of Tradition* (Cambridge: Cambridge University Press, 1983).

HOGG, GARY, *Customs and Traditions of England* (Newton Abbot: David & Charles, 1971).

HOLE, CHRISTINA, *Traditions and Customs of Cheshire* (London: Williams and Norgate, 1937).

—— *English Sports and Pastimes* (London: Batsford, 1949).

—— 'Some Instances of Image-Magic in Great Britain', in: *The Witch Figure*, ed. V. Newall (London: Routledge & Kegan Paul, 1973), 80-94.

—— *English Traditional Customs* (London: Batsford, 1975).

—— *British Folk Customs* (London: Hutchinson, 1976).

—— *Dictionary of British Folk Customs* (London: Granada, 1978).

HOLLAND, WILLIAM, *Paupers and Pig Killers: The Diary of William Holland, a Somerset Parson, 1799-1818*, ed. Jack Ayres (Gloucester: Sutton, 1984).

HOLT, ALAN, *Folklore of Somerset* (Stroud: Alan Sutton, 1992).

HOLT, J. C., *Robin Hood* (London: Thames & Hudson, 1982).

HONE, WILLIAM, *The Every-Day Book*, 2 vols. (London: Thomas Tegg, 1827).

—— *The Table Book* (London: Thomas Tegg, 1827).

—— *The Year-Book* (London: Thomas Tegg, 1832).

HOPE, R. C. *The Legendary Lore of the Holy Wells of England* (London: Elliot Stock, 1893; reprint, Detroit: Singing Tree Press, 1968).

HOWARD, ALEXANDER, *Endless Cavalcade: A Diary of British Festivals and Customs* (London: Barker, 1964).

HUNT, ROBERT, *Popular Romances of the West of England*, 2 vols. (London: Chatto and Windus, 1865/1881).

HUNT, TONY, *Popular Medicine in Thirteenth-Century England* (London: Brewer, 1990).

HUTTON, RONALD, *The Pagan Religions of the Ancient British Isles* (Oxford: Blackwell, 1991).

—— *The Rise and Fall of Merry England: The Ritual Year 1400-1700* (Oxford: Oxford University Press, 1994).

—— *The Stations of the Sun: A History of the Ritual Year in Britain* (Oxford: Oxford University Press, 1996).

—— *The Triumph of the Moon: A History of Modern Pagan Witchcraft* (Oxford: Oxford University Press, 1999).

IGGLESDEN, CHARLES, *Those Superstitions* (London: Jarrolds, [c.1932]).

JACOBS, JOSEPH, *English Fairy Tales* (London: Nutt, 1890 (rev. 1898); reprint, London: Bodley Head, 1968).

—— *More English Fairy Tales* (London: David Nutt, 1894; reprint, London: Bodley Head, 1968).

JAMES, M. R., 'Twelve Medieval Ghost Stories', *English Historical Review* 37 (1922), 413–22.

JEFFREY, SHAW, *Whitby Lore and Legend* (2nd edn., Whitby: Horne, 1923).

JENKIN, A. K. HAMILTON, *Cornish Homes and Customs* (London: Dent, 1934).

JONES-BAKER, DORIS, *The Folklore of Hertfordshire* (London: Batsford, 1977).

JUDGE, ROY, *The Jack in the Green* (Cambridge: Brewer, 1979); rev. edn., London: Folklore Society, 2000.

—— 'Changing Attitudes to May Day 1844–1914', unpublished Ph.D. thesis, University of Leeds, 1987.

—— 'May Day and Merrie England', *Folklore* 102 (1991), 131–48.

—— 'Merrie England and the Morris', *Folklore* 104 (1993), 124–33.

KEEN, MAURICE, *The Outlaws of Medieval Legend* (London: Routledge & Kegan Paul, 1961; revised edn., 1977).

KEIGHTLEY, THOMAS, *The Fairy Mythology* (London: Ainsworth, 1828; revised and enlarged edn., London: Bohn Library, 1889).

KIGHTLY, CHARLES, *The Customs and Ceremonies of Britain: An Encyclopaedia of Living Traditions* (London: Thames & Hudson, 1986).

KNIGHT, STEPHEN, *Robin Hood: A Complete Study of the English Outlaw* (Oxford: Blackwell, 1994).

—— *Robin Hood: An Anthology of Scholarship and Criticism* (Cambridge: Brewer, 1999).

KRAMER, HEINRICH and SPRANGER, JAMES, *Malleus Maleficarum*, trans. Montague Summers (1486; reprint, London: Bracken, 1996).

LAMBERT, MARGARET, and MARX, ENID, *English Popular Art* (London: Merlin Press (revised and enlarged edn.), 1989).

Lancashire Lore (Preston: Lancashire Fed. of Women's Institutes, 1971).

LARWOOD, JOHN, and HOTTON, J. C., *The History of Signboards* (London: Hotton, 1866; revised and reissued as *English Inn Signs* (Exeter: Blaketon Hall, 1985)).

LATHAM, CHARLOTTE, 'Some West Sussex Superstitions Lingering in 1868', *Folk-Lore Record* 1 (1878), 1–67.

LEACH, ROBERT, *The Punch and Judy Show: History, Tradition and Meaning* (London: Batsford, 1985).

LEAN, VINCENT STUCKEY, *Lean's Collectanea*, 5 vols. (Bristol: Arrowsmith, 1902–4).

LEATHER, ELLA MARY, *The Folk-Lore of Herefordshire* (London: Sidgwick and Jackson, 1912).

LITTEN, JULIAN, *The English Way of Death* (London: Robert Hale, 1991).

LLOYD, VIRGINIA, *The Ritual Protection of Post-Medieval Houses in East Anglia* (London: The Folklore Society, 1999).

LOVETT, EDWARD, *Magic in Modern London* (Croydon: Croydon Advertiser, 1925).

—— *Folk-Lore and Legend of the Surrey Hills and the Sussex Downs and Forest* (Caterham: The Author, 1928).

LUPTON, THOMAS, *A Thousand Notable Things of Sundry Sortes* (London, 1579; enlarged 1660).

McCOSH, SANDRA, *Children's Humour* (London: Panther, 1979).

MACDONALD, MICHAEL, and MURPHY, TERENCE R., *Sleepless Souls: Suicide in Early Modern England* (Oxford: Oxford University Press, 1990).

MACFARLANE, ALAN, *Witchcraft in Tudor and Stuart England* (London: Routledge & Kegan Paul, 1970; reprint, 1999).

McLEAN, TERESA, *The English at Play in the Middle Ages* (Windsor: Kensal Press [n.d.]).

MALCOLMSON, ROBERT W., *Popular Recreations in English Society 1700–1850* (Cambridge: Cambridge University Press, 1973).

MAPLE, ERIC, 'Cunning Murrell', *Folklore* 71 (1960), 37–43.

—— 'The Witches of Canewdon', *Folklore* 71 (1960), 241–50.

—— 'The Witches of Dengie', *Folklore* 73 (1962), 178–84.

—— 'Witchcraft and Magic in the Rochford Hundred', *Folklore* 76 (1965), 213–24.

MARPLES, MORRIS, *White Horses and Other Hill Figures* (London: Country Life, 1949).

MATTHEWS, W. H., *Mazes and Labyrinths: Their History and Development* (London: Longman, 1922).

MAYLAM, PERCY, *The Hooden Horse: An East Kent Custom* (Canterbury: The Author, 1909).

MELTON, JOHN, *Astrologaster, or the Figurecaster* (1620; reprint, Los Angeles: Augustin Reprint Society, 1975).

MERRIFIELD, RALPH, *The Archaeology of Ritual and Magic* (London: Batsford, 1987).

MICHELL, JOHN and RICKARD, ROBERT J. M., *Phenomena: A Book of Wonders* (London: Thames & Hudson, 1977).

—— and —— *Living Wonders: Mysteries and Curiosities of the Animal World* (London: Thames & Hudson, 1982).

MIRK, JOHN, *Mirk's Festial: A Collection of Homilies*, ed. Theodor Erbe (London: Early English Text Society, 1905).

MOOR, EDWARD, *Suffolk Words and Phrases* (Woodbridge: Loder, 1823).

MORRIS, DESMOND, *Gestures: Their Origins and Distribution* (London: Cape, 1979).

MORRIS, M. C. F., *Yorkshire Folk-Talk* (2nd edn., London: A. Brown, 1911).

MORSLEY, CLIFFORD, *News from the English Countryside 1750–1850* (London: Harrap, 1979).

MOSS, FLETCHER, *Folklore: Old Customs and Tales of my Neighbours* (Didsbury: The Author, 1898).

MURFIN, LYNN, *Popular Leisure in the Lake Counties* (Manchester: Manchester University Press, 1990).

NARES, ROBERT, *A Glossary, or Collection of Words, Phrases, Names and Allusions to Customs, Proverbs, etc.*, new edn. ed. James O. Halliwell and Thomas Wright (London: Reeves & Turner, 1888).

NARVÁEZ, PETER (ed.), *The Good People: New Fairylore Essays* (New York: Garland, 1991).

NEWALL, VENETIA, *Discovering the Folklore of Birds and Beasts* (Tring: Shire, 1971).

NEWALL, VENETIA, *An Egg at Easter* (London: Routledge & Kegan Paul, 1971).

NICHOLSON, JOHN, *Folk Lore of East Yorkshire* (London: Simpkin Marshall, 1890; reprint, Felinfach: Llanerch, 1998).

NORTHALL, G. F., *English Folk Rhymes* (London: Kegan Paul, 1892).

OPIE, IONA, and OPIE, PETER, *The Lore and Language of Schoolchildren* (Oxford: Oxford University Press, 1959).

—— and —— *Children's Games in Street and Playground* (Oxford: Oxford University Press, 1969).

—— and —— *The Classic Fairy Tales* (Oxford: Clarendon Press, 1974).

—— and —— *The Singing Game* (London: Oxford University Press, 1985).

—— and —— *Children's Games With Things* (Oxford: Oxford University Press, 1997).

—— and —— *The Oxford Dictionary of Nursery Rhymes* (Oxford: Clarendon Press, 1951 (2nd edn. 1997).

—— and TATEM, MOIRA, *A Dictionary of Superstitions* (Oxford: Oxford University Press, 1989).

PALMER, KINGSLEY, *Oral Folk-Tales of Wessex* (Newton Abbot: David & Charles, 1973).

—— *The Folklore of Somerset* (London: Batsford, 1976).

PALMER, ROY, *The Folklore of Warwickshire* (London: Batsford, 1976).

—— *The Folklore of Leicestershire and Rutland* (Wymondham: Sycamore Press, 1985).

—— *Britain's Living Folklore* (Newton Abbott: David & Charles, 1991).

—— *The Folklore of Gloucestershire* (Tiverton: Westcountry Books, 1994).

PATTEN, BOB, and PATTEN, JACQUELINE, 'Rab Channing: Life and Legends', *Folklore* 97 (1986), 56–62.

PATTEN, R. W., *Exmoor Custom and Song* (Dulverton: Exmoor Press, 1974).

PEGG, BOB, *Rites and Riots: Folk Customs of Britain and Europe* (Poole: Blandford 1981).

PENNICK, NIGEL, *Mazes and Labyrinths* (London: Robert Hale, 1990).

PETRY, MICHAEL JOHN, *Herne the Hunter: A Berkshire Legend* (Reading: William Smith, 1972).

PHILIP, NEIL, *The Penguin Book of English Folktales* (London: Penguin, 1992).

PICARD, LIZA, *Restoration London* (London: Weidenfeld & Nicholson, 1997).

PIMLOTT, J. A. R. *The Englishman's Holiday: A Social History* (London: Faber, 1947).

PLOT, ROBERT, *The Natural History of Staffordshire* (1686).

PORTER, ENID, 'Some Folk Beliefs of the Fens', *Folklore* 69 (1958), 112–22.

—— *Cambridgeshire Customs and Folklore* (London: Routledge & Kegan Paul, 1969).

—— *The Folklore of East Anglia* (London: Batsford, 1974).

PORTER, JAMES, *The Traditional Music of Britain and Ireland: A Research and Information Guide* (New York: Garland, 1989).

PUCKLE, BERTRAM, *Funeral Customs: Their Origin and Development* (London: Werner Laurie, 1926).

RADFORD, E., RADFORD, M. A., and HOLE, CHRISTINA, *The Encyclopedia of Superstitions* (London: Hutchinson, 1961; reprinted 1980).

RAHTZ, PHILIP, *The English Heritage Book of Glastonbury* (London: Batsford, 1993).

RAWE, DONALD R., *Padstow's Obby Oss and May Day Festivities* (Padstow: Lodenek, 1971).

READER, IAN, and WALTER, TONY, *Pilgrimage in Popular Culture* (London: Macmillan, 1993).

RICHARDSON, RUTH, *Death, Dissection and the Destitute* (London: Routledge & Kegan Paul, 1987).

RICHMOND, W. EDSON, *Ballad Scholarship: An Annotated Bibliography* (New York: Garland, 1989).

ROWE, DOC, *We'll Call Once More Unto Your House* (Padstow: Padstow Echo, 1982).

ROWLING, MARJORIE, *The Folklore of the Lake District* (London: Batsford, 1976).

RUDKIN, E. H., *Lincolnshire Folklore* (Gainsborough, 1936; reprint, EP Publications, 1973).

RUSSELL, JEFFREY B., *A History of Witchcraft* (London: Thames & Hudson, 1980).

SCOT, REGINALD, *The Discoverie of Witchcraft* (1584; reprint, New York: Dover, 1972).

SHARP, CECIL, *The Country Dance Book* (London: Novello, 1909–22).

—— *English Folk Song: Some Conclusions* (London: Simpkin & Novello, 1907).

—— *Folk Songs from Somerset* (London: Simpkin, Marshall, 1904–9).

—— *The Morris Book* (London: Novello, 1907–13).

—— *The Sword Dances of Northern England* (London: Novello, 1911–13).

SHARPE, JAMES, *Instruments of Darkness: Witchcraft in England 1550–1750* (London: Hamish Hamilton, 1996).

SHEPARD, ODELL, *The Lore of the Unicorn* (London: Allen and Unwin, 1930; Random House, 1996).

SHERIDAN, RONALD, and ROSS, ANNE, *Grotesques and Gargoyles: Paganism in the Medieval Church* (Newton Abbot: David & Charles, 1975).

SHUEL, BRIAN, *The National Trust Guide to Traditional Customs of Britain* (Exeter: Webb & Bower, 1985).

SIKES, WIRT, *British Goblins* (Boston: Osgood, 1881).

SIMONS, JOHN, *Guy of Warwick and Other Chapbook Romances* (Exeter: University of Exeter Press, 1998).

SIMPSON, JACQUELINE, 'The Legends of Chanctonbury Ring', *Folklore* 80 (1969), 122–31.

—— *The Folklore of Sussex* (London: Batsford, 1973).

—— *The Folklore of the Welsh Border* (London: Batsford, 1976).

—— *British Dragons* (London: Batsford, 1980).

—— 'Multi-Purpose Treacle Mines in Sussex and Surrey', *Lore and Language* 3:1 (1982), 61–73.

—— 'Beyond Etiology: Interpreting Local Legends', *Fabula* 24 (1983), 223–32.

—— 'The Lost Slinfold Bell: Some Functions of a Local Legend', *Lore and Language* 4:1 (1985), 57–67.

—— 'God's Visible Judgements: The Christian

Dimension of Landscape Legends', *Landscape History* 8 (1987), 53–8.

—— 'The Local Legend: A Product of Popular Culture', *Rural History* 2:1 (1991), 25–35.

SIMPSON, JOHN, and SPEAKE, JENNIFER, *The Concise Oxford Dictionary of Proverbs* (Oxford: Oxford University Press, 1992).

SKINNER, BOB, *Toad in the Hole* (London: Fortean Times, 1985).

SLUCKIN, ANDY, *Growing up in the Playground: The Social Development of Children* (London: Routledge & Kegan Paul, 1981).

SMITH, ALAN, *Discovering Folklore in Industry* (Tring: Shire, 1969).

SMITH, JULIA, *Fairs, Feasts and Frolics: Customs and Traditions in Yorkshire* (Otley: Smith Settle, 1989).

SMITH, PAUL, *The Book of Nasty Legends* (London: Routledge & Kegan Paul, 1983).

—— *The Complete Book of Office Mis-Practice* (London: Routledge & Kegan Paul, 1984).

—— *Perspectives on Contemporary Legend* (I) (Sheffield: CECTAL, 1984).

—— *More Nasty Legends* (London: Routledge & Kegan Paul, 1986).

SPEAIGHT, G., *Punch and Judy: A History* (London: Studio Vista, 1970).

—— *The History of the English Puppet Theatre* (London: Harrap, 1955; Robert Hale, 1990).

STERNBERG, THOMAS, *The Dialect and Folk-Lore of Northamptonshire* (London: Russell Smith, 1851).

STONE, BENJAMIN, *Sir Benjamin Stone's Pictures: Festivals, Ceremonies, and Customs* (London: Cassell, 1906).

STORCH, ROBERT D., *Popular Culture and Custom in Nineteenth Century England* (London: Croom Helm, 1982).

STORMS, G., *Anglo-Saxon Magic* (The Hague: Nijhoff, 1948).

STOW, JOHN, *A Survey of London* (1598; 2nd edn., 1602; reprint, Stroud: Alan Sutton, 1994).

STRUTT, JOSEPH, *Glig-Gamena Angel-Deod, or The Sports and Pastimes of the People of England* (1801); later edition: as *The Sports and Pastimes of the People of England*, ed. William Hone (London: Chatto & Windus, 1876).

STUBBES, PHILIP, *Anatomy of Abuses* (1583, Reprinted, London: New Shakespeare Society, 1877, 1882).

SUTTON, MAUREEN, *We Didn't Know Aught* (Stamford: Paul Watkins, 1992).

—— *A Lincolnshire Calendar* (Stamford: Paul Watkins, 1997).

SUTTON-SMITH, BRIAN, *The Folkgames of Children* (Austin, Tex.: University of Texas Press, 1972).

—— *Children's Folklore: A Source Book* (New York: Garland, 1995).

SWAINSON, Revd CHARLES, *Provincial Names and Folk Lore of British Birds* (London: Folklore Society, 1886; reprint, Nedeln/Lichtenstein: Kraus Reprints, 1969).

SYKES, HOMER, *Once a Year: Some Traditional British Customs* (London: Gordon Fraser, 1977).

TEBBUTT, C. F., *Huntingdonshire Folklore* (St. Neots: Tomson & Lendrum, 1952).

—— *Huntingdonshire Folklore* (St Ives: Friends of Norris Museum, 1984).

THOMAS, KEITH, *Religion and the Decline of Magic* (London: Weidenfeld & Nicolson, 1971).

—— *Man and the Natural World* (London: Allen Lane, 1983).

TIDDY, R. J. E., *The Mummers' Play* (Oxford: Oxford University Press, 1923).

TONGUE, RUTH L., *Somerset Folklore* (London: The Folklore Society, 1965).

—— *Forgotten Folktales of the English Counties* (London: Routledge & Kegan Paul, 1970).

TUSSER, THOMAS, *Five Hundred Points of Good Husbandrie* (1580; new edn., London: Trubner, 1878).

UDAL, J. S., *Dorsetshire Folk-Lore* (Hertford: Stephen Austin & Sons, 1922).

UNDERDOWN, DAVID, *Revel, Riot and Rebellion: Popular Politics and Culture in England 1603–1660* (Oxford: Oxford University Press, 1985).

VALIENTE, DOREEN, *An ABC of Witchcraft Past and Present* (London, Robert Hale, 1973).

—— *The Rebirth of Witchcraft* (London: Robert Hale, 1989).

VICKERY, ROY, *Unlucky Plants* (London: Folklore Society, 1985)

—— *A Dictionary of Plant Lore* (Oxford: Oxford University Press, 1995).

WALES, TONY, *A Sussex Garland* (Newbury: Countryside Books, 1979).

—— *Sussex Customs, Curiosities and Country Lore* (Southampton: Ensign, 1990).

WALTER, TONY, *Funerals and How to Improve Them* (London: Hodder & Stoughton, 1990).

WEIGHTMAN, GAVIN, and HUMPHRIES, STEVE, *Christmas Past* (London: Sidgwick & Jackson, 1987).

WEIR, ANTHONY, and JERMAN, JAMES, *Images of Lust: Sexual Carvings on Medieval Churches* (London: Batsford, 1986).

WELSFORD, ENID, *The Fool: His Social and Literary History* (London: Faber, 1935).

WESTWOOD, JENNIFER, *Albion: A Guide to Legendary Britain* (London: Granada Publishing, 1985).

WHERRY, B. A., 'Wizardry on the Welsh Border', *Folk-Lore* 15 (1904), 75–86.

WHITE, GILBERT, *The Natural History and Antiquities of Selborne* (Benjamin White, 1788/9).

WHITLOCK, RALPH, *The Folklore of Wiltshire* (London: Batsford, 1976).

—— *The Folklore of Devon* (London: Batsford, 1977).

—— *A Calendar of Country Customs* (London: Batsford, 1978).

WILES, DAVID, *The Early Plays of Robin Hood* (Cambridge: Brewer, 1981).

WILGUS, D. K., *Anglo-American Folksong Scholarship since 1898* (New Brunswick: Rutgers University Press, 1959).

WILSON, DAVID, *Anglo-Saxon Paganism* (London: Routledge & Kegan Paul, 1992).

WILSON, MICHAEL, *Performance and Practice: Oral Narrative Traditions Among Teenagers in Britain and Ireland* (Aldershot: Ashgate Publishing, 1997).

WILTSHIRE, KATHLEEN, *Wiltshire Folklore* (Salisbury: Compton Russell, 1975).

WOOTTON, ANTHONY, *Animal Folklore, Myth and Legend* (Poole: Blandford, 1986).

WRIGHT, A. R., *English Folklore* (London: Benn, 1928).

—— and LONES, T. E., *British Calendar Customs: England*, 3 vols. (London: Folklore Society, 1936–40).

WRIGHT, E. M., *Rustic Speech and Folk-Lore* (Oxford: Oxford University Press, 1913).

Oxford Paperback Reference

The Kings of Queens of Britain
John Cannon and Anne Hargreaves

A detailed, fully-illustrated history ranging from mythical and pre-conquest rulers to the present House of Windsor, featuring regional maps and genealogies.

A Dictionary of Dates
Cyril Leslie Beeching

Births and deaths of the famous, significant and unusual dates in history – this is an entertaining guide to each day of the year.

'a dipper's blissful paradise ... Every single day of the year, plus an index of birthdays and chronologies of scientific developments and world events.'

Observer

A Dictionary of British History
Edited by John Cannon

An invaluable source of information covering the history of Britain over the past two millennia. Over 3,600 entries written by more than 100 specialist contributors.

Review of the parent volume
'the range is impressive ... truly (almost) all of human life is here'
Kenneth Morgan, *Observer*

Oxford Paperback Reference

The Concise Oxford Dictionary of English Etymology
T. F. Hoad

A wealth of information about our language and its history, this reference source provides over 17,000 entries on word origins.

'A model of its kind'

Daily Telegraph

A Dictionary of Euphemisms
R. W. Holder

This hugely entertaining collection draws together euphemisms from all aspects of life: work, sexuality, age, money, and politics.

Review of the previous edition
'This ingenious collection is not only very funny but extremely instructive too'

Iris Murdoch

The Oxford Dictionary of Slang
John Ayto

Containing over 10,000 words and phrases, this is the ideal reference for those interested in the more quirky and unofficial words used in the English language.

'hours of happy browsing for language lovers'

Observer

Oxford Paperback Reference

The Concise Oxford Companion to English Literature
Margaret Drabble and Jenny Stringer

Based on the best-selling *Oxford Companion to English Literature*, this is an indispensable guide to all aspects of English literature.

Review of the parent volume
'a magisterial and monumental achievement'

Literary Review

The Concise Oxford Companion to Irish Literature
Robert Welch

From the ogam alphabet developed in the 4th century to Roddy Doyle, this is a comprehensive guide to writers, works, topics, folklore, and historical and cultural events.

Review of the parent volume
'Heroic volume ... It surpasses previous exercises of similar nature in the richness of its detail and the ecumenism of its approach.'

Times Literary Supplement

A Dictionary of Shakespeare
Stanley Wells

Compiled by one of the best-known international authorities on the playwright's works, this dictionary offers up-to-date information on all aspects of Shakespeare, both in his own time and in later ages.

Oxford Paperback Reference

The Concise Oxford Dictionary of Quotations
Edited by Elizabeth Knowles

Based on the highly acclaimed *Oxford Dictionary of Quotations*, this paperback edition maintains its extensive coverage of literary and historical quotations, and contains completely up-to-date material. A fascinating read and an essential reference tool.

The Oxford Dictionary of Humorous Quotations
Edited by Ned Sherrin

From the sharply witty to the downright hilarious, this sparkling collection will appeal to all senses of humour.

Quotations by Subject
Edited by Susan Ratcliffe

A collection of over 7,000 quotations, arranged thematically for easy look-up. Covers an enormous range of nearly 600 themes from 'The Internet' to 'Parliament'.

The Concise Oxford Dictionary of Phrase and Fable
Edited by Elizabeth Knowles

Provides a wealth of fascinating and informative detail for over 10,000 phrases and allusions used in English today. Find out about anything from the 'Trojan house' to 'ground zero'.

More Art Reference from Oxford

The Grove Dictionary of Art

The 34 volumes of *The Grove Dictionary of Art* provide unrivalled coverage of the visual arts from Asia, Africa, the Americas, Europe, and the Pacific, from prehistory to the present day.

'succeeds in performing the most difficult of balancing acts, satisfying specialists while ... remaining accessible to the general reader'

The Times

The Grove Dictionary of Art – Online
www.groveart.com

This immense cultural resource is now available online. Updated regularly, it includes recent developments in the art world as well as the latest art scholarship.

'a mammoth one-stop site for art-related information'

Antiques Magazine

The Oxford History of Western Art
Edited by Martin Kemp

From Classical Greece to postmodernism, *The Oxford History of Western Art* is an authoritative and stimulating overview of the development of visual culture in the West over the last 2,700 years.

'here is a work that will permanently alter the face of art history ... a hugely ambitious project successfully achieved'

The Times

The Oxford Dictionary of Art
Edited by Ian Chilvers

The Oxford Dictionary of Art is an authoritative guide to the art of the western world, ranging across painting, sculpture, drawing, and the applied arts.

'the best and most inclusive single-volume available'

Marina Vaizey, *Sunday Times*

Oxford Paperback Reference

The Concise Oxford Dictionary of Art & Artists
Ian Chilvers

Based on the highly praised *Oxford Dictionary of Art*, over 2,500 up-to-date entries on painting, sculpture, and the graphic arts.

'the best and most inclusive single volume available, immensely useful and very well written'

Marina Vaizey, *Sunday Times*

The Concise Oxford Dictionary of Art Terms
Michael Clarke

Written by the Director of the National Gallery of Scotland, over 1,800 entries cover periods, styles, materials, techniques, and foreign terms.

A Dictionary of Architecture
James Stevens Curl

Over 5,000 entries and 250 illustrations cover all periods of Western architectural history.

'splendid ... you can't have a more concise, entertaining, and informative guide to the words of architecture'

Architectural Review

'excellent, and amazing value for money ... by far the best thing of its kind'

Professor David Walker

AskOxford.COM
Oxford Dictionaries Passionate about language

For more information about the background to Oxford Quotations and Language Reference Dictionaries, and much more about Oxford's commitment to language exploration, why not visit the world's largest language learning site, www.AskOxford.com

Passionate about English?

What were the original 'brass monkeys'? **Ask**Oxford.COM

How do new words enter the dictionary? **Ask**Oxford.COM

How is 'whom' used? **Ask**Oxford.COM

Who said, 'For also knowledge itself is power?' **Ask**Oxford.COM

How can I improve my writing? **Ask**Oxford.COM

If you have a query about the English language, want to look up a word, need some help with your writing skills, are curious about how dictionaries are made, or simply have some time to learn about the language, bypass the rest and ask the experts at www.AskOxford.com.

Passionate about language?

If you want to find out about writing in French, German, Spanish, or Italian, improve your listening and speaking skills, learn about other cultures, access resources for language students, or gain insider travel tips from those **Ask**Oxford.COM in the know, ask the experts at

OXFORD

Oxford Companions

'Opening such books is like sitting down with a knowledgeable friend. Not a bore or a know-all, but a genuinely well-informed chum ... So far so splendid.'

Sunday Times [of *The Oxford Companion to Shakespeare*]

For well over 60 years Oxford University Press has been publishing Companions that are of lasting value and interest, each one not only a comprehensive source of reference, but also a stimulating guide, mentor, and friend. There are between 40 and 60 Oxford Companions available at any one time, ranging from music, art, and literature to history, warfare, religion, and wine.

Titles include:

The Oxford Companion to English Literature
Edited by Margaret Drabble
'No guide could come more classic.'

Malcolm Bradbury, *The Times*

The Oxford Companion to Music
Edited by Alison Latham
'probably the best one-volume music reference book going'
Times Educational Supplement

The Oxford Companion to Western Art
Edited by Hugh Brigstocke
'more than meets the high standard set by the growing number of Oxford Companions'

Contemporary Review

The Oxford Companion to Food
Alan Davidson
'the best food reference work ever to appear in the English language'
New Statesman

The Oxford Companion to Wine
Edited by Jancis Robinson
'the greatest wine book ever published'
Washington Post

OXFORD

Oxford Paperback Reference

The Concise Oxford Dictionary of World Religions
Edited by John Bowker

Over 8,200 entries containing unrivalled coverage of all the major world religions, past and present.

'covers a vast range of topics ... is both comprehensive and reliable'
The Times

The Oxford Dictionary of Saints
David Farmer

From the famous to the obscure, over 1,400 saints are covered in this acclaimed dictionary.

'an essential reference work'
Daily Telegraph

The Concise Oxford Dictionary of the Christian Church
E. A. Livingstone

This indispensable guide contains over 5,000 entries and provides full coverage of theology, denominations, the church calendar, and the Bible.

'opens up the whole of Christian history, now with a wider vision than ever'

Robert Runcie, former Archbishop of Canterbury